The Edinburgh Anthology of Scottish Literature
Volume 1

The Edinburgh Anthology of Scottish Literature

VOLUME 1

Edited by Robert Irvine

Kennedy & Boyd

Kennedy & Boyd
an imprint of
Zeticula
57 St Vincent Crescent
Glasgow
G3 8NQ
Scotland.

http://www.kennedyandboyd.co.uk
admin@kennedyandboyd.co.uk

First published in 2009
Reprinted 2010
Copyright © Zeticula 2009
Introduction and notes © Robert Irvine 2009.
Cover image: 'The Scott Monument under construction' by David Octavius Hill
and Robert Adamson (1843) Copyright © National Galleries of Scotland

ISBN-13 978-1-84921-003-4 Paperback

Acknowledgements

Many thanks are due to Anne Mason for her help in producing this volume, and to Tricia Boyd for her assistance with the cover image.

A grant from Edinburgh University's School of Languages, Literatures and Cultures supported the preparation of some of these texts.

A note on the texts

All texts here are based on their first editions, with the exception of *Fragments of Ancient Poetry* and *The Lay of the Last Minstrel*, which are based on their second editions. Obvious errors have been silently amended; a few significant changes in later editions are identified in footnotes.

In the case of *Annals of the Parish*, I have also adopted changes made by Galt in the second edition of 1822, where these corrected the first edition's anglicisations of Scots words, or, on a couple of occasions, particularly gross stylistic slips. For a list of variant readings between the first and second editions see John Galt, *Annals of the Parish* ed. James Kinsley (Oxford: The World's Classics, 1986).

As well as referring to the *Oxford English Dictionary* (OED), footnotes glossing Scots words and phrases (marked Sc.) in Galt and Hogg cite the *Scottish National Dictionary* (SND) and the *Dictionary of the Older Scottish Tongue* (DOST). These can be most conveniently consulted through the Dictionary of the Scots Language website: www.dsl.ac.uk.

Contents

Introduction

The texts assembled in this volume are drawn from a period in which Scottish writing enjoyed unparalleled success and influence across the western world. The national epic of 'Ossian', the poetry of Robert Burns, and the poems and novels of Walter Scott were celebrated and imitated all across Europe and the English-speaking world, building on Scotland's established reputation for the historical and philosophical writing of the Scottish Enlightenment. No other European nation of comparable size has ever had this level of international impact. This introduction will sketch some of the issues raised by this remarkable flourishing.

Eighteenth- and early nineteenth-century Scotland was a country going through a historical process we can most conveniently label 'modernisation'. The 'modern' in this sense might be thought of in terms of three developments: the centralisation of political power in a bureaucratic state; the development of a capitalist economy, with banks, joint-stock companies and so on; and the emergence of a public sphere of information exchange and debate mediated by print. By the end of the century, Edinburgh boasted a particularly innovative publishing industry, and Glasgow had become a commercial powerhouse, first as a major centre of trade across the North Atlantic, principally in tobacco, and then, from the end of the eighteenth century, as a centre of industrial production. In the realm of politics, Scotland's 'modernisation' took a slightly unusual form. Certainly, power was increasingly consolidated in a centralised state in this period. The last Jacobite rebellion provides a particularly acute instance of this. In 1745–6, a largely Highland army waged a civil war to restore the (Catholic) Stuart dynasty to the throne, from which it had been excluded by the (Protestant) House of Hanover since 1714. This rebellion was mostly Highland, and indeed only possible, because Highland clan chiefs were able to raise private armies from their dependents, a type of military service long since abolished in the lowlands. The defeat of the Jacobites meant the final destruction of this last vestige of feudal autonomy. Government soldiers imposed government rule across the Highlands, reducing those chiefs who remained to mere landowners on the lowland model. But of course the state that asserted this power was not Scottish, but British; the Jacobites themselves wanted to restore the Stuarts to the throne of England and Ireland, as well as to that of Scotland. Scotland had lost its court, and the aristocratic literary culture that went with it, in 1603, when James VI of Scotland went to London to become James I of England as well. Scotland remained an independent kingdom, albeit one whose king was permanently somewhere else, until 1707. Then, a variety of political and economic pressures persuaded the Scottish parliament to enter a union with the English parliament, dissolving Scotland's political sovereignty in that of a new state, Great Britain.

Scottish aristocrats (the big landowners who inherited political power as dukes or earls) had no remaining reason to make Edinburgh, rather than London, the base of their political operations. Their absence meant that much of Scottish life was governed by the smaller landowners in the countryside, and the business, ecclesiastical and legal elites in the cities. This ruling class was vigorous in the pursuit of those types of modernisation, economic and cultural, open to it in the absence of a state. More than this: it was also highly conscious of this modernisation as constituting a radical break with the past. Its writers and thinkers, in the movement we now celebrate as the Scottish Enlightenment, developed concepts to explain how a society based on trade and manufactures differed from earlier types of society. Economic activity, they speculated, is more than one social practice among others. As its material basis, that which allows it to survive, a society's type of economy determines the nature of many of its other institutions. Modern Britain's foundation in trade required, not only banks and stock-exchanges, but a set of laws protecting property defined in terms of money, and a parliamentary system to make them. As long as its economy had been primarily agricultural, and property meant land, a different type of legal and political system had been required, the one that the historians retrospectively named 'feudal'. In the earliest, 'primitive' or 'savage' ages of humankind, the Scottish historians envisioned hunter-gathers organised in tribes of the kind encountered in North America. Because it thought of human history as progressing though a series of distinct stages, we refer to this model as the 'stadial' theory of history.

A commercial society also required a distinctly modern set of social relations. In particular, it required a means whereby those who had become wealthy through trade could be integrated into the country's elite, one broader than, but incorporating, the old ruling class, whose power was based on their possession of land. Taking their cue from Joseph Addison and Richard Steele's campaign for the reformation of manners in the *Spectator* (1711–12, 1714), some of Scotland's self-consciously modernising elite promoted a model of sociability named 'polite' to this end. This can be defined in terms of its rejection of violence: not just the physical violence associated with a feudal ruling class, but violent attachment to a political party or a religious denomination. Polite 'manners' (the latter term having a broader meaning than today, to signify something like 'cultural norms') were accordingly those thought to mitigate the threat of civil conflict that had torn Britain apart in the previous century (and briefly recurred in 1745–6). Print culture was central to the promotion of this agenda. The nation was to be united, not by a dynasty or a religion, but through the peaceful exchange of ideas through books and journals on the model of a conversation. This meant that polite writing had to avoid reference to sex and the body, to avoid alienating female readers, as well as political and religious controversy. So, for example, the satire of Alexander Pope and Jonathan Swift, often ferociously partisan and sometimes bawdy, was excluded from the canon of the polite: this type of writing largely vanished in English from the 1740s onwards. But the polite encoded its own politics: the vast majority of the population who owned no property, and thus did not have the leisure to take part, were excluded from the conversation.

The new historical thinking also postulated what had been *lost* in the shift to the modern. While they emphasised that political and legal institutions changed to fit the developing economic basis of a society, the enlightenment philosophers were also deeply interested in what they thought did *not* change in the course of history: the underlying structures of the human mind and the nature of perception, both physical and moral. Morality, they thought, was produced by sympathetic instincts, feelings embedded in our human nature, rather than a civilizing education. The very containment of passion required by modern sociability might erode these instincts. Earlier, more 'primitive' forms of social organisation might accordingly allow more direct, more spontaneous expression of 'natural' feeling than is possible in modern society. And this meant that less-developed societies might retain a higher capacity for *poetry* than commercial ones. For poetry, on this view, was the sincere expression of individual feeling (as it was to be for Wordsworth) rather than a mode of social criticism (as it had been for Pope). At the same time, this definition includes under 'poetry' types of expression that are not, originally, written down at all, such as ballads transmitted by word-of-mouth.

This understanding of the place of poetry in history was a major factor in the astonishing success, in the 1760s, of the works of 'Ossian', as 'collected' and published by James Macpherson. Presented as translations of ancient Gaelic verse, composed by a Highland bard in the third century, their authenticity was soon called into doubt, most vociferously by Samuel Johnson. Today it is accepted that, at least in the initial volume, *Fragments of Ancient Poetry* (1760; extracted in this anthology), Macpherson did draw on traditional Gaelic ballads which he and his contacts collected in the Highlands. These ballads were first composed perhaps a thousand years later than Macpherson claimed, however, and were certainly not the remains of a single epic poem composed by a single poet as he assumed. Hugh Blair, in the essay extracted in this volume, provided an influential explanation of the origins of Ossian's poetry in terms of the stadial theory of history. But Macpherson's 'translations', re-creations and inventions were shaped from the start by his knowledge of what a polite eighteenth-century readership would expect of a 'primitive' bard; anticipating the critical response, not only of academics like Blair, but of the periodical journals like the *Gentleman's Magazine* or the *Scots Magazine* which set the standard of polite taste in literature.

A large part of that anticipation meant distancing these works from the actually-existing Highland culture in which Macpherson claimed to have found them. By locating them in the third century, he can insist that Fingal and his heroes lived before the coming of Christianity to Scotland, and before the establishment of the clan system in the Highlands. They are thus not immediately identifiable with the often Catholic Highland warriors who invaded lowland Scotland and England in a Jacobite rebellion that was only 15 years in the past when *Fragments* was published. Fingal's people, indeed, do not even identify themselves as *Scottish*: their distant historical period is prior to the establishment of the rival kingdoms of England and Scotland. Rather, they are Celts on the island of Britain who have escaped Roman conquest. To that extent, they can be understood as the original free *Britons*, providing a reassuringly ancient and heroic precedent for the political identity of Macpherson's modern readers.

Yet if the Preface and footnotes to *Fragments of Ancient Poetry* insist on the difference between the tribe of Fingal and the eighteenth-century clans, the poems themselves might now seem to us haunted by the recent historical experience of the Highlands. Ossian mourns the absolute defeat of his people, the destruction of tribal continuity, the end of a family line; a mourning that makes perfect sense as a response to the brutal collective punishment of the rebel clans by the government army, the execution of their chiefs and government appropriation of their estates, the banning of plaid and bagpipes and weaponry. To all this Macpherson had a personal connection, as the nephew of a clan chief and leader in the rebellion who spent nine years in hiding after 1746 before escaping to exile in France. But *Fragments* mounts no resistance to the forcible integration of his homeland into modern Britain; rather, it is complicit in it. Stripped of their political structures, the Highlands become available to lowland investors as an economic opportunity; stripped of their political associations, they become available to Macpherson's readers as a landscape of pure feeling, where no historical reality will obstruct the pleasurable indulgence of melancholy and the sublime. This is what Blair means when he calls the works of Ossian 'the Poetry of the Heart'.

In 'Ossian', the Enlightenment's postulation of a primitive 'other' as the location of sincere feeling found its perfect confirmation. In Robert Burns, a polite readership found something very similar. Since the labouring poor were by definition excluded from the 'polite', they too could be understood as a repository of natural feeling undiluted by the necessary accommodations of modern society, making them imaginable as an origin for poetry. In the framing material of his first published collection, the Kilmarnock *Poems* of 1786, Burns to a certain extent collaborates in this view of his place as a poet. Some of the poems, too, lend themselves to this kind of reading. Henry Mackenzie's influential review of the Kilmarnock edition in *The Lounger* (a periodical modelled on *The Spectator*) selects for praise the sentimental moralising of, for example, 'The Cotter's Saturday Night', 'To a Mouse', and 'To a Mountain Daisy'. In such poems, the poverty and hard labour of the rural poor act to confirm the naturalness of the conventional piety and domestic morality to which they apparently adhere. These poems thus tend to confirm rather than challenge the values of their propertied readers. Indeed the first of these, dedicated to Burns's lawyer friend Robert Aiken, includes a moment of recognition of this mechanism at work. The poem's description of a labouring family will also, the first stanza tells us, imagine 'what Aiken in a *Cottage* would have been' (1.8), suggesting that the poem reflects the virtues of its propertied reader as much as the life of the people he is reading about. As in Macpherson, the effect is to empty a scene of human suffering of its political meaning. The social difference between the subject of the poetry and its reader generates the pleasures of sympathetic identification rather than the discomfort of political critique.

However, most of Burns's poetry resists this sort of genteel appropriation of labouring-class experience. His use of Scots itself defies the imposition of a standardised, polite English as the only acceptable medium of literary expression. He also revels in satire, that Augustan genre excluded from the improving agenda of polite culture. In the verse epistles, indeed, Burns goes beyond a commitment to an older, politically and socially critical ideal of poetry. If 'A Cotter's Saturday Night' offers up the manners of his own rank for the cultural consumption of the polite, the 'Epistles to Lapraik', for example, do the reverse, appropriating the modes of polite culture for the use of the labouring poor themselves. Here the tenant-farmer poet addresses, not a property-owning audience above him, but one on his own level, and the discursive ideal is the Enlightenment one of mutually-improving conversation, with poetry serving as a medium for this specific type of sociability. The politics of such poems lies not in any overt criticism of the ruling class, but in the cultural autonomy from that class that they implicitly assert. In the first 'Epistle to Lapraik', Burns stakes his claim to a poetic vocation on 'Nature' and 'the Heart', rather than on any literary training, just as he had on the Kilmarnock edition's title-page, and in its preface. But there it had served to gratify the Hugh Blairs and Henry Mackenzies of the period in their desire to find untutored inspiration in a son of the soil; in the verse epistles it expresses indifference to the literary expectations of such 'Critic-folk', his 'learned foes', made possible by an alternative readership among the poet's social peers.

That the new modes of modern print culture might be taken over by those ranks they had been designed to exclude had always been a possibility. In England, it had been assumed that their general illiteracy, as well as their lack of access to books, sealed off the Enlightenment from the poor. In Scotland, where the Presbyterian church had established a network of parish schools, basic literacy was more common; but here it was assumed that the reading of the poor would restrict itself to the Bible and other religious materials. The 1790s proved these assumptions to be quite wrong, in the context of the 1789 revolution in France. The British government was horrified at the extent to which sympathy with the French Revolution energised many British working people and revealed a passion for reading and ideas among them that it had previously been safe to deny or ignore. Thomas Paine's defence of the Revolution, *Rights of Man*, sold perhaps 200,000 copies in the two years after its publication in 1791. Even more worrying than this number was the means of its distribution. Radicals had formed themselves into local 'Constitutional Societies' and 'Corresponding Societies' in which to discuss political ideas and, as the latter title suggests, these were in touch with one another, by letter, on a national level. It was through this network that Paine's book was dispersed, allowing many people to read it, or hear it read, who could not afford to buy it. The nation as a conversation held through the medium of print, grounded on a common 'human nature': the ideal of polite sociability, which had evolved to efface the difference between one group of propertied people and another, had now been seized by many among the propertyless majority. What had been understood as a way of evading political difference was revealed as a political weapon. Literacy itself was now a political issue.

The government response in Scotland was particularly ruthless. Thomas Muir, himself a lawyer, was found guilty of circulating, reading out and encouraging others to read 'seditious' texts such as *Rights of Man* in August 1793, and sentenced to 14 years transportation to the penal colony of Botany Bay in Australia. Over the next seven months, the Scottish courts sentenced another four men to transportation for similar 'crimes'. The 'Treason Trials' which followed in London, in contrast, led only to acquittals. It is in this context that one must read Burns's poems of the 1790s: both their anger and despair, and the fact that they generally evoke the French Revolution indirectly, by reference to the Scottish or American wars of independence, rather than explicitly. Many, such as the Washington 'Ode', were not published until long after Burns's death in 1795. The politics of culture revealed by the conflicts of the 1790s continued to shape Scottish writing in the decades that followed.

It is in this context, for example, that we can understand Walter Scott's reactionary enthusiasm for the orally-transmitted culture of the rural poor. His collection of ballads, *Minstrelsy of the Scottish Border* (1802–3), implicitly identifies the national poetic tradition with a *pre*-literate society, whose songs and stories can be transferred into print culture only by polite Edinburgh gentlemen like himself. In fact the Borders glens where Scott found his originals were just as literate as Burns's Ayrshire. Scott's work tends to efface the literacy of working people because the 1790s had revealed it to be a political threat. Scott's first great poetic composition, *The Lay of the Last Minstrel* (1805), also emerges from this cultural politics. The *Lay* is, in one way, an extended version of the 'modern imitations' of traditional ballads that Scott included in the *Minstrelsy*. Scott had learned from the Ossian controversy that the claim to historical authenticity is not actually required for aesthetic success; all that is needed is the *effect* of antiquity, produced here by the short lines, simple imagery, and rough-and-ready meter of the ballads. Like Ossian, Scott's minstrel is the last of his line, having lost his son in battle as Ossian had lost his; but he has an appreciative audience as Ossian has not. The border ballads, of course, were sung by the rural poor to each other; Scott instead makes his singer a courtly performer, enjoying the aristocratic patronage of Anne Scott, Duchess of Buccleuch. Indeed, the dedication of the whole poem to Charles Scott, the current heir to the Buccleuch dukedom, aligns Scott the poet with the minstrel in this regard. It thus asserts the continuity down to the present time of the hierarchical social relations of the seventeenth century (when the minstrel is singing), a continuity apparently untroubled by the revolutionary turmoil of the preceding decade. But it is important to realise that Scott is publishing the *Lay* as a private enterprise in partnership with his publisher, James Ballantyne. The radical Burns depended on the support of wealthy landowners to get his first volumes into print, but not the reactionary Scott, who was from the start a literary entrepreneur. The dedication to the *Lay* thus papers over the absolute historical break between the minstrel's era and Scott's, a break constituted, not by the French Revolution, or even by the shift from an oral culture to a literate one, but by a capitalist mode of production which frees literature from the need for aristocratic patronage.

Complicating the politics of the poem, however, is the presence in the story that the minstrel tells of a book; and a book, the reading of which lends the reader enormous power. This book is meant for aristocratic eyes only, but it comes into the possession of a wicked goblin, whose only intention is to use this power to do evil. As far as that goes, the story might be a parable of the dangerous power of literacy, and the necessity of keeping it under the control of the ruling class. However, the intentions of the aristocrat for whom the book is originally destined are hardly laudable either: this earlier Lady Scott wants to use its power to pursue a blood-feud with a rival clan who have murdered her husband. Although the goblin intends only evil, its diversion into his hands eventually results in the peaceful resolution of this feud. If this is indeed a parable about literacy, it might suggest that its free circulation will lead to happy historical outcomes, despite, not because of, the intentions of all involved.

The British response to the French Revolution also shaped the context in which women writers had access to the market. Polite culture had a quite specific role for propertied women. Their presence in social life was deemed an important way of moderating the political and religious passions of their menfolk. By extension, women's writing had gained a certain amount of cultural authority, although the price for this was a severe narrowing of its subject matter to the moral and domestic. The threat from France was quickly translated by reactionary writers into a threat to the private life of the family and the sexual regulation that supported it (although in fact the Revolution itself was not at all radical in this respect); and so, in the 1790s, the woman writer's role in defending domestic morality assumed a new, and overtly political, importance.

It is striking, then, that Joanna Baillie's remarkable, decades-long project, *A Series of Plays: in which it is attempted to delineate the stronger passions of the mind* claims its literary authority in other ways, by placing itself in relation to genres gendered masculine. The systematic exploration of the psychology of feeling announced on the title page of the 1798 volume, and explained in the 'Introductory Discourse', is a clear continuation of Scottish Enlightenment concerns. In that discourse, the people among whom our 'human nature' is to be 'discovered by stronger and more unequivocal marks' than elsewhere has broadened to encompass all of 'the middling and lower classes of society' and not only the uneducated primitive or ploughman. Still, this could have seemed politically radical in the ideologically-saturated atmosphere of the 1790s, as not before. It could no longer be assumed that crediting the lower classes with a specific claim to 'human nature' did no more than make their songs and poems available for the aesthetic appreciation of their superiors; it could also ground a demand on their part for political rights. When William Wordsworth made an almost identical claim in the 'Preface' to *Lyrical Ballads* two years later it was certainly interpreted in this way. But no one seems to have mistaken Baillie for a dangerous subversive. Her interest in natural feeling is contained within the terms of enlightenment science, rather than, as in Wordsworth, part of a wider social critique. It also helps that the plays themselves so clearly evoke an icon of English national culture, William Shakespeare. Wordsworth's claim to be writing in 'the real language of men' is not realised in his actual verse any more than Baillie's, but it does provide an impetus to formal experiment. Baillie's enlightenment interest in human psychology is realised in a five-act structure, iambic pentameter, and a linguistic register, all borrowed from two hundred years before. In this respect, Baillie is engaged in recovering and reinventing 'ancient' poetic forms within an enlightenment context just as much as Macpherson or Scott, but rather than raiding the cultural resources of the rural poor, she appropriates the body of texts at the pinnacle of the English literary canon.

Yet Baillie's plays cannot simply evade the politics of their time. *De Monfort*'s anti-hero is an aristocrat who is incapable of containing his own passion for the sake of polite sociability; and the passion that cannot be contained is hatred for a fellow-aristocrat who is a consummate performer in this regard. The hero of the play is Jane de Monfort, the anti-hero's sister. She perfectly embodies conventional feminine moral authority: devoted to the family, self-sacrificing, and defined entirely by the good effect she has on others. To that extent Jane is a familiar conservative ideal. Yet the breakdown of social order with which she is faced does not come from the democratic demands of the lower orders, but from the unconstrained rage of a male member of the ruling class. If this is a play about its own time and place (and its German setting serves to safely distance it from events in Britain), it suggests that the danger to British society comes not from the French Republic or its British sympathisers, but from the immoderate reaction to them on the part of the authorities.

Some of the heat went out of the Revolution controversy in the first decade of the nineteenth century, as government censorship had its effect, the government's supporters realised that a British revolution was not imminent after all, and the French Republic was turned into an authoritarian empire by Napoleon Bonaparte. But there was no going back. Ideas that had looked like an evasion of politics, such as the association of natural feeling with the poor, now seemed themselves deeply political. An instance of this was the place of the Covenanters in Scottish national culture. In 1638, in the early stages of the civil wars, Scotland's rulers had committed themselves, in a 'National Covenant' with God, to a national church organised along Presbyterian lines: that is, without a hierarchy of bishops and archbishops ('prelates') on the English model, and thus independent of royal authority. In the 1660s, 70s, and 80s Charles II and his successor James VII imposed just such a hierarchy ('prelacy' or 'episcopacy') on the Kirk; ministers who did not accept this (around a third of them) were forced out of their churches, continuing to preach to their congregations in inaccessible hill country. These 'covenanting' congregations eventually rose in a series of armed revolts, to which the government responded with increasingly brutal military repression, especially in South-West Scotland, the heartland of the movement. Peace came only with the Catholic James's deposition in 1688 and replacement on the throne by his Protestant daughter Mary and her husband, the Dutch Prince William of Orange. Under William and Mary, the Presbyterian church was re-established, although an Episcopal Church of Scotland continued in parallel as part of the Anglican communion. The Covenanters who had died continued to be remembered as martyrs for their religion, but also as rebels who had asserted the rights of their nation. Their story provided a powerful myth of Scottish national identity in the century that followed; but because the British crown had restored Presbyterianism, and the Union of 1707 had guaranteed the continued independence of the Kirk, this story did not offer any resistance to the political status quo. It was assumed that Protestantism, of any shade, entailed loyalty to the Hanoverian regime.

In the decades after the French Revolution, Scotland's Covenanting heritage appeared in a different light. The Covenanting movement of the 1670s and 80s had been primarily a cause of the common people. As the ideological struggle of the 1790s hardened into class conflict after the final defeat of Napoleon in 1815, the Covenanters looked increasingly like a precedent for popular national revolt incubating at the very heart of (one version of) Scottish national identity. The industrial revolution was filling the towns and cities with workers who, following the example set by the Corresponding Societies of the 1790s, thought of themselves as a class, at a national level, freed as they were from the local identities that structured life in a country parish. And in Scotland, most of the new industrial towns and cities were in the South West, precisely the areas where the martyrs of the Covenant were most celebrated. Then, in August 1819, a rally to demand parliamentary reform was charged by cavalry in Manchester, killing 15 people (the 'Peterloo Massacre'); this, and the government crackdown that followed, sparked riots in Paisley the following month. The stand-off between government and the west of Scotland working class eventually came to a head in the 'Radical War' of April 1820, when radical groups in Glasgow and elsewhere attempted armed rebellion (prompted, it seems clear, by government *agent provocateurs*). This was put down, three of its leaders hanged, and 20 others sentenced to transportation.

It is in this context that we have to understand the fiction of John Galt in this period, including his second novel *Annals of the Parish* (1821). This begins with the narrator, the minister of an Ayrshire parish for half a century, giving his farewell sermon in 1810. In it, he warns against taking the example of the Covenanters as a legitimation for rebellion in the name of anything other than religious freedom. But the novel does not make clear what function Presbyterianism *should* play in modern Scotland, if not this one.

Balwhidder's chronicle of his ministry faithfully registers the process of modernisation in both its forms. The progress of politeness is most noticeable in Mrs Malcolm's daughter Kate. Although her mother is Scots-speaking, devout, and the widow of a sea-captain, Kate Malcolm is educated in metropolitan ways by Lady Macadam, an education she crowns by marrying Lady Macadam's son and heir. Thus do the commercial classes gain social recognition from old wealth in return for accepting their tutelage in polite manners. The progress of commerce, meanwhile, produces more abrupt changes. Social leadership is provided in the first half of the book by the benevolent patronage of Lord Eglesham; in the second half, the central figure in the parish is Mr Cayenne, the mill-owner, whose talent is for confrontation and conflict. Balwhidder is able to do much good as a conduit between the parish poor and their aristocratic overlord, but with the coming of the mill, this local and vertical social organisation is replaced by the national, horizontal stratification and antagonisms of class. The mill-workers set up their own church, the mill-owner is essentially an atheist, and Balwhidder has no role in mediating between the two.

It has sometimes been suggested that *Annals of the Parish* is a satire on the narrow historical perspective of a provincial parish minister; one who can write of the year of the French Revolution, for example, that it 'was not remarkable for any extraordinary occurrence'. This is to forget that, for the historians and philosophers of the Scottish Enlightenment, the incremental changes in society produced by technological developments (a mill, a new farming technique, a new trade route) *are* history; because those changes are fundamental and lasting, while the actions of kings and generals and politicians are so much sound and fury on the surface of things. From this point of view, the new stage-coach to Glasgow that allows Mrs Balwhidder to sell her butter there *is* more important than the storming of the Bastille; not on its own, but as part of a process of improvement that will continue when the French Republic has long disappeared. But if the intentions of statesmen are doomed to frustration if they try to swim against the steady current of historical change, what of the intentions of parish ministers? There are moments in the novel where a new historical context gives Balwhidder's old-style Presbyterian rhetoric radical meanings that he does not intend. He preaches on David and Goliath to British officers on the eve of the American Revolution, apparently unaware of the biblical legitimacy this lends the colonial David in its struggle with the empire that they serve; in the General Assembly, in the presence of the representative of the King, he preaches on a text which seems to breathe seventeenth-century hostility to the crown. He is also impressed with the radicals he encounters early in the 1790s, a bookshop-keeper and some young weavers. There is plenty here to suggest that the rebels of 1820, the year before *Annals* was published, *are* the true heirs of the Covenanters' spirit of resistance, even if Balwhidder remains unconscious of such indications.

It was still possible, however, to see in Scotland's religious inheritance a bulwark *against* democratic agitation. Writers like Scott certainly remained committed to the principle that economic improvement and the cultivation of literature could be maintained while closing down the potential for enlightenment ideas to threaten the political status quo. But an alternative conservative strategy was to dump the enlightenment project altogether. Implicit in James Hogg's writing is the assumption that the modern propertied classes are in effect their own worst enemies, for only faith can underpin a natural social order, and the propertied classes have abandoned what Hogg considers faith. Hogg's mother was one of Scott's sources for the ballads of the *Minstrelsy*, and he was acutely conscious of the losses involved in the refinement of such material for a polite audience. Hogg's answer was in effect to take over this project himself, building a literary career on his inside knowledge, as a member of the rural working class, of the folk-culture that Scott had raided. But Hogg's versions of folk-tale and imitation ballad resist their easy assimilation to the sceptical world-view of an enlightened readership. For one thing, Christian faith, and encounters with faeries, kelpies, brownies and the rest, are not only understood to be consistent with one another, but part of the same continuum of belief, as they were in Hogg's community. Hence there is no contradiction in a brownie coming to enact revenge on a landowning persecutor of the Covenanters, as happens in 'The Brownie of the Black Haggs'. For Hogg, supernatural agency cannot be lifted out of the cultural context in which it is implicitly believed in, and repackaged as a purely aesthetic experience for the wealthy. In Hogg, the original context follows the tale, rather as the real ghost follows the ghost-story in 'The Barber of Duncow'. But this literary strategy depended on selling stories to a polite readership in order to frustrate that readership's expectations, which was a hard trick to pull off; and in the process, Hogg encountered the same condescension and stereotyping that had frustrated Burns a generation before.

Thomas Carlyle, on the other hand, had abandoned orthodox religious faith, but had also abandoned the enlightenment version of history, whose faith in the necessary benefits of incremental progress looked to him equally irrational from the perspective of 1829. What 'Signs of the Times' calls 'machinery' is, among other things, that version of history that imagines individuals to be the effects, rather than the causes, of social change. In place of the Scottish Enlightenment's conception that legal and political systems are the products of a society's *material* basis, Carlyle (following the German philosopher Hegel, among others) sees human society, including its technology, as the realisation of *ideas*, the expression of great creative concepts forged in the souls of heroic individuals. Even the French Revolution was an example of this, 'an Idea: a Dynamic, not a Mechanic force'. This return of historical agency to the individual is of course potentially politically radical. But Carlyle preaches it in a rhetoric that recalls the Presbyterian pulpit that had he renounced for print culture, with a blizzard of historical examples taking the place of quotation from the bible; and there is a hint that Carlyle want to close down a radical interpretation of his text, when he writes that 'it is towards a higher freedom than mere freedom from oppression by his fellow-mortal, that man dimly aims'. But as the history of the enlightenment itself had shown, no text can wholly determine the use that is made of it, or by whom.

FRAGMENTS

OF

ANCIENT POETRY,

Collected in the HIGHLANDS of SCOTLAND,

AND

Translated from the GALIC or ERSE Language.
The SECOND EDITION.

Vos quoque qui fortes animas, belloque peremtas
Laudibus in longum vates dimittitis aevum,
Plurima securi fudistis carmina Bardi.

LUCAN[1]

EDINBURGH
Printed for G. HAMILTON and J. BALFOUR
MDCCLX

PREFACE

The Public may depend on the following fragments as genuine remains of ancient Scottish poetry. The date of their composition cannot be exactly ascertained. Tradition, in the country where they were written, refers them to an æra of the most remote antiquity; and this tradition is supported by the spirit and strain of the poems themselves; which abound in those ideas, and paint those manners, that belong to the most early state of society. The diction too, in the original, is very obsolete; and differs widely from the style of such poems as have been written in the same language two or three centuries ago. They were certainly composed before the establishment of clanship in the northern part of Scotland, which is itself very ancient; for had clans been then formed and known, they must have made a considerable figure in the work of a Highland Bard; whereas there is not the least mention of them in these poems. It is remarkable that there are found in them no allusions to the Christian religion or worship; indeed, few traces of religion of any kind. One circumstance seems to prove them to be coeval with the very infancy of Christianity in Scotland. In a fragment of the same poems, which the translator has seen, a Culdee or Monk is represented as desirous to take down in writing from the mouth of Oscian, who is the principal personage in several of the following fragments, his warlike atchievements and those of his family. But Oscian treats the Monk and his religion with disdain, telling him, that the deeds of such great men were subjects too high to be recorded by him, or by any of his religion: A full proof that Christianity was not as yet established in the country.

Though the poems now published appear as detached pieces in this collection, there is ground to believe that most of them were originally episodes of a greater work which related to the wars of Fingal. Concerning this hero innumerable traditions remain, to this day, in the Highlands of Scotland. The story of Oscian, his son, is so generally known, that to describe one in whom the race of a great family ends, it has passed into a proverb; "Oscian the last of the heroes."

---

1 These lines are from the *Pharsalia*, an epic poem of the Civil War between Caesar and Pompey by the Roman poet Marcus Annaeus Lucanus (A.D. 39–65): 'You too, ye Bards! whom sacred Raptures fire, / To chaunt your Heroes to your Country's Lyre; / Who consecrate in your immortal Strain, / Brave Patriot Souls in righteous Battle slain; / Securely now the tuneful Task renew, / And noblest Themes in deathless Songs pursue' (a contemporary translation by Nicholas Rowe).

1

There can be no doubt that these poems are to be ascribed to the Bards; a race of men well known to have continued throughout many ages in Ireland and the north of Scotland. Every chief or great man had in his family a Bard or poet, whose office it was to record in verse, the illustrious actions of that family. By the succession of these Bards, such poems were handed down from race to race; some in manuscript, but more by oral tradition. And tradition, in a country so free of intermixture with foreigners, and among a people so strongly attached to the memory of their ancestors, has preserved many of them in a great measure incorrupted to this day.

They are not set to music, or sung. The versification in the original is simple; and to such as understand the language, very smooth and beautiful. Rhyme is seldom used: but the cadence, and the length of the line varied, so as to suit the sense. The translation is extremely literal. Even the arrangement of the words in the original has been imitated; to which must be imputed some inversions in the style, that otherwise would not have been chosen.

Of the poetical merit of these fragments nothing shall here be said. Let the public judge, and pronounce. It is believed, that, by a careful inquiry, many more remains of ancient genius, no less valuable than those now given to the world, might be found in the same country where these have been collected. In particular there is reason to hope that one work of considerable length, and which deserves to be styled an heroic poem, might be recovered and translated, if encouragement were given to such an undertaking. The subject is, an invasion of Ireland by Swarthan King of Lochlyn; which is the name of Denmark in the Erse language. Cuchulaid, the General or Chief of the Irish tribes, upon intelligence of the invasion, assembles his forces; councils are held; and battles fought. But after several unsuccessful engagements, the Irish are forced to submit. At length, Fingal King of Scotland, called in this poem, "The Desert of the hills," arrives with his ships to assist Cuchulaid. He expels the Danes from the country; and returns home victorious. This poem is held to be of greater antiquity than any of the rest that are preserved: And the author speaks of himself as present in the expedition of Fingal. The three last poems in the collection are fragments which the translator obtained of this Epic poem; and tho' very imperfect, they were judged not unworthy of being inserted. If the whole were recovered, it might serve to throw considerable light upon the Scottish and Irish antiquities.

FRAGMENT I.
SHILRIC, VINVELA.

VINVELA
My love is a son of the hill. He pursues the flying deer. His gray dogs are panting around him; his bow-string sounds in the wind. Whether by the fount of the rock, or by the stream of the mountain thou liest; when the rushes are nodding with the wind, and the mist is flying over thee, let me approach my love unperceived, and see him from the rock. Lovely I saw thee first by the aged oak of Branno; thou wert returning tall from the chace; the fairest among thy friends.

SHILRIC
What voice is that I hear? that voice like the summer-wind. — I sit not by the nodding rushes; I hear not the fount of the rock. Afar, Vinvela, afar I go to the wars of Fingal. My dogs attend me no more. No more I tread the hill. No more from on high I see thee, fair moving by the stream of the plain; bright as the bow of heaven; as the moon on the western wave.

VINVELA

Then thou art gone, O Shilric! and I am alone on the hill. The deer are seen on the brow; void of fear they graze along. No more they dread the wind; no more the rustling tree. The hunter is far removed; he is in the field of graves. Strangers! sons of the waves! spare my lovely Shilric.

SHILRIC

If fall I must in the field, raise high my grave, Vinvela. Grey stones, and heaped-up earth, shall mark me to future times. When the hunter shall sit by the mound, and produce his food at noon, "Some warrior rests here," he will say; and my fame shall live in his praise. Remember me, Vinvela, when low on earth I lie!

VINVELA

Yes!—I will remember thee—indeed my Shilric will fall. What shall I do, my love! when thou art gone for ever? Through these hills I will go at noon: I will go through the silent heath. There I will see the place of thy rest, returning from the chace. Indeed, my Shilric will fall; but I will remember him.

II.

I sit by the mossy fountain; on top of the hill of winds. One tree is rustling above me. Dark waves roll over the heath. The lake is troubled below. The deer descend from the hill. No hunter at a distance is seen; no whistling cow-herd is nigh. It is mid-day: but all is silent. Sad are my thoughts alone. Didst thou but appear, O my love, a wanderer on the heath! thy hair floating on the wind behind thee; thy bosom heaving on the sight; thine eyes full of tears for thy friends, whom the mist of the hill had concealed! Thee I would comfort, my love, and bring thee to thy father's house.

But is it she that there appears, like a beam of light on the heath? bright as the moon in autumn, as the sun in the summer-storm, comest thou lovely maid over rocks, over mountains to me?—She speaks: but how weak her voice! like the breeze in the reeds of the pool. Hark!

Returnest thou safe from the war? Where are thy friends, my love? I heard of thy death on the hill; I heard and mourned thee, Shilric!

Yes, my fair, I return; but I alone of my race. Thou shalt see them no more: their graves I raised on the plain. But why art thou on the desert hill? why on the heath, alone?

Alone I am, O Shilric! alone in the winter-house. With grief for thee I expired. Shilric, I am pale in the tomb.

She fleets, she sails away; as grey mist before the wind!—and, wilt thou not stay, my love? Stay and behold my tears? fair thou appearest, my love! fair thou wast, when alive!

By the mossy fountain I will sit; on the top of the hill of winds. When mid-day is silent around, converse, O my love, with me! come on the wings of the gale! on the blast of the mountain, come! Let me hear thy voice, as thou passest, when mid-day is silent around.

III.

Evening is grey on the hills. The north wind resounds through the woods. White clouds rise on the sky: the thin-wavering snow descends. The river howls afar, along its winding course. Sad, by a hollow rock, the grey-hair'd Carryl sat. Dry fern waves over his head; his seat is an aged birch. Clear to the roaring winds he lifts his voice of woe.

Tossed on the wavy ocean is He, the hope of the isles; Malcolm, the support of the poor; foe to the proud in arms! Why hast thou left us behind? why live we to mourn thy fate? We might have heard, with thee, the voice of the deep; have seen the oozy rock.

Sad on the sea-beat shore thy spouse looketh for thy return. The time of thy promise is come; the night is gathering around. But no white sail is on the sea; no voice but the blustering winds. Low is the soul of the war! Wet are the locks of youth! By the foot of some rock thou liest; washed by the waves as they come. Why, ye winds, did ye bear him on the desert rock? Why, ye waves, did ye roll over him?

But, Oh! what voice is that? Who rides on that meteor of fire! Green are his airy limbs. It is he! it is the ghost of Malcolm!—Rest, lovely soul, rest on the rock; and let me hear thy voice—He is gone, like a dream of the night. I see him through the trees. Daughter of Reynold! he is gone. Thy spouse shall return no more. No more shall his hounds come from the hill, forerunners of their master. No more from the distant rock shall his voice greet thine ear. Silent is he in the deep, unhappy daughter of Reynold!

I will sit by the stream of the plain. Ye rocks! hang over my head. Hear my voice, ye trees! as ye bend on the shaggy hill. My voice shall preserve the praise of him, the hope of the isles.

IV.
CONNAL, CRIMORA.

CRIMORA.

Who cometh from the hill, like a cloud tinged with the beam of the west? Whose voice is that, loud as the wind, but pleasant as the harp of Carryl? It is my love in the light of steel; but sad is his darkened brow. Live the mighty race of Fingal? or what disturbs my Connal?

CONNAL.

They live. I saw them return from the chace, like a stream of light. The sun was on their shields: Like a ridge of fire they descended the hill. Loud is the voice of the youth; the war, my love, is near. To-morrow the enormous Dargo comes to try the force of our race. The race of Fingal he defies; the race of battle and wounds.

CRIMORA.

Connal, I saw his sails like grey mist on the sable wave. They slowly came to land. Connal, many are the warriors of Dargo!

CONNAL.

Bring me thy father's shield; the iron shield of Rinval; that shield like the full moon when it is darkened in the sky.

CRIMORA.

That shield I bring, O Connal; but it did not defend my father. By the spear of Gauror he fell. Thou mayst fall, O Connal!

CONNAL.

Fall indeed I may: But raise my tomb, Crimora. Some stones, a mound of earth, shall keep my memory. Bend thy red eye over my tomb, and beat thy breast of sighs. Though fair thou art, my love, as the light; more pleasant than the gale of the hill; yet I will not stay. Raise my tomb, Crimora.

4

Then give me those arms of light; that sword, and that spear of steel. I shall meet Dargo with thee, and aid my lovely Connal. Farewell, ye rocks of Ardven! ye deer! and ye streams of the hill! — We shall return no more. Our tombs are distant far.

V.

Autumn is dark on the mountains; grey mist rests on the hills. The whirlwind is heard on the heath. Dark rolls the river thro' the narrow plain. A tree stands alone on the hill, and marks the grave of Connal. The leaves whirl round with the wind, and strew the grave of the dead. At times are seen here the ghosts of the deceased, when the musing hunter alone stalks slowly over the heath. Appear in thy armour of light, thou ghost of the mighty Connal! Shine, near thy tomb, Crimora! like a moon-beam from a cloud.

Who can reach the source of thy race, O Connal? and who recount thy Fathers? Thy family grew like an oak on the mountain, which meeteth the wind with its lofty head. But now it is torn from the earth. Who shall supply the place of Connal?

Here was the din of arms; and here the groans of the dying. Mournful are the wars of Fingal! O Connal! it was here thou didst fall. Thine arm was like a storm; thy sword, a beam of the sky; thy height, a rock on the plain; thine eyes, a furnace of fire. Louder than a storm was thy voice, when thou confoundedst the field. Warriors fell by thy sword, as the thistle by the staff of a boy.

Dargo the mighty came on, like a cloud of thunder. His brows were contracted and dark. His eyes like two caves in a rock. Bright rose their swords on each side; dire was the clang of their steel.

The daughter of Rinval was near; Crimora, bright in the armour of man; her hair loose behind, her bow in her hand. She followed the youth to the war, Connal her much-beloved. She drew the string on Dargo; but erring pierced her Connal. He falls like an oak on the plain; like a rock from the shaggy hill. What shall she do, hapless maid! — He bleeds; her Connal dies. All the night long she cries, and all the day, O Connal, my love, and my friend! With grief the sad mourner died.

Earth here incloseth the loveliest pair on the hill. The grass grows between the stones of their tomb; I sit in the mournful shade. The wind sighs through the grass; and their memory rushes on my mind. Undisturbed you now sleep together; in the tomb of the mountain you rest alone.

VI.

Son of the noble Fingal, Oscian, Prince of men! what tears run down the cheeks of age? what shades thy mighty soul?

Memory, son of Alpin, memory wounds the aged. Of former times are my thoughts; my thoughts are of the noble Fingal. The race of the king return into my mind, and wound me with remembrance.

One day, returned from the sport of the mountains, from pursuing the sons of the hill, we covered this heath with our youth. Fingal the mighty was here, and Oscur, my son, great in war. Fair on our sight from the sea, at once, a virgin came. Her breast was like the snow of one night. Her cheek like the bud of the rose. Mild was her blue rolling eye: but sorrow was big in her heart.

Fingal renowned in war! she cries, sons of the king, preserve me! Speak secure, replies the king, daughter of beauty, speak: our ear is open to all: our swords redress the injured. I fly from Ullin, she cries, from Ullin famous in war. I fly from the embrace of him who would debase my blood. Cremor, the friend of men, was my father; Cremor the Prince of Inverne.

Fingal's younger sons arose; Carryl expert in the bow; Fillan beloved of the fair; and Fergus first in the race. — Who from the farthest Lochlyn? who to the seas of Molochasquir? who dares hurt the maid whom the sons of Fingal guard? Daughter of beauty, rest secure; rest in peace, thou fairest of women.

Far in the blue distance of the deep, some spot appeared like the back of the ridge-wave. But soon the ship increased on our sight. The hand of Ullin drew her to land. The mountains trembled as he moved. The hills shook at his steps. Dire rattled his armour around him. Death and destruction were in his eyes. His stature like the oak of Morven. He moved in the lightning of steel.

Our warriors fell before him, like the field before the reapers. Fingal's three sons he bound. He plunged his sword into the fair-one's breast. She fell as a wreath of snow before the sun in spring. Her bosom heaved in death; her soul came forth in blood.

Oscur my son came down; the mighty in battle descended. His armour rattled as thunder; and the lightning of his eyes was terrible. There, was the clashing of swords; there, was the voice of steel. They struck and they thrust; they digged for death with their swords. But death was distant far, and delayed to come. The sun began to decline; and the cow-herd thought of home. Then Oscur's keen steel found the heart of Ullin. He fell like a mountain-oak covered over with glistering frost: He shone like a rock on the plain. — Here the daughter of beauty lieth; and here the bravest of men. Here one day ended the fair and the valiant. Here rest the pursuer and the pursued.

Son of Alpin, the woes of the aged are many: their tears are for the past. This raised my sorrow, warrior; memory awaked my grief. Oscur my son was brave, but Oscur is now no more. Thou hast heard of my grief, O son of Alpin; forgive the tears of the aged.

VII.[2]

Why openest thou afresh the spring of my grief, O son of Alpin, inquiring how Oscur fell? My eyes are blind with tears; but memory beams on my heart. How can I relate the mournful death of the head of the people! Prince of the warriors, Oscur, my son, shall I see thee no more!

He fell as the moon in a storm; as the sun from the midst of his course, when clouds rise from the waste of the waves, when the blackness of the storm inwraps the rocks of Ardanidder. I, like an ancient oak on Morven, I moulder alone in my place. The blast hath lopped my branches away; and I tremble at the wings of the north. Prince of the warriors, Oscur, my son! shall I see thee no more!

Dermid and Oscur were one: They reaped the battle together. Their friendship was strong as their steel; and death walked between them to the field. They came on the foe like two rocks falling from the brow of Ardven. Their swords were stained with the blood of the valiant: warriors fainted at their names. Who was a match for Oscur, but Dermid? and who for Dermid, but Oscur!

They killed mighty Dargo in the field; Dargo before invincible. His daughter was fair as the morn; mild as the beam of night. Her eyes, like two stars in a shower: her breath, the gale of spring: her breasts, as the new-fallen snow floating on the moving heath. The warriors saw her, and loved; their souls were fixed on the maid. Each loved her, as his fame; each must possess her or die. But her soul was fixed on Oscur; my son was the youth of her love. She forgot the blood of her father; and loved the hand that slew him.

Son of Oscian, said Dermid, I love; O Oscur, I love this maid. But her soul cleaveth unto thee; and nothing can heal Dermid. Here, pierce this bosom, Oscur; relieve me,

2 This fragment was the one originally shown by Macpherson to John Home, famous as the
   playwright of *Douglas* (1756), in 1759: Home strongly encouraged publishing this collection.

my friend, with thy sword.

My sword, son of Morny, shall never be stained with the blood of Dermid.

Who then is worthy to slay me, O Oscur son of Oscian? Let not my life pass away unknown. Let none but Oscur slay me. Send me with honour to the grave, and let my death be renowned.

Dermid, make use of thy sword; son of Morny, wield thy steel. Would that I fell with thee! that my death came from the hand of Diarmid!

They fought by the brook of the mountain, by the streams of Branno. Blood tinged the silvery stream, and crudled round the mossy stones. Dermid the graceful fell; fell, and smiled in death.

And fallest thou, son of Morny; fallest thou by Oscur's hand! Dermid invincible in war, thus do I see thee fall! — He went, and returned to the maid whom he loved; returned, but she perceived his grief.

Why that gloom, son of Oscur? what shades thy mighty soul?

Though once renowned for the bow, O maid, I have lost my fame. Fixed on a tree by the brook of the hill, is the shield of Gormur the brave, whom in battle I slew. I have wasted the day in vain, nor could my arrow pierce it.

Let me try, son of Oscian, the skill of Dargo's daughter. My hands were taught the bow: my father delighted in my skill.

She went. He stood behind the shield. Her arrow flew and pierced his breast.[3]

Blessed be that hand of snow; and blessed be thy bow of yew! I fall resolved on death: and who but the daughter of Dargo was worthy to slay me? Lay me in the earth, my fair-one; lay me by the side of Dermid.

Oscur! I have the blood, the soul of the mighty Dargo. Well pleased I can meet death. My sorrow I can end thus. — She pierced her white bosom with steel. She fell; she trembled; and died.

By the brook of the hill their graves are laid; a birch's unequal shade covers their tomb. Often on their green earthen tombs the branchy sons of the mountain feed, when mid-day is all in flames, and silence is over all the hills.

VIII.

By the side of a rock on the hill, beneath the aged trees, old Oscian sat on the moss; the last of the race of Fingal. Sightless are his aged eyes; his beard is waving in the wind. Dull through the leafless trees he heard the voice of the north. Sorrow revived in his soul: he began and lamented the dead.

How hast thou fallen like an oak, with all thy branches round thee! Where is Fingal the King? where is Oscur my son? where are all my race? Alas! in the earth they lie. I feel their tombs with my hands. I hear the river below murmuring hoarsely over the stones. What dost thou, O river, to me? Thou bringest back the memory of the past.

The race of Fingal stood on thy banks, like a wood in a fertile soil. Keen were their spears of steel. Hardy was he who dared to encounter their rage. Fillan the great was there. Thou Oscur wert there, my son! Fingal himself was there, strong in the grey locks of years. Full rose his sinewy limbs; and wide his shoulders spread. The unhappy met with his arm, when the pride of his wrath arose.

---

3 Nothing was held by the ancient Highlanders more essential to their glory, than to die by the hand of some person worthy or renowned. This was the occasion of Oscur's contriving to be slain by his mistress, now that he was weary of life. In those early times, suicide was utterly unknown among that people, and no traces of it are found in the old poetry. Whence the translator suspects the account that follows of the daughter of Dargo killing herself, to be the interpolation of some later Bard. [Macpherson's note]

The son of Morny came; Gaul, the tallest of men. He stood on the hill like an oak; his voice was like the streams of the hill. Why reigneth alone, he cries, the son of the mighty Corval? Fingal is not strong to save: he is no support for the people. I am strong as a storm in the ocean; as a whirlwind on the hill. Yield, son of Corval; Fingal, yield to me. He came like a rock from the hill, resounding in his arms.

Oscur stood forth to meet him; my son would meet the foe. But Fingal came in his strength, and smiled at the vaunter's boast. They threw their arms round each other; they struggled on the plain. The earth is ploughed with their heels. Their bones crack as the boat on the ocean, when it leaps from wave to wave. Long did they toil; with night, they fell on the sounding plain; as two oaks, with their branches mingled, fall crashing from the hill. The tall son of Morny is bound; the aged overcame.

Fair with her locks of gold, her smooth neck, and her breasts of snow; fair, as the spirits of the hill when at silent noon they glide along the heath; fair, as the rain-bow of heaven; came Minvane the maid. Fingal! she softly saith, loose me my brother Gaul. Loose me the hope of my race, the terror of all but Fingal. Can I, replies the King, can I deny the lovely daughter of the hill? Take thy brother, O Minvane, thou fairer than snow of the north!

Such, Fingal! were thy words; but thy words I hear no more. Sightless I sit by thy tomb. I hear the wind in the wood; but no more I hear my friends. The cry of the hunter is over. The voice of war is ceased.

* * * * *

XIV.[4]

Cuchulaid sat by the wall; by the tree of the rustling leaf.[5] His spear leaned against the mossy rock. His shield lay by him on the grass. Whilst he thought on the mighty Carbre whom he slew in battle, the scout of the ocean came, Moran the son of Fithil.

Rise, Cuchulaid, rise! I see the ships of Garve. Many are the foe, Cuchulaid; many the sons of Lochlyn.

Moran! thou ever tremblest; thy fears increase the foe. They are the ships of the Desert of hills arrived to assist Cuchulaid.

I saw their chief, says Moran, tall as a rock of ice. His spear is like that fir; his shield like the rising moon. He sat upon a rock on the shore, as a grey cloud upon the hill. Many, mighty man! I said, are our heroes; Garve, well art thou named,[6] many are the sons of our king.

He answered like a wave on the rock; who is like me here? The valiant live not with me; they go to the earth from my hand. The king of the Desert of hills alone can fight with Garve. Once we wrestled on the hill. Our heels overturned the wood. Rocks fell from their place, and rivulets changed their course. Three days we strove together; heroes stood at a distance, and feared. On the fourth, the King saith that I fell; but Garve saith, he stood. Let Cuchulaid yield to him that is strong as a storm.

No. I will never yield to man. Cuchulaid will conquer or die. Go, Moran, take my spear; strike the shield of Caithbait with hangs before the gate. It never rings in peace. My heroes shall hear on the hill. —

---

4   This is the opening of the epic poem mentioned in the preface. The two following fragments [not given here] are parts of some episodes of the same work. [Macpherson's note. These three fragments, with an advertisement for the forthcoming publication of this epic, close the 1760 volume.]

5   The aspen or poplar tree. [Macpherson's note]

6   Garve signifies a man of great size. [Macpherson's note]

A

CRITICAL DISSERTATION

ON THE

POEMS OF OSSIAN,

THE

SON OF FINGAL.

LONDON:
printed for T. BECKET and P. A. DE HONDT, at *Tully's–*
Head, in the *Strand*. MDCCLXIII.

Advertisement.

The Substance of the following Dissertation was delivered by the Author in the Course of his Lectures on Rhetorick and Belles-Lettres, in the University of Edinburgh. At the Desire of several of his Hearers, he has enlarged, and given it to the Publick, in its present Form.[1]

In this Dissertation, it is proposed, to make some Observations on the ancient Poetry of Nations, particularly the Runic and the Celtic;[2] *to point out those characters of Antiquity, which the Works of Ossian bear; to give an Idea of the Spirit and Strain of his Poetry; and after applying the Rules of Criticism to Fingal, as an Epic Poem, to examine the Merit of Ossian's Compositions in general, with Regard to Description, Imagery, and Sentiment.*

AMONG the monuments remaining of the ancient state of nations, few are more valuable than their poems or songs. History, when it treats of remote and dark ages, is seldom very instructive. The beginnings of society, in every country, are involved in fabulous confusion; and though they were not, they would furnish few events worth recording. But, in every period of society, human manners are a curious spectacle; and the most natural pictures of ancient manners are exhibited in the ancient poems of nations. These present to us, what is much more valuable than the history of such transactions as a rude age can afford, the history of human imagination and passion. They make us acquainted with the notions and feelings of our fellow-creatures in the most artless ages; discovering what objects they admired, and what pleasures they pursued, before those refinements of society had taken place, which enlarge indeed, and diversify the transactions, but disguise the manners of mankind.

Besides this merit, which ancient poems have with philosophical observers of human nature, they have another with persons of taste. They promise some of the highest beauties of poetical writing. Irregular and unpolished we may expect the productions

---

1   The author is Hugh Blair (1718–1800), minister and professor of Rhetoric and Belles-Lettres at Edinburgh. The *Dissertation* appeared after the publication of the coherent epic *Fingal* in 1761–2, promised in the Preface to *Fragments of Ancient Poetry* and advertised at the end of that volume: I have omitted the sections which deal specifically and in depth with *Fingal*. The 'present Form' of the *Dissertation* was the same quarto format as *Fingal* and indeed the later *Works of Ossian* (1765) which included a second epic, *Temora*. As books were usually bought unbound, this allowed purchasers to have the criticism bound in one volume with the poems, and most copies of the *Dissertation* in libraries are found like this.

2   By 'Runic' Blair refers to old Germanic and Scandinavian literatures. I have omitted the sections which develop the comparison between these and Ossian.

of uncultivated ages to be; but abounding, at the same time, with that enthusiasm, that vehemence and fire, which are the soul of poetry. For many circumstances of those times which we call barbarous, are favourable to the poetical spirit. That state, in which human nature shoots wild and free, though unfit for other improvements, certainly encourages the high exertions of fancy and passion.

In the infancy of societies, men live scattered and dispersed, in the midst of solitary rural scenes, where the beauties of nature are their chief entertainment. They meet with many objects, to them new and strange; their wonder and surprize are frequently excited; and by the sudden changes of fortune occurring in their unsettled state of life, their passions are raised to the utmost. Their passions have nothing to restrain them: their imagination has nothing to check it. They display themselves to one another without disguise: and converse and act in the uncovered simplicity of nature. As their feelings are strong, so their language, of itself, assumes a poetical turn. Prone to exaggerate, they describe every thing in the strongest colours; which of course renders their speech picturesque and figurative. Figurative language owes its rise chiefly to two causes; to the want of proper names for objects, and to the influence of imagination and passion over the form of expression. Both these causes concur in the infancy of society. Figures are commonly considered as artificial modes of speech, devised by orators and poets, after the world had advanced to a refined state. The contrary of this is the truth. Men never have used so many figures of style, as in those rude ages when, besides the power of a warm imagination to suggest lively images, the want of proper and precise terms for the ideas they would express, obliged them to have recourse to circumlocution, metaphor, comparison, and all those substituted forms of expression, which give a poetical air to language. An American chief, at this day, harangues at the head of his tribe, in a more bold metaphorical style, than a modern European would adventure to use in an Epic poem.

In the progress of society, the genius and manners of men undergo a change more favourable to accuracy than to sprightliness and sublimity. As the world advances, the understanding gains ground upon the imagination; the understanding is more exercised; the imagination, less. Fewer objects occur that are new or surprizing. Men apply themselves to trace the causes of things; they correct and refine one another; they subdue or disguise their passions; they form their exterior manners upon one uniform standard of politeness and civility. Human nature is pruned according to method and rule. Language advances from sterility to copiousness, and at the same time, from fervour and enthusiasm, to correctness and precision. Style becomes more chaste; but less animated. The progress of the world in this respect resembles the progress of age in man. The powers of imagination are most vigorous and predominant in youth; those of the understanding ripen more slowly, and often attain not their maturity, till the imagination begin to flag. Hence, poetry, which is the child of imagination, is frequently most glowing and animated in the first ages of society. As the ideas of our youth are remembered with a peculiar pleasure on account of their liveliness and vivacity; so the most ancient poems have often proved the greatest favourites of nations.

Poetry has been said to be more ancient than prose: and however paradoxical such an assertion may seem, yet, in a qualified sense, it is true. Men certainly never conversed with one another in regular numbers; but even their ordinary language would, in ancient times, for the reasons before assigned, approach to a poetical style; and the first compositions transmitted to posterity, beyond doubt, were, in a literal sense, poems; that is, compositions in which imagination had the chief hand, formed into some kind of numbers, and pronounced with a musical modulation or tone. Music or song has been found coæval with society among the most barbarous nations. The only subjects which could prompt men, in their first rude state, to utter their thoughts in compositions of any length, were such as naturally assumed the tone of poetry; praises of their gods, or of their ancestors; commemorations of their own warlike exploits; or lamentations over their misfortunes. And before writing was invented, no other compositions, except songs and poems, could take such hold of the imagination and memory, as to be preserved by oral tradition, and handed down from one race to another.

Hence we may expect to find poems among the antiquities of all nations. It is probable too, that an extensive search would discover a certain degree of resemblance among all the most ancient poetical productions, from whatever country they have proceeded. In a similar state of manners, similar objects and passions operating upon the imaginations of men, will stamp their productions with the same general character. Some diversity will, no doubt, be occasioned by climate and genius. But mankind never bear such resembling features, as they do in the beginnings of society. Its subsequent revolutions give rise to the principal distinctions among nations; and divert, into channels widely separated, that current of human genius and manners, which descends originally from one spring. What we have been long accustomed to call the oriental vein of poetry, because some of the earliest poetical productions have come to us from the East, is probably no more oriental than occidental; it is characteristical of an age rather than a country; and belongs, in some measure, to all nations at a certain period. Of this the works of Ossian seem to furnish a remarkable proof.

*****

Now when we consider a college or order of men [the Bards], who, cultivating poetry throughout a long series of ages, had their imaginations continually employed on the ideas of heroism; who had all the poems and panegyricks, which were composed by their predecessors, handed down to them with care; who rivalled and endeavoured to outstrip those who had gone before them, each in the celebration of his particular hero; is it not natural to think, that at length the character of a hero would appear in their songs with the highest lustre, and be adorned with qualities truly noble? Some of the qualities indeed which distinguish a Fingal, moderation, humanity, and clemency, would not probably be the first ideas of heroism occurring to a barbarous people: But no sooner had such ideas begun to dawn on the minds of poets, than, as the human mind easily opens to the native representations of human perfection, they would be seized and embraced; they would enter into their panegyricks; they would afford materials for succeeding bards to work upon, and improve; they would contribute not a little to exalt the publick manners. For such songs as these, familiar to the Celtic warriors from their childhood, and throughout their whole life, both in war and in peace, their principal entertainment, must have had a very considerable influence in propagating among them real manners nearly approaching to the poetical; and in forming even such a hero as Fingal. Especially when we consider that among their limited objects of ambition, among the few advantages which in a savage state, man could obtain over man, the chief was Fame, and that Immortality which they expected to receive from their virtues and exploits, in the songs of the bards.

*****

The compositions of Ossian are so strongly marked with characters of antiquity, that although there were no external proof to support that antiquity, hardly any reader of judgment and taste, could hesitate in referring them to a very remote æra. There are four great stages through which men successively pass in the progress of society.

The first and earliest is the life of hunters; pasturage succeeds to this, as the ideas of property begin to take root; next agriculture; and lastly, commerce.[3] Throughout Ossian's poems, we plainly find ourselves in the first of these periods of society; during which, hunting was the chief employment of men, and their principal method of their procuring subsistence. Pasturage was not indeed wholly unknown; for we hear of dividing the herd in the case of divorce; but the allusions to herds and to cattle are not many; and of agriculture, we find no traces. No cities appear to have been built in the territories of Fingal. No arts are mentioned except that of navigation and working in iron.[4] Every thing presents to us the most simple and unimproved manners. At their feasts, the heroes prepared their own repast; they sat round the light of the burning oak; the winds lifted their locks, and whistled through their open halls. Whatever was beyond the necessities of life was known to them only as the spoil of the Roman province; "the gold of the stranger; the lights of the stranger; the steeds of the stranger, the children of the rein."

*****

The manner of composition bears all the marks of the greatest antiquity. No artful transitions; nor full and extended connection of parts; such as we find among the poets of later times, when order and regularity of composition were more studied and known; but a style always rapid and vehement; in narration concise even to abruptness, and leaving several circumstances to be supplied by the reader's imagination. The language has all that figurative cast, which, as I before shewed, partly a glowing and undisciplined imagination, partly the sterility of language and the want of proper terms, have always introduced into the early speech of nations; and in several respects, it carries a remarkable resemblance to the style of the Old Testament. It deserves particular notice, that as one of the most genuine and decisive characters of antiquity, that very few general terms or abstract ideas, are to be met with in the whole collection of Ossian's works. The ideas of men, at first, were all particular. They had not words to express general conceptions. These were the consequence of more profound reflection, and longer acquaintance with the arts of thought and of speech.[5] Ossian, accordingly, almost never expresses himself in the abstract. His ideas extended little farther than to the objects he saw around him. A public, a community, the universe, were conceptions beyond his sphere. Even a mountain, a sea, or a lake, which he has occasion to mention, though only in a simile, are for the most part particularized; it is the hill of Cromla, the storm of the sea of Malmor, or the reeds of the lake of Lego. A mode of expression, which whilst it is characteristical of ancient ages, is at the same time highly favourable to descriptive poetry. For the same reasons, personification is a poetical figure not very common with Ossian. Inanimate objects, such as winds, trees, flowers, he sometimes personifies with great beauty. But the personifications which are so familiar to later poets of Fame, Time, Terror, Virtue, and the rest of that class, were unknown to our Celtic bard. These were modes of conception too abstract for his age.

3   This 'four-stages' model of history is an influential one in Scottish thinking of the period: it appears, for example, in Book V of Adam Smith's *Wealth of Nations* (1776) and received fuller treatment in Smith's *Lectures on Jurisprudence* (delivered in the University of Glasgow in 1763–4).

4   Blair adds a footnote here giving evidence for these claims.

5   That human knowledge derives in the first place from our encounters with particular things, from which the mind by a secondary operation constructs general or abstract ideas, is fundamental to the empirical philosophy underpinning much enlightenment thought, especially in its crucial formulation by John Locke in *An Essay Concerning Human Understanding* (1690): see especially Book III, 'Of Words', chapter iii, 'Of General Terms'.

*****

Assuming it, then, as we well may, for certain, that the poems now under consideration, are genuine venerable monuments of very remote antiquity; I proceed to make some remarks upon their general spirit and strain. The two great characteristics of Ossian's poetry are, tenderness and sublimity. It breathes nothing of the gay and chearful kind; an air of solemnity and seriousness is diffused over the whole. Ossian is perhaps the only poet who never relaxes, or lets himself down into the light and amusing strain; which I readily admit to be no small disadvantage to him, with the bulk of readers. He moves perpetually in the high region of the grand and the pathetick. One key note is struck at the beginning, and supported to the end; nor is any ornament introduced, but what is perfectly concordant with the general tone or melody. The events recorded, are all serious and grave; the scenery throughout, wild and romantic. The extended heath by the sea shore; the mountain shaded with mist; the torrent rushing through a solitary valley; the scattered oaks, and the tombs of warriors overgrown with moss; all produce a solemn attention in the mind, and prepare it for great and extraordinary events. We find not in Ossian, an imagination that sports itself, and dresses out gay trifles to please the fancy. His poetry, more perhaps than that of any other writer, deserves to be styled, *The Poetry of the Heart*. It is a heart penetrated with noble sentiments, and with sublime and tender passions; a heart that glows, and kindles the fancy; a heart that is full, and pours itself forth. Ossian did not write, like modern poets, to please readers and critics. He sung from the love of poetry and song. His delight was to think of the heroes among whom he had flourished; to recall the affecting incidents of his life; to dwell upon his past wars and loves and friendships; till, as he expresses it himself, "the light of his soul arose; the days of other years rose before him;" and under this true poetic inspiration, giving vent to his genius, no wonder we should often hear, and acknowledge in his strains, the powerful and ever-pleasing voice of nature.

— Arte, natura potentior omni. —

Est Deus in nobis, agitante calescimus illo. [Ovid, *Fasti*, 6.][6]

It is necessary here to observe, that the beauties of Ossian's writings cannot be felt by those who have given them only a single or hasty perusal. His manner is so different from that of the poets, to whom we are most accustomed; his style is so concise, and so much crowded with imagery; the mind is kept at such a stretch in accompanying the author; that an ordinary reader is at first apt to be dazzled and fatigued, rather than pleased. His poems require to be taken up at intervals, and to be frequently reviewed; and then it is impossible but his beauties must open to every reader who is capable of sensibility. Those who have the highest degree of it, will relish them the most.

As Homer is of all the great poets, the one whose manner, and whose times come the nearest to Ossian's, we are naturally led to run a parallel in some instances between the Greek and the Celtic bard. For though Homer lived more than a thousand years before Ossian, it is not from the age of the world, but from the state of society, that we are to judge of resembling times. The Greek has, in several points, a manifest superiority. He introduces a greater variety of incidents; he possesses a larger compass of ideas; has

---

6   The last line reads, 'There is a god within us. It is when he stirs us that our bosom warms'; and the next line continues 'it is his impulse that sows the seeds of inspiration' (ll.5–6) in J.G. Frazer's 1931 translation of the unfinished poetic calendar of the Roman year by Ovid (43 B.C.–17/18 A.D.). The first line here adapts l.302–3 of the tenth satire of Juvenal (c.60–c.130 A.D.): 'quid enim puero conferre potest plus / custode et cura natura potentior omni' ('For Nature is a better Guardian far, / Than Sawcy Pedants, or dull Tutors are' [Dryden's translation ll.466–7]).

more diversity in his characters; and a much deeper knowledge of human nature. It was not to be expected, that in any of these particulars, Ossian could equal Homer. For Homer lived in a country where society was much further advanced; he had beheld

many more objects; cities built and flourishing; laws instituted; order, discipline, and arts begun. His field of observation was larger and more splendid; his knowledge, of course, more extensive; his mind also, it shall be granted, more penetrating. But if Ossian's ideas and objects be less diversified than those of Homer, they are all, however, of the kind fittest for poetry: The bravery and generosity of heroes, the tenderness of lovers, the attachment of friends, parents, and children. In a rude age and country, though the events that happen be few, the undissipated mind broods over them more; they strike the imagination, and fire the passions in a higher degree; and of consequence become happier materials to a poetical genius, than the same events when scattered through the wide circle of more varied action, and cultivated life.

Homer is more cheerful and sprightly than Ossian. You discern in him all the Greek vivacity; whereas Ossian uniformly maintains the gravity and solemnity of a Celtic hero. This too is in a great measure to be accounted for from the different situations in which they lived, partly personal, and partly national. Ossian had survived all his friends,[7] and was disposed to melancholy by the incidents of his life. But besides this, chearfulness is one of the many blessings which we owe to formed society. The solitary wild state is always a serious one. Bating the sudden and violent bursts of mirth, which sometimes break forth at their dances and feasts; the savage American tribes have been noted by all travellers for their gravity and taciturnity. Somewhat of this taciturnity may be also remarked in Ossian. On all occasions he is frugal of his words; and never gives you more of an image or description, than is just sufficient to place it before you in one clear point of view. . . .

---

7   See *Fragments* VI–VIII.

POEMS,

CHIEFLY IN THE

SCOTTISH DIALECT,

BY

ROBERT BURNS.

THE Simple Bard, unbroke by rules of Art,
He pours his wild effusions of the heart:
And if inspir'd, 'tis Nature's pow'rs inspire;
Her's all the melting thrill, and her's the kindling fire.
                                        ANONYMOUS

KILMARNOCK:
PRINTED BY JOHN WILSON.
MDCCLXXXVI.[1]

PREFACE.

THE following trifles are not the production of a Poet, who, with all the advantages of learned art, and perhaps amid the elegancies and idlenesses of upper life, looks for a rural theme, with an eye to Theocrites or Virgil.[2] To the Author of this, these and other celebrated names their countrymen are, in their original languages, 'A fountain shut up, and a book sealed.' Unacquainted with the necessary requisites for commencing Poet by rule, he sings the sentiments and manners, he felt and saw in himself and his rustic compeers around him, in his and their native language. Though a Rhymer from his earliest years, at least from the earliest impulses of the softer passions, it was not till very lately, that the applause, perhaps the partiality, of Friendship, wakened his vanity so far as to make him think any thing of his was worth showing; and none of the following works were ever composed with a view to the press. To amuse himself with the little creations of his own fancy, amid the toil and fatigues of a laborious life; to transcribe the various feelings, the loves, the griefs, the hopes, the fears, in his own breast; to find some kind of counterpoise to the struggles of a world, always an alien scene, a task uncouth to the poetical mind; these were his motives for courting the Muses, and in these he found Poetry to be it's own reward.

Now that he appears in the public character of an Author, he does it with fear and trembling. So dear is fame to the rhyming tribe, that even he, an obscure, nameless Bard, shrinks aghast, at the thought of being branded as 'An impertinent blockhead, obtruding his nonsense on the world; and because he can make a shift to jingle a few doggerel, Scotch rhymes together, looks upon himself as a Poet of no small consequence forsooth.'

It is an observation of the celebrated Poet,[3] whose divine Elegies do honor to our

---

1   This volume, Burns's first, is usually referred to as the 'Kilmarnock edition': later, enlarged editions of the *Poems* were published in Edinburgh. The epigraph is Burns's own.

2   Virgil: Publius Vergilius Maro (70–19 B.C.), whose poems describing the routines of rural life, the *Georgics*, were an important model and source of legitimacy for descriptive poetry in the eighteenth century. Theocritus (c.300–c.260 B.C.), Greek pastoral poet.

3   Shenstone [Burns's note. William Shenstone (1714–63), nature-poet and essayist.]

language, our nation, and our species, that 'Humility has depressed many a genius to a hermit, but never raised one to fame.' If any Critic catches at the word *genius*, the Author tells him, once for all, that he certainly looks upon himself as possest of some poetic abilities, otherwise his publishing in the manner he has done, would be a manoeuvre below the worst character, which, he hopes, his worst enemy will never give him: but to the genius of a Ramsay, or the glorious dawnings of the poor, unfortunate Ferguson,[4] he, with equal unaffected sincerity, declares, that, even in his highest pulse of vanity, he has not the most distant pretentions. These two justly admired Scotch Poets he has often had in his eye in the following pieces; but rather with a view to kindle at their flame, than for servile imitation.

To his Subscribers, the Author returns his most sincere thanks.[5] Not the mercenary bow over a counter, but the heart-throbbing gratitude of the Bard, conscious how much he is indebted to Benevolence and Friendship, for gratifying him, if he deserves it, in that dearest wish of every poetic bosom—to be distinguished. He begs his readers, particularly the Learned and Polite, who may honor him with a perusal, that they will make every allowance for Education and Circumstances of Life: but, if after a fair, candid, and impartial criticism, he shall stand convicted of Dulness and Nonsense, let him be done by, as he would in that case do by others—let him be condemned, without mercy, to contempt and oblivion.

---

4   Allan Ramsay (1684–1758), the most successful of the post-Union revivalists of poetry in Scots; Robert Fergusson (1750–74), vivid lyricist of the urban (Edinburgh) scene who died in poverty. Burns arranged and paid for a stone to mark Fergusson's grave on his first visit to Edinburgh in 1786–7.
5   Publication by Subscription involved getting potential readers to promise in advance to purchase a copy once it appeared, reducing the financial risk to both publisher and author. In return, a subscriber's name would appear in a list in the front of the volume.

ADDRESS TO THE DEIL.

O Prince, O chief of many throned pow'rs,
That led th' embattl'd Seraphim to war –
MILTON[1]

O Thou, whatever title suit thee!
Auld Hornie, Satan, Nick, or Clootie,
Wha in yon cavern grim and sootie   who
        Clos'd under hatches,
Spairges about the brunstane cootie,   5   splashes; brimstone dish
        To scaud poor wretches!   scald

Hear me, *auld Hangie*, for a wee,
An' let poor *damned bodies* bee;
I'm sure sma' pleasure it can gie,
        Ev'n to a *deil*,   10
To skelp an' scaud poor dogs like me,   slap and scald
        An' hear us squeel!

Great is thy pow'r, an' great thy fame;
Far ken'd, an' noted is thy name;
An' tho' yon *lowan heugh*'s thy hame,   15   that blazing pit
        Thou travels far;
An' faith! thou's neither lag nor lame,
        Nor blate nor scaur.   bashful; timid

Whyles, ranging like a roaran lion,
For prey, a' holes an' corners tryin;   20
Whyles, on the strong-wing'd Tempest flyin,
        Tirlan the *kirks*;   shaking
Whyles, in the human bosom pryin,
        Unseen thou lurks.

I've heard my rev'rend *Graunie* say,   25
In lanely glens ye like to stray;
Or where auld, ruin'd castles, gray,
        Nod to the moon,
Ye fright the nightly wand'rer's way,
        Wi' eldritch croon.   30   uncanny

When twilight did my *Graunie* summon,
To say her pray'rs, douse, honest woman!   sedate and kindly
Aft 'yont the dyke she's heard you bumman,   often beyond; humming
        Wi' eerie drone;
Or, rustling, thro' the boortries coman,   35   elder-hedges
        Wi' heavy groan.

---

1   Beelzebub's address to Satan in Book I, ll.128–9 of *Paradise Lost* (1667).

Ae dreary, windy, winter night,
The stars shot down wi' sklentan light,   *slanting*
Wi' you, *mysel*, I gat a fright
          Ayont the lough;   40   *beyond*
Ye, like a *rash-buss*, stood in sight,   *clump of rushes*
          Wi' waving sugh: *wind*

The cudgel in my nieve did shake,   *fist*
Each bristl'd hair stood like a stake,
When wi' an eldritch, stoor, *quaick, quaick*,   45   *tumultuous*
          Amang the springs,
Awa ye squatter'd like a *drake*,
          On whistling wings.

Let *Warlocks* grim, an' wither'd *Hags*,
Tell, how wi' you on ragweed nags,   50
They skim the muirs an' dizzy crags,
          Wi' wicked speed;
And in kirk-yards renew their leagues,
          Owre howcket dead.   *dug-up*

Thence, countra wives, wi' toil an' pain,   55
May plunge an' plunge the *kirn* in vain;   *churn*
For Oh! the yellow treasure 's taen   *taken*
          By witching skill;
An' dawtet, twal-pint *Hawkie* 's gane[2]   *treasured; twelve*
          As yell 's the Bill.   60   *dry as the bull*

Thence, mystic knots mak great abuse,
On *Young-Guidmen*, fond, keen an' croose;   *husbands; cocksure*
When the best *wark-lume* i' the house,   *tool (or penis) in*
          By cantraip wit,   *magic*
Is instant made no worth a louse,   65
          Just at the bit.   *crucial moment*

When thowes dissolve the snawy hoord,   *thaws; hoard*
An' float the jinglan icy boord,
Then, *Water-kelpies* haunt the foord,
          By your direction,   70
An' nighted Trav'llers are allur'd
          To their destruction.

An' aft your moss-traversing *Spunkies*   *often; sparks*
Decoy the wight that late an' drunk is: *fellow*
The bleezan, curst, mischievous monkies   75
          Delude his eyes,
Till in some miry slough he sunk is,
          Ne'er mair to rise.

---

2   'Hawkie' is a traditional name for a cow.

When MASONS' mystic *word* an' *grip*,
In storms an' tempests raise you up,   80
Some cock or cat, your rage maun stop,   *must*
        Or, strange to tell!
The *youngest Brother* ye wad whip
        Aff straught to *H–ll.*

Lang syne in EDEN'S bonie yard,   85   *long since*
When youthfu' lovers first were pair'd,
An' all the Soul of Love they shar'd,
        The raptur'd hour,
Sweet on the fragrant, flow'ry swaird,
        In shady bow'r.   90

Then you, ye auld, snick-drawing dog!   *crafty*
Ye cam to Paradise incog,   *incognito*
An' play'd on man a cursed brogue,   *trick*
        (Black be your fa'!)   *fall*
An' gied the infant warld a shog,   95   *jolt*
        'Maist ruin'd a'.   *Almost*

D'ye mind that day, when in a bizz,   *flurry*
Wi' reeket duds, an' reestet gizz,   *smoky clothes; scorched wig*
Ye did present your smoutie phiz   *smutty face*
        'Mang better folk,   100   *among*
An' sklented on the *man of Uzz*[3]   *threw*
        Your spitefu' joke?

An' how ye gat him i' your thrall,
An' brak him out o' house an' hal',
While scabs an' botches did him gall,   105   *tumours*
        Wi' bitter claw,
An' lows'd his ill-tongu'd, wicked *Scawl*   *let loose; scold (i.e. wife)*
        Was worst ava?   *of all*

But a' your doings to rehears,
Your wily snares an' fechtin fierce,   110   *fighting*
Sin' that day MICHAEL did you pierce,[4]
        Down to this time,
Wad ding a *Lallan* tongue, or *Erse,*[5]
        In prose or Rhyme.

---

3   The Man of Uz is Job, 'perfect and upright', and very rich: the Book of Job begins when God puts everything of Job's in Satan's power to prove that His servant does not only obey Him because he is rewarded for it. Satan proceeds to visit every kind of devastation on Job's household, family, and body.

4   Vide Milton, Book 6th. [Burns's note. Satan 'first knew pain' when the Archangel Michael cuts him with a sword during the War in Heaven in *Paradise Lost* Book VI ll.325–8].

5   I.e. would defeat both Scots and Gaelic to express.

An' now, auld *Cloots*, I ken ye're thinkan,   115
A certain *Bardie*'s rantin, drinkin,
Some luckless hour will send him linkan,   tripping
        To your black pit;
But faith! he'll turn a corner jinkan,   dodging
        An' cheat you yet.   120

But fare-you-weel, auld *Nickie-ben*!
O wad ye tak a thought an' men'!   mend (your ways)
Ye aiblins might—I dinna ken—   perhaps; don't
        Still hae a *stake*—
I'm wae to think upo' yon den,   125   woe; upon that
        Ev'n for your sake!

THE VISION.
DUAN FIRST.[1]

THE sun had clos'd the *winter-day*,
The Curlers quat their roaring play,
And hunger'd Maukin taen her way,   a hare; taken
        To kail-yards green,   cabbage-patches
While faithless snaws ilk step betray   5   each
        Whare she has been.

The thresher's weary *flingin-tree*,   flail
The lee-lang day had tir'd me;
And when the Day had clos'd his e'e,   eye
        Far i' the West,   10
Ben i' the *Spence*, right pensivelie,   through in; parlour
        I gaed to rest.   went

There, lanely, by the ingle-cheek,   fireplace
I sat and ey'd the spewing reek,   smoke
That fill'd, wi' hoast-provoking smeek,   15   cough-
        The auld, clay biggin;   building
And heard the restless rattons squeak   rats
        About the riggin.   roof

All in this mottie, misty clime,   dusty
I backward mus'd on wasted time,   20
How I had spent my *youthfu' prime*,
        An' done nae-thing,
But stringing blethers up in rhyme   nonsense
        For fools to sing.

Had I to guid advice but harket,   25
I might, by this, hae led a market,
Or strutted in a Bank and clarket
        My *Cash-Account*;
While here, half-mad, half-fed, half-sarket,   half-clothed (shirted)
        Is a' th' amount.   30

I started, mutt'ring blockhead! coof!   fool
And heav'd on high my waukit loof,   calloused palm
To swear by a' yon starry roof,   that
        Or some rash aith,
That I, henceforth, wad be *rhyme-proof*   35
        Till my last breath—

When click! the *string* the *snick* did draw;
And jee! the door gaed to the wa';   went; wall

---

1   Duan, a term of Ossian's for the different divisions of a digressive Poem. See his Cath-Loda, Vol. 2 of M'Pherson's translation. [Burns's note. 'Cath-Loda' appears in the 1765 *Works of Ossian*.]

And by my ingle-lowe I saw,   fireplace-glow
     Now bleezin bright, 40 blazing
A tight, outlandish *Hizzie*, braw,   young woman; fine
     Come full in sight.

Ye need na doubt, I held my whisht;   kept quiet
The infant aith, half-form'd, was crusht;
I glowr'd as eerie's I'd been dusht,[2] 45 apprehensive as if
     In some wild glen;
When sweet, like *modest Worth*, she blusht,
     An' stepped ben.   within

Green, slender, leaf-clad *Holly-boughs*
Were twisted, gracefu', round her brows, 50
I took her for some SCOTTISH MUSE,
     By that same token;
And come to stop those reckless vows,
     Would soon been broken.

A "hair-brain'd, sentimental trace" 55
Was strongly marked in her face;
A wildly-witty, rustic grace
     Shone full upon her;
Her *eye*, ev'n turn'd on empty space,
     Beam'd keen with *Honor*. 60

Down flow'd her robe, a *tartan* sheen,
Till half a leg was scrimply seen;   scarcely
And such a *leg*! my BESS, I wean,[3] believe
     Could only peer it; match
Sae straught, sae taper, tight and clean — 65
     Nane else came near it.

Her *Mantle* large, of greenish hue,
My gazing wonder chiefly drew;
Deep *lights* and *shades*, bold-mingling, threw
     A lustre grand; 70
And seem'd, to my astonish'd view,
     A *well-known* Land.

Here, rivers in the sea were lost;
There, mountains to the skies were tost:
Here, tumbling billows mark'd the coast, 75
     With surging foam;
There, distant shone, *Art*'s lofty boast,
     The lordly dome.

---

2 Burns translates 'dusht' as 'pushed by a ram, ox, &c.'
3 'My BESS, I wean' in the Kilmarnock edition is replaced by 'my bonny *Jean*' in the Edinburgh
 edition of the following year, 1787. This refers to Jean Armour, who had twins to Burns in the
 meantime. He married her in 1788 (after another set of twins).

Here, DOON pour'd down his far-fetch'd floods;
There, well-fed IRWINE stately thuds: 80
Auld hermit AIRE staw thro' his woods,[4]   stole
        On to the shore;
And many a lesser torrent scuds,
        With seeming roar.

Low, in a sandy valley spread,   85
An ancient BOROUGH rear'd her head;[5]
Still, as in *Scottish Story* read,
        She boasts a *Race*
To ev'ry nobler virtue bred,
        And polish'd grace. [6]   90

DUAN SECOND.

With musing-deep, astonish'd stare,
I view'd the heavenly-seeming *Fair*;
A whisp'ring *throb* did witness bear
        Of kindred sweet,
When with an elder Sister's air   95
        She did me greet.

'All hail! *my own* inspired Bard!
'In me thy native Muse regard!
'Nor longer mourn thy fate is hard,
        'Thus poorly low!   100
'I come to give thee such *reward*,
        'As *we* bestow.

'Know, the great *Genius* of this Land,
'Has many a light, aerial band,
'Who, all beneath his high command,   105
        'Harmoniously,
'As *Arts* or *Arms* they understand,
        'Their labors ply.

'They SCOTIA'S Race among them share;
'Some fire the *Sodger* on to dare;   110   soldier
'Some rouse the *Patriot* up to bare
        'Corruption's heart:
'Some teach the *Bard*, a darling care,
        The tuneful art.

---

4   The Doon, Irvine and Ayr are all rivers in Ayrshire; Burns's muse is named after another, the Coyle.

5   I.e. Ayr, a Royal Burgh since 1205.

6   In the Edinburgh Edition of 1787, after Burns's fame had won him access to the highest levels of Scottish society, he added a further seven stanzas at this point, singing the praises of several members of the local gentry.

''Mong swelling floods of reeking gore,   115
'They ardent, kindling spirits pour;
'Or, mid the venal Senate's roar,
                    'They, sightless, stand,
'To mend the honest *Patriot-lore*,
                    'And grace the hand.   120

'Hence, FULLARTON, the brave and young;
'Hence, DEMPSTER'S truth-prevailing tongue;[7]
'Hence, sweet harmonious BEATTIE sung
                    'His "Minstrel lays;"
'Or tore, with noble ardour stung,   125
                    The *Sceptic's* bays.[8]

'To lower Orders are assign'd
'The humbler ranks of Human-kind,
'The rustic Bard, the lab'ring Hind,
                    'The Artisan;   130
'All chuse, as, various they're inclin'd,
                    'The various man.

'When yellow waves the heavy grain,
'The threat'ning *Storm*, some, strongly, rein;
'Some teach to meliorate the plain   135
                    'With *tillage-skill*;
'And some instruct the Shepherd-train,
                    'Blythe o'er the hill.

'Some hint the Lover's harmless wile;
'Some grace the Maiden's artless smile;   140
'Some soothe the Lab'rer's weary toil,
                    'For humble gains,
'And make his *cottage-scenes* beguile
                    'His cares and pains.

'Some, bounded to a district-space   145
'Explore at large Man's *infant race*,
'To mark the embryotic trace,
                    'Of *rustic Bard*;
'And careful note each op'ning grace,
                    'A guide and guard.   150

7   Burns names two prominent Scottish landowners. Colonel William Fullarton (1754–1808) had led troops, partly raised on his Ayrshire estates, in the Second Mysore War (1780–84) in India, and been an actively 'improving' landlord since his return. George Dempster (1732–1818), another agriculturalist, and M.P. for the Fife and Forfar burghs, was a Whig with a reputation for independence and critical of government on issues such the American War and the East India Company.

8   James Beattie (1735 –1803), now best remembered for his influential poem on the education of a poet, *The Minstrel* (1771, 1774), was in his own time also celebrated as the author of *Essay on the Nature and Immutability of Truth* (1770), a scathing (though incoherent) rebuttal of the scepticism of David Hume's *Treatise of Human Nature* (1739-40).

'*Of these am I*—COILA my name;
'And this district as mine I claim,
'Where once the *Campbells*, chiefs of fame,
          'Held ruling pow'r:
'I mark'd thy embryo-tuneful flame,   155
          'Thy natal hour.

'With future hope, I oft would gaze,
'Fond, on thy little, early ways,
'Thy rudely-caroll'd, chiming phrase,
          'In uncouth rhymes,   160
'Fir'd at the simple, artless lays
          'Of other times.

'I saw thee seek the sounding shore,
'Delighted with the dashing roar;
'Or when the *North* his fleecy store   165
          'Drove thro' the sky,
'I saw grim Nature's visage hoar,
          'Struck thy young eye.

'Or when the deep-green-mantl'd Earth,
'Warm-cherish'd ev'ry floweret's birth,   170
'And joy and music pouring forth,
          'In ev'ry grove,
'I saw thee eye the gen'ral mirth
          'With boundless love.

'When ripen'd fields, and azure skies,   175
'Call'd forth the *Reaper's* rustling noise,
'I saw thee leave their ev'ning joys,
          'And lonely stalk,
'To vent thy bosom's swelling rise,
          'In pensive walk.   180

'When *youthful Love*, warm-blushing, strong,
'Keen-shivering shot thy nerves along,
'Those accents, grateful to thy tongue,
          'Th' adored *Name*,
'I taught thee how to pour in song,   185
          'To soothe thy flame.

'I saw thy pulse's maddening play,
'Wild-send thee Pleasure's devious way,
'Misled by Fancy's *meteor-ray*,
          'By Passion driven;   190
'But yet the *light* that led astray,
          'Was *light* from Heaven.

'I taught thy manners-painting strains,
'The *loves*, the *ways*, of simple swains,
'Till now, o'er all my wide domains   195
                    'Thy fame extends;
'And some, the pride of *Coila*'s plains,
                    'Become thy friends.

'Thou canst not learn, nor I can show,
'To paint with *Thomson*'s landscape-glow;   200
'Or wake the bosom-melting throe,
                    'With Shenstone's art;
'Or pour, with *Gray*, the moving flow,
                    'Warm on the heart.[9]

'Yet all beneath th'unrivall'd Rose,   205
'The lowly Daisy sweetly blows;
'Tho' large the forest's Monarch throws
                    'His army shade,
Yet green the juicy Hawthorn grows,
                    'Adown the glade.   210

'Then never murmur nor repine;
'Strive in thy *humble sphere* to shine;
'And trust me, not *Potosi's mine*,[10]
                    'Nor *King's regard*,
'Can give a bliss o'ermatching thine,   215
                    'A *rustic Bard*.

'To give my counsels all in one,
'Thy *tuneful flame* still careful fan;
'Preserve *the dignity of Man*,
                    'With Soul erect;   220
'And trust, the UNIVERSAL PLAN
                    'Will all protect.

'*And wear thou this*' —She solemn said,
And bound the *Holly* round my head:
The polish'd leaves, and berries red,   225
                    Did rustling play;
And, like a passing thought, she fled,
                    In light away.

---

9   Burns acknowledges some of the major poets of the previous generation: James Thomson (1700–48), Scottish-born member of Pope's circle and author of the nature-descriptive *The Seasons*; for Shenstone see note 3 to 'Preface'; Thomas Gray (1716–71) author of elegies, odes, and Bardic verse.

10 Potosi was a silver mine in what is now Bolivia, and a major source of wealth for the Spanish Empire.

THE COTTER'S SATURDAY NIGHT.
INSCRIBED TO R. A****, Esq.[1]

Let not Ambition mock their useful toil,
Their homely joys, and destiny obscure;
Nor Grandeur hear, with a disdainful smile,
The short and simple annals of the Poor.
                                                        GRAY[2]

I.

My lov'd, my honor'd, much respected friend,
  No mercenary Bard his homage pays;
With honest pride, I scorn each selfish end,
  My dearest meed, a friend's esteem and praise:
To you I sing, in simple Scottish lays,
  The *lowly train* in life's sequester'd scene;
The native feelings strong, the guileless ways,
  What A**** in a *Cottage* would have been;
Ah! tho' his worth unknown, far happier there I ween!

II.

November chill blaws loud wi' angry sugh;   rush of wind
  The short'ning winter-day is near a close;
The miry beasts retreating frae the pleugh;   from the plough
  The black'ning trains o' craws to their repose:
The toil-worn COTTER frae his labor goes,[3]   from
  This night his weekly moil is at an end,
Collects his *spades*, his *mattocks* and his *hoes*,
  Hoping the *morn* in ease and rest to spend,
And weary, o'er the moor, his course does hameward bend.[4]

III.

At length his lonely *Cot* appears in view,
  Beneath the shelter of an aged tree;
The expectant *wee-things*, toddlan, stacher through   totter
  To meet their *Dad*, wi' flichterin noise and glee.   fluttering
His wee-bit ingle, blinkan bonilie,   fireplace
  His clean hearth-stane, his thrifty *Wifie's* smile,
The *lisping infant*, prattling on his knee,
  Does a' his weary *kiaugh* and care beguile,   anxiety
And makes him quite forget his labor and his toil.

---

1 Robert Aiken (1739–1807), the prosperous Ayr lawyer who gathered almost a quarter of the subscriptions (see note 5 to 'Preface') that made the Kilmarnock edition possible, Aiken was also involved in the case behind 'Holy Willie's Prayer': see below.

2 Thomas Gray, *Elegy written in a Country Church-Yard* (1751) st.8.

3 A cotter is a tenant of a cottage with a small piece of land, originally paying rent in the form of service on a larger farm to which it was attached.

4 Echoes the opening stanza of Gray's *Elegy*: 'The plowman homeward plods his weary way, / And leaves the world to darkness and to me.'

IV.

Belyve, the *elder bairns* come drapping in,   soon; children
     At *Service* out, amang the Farmers roun';
Some ca' the pleugh, some herd, some tentie rin   drive; careful run
     A cannie errand to a neebor toun:
Their eldest hope, their *Jenny*, woman-grown,
     In youthfu' bloom, Love sparkling in her e'e,   eye
Comes hame, perhaps, to shew a braw new gown,   fine
     Or deposite her sair-won penny-fee,   hard-won
To help her *Parents* dear, if they in hardship be.

V.

With joy unfeign'd, *brothers* and *sisters* meet,
     And each for other's weelfare kindly spiers: asks
The social hours, swift-wing'd, unnotic'd fleet;
     Each tells the uncos that he sees or hears.   news
The Parents partial eye their hopeful years;
     Anticipation forward points the view;
The *Mother* wi' her needle and her sheers
     Gars auld claes look amaist as weel's the new;   makes; almost
The *Father* mixes a' wi' admonition due.

VI.

Their Master's and their Mistress's command,
     The *youngkers* a' are warned to obey;
And mind their labors wi' an eydent hand,
     And ne'er, tho' out o' sight, to jauk or play:
'And O! be sure to fear the LORD alway!
     'And mind your *duty*, duely, morn and night!
'Lest in temptation's path ye gang astray,   go
     'Implore his *counsel* and assisting *might*:
'They never sought in vain, that sought the LORD aright.'

VII.

But hark! a rap comes gently to the door;
     Jenny, wha kens the meaning o' the same,
Tells how a neebor lad came o'er the muir,
     To do some errands, and convoy her hame.
The wily Mother sees the *conscious flame*
     Sparkle in *Jenny*'s e'e, and flush her cheek,   eye
With heart-struck, anxious care enquires his name,
     While Jenny hafflins is afraid to speak;   nearly
Weel-pleas'd the Mother hears, it's nae wild, worthless *Rake*.[5]

VIII.

With kindly welcome, *Jenny* brings him ben;   within
     A *strappan youth*; he takes the Mother's eye;
Blythe *Jenny* sees the *visit*'s no ill-taen;   ill-taken
     The Father cracks of horses, pleughs and kye.   chats; cattle

---

5   I.e. a seducer from the gentry class.

The *Youngster's* artless heart o'erflows wi' joy,
    But blate and laithfu', scarce can weel behave;   bashful
The Mother, wi' a woman's wiles, can spy
    What makes the *youth* sae bashfu' and sae grave;
Weel-pleas'd to think her *bairn's* respected like the lave.   the rest

IX.

O happy love! where love like this is found!
    O heart-felt raptures! bliss beyond compare!
I've paced much this weary, *mortal round*,
    And sage EXPERIENCE bids me this declare—
'If Heaven a draught of heavenly pleasure spare,
    'One *cordial* in this melancholly *Vale*,
''Tis when a youthful, loving, *modest* Pair,
    'In other's arms, breathe out the tender tale,
'Beneath the milk-white thorn that scents the ev'ning gale.'

X.

Is there, in human form, that bears a heart—
    A Wretch! a Villain! lost to love and truth!
That can, with studied, sly, ensnaring art,
    Betray sweet *Jenny's* unsuspecting youth?
Curse on his perju'd arts! dissembling smooth!
    Are *Honor, Virtue, Conscience*, all exil'd?
Is there no Pity, no relenting Ruth,
    Points to the Parents fondling o'er their Child?
Then paints the *ruin'd Maid*, and *their* distraction wild!

XI.

But now the Supper crowns their simple board,
    The healsome *Porritch*, chief of SCOTIA'S food:
The soupe their *only Hawkie* does afford,   (their cow)
    That 'yont the hallan snugly chows her cood: beyond; partition
The *Dame* brings forth, in complimental mood,
    To grace the lad, her weel-hain'd kebbuck, fell;   hoarded cheese; pungent
And aft he's prest, and aft he ca's it guid;   often; calls
    The frugal *Wifie*, garrulous, will tell,
How 'twas a towmond auld, sin' Lint was i' the bell. twelvemonth; flax; in flower

XII.

The chearfu' Supper done, wi' serious face,
    They, round the ingle, form a circle wide;   fireplace
The Sire turns o'er, with patriarchal grace,
    The big *ha'-Bible*, ance his *Father's* pride: hall (family) Bible
His bonnet rev'rently laid aside,
    His *lyart haffets* wearing thin and bare;   grizzled temple-hair
Those strains that once did sweet in ZION glide,
    He wales a portion with judicious care;   chooses
'And let us worship GOD!' he says with solemn air.

XIII.

They chant their artless notes in simple guise;
    They tune their hearts, by far the noblest aim:
Perhaps *Dundee's* wild-warbling measures rise,
    Or plaintive *Martyrs*, worthy of the name;
Or noble *Elgin* beets the heaven-ward flame,   fans
    The sweetest far of SCOTIA'S holy lays:[6]
Compar'd with these, *Italian trills* are tame;
    The tickl'd ears no heart-felt raptures raise;
Nae unison hae they, with our CREATOR'S praise.

XIV.

The priest-like Father reads the sacred page,
    How *Abram* was the Friend of GOD on high;
Or, *Moses* bade eternal warfare wage,
    With *Amalek's* ungracious progeny;[7]
Or how the *royal Bard* did groaning lye,
    Beneath the stroke of Heaven's avenging ire;[8]
Or *Job's* pathetic plaint, and wailing cry;
    Or rapt *Isaiah's* wild, seraphic fire;
Or other *Holy Seers* that tune the *sacred lyre.*

XV.

Perhaps the *Christian Volume* is the theme;
    How *guiltless blood* for *guilty man* was shed;
How HE, who bore in heaven the second name,
    Had not on Earth whereon to lay His head:
How His first *followers* and *servants* sped;
    The *Precepts sage* they wrote to many a land:
How *he*, who lone in *Patmos* banished,
    Saw in the sun a mighty angel stand;
And heard great *Bab'lon's* doom pronounc'd by Heaven's command.[9]

XVI.

Then kneeling down to HEAVEN'S ETERNAL KING,
    The *Saint*, the *Father*, and the *Husband* prays:
Hope 'springs exulting on triumphant wing,'[10]
    That *thus* they all shall meet in future days:
There, ever bask in *uncreated rays,*

---

6   These are the names of old Common Metre psalm tunes.

7   Amalek, a Duke of Edom, is defeated by Joshua in Exodus 17; but his descendents keep coming back for more, on and off, throughout the first half of the Old Testament.

8   When David (author of the Psalms) gets another man's wife pregnant, and arranges for her husband to die in battle, God punishes him by having the child die (2 Samuel 11–12).

9   It was on Patmos that St John the Divine had the visions recorded in the Book of Revelation. He sees an angel standing in the sun at 19.17; the final pronouncement of Babylon's destruction comes at 18.21.

10   Pope's *Windsor Forest.* [Burns's note. 'See! from the Brake the whirring Pheasant springs, / And mounts exulting on triumphant Wings' (ll. 111–12). The pheasant is shot in the following couplet.]

No more to sigh, or shed the bitter tear,
    Together hymning their CREATOR'S praise
        In *such society*, yet still more dear;
While circling Time moves round in an eternal sphere.

XVII.

Compar'd with *this*, how poor Religion's pride,
    In all the pomp of *method*, and of *art*,
When men display to congregations wide,
    Devotion's ev'ry grace, except the *heart!*
The POWER, incens'd, the Pageant will desert,
    The pompous strain, the sacredotal stole;
But haply, in some *Cottage* far apart,
    May hear, well pleas'd, the language of the *Soul*;
And in His *Book of Life* the Inmates poor enroll.

XVIII.

Then homeward all take off their sev'ral way;
    The youngling *Cottagers* retire to rest:
The Parent-pair their *secret homage* pay,
    And proffer up to Heaven the warm request,
That HE who stills the *raven's* clam'rous nest,
    And decks the *lily* fair in flow'ry pride,
Would, in the way His *Wisdom* sees the best,
    For them and for their *little ones* provide;
But chiefly, in their hearts with *Grace divine* preside.

XIX.

From scenes like these, old SCOTIA'S grandeur springs,
    That makes her lov'd at home, rever'd abroad:
Princes and lords are but the breath of kings,
    'An honest man 's the noble work of GOD:'[11]
And *certes*, in fair Virtue's heavenly road,
    The *Cottage* leaves the *Palace* far behind:
What is a lordling's pomp? a cumbrous load,
    Disguising oft the *wretch* of human kind;
Studied in arts of Hell, in wickedness refin'd!

XX.

O SCOTIA! my dear, my native soil!
    For whom my warmest wish to heaven is sent!
Long may thy hardy sons of *rustic toil*
    Be blest with health and peace and sweet content!
And O may Heaven their simple lives prevent
    From *Luxury's* contagion, weak and vile!
Then howe'er *crowns* and *coronets* be rent,
    A *virtuous Populace* may rise the while;

---

11 Another (mis)quote from Pope, which Burns clearly expected his readers to identify, from
    the *Essay on Man* Epistle IV: 'A Wit's a feather, and a Chief a rod; / An honest Man's the
    noblest work of God' (ll.247–8).

And stand a wall of fire, around their much-lov'd ISLE.

XXI.

O THOU! who pour'd the *patriotic tide*,
     That stream'd thro' great, unhappy WALLACE' heart;
Who dar'd to, nobly, stem tyrannic pride,
     Or *nobly die*, the second glorious part:
(The Patriot's GOD, peculiarly thou art,
     His *friend, inspirer, guardian* and *reward!*)
O never, never SCOTIA'S realm desert,
     But still the *Patriot*, and the *Patriot-Bard*,
In bright succesion raise, her *Ornament* and *Guard!*

TO A MOUSE,

On turning her up in her Nest, with the Plough, November, 1785.

WEE, sleeket, cowran, tim'rous *beastie*,	glossy, cringing
O, what a panic's in thy breastie!	
Thou need na start awa sae hasty,	
Wi' bickering brattle!	scurrying hurry
I wad be laith to rin an' chase thee, 5	
Wi' murd'ring *pattle!*	small spade

I'm truly sorry Man's dominion
Has broken Nature's social union,
An' justifies that ill opinion,
        Which makes thee startle,   10
At me, thy poor, earth-born companion,
        An' *fellow-mortal!*

I doubt na, whyles, but thou may *thieve*;	
What then? poor beastie, thou maun live!	must
A *daimen-icker* in a *thrave* 15	odd ear in a sheaf
'S a sma' request:	
I'll get a blessin wi' the lave,	with the rest
An' never miss't!	

Thy wee-bit *housie*, too, in ruin!	
It's silly wa's the win's are strewin! 20	walls; winds
An' naething, now, to big a new ane,	build
O' foggage green!	tall grass
An' bleak *December's winds* ensuin,	
Baith snell an' keen!	both bitter

Thou saw the fields laid bare an' wast, 25	
An' weary *Winter* comin fast,	
An' cozie here, beneath the blast,	
Thou thought to dwell,	
Till crash! the cruel *coulter* past	plough-blade
Out thro' thy cell. 30	

That wee-bit heap o' leaves an' stibble,	
Has cost thee monie a weary nibble!	
Now thou's turn'd out, for a' thy trouble,	
But house or hald,	refuge
To thole the Winter's *sleety dribble*, 35	endure
An' *cranreuch* cauld!	hoar-frost

But Mousie, thou art no thy-lane,	on your own
In proving *foresight* may be vain:	
The best laid schemes o' *Mice* an' *Men*,	
Gang aft agley, 40	go often awry

An' lae'e us nought but grief an' pain,
            For promis'd joy!   leave

Still, thou art blest, compar'd wi' *me!*
The *present* only toucheth thee:
But Och! I *backward* cast my e'e,   45   eye
            On prospects drear!
An' *forward*, tho' I canna *see,*   cannot
            I *guess* an' *fear!*

TO A MOUNTAIN-DAISY,
On turning one down, with the Plough, in April — 1786.

WEE, modest, crimson-tipped flow'r,
Thou's met me in an evil hour;
For I maun crush amang the stoure   *must; dust*
        Thy slender stem:
To spare thee now is past my pow'r,   5
        Thou bonie gem.

Alas! it's no thy neebor sweet,
The bonie *Lark*, companion meet!
Bending thee 'mang the dewy weet!   *among*
        Wi's spreckl'd breast,   10
When upward-springing, blythe, to greet
        The purpling East.

Cauld blew the bitter-biting *North*   *cold*
Upon thy early, humble birth;
Yet cheerfully thou glinted forth   15
        Amid the storm,
Scarce rear'd above the *Parent-earth*
        Thy tender form.

The flaunting *flow'rs* our Gardens yield,
High-shelt'ring woods and wa's maun shield,   20   *walls must*
But thou, beneath the random bield   *shelter*
        O' clod or stane,
Adorns the histie *stibble-field*,   *dry*
        Unseen, alane.

There, in thy scanty mantle clad,   25
Thy snawie bosom sun-ward spread,
Thou lifts thy unassuming head
        In humble guise;
But now the *share* uptears thy bed,
        And low thou lies!   30

Such is the fate of artless Maid,
Sweet *flow'ret* of the rural shade!
By Love's simplicity betray'd,
        And guileless trust,
Till she, like thee, all soil'd, is laid   35
        Low i' the dust!

Such is the fate of simple Bard,
On Life's rough ocean luckless starr'd!
Unskilful he to note the card
        Of *prudent Lore*,   40

Till billows rage, and gales blow hard,
        And whelm him o'er!

Such fate to *suffering worth* is giv'n,
Who long with wants and woes has striv'n,
By human pride or cunning driv'n   45
        To Mis'ry's brink,
Till wrench'd of ev'ry stay but HEAV'N,
        He, ruin'd, sink!

Ev'n thou who mourn'st the *Daisy's* fate,
That fate is thine—no distant date;   50
Stern Ruin's *plough-share* drives, elate,
        Full on thy bloom,
Till crush'd beneath the *furrow's* weight,
        Shall be thy doom!

A DEDICATION TO G**** H*******, Esq. [1]

EXPECT na, sir, in this narration,
A fleechin, fleth'rin *Dedication*,   flattering, wheedling
To roose you up, an' ca' you guid,   praise; call
An' sprung o' great an' noble bluid;
Because ye're surnam'd like *His Grace*,[2]   5
Perhaps related to the race:
Then when I'm tir'd—and sae are ye,
Wi' mony a fulsome, sinfu' lie,
Set up a face, how I stop short,   make a pretence
For fear your modesty be hurt.   10

    This may do—maun do, Sir, wi' them wha   must
Maun please the Great-folk for a wamefou;   stomach-full
For me! sae laigh I need na bow,   low
For, LORD be thanket, *I can plough*;
And when I downa yoke a naig,   15   cannot
Then, LORD be thanket, *I can beg*;
Sae I shall say, an' that's nae flatt'rin,
It's just *sic Poet* an' *sic Patron*.   such a

    The Poet, some guid Angel help him,
Or else, I fear, some *ill ane* skelp him!   20   slap
He may do weel for a' he's done yet,
But only—he's no just begun yet.

    The Patron, (sir, ye maun forgie me,   must forgive
I winna lie, come what will o' me)   will not
On ev'ry hand it will allow'd be,   25
He's just—nae better than he should be.

    I readily and freely grant,
He downa see a poor man want;   cannot
What's no his ain, he winna tak it;   own; will not
What ance he says, he winna break it;   30   once
Ought he can lend he'll no refus't,
Till aft his guidness is abus'd;   often
And rascals whyles that do him wrang,   sometimes
Ev'n *that*, he does na mind it lang:
As Master, Landlord, Husband, Father,[3]   35
He does na fail his part in either.

---

1   Gavin Hamilton (1751–1805), landowner, Mauchline solicitor, and fellow freemason; like
    Aiken, instrumental in getting the Kilmarnock *Poems* published; and one of Burns's best
    friends until a disagreement over money matters in 1788. See note to 'Holy Willie's Prayer'
    below.
2   I.e. like the Duke of Hamilton, one of the most powerful noblemen in the region.
3   Hamilton was in one sense Burns's landlord: he had subleased the farm at Mossgiel to Burns
    and his brother since 1783.

But then, nae thanks to him for a' that;
Nae *godly symptom* ye can ca' that;   call
It's naething but a milder feature,
Of our poor, sinfu', corrupt Nature: 40
Ye'll get the best o' moral works,
'Mang black *Gentoos*, and Pagan *Turks*,   among
Or Hunters wild on *Ponotaxi*,
Wha never heard of Orth–d–xy.[4]
That he's the poor man's friend in need,   45
The GENTLEMAN in word and deed,
It's no thro' terror of D–mn–t–n;
It's just a carnal inclination,
And Och! that's nae r–g–n–r–t–n![5]

   Morality, thou deadly bane,   50
Thy tens o' thousands thou hast slain!
Vain is his hope, whase stay an' trust is,
In *moral* Mercy, Truth, and Justice!

   No — stretch a point to catch a plack;[6]   farthing
Abuse a Brother to his back;   55
Steal through the *winnock* frae a wh–re,   window from
But point the Rake that taks the *door*;
Be to the Poor like onie whunstane,   any whinstone
And haud their noses to the grunstane;   grindstone
Ply ev'ry art o' *legal* thieving;   60
No matter — stick to *sound believing*.

   Learn three-mile pray'rs, an' half-mile graces,
Wi' weel-spread looves, an' lang, wry faces;   palms
Grunt up a solemn, lengthen'd groan,
And damn a' Parties but your own;   65
I'll warrant then, ye're nae Deceiver,
A steady, sturdy, staunch *Believer*.

   O ye wha leave the springs o' C–lv–n,
For *gumlie dubs* of your ain delvin!   muddy pools of your own digging
Ye sons of Heresy and Error,   70
Ye'll *some day* squeel in quaking terror!
When Vengeance draws the sword in wrath,
And in the fire throws the *sheath*;
When Ruin, with his sweeping *besom*,   broom
Just frets till Heav'n commission gies him;   75
While o'er the *Harp* pale Misery moans,
And strikes the ever-deep'ning tones,
Still louder shrieks, and heavier groans!

---

4   I.e. the orthodox Calvinism of the Church of Scotland. 'Gentoos' are Hindus, and 'Ponotaxi'
   sounds like a generic South American location.
5   Regeneration: i.e., the work of God within the believer's soul.
6   A traditional expression: 'bend the truth if you can make money out of it'.

Your pardon, Sir, for this digression,
I maist forgat my *Dedication*;   80   almost
But when Divinity comes cross me,
My readers then are sure to lose me.[7]

So, Sir, you see 'twas nae daft vapour;
But I maturely thought it proper,
When a' my works I did review,   85
To *dedicate* them, sir, to YOU:
Because (ye need na tak it ill)
I thought them something like *yoursel*.

Then patronize them wi' your favor,
And your Petitioner shall ever —   90
I had amaist said, *ever pray*,   almost
But that's a word I need na say:
For prayin I hae little skill o't;
I'm baith dead-sweer, an' wretched ill o't;   both quite disinclined
But I'se repeat each poor man's *pray'r*,   95   I shall
That kens or hears about you, Sir —

   'May ne'er Misfortune's gowling bark,   howling
'Howl thro' the dwelling o' the CLERK!
'May ne'er his gen'rous, honest heart,
'For that same gen'rous spirit smart!   100
'May K******'s far-honour'd name[8]
'Lang beet his hymeneal flame,   long fan
'Till H*******'s, at least a diz'n,
'Are frae their nuptial labors risen: from
'Five bonie Lasses round their table,   105
'And sev'n braw fellows, stout an' able,   fine
'To serve their King an' Country weel,
'By word, or pen, or pointed steel!
'May Health and Peace, with mutual rays,
'Shine on the ev'ning o' his days;   110
'Till his wee, curlie *John's* ier-oe,   great-grandchild
'When ebbing life nae mair shall flow,
'The last, sad, mournful rites bestow!'

   I will not wind a lang conclusion,
With complimentary effusion;   115
But, whilst your wishes and endeavours
Are blest with Fortune's smiles and favours,
I am, Dear Sir, with zeal most fervent,
Your much indebted, humble servant.

---

7   For the specific context of the anti-clericalism shared by Burns and Hamilton, see also under
    'Holy Willie's Prayer' below.
8   Hamilton's wife Helen Kennedy.

But if, which Pow'rs above prevent,   120
That iron-hearted Carl, *Want*,
Attended, in his grim advances,
By *sad mistakes*, and *black mischances*,
While hopes, and joys, and pleasures fly him,
Make you as poor a dog as I am,   125
Your *humble servant* then no more;
For who would humbly serve the Poor?
But, by a poor man's hopes in Heav'n!
While recollection's pow'r is giv'n,
If, in the vale of humble life,   130
The victim sad of Fortune's strife,
I, through the tender-gushing tear,
Should recognise my *Master dear*,
If friendless, low, we meet together,
Then, sir, your hand—my FRIEND and BROTHER.

EPISTLE TO J. L*****K,
AN OLD SCOTCH BARD.[1]

April 1st, 1785

WHILE briers an' woodbines budding green,
An' Paitricks scraichan loud at e'en,   corncrakes; evening
And morning Poossie whiddan seen,   hare running easily
         Inspire my Muse,
This freedom, in an *unknown* frien',   5
         I pray excuse.

On Fasteneen we had a rockin,[2]   spinning party
To ca' the crack and weave our stockin;   gossip
And there was muckle fun and jokin,   lots of
         Ye need na doubt;   10
At length we had a hearty yokin,   took turns
         At *sang about.*

There was ae *sang*, amang the rest,
Aboon them a' it pleas'd me best,   above
That some kind husband had addrest,   15
         To some sweet wife:
It thirl'd the heart-strings thro' the breast,   pierced
         A' to the life.

I've scarce heard ought describ'd sae weel,
What gen'rous, manly bosoms feel;   20
Thought I , 'Can this be *Pope*, or *Steele*,
         Or *Beattie*'s wark;'[3]
They tald me 'twas an odd kind chiel   bloke
         About *Muirkirk.*

It pat me fidgean-fain to hear't,   25   made me restlessly eager
An' sae about him there I spier't;   asked
Then a' that kent him round declar'd,
         He had *ingine*,   genius
That nane excell'd it, few cam near 't ,
         It was sae fine.   30

That set him to a pint of ale,
An' either douse or merry tale,   sober
Or rhymes an' sangs he'd made himsel,
         Or witty catches,
'Tween Inverness and Tiviotdale,   35
         He had few matches.

---

1   John Lapraik (1727–1807) went on to publish *Poems on Several Occasions* in 1788 after losing his farm in a bank-crash.

2   Fasteneen is Shrove Tuesday.

3   Alexander Pope (1688–1744), the greatest English poet of his time; Richard Steele (1672–1796), poet, playwright and essayist. For Beattie see note 8 to 'The Vision'.

Then up I gat, an' swoor an aith,
Tho' I should pawn my pleugh an' graith,   tools
Or die a cadger pownie's death,   pedlar's pony's
        At some dyke-back,   40
A *pint* an' *gill* I'd gie them *baith*,   measure of whisky
        To hear your crack.   chat

But first an' foremost, I should tell,
Amaist as soon as I could spell,   almost
I to the *crambo-jingle* fell,   45   doggerel
        Tho' rude and rough,
Yet crooning to a body's sel,   self
        Does weel eneugh.

I am nae *Poet*, in a sense,
But just a *Rhymer* like by chance,   50
An' hae to Learning nae pretence,
        Yet, what the matter?
Whene'er my Muse does on me glance,
        I jingle at her.

Your Critic-folk may cock their nose,   55
And say, 'How can you e'er propose,
'You wha ken hardly *verse* frae *prose*,   from
        'To mak a *sang*?'
Yet by your leaves, my learned foes,
        Ye're maybe wrang.   60

What's a' your jargon o' your Schools,
Your Latin names for horns an' stools;
If honest Nature made you *fools*,
        What sairs your Grammars?   serves
Ye'd better taen up *spades* and *shools*,   65   taken; shovels
        Or *knappin-hammers*.   for breaking stones

A set o' dull, conceited Hashes,   wasters
Confuse their brains in *Colledge-classes*!
They *gang in* Stirks, and *come out* Asses,   go in bullocks
        Plain truth to speak;   70
An' syne they think to climb Parnassus[4]   then
        By dint o' Greek!

Gie me ae spark o' Nature's fire,
That's a' the learning I desire;
Then tho' I drudge thro' dub an' mire   75   mud
        At pleugh or cart,
My Muse, tho' hamely in attire,
        May touch the heart.

---

4   The mythical mountain home of the muses.

O for a spunk o' ALLAN'S glee,   spark
Or FERGUSON'S, the bauld an' slee,[5]   80   bold and sly
Or bright L*****K'S, my friend to be,
            If I can hit it!
That would be *lear* eneugh for me,   learning
            If I could get it.

Now, Sir, if ye hae friends enow,   85   enough
Tho' *real friends* I b'lieve are few,
Yet, if your catalogue be fow,   full
            I'se no insist;   I shall
But gif ye want ae friend that's true,   if
            I'm on your list.   90

I winna blaw about *mysel*,   will not
As ill I like my fauts to tell;   fauts
But friends an' folk that wish me well,
            They sometimes roose me;   praise
Tho' I maun own, as monie still,   95   must
            As far abuse me.

There's ae *wee faut* they whiles lay to me,
I like the lasses—Gude forgie me!
For mony a Plack they wheedle frae me,   farthing; from
            At dance or fair: 100
Maybe some *ither thing* they gie me
            They weel can spare.

But MAUCHLINE Race or MAUCHLINE Fair,[6]
I should be proud to meet you there;
We'se gie ae nights's discharge to *care*,   105   we shall
            If we forgather,   meet up
An' hae a swap o' *rhymin-ware*,
            Wi' ane anither.

The *four-gill chap*, we'se gar him clatter,   half-pint measure
An kirs'n him wi' reekin water;   110   christen; smoking
Syne we'll sit down an' tak our whitter,   then; draught
            To chear our heart;
An' faith, we'se be *acquainted* better   we shall
            Before we part.

Awa ye selfish, warly race,   115   worldly
Wha think that havins, sense an' grace,   manners
Ev'n love an' friendship should give place
            To *catch-the-plack*!   farthing
I dinna like to see your face,   don't
            Nor hear your crack.   120

---

5   See note 4 to 'Preface'.
6   Mauchline was the parish where Robert and Gilbert Burns were renting Mossgiel farm at
    this time.

But ye whom social pleasure charms,
Whose hearts the *tide of kindness* warms,
Who hold your *being* on the terms,
        'Each aid the others,'
Come to my bowl, come to my arms,   125
        My friends, my brothers!

But to conclude my lang epistle,
As my auld pen's worn to the grissle;
Twa lines frae you wad gar me fissle,   from; make; excited
        Who am, most fervent,   130
While I can either sing, or whistle,
        Your friend and servant.

TO THE SAME.[1]

April 21st, 1785.

WHILE new-ca'd kye rowte at the stake,   driven; cattle; bellow
An' pownies reek in pleugh or braik,   smoke; harrow
This hour on e'enin's edge I take,   evening
        To own I'm debtor,
To honest-hearted, auld L*****K,   5
        For his kind *letter.*

Forjesket sair, with weary legs,   worn out
Rattlin the corn out-owre the rigs,   casting seed-corn
Or dealing thro' amang the naigs   horses
        Their ten-hours' bite,   10
My awkart Muse sair pleads and begs,   obstinate
        I would na write.

The tapetless, ramfeezl'd hizzie,   heedless; exhausted
She's saft at best an' something lazy,
Quo' she, 'Ye ken we've been sae busy   15
        'This month an' mair,
'That trouth, my head is grown right dizzie,
        'An' something sair.'

Her dowf excuses pat me mad;   feeble; made
'Conscience,' says I, 'ye thowless jad!   20   spiritless jade
'I'll write, an' that a hearty blaud,   specimen
        'This vera night;
'So dinna ye affront your trade,   don't
        'But rhyme it right.

'Shall bauld L*****K, the *king o' hearts*,   25   bold
'Tho' mankind were a *pack o' cartes*,
'Roose you sae weel for your deserts,   praise; well
        'In terms sae friendly,
'Yet ye'll neglect to shaw your parts
        'An' thank him kindly?'   30

Sae I gat paper in a blink,
An' down gaed *stumpie* in the ink: went; [his pen]
Quoth I, 'Before I sleep a wink,
        'I vow I'll close it;
'An' if ye winna mak it clink,   35   will not
        'By Jove I'll prose it!'

---

1   Usually known as the 'Second Epistle to Lapraik'.

Sae I've begun to scrawl, but whether
In rhyme, or prose, or baith thegither,
Or some hotch-potch that's rightly neither,
   Let time mak proof;   40
But I shall scribble down some blether   *nonsense*
   Just clean aff-loof.   *off the cuff*

My worthy friend, ne'er grudge an' carp,
Tho' fortune use you hard an' sharp;
Come, kittle up your *moorlan harp*[2]   45   *tune up*
   Wi' gleesome touch!
Ne'er mind how Fortune *waft* an' *warp*;
   She's but a b–tch.

She's gien me mony a jirt an' fleg,   *given; jerk and scare*
Sin' I could striddle owre a rig;   50
But, by the L—d, tho' I should beg
   Wi' lyart pow,   *grizzled head*
I'll laugh, an' sing, an' shake my leg,
   As lang's I dow!   *dare*

Now comes the *sax an' twentieth* simmer,   55
I've seen the bud upo' the timmer,   *on the wood*
Still persecuted by the limmer   *jade*
   Frae year to year;   *from*
But yet, despite the kittle kimmer,   *fickle wench*
   I, Rob, am here.   60

Do ye envy the *city-gent*,
Behint a kist to lie an' sklent;   *chest; squint greedily*
Or purse-proud, big wi' cent per cent,
   An' muckle wame,   *big belly*
In some bit *Brugh* to represent   65
   A *Baillie's* name?[3]

Or is't the paughty, feudal *Thane*,   *insolent*
Wi' ruffl'd sark an' glancing cane,   *shirt*
Wha thinks himsel nae *sheep-shank bane*,
   But lordly stalks,   70
While caps and bonnets aff are taen,   *taken*
   As by he walks?

'O *Thou* wha gies us each guid gift!
'Gie me o' *wit* an' *sense* a lift,   *large amount*
'Then turn me, if *Thou* please, *adrift*,   75
   'Thro' Scotland wide;
'Wi' *cits* nor *lairds* I wadna shift,   *change places*
   'In a' their pride!'

---

2 Lapraik's farm was near Muirkirk ('Epistle to Lapraik' l.24), twelve miles further up the
 valley of the River Ayr from Mauchline; as its name suggests, this is an upland area.
3 Brugh: a burgh, a market-town. A baillie is a local magistrate in a burgh.

Were this the *charter* of our state,
'On pain o' *hell* be rich an' great,'   80
Damnation then would be our fate,
        Beyond remead;
But, thanks to *Heav'n*, that's no the gate   way
        We learn our *creed*.

For thus the royal *Mandate* ran,   85
When first the human race began,
'The social, friendly, honest man,
        'Whate'er he be,
''Tis *he* fulfils *great Nature's plan*,
        And none but *he*.'   90

O *Mandate*, glorious and divine!
The followers o' the ragged Nine,[4]
Poor, thoughtless devils! yet may shine
        In glorious light,
While sordid sons o' Mammon's line   95
        Are dark as night!

Tho' here they scrape, an' squeeze, an' growl,
Their worthless nievefu' of a *soul*,   fistful
May in some *future carcase* howl,
        The forest's fright;   100
Or in some day-detesting *owl*
        May shun the light.

Then may L*****K and B**** arise,
To reach their native, kindred skies,
And *sing* their pleasures, hopes an' joys,   105
        In some mild sphere,
Still closer knit in friendship's ties
        Each passing year!

---

4   'The Nine' are the Muses, goddesses responsible for the various arts.

TAM O' SHANTER: A TALE.[1]

Of Brownyis and of Bogillis full is this Buke.

GAWIN DOUGLAS.[2]

WHEN chapman billies leave the street,		pedlars
And drouthy neebors, neebors meet,		thirsty
As market-days are wearing late,		
And folk begin to tak the gate;		take the road
While we sit bousing at the nappy,	5	ale
An' getting fou and unco happy,		drunk; very
We think na on the lang Scots miles,		
The mosses, waters, slaps and styles,		gap in a dyke
That lie between us and our hame,		
Where sits our sulky, sullen dame,	10	
Gathering her brows like gathering storm,		
Nursing her wrath to keep it warm.		

This truth fand honest *Tam o' Shanter*,   found
As he frae Ayr ae night did canter: from
(Auld Ayr, wham ne'er a town surpasses,   15
For honest men and bonny lasses).

O *Tam*! hadst thou but been sae wise,
As taen thy ain wife *Kate*'s advice!   taken your own
She tauld thee weel thou was a skellum,   rascal
A blethering, blustering, drunken blellum;   20   blusterer
That frae November till October,   from
Ae market-day thou was nae sober;
That ilka melder,[3] wi' the miller,   each
Thou sat as lang as thou had siller;   silver
That ev'ry naig was ca'd a shoe on,   25   horse; hammered
The smith and thee gat roaring fou on;   drunk
That at the L—d's house, even on Sunday,
Thou drank wi' Kirkton Jean till Monday.
She prophesied that late or soon,
Thou wad be found, deep drown'd in Doon;   30
Or catch'd wi' warlocks in the mirk,
By Alloway's auld, haunted kirk.

Ah, gentle dames! it gars me greet,   makes me weep
To think how mony counsels sweet,
How mony lengthen'd sage advices,   35
The husband frae the wife despises!   from

---

1 First published in the *Edinburgh Herald* 18th March 1791.
2 From Douglas's *Eneados*, his translation of Virgil's *Aeneid* into Scots (completed 1513), book VI, Prologue, l.18.
3 The occasion of getting your corn ground by the miller.

But to our tale: Ae market-night,
Tam had got planted unco right;   very well
Fast by an ingle, bleezing finely,   fireplace
Wi reaming swats, that drank divinely;   40   foaming new beer
And at his elbow, Souter *Johnny*,   cobbler
His ancient, trusty, drouthy crony;   thirsty
Tam lo'ed him like a vera brither;   loved
They had been fou for weeks thegither.   drunk
The night drave on wi' sangs and clatter;   45
And ay the ale was growing better:
The landlady and *Tam* grew gracious,
Wi' favours, secret, sweet, and precious:
The Souter tauld his queerest stories;
The landlord's laugh was ready chorus: 50
The storm without might rair and rustle,   roar
Tam did na mind the storm a whistle.

   Care, mad to see a man sae happy,
E'en drown'd himsel amang the nappy: ale
As bees flee hame wi' lades o' treasure,   55   loads
The minutes wing'd their way wi' pleasure:
Kings may be blest, but *Tam* was glorious,
O'er a' the ills o' life victorious!

   But pleasures are like poppies spread,
You seize the flower, its bloom is shed;   60
Or like the snow falls in the river,
A moment white—then melts for ever;
Or like the borealis race,
That flit ere you can point their place;
Or like the rainbow's lovely form   65
Evanishing amid the storm.—
Nae man can tether time or tide,
The hour approaches *Tam* maun ride;   must
That hour, o' night's black arch the key-stane,
That dreary hour he mounts his beast in;   70
And sic a night he taks the road in,   such
As ne'er poor sinner was abroad in.

   The wind blew as 'twad blawn its last;   if it would have
The rattling showers rose on the blast;
The speedy gleams the darkness swallow'd;   75
Loud, deep, and lang, the thunder bellow'd:
That night, a child might understand,
The deil had business on his hand.

Weel mounted on his grey mare, *Meg*,
A better never lifted leg,   80
Tam skelpit on thro' dub and mire,   belted; mud
Despising wind, and rain, and fire;
Whiles holding fast his gude blue bonnet;
Whiles crooning o'er some auld Scots sonnet;
Whiles glowring round wi' prudent cares,   85
Lest bogles catch him unawares: ghosts/goblins
Kirk-Alloway was drawing nigh,
Where ghaists and houlets nightly cry.   owls

By this time he was cross the ford,
Whare, in the snaw, the chapman smoor'd;   90   pedlar; smothered
And past the birks and meikle stane,   birches; big
Whare drunken *Charlie* brak 's neck-bane;   broke his
And thro' the whins, and by the cairn,
Whare hunters fand the murder'd bairn;   found
And near the thorn, aboon the well,   95   above
Whare *Mungo*'s mither hang'd hersel. —
Before him *Doon* pours all his floods;
The doubling storm roars thro' the woods;
The lightnings flash from pole to pole;
Near and more near the thunders roll: 100
When, glimmering thro' the groaning trees,
Kirk-Alloway seem'd in a bleeze;   blaze
Thro' ilka bore the beams were glancing;   every crack
And loud resounded mirth and dancing. —

Inspiring bold *John Barleycorn*!   105
What dangers thou canst make us scorn!
Wi' tippeny, we fear nae evil;   small beer
Wi' usquabae, we'll face the devil! —   whisky
The swats sae ream'd in *Tammie*'s noddle,   beer so foamed
Fair play, he car'd na deils a boddle.   110   did not care for; penny
But *Maggie* stood right sair astonish'd,
Till, by the heel and hand admonish'd,
She ventured forward on the light;
And, wow! *Tam* saw an unco sight!   strange
Warlocks and witches in a dance;   115
Nae cotillion brent new frae *France*,[4]   brand new from
But hornpipes, jigs, strathspeys, and reels,
Put life and mettle in their heels.
A winnock-bunker in the east,   window seat
There sat auld Nick, in shape o' beast;   120
A towzie tyke, black, grim, and large,   shaggy mongrel
To gie them music was his charge:
He screw'd the pipes and gart them skirl,   made
Till roof and rafters a' did dirl. —   shake

---

4   *Cotillion* could name several types of fashionable dance.

Coffins stood round, like open presses,	125	cupboards
That shaw'd the dead in their last dresses;		showed
And by some devilish cantraip slight		magic
Each in its cauld hand held a light. —		
By which heroic *Tam* was able		
To note upon the haly table,	130	altar
A murderer's banes in gibbet airns;		bones; irons
Twa span-lang, wee, unchristen'd bairns;		
A thief, new-cutted frae a rape,		from a rope
Wi' his last gasp his gab did gape;		mouth
Five tomahawks, wi' blude red-rusted:	135	
Five scymitars, wi' murder crusted;		
A garter which a babe had strangled;		
A knife, a father's throat had mangled,		
Whom his ain son o' life bereft,		own
The grey hairs yet stack to the heft;	140	
Three Lawyers' tongues, turned inside out,		
Wi' lies seamed like a beggar's clout;		cloth
Three Priests' hearts, rotten black as muck,		
Lay stinking, vile, in every neuk.[5]		corner

As *Tammie* glow'rd, amaz'd, and curious, 145
The mirth and fun grew fast and furious:
The piper loud and louder blew;
The dancers quick and quicker flew;

They reel'd, they set, they cross'd, they cleekit,		linked arms
Till ilka carlin swat and reekit,	150	woman; steamed
And coost her duddies to the wark,		cast; clothes
And linkit at it in her sark!		tripped; shift

Now *Tam*, O *Tam*! had they been queans,
A' plump and strapping in their teens,

Their sarks, instead o' creeshie flannen,	155	shifts; greasy flannel
Been snaw-white seventeen hunder linnen!		
Thir breeks o' mine, my only pair,		these trousers
That ance were plush, o' guid blue hair,		once
I wad hae gien them off my hurdies,		given
For ae blink o' the bonie burdies!	160	

But wither'd beldams, auld and droll,

Rigwoodie hags wad spean a foal,		withered; wean
Louping and flinging on a crummock,		jumping; stick
I wonder didna turn thy stomach.		

5   On the advice of Alexander Fraser Tytler, Edinburgh historian and lawyer, Burns cut lines 141-144 when the poem was republished in an edition of his poems in 1793. He replaced them with this couplet: 'Wi' mair o' horrible and awefu', / Which even to name wad be unlawfu'.'

But *Tam* kent what was what fu' brawlie,   165   full well
There was ae winsome wench and wawlie,   handsome
That night enlisted in the core,   company
(Lang after kend on *Carrick* shore;[6]
For mony a beast to dead she shot,
And perish'd mony a bony boat,   170
And shook baith meikle corn and bear,   much; barley
And kept the country-side in fear:)
Her cutty sark, o' Paisley harn,   short shift; linen
That while a lassie she had worn,
In longitude tho' sorely scanty,   175
It was her best, and she was vauntie. —   vain
Ah! little kend thy reverend grannie,
That sark she coft for her wee Nannie,   shift; bought
Wi' twa pund Scots ('twas a' her riches),
Wad ever grac'd a dance of witches!   180

But here my Muse her wing maun cour;   must fold
Sic flights are far beyond her pow'r;   such
To sing how Nannie lap and flang,   jumped
(A souple jade she was and strang),
And how *Tam* stood, like ane bewitch'd,   185
And thought his very een enrich'd;   eyes
Even Satan glowr'd, and fidg'd fu' fain,   twitched with excitement
And hotch'd and blew wi' might and main: jerked
Till first ae caper, syne anither,   then another
Tam tint his reason a' thegither,   190   lost; altogether
And roars out, 'Weel done, Cutty-sark!'
And in an instant all was dark:
And scarcely had he Maggie rallied,
When out the hellish legion sallied.

As bees bizz out wi' angry fyke,   195   fuss
When plundering herds assail their byke;
As open pussie's mortal foes,   a hare's
When, pop! she starts before their nose;
As eager runs the market-crowd,
When 'Catch the thief!' resounds aloud;   200
So Maggie runs, the witches follow,
Wi' mony an eldritch skreich and hollow.   uncanny

Ah, *Tam*! Ah, *Tam*! thou'll get thy fairin!   reward, deserts
In hell, they'll roast thee like a herrin!
In vain thy *Kate* awaits thy comin!   205
Kate soon will be a woefu' woman!
Now, do thy speedy utmost, Meg,

---

6   I.e. the coast south of Ayr.

And win the key-stane⁷ o' the brig;
There, at them thou thy tail may toss,
A running stream they dare na cross.   210
But ere the keystane she could make,
The fient a tail she had to shake!   The devil a
For Nannie, far before the rest,
Hard upon noble Maggie prest,
And flew at *Tam* wi' furious ettle;   215   purpose
But little wist she Maggie's mettle—
Ae spring brought off her master hale,
But left behind her ain grey tail: own
The carlin claught her by the rump,   old woman
And left poor Maggie scarce a stump.   220

   Now, wha this tale o' truth shall read,
Ilk man and mother's son, take heed: every
Whene'er to drink you are inclin'd,
Or cutty-sarks run in your mind,
Think, ye may buy the joys o'er dear,   225
Remember Tam o' Shanter's mare.

---

7   It is a well known fact that witches, or any evil spirits, have no power to follow a poor
wight any farther than the middle of the next running stream.—It may be proper likewise to
mention to the benighted traveller, that when he falls in with *bogles*, whatever danger may be
in his going forward, there is much more hazard in turning back. [Burns's note]

POEMS AND SONGS PUBLISHED ANONYMOUSLY
OR POSTHUMOUSLY.

Robert Bruce's March to Bannockburn — [1]

SCOTS, wha hae wi' WALLACE bled,   who have with
Scots, wham Bruce has aften led,
Welcome to your gory bed, —
  Or to victorie. —

Now 's the day, and now 's the hour;   5
See the front o' battle lour;
See approach proud EDWARD's power,
  Chains and Slaverie.

Wha will be a traitor-knave?
Wha will fill a coward's grave?   10
Be sae base as be a Slave?
  — Let him turn and flie: —

Wha for SCOTLAND's king and law,
Freedom's sword will strongly draw,
FREE-MAN stand, or FREE-MAN fa',   15 fall
  Let him follow me. —

By Oppression's woes and pains!
By your Sons in servile chains!
We will drain our dearest veins,
  But they *shall* be free!   20

Lay the proud Usurpers low!
Tyrants fall in every foe!
LIBERTY's in every blow!
  Let us DO — OR DIE!!!

---

1 First published anonymously in the London *Morning Chronicle*, May 1794. Also known as
 'Scots wha hae'; sung to the tune 'Hey tuti tatey'.

Song — For a' that and a' that — [1]

Is there, for honest Poverty
    That hings his head, and a' that;   hangs
The coward-slave, we pass him by,
    We dare be poor for a' that!
For a' that, and a' that,   5
    Our toils obscure and a' that,
The rank is but the guinea's stamp,
    The Man's the gowd for a' that. —   gold

What though on hamely fare we dine,
    Wear hoddin grey,[2] and a' that?   10
Gie fools their silks, and knaves their wine,
    A Man's a Man for a' that.
For a' that, and a' that,
    Their tinsel show, and a' that;
The honest man, tho' e'er sae poor,   15
    Is king o' men for a' that. —

Ye see yon birkie ca'd, a lord,   that fellow called
    Wha struts, and stares, and a' that,
Though hundreds worship at his word,
    He 's but a coof for a' that.   20   fool
For a' that, and a' that,
    His ribband, star and a' that,
The man of independent mind,
    He looks and laughs at a' that. —

A prince can mak a belted knight,   25
    A marquise, duke, and a' that;
But an honest man's aboon his might,   above
    Gude faith, he mauna fa' that!   must not lay claim to
For a' that, and a' that,
    Their dignities and a' that,   30
The pith o' Sense, and pride o' Worth,
    Are higher rank than a' that. —

Then let us pray that come it may,
    As come it will for a' that,
That Sense and Worth, o'er a' the earth   35
    Shall bear the gree, and a' that.
For a' that, and a' that,
    It's comin yet for a' that,
That Man to Man the warld o'er,
    Shall brothers be for a' that. —   40

---

1   First published anonymously in the *Glasgow Magazine*, August 1795 (although the first stanza given here was added later from the MS). Also known as 'A Man's a Man for a' That': strictly speaking, 'For a' that and a' that' is the name of the tune Burns was writing for.

2   Coarse woollen cloth used for work-clothes.

Holy Willie's Prayer[1]

And send the Godly in a pet to pray —
POPE[2]

Argument.

Holy Willie was a rather oldish batchelor Elder in the parish of Mauchline, and much and justly famed for that polemical chattering which ends in tippling Orthodoxy, and for that Spiritualized Bawdry which refines to Liquorish Devotion. — In a Sessional process with a gentleman in Mauchline, a Mr. Gavin Hamilton, Holy Willie, and his priest, father Auld, after full hearing of the Presbytry of Ayr, came off but second best; owing partly to the oratorical powers of Mr. Robt. Aiken, Mr. Hamilton's Counsel; but chiefly to Mr. Hamilton's being one of the most irreproachable and truly respectable characters in the country. — On losing his Process, the Muse overheard him at his devotions as follows —

O THOU that in the heavens does dwell!
Wha, as it pleases best thysel,
Sends ane to heaven and ten to h-ll,
    A' for thy glory!
And no for ony gude or ill   5
    They've done before thee. —

I bless and praise thy matchless might,
When thousands thou hast left in night,
That I am here before thy sight,
    For gifts and grace,   10
A burning and a shining light
    To a' this place. —

What was I, or my generation,
That I should get such exaltation?
I, wha derserv'd most just damnation,   15
    For broken laws
Sax thousand years ere my creation,
    Thro' Adam's cause!

When from my mother's womb I fell,
Thou might hae plunged me in hell,   20
To gnash my gooms, and weep, and wail,
    In burning lakes,
Where damned devils roar and yell
    Chain'd to their stakes. —

---

1   First printed in pamphlet form in 1799 (without the 'Argument' at its head), but written in 1785, at the time of the events alluded to in the poem, and circulated privately. The charges, a vehicle for Rev. Auld's personal animus against Hamilton, were: '1. Unnecessary absence from church two Sabbaths in December and three Sabbaths in January together; 2. Setting out on a journey to Carrick on the third Sabbath in January; 3. Habitual if not total neglect of family worship; 4. Abusive letter to [Mauchline Kirk] Session dated 13th Nov. 1784.' Session appealed to the Synod of Glasgow and Ayr but Hamilton was again exonerated.

2   In Pope's *The Rape of the Lock* canto IV it is the spleen, understood as producing caprice and ill-humour, which has this effect (among various others).

Yet I am here, a chosen sample,   25
To shew thy grace is great and ample:
I'm here, a pillar o' thy temple
          Strong as a rock,
A guide, a ruler and example
          To a' thy flock. —   30

O L—d thou kens what zeal I bear,
When drinkers drink, and swearers swear,
And singin' there, and dancin' here,
          Wi' great an' sma';
For I am keepet by thy fear,   35
          Free frae them a'. —   from

But yet—O L—d—confess I must—
At times I'm fash'd wi' fleshly lust;   troubled with
And sometimes too, in warldly trust
          Vile Self gets in;   40
But thou remembers we are dust,
          Defil'd wi' sin. —

O L—d—yestreen—thou kens—wi' Meg—   yesterday evening
Thy pardon I sincerely beg!
O may't ne'er be a living plague,   45
          To my dishonor!
And I'll ne'er lift a lawless leg
          Again upon her. —

Besides, I farther maun avow,   must
Wi' Leezie's lass, three times—I trow—   50
But L—d, that friday I was fou   drunk
          When I cam near her;
Or else, thou kens, thy servant true
          Wad never steer her. —   afflict

Maybe thou lets this fleshly thorn   55
Buffett thy servant night and morn,
Lest he o'er proud and high should turn,
          That he 's sae gifted;
If sae, thy hand maun e'en be borne   must
          Untill thou lift it. —   60

L—d bless thy Chosen in this place,
For here thou has a chosen race:
But G—d, confound their stubborn face,
          And blast their name,
Wha bring thy rulers to disgrace   65
          And open shame. —

L—d mind Gaun Hamilton's deserts!
He drinks, and swears, and plays at cartes,
Yet has sae mony taking arts
            Wi' Great and Sma',   70
Frae G–d's ain priest the people's hearts   *from God's own*
            He steals awa. —

And when we chasten'd him therefore,
Thou kens how he bred sic a splore,   *such an uproar*
And set the warld in a roar   75
            O' laughin at us:
Curse thou his basket and his store,
            Kail and potatoes. —   *cabbage*

L—d hear my earnest cry and prayer
Against that Presbytry of Ayr!   80
Thy strong right hand, L—d, make it bare
            Upon their heads!
L—d visit them, and dinna spare   *don't*
            For their misdeeds!

O L—d my G–d, that glib-tongued Aiken!   85
My very heart and flesh are quaking
To think how I sat, sweating, shaking,
            And p–ss'd wi' dread,
While Auld wi' hingin lip gaed sneaking   *hanging; went*
            And hid his head!   90

L—d, in thy day o' vengeance try him!
L—d visit him that did employ him!
And pass not in thy mercy by them,
            Nor hear their prayer;
But for thy people's sake destroy them,   95
            And dinna spare!   *don't*

But L—d, remember me and mine
Wi' mercies temporal and divine!
That I for grace and gear may shine,   *property*
            Excell'd by nane!   100
And a' the glory shall be thine!
            AMEN! AMEN!

Love and Liberty—A Cantata[1]

Recitativo—[1][2]

WHEN lyart leaves bestrow the yird,	grey; earth
Or wavering like the Bauckie-bird,[3]	
Bedim cauld Boreas' blast;[4]	
When hailstanes drive wi' bitter skyte,	sudden blow
And infant Frosts begin to bite,	
In hoary cranreuch drest;	hoar-frost
Ae night at e'en a merry core	company
O' randie, gangrel bodies,	rude vagrant
In Poosie Nansie's[5] held the splore,	carousal
To drink their orra dudies:	spare clothes
Wi' quaffing, and laughing,	
They ranted an' they sang,	
Wi' jumping, an' thumping,	
The vera girdle rang.	griddle (on the fire)
First, niest the fire, in auld, red rags,	next to
Ane sat; weel braced wi' mealy bags	
And knapsack a' in order;	
His doxy lay within his arm;	tart
Wi' USQEBAE an' blankets warm,	whisky
She blinket on her Sodger:	
An' ay he gies the tozie drab	tipsy
The tither skelpan kiss,	Another smacking
While she held up her greedy gab,	mouth
Just like an aumous dish:	alms dish
Ilk smack still, did crack still,	each
Just like a cadger's whip;	pedlar's
Then staggering, an' swaggering,	
He roar'd this ditty up—	

---

1   This series of poems and songs is also known as *The Jolly Beggars*; not Burns's title, but suggestive of the obvious precedent for this kind of work, John Gay's *Beggar's Opera* of 1728. It was written in 1785–6 and published in 1799. For the tunes to the songs, see James Kinsley's edition of the *Poems and Songs* (OUP 1969).

2   *Recitative* is the type of delivery, between speaking and singing, used to fill in the dialogue and narration between songs in eighteenth-century opera.

3   The old Scotch name for the Bat. [Burns's note]

4   Boreas is the North Wind.

5   The Hostess of a noted Caravansary in M—, well known to and much frequented by the lowest orders of Travellers and Pilgrims. [Burns's note: i.e., an inn in Mauchline.]

Air [1]. *Tune, Soldier's joy*

I AM a son of Mars who have been in many wars,
    And show my cuts and scars wherever I come;
This here was for a wench, and that other in a trench,
    When welcoming the French at the sound of the drum.
                  [Chorus:] Lal de daudle &c.

My Prenticeship I past where my LEADER breath'd his last,
    When the bloody die was cast on the heights of ABRAM;
And I served out my TRADE when the gallant *game* was play'd,
    And the MORO low was laid at the sound of the drum.

I lastly was with Curtis among the *floating batt'ries*,
    And there I left for witness, an arm and a limb;
Yet let my Country need me, with ELLIOT to head me,
    I'd clatter on my stumps at the sound of a drum.[6]

And now tho' I must beg, with a wooden arm and leg,
    And many a tatter'd rag hanging over my bum,
I'm as happy with my wallet, my bottle, and my Callet,
    As when I us'd in scarlet to follow a drum.

What tho', with hoary locks, I must stand the winter shocks,
    Beneath the woods and rocks oftentimes for a home,
When the tother bag I sell and the tother bottle tell,
    I could meet a troop of HELL at the sound of a drum.

Recitativo — [2]

He ended; and the kebars sheuk,	rafters
Aboon the chorus roar;	above
While frighted rattons backward leuk,	rats
An' seek the benmost bore:	furthest in crack
A fairy FIDDLER frae the neuk,	corner
He skirl'd out, ENCORE.	
But up arose the martial CHUCK,	sweetheart
An' laid the loud uproar —	

---

6   The soldier has fought in some of the campaigns that established Britain's global dominance
in the mid-eighteenth century: on the Heights of Abraham (13th September 1759), where Gen.
Woolfe's victory over the French (achieved in part by his use of Highland troops) established
British control in Canada, but at which Woolfe himself was killed; at the storming of El Moro,
the Spanish fortress on Cuba, that secured Havana for British troops in 1762 (the ensuing
treaty granted Florida to the UK instead); and in Gibralter, where Gen. Sir George Eliot held
out against a three-year Spanish seige, aided by Rear Admiral Roger Curtis's supplies and
destruction of the naval batteries bombarding the peninsula in 1782.

Air [2]. *Tune, Sodger laddie*

I ONCE was a Maid, tho' I cannot tell when,
And still my delight is in proper young men:
Some one of a troop of DRAGOONS was my dadie,
No wonder I'm fond of a SODGER LADDIE.   soldier
            [Chorus:] Sing, lal de lal, &c.

The first of my LOVES was a swaggering blade,
To rattle the thundering drum was his trade;
His leg was so tight and his cheek was so ruddy,
Transported I was with my SODGER LADDIE.

But the godly old Chaplain left him in the lurch,
The sword I forsook for the sake of the church;
He ventur'd the SOUL, and I risked the BODY,
'Twas then I proved false to my SODGER LADDIE.

Full soon I grew sick of my sanctified *Sot*,
The Regiment AT LARGE for a HUSBAND I got;
From the gilded SPONTOON to the FIFE I was ready;[7]
I asked no more but a SODGER LADDIE.

But the PEACE it reduc'd me to beg in despair,[8]
Till I met my old boy in a CUNNINGHAM fair;
His RAGS REGIMENTAL they flutter'd so gaudy,
My heart it rejoic'd at a SODGER LADDIE.

And now I have lived — I know not how long,
And still I can join in a cup and a song;
But whilst with both hands I can hold the glass steady,
Here's to thee, MY HERO, my SODGER LADDIE.

Recitativo — [3]

Then niest outspak a raucle Carlin,   course old woman
Wha ken't fu' weel to cleek the Sterlin;   pilfer
For monie a pursie she had hooked,
An' had in mony a well been douked: ducked
Her LOVE had been a HIGHLAND LADDIE,
But weary fa' the waefu' woodie!   a curse on; noose
Wi' sighs an' sobs she thus began
To wail her braw JOHN HIGHLANDMAN —   fine

---

7   As spontoon is a halberd carried by infantry officers; the fife would have been played by a
     boy.
8   Presumably the Peace of Paris, in 1782, that ended the War of Independence in North
     America and the war with France that accompanied it.

Air [3]. *Tune, O an' ye were dead Gudeman*

A HIGHLAND lad my love was born,
The lalland laws he held in scorn;   lowland
But he still was faithfu' to his clan,
My gallant, braw JOHN HIGHLANDMAN.

> Chorus—Sing, hey my braw John Highlandman!
> Sing ho my braw John Highlandman!
> There's not a lad in a' the lan'
> Was match for my John Highlandman.

With his Philabeg, an' tartan Plaid,   kilt
An' guid Claymore down by his side,   broadsword
The ladies' hearts he did trepan,   buguile
My gallant, braw JOHN HIGHLANDMAN.
> Sing hey &c.

We ranged a' from Tweed to Spey,
An' liv'd like lords an' ladies gay:
For a lalland face he feared none,
My gallant, braw JOHN HIGHLANDMAN.
> Sing hey &c.

They banish'd him beyond the sea,
But ere the bud was on the tree,
Adown my cheeks the pearls ran,
Embracing my JOHN HIGHLANDMAN.
> Sing hey &c.

But Och! they catch'd him at the last,
And bound him in a dungeon fast,
My curse upon them every one,
They've hang'd my braw JOHN HIGHLANDMAN.
> Sing hey &c.

And now a Widow I must mourn
The Pleasures that will ne'er return;
No comfort but a hearty can,
When I think on JOHN HIGHLANDMAN.
> Sing hey &c.

Recitativo — [4]

A pigmy Scraper wi' his Fiddle,
Wha us'd to trystes an' fairs to driddle,   markets; dawdle
Her strappan limb an' gausy middle,   ample
    (He reach'd nae higher)
Had hol'd his HEARTIE like a riddle,
    An' blawn't on fire.

Wi' hand on hainch, and upward e'e,   hip; eye
He croon'd his gamut, ONE, TWO, THREE,
Then in an ARIOSO key,
    The wee Apollo
Set off wi' ALLEGRETTO glee
    His GIGA⁹ SOLO —

Air [4]. *Tune, Whistle owre the lave o't*

Let me ryke up to dight that tear,
An' go wi' me an' be my DEAR;
An' then your every CARE an' FEAR
       May whistle owre the lave o't.   over the rest of it

   Chorus — I am a Fiddler to my trade,
       An' a' the tunes that e'er I play'd,
       The sweetest still to WIFE or MAID,
       Was whistle owre the lave o't.

At KIRNS an' WEDDINS we'se be there,   harvest-homes; we shall
An' O sae nicely 's we will fare!
We'll bowse about till Dadie CARE   booze
       Sing, Whistle owre the lave o't.
       I am &c.

Sae merrily 's the banes we'll pyke,   bones we'll pick
An' sun oursels about the dyke;
An' at our leisure, when ye like
       We'll whistle owre the lave o't.
       I am &c.

But bless me wi' your heav'n o' charms,
An' while I kittle hair on thairms,   tickle; fiddle-strings
HUNGER, CAULD, an' a' sic harms   such
       May whistle owre the lave o't.
       I am &c.

---

9   A *gigue* is a lively piece in two sections, each repeated. 'Arioso' instrumental playing is in a
sustained, vocal style. 'Allegretto' playing is brisk. Apollo is god of music.

Recitativo — [5]

Her charms had struck a sturdy CAIRD,   tinker
        As weel as poor GUTSCRAPER;
He taks the Fiddler by the beard,
        An' draws a roosty rapier—
He swoor by a' was swearing worth
        To speet him like a Pliver,   spit; plover
Unless he would from that time forth
        Relinquish her for ever:

Wi' ghastly e'e poor TWEEDLEDEE   eye
        Upon his hunkers bended,   squatted
An' pray'd for grace wi' ruefu' face,
        An' so the quarrel ended;
But tho' his little heart did grieve,
        When round the TINKLER prest her,
He feign'd to snirtle in his sleeve   snigger
        When thus the CAIRD address'd her—

Air [5]. *Tune, Clout the Caudron*

My bonie lass I work in brass,
        A TINKLER is my station;
I've travell'd round all Christian ground
        In this my occupation;
I've ta'en the gold, an' been enroll'd
        In many a noble squadron:
But vain they search'd, when off I march'd
        To go an' clout the CAUDRON.   patch
                I've ta'en the gold, &c.

Despise that SHRIMP, that withered IMP,
        With a' his noise an' cap'rin;
An' take a share, with those that bear
        The *budget* and the *apron*!   leather bag
And *by* that STOWP! my faith an' houpe,   tankard
        And by that dear KILBAIGIE,[10]
If e'er ye want, or meet with scant,   poverty
        May I ne'er weet my CRAIGIE!   wet; throat
                And by that Stowp, &c.

---

10 A peculiar sort of Whiskie so called: a great favorite with Poosie Nansie's Clubs. [Burns's note]

The Caird prevail'd — th' unblushing fair
    In his embraces sunk;
Partly wi' LOVE o'ercome sae sair,
    An' partly she was drunk:
Sir VIOLINO with an air,
    That show'd a man o' spunk,   spirit
Wish'd UNISON between the PAIR,
    An' made the bottle clunk
            To their health that night.

But hurchin Cupid shot a shaft,   urchin
    That play'd a DAME a shavie —   trick
The Fiddler RAK'D her FORE AND AFT,
    Behint the chicken cavie: hen-coop
Her lord, a wight of HOMER's craft[11]   fellow
    Tho' limpan wi' the Spavie,   spavin, leg-tumour
He hirpl'd up and lap like daft,   hobbled; leapt
    An' shor'd them DAINTY DAVIE   offered them
            O' *boot* that night.   into the bargain

He was a care-defying blade,
    As ever BACCHUS listed!   enlisted
Tho' Fortune sair upon him laid,
    His heart she ever miss'd it.
He had no WISH but — to be glad,
    Nor WANT but — when he thristed;   thirsted
He hated nought but — to be sad,
    An' thus the Muse suggested
            His sang that night.

Air [6]. *Tune, For a' that an' a' that*

I AM a BARD, of no regard
    Wi' gentle folks an' a' that;
But HOMER LIKE the glowran byke,   gazing crowd
    Frae town to town I draw that.   from

Chorus —   For a' that, an' a' that,
            An' twice as muckle's a' that,   much as
            I've lost but ANE, I've TWA behin',
            I've WIFE ENEUGH for a' that.

I never drank the Muses' STANK,   pond
    Castalia's burn an' a' that,
But there it streams an' richly reams,   foams

---

11 Homer is allowed to be the eldest Ballad singer on record. [Burns's note]

My HELICON I ca' that.[12]   call
     For a' that &c.

Great love I bear to all the FAIR,
     Their humble slave an' a' that;
But lordly WILL, I hold it still
     A mortal sin to thraw that.   frustrate
     For a' that &c.

In raptures sweet this hour we meet
     Wi' mutual love an' a' that;
But for how lang the FLIE MAY STANG,
     Let INCLINATION law that.
     For a' that &c.

Their tricks an' craft hae put me daft,
     They've ta'en me in, an' a' that,
But clear your decks an' here 's the SEX!   [a toast]
     I like the jads for a' that.

        For a' that, an' a' that,
        An' twice as muckle's a' that,
        My DEAREST BLUID to do them guid,
        They're welcome till't for a' that.   to it

Recitativo — [7]

So sung the BARD — and Nansie's waw's   walls
Shook with a thunder of applause
     Re-echo'd from each mouth!
They toom'd their pocks, they pawn'd their duds,   emptied pockets; clothes
They scarcely left to coor their fuds   cover; tails
     To quench their lowan drouth: glowing thirst
Then owre again, the jovial thrang
     The Poet did request
To lowse his PACK an' wale a sang,   choose
     A BALLAD o' the best.
       He rising, rejoicing,
          Between his TWA DEBORAHS,
       Looks round him an' found them
          Impatient for the Chorus:

---

12 Castalia is a spring on Mount Parnassus, sacred to the Muses; Helicon another mountain, with similar springs.

Air [7]. *Tune, Jolly Mortals fill your glasses*

SEE the smoking bowl before us,
    Mark our jovial, ragged ring!
Round and round take up the Chorus,
    And in raptures let us sing —

    Chorus —   A fig for those by law protected!
              LIBERTY'S a glorious feast!
              Courts for cowards were erected,
              Churches built to please the PRIEST.

What is TITLE, what is TREASURE,
    What is REPUTATION's care?
If we lead a life of pleasure,
    'Tis no matter HOW or WHERE.
              A fig, &c.

With the ready trick and fable
    Round we wander all the day;
And at night, in barn or stable,
    Hug our doxies on the hay.
              A fig, &c.

Does the train-attended CARRIAGE
    Thro' the country lighter rove?
Does the sober bed of MARRIAGE
    Witness brighter scenes of love?
              A fig, &c.

Life is all a VARIORUM,
    We regard not how it goes;
Let them cant about DECORUM,
    Who have character to lose.
              A fig, &c.

Here's to BUDGETS, BAGS and WALLETS!
    Here's to all the wandering train!
Here's our ragged BRATS and CALLETS!   wenches
    One and all, cry out, AMEN!

              A fig for those by LAW protected!
              LIBERTY'S a glorious feast!
              COURTS for cowards were erected,
              CHURCHES built to please the Priest.

ADDRESS OF BEELZEBUB.[1]

To the Rt. Hon.ble JOHN, EARL OF BREADALBANE, President of the Rt. Hon.ble the HIGHLAND SOCIETY, which met, on the 23d of May last, at the Shakespeare, Covent garden, to concert ways and means to frustrate the designs of FIVE HUNDRED HIGHLANDERS, who, as the Society were informed by Mr. McKenzie of Applecross, were so audacious as to attempt an escape from their lawful lords and masters whose property they were, by emigrating from the lands of Mr. Mcdonald of Glengary to the wilds of CANADA, in search of that fantastic thing — LIBERTY —

LONG LIFE, my Lord, an' health be yours,
Unskaith'd by hunger'd HIGHLAN BOORS!
Lord grant, nae duddie, desp'rate beggar,   *ragged*
Wi' durk, claymore, or rusty trigger
May twin auld SCOTLAND o' a LIFE,   5   *deprive*
She likes — as BUTCHERS like a KNIFE!

Faith, you and Applecross were right
To keep the highlan hounds in sight!
I doubt na! they wad bid nae better,   *ask*
Than let them ance out owre the water;   10   *once*
Then up amang thae lakes an' seas
They'll mak what rules an' laws they please.

Some daring Hancocke, or a Frankline,
May set their HIGHLAN bluid a ranklin;
Some Washington again may head them,   15
Or some MONTGOMERY, fearless, lead them;[2]
Till God knows what may be effected,
When by such HEADS an' HEARTS directed:
Poor, dunghill sons of dirt an' mire,
May to PATRICIAN RIGHTS ASPIRE;   20
Nae sage North, now, nor sager Sackville,[3]
To watch an' premier owre the pack vile!
An' whare will ye get Howes an' Clintons
To bring them to a right repentance
To cowe the rebel generation,   25
An' save the honor o' the NATION?

---

1   Written in 1790; first published in the *Scots Magazine*, February 1818.
2   John Hancock (1737–93), President of the Continental Congress at the signing of the Declaration of Independence in 1776; Benjamin Franklin (1706–90), scientist, inventor and writer who helped draft the declaration; George Washington (1732–99), commander in the war with Britain and first President of the new state; Richard Montgomery (1738–75), a retired British soldier who led a rebel unit to capturing Montreal but was killed attacking Quebec.
3   Frederick, Lord North (1713–92), premier 1770–82 and thus responsible for the failure in America; George, 1st Viscount Sackville (1716–85), Secretary of State for American Affairs during the war; William, 5th Viscount Howe (1729–1814), the general in charge of British forces; Sir Henry Clinton (1738–95), general whose inability to relieve the seige of Gen. Cornwallis's army at Yorktown led to its surrender and the final British collapse in 1781.

THEY! an' be d—mn'd! what right hae they
To Meat, or Sleep, or light o' day,
Far less to riches, pow'r, or freedom,
But what your lordships PLEASE TO GIE THEM?

But, hear me, my lord! Glengary, hear!
Your HAND 'S OWRE LIGHT ON THEM, I fear;   too
Your FACTORS, GRIEVES, TRUSTEES and BAILIES,
I canna say but they do gailies;   cannot; well enough
They lay aside a' tender mercies   35
An' tirl the HALLIONS to the BIRSIES;   strip; rascals; bristles
Yet, while they're only poin'd and herriet,   distrained (for debt); harried
They'll keep their stubborn Highlan spirit.
But smash them! crush them a' to spails!   splinters
An' rot the DYVORS i' the JAILS!   40   bankrupts
The young dogs, swinge them to the labour,   flog
Let WARK an' HUNGER mak them sober!
The HIZZIES, if they're oughtlins fausont,   trollops; decent
Let them in DRURY LANE be lesson'd!⁴
An' if the wives, an' dirty brats,   45
Come thiggan at your doors an' yets,   begging; gates
Flaffan wi' duds, an' grey wi' beese,   flapping; rags; vermin
Frightan awa your deucks an' geese;
Get out a HORSE-WHIP, or a JOWLER,
The langest thong, the fiercest growler,   50
An' gar the tatter'd gipseys pack   make
Wi' a' their bastarts on their back!

Go on, my lord! I lang to meet you,
An' in my HOUSE AT HAME to greet you;
Wi' COMMON LORDS ye shanna mingle,   55
The benmost neuk, beside the ingle   furthest-in corner; fireplace
At my right hand, assign'd your seat,
'Tween HEROD's hip an' POLYCRATE;
Or, if ye on your station tarrow,   hesitate
Between ALMAGRO and PIZARRO,⁵   60
A seat, I'm sure ye're weel deservin 't;
An' till ye come—your humble servant,
                              BEELZEBUB
HELL 1st June Anno Mundi 5790⁶

---

4   London's Drury Lane was a notorious haunt of prostitutes.
5   Herod, king of Judea under Rome at the time of Christ; Polycrates, king of Samos in the
    Aegean in the mid sixth century B.C.; Diego D'Almargo (1475–1538) and Francisco Pizarro
    (1478–1541) leaders of the brutal Spanish conquest of Peru.
6   That is, 1790, plus the 4000 years calculated to have elapsed between the creation of the Earth
    and the birth of Christ: Satan of course does not count years from the latter.

ODE [For General Washington's Birthday].[1]

No Spartan tube, no Attic shell,
   No lyre Eolian I awake;
'Tis Liberty's bold note I swell,
   Thy harp, Columbia, let me take.[2]
See gathering thousands, while I sing,   5
A broken chain, exulting, bring,
   And dash it in a tyrant's face!
And dare him to his very beard,
And tell him, he no more is feared,
No more the Despot of Columbia's race.   10
A tyrant's proudest insults braved,
They shout, a People freed! They hail an Empire saved.

   Where is Man's godlike form?
Where is that brow erect and bold,
That eye that can, unmoved, behold   15
The wildest rage, the loudest storm,
That e'er created fury dared to raise!
Avaunt! thou caitiff, servile, base,
That tremblest at a Despot's nod,
Yet, crouching under th' iron rod,   20
Canst laud the hand that struck th' insulting blow!
Art thou of man's imperial line?
Dost boast that countenance divine?
Each skulking feature answers, No!
But come, ye sons of Liberty,   25
Columbia's offspring, brave as free,
  In danger's hour still flaming in the van:
Ye know, and dare maintain, The Royalty of Man.

   Alfred, on thy starry throne,
   Surrounded by the tuneful choir,   30
The Bards that erst have struck the patriot lyre,
And rous'd the freeborn Briton's soul of fire,
   No more thy England own. —[3]
Dare injured nations form the great design,
   To make detested tyrants bleed?[4]   35
Thy England execrates the glorious deed!
   Beneath her hostile banners waving,
   Every pang of honor braving,

---

1   Written in 1794; not published until 1874.
2   'Columbia' here meaning the Americas in general: that continent discovered by Christopher
     Columbus.
3   Taking Alfred the Great (848–99) as England's great liberator (from the Danes).
4   The French Republic had executed the erstwhile Louis XVI in January 1793.

England in thunder calls—'The Tyrant's cause is mine!'[5]
    That hour accurst, how did the fiends rejoice,   40
And hell thro' all her confines raise th' exulting voice,
    That hour which saw the generous English name
Linkt with such damned deeds of everlasting shame!

    Thee, Caledonia, thy wild heaths among,   45
    Famed for the martial deed, the heaven-taught song,
        To thee I turn with swimming eyes.—
        Where is that soul of Freedom fled?
        Immingled with the mighty Dead!
    Beneath that hallow'd turf where WALLACE lies!
    Hear it not, Wallace, in thy bed of death!   50
        Ye babbling winds in silence sweep;
        Disturb not ye the hero's sleep,
        Nor give the coward secret breath.—
    Is this the ancient Caledonian form,
    Firm as her rock, resistless as the storm?   55
    Shew me that eye which shot immortal hate,
        Blasting the Despot's proudest bearing:
    Shew me that arm which, nerved with thundering fate,
        Braved Usurpation's boldest daring!
        Dark-quenched as yonder sinking star,   60
        No more that glance lightens afar;
That palsied arm no more whirls on the waste of war.

---

5   When Britain went to war with the French Republic in February, it was entering a military and political alliance with absolutist monarchies such as Prussia, Austria and Spain. The U.S. government was of course sympathetic to the Republic.

The Fornicator. A New Song—[1]

Tune, Clout the Caldron.

YE jovial boys who love the joys,
    The blissful joys of Lovers;
Yet dare avow with dauntless brow,
    When the bony lass discovers;   *i.e. reveals her pregnancy*
I pray draw near and lend an ear,   5
    And welcome in a Frater,   *brother*
For I've lately been on quarantine,
    A proven Fornicator.

Before the Congregation wide
    I pass'd the muster fairly,   10
My handsome Betsey by my side,
    We gat our ditty rarely;[2]
But my downcast eye by chance did spy
    What made my lips to water,
Those limbs so clean where I, between,   15
    Commence'd a Fornicator.

With rueful face and signs of grace
    I pay'd the buttock-hire,[3]
The night was dark and thro' the park
    I could not but convey her;   20
A parting kiss, what could I less,
    My vows began to scatter,
My Betsey fell—lal de dal lal lal,
    I am a Fornicator.

But for her sake this vow I make,   25
    And solemnly I swear it,
That while I own a single crown,
    She's welcome for to share it;
And my rogueish boy his Mother's joy,
    And darling of his Pater,   30   *father*
For him I boast my pains and cost,
    Although a Fornicator.

Ye wenching blades whose hireling jades
    Have tipt you off blue-boram,[4]
I tell you plain, I do disdain   35

---

1   Written in 1784–5. As well as collecting, arranging and writing traditional folk-songs, Burns also collected and wrote bawdy lyrics. This collection came to be known as *The Merry Muses of Caledonia* and, after many years unofficial circulation, were eventually published in 1965, in the era of the Lady Chatterley trial. This and the following lyric are from this source.
2   'Received our reproof', i.e. from the minister in church, in the 'stool of repentance'.
3   The church fine for fornication.
4   I.e. whose whores have given them pox.

          To rank you with the Quorum;
But a bony lass upon the grass
          To teach her esse Mater,   to become a mother
And no reward but for regard,
          O that's a Fornicator.   40

Your warlike Kings and Heros bold,
          Great Captains and Commanders;
Your mighty Cèsars fam'd of old,
          And Conquering Alexanders;
In fields they fought and laurels bought   45
          And bulwarks strong did batter,
But still they grac'd our noble list
          And ranked Fornicator!!!

Why should na poor folk mowe.[1]

Tune, The Campbells are Coming.

WHEN Princes and Prelates and het-headed zealots
    All Europe hae set in a lowe,   blaze
The poor man lies down, nor envies a crown,
    And comforts himsel with a mowe. —   fuck

Chorus
And why shouldna poor folk mowe, mowe, mowe,
    And why shouldna poor folk mowe:
The great folk hae siller, and houses and lands,   silver
    Poor bodies hae naething but mowe. —

2
When Br–nsw–ck's great Prince cam a cruising to Fr–nce
    Republican billies to cowe,[2]
Bauld Br–nsw–c's great Prince wad hae shawn better sense,   bold
    At hame with his Princess to mowe. —
        And why should na &c. —

3
Out over the Rhine proud Pr–ss–a wad shine,
    To *spend* his best blood he did vow;
But Frederic had better ne'er forded water,[3]
    But *spent* as he docht in a mowe. —   as he planned [?]
        And why &c. —

4
By sea and by shore! the Emp–r–r swore,[4]
    In Paris he'd kick up a row;
But Paris sae ready just leugh at the laddie   laughed
    And bade him gae tak him a mowe. —
        And why &c. —

5
Auld Kate laid her claws on poor Stanislaus,[5]
    And Poland has bent like a bow:
May the deil in her a— ram a huge pr–ck o' brass!
    And damn her in h–ll with a mowe!
        And why &c. —

---

1   Written in 1792.
2   Charles William Ferdinand, Duke of Brunswick and brother-in-law to George III, invaded France with a mostly Prussian and Austrian army in August 1792, aiming to overthrow the revolution. It was defeated at Valmy.
3   Frederick-William II was King of Prussia.
4   Francis II, Holy Roman Emperor, another member of the coalition against France.
5   Catherine the Great, Empress of Russia; and Stanisław August Poniatowski, last King of the Polish-Lithuanian Commonwealth. Stanisław had sided with his reformist parliament to produce a modernising Constitution for Poland, partly inspired by events in France, in 1791. The following year Russia invaded to reassert its hegemony, and defeated the new state.

6

But truce with commotions and new-fangled notions,
    A bumper I trust you'll allow:
Here's George our gude king and Charlotte his queen,
    And lang may they tak a gude mowe!

A

SERIES OF PLAYS:

IN WHICH
IT IS ATTEMPTED TO DELINIATE

THE STRONGER PASSIONS OF THE MIND.

EACH PASSION BEING THE SUBJECT
OF

A TRAGEDY AND A COMEDY.[1]

LONDON:
PRINTED FOR T. CADELL, JUN. AND W.DAVIES, IN THE STRAND.

1798

[from] INTRODUCTORY DISCOURSE[2]

IT is natural for a writer, who is about to submit his works to the Publick, to feel a strong inclination, by some Preliminary Address, to conciliate the favour of his reader, and dispose him, if possible, to peruse them with a favourable eye. I am well aware, however, that his endeavours are generally fruitless: in his situation our hearts revolt from all appearance of confidence, and we consider his diffidence as hypocrisy. Our own word is frequently taken for what we say of ourselves, but very rarely for what we say of our works. Were these three plays, which this small volume contains, detached pieces only, and unconnected with others that do not yet appear, I should have suppressed this inclination altogether;[3] and have allowed my reader to begin what

---

1   By Joanna Baillie (1762–1851). This volume is usually referred to as the 1798 *Plays on the Passions*. Other volumes followed.

2   What follows are extracts only. I have omitted all of Baillie's own footnotes. Where sections of paragraphs have been elided, this is marked thus: […]; where whole paragraphs have been elided, this is marked with asterisks. The complete text can be conveniently read on Google Books, in an 1821 edition of this volume.

3   The three plays are *Count Basil* and *The Tryal*, respectively a tragedy and a comedy delineating the passion of love; and *De Monfort*, representing the passion of hate. *De Monfort*'s partner comedy on hate is *The Election*, included in the second volume of *Plays on the Passions*, published in 1802. Baillie's original plan was for a pair of plays to address, as well as love and hate, ambition, fear, hope, remorse, jealousy, pride, envy, revenge, anger, joy, and grief. This plan was subsequently revised, and having got as far as remorse and jealousy in the

is before him, and to form what opinion of it his taste or his humour might direct, without any previous trespass upon his time or his patience. But they are part of an extensive design: of one which, as far as my information goes, has nothing exactly similar to it in the language: of one which a whole life time will be limited enough to accomplish; and which has, therefore, a considerable chance of being cut short by that hand which nothing can resist.

Before I explain the plan of this work, I must make a demand upon the patience of my reader, whilst I endeavour to communicate to him those ideas regarding human nature, as they in some degree affect almost every species of moral writings, but particularly the Dramatic, that induced me to attempt it; and, as far as my judgment enabled me to apply them, has directed me in the execution of it.

From that strong sympathy which most creatures, but the human above all, feel for others of their kind, nothing has become so much an object of man's curiosity as man himself. We are all conscious of this within ourselves, and so constantly do we meet with it in others, that like every circumstance of continually repeated occurrence, it thereby escapes observation. Every person, who is not deficient in intellect, is more or less occupied in tracing, amongst the individuals he converses with, the varieties of understanding and temper which constitute the characters of men; and receives great pleasure from every stroke of nature that points out to him those varieties. This is, much more than we are aware of, the occupation of children, and of grown people also, whose penetration is but lightly esteemed; and that conversation which degenerates with them into trivial and mischievous tattling, takes its rise not unfrequently from the same source that supplies the rich vein of the satirist and the wit. That eagerness so universally shewn for the conversation of the latter, plainly enough indicates how many people have been occupied in the same way with themselves. Let any one, in a large company, do or say what is strongly expressive of his particular character, or of some passion or humour of the moment, and it will be detected by almost every person present. How often may we see a very stupid countenance animated with a smile, when the learned and the wise have betrayed some native feature of their own minds! And how often will this be the case when they have supposed it to be concealed under a very different disguise! From this constant employment of their minds, most people, I believe, without being conscious of it, have stored up in idea the greater part of those strongly marked varieties of human character, which may be said to divide it into classes;[4] and in one of those classes they involuntarily place every new person they become acquainted with.

* * * * *

In our ordinary intercourse with society, this sympathetick propensity of our minds is exercised upon men, under the common occurrences of life, in which we have often observed them. Here vanity and weakness put themselves forward to view, more conspicuously than the virtues: here men encounter those smaller trials, from which they are not apt to come off victorious; and here, consequently, that which is marked with the whimsical and ludicrous will strike us most forcibly, and make the strongest impression on our memory. To this sympathetick propensity of our minds, so exercised, the genuine and pure comick of every composition, whether drama, fable, story, or satire is addressed.

1836 *Miscellaneous Plays*, Baillie regarded the project as complete.

4   It is perhaps worth pointing out that Baillie does not mean *social* classes: the use of 'class' in the formulations 'working class', 'middle class' etc was just coming into currency around this time.

If man is an object of so much attention to man, engaged in the ordinary occurrences of life, how much more does he excite his curiosity and interest when placed in extraordinary situations of difficulty and distress? It cannot be any pleasure we receive from the sufferings of a fellow-creature which attracts such multitudes of people to a publick execution, though it is the horrour we conceive for such a spectacle that keeps so many away. To see a human being bearing himself up under such circumstances, or struggling with the terrible apprehensions which such a situation impresses, must be the powerful incentive, which makes us press forward to behold what we shrink from, and wait with trembling expectation for what we dread. For though few at such a spectacle can get near enough to distinguish the expression of face, or the minuter parts of a criminal's behaviour, yet from a considerable distance will they eagerly mark whether he steps firmly; whether the motions of his body denote agitation or calmness; and if the wind does but ruffle his garment, they will, even from that change upon the outline of his distant figure, read some expression connected with his dreadful situation. Though there is a greater proportion of people in whom this strong curiosity will be overcome by other dispositions and motives; though there are many more who will stay away from such a sight than will go to it; yet there are very few who will not be eager to converse with a person who has beheld it; and to learn, very minutely, every circumstance connected with it, except the very act itself of inflicting death. To lift up the roof of his dungeon, like the *Diable boiteux*,[5] and look upon a criminal the night before he suffers, in his still hour of privacy, when all that disguise, which respect for the opinion of others, the strong motive by which even the lowest and wickedest of men continue to be moved, would present an object to the mind of every person, not withheld from it by great timidity of character, more powerfully attractive than almost any other.

* * * * *

But it is not in situations of difficulty and distress alone, that man becomes the object of this sympathetick curiosity; he is no less so when the evil he contends with arises in his own breast, and no outward circumstance connected with him either awakens our attention or our pity. What human creature is there, who can behold a being like himself under the violent agitation of those passions which all have, in some degree, experienced, without feeling himself most powerfully excited by the sight? I say, all have experienced, for the bravest man on earth knows what fear is as well as the coward; and will not refuse to be interested for one under the dominion of this passion, provided there be nothing in the circumstances attending it to create contempt. Anger is a passion that attracts less sympathy than any other, yet the unpleasing and distorted features of an angry man will be more eagerly gazed upon, by those who are no wise concerned with his fury or the objects of it, than the most amiable placid countenance in the world. Every eye is directed to him; every voice is hushed to silence in his presence; even children will leave off their gambols as he passes, and gaze after him more eagerly than the gaudiest equipage. The wild tossings of despair; the gnashing of hatred and revenge; the yearnings of affection, and the softened mien of love; all that language of the agitated soul, which every age and nation understands, is never addressed to the dull nor inattentive.

It is not merely under the violent agitations of passion, that man so rouses and interests us; even the smallest indications of an unquiet mind, the restless eye, the muttering lip, the half-checked exclamation, and the hasty start, will set our attention

---

5 *Le Diable boiteux* (1707) is a picaresque novel by French author Alain René Lesage in which a devil reveals to the hero various types of human depravity by lifting the roofs of houses to reveal the private behaviour going on within.

as anxiously upon the watch, as the first distant flashes of a gathering storm. When some great explosion of passion bursts forth, and some consequent catastrophe happens, if we are at all acquainted with the unhappy perpetrator, how minutely will we endeavour to remember every circumstance of his past behaviour! And with what avidity will we seize upon every recollected word or gesture, that is in the smallest degree indicative of the supposed state of his mind, at the time when they took place. If we are not acquainted with him, how eagerly will we listen to similar recollections from another! Let us understand, from observation or report, that any person harbours in his breast, concealed from the world's eye, some powerful rankling passion of what kind soever it be, we will observe every word, every motion, every look, even the distant gait of such a man, with a constancy and attention bestowed upon no other. Nay, should we meet him unexpectedly on our way, a feeling will pass across our minds as though we found ourselves in the neighbourhood of some secret and fearful thing. If invisible, would we not follow him into his lonely haunts, into his closet, into the midnight silence of his chamber? There is, perhaps, no employment which the human mind will with so much avidity pursue, as the discovery of concealed passion, as the tracing the varieties and progress of a perturbed soul.

It is to this sympathetick curiosity of our nature, exercised upon mankind in great and trying occasions, and under the influence of the stronger passions, when the grand, the generous, the terrible attract our attention far more than the base and depraved, that the high and powerfully tragick, of every composition, is addressed.

This propensity is universal. Children begin to shew it very early; it enters into many of their amusements, and that part of them too, for which they shew the keenest relish. It tempts them many times, as well as the mature in years, to be guilty of tricks, vexations, and cruelty; yet God Almighty has implanted it within us, as well as all our other propensities and passions, for wise and good purposes. It is our best and most powerful instructor. From it we are taught the proprieties and decencies of ordinary life, and are prepared for distressing and difficult situations. In examining others we know ourselves. With limbs untorn, with head unsmitten, with senses unimpaired by despair, we know what we ourselves might have been on the rack, on the scaffold, and in the most afflicting circumstances of distress. Unless when accompanied with passions of the dark and malevolent kind, we cannot well exercise this disposition without becoming more just, more merciful, more compassionate; and as the dark and malevolent passions are not the predominant inmates of the human breast, it hath produced more deeds—O many more! of kindness than of cruelty. It holds up for our example a standard of excellence, which, without its assistance, our inward consciousness of what is right and becoming might never have dictated. It teaches us, also, to respect ourselves, and our kind; for it is a poor mind, indeed, that from this employment of its faculties, learns not to dwell upon the noble view of human nature rather than the mean.

Universal, however, as this disposition undoubtedly is, with a generality of mankind it occupies itself in a passing and superficial way. Though a native trait of character or of passion is obvious to them as well as to the sage, yet to their minds it is but the visitor of a moment; they look upon it singly and unconnected: and though this disposition, even so exercised, brings instruction as well as amusement, it is chiefly by storing up in their minds those ideas to which the instructions of others refer, that it can be eminently useful. Those who reflect and reason upon what human nature holds out to their observation, are comparatively but few. No stroke of nature which engages their attention stands insulated and alone. Each presents itself to them with many varied connections; and they comprehend not merely the immediate feeling which gave rise to it, but the relation of that feeling to others which are concealed. We wonder at the changes and caprices of men; they see in them nothing but what is natural and accountable. We stare upon some dark catastrophe of passion, as the Indians did stare upon an eclipse of the moon; they, conceiving the track of ideas through which an impassioned mind has passed, regard it like the philosopher who foretold the phenomenon. Knowing what situation of life he is about to be thrown into, they perceive in the man, who, like Hazael, says, "is thy servant a dog that he should do this thing?" the foul and ferocious murderer.[6] A man of this contemplative character partakes, in some degree, of the entertainment of the Gods, who were supposed to look down upon this world and the inhabitants of it, as we do upon a theatrical exhibition; and if he is of a benevolent disposition, a good man struggling with, and triumphing over adversity, will be to him, also, the most delightful spectacle. But though this eagerness to observe their fellow-creatures in every situation, leads not the generality of mankind to reason and reflect; and those strokes of nature which they are so ready to remark, stand single and unconnected in their minds, yet they may be easily induced to do both: and there is no mode of instruction which they will so eagerly pursue, as that which lays open before them, in a more enlarged and connected view, than their individual observations are capable of supplying, the varieties of the human mind. Above all, to be well exercised in this study will fit a man more particularly for the most important situations of life. He will prove for it the better Judge, the better Magistrate, the better Advocate; and as a ruler or conductor of other men, under every occurring circumstance, he will find himself the better enabled to fulfil his duty, and accomplish his designs. He will perceive the natural effect of every order that he issues upon the minds of his soldiers, his subjects, or his followers; and he will deal to others judgment tempered with mercy; that is to say truly just; for justice appears to us severe only when it is imperfect.

In proportion as moral writers of every class have exercised within themselves this sympathetick propensity of our nature, and have attended to it in others, their works have been interesting and instructive. They have struck the imagination more forcibly, convinced the understanding more clearly, and more lastingly impressed the memory. If unseasoned with any reference to this, the fairy bowers of the poet, with all his gay images of delight, will be admired and forgotten; the important relations of the historian, and even the reasonings of the philosopher will make a less permanent impression.

* * * * *

Our desire to know what men are in the closet as well as in the field, by the blazing hearth, and at the social board, as well as in the council and the throne, is very imperfectly gratified by real history; romance writers, therefore, stepped boldly forth to supply the deficiency; and tale writers, and novel writers, of many descriptions, followed after. If they have not been very skilful in the delineations of nature; if they have represented men and women speaking and acting as men and women never did speak or act; if they have caricatured both our virtues and our vices; if they have given us such pure and unmixed, or such heterogeneous combinations of character as real life never presented, and yet have pleased and interested us, let it not be imputed to the dulness of man in discerning what is genuinely natural in himself. There are many inclinations belonging to us, besides this great master-propensity of which I am treating. Our love of the grand, the beautiful, the novel, and above all of the marvellous, is very strong; and if we are richly fed with what we have a good relish for, we may be weaned to forget our native and favourite aliment. Yet we can never so far

6   See 2 Kings 8:13.

forget it, but we will cling to, and acknowledge it again, whenever it is presented before us. In a work abounding with the marvellous and unnatural, if the author has any how stumbled upon an unsophisticated genuine stroke of nature, we will immediately perceive and be delighted with it, though we are foolish enough to admire at the same time, all the nonsense with which it is surrounded. After all the wonderful incidents, dark mysteries, and secrets revealed, which eventful novel[7] so liberally presents to us; after the beautiful fairy ground, and even the grand and sublime scenes of nature with which descriptive novel so often enchants us; those works which most strongly characterize human nature in the middling and lower classes of society, where it is to be discovered by stronger and more unequivocal marks, will ever be the most popular. For though great pains have been taken in our higher sentimental novels to interest us in the delicacies, embarrassments, and artificial distresses of the more refined part of society, they have never been able to cope in the public opinion with these. The one is a dressed and beautiful pleasure-ground, in which we are enchanted for a while, amongst the delicate and unknown plants of cultivation; the other is a rough forest of our native land; the oak, the elm, the hazle, and the bramble are there; and amidst the endless varieties of its paths we can wander for ever. Into whatever scenes the novelist may conduct us, what object soever he may present to our view, still is our attention most sensibly awake to every touch faithful to nature; still are we upon the watch for every thing that speaks to us of ourselves.

The fair field of what is properly called poetry, is enriched with so many beauties, that in it we are often tempted to forget what we really are, and what kind of beings we belong to. Who in the enchanted regions of simile, metaphor, allegory and description, can remember the plain order of things in this every-day world? From heroes whose majestick forms rise like a lofty tower, whose eyes are lightening, whose arms are irresistible, whose course is like the storms of heaven, bold and exalted sentiments we will readily receive; and will not examine them very accurately by that rule of nature which our own breast prescribes to us. A shepherd whose sheep, with fleeces of the purest snow, browse the flowery herbage of the most beautiful vallies; whose flute is ever melodious, and whose shepherdess is ever crowned with roses; whose every care is love, will not be called very strictly to account for the loftiness and refinement of his thoughts. The fair Nymph, who sighs out her sorrows to the conscious and compassionate wilds; whose eyes gleam like the bright drops of heaven; whose loose tresses stream to the breeze, may say what she pleases with impunity. I will venture, however, to say, that amidst all this decoration and ornament, all this loftiness and refinement, let one simple trait of the human heart, one expression of passion genuine and true to nature, be introduced, and it will stand forth alone in the boldness of reality, whilst the false and unnatural around it, fades away upon every side, like the rising exhalations of the morning. With admiration, and often with enthusiasm we proceed on our way through the grand and the beautiful images, raised to our imagination by the lofty Epic muse; but what even here are those things that strike upon the heart; that we feel and remember? Neither the descriptions of war, the sound of the trumpet, the clanging of arms, the combat of heroes, nor the death of the mighty, will interest our minds like the fall of the feeble stranger, who simply expresses the anguish of his soul, at the thoughts of that far-distant home which he must never return to again, and closes his eyes, amongst the ignoble and forgotten; like the timid stripling goaded by the shame of reproach, who urges his trembling steps to the fight, and falls like a

---

7   This odd usage, repeated in the next clause, omitting the article from the expected 'the eventful novel', is not mentioned in OED, but it remains uncorrected in subsequent editions.

tender flower before the first blast of winter. How often will some simple picture of this kind be all that remains upon our minds of the terrifick and magnificent battle, whose description we have read with admiration! How comes it that we relish so much the episodes of an heroic poem?[8] It cannot merely be that we are pleased with a resting place, where we enjoy the variety of contrast; for were the heroic style introduced into it, ninety readers out of an hundred would pass over it altogether. It is not that we meet such a story, so situated, with a kind of sympathetic good will, as in passing through a country of castles and of palaces, we should pop unawares upon some humble cottage, resembling the dwellings of our native land, and gaze upon it with affection. The highest pleasures which we receive from poetry, as well as from the real objects which surround us in the world, are derived from the sympathetick interest we all take in beings like ourselves; and I will even venture to say, that were the grandest scenes which can enter into the imagination of man, presented to our view, and all reference to man completely shut out from our thoughts, the objects that composed it would convey to our minds little better than dry ideas of magnitude, colour, and form; and the remembrance of them would rest upon our minds like the measurement and distances of the planets.

If the study of human nature then, is so useful to the poet, the novelist, the historian, and the philosopher, of how much greater importance must it be to the dramatick writer? To them it is a powerful auxiliary, to him it is the centre and strength of the battle. If characteristick views of human nature enliven not their pages, there are many excellencies with which they can, in some degree, make up for the deficiency, it is what we receive from them with pleasure rather than demand. But in his works no richness of invention, harmony of language, nor grandeur of sentiment will supply the place of faithfully delineated nature. The poet and the novelist may represent to you their great characters from the cradle to the tomb. They may represent them in any mood or temper, and under the influence of any passion which they see proper, without being obliged to put words into their mouths, those great betrayers of the feigned and adopted. They may relate every circumstance however trifling and minute, that serves to develop their tempers and dispositions. They tell us what kind of people they intend their men and women to be, and as such we receive them. If they are to move us in any scene of distress, every circumstance regarding the parties concerned in it, how they looked, how they moved, how they sighed, how the tears gushed from their eyes, how the very light and shadow fell upon them, is carefully described, and the few things that are given them to say along with all this assistance, must be very unnatural indeed if we refuse to sympathize with them. But the characters of the drama must speak directly for themselves. Under the influence of every passion, humour, and impression; in the artificial veilings of hypocrisy and ceremony, in the openness of freedom and confidence, and in the lonely hour of meditation they speak. He who made us hath placed within our breast a judge that judges instantaneously of every thing they say. We expect to find them creatures like ourselves; and if they are untrue to nature, we feel that we are imposed upon; as though the poet had introduced to us for brethren, creatures of a different race, beings of another world.

* * * * *

[…] But in presenting to us those views of great characters, and of the human mind in difficult and trying situations which particularly belong to Tragedy, the far greater proportion, even of those who may be considered as respectable dramatick poets, have very much failed. From the beauty of those original dramas to which they have ever

---

8   Baillie is using 'episode' its older sense of 'digression' or 'interpolated narrative'.

looked back with admiration, they have been tempted to prefer the embellishments of poetry to faithfully delineated nature. They have been more occupied in considering the works of the great Dramatists who have gone before them, and the effects produced by their writings, than the varieties of human character which first furnished materials for those works, or those principles in the mind of man by means of which such effects were produced. Neglecting the boundless variety of nature, certain strong outlines of character, certain bold features of passion, certain grand vicissitudes and striking dramatick situations have been repeated from one generation to another; whilst a pompous and solemn gravity, which they have supposed to be necessary for the dignity of tragedy, has excluded almost entirely from their works those smaller touches of nature, which so well develop the mind; and by showing men in their hours of state and exertion only, they have consequently shewn them imperfectly. Thus, great and magnanimous heroes, who bear with majestick equanimity every vicissitude of fortune; who in every temptation and trial stand forth in unshaken virtue, like a rock buffeted by the waves; who encompast with the most terrible evils, in calm possession of their souls, reason upon the difficulties of state; and, even upon the brink of destruction, pronounce long eulogiums on virtue, in the most eloquent and beautiful language, have been held forth to our view as objects of imitation and interest; as though they had entirely forgotten that it is only from creatures like ourselves that we feel, and therefore, only from creatures like ourselves that we receive the instruction of example. [...]

* * * * *

They have, indeed, from this regard to the works of preceding authors, and great attention to the beauties of composition, and to dignity of design, enriched their plays with much striking, and sometimes sublime imagery, lofty thoughts, and virtuous sentiments; but in striving so eagerly to excel in those things that belong to tragedy in common with many other compositions, they have very much neglected those that are peculiarly her own. [...] Every species of moral writing has its own way of conveying instruction, which it can never, but with disadvantage, exchange for any other. The Drama improves us by the knowledge we acquire of our own minds, from the natural desire we have to look into the thoughts, and observe the behaviour of others. Tragedy brings to our view men placed in those elevated situations, exposed to those great trials, and engaged in those extraordinary transactions, in which few of us are called upon to act. As examples applicable to ourselves, therefore, they can but feebly affect us; it is only from the enlargement of our ideas in regard to human nature, from that admiration of virtue, and abhorrence of vice which they excite, that we can expect to be improved by them. But if they are not represented to us as real and natural characters, the lessons we are taught from their conduct and sentiments will be no more to us than those which we receive from the pages of the poet or the moralist.

But the last part of the task which I have mentioned as peculiarly belonging to tragedy, unveiling the human mind under the dominion of those strong and fixed passions, which seemingly unprovoked by outward circumstances, will from small beginnings brood within the breast, till all the better dispositions, all the fair gifts of nature are borne down before them, her poets in general have entirely neglected, and even her first and greatest have but imperfectly attempted. They have made use of the passions to mark their several characters, and animate the scenes, rather than to open to our view the nature and portraitures of those great disturbers of the human breast, with whom we are all, more or less, called upon to contend. [...] The impassioned character is generally brought into view under those irresistible attacks of their power, which it is impossible to repell; whilst those gradual steps that led him to this state, in some of which a stand might have been made against the foe, are left entirely in the shade. [...]

It is characteristick of the more powerful passions that they will encrease and nourish themselves on very slender aliment; it is from within that they are chiefly supplied with what they feed on; and it is in contending with opposite passions and affections of the mind that we best[9] discover their strength, not with events. But in tragedy it is events more frequently than opposite affections which are opposed to them; and those of such force and magnitude that the passions themselves are almost obscured by the spendour and importance of the transactions to which they are attached. [...]

From this general view, which I have endeavoured to communicate to my reader, of tragedy, and those principles in the human mind upon which the success of her efforts depends, I have been led to believe, that an attempt to write a series of tragedies, of simpler construction, less embellished with poetical decorations, less constrained by that lofty seriousness which has so generally been considered as necessary for the support of tragick dignity, and in which the chief object should be to delineate the progress of the higher passions in the human breast, each play exhibiting a particular passion, might not be unacceptable to the publick. And I have been the more readily induced to act upon this idea, because I am confident, that tragedy, written upon this plan, is fitter to produce stronger moral effect than upon any other. [...] We cannot, it is true, amidst its wild uproar [of the 'tempest' of passion], listen to the voice of reason, and save ourselves from destruction; but we can foresee its coming, we can mark its rising signs, we can know the situations that will most expose us to its rage, and we can shelter our heads from the coming blast. [...] Above all, looking back to the first rise, and tracing the progress of passion, points out to us those stages in the approach of the enemy, when he might have been combated most successfully; and where the suffering him to pass may be considered as occasioning all the misery that ensues.

* * * * *

It was the saying of a sagacious Scotchman, 'let who will make the laws of a nation, if I may have the writing of its ballads.'[10] Something similar may be said in regard to the Drama. Its lessons reach not, indeed, to the lowest classes of the labouring people, who are the broad foundation of society, which can generally never be moved without endangering every thing that is constructed upon it, and who are our potent and formidable ballad readers; but they reach to the classes next in order to them, and who will always have over them no inconsiderable influence. The impressions made by it are communicated, at the same instant of time, to a greater number of individuals, than those of any other species of writing; and they are strengthened in every spectator, by observing their effects upon those who surround him. From this observation, the mind of the reader will suggest of itself, what it would be unnecessary, and, perhaps, improper in me here to enlarge upon. The theatre is a school in which much good or evil may be learned. At the beginning of its career the Drama was employed to mislead and excite; and were I not unwilling to refer to transactions of the present times, I might abundantly confirm what I have said by recent examples. The authour, therefore, who aims in any degree to improve the mode of its instruction, and point to more useful lessons than it is generally employed to dispense, is certainly praiseworthy, though want of abilities may unhappily prevent him from being successful in his efforts.

* * * * *

9   The first edition reads 'least' here, which makes no sense; later editions correct this and I follow them at this point.

10   This is a paraphrase from *An Account of a Conversation Concerning a Right Regulation of Governments* (1704) by Andrew Fletcher of Saltoun, political theorist and member of the last Scottish parliament before the Union.

It may, perhaps, be supposed from my publishing these plays, that I have written them for the closet rather than the stage. If upon perusing them with attention, the reader is disposed to think they are better calculated for the first than the last, let him impute it to want of skill in the authour, and not to any previous design. A play, but of small poetical merit, that is suited to strike and interest the spectator, to catch the attention of him who will not, and of him who cannot read, is a more valuable and useful production than one whose elegant and harmonious pages are admired in the libraries of the tasteful and refined. To have received approbation from an audience of my countrymen, would have been more pleasing to me than any other praise. A few tears from the simple and young would have been, in my eyes, pearls of great price; and the spontaneous, untutored plaudits of the rude and uncultivated would have come to my heart as offerings of no mean value. I should, therefore, have been better pleased to have introduced them to the world from the stage than from the press. I possess, however, no likely channel to the former mode of publick introduction; and upon further reflection it appeared to me that by publishing them in this way, I have an opportunity afforded me of explaining the design of my work, and enabling the publick to judge, not only of each play by itself, but as making a part likewise of the whole; an advantage which, perhaps, does more than over-balance the splendour and effect of theatrical representation.

It may be thought that with this extensive plan before me, I should not have been in a hurry to publish, but have waited to give a larger portion of it to the publick, which would have enabled them to make a truer estimate of its merit. To bring forth only three plays of the whole, and the last without its companion, may seem like the haste of those vain people, who as soon as they have written a few pages of a discourse, or a few couplets of a poem, cannot be easy till every body has seen them. I do protest, in honest simplicity! It is distrust and not confidence, that has led me at this early stage of an undertaking, to bring it before the publick. [...] I have not proceeded so far, indeed, merely upon the strength of my own judgment; but the friends to whom I have shewn my manuscripts are partial to me, and their approbation which in the case of any indifferent person would be in my mind absolutely decisive, goes but a little way in relieving me from these apprehensions. To step beyond the circle of my own immediate friends in quest of opinion, from the particular temper of my mind I feel an uncommon repugnance: I can with less pain to myself bring them before the publick at once, and submit to its decision. It is to my countrymen at large that I call for assistance. If this work is fortunate enough to attract their attention, let their strictures as well as their praise come to my aid: the one will encourage me in a long and arduous undertaking, the other will teach me to improve it as I advance. For there are many errours that may be detected, and improvements that may be suggested in the prosecution of this work, which from the observations of a great variety of readers are more likely to be pointed out to me, than from those of a small number of persons, even of the best judgment. I am not possessed of that confidence in mine own powers, which enables the concealed genius, under the pressure of present discouragement, to pursue his labours in security, looking firmly forward to other more enlightened times for his reward. If my own countrymen with whom I live and converse, who look upon the same race of men, the same state of society, the same passing events with myself, receive not my offering, I presume not to look to posterity.

Before I close this discourse, let me crave the forbearance of my reader, if he has discovered in the course of it any unacknowledged use of the thoughts of other authours, which he thinks ought to have been noticed; and let me beg the same favour, if in reading the following plays, any similar neglect seems to occur. There are few writers who have sufficient originality of thought to strike out for themselves new ideas upon every occasion. When a thought presents itself to me, as suited to the purpose I am aiming at, I would neither be thought proud enough to reject it, on finding that another has used it before me, nor mean enough to make use of it without acknowledging the obligation, when I can at all guess to whom such acknowledgments are due. But I am situated where there is no library to consult; my reading through the whole of my life has been of a loose, scattered, unmethodical kind, with no determined direction, and I have not been blessed by nature with the advantages of a retentive or accurate memory. Do not, however, imagine from this, I at all wish to insinuate that I ought to be acquitted of every obligation to preceding authours; and that when a palpable similarity of thought and expression is observable between us, it is a similarity produced by accident alone, and with perfect unconsciousness on my part. I am frequently sensible, from the manner in which an idea arises to my imagination, and the readiness with which words, also, present themselves to clothe it in, that I am only making use of some dormant part of that hoard of ideas which the most indifferent memories lay up, and not the native suggestions of my own mind. […] If this volume should appear, to any candid and liberal critick, to merit that he should take the trouble of pointing out to me in what parts of it I seem to have made use of other authours' writings, which according to the fair laws of literature ought to have been acknowledged, I shall think myself obliged to him. I shall examine the sources he points out as having supplied my own lack of ideas; and if this book should have the good fortune to go through a second edition, I shall not fail to own my obligations to him, and the authours from whom I may have borrowed.

How little credit soever, upon perusing these plays, the reader may think me entitled to in regard to the execution of the work, he will not, I flatter myself, deny me some credit in regard to the plan. I know of no series of plays, in any language, expressly descriptive of the different passions; and I believe there are few plays existing in which the display of one strong passion is the chief business of the drama, so written that they could properly make part of such a series. […]

I have now only to thank my reader, whoever he may be, who has followed me through the pages of this discourse, for having had the patience to do so. May he, in going through what follows (a wish the sincerity of which he cannot doubt) find more to reward his trouble than I dare venture to promise him; and for the pains he has already taken, and that, which he intends to take for me, I request that he will accept of my grateful acknowledgments.

DE MONFORT:

A TRAGEDY

PERSONS OF THE DRAMA.

MEN.

DE MONFORT.
REZENVELT.
COUNT FREBERG, *Friend to* De Monfort *and* Rezenvelt.
MANUEL, *Servant to* De Monfort.
JEROME, De Monfort's *old Landlord.*
GRIMBALD, *an artful knave.*
BERNARD, *a Monk.*
Monks, Gentlemen, Officers, Page, &c. &c.

WOMEN.

JANE DE MONFORT, *sister to* De Monfort.
COUNTESS FREBERG, *Wife to* Freberg.
THERESA, *Servant to the* Countess.
Abbess, Nuns, *and a* Lay Sister, Ladies, &c.

Scene, a Town in Germany.

ACT I.—SCENE I.

JEROME's *House. A large old-fashioned Chamber.*

Jer. (*speaking without.*) This way, good masters.

Enter JEROME, *bearing a light, and followed by* Manuel, *and* Servants *carrying luggage.*

	Rest your burdens here.
	This spacious room will please the Marquis best.
	He takes me unawares; but ill prepar'd:
	If he had sent, e'en tho' a hasty notice,
	I had been glad.
Man.	Be not disturb'd, good Jerome;
	Thy house is in most admirable order;
	And they who travel o'cold winter nights
	Think homeliest quarters good.
Jer.	He is not far behind?
Man.	A little way.
	(*To the servants.*) Go you and wait below till he arrive.

Jer.	(*Shaking* Manuel *by the hand.*)
	Indeed, my friend, I'm glad to see you here,
	Yet marvel wherefore.
Man.	I marvel wherefore too, my honest Jerome:
	But here we are, pri'thee be kind to us.
Jer.	Most heartily I will. I love your master:
	He is a quiet and a lib'ral man:
	A better inmate never cross'd my door.
Man.	Ah! but he is not now the man he was.
	Lib'ral he'll be, God grant he may be quiet.
Jer.	What has befallen him?
Man.	I cannot tell thee;
	But faith, there is no living with him now.
Jer.	And yet, methinks, if I remember well,
	You were about to quit his service, Manuel,
	When last he left this house. You grumbled then.
Man.	I've been upon the eve of leaving him
	These ten long years; for many times is he
	So difficult, capricious, and distrustful,
	He galls my nature — yet, I know not how,
	A secret kindness binds me to him still.
Jer.	Some, who offend from a suspicious nature,
	Will afterwards such fair confession make
	As turns e'en the offence into a favour.
Man.	Yes, some indeed do so: so will not he;
	He'd rather die than such confession make.
Jer.	Ay, thou art right, for now I call to mind
	That once he wrong'd me with unjust suspicion,
	When first he came to lodge beneath my roof;
	And when it so fell out that I was proved
	Most guiltless of the fault, I truly thought
	He would have made profession of regret;
	But silent, haughty, and ungraciously
	He bore himself as one offended still.
	Yet shortly after, when unwittingly
	I did him some slight service, o' the sudden
	He overpower'd me with his grateful thanks;
	And would not be restrain'd from pressing on me
	A noble recompense. I understood
	His o'erstrain'd gratitude and bounty well,
	And took it as he meant.
Man.	'Tis often thus.
	I would have left him many years ago,
	But that with all his faults there sometimes come
	Such bursts of natural goodness from his heart,
	As might engage a harder churl than I
	To serve him still. — And then his sister too,
	A noble dame, who should have been a queen:

	The meanest of her hinds, at her command,[1]
	Had fought like lions for her, and the poor,
	E'en o'er their bread of poverty had bless'd her—
	She would have griev'd if I had left my Lord.
Jer.	Comes she along with him?
Man.	No, he departed all unknown to her,
	Meaning to keep conceal'd his secret route;
	But well I knew it would afflict her much,
	And therefore left a little nameless billet,
	Which after our departure, as I guess,
	Would fall into her hands, and tell her all.
	What could I do! O 'tis a noble lady!
Jer.	All this is strange—something disturbs his mind—
	Belike he is in love.
Man.	No, Jerome, no.
	Once on a time I serv'd a noble master,
	Whose youth was blasted with untoward love,
	And he with hope and fear and jealousy
	For ever toss'd, led an unquiet life:
	Yet, when unruffled by the passing fit,
	His pale wan face such gentle sadness wore
	As mov'd a kindly heart to pity him;
	But Monfort, even in his clamest hour,
	Still bears that gloomy sternness in his eye
	Which sullenly repells all sympathy.
	O no! good Jerome, no, it is not love.
Jer.	Hear I not horses trampling at the gate?
	(*Listening.*)
	He is arriv'd—stay thou—I had forgot—
	A plague upon't! my head is so confus'd—
	I will return i'the instant to receive him.

(EXIT *hastily.*)

(*A great bustle without.* EXIT Manuel *with lights, and returns again, lighting in* De Monfort, *as if just alighted from his journey.*)

Man.	Your ancient host, my lord, receives you gladly,
	And your apartment will be soon prepar'd.
De Mon.	'Tis well.
Man.	Where shall I place the chest you gave in charge?
	So please you, say my lord.
De Mon.	(*Throwing himself into a chair.*) Where-e'er thou wilt.
Man.	I would not move that luggage till you came.
	(*Pointing to certain things.*)
De Mon.	Move what thou wilt, and trouble me no more.
	(Manuel, *with the assistance of other Servants, sets about putting the things in order, and* De Monfort *remains sitting in a thoughtful posture.*)

Enter JEROME, *bearing wine, &c. on a salver. As he approaches* DE MONFORT, MANUEL *pulls him by the sleeve.*

---

1   Hinds: farm labourers.

Man.	(*Aside to* Jerome.) No, do not now; he will not be disturb'd.
Jer.	What! not to bid him welcome to my house,
	And offer some refreshment?
Man.	No, good Jerome.
	Softly, a little while: I pri'thee do.
	(Jerome *walks softly on tip-toes, till he gets near* De Monfort, *behind backs,*
	then peeping on one side to see his face.)
Jer.	(*Aside to* Manuel) Ah, Manuel, what an alter'd man is here!
	His eyes are hollow, and his cheeks are pale—
	He left this house a comely gentleman.
De Mon.	Who whispers there?
Man.	'Tis your old landlord, sir.
Jer.	I joy to see you here—I crave your pardon—
	I fear I do intrude—
De Mon.	No, my kind host, I am oblig'd to thee.
Jer.	How fares it with your honour?
De Mon.	Well enough.
Jer.	Here is a little of the fav'rite wine
	That you were wont to praise. Pray honour me.
	(*Fills a glass.*)
De Mon.	(*After drinking*) I thank you, Jerome, 'tis delicious.
Jer.	Ay, my dear wife did ever make it so.
De Mon.	And how does she?
Jer.	Alas, my lord! she's dead.
De Mon.	Well, then she is at rest.
Jer.	How well, my lord?
De Mon.	Is she not with the dead, the quiet dead,
	Where all is peace. Not e'en the impious wretch,
	Who tears the coffin from its earthy vault,
	And strews the mould'ring ashes to the wind
	Can break their rest.
Jer.	Woe's me! I thought you would have griev'd for her.
	She was a kindly soul! Before she died,
	When pining sickness bent her cheerless head,
	She set my house in order—
	And but the morning ere she breath'd her last,
	Bade me preserve some flaskets of this wine,
	That should the Lord de Monfort come again
	His cup might sparkle still.
	(De Monfort *walks across the stage, and wipes his eyes.*)
	Indeed I fear I have distress'd you, sir;
	I surely thought you would be griev'd for her.
De Mon.	(*Taking* Jerome's *hand.*) I am, my friend. How long has she been dead?
Jer.	Two sad long years.
De Mon.	Would she were living still!
	I was too troublesome, too heedless of her.
Jer.	O no! she lov'd to serve you.
	(*Loud knocking without.*)

De Mon.	What fool comes here, at such untimely hours,
	To make this cursed noise. (*To* Manuel.) Go to the gate.

[EXIT Manuel.

	All sober citizens are gone to bed;
	It is some drunkards on their nightly rounds,
	Who mean it but in sport.
Jer.	I hear unusual voices—here they come.

Re-enter MANUEL, *shewing in Count* FREBERG *and his* LADY.

Freb.	(*Running to embrace* De Monfort.)
	My dearest Monfort! most unlook'd for pleasure!
	Do I indeed embrace thee here again?
	I saw thy servant standing by the gate,
	His face recall'd, and learnt the joyful tidings.
	Welcome, thrice welcome here!
De Mon.	I thank thee, Freberg, for this friendly visit,
	And this fair Lady too. (*Bowing to the* LADY.)
Lady.	I fear, my Lord,
	We do intrude at an untimely hour:
	But now, returning from a midnight mask,
	My husband did insist that we should enter.
Freb.	No, say not so; no hour untimely call,
	Which doth together bring long absent friends.
	Dear Monfort, why hast thou play'd so sly,
	To come upon us thus so suddenly?
De Mon.	O! many varied thoughts do cross our brain,
	Which touch the will, but leave the memory trackless;
	And yet a strange compounded motive make,
	Wherefore a man should bend his evening walk
	To th' east or west, the forest or the field.
	Is it not often so?
Freb .	I ask no more, happy to see you here
	From any motive. There is one behind,
	Whose presence would have been a double bliss:
	Ah! how is she? The noble Jane De Monfort.
De Mon.	(*Confused.*) She is—I have—I left my sister well.
Lady.	(*to* Freberg.) My Freberg, you are heedless of respect.
	You surely mean to say the Lady Jane.
Freb.	Respect! No, madam; Princess, Empress, Queen,
	Could not denote a creature so exalted
	As this plain appellation doth,
	The noble Jane De Monfort.
Lady.	(*Turning from him displeased to* Monfort.)
	You are fatigued, my Lord; you want repose;
	Say, should we not retire?
Freb.	Ha! is it so?
	My friend, your face is pale; have you been ill?
De Mon.	No, Freberg, no; I think I have been well.

91

Freb.	(*Shaking his head.*) I fear thou hast not, Monfort—Let it pass.
	We'll re-establish thee: we'll banish pain.
	I will collect some rare, some cheerful friends,
	And we shall spend together glorious hours,
	That gods might envy. Little time so spent
	Doth far outvalue all our life beside.
	This is indeed our life, our waking life,
	The rest dull breathing sleep.
De Mon.	Thus, it is true, from the sad years of life
	We sometimes do short hours, yea minutes strike,
	Keen, blissful, bright, never to be forgotten;
	Which, through the dreary gloom of time o'erpast
	Shine like fair sunny spots on a wild waste.
	But few they are, as few the heaven-fir'd souls
	Whose magick power creates them. Bless'd art thou,
	If in the ample circle of thy friends
	Thou canst but boast a few.
Freb.	Judge for thyself: in truth I do not boast.
	There is amongst my friends, my later friends,
	A most accomplish'd stranger. New to Amberg,
	But just arriv'd; and will ere long depart.
	I met him in Franconia two years since.[2]
	He is so full of pleasant anecdote,
	So rich, so gay, so poignant is his wit,
	Time vanishes before him as he speaks,
	And ruddy morning thro' the lattice peeps
	Ere night seems well begun.
De Mon.	How is he call'd?
Freb .	I will surprise thee with a welcome face:
	I will not tell thee now.
Lady.	(*to* Mon.) I have, my lord, a small request to make,
	And must not be denied. I too may boast
	Of some good friends, and beauteous countrywomen:
	To-morrow night I open wide my doors
	To all the fair and gay: beneath my roof
	Musick, and dance, and revelry shall reign.
	I pray you come and grace it with your presence.
De Mon.	You honour me too much to be denied.
Lady.	I thank you, sir; and in return for this,
	We shall withdraw, and leave you to repose.
Freb.	Must it be so? Good night—sweet sleep to thee.
	(*To* De Monfort.)
De Mon.	(*to* Freb.) Good night. (*To Lady.*) Good night, fair Lady.
Lady.	Farewel!
	[EXEUNT Freberg *and* Lady.]
De Mon.	(*to* Jer.) I thought Count Freberg had been now in France.
Jer.	He meant to go, as I have been inform'd.

---

2   Franconia (Franken) is an ancient Duchy in south-east Germany, now mostly part of Bavaria, centred on the cities of Bamberg and Nuremberg. Amberg is an old town immediately to the East.

De Mon.	Well, well, prepare my bed; I will to rest.

[EXIT Jerome.

De Mon.	(*alone*) I know not how it is, my heart stands back,
	And meets not this man's love. — Friends! rarest friends!
	Rather than share his undiscerning praise
	With every table-wit, and book-form'd sage,
	And paltry poet puling to the moon,
	I'd court from him proscription, yea abuse,
	And think it proud distinction.

[EXIT.

SCENE II.

A Small Apartment in JEROME's *House: a table and breakfast set out. Enter* DE MONFORT, *followed by* MANUEL, *and sits down by the table, with a cheerful face.*

De Mon.	Manuel, this morning's sun shines pleasantly:
	These old apartments too are light and cheerful.
	Our landlord's kindness has reviv'd me much;
	He serves as though he lov'd me. This pure air
	Braces the listless nerves, and warms the blood:
	I feel in freedom here.
	(*Filling a cup of coffee, and drinking.*)
Man.	Ah! sure, my Lord,
	No air is purer than the air at home.
De Mon.	Here can I wander with assured steps,
	Nor dread, at every winding of the path,
	Lest an abhorred serpent cross my way,
	To move — (*Stopping short.*)
Man.	What says your honour?
	There are no serpents in our pleasant fields.
De Mon.	Thinkst thou there are no serpents in the world,
	But those who slide along the grassy sod,
	And sting the luckless foot that presses them?
	There are who in the path of social life
	Do bask their spotted skins in Fortune's sun,
	And sting the soul — Ay, till its healthful frame
	Is chang'd to secret, fest'ring, sore disease,
	So deadly is the wound.
Man.	Heav'n guard your honour from such horrid skathe:
	They are but rare, I hope?
De Mon.	(*Shaking his head.*) We mark the hollow eye, the wasted frame,
	The gait disturb'd of wealthy honour'd men,
	But do not know the cause.
Man.	'Tis very true. God keep you well, my lord!
De Mon.	I thank thee, Manuel, I am very well.
	I shall be gay too, by the setting sun.
	I go to revel it with sprightly dames,

	And drive the night away.
	(*Filling another cup and drinking.*)
Man.	I should be glad to see your honour gay.
De Mon.	And thou too shalt be gay. There, honest Manuel,
	Put these broad pieces in thy leathern purse,
	And take at night a cheerful jovial glass.
	Here is one too, for Bremer; he loves wine;
	And one for Jacques: be joyful altogether.

Enter SERVANT.

Ser.	My Lord, I met e'en now, a short way off,
	Your countryman the Marquis Rezenvelt.
De Mon.	(*Starting from his seat, and letting the cup fall from his hand.*)
	Who, sayst thou?
Ser.	Marquis Rezenvelt, an' please you.
De Mon.	Thou ly'st—it is not so—it is impossible.
Ser.	I saw him with these eyes, plain as yourself.
De Mon.	Fool! 'tis some passing stranger thou hast seen,
	And with a hideous likeness been deceiv'd.
Ser.	No other stranger could deceive my sight.
De Mon.	(*Dashing his clenched hand violently upon the table, and overturning every thing.*)
	Heaven blast thy sight! it lights on nothing good.
Ser.	I surely thought no harm to look upon him.
De Mon.	What, dost thou still insist? He must it be?
	Does it so please thee well? (Servant *endeavours to speak.*)
	Hold thy damn'd tongue.
	By heaven I'll kill thee. (*Going furiously up to him.*)
Man.	(*In a soothing voice.*)
	Nay, harm him not, my lord; he speaks the truth;
	I've met his groom, who told me certainly
	His Lord is here. I should have told you so,
	But thought, perhaps, it might displease your honour.
De Mon.	(*Becoming all at once calm, and turning sternly to* Manuel.)
	And how dar'st thou to think it would displease me?
	What is't to me who leaves or enters Amberg?
	But it displeases me, yea e'en to frenzy,
	That every idle fool must hither come,
	To break my leisure with the paltry tidings
	Of all the cursed things he stares upon.
	(Servant *attempts to speak*—De Monfort *stamps with his foot.*)
	Take thine ill-favour'd visage from my sight,
	And speak of it no more.

[EXIT Servant.

And go thou too; I choose to be alone.

[EXIT Manuel.

(De Monfort *goes to the door by which they went out; opens it, and looks.*)
But is he gone indeed? Yes, he is gone.

(*Goes to the opposite door, opens it, and looks: then gives loose to all the fury of gesture, and walks up and down in great agitation*)
It is too much: by heaven it is too much!
He haunts me — stings me — like a devil haunts —
He'll make a raving maniac of me — Villain!
The air wherein thou draw'st thy fulsome breath
Is poison to me — Oceans shall divide us! (*Pauses.*)
But no; thou thinkst I fear thee, cursed reptile!
And hast a pleasure in the damned thought.
Though my heart's blood should curdle at thy sight,
I'll stay and face thee still.
(*Knocking at the chamber door.*)
                      Ha! Who knocks there?

Freb.	(*Without.*) It is thy friend, De Monfort.
De Mon.	(Opening the door). Enter, then.

Enter FREBERG.

Freb.	(*Taking his hand kindly.*)
	How art thou now? How hast thou pass'd the night?
	Has kindly sleep refresh'd thee?
De Mon.	Yes, I have lost an hour or two in sleep,
	And so should be refresh'd.
Freb.	And art thou not?
	Thy looks speak not of rest. Thou art disturb'd.
De Mon.	No, somewhat ruffled from a foolish cause,
	Which soon will pass away.
Freb.	(*Shaking his head.*) Ah no, De Monfort! something in thy face
	Tells me another tale. Then wrong me not:
	If any secret grief distract thy soul,
	Here am I all devoted to thy love;
	Open thy heart to me. What troubles thee?
De Mon.	I have no grief: distress me not, my friend.
Freb.	Nay, do not call me so. Wert thou my friend,
	Wouldst thou not open all thine inmost soul,
	And bid me share its every consciousness?
De Mon.	Freberg, thou knowst not man; not nature's man,
	But only him who, in smooth studied works
	Of polish'd sages, shines deceitfully
	In all the splendid foppery of virtue.
	That man was never born whose secret soul
	With all its motley treasure of dark thoughts,
	Foul fantasies, vain musings, and wild dreams,
	Was ever open'd to another's scan.
	Away, away! it is delusion all.
Freb.	Well, be reserved then: perhaps I'm wrong.
De Mon.	How goes the hour?
Freb.'	Tis early: a long day is still before us,
	Let us enjoy it. Come along with me;

	I'll introduce you to my pleasant friend.

De Mon. Your pleasant friend?

Freb.   Yes, he of whom I spake.

    (*Taking his hand.*)

    There is no good I would not share with thee,

    And this man's company, to minds like thine,

    Is the best banquet feast I could bestow.

    But I will speak in mystery no more,

    It is thy townsman, noble Rezenvelt.

    (De Mon. *pulls his hand hastily from Freberg, and shrinks back.*)

    Ha! what is this? Art thou pain-stricken, Monfort?

    Nay, on my life, thou rather seem'st offended:

    Does it displease thee that I call him friend?

De Mon. No, all men are thy friends.

Freb.   No, say not all men. But thou art offended.

    I see it well. I thought to do thee pleasure.

    But if his presence is not welcome here,

    He shall not join our company to-day.

De Mon. What dost thou mean to say? What is't to me

    Whether I meet with such a thing as Rezenvelt

    To-day, to-morrow, every day, or never.

Freb .   In truth, I thought you had been well with him.

    He prais'd you much.

De Mon. I thank him for his praise—Come, let us move:

    This chamber is confin'd and airless grown.

    (*Starting.*)

    I hear a stranger's voice!

Freb.   'Tis Rezenvelt.

    Let him be told that we are gone abroad.

De Mon. (*Proudly.*) No! let him enter. Who waits there? Ho! Manuel!

Enter MANUEL.

    What stranger speaks below?

Man.   The Marquis Rezenvelt.

    I have not told him that you are within.

De Mon. (*Angrily.*) And wherefore did'st thou not? Let him ascend.

    (*A long pause.* De Montfort *walking up and down with a quick pace.*)

Enter REZENVELT, *and runs freely up to* De Monfort.

Rez.   (*to* De Mon.) My noble Marquis, welcome.

De Mon.   Sir, I thank you.

Rez. (*to* Freb.) My gentle friend, well met. Abroad so early?

Freb.   It is indeed an early hour for me.

    How sits thy last night's revel on thy spirits?

Rez.   O, light as ever. On my way to you

    E'en now I learnt De Montfort was arriv'd,

    And turn'd my steps aside; so here I am.

	(*Bowing gaily to* De Monfort.)
De Mon.	(*Proudly.*) I thank you, Sir; you do me too much honour.
Rez.	Nay, say not so; not too much honour, Marquis,
	Unless, indeed, 'tis more than pleases you.
De Mon.	(*Confused.*) Having no previous notice of your coming,
	I look'd not for it.
Rez.	Ay, true indeed; when I approach you next,
	I'll send a herald to proclaim my coming,
	And bow to you by sound of trumpet, marquis.
De Mon.	(*to* Freb.) (*Turning haughtily from* Rezenvelt *with affected indifference.*)
	How does your cheerful friend, that good old man?
Freb.	My cheerful friend? I know not whom you mean.
De Mon.	Count Waterlan.
Freb.	I know not one so nam'd.
De Mon.	(*Very confused.*) O pardon me—it was at Bâle I knew him.[3]
Freb.	You have not yet inquir'd for honest Reisdale.
	I met him as I came, and mention'd you.
	He seem'd amaz'd; and fain he would have learnt
	What cause procur'd us so much happiness.
	He question'd hard, and hardly would believe;
	I could not satisfy his strong desire.
Rez.	And know you not what brings De Montfort here?
Freb.	Truly, I do not.
Rez.	O! 'tis love of me.
	I have but two short days in Amberg been,
	And here with postman's speed he follows me,
	Finding his home so dull and tiresome grown.
Freb.	(*to* De Mon.) Is Rezenvelt so sadly miss'd with you?
	Your town so chang'd?
De Mon.	Not altogether so:
	Some witlings and jest-mongers still remain
	For fools to laugh at.
Rez.	But he laughs not, and therefore he is wise.
	He ever frowns on them with sullen brow
	Contemptuous; therefore he is very wise;
	Nay, daily frets his most refined soul
	With their poor folly to its inmost core;
	Therefore he is most eminently wise.
Freb.	Fy, Rezenvelt! You are too early gay;
	Such spirits rise but with the ev'ning glass.
	They suit not placid morn.
	(*To* De Monfort, *who after walking impatiently up and down, comes close to his ear, and lays hold of his arm.*)
	What would you, Monfort?
De Mon.	Nothing—Yet, what is't o'clock?
	No, no—I had forgot—'tis early still.
	(*Turns away again.*)
Freb. (*to* Rez.)	Waltser informs me that you have agreed

---

3   The French name for the Swiss city more often called Basel..

	To read his verses o'er, and tell the truth.
	It is a dangerous task.
Rez.	Yet I'll be honest:
	I can but lose his favour and a feast.

(*Whilst they speak*, De Monfort *walks up and down impatiently and irresolute; at last pulls the bell violently.*)

Enter SERVANT.

De Mon.	(*to* Ser.) What dost thou want? —
Ser.	I thought your honour rung.
De Mon.	I have forgot — Stay; are my horses saddled?
Ser.	I thought, my Lord, you would not ride to-day,
	After so long a journey.
De Mon.	(*Impatiently.*) Well — 'tis good.
	Begone! — I want thee not.

[EXIT Servant.

Rez.	(*Smiling significantly.*) I humbly crave your pardon, gentle Marquis.
	It grieves me that I cannot stay with you,
	And make my visit of a friendly length.
	I trust your goodness will excuse me now;
	Another time I shall be less unkind.
	(*To* Freberg.) Will you not go with me?
Freb.	Excuse me, Monfort, I'll return again.

[EXEUNT Rezenvelt *and* Freberg.

De Mon.	(*Alone, tossing his arms distractedly.*)
	Hell hath no greater torment for th' accurs'd
	Than this man's presence gives —
	Abhorred fiend! he hath a pleasure too,
	A damned pleasure in the pain he gives!
	Oh! the side glance of that detested eye!
	That conscious smile! that full insulting lip!
	It touches every nerve: it makes me mad.
	What, does it please thee? Dost thou woo my hate?
	Hate shalt thou have! determin'd, deadly hate,
	Which shall awake no smile. Malignant villain!
	The venom of thy mind is rank and devilish,
	And thin the film that hides it.
	Thy hateful visage ever spoke thy worth:
	I loath'd thee when a boy.
	That men should be besotted with him thus![4]
	And Freberg likewise so bewitched is,
	That like a hireling flatt'rer, at his heels
	He meanly paces, off'ring brutish praise.
	O! I could curse him too.

[EXIT.

---

4   The first two editions have 'That — — should be besotted with him thus!' The blank is filled
    with 'men' in the third edition (1800).

A very splendid apartment in Count FREBERG's *house, fancifully decorated. A wide folding door opened, shews another magnificent room lighted up to receive company. Enter through the folding doors the* Count *and* Countess, *richly dressed.*

Freb.	(*Looking round.*) In truth, I like those decorations well:
	They suit those lofty walls. And here, my love,
	The gay profusion of a woman's fancy
	Is well display'd. Noble simplicity
	Becomes us less, on such a night as this
	Than gaudy show.
Lady.	Is it not noble then? (*He shakes his head.*) I thought it so;
	And as I know you love simplicity,
	I did intend it should be simple too.
Freb.	Be satisfied, I pray; we want to-night
	A cheerful banquet-house, and not a temple.
	How runs the hour?
Lady.	It is not late, but soon we shall be rous'd
	With the loud entry of our frolick guests.

Enter a PAGE, *richly dressed.*

Page.	Madam, there is a Lady in your hall,
	Who begs to be admitted to your presence.
Lady.	Is it not one of our invited friends?
Page.	No, far unlike to them; it is a stranger.
Lady.	How looks her countenance?
Page.	So queenly, so commanding, and so noble,
	I shrunk at first in awe; but when she smil'd,
	For so she did to see me thus abash'd,
	Methought I could have compass'd sea and land
	To do her bidding.
Lady.	Is she young or old?
Page.	Neither, if right I guess; but she is fair;
	For time hath laid his hand so gently on her,
	As he too had been aw'd.
Lady.	The foolish stripling!
	She has bewitch'd thee. Is she large in stature?
Page.	So stately and so graceful is her form,
	I thought at first her stature was gigantick,
	But on a near approach I found, in truth,
	She scarcely does surpass the middle size.
Lady.	What is her garb?
Page.	I cannot well describe the fashion of it.
	She is not deck'd in any gallant trim,
	But seems to me clad in the usual weeds
	Of high habitual state; for as she moves
	Wide flows her robe in many a waving fold,

	As I have seen unfurled banners play
	With a soft breeze.
Lady.	Thine eyes deceive thee, boy,
	It is an apparition thou hast seen.
Freb.	(*Starting from his seat, where he has been sitting during the conversation between* the Lady *and the* Page.)
	It is an apparition he has seen.
	Or it is Jane De Monfort.

                  [EXIT, *hastily.*

Lady.	(*Displeased.*) No; such description surely suits not her.
	Did she enquire for me?
Page.	She ask'd to see the lady of Count Freberg.
Lady.	Perhaps it is not she—I fear it is—
	Ha! here they come. He has but guess'd too well.

    Enter FREBERG, *leading in* JANE DE MONFORT.

Freb.	(*Presenting her to* Lady.) Here, madam, welcome a most worthy guest.
Lady.	Madam, a thousand welcomes. Pardon me;
	I could not guess who honour'd me so far;
	I should not else have waited coldly here.
Jane.	I thank you for this welcome, gentle Countess.
	But take those kind excuses back again;
	I am a bold intruder on this hour,
	And am entitled to no ceremony.
	I came in quest of a dear truant friend,
	But Freberg has inform'd me—
	(*To* Freberg.) And he is well, you say?
Freb.	Yes, well, but joyless.
Jane .	It is the usual temper of his mind:
	It opens not, but with the thrilling touch
	Of some strong heart-string o' the sudden press'd.
Freb.	It may be so, I've known him otherwise:
	He is suspicious grown.
Jane.	Not so, Count Freberg, Monfort is too noble.
	Say rather, that he is a man in grief,
	Wearing at times a strange and scowling eye;
	And thou, less generous than beseems a friend,
	Hast thought too hardly of him.
Freb.	(*Bowing with great respect.*) So will I say;
	I'll own nor word nor will, that can offend you.
Lady.	De Monfort is engag'd to grace our feast,
	Ere long you'll see him here.
Jane .	I thank you truly, but this homely dress
	Suits not the splendour of such scenes as these.
Freb .	(*Pointing to her dress.*) Such artless and majestick elegance,
	So exquisitely just, so nobly simple,
	Will make the gorgeous blush.
Jane.	(*Smiling.*) Nay, nay, be more consistent, courteous knight,

	And do not praise a plain and simple guise
	With such profusion of unsimple words.
	I cannot join your company to-night.
Lady.	Not stay to see your brother?
Jane.	Therefore it is I would not, gentle hostess.
	Here will he find all that can woo the heart
	To joy and sweet forgetfulness of pain;
	The sight of me would wake his feeling mind
	To other thoughts. I am no doting mistress,
	No fond distracted wife, who must forthwith
	Rush to his arms and weep. I am his sister:
	The eldest daughter of his father's house:
	Calm and unwearied is my love for him;
	And having found him, patiently I'll wait,
	Nor greet him in the hour of social joy,
	To dash his mirth with tears. —
	The night wears on; permit me to withdraw.
Freb.	Nay, do not, do not injure us so far!
	Disguise thyself, and join our friendly train.
Jane.	You wear not masks to-night?
Lady.	We wear not masks, but you may be conceal'd
	Behind the double foldings of a veil.
Jane.	(*After pausing to consider.*) In truth, I feel a little so inclin'd.
	Methinks unknown, I e'en might speak to him,
	And gently prove the temper of his mind:
	But for the means I must become your debtor.
	(*To* Lady.)
Lady.	Who waits? (*Enter her* Woman.) Attend this lady to my wardrobe,
	And do what she commands you.

[EXEUNT Jane *and* Waiting-woman.

Freb.	(*Looking after* Jane, *as she goes out, with admiration.*)
	Oh! what a soul she bears! see how she steps!
	Nought but the native dignity of worth
	E'er taught the moving form such noble grace.
Lady.	Such lofty mien, and high assumed gait
	I've seen ere now, and men have call'd it pride.
Freb.	No, 'faith! thou never didst, but oft indeed
	The paltry imitation thou hast seen.
	(*Looking at her.*) How hang those trappings on thy motly gown?
	They seem like garlands on a May-day queen,
	Which hinds have dress'd in sport.
Lady.	I'll doff it, then, since it displeases you.
Freb.	No, no, thou art lovely still in every garb.
	But see the guests assemble.

Enter groups of well dressed people, who pay their compliments to Freberg *and his* Lady; *and followed by her pass into the inner apartment, where more company appear assembling, as if by another entry.*

Freb.	(*Who remains on the front of the stage, with a friend or two.*)
	How loud the hum of this gay-meeting crowd!
	'Tis like a bee-swarm in the noonday sun.
	Musick will quell the sound. Who waits without?
	Musick strike up.
	(*A grand piece of musick is playing, and when it ceases, enter from the inner apartment* REZENVELT, *with several gentlemen, all richly dressed.*)
Freb.	(*to those just entered.*)
	What lively gallants quit the field so soon?
	Are there no beauties in that moving crowd
	To fix your fancy?
Rez.	Ay, marry, are there! men of ev'ry mind
	May in that moving crowd some fair one find,
	To suit their taste, though whimsical and strange,
	As ever fancy own'd.
	Beauty of every cast and shade is there,
	From the perfection of a faultless form,
	Down to the common, brown, unnoted maid,
	Who looks but pretty in her Sunday gown.
1st Gent.	There is, indeed, a gay variety.
Rez.	And if the liberality of nature
	Suffices not, there's store of grafted charms,
	Blending in one the sweets of many plants
	So obstinately, strangely opposite,
	As would have well defied all other art
	But female cultivation. Aged youth,
	With borrow'd locks in rosy chaplets bound,
	Cloathes her dim eye, parch'd lip, and skinny cheek
	In most unlovely softness.
	And youthful age, with fat round trackless face,
	The down-cast look of contemplation deep,
	Most pensively assumes.
	Is it not even so? The native prude,
	With forced laugh, and merriment uncouth,
	Plays off the wild coquet's successful charms
	With most unskilful pains; and the coquet,
	In temporary crust of cold reserve,
	Fixes her studied looks upon the ground
	Forbiddingly demure.
Freb.	Fy! thou art too severe.
Rez.	Say, rather, gentle.
	I' faith! the very dwarfs attempt to charm
	With lofty airs of puny majesty,
	While potent damsels, of a portly make,
	Totter like nurselings, and demand the aid
	Of gentle sympathy.
	From all those diverse modes of dire assault,
	He owns a heart of hardest adamant,
	Who shall escape to-night.

Freb.	(*to* De Monfort, *who has entered during* Rezenvelt's *speech, and heard the greatest part of it.*) Ha, ha, ha, ha!
	How pleasantly he gives his wit the rein,
	Yet guides its wild career!
	(De Monfort *is silent.*)
Rez.	(*Smiling archly.*) What, think you, Freberg, the same powerful spell
	Of transformation reigns o'er all to-night?
	Or that De Monfort is a woman turn'd,
	So widely from his native self to swerve,
	As grace my gai'ty with a smile of his?
De Mon.	Nay, think not, Rezenvelt, there is no smile
	I can bestow on thee. There is a smile,
	A smile of nature too, which I can spare,
	And yet, perhaps, thou wilt not thank me for it.
	(*Smiles contemptuously.*)
Rez.	Not thank thee! It were surely most ungrateful
	No thanks to pay for nobly giving me
	What, well we see, has cost thee so much pain.
	For nature hath her smiles, of birth more painful
	Than bitt'rest execrations.
Freb.	These idle words will lead us to disquiet:
	Forbear, forbear, my friends. Go, Rezenvelt,
	Accept the challenge of those lovely dames,
	Who through the portal come with bolder steps
	To claim your notice.
	(*Enter a group of Ladies from the other apartment.* Rezenvelt *shrugs up his shoulders, as if unwilling to go.*)
1st Gent.	(*to* Rez.) Behold in sable veil a lady comes,
	Whose noble air doth challenge fancy's skill
	To suit it with a countenance as goodly.
	(*Pointing to* Jane De Monfort, *who now enters in a thick black veil.*)
Rez.	Yes, this way lies attraction. (*To* Freberg.) With permission,
	(*Going up to* Jane.)
	Fair lady, though within that envious shroud
	Your beauty deigns not to enlighten us,
	We bid you welcome, and our beauties here
	Will welcome you the more for such concealment.
	With the permission of our noble host—
	(*Taking her hand, and leading her to the front of the stage.*)
Jane .	(*to* Freb.) Pardon me this presumption, courteous sir:
	I thus appear, (*pointing to her veil*), not careless of respect
	Unto the generous lady of the feast.
	Beneath this veil no beauty shrouded is,
	That, now, or pain, or pleasure can bestow.
	Within the friendly cover of its shade
	I only wish, unknown, again to see
	One who, alas! is heedless of my pain.
De Mon.	Yes, it is ever thus. Undo that veil,
	And give thy count'nance to the cheerful light.

	Men now all soft, and female beauty scorn,

Men now all soft, and female beauty scorn,
And mock the gentle cares which aim to please.
It is most damnable! undo thy veil,
And think of him no more.

Jane.   I know it well, e'en to a proverb grown,
Is lovers' faith, and I had borne such slight:
But he who has, alas! forsaken me,
Was the companion of my early days,
My cradle's mate, mine infant play-fellow.
Within our op'ning minds with riper years,
The love of praise and gen'rous virtue sprung:
Thro' varied life our pride, our joys, were one;
At the same tale we wept: he is my brother.

De Mon.   And he forsook thee? — No, I dare not curse him:
My heart upbraids me with a crime like his.

Jane.   Ah! do not thus distress a feeling heart.
All sisters are not to the soul entwin'd
With equal bands; thine has not watch'd for thee,
Weep'd for thee, cheer'd thee, shar'd thy weal and woe,
As I have done for him.

De Mon.   (*Eagerly.*) Ha! has she not?
By heaven! the sum of all thy kindly deeds
Were but as chaff pois'd against massy gold,
Compar'd to that which I do owe her love.
Oh, pardon me! I mean not to offend —
I am too warm — but she of whom I speak
Is the dear sister of my earliest love;
In noble, virtuous worth to none a second:
And though behind those sable folds were hid
As fair a face as ever woman own'd,
Still would I say she is as fair as thee.
How oft amidst the beauty-blazing throng,
I've proudly to th' inquiring stranger told
Her name and lineage! yet within her house,
The virgin mother of an orphan race
Her dying parents left, this noble woman
Did, like a Roman matron, proudly sit,
Despising all the blandishments of love;
While many a youth his hopeless love conceal'd,
Or, humbly distant, woo'd her like a queen.
Forgive, I pray you! O forgive this boasting!
In faith! I mean you no discourtesy.

Jane.   (*Off her guard, in a soft natural tone of voice.*) Oh no! nor do me any.

De Mon.   What voice speaks now? Withdraw, withdraw this shade!
For if thy face bear semblance to thy voice,
I'll fall and worship thee. Pray! pray undo!
(*Puts forth his hand eagerly to snatch away the veil, whilst she shrinks back, and* Rezenvelt *steps between to prevent him.*)

Rez.   Stand off: no hand shall lift this sacred veil.

De Mon.	What, dost thou think De Monfort fall'n so low,
	That there may live a man beneath heav'n's roof,
	Who dares to say he shall not?
Rez.	He lives who dares to say —
Jane.	(*Throwing back her veil, much alarmed, and rushing between them.*)
	Forbear, forbear!

(Rezenvelt, *very much struck, steps back respectfully, and makes her a very low bow. De Monfort stands for a while motionless, gazing upon her, till she, looking expressively to him, extends her arms, and he, rushing into them, bursts into tears. Freberg seems very much pleased. The company then advancing from the inner apartment, gather about them, and the Scene closes.*)

SCENE II.

De Monfort's *apartments. Enter* DE MONFORT, *with a disordered air, and his hand pressed upon his forehead, followed by* JANE.

De Mon.	No more, my sister, urge me not again:
	My secret troubles cannot be reveal'd.
	From all participation of its thoughts
	My heart recoils: I pray thee be contented.
Jane.	What, must I, like a distant humble friend,
	Observe thy restless eye, and gait disturb'd,
	In timid silence, whilst with yearning heart
	I turn aside to weep? O no! De Monfort!
	A nobler task thy noble mind will give;
	Thy true entrusted friend I still shall be.
De Mon.	Ah, Jane, forbear! I cannot e'en to thee.
Jane .	Then, fy upon it! fy upon it, Monfort!
	There was a time when e'en with murder stain'd,
	Had it been possible that such dire deed
	Could e'er have been the crime of one so piteous,
	Thou wouldst have told it me.
De Mon.	So would I now — but ask of this no more.
	All other trouble but the one I feel
	I had disclos'd to thee. I pray thee spare me.
	It is the secret weakness of my nature.
Jane.	Then secret let it be; I urge no farther.
	The eldest of our valiant father's hopes,
	So sadly orphan'd, side by side we stood,
	Like two young trees, whose boughs, in early strength
	Screen the weak saplings of the rising grove,
	And brave the storm together —
	I have so long, as if by nature's right,
	Thy bosom's inmate and adviser been,
	I thought through life I should have so remain'd,
	Nor ever known a change. Forgive me, Monfort,
	A humbler station will I take by thee:

	The close attendant of thy wand'ring steps;
	The cheerer of this home, with strangers sought;
	The soother of those griefs I must not know,
	This is mine office now: I ask no more.
De Mon.	Oh, Jane! thou dost constrain me with thy love!
	Would I could tell it thee!
Jane.	Thou shalt not tell me. Nay I'll stop mine ears,

De Mon. Oh, Jane! thou dost constrain me with thy love!
Would I could tell it thee!

Jane. Thou shalt not tell me. Nay I'll stop mine ears,
Nor from the yearnings of affection wring
What shrinks from utt'rance. Let it pass, my brother.
I'll stay by thee; I'll cheer thee, comfort thee:
Pursue with thee the study of some art,
Or nobler science, that compels the mind
To steady thought progressive, driving forth
All floating, wild, unhappy fantasies;
Till thou, with brow unclouded, smil'st again,
Like one who from dark visions of the night,
When th' active soul within its lifeless cell
Holds it own world, with dreadful fancy press'd
Of some dire, terrible, or murd'rous deed,
Wakes to the dawning morn, and blesses heaven.

De Mon. It will not pass away; 'twill haunt me still.

Jane. Ah! say not so, for I will haunt thee too;
And be to it so close an adversary,
That, though I wrestle darkling with the fiend,
I shall o'ercome it.

De Mon.   Thou most gen'rous woman!
Why do I treat thee thus? It should not be—
And yet I cannot—O that cursed villain!
He will not let me be the man I would.

Jane. What sayst thou, Monfort? Oh! what words are these?
They have awak'd my soul to dreadful thoughts.
I do beseech thee, speak!
(*He shakes his head, and turns from her; she following him.*)
By the affection thou didst ever bear me;
By the dear mem'ry of our infant days;
By kindred living ties, ay, and by those
Who sleep i' the tomb, and cannot call to thee,
I do conjure thee speak.
(*He waves her off with his hand and covers his face with the other, still turning from her.*)
               Ha! wilt thou not?
(*Assuming dignity.*)
Then, if affection, most unwearied love,
Tried early, long, and never wanting found,
O'er gen'rous man hath more authority,
More rightful power than crown or sceptre give,
I do command thee.
(*He throws himself into a chair, greatly agitated.*)
De Monfort, do not thus resist my love.

	Here I entreat thee on my bended knees.
	(*Kneeling.*)
	Alas! my brother!
	(De Monfort *starts up, and catching her in his arms, raises her up, then placing her in the chair, kneels at her feet.*)
De Mon.	Thus let him kneel who should the abased be,
	And at thine honour'd feet confession make!
	I'll tell thee all—but, oh! thou wilt despise me.
	For in my breast a raging passion burns,
	To which thy soul no sympathy will own.
	A passion which hath made my nightly couch
	A place of torment; and the light of day,
	With the gay intercourse of social man
	Feel like th' oppressive airless pestilence.
	O Jane! thou wilt despise me.
Jane.	Say not so:
	I never can despise thee, gentle brother.
	A lover's jealousy and hopeless pangs
	No kindly heart contemns.
De Mon.	A lover, sayst thou?
	No, it is hate! black, lasting, deadly hate;
	Which thus hath driven me forth from kindred peace,
	From social pleasure, from my native home,
	To be a sullen wand'rer on the earth,
	Avoiding all men, cursing and accurs'd.
Jane.	De Monfort, this is fiend-like, frightful, terrible!
	What being, by th'Almighty Father form'd,
	Of flesh and blood, created even as thou,
	Could in thy breast such horrid tempest wake,
	Who art thyself his fellow?
	Unknit thy brows, and spread those wrath-clench'd hands.
	Some sprite accurst within thy bosom mates
	To work thy ruin. Strive with it, my brother!
	Strive bravely with it; drive it from thy breast:
	'Tis the degrader of a noble heart;
	Curse it, and bid it part.
De Mon.	It will not part. (*His hand on his breast.*)
	I've lodged it here too long;
	With my first cares I felt its rankling touch,
	I loath'd him when a boy.
Jane.	Who did'st thou say?
De Mon.	Oh! that detested Rezenvelt!
	E'en in our early sports, like two young whelps
	Of hostile breed, instinctively reverse,
	Each 'gainst the other pitch'd his ready pledge,
	And frown'd defiance. As we onward pass'd
	From youth to man's estate, his narrow art
	And envious gibing malice, poorly veil'd
	In the affected carelessness of mirth,

Still more detestable and odious grew.
There is no living being on this earth
Who can conceive the malice of his soul,
With all his gay and damned merriment,
To those, by fortune or by merit plac'd
Above his paltry self. When, low in fortune,
He look'd upon the state of prosp'rous men,
As nightly birds, rous'd from their murky holes,
Do scowl and chatter at the light of day,
I could endure it; even as we bear
Th' impotent bite of some half-trodden worm,
I could endure it. But when honours came,
And wealth and new-got titles fed his pride;
Whilst flatt'ring knaves did trumpet forth his praise,
And grov'ling idiots grinn'd applauses on him;
Oh! then I could no longer suffer it!
It drove me frantic. — What! what would I give!
What would I give to crush the bloated toad,
So rankly do I loathe him!

Jane. And would thy hatred crush the very man
Who gave to thee that life he might have ta'en?
That life which thou so rashly didst expose
To aim at his! Oh! this is horrible!

De Mon. Ha! thou hast heard it, then? From all the world,
But most of all from thee, I thought it hid.

Jane. I heard a secret whisper, and resolv'd
Upon the instant to return to thee.
Did'st thou receive my letter?

De Mon. I did! I did! 'twas that which drove me hither.
I could not bear to meet thine eye again.

Jane. Alas! that, tempted by a sister's tears,
I ever left thy house! these few past months,
These absent months, have brought us all this woe.
Had I remain'd with thee it had not been.
And yet, methinks, it should not move you thus.
You dar'd him to the field; both bravely fought;
He more adroit disarm'd you; courteously
Return'd the forfeit sword, which, so return'd,
You did refuse to use against him more;
And then, as says report, you parted friends.

De Mon. When he disarm'd this curs'd, this worthless hand
Of its most worthless weapon, he but spar'd
From dev'lish pride, which now derives a bliss
In seeing me thus fetter'd, sham'd, subjected
With the vile favour of his poor forbearance;
While he securely sits with gibing brow,
And basely bates me, like a muzzled cur
Who cannot turn again. —
Until that day, till that accursed day,

	I knew not half the torment of this hell,
	Which burns within my breast. Heaven's lightnings blast him!
Jane.	O this is horrible! Forbear, forbear!
	Lest heaven's vengeance light upon thy head,
	For this most impious wish.
De Mon.	Then let it light.
	Torments more fell than I have felt already
	It cannot send. To be annihilated;
	What all men shrink from; to be dust, be nothing,
	Were bliss to me, compar'd to what I am.
Jane.	Oh! wouldst thou kill me with these dreadful words?
De Mon.	(*Raising his hands to heaven.*) Let me but once upon his ruin look,
	Then close mine eyes for ever!

(Jane, *in great distress, staggers back, and supports herself upon the side
scene. De Monfort, alarm'd, runs up to her with a softened voice.*)

	Ha! how is this? thou'rt ill; thou'rt very pale.
	What have I done to thee? Alas, alas!
	I meant not to distress thee. —O my sister!
Jane.	(*Shaking her head.*) I cannot speak to thee.
De Mon.	I have kill'd thee.
	Turn, turn thee not away! look on me still!
	Oh! droop not thus, my life, my pride, my sister!
	Look on me yet again.
Jane.	Thou too, De Monfort,
	In better days, wert wont to be my pride.
De Mon.	I am a wretch, most wretched in myself,
	And still more wretched in the pain I give.
	O curse that villain! that detested villain!
	He has spread mis'ry o'er my fated life:
	He will undo us all.
Jane.	I've held my warfare through a troubled world,
	And borne with steady mind my share of ill;
	For then the helpmate of my toil wert thou.
	But now the wane of life comes darkly on,
	And hideous passion tears me from thy heart,
	Blasting thy worth. —I cannot strive with this.
De Mon.	(*Affectionately.*) What shall I do?
Jane.	Call up thy noble spirit;
	Rouse all the gen'rous energy of virtue;
	And with the strength of heaven-endued man,
	Repel the hideous foe. Be great; be valiant.
	O, if thou couldst! e'en shrouded as thou art
	In all the sad infirmities of nature,
	What a most noble creature wouldst thou be!
De Mon.	Ay, if I could: alas! alas! I cannot.
Jane.	Thou canst, thou mayst, thou wilt.
	We shall not part till I have turn'd thy soul.

Enter MANUEL.

De Mon.	Ha! some one enters. Wherefore com'st thou here?
Man.	Count Freberg waits your leisure.
De Mon.	(*Angrily.*) Be gone, be gone. — I cannot see him now.

[EXIT Manuel.

Jane.	Come to my closet; free from all intrusion,
	I'll school thee there; and thou again shalt be
	My willing pupil, and my gen'rous friend;
	The noble Monfort I have lov'd so long,
	And must not, will not lose.
De Mon.	Do as thou wilt; I will not grieve thee more.

[EXEUNT.

SCENE III.

Count FREBERG's *House. Enter the* COUNTESS, *followed by the* PAGE, *and speaking as she enters.*

Lady.	Take this and this. (*Giving two packets.*)
	And tell my gentle friend,
	I hope to see her ere the day be done.
Page.	Is there no message for the Lady Jane?
Lady.	No, foolish boy, that would too far extend
	Your morning's route, and keep you absent long.
Page.	O no, dear Madam! I'll the swifter run.
	The summer's light'ning moves not as I'll move,
	If you will send me to the Lady Jane.
Lady.	No, not so slow, I ween. The summer's light'ning!
	Thou art a lad of taste and letters grown:
	Would'st poetry admire, and ape they master.
	Go, go; my little spaniels are unkempt;
	My cards unwritten, and my china broke:
	Thou art too learned for a lady's page.
	Did I not bid thee call Theresa here?
Page.	Madam she comes.

Enter THERESA, *carrying a robe over her arm.*

Lady.	(*to* Ther.) What has employ'd you all this dreary while?
	I've waited long.
Ther.	Madam, the robe is finish'd.
Lady.	Well, let me see it.
	(Theresa *spreads out the robe.*)
	(*Impatiently to the* Page.) Boy, hast thou ne'er a hand to lift that fold?
	See where it hangs.
	(Page *takes the other side of the robe, and spreads it out to its full extent before her, whilst she sits down and looks at it with much dissatisfaction.*)
Ther.	Does not my lady like this easy form?

110

Lady.	That sleeve is all awry.
Ther.	Your pardon, madam;
	'Tis but the empty fold that shapes it thus.
	I took the pattern from a graceful shape;
	The Lady Jane De Monfort wears it so.
Lady.	Yes, yes, I see 'tis thus with all of you.
	Whate'er she wears is elegance and grace,
	Whilst ev'ry ornament of mine, forsooth,
	Must hang likfe trappings on a May-day queen.
	(*Angrily to the* Page, *who is smiling to himself.*)
	Youngster be gone. Why do you loiter here?

[EXIT Page.

Ther .	What would you, madam, chuse to wear to-night?
	One of your newest robes?
Lady.	I hate them all.
Ther .	Surely, that purple scarf became you well,
	With all those wreaths of richly hanging flowers.
	Did I not overhear them say, last night,
	As from the crouded ball-room ladies past,
	How gay and handsome, in her costly dress,
	The Countess Freberg look'd.
Lady.	Did'st thou o'erhear it?
Ther.	I did, and more than this.
Lady.	Well, all are not so greatly prejudic'd;
	All do not think me like a May-day queen,
	Which peasants deck in sport.
Ther.	And who said this?
Lady.	(*Putting her handkerchief to her eyes.*) E'en my good lord, Theresa.
Ther.	He said it but in jest. He loves you well.
Lady.	I know as well as thee he loves me well;
	But what of that? he takes no pride in me.
	Elsewhere his praise and admiration go,
	And Jane De Monfort is not mortal woman.
Ther.	The wond'rous character this lady bears
	For worth and excellence; from early youth
	The friend and mother of her younger sisters
	Now greatly married, as I have been told,
	From her most prudent care, may well excuse
	The admiration of so good a man
	As my good master is. And then, dear madam,
	I must confess, when I myself did hear
	How she was come thro' the rough winter's storm,
	To seek and comfort an unhappy brother,
	My heart beat kindly to her.
Lady.	Ay, ay, there is a charm in this I find:
	But wherefore may she not have come as well
	Through wintery storms to seek a lover too?
Ther .	No, madam, no, I could not think of this.
Lady.	That would reduce her in your eyes, mayhap,

To woman's level. — Now I see my vengeance!
I'll tell it round that she is hither come,
Under pretence of finding out De Monfort,
To meet with Rezenvelt. When Freberg hears it
'Twill help, I ween, to break this magick charm.

Ther.   Ah no! there is —

Lady.   Well, hold thy foolish tongue.
Carry that robe into my chamber, do:
I'll try it there myself.

                                                [EXEUNT.

ACT III. — SCENE I.

De Monfort discovered sitting by a table reading. After a little time he lays down his book, and continues in a thoughtful posture. Enter to him Jane De Monfort.

Jane.	Thanks, gentle brother. —
	(*Pointing to the book.*)
	Thy willing mind has rightly been employ'd:
	Did not thy heart warm at the fair display
	Of peace and concord and forgiving love?
De Mon.	I know resentment may to love be turn'd;
	Tho' keen and lasting, into love as strong:
	And fiercest rivals in th'ensanguin'd field
	Have cast their brandish'd weapons to the ground,
	Joining their mailed breasts in close embrace,
	With gen'rous impulse fir'd. I know right well
	The darkest, fellest wrongs have been forgiven
	Seventy times o'er from blessed heavenly love:
	I've heard of things like these; I've heard and wept.
	But what is this to me?
Jane.	All, all, my brother!
	It bids thee too that noble precept learn,
	To love thine enemy.
De Mon.	Th' uplifted stroke that would a wretch destroy
	Gorg'd with my richest spoil, stain'd with my blood,
	I would arrest, and cry, hold! hold! have mercy:
	But when the man most adverse to my nature,
	Who e'en from childhood hath, with rude malevolence,
	Withheld the fair respect all paid beside,
	Turning my very praise into derision;
	Who galls and presses me where'er I go,
	Would claim the gen'rous feelings of my heart,
	Nature herself doth lift her voice aloud,
	And cries, it is impossible.
Jane. (	*Shaking her head.*) — Ah, Monfort, Monfort!
De Mon.	I can forgive th' envenom'd reptile's sting,
	But hate his loathsome self.
Jane.	And canst thou do no more for love of heaven?
De Mon.	Alas! I cannot now so school my mind
	As holy men have taught, nor search it truly:
	But this, my Jane, I'll do for love of thee;
	And more it is than crowns could win me to,
	Or any power but thine. I'll see the man.
	Th' indignant risings of abhorrent nature;
	The stern contraction of my scowling brows,
	That, like the plant, whose closing leaves do shrink
	At hostile touch, still knit at his approach;
	The crooked curving lip, by instinct taught,
	In imitation of disgustful things

	To pout and swell, I strictly will repress;
	And meet him with a tamed countenance,
	E'en as a townsman, who would live at peace,
	And pay him the respect his station claims.
	I'll crave his pardon too for all offence
	My dark and wayward temper may have done;
	Nay more, I will confess myself his debtor
	For the forbearance I have curs'd so oft.
	Life spar'd by him, more horrid than the grave
	With all its dark corruption! This I'll do.
	Will it suffice thee? More than this I cannot.
Jane.	No more than this do I require of thee
	In outward act, tho' in thy heart, my friend,
	I hop'd a better change, and yet will hope.
	I told thee Freberg had propos'd a meeting.
De Mon.	I know it well.
Jane.	And Rezenvelt consents.
	He meets you here; so far he shews respect.
De Mon.	Well, let it be; the sooner past the better.
Jane .	I'm glad to hear you say so, for, in truth,
	He has propos'd for it an early hour.
	'Tis almost near his time; I came to tell you.
De Mon.	What, comes he here so soon? shame on his speed!
	It is not decent thus to rush upon me.
	He loves the secret pleasure he will feel
	To see me thus subdued.
Jane.	O say not so! he comes with heart sincere.
De Mon.	Could we not meet elsewhere? from home — i' the fields,
	Where other men — must I alone receive him?
	Where is your agent, Freberg, and his friends,
	That I must meet him here?
	(*Walks up and down, very much disturbed.*)
	Now didst thou say? — how goes the hour? — e'en now!
	I would some other friend were first arriv'd.
Jane.	See, to thy wish comes Freberg and his dame.
De Mon.	His lady too! why comes he not alone?
	Must all the world stare upon our meeting?

Enter COUNT FREBERG *and his* COUNTESS.

Freb.	A happy morrow to my noble marquis
	And his most noble sister.
Jane.	Gen'rous Freberg,
	Your face, methinks, forebodes a happy morn
	Open and cheerful. What of Rezenvelt?
Freb.	I left him at his home, prepar'd to follow:
	He'll soon appear. (*To* De Monfort.) And now, my worthy friend,
	Give me your hand; this happy change delights me.
	(De Monfort *gives him his hand coldly, and they walk to the bottom of the*
	stage together, in earnest discourse, whilst Jane *and the* Countess *remain*

	in the front.)
Lady.	My dearest madam, will you pardon me?
	I know Count Freberg's bus'ness with De Monfort,
	And had a strong desire to visit you,
	So much I wish the honour of your friendship.
	For he retains no secret from mine ear.
Jane.	(*archly.*) Knowing your prudence. — You are welcome, madam,
	So shall Count Freberg's lady ever be.
	(De Monfort *and* Freberg *returning towards the front of the stage, still*
	engaged in discourse.)
Freb.	He is indeed a man, within whose breast,
	Firm rectitude and honour hold their seat,
	Tho' unadorned with that dignity
	Which were their fittest garb. Now, on my life!
	I know no truer heart than Rezenvelt.
De Mon.	Well, Freberg, well, — there needs not all this pains
	To garnish out his worth; let it suffice;
	I am resolv'd I will respect the man,
	As his fair station and repute demand.
	Methinks I see not at your jolly feasts
	The youthful knight, who sang so pleasantly.
Freb.	A pleasant circumstance detains him hence;
	Pleasant to those who love high gen'rous deeds
	Above the middle pitch of common minds;
	And, tho' I have been sworn to secrecy,
	Yet must I tell it thee.
	This knight is near akin to Rezenvelt
	To whom an old relation, short while dead,
	Bequeath'd a good estate, some leagues distant.
	But Rezenvelt, now rich in fortune's store,
	Disdain'd the sordid love of further gain,
	And gen'rously the rich bequest resign'd
	To this young man, blood of the same degree
	To the deceas'd, and low in fortune's gifts,
	Who is from hence to take possession of it:
	Was it not nobly done?
De Mon.	'Twas right and honourable.
	This morning is oppressive, warm, and heavy:
	There hangs a foggy closeness in the air;
	Dost thou not feel it?
Freb.	O no! to think upon a gen'rous deed
	Expands my soul, and makes me lightly breath.
De Mon.	Who gives the feast to night? His name escapes me.
	You say I am invited.
Freb.	Old Count Waterlan.
	In honour of your townsman's gen'rous gift
	He spreads the board.
De Mon.	He is too old to revel with the gay.
Freb.	But not too old is he to honour virtue.

	I shall partake of it with open soul;
	For, on my honest faith, of living men
	I know not one, for talents, honour, worth,
	That I should rank superior to Rezenvelt.
De Mon.	How virtuous he hath been in three short days!
Freb.	Nay, longer, Marquis, but my friendship rests
	Upon the good report of other men;
	And that has told me much.

(De Monfort *aside, going some steps hastily from* Freberg, *and rending his cloak with agitation as he goes.*)

Would he were come! by heaven I would he were!
This fool besets me so.

(*Suddenly correcting himself, and joining the* Ladies, *who have retired to the bottom of the stage, he speaks to* Countess Freberg *with affected cheerfulness.*)

The sprightly dames of Amberg rise by times,
Untarnish'd with the vigils of the night.

Lady.	Praise us not rashly, 'tis not always so.
De Mon.	He does not rashly praise who praises you;
	For he were dull indeed —

(*Stopping short, as if he heard something.*)

Lady.	How dull indeed?
De Mon.	I should have said — It has escap'd me now —

(*Listening again, as if he heard something.*)

Jane.	(*to* De Mon.) What, hear you aught?
De Mon.	(*hastily.*) 'Tis nothing.
Lady.	(*to* De Mon.) Nay, do not let me lose it so, my lord.
	Some fair one has bewitch'd your memory,
	And robs me of the half-form'd compliment.
Jane.	Half-utter'd praise is to the curious mind,
	As to the eye half-veiled beauty is,
	More precious than the whole. Pray pardon him.
	Some one approaches. (*Listening.*)
Freb.	No, no, it is a servant who ascends;
	He will not come so soon.
De Mon.	(*Off his guard.*) 'Tis Rezenvelt: I heard his well-known foot!
	From the first stair-case, mounting step by step.
Freb.	How quick an ear thou hast for distant sound!
	I heard him not.

(De Monfort *looks embarrassed, and is silent.*)

Enter REZENVELT.

(De Monfort, *recovering himself, goes up to receive* Rezenvelt, *who meets him with a cheerful countenance.*)

De Mon.	(*to* Rez.) I am, my lord, beholden to you greatly.
	This ready visit makes me much your debtor.
Rez.	Then may such debts between us, noble marquis,
	Be oft incurr'd, and often paid again.
	(*To* Jane.) Madam, I am devoted to your service,

	And ev'ry wish of yours commands my will.
	(*To* Countess.) Lady, good morning. (*To* Freb.) Well, my gentle friend,
	You see I have not linger'd long behind.
Freb.	No, thou art sooner than I look'd for thee.
Rez.	A willing heart adds feather to the heel,
	And makes the clown a winged mercury.
De Mon.	Then let me say, that with a grateful mind
	I do receive these tokens of good will;
	And must regret that, in my wayward moods,
	I have too oft forgot the due regard
	Your rank and talents claim.
Rez.	No, no, De Monfort,
	You have but rightly curb'd a wanton spirit,
	Which makes me too neglectful of respect.
	Let us be friends, and think of this no more.
Freb.	Ay, let it rest with the departed shades
	Of things which are no more; whilst lovely concord,
	Follow'd by friendship sweet, and firm esteem,
	Your future days enrich. O heavenly friendship!
	Thou dost exalt the sluggish souls of men,
	By thee conjoin'd, to great and glorious deeds;
	As two dark clouds, when mix'd in middle air,
	With vivid lightnings flash, and roar sublime.
	Talk not of what is past, but future love.
De Mon.	(*With dignity.*) No, Freberg, no, it must not. (*To* Rezenvelt.) No, my lord,
	I will not offer you an hand of concord,
	And poorly hide the motives which constrain me.
	I would that, not alone these present friends,
	But ev'ry soul in Amberg were assembled,
	That I, before them all, might here declare
	I owe my spared life to your forbearance.
	(*Holding out his hand.*) Take this from one who boasts no feeling warmth,
	But never will deceive.
	(Jane *smiles upon* De Monfort *with great approbation, and* Rezenvelt *runs up to him with open arms.*)
Rez.	Away with hands! I'll have thee to my breast.
	Thou art, upon my faith, a noble spirit!
De Mon.	(*Shrinking back from him.*)
	Nay, if you please, I am not so prepar'd—
	My nature is of temp'rature too cold—
	I pray you pardon me. (Jane's *countenance changes.*)
	But take this hand, the token of respect;
	The token of a will inclin'd to concord;
	The token of a mind that bears within
	A sense impressive of the debt it owes you:
	And cursed be its power, unnerv'd its strength,
	If e'er again it shall be lifted up
	To do you any harm.
Rez.	Well, be it so, De Monfort, I'm contented;

	I'll take thy hand, since I can have no more.
	(*Carelessly*.) I take of worthy men whate'er they give.
	Their heart I gladly take; if not, their hand:
	If that too is withheld, a courteous word,
	Or the civility of placid looks;
	And, if e'en these are too great favours deem'd,
	'Faith, I can set me down contentedly
	With plain and homely greeting, or, God save ye!
De Mon.	(*Aside, starting away from him some paces*.)
	By the good light, he makes a jest of it!
	(Jane *seems greatly distressed, and* Freberg *endeavours to cheer her*.)
Freb.	(*to* Jane.) Cheer up, my noble friend; all will go well;
	For friendship is no plant of hasty growth.
	Though rooted in esteem's deep-fixed soil,
	The gradual culture of kind intercourse
	Must bring it to perfection.
	(*To the* Countess.) My love, the morning, now, is far advanced;
	Our friends elsewhere expect us; take your leave.
Lady.	(*to* Jane.) Farewell! dear madam, till the ev'ning hour.
Freb.	(*to* De Mon.) Good day, De Monfort. (*To* Jane.) Most devoutly yours.
Rez.	(*to* Freb.) Go not too fast, for I will follow you.

[EXEUNT Freberg *and his* Lady.

	(*To* Jane.) The Lady Jane is yet a stranger here:
	She might, perhaps, in the purlieus of Amberg
	Find somewhat worth her notice.
Jane.	I thank you, Marquis, I am much engag'd;
	I go not out to-day.
Rez.	Then fare ye well! I see I cannot now
	Be the proud man who shall escort you forth,
	And show to all the world my proudest boast,
	The notice and respect of Jane De Monfort.
De Mon.	(*Aside, impatiently*.) He says farewell, and goes not!
Jane.	(*to* Rez.) You do me honour.
Rez.	Madam, adieu! (*To* Jane.) Good morning, noble marquis.

[EXIT

(Jane *and* De Monfort *look expressively to one another, without speaking, and then*
EXEUNT, *severally*.)

SCENE II.

A splendid Banquetting Room. DE MONFORT, REZENVELT, FREBERG, MASTER OF THE
HOUSE, *and* GUESTS, *are discovered sitting at table, with wine, &c. before them.*

SONG. — A GLEE.[1]

Pleasant is the mantling bowl,
And the song of merry soul;

---

1   A glee is an unaccompanied song for three or more voices.

And the red lamps cheery light,
And the goblet glancing bright;
Whilst many a cheerful face, around,
Listens to the jovial sound.
Social spirits, join with me;
Bless the God of jollity.

Freb.   (*to* De Mon.) (*Who rises to go away.*)
          Thou wilt not leave us, Monfort? wherefore so?

De Mon.   (*Aside to* Freberg.) I pray thee take no notice of me now.
          Mine ears are stunned with these noisy fools;
          Let me escape.

                                      [EXIT, hastily.

Master of the House. What, is De Monfort gone?

Freb.   Time presses him.

Rez.   It seem'd to sit right heavily upon him,
          We must confess.

Mast.   (*to* Freb.) How is your friend? he wears a noble mien,
          But most averse, methinks, from social pleasure.
          Is this his nature?

Freb.   No, I've seen him cheerful,
          And at the board, with soul-enliven'd face,
          Push the gay goblet round. — But it wears late.
          We shall seem topers more than social friends,
          If the returning sun surprise us here.
          (*To* Mast.) Good rest, my gen'rous host; we will retire.
          You wrestle with your age most manfully,
          But brave it not too far. Retire to sleep.

Mast.   I will, my friend, but do you still remain,
          With noble Rezenvelt, and all my guests.
          Ye have not fourscore years upon your head;
          Do not depart so soon. God save you all!

                            [EXIT Master, *leaning upon a* Servant.

Freb.   (*to the Guests.*) Shall we resume?

Guests.   The night is too far spent.

Freb.   Well then, good rest to you.

Rez.   (*to Guests.*) Good rest, my friends.

                      [EXEUNT *all but* Freberg *and* Rezenvelt.

Freb.   Alas, my Rezenvelt!
          I vainly hop'd the hand of gentle peace,
          From this day's reconciliation sprung,
          These rude unseemly jarrings had subdu'd;
          But I have mark'd, e'en at the social board,
          Such looks, such words, such tones, such untold things,
          Too plainly told, 'twixt you and Monfort pass,
          That I must now despair.
          Yet who could think, two minds so much refin'd,
          So near in excellence, should be remov'd,
          So far remov'd, in gen'rous sympathy?

Rez.	Ay, far remov'd indeed.
Freb.	And yet, methought, he made a noble effort,
	And with a manly plainness bravely told
	The galling debt he owes to your forbearance.
Rez.	'Faith! so he did, and so did I receive it;
	When, with spread arms, and heart e'en mov'd to tears,
	I frankly proffer'd him a friend's embrace:
	And, I declare, had he as such receiv'd it,
	I from that very moment had forborne
	All opposition, pride-provoking jest,
	Contemning carelessness, and all offence;
	And had caress'd him as a worthy heart,
	From native weakness such indulgence claiming:
	But since he proudly thinks that cold respect,
	The formal tokens of his lordly favour,
	So precious are, that I would sue for them
	As fair distinction in the world's eye,
	Forgetting former wrongs, I spurn it all;
	And but that I do bear the noble woman,
	His worthy, his incomparable sister,
	Such fix'd, profound regard, I would expose him;
	And, as a mighty bull, in senseless rage,
	Rous'd at the baiter's will, with wretched rags
	Of ire-provoking scarlet, chaffs and bellows,
	I'd make him at small cost of paltry wit,
	With all his deep and manly faculties,
	The scorn and laugh of fools.
Freb.	For heaven's sake, my friend! restrain your wrath!
	For what has Monfort done of wrong to you,
	Or you to him, bating one foolish quarrel,
	Which you confess from slight occasion rose,
	That in your breasts such dark resentment dwells,
	So fix'd, so hopeless?
Rez.	O! from our youth he has distinguish'd me
	With ev'ry mark of hatred and disgust.
	For e'en in boyish sports I still oppos'd
	His proud pretensions to pre-eminence;
	Nor would I to his ripen'd greatness give
	That fulsome adulation of applause
	A senseless crowd bestow'd. Tho' poor in fortune,
	I still would smile at vain-assuming wealth:
	But when unlook'd-for fate on me bestow'd
	Riches and splendour equal to his own,
	Tho' I, in truth, despise such poor distinction,
	Feeling inclin'd to be at peace with him,
	And with all men beside, I curb'd my spirit,
	And sought to soothe him. Then, with spiteful rage,
	From small offence he rear'd a quarrel with me,
	And dar'd me to the field. The rest you know.

	In short, I still have been th' opposing rock,
	O'er which the stream of his o'erflowing pride
	Hath foam'd and bellow'd. Seest thou how it is?
Freb.	Too well I see, and warn thee to beware.
	Such streams have oft, by swelling floods surcharg'd,
	Borne down with sudden and impetuous force,
	The yet unshaken stone of opposition,
	Which had for ages stopp'd their flowing course.
	I pray thee, friend, beware.
Rez.	Thou canst not mean—he will not murder me?
Freb.	What a proud heart, with such dark passion toss'd,
	May, in the anguish of its thoughts, conceive,
	I will not dare to say.
Rez.	Ha, ha! thou knowst him not.
	Full often have I mark'd it in his youth,
	And could have almost lov'd him for the weakness;
	He's form'd with such antipathy, by nature,
	To all infliction of corporeal pain,
	To wounding life, e'en to the sight of blood,
	He cannot if he would.
Freb.	Then fy upon thee!
	It is not gen'rous to provoke him thus.
	But let us part: we'll talk of this again.
	Something approaches.—We are here too long.
Rez.	Well, then, to-morrow I'll attend your call.
	Here lies my way. Good night.

[EXIT.

Enter GRIMBALD.

Grim.	Forgive, I pray, my lord, a stranger's boldness.
	I have presum'd to wait your leisure here,
	Though at so late an hour.
Freb.	But who art thou?
Grim.	My name is Grimbald, sir,
	A humble suitor to your honour's goodness,
	Who is the more embolden'd to presume,
	In that the noble Marquis of De Monfort
	Is so much fam'd for good and gen'rous deeds.
Freb.	You are mistaken, I am not the man.
Grim.	Then, pardon me; I thought I could not err.
	That mien so dignified, that piercing eye
	Assur'd me it was he.
Freb.	My name is not De Monfort, courteous stranger;
	But, if you have a favour to request,
	I may, with him, perhaps, befriend your suit.
Grim.	I thank your honour, but I have a friend
	Who will commend me to De Monfort's favour:
	The Marquis Rezenvelt has known me long,
	Who, says report, will soon become his brother.

Freb.	If thou wouldst seek thy ruin from De Monfort,
	The name of Rezenvelt employ, and prosper;
	But, if aught good, use any name but his.
Grim.	How may this be?
Freb.	I cannot now explain.
	Early to-morrow call upon Count Freberg;
	So am I call'd, each burgher knows my house,
	And there instruct me how to do you service.
	Good-night.

                                             [EXIT.

Grim.	(*Alone.*) Well, this mistake may be of service to me:
	And yet my bus'ness I will not unfold
	To this mild, ready, promise-making courtier;
	I've been by such too oft deceiv'd already:
	But if such violent enmity exist
	Between De Monfort and this Rezenvelt,
	He'll prove my advocate by opposition.
	For, if De Monfort would reject my suit,
	Being the man whom Rezenvelt esteems,
	Being the man he hates, a cord as strong,
	Will he not favour me? I'll think of this.

                                             [EXIT.

SCENE III.

A lower Apartment in JEROME'S *house, with a wide folding glass door, looking into a garden, where the trees and shrubs are brown and leafless. Enter* DE MONFORT *with his arms crossed, with a thoughtful frowning aspect, and paces slowly across the stage,* Jerome *following behind him, with a timid step.* De Monfort *hearing him, turns suddenly about.*

De Mon.	(*Angrily.*) Who follows me to this sequester'd room?
Jer .	I have presum'd, my lord. 'Tis somewhat late:
	I am inform'd you eat at home to-night;
	Here is a list of all the dainty fare
	My busy search has found; please to peruse it.
De Mon.	Leave me: begone! Put hemlock in thy soup,
	Or deadly night-shade, or rank hellebore,[2]
	And I will mess upon it.
Jer.	Heaven forbid!
	Your honour's life is all too precious, sure—
De Mon.	(*Sternly.*) Did I not say begone?
Jer.	Pardon, my lord, I'm old, and oft forget.

                                           [EXIT.

De Mon.	(*Looking after him, as if his heart smote him.*)
	Why will they thus mistime their foolish zeal,
	That I must be so stern?

---

2   All of these are of course highly poisonous plants, also used in tiny quantities for medicinal purposes.

O, that I were upon some desert coast!
Where howling tempests and the lashing tide
Would stun me into deep and senseless quiet;
As the storm-beaten trav'ller droops his head,
In heavy, dull, lethargic weariness,
And, 'midst the roar of jarring elements,
Sleeps to awake no more.
What am I grown? all things are hateful to me.

Enter MANUEL.

	(Stamping with his foot.) Who bids thee break upon my privacy?
Man.	Nay, good my lord! I heard you speak aloud,
	And dreamt not surely that you were alone.
De Mon.	What, dost thou watch, and pin thine ears to holes,
	To catch those exclamations of the soul,
	Which heaven alone should hear? Who hir'd thee, pray?
	Who basely hir'd thee for a task like this?
Man.	My lord, I cannot hold. For fifteen years,
	Long-troubled years, I have your servant been,
	Nor hath the proudest lord in all the realm,
	With firmer, with more honourable faith
	His sov'reign serv'd, than I have served you;
	But if my honesty be doubted now,
	Let him who is more faithful take my place,
	And serve you better.
De Mon.	Well, be it as thou wilt. Away with thee.
	Thy loud-mouth'd boasting is no rule for me
	To judge thy merit by.

Enter JEROME *hastily, and pulls* MANUEL *away.*

Jer.	Come, Manuel, come away; thou art not wise.
	The stranger must depart and come again,
	For now his honour will not be disturb'd.

[EXIT Manuel *sulkily.*

De Mon.	A stranger, said'st thou.
	(Drops his handkerchief.)
Jer.	I did, good sir, but he shall go away;
	You shall not be disturb'd.
	(Stooping to lift the handkerchief.)
	You have dropp'd somewhat.
De Mon.	*(Preventing him.)* Nay, do not stoop, my friend! I pray thee not!
	Thou art too old to stoop. —
	I'm much indebted to thee. — Take this ring —
	I love thee better than I seem to do.
	I pray thee do it — thank me not. — What stranger?
Jer.	A man who does most earnestly entreat
	To see your honour; but I know him not.

De Mon.	Then let him enter.

[EXIT Jerome.

A pause. Enter GRIMBALD.

De Mon.	You are the stranger who would speak with me?
Grim.	I am so far unfortunate, my lord.
	That, though my fortune on your favour hangs,
	I am to you a stranger.
De Mon.	How may this be? What can I do for you?,
Grim.	Since thus your lordship does so frankly ask,
	The tiresome preface of apology
	I will forbear, and tell my tale at once. —
	In plodding drudgery I've spent my youth,
	A careful penman in another's office;
	And now, my master and employer dead,
	They seek to set a stripling o'er my head,
	And leave me on to drudge, e'en to old age,
	Because I have no friend to take my part.
	It is an office in your native town,
	For I am come from thence, and I am told
	You can procure it for me. Thus, my lord,
	From the repute of goodness which you bear,
	I have presum'd to beg.
De Mon.	They have befool'd thee with a false report.
Grim.	Alas! I see it is in vain to plead.
	Your mind is pre-possess'd against a wretch,
	Who has, unfortunately for his weal,
	Offended the revengeful Rezenvelt.
De Mon.	What dost thou say?
Grim.	What I, perhaps, had better leave unsaid.
	Who will believe my wrongs if I complain?
	I am a stranger, Rezenvelt my foe,
	Who will believe my wrongs?
De Mon.	(*Eagerly catching him by the coat.*)

I will believe them!

	Though they were base as basest, vilest deeds,
	In ancient record told, I would believe them.
	Let not the smallest atom of unworthiness
	That he has put upon thee be conceal'd.
	Speak boldly, tell it all; for, by the light!
	I'll be thy friend, I'll be thy warmest friend,
	If he has done thee wrong.
Grim.	Nay, pardon me, it were not well advis'd,
	If I should speak so freely of the man,
	Who will so soon your nearest kinsman be.
De Mon.	What canst thou mean by this?
Grim.	That Marquis Rezenvelt
	Has pledg'd his faith unto your noble sister,
	And soon will be the husband of her choice.

	So I am told, and so the world believes.
De Mon.	'Tis false! 'tis basely false!
	What wretch could drop from his envenom'd tongue
	A tale so damn'd? — It chokes my breath —
	(*Stamping with his foot.*) What wretch did tell it thee?
Grim.	Nay, every one with whom I have convers'd
	Has held the same discourse. I judge it not.
	But you, my lord, who with the lady dwell.
	You best can tell what her deportment speaks;
	Whether her conduct and unguarded words
	Belie such rumour.
	(De Monfort *pauses, staggers backwards, and sinks into a chair; then starting up hastily.*)
De Mon.	Where am I now? 'midst all the cursed thoughts
	That on my soul like stinging scorpions prey'd,
	This never came before — Oh, if it be!
	The thought will drive me mad. — Was it for this
	She urg'd her warm request on bended knee?
	Alas! I wept, and thought of sister's love,
	No damned love like this.
	Fell devil! 'tis hell itself has lent thee aid
	To work such sorcery! (*Pauses.*) I'll not believe it.
	I must have proof clear as the noon-day sun
	For such foul charge as this! Who waits without!
	(*Paces up and down, furiously agitated.*)
Grim.	(*Aside.*) What have I done? I've carried this too far.
	I've rous'd a fierce ungovernable madman.

Enter JEROME.

De Mon.	(*In a loud angry voice.*) Where did she go, at such an early hour,
	And with such slight attendance?
Jer.	Of whom inquires your honour?
De Mon.	Why, of your lady. Said I not my sister?
Jer.	The Lady Jane, your sister?
De Mon.	(*In a faltering voice.*) Yes, I did call her so.
Jer .	In truth, I cannot tell you where she went.
	E'en now, from the short-beechen walk hard-by,
	I saw her through the garden-gate return.
	The Marquis Rezenvelt, and Freberg's Countess,
	Are in her company. This way they come,
	As being nearer to the back apartments;
	But I shall stop them, if it be your will,
	And bid them enter here.
De Mon.	No, stop them not. I will remain unseen,
	And mark them as they pass. Draw back a little.
	(Grimbald *seems alarm'd, and steals off unnoticed.* De Monfort *grasps* Jerome *tightly by the hand, and drawing back with him two or three steps, not to be seen from the garden, waits in silence with his eyes fixed on the*

glass-door.)

De Mon.	I hear their footsteps on the grating sand.
	How like the croaking of a carrion bird,
	That hateful voice sounds to the distant ear!
	And now she speaks—her voice sounds cheerly too—
	O curse their mirth!—
	Now, now, they come; keep closer still! keep steady!
	(*Taking hold of* Jerome *with both hands.*)
Jer.	My lord, you tremble much.
De Mon.	What, do I shake?
Jer.	You do, in truth, and your teeth chatter too.
De Mon.	See! see they come! he strutting by her side.

(Jane, Rezenvelt, *and* Countess Freberg *appear through the glass-door,
pursuing their way up a short walk leading to the other wing of the house.*)

	See how he turns his odious face to her's!
	Utt'ring with confidence some nauseous jest.
	And she endures it too—Oh! this looks vilely!
	Ha! mark that courteous motion of his arm—
	What does he mean?—He dares not take her hand!
	(*Pauses and looks eagerly.*) By heaven and hell he does!

(*Letting go his hold of* Jerome, *he throws out his hands vehemently, and
thereby pushes him against the scene.*)

Jer.	Oh! I am stunn'd! my head is crack'd in twain:
	Your honour does forget how old I am.
De Mon.	Well, well, the wall is harder than I wist.
	Begone, and whine within.

[Exit Jerome, *with a sad rueful countenance.*
(De Monfort *comes forward to the front of the stage, and makes a long pause,
expressive of great agony of mind.*)

It must be so: each passing circumstance;
Her hasty journey here; her keen distress
Whene'er my soul's abhorrence I express'd;
Ay, and that damned reconciliation,
With tears extorted from me: Oh, too well!
All, all too well bespeak the shameful tale.
I should have thought of heav'n and hell conjoin'd,
The morning star mix'd with infernal fire,
Ere I had thought of this—
Hell's blackest magick, in the midnight hour,
With horrid spells and incantation dire,
Such combination opposite, unseemly,
Of fair and loathsome, excellent and base,
Did ne'er produce.—But every thing is possible,
So as it may my misery enhance!
Oh! I did love her with such pride of soul!
When other men, in gay pursuit of love,
Each beauty follow'd, by her side I stay'd;
Far prouder of a brother's station there,
Than all the favours favour'd lovers boast.

We quarrell'd once, and when I could no more
The alter'd coldness of her eye endure,
I slipp'd o'tip-toe to her chamber-door;
And when she ask'd who gently knock'd—Oh! oh!
Who could have thought of this?
(*Throws himself into a chair, covers his face with his hand, and bursts into*
tears. After some time, he starts up from his seat furiously.)
Hell's direst torment seize th' infernal villain!
Detested of my soul! I will have vengeance!
I'll crush thy swelling pride—I'll still thy vaunting—
I'll do a deed of blood—Why shrink I thus?
If by some spell or magick sympathy,
Piercing the lifeless figure on that wall
Could pierce his bosom too, would I not cast it?
(*Throwing a dagger against the wall.*)
Shall groans and blood affright me? No, I'll do it.
Tho' gasping life beneath my pressure heav'd,
And my soul shudder'd at the horrid brink,
I would not flinch.—Fie, this recoiling nature!
O that his sever'd limbs were strew'd in air,
So as I saw it not!
(*Enter* Rezenvelt *behind, from the glass door. De Monfort* turns round, and on seeing him,
starts back, then drawing his sword, rushes furiously upon him.*)
Detested robber; now all forms are over:
Now open villainy, now open hate!
Defend thy life.

Rez.	De Monfort, thou art mad.
De Mon.	Speak not, but draw. Now for thy hated life!

(*They fight:* Rezenvelt *parries his thrusts with great skill, and at last*
disarms him.)
Then take my life, black fiend, for hell assists thee.

Rez.	No, Monfort, but I'll take away your sword,

Not as a mark of disrespect to you,
But for your safety. By to-morrow's eve
I'll call on you myself and give it back;
And then, if I am charg'd with any wrong,
I'll justify myself. Farewell, strange man!

[EXIT.

(De Monfort *stands for some time quite motionless, like one stupified. Enter to him a*
SERVANT: *he starts.*)

De Mon.	Ha! who art thou?
Ser.	'Tis I, an' please your honour.
De Mon.	(*Staring wildly at him.*) Who art thou?
Ser.	Your servant Jacques.
De Mon.	Indeed I knew thee not.

Leave me, and when Rezenvelt is gone,
Return and let me know.

Ser.	He's gone already, sir.
De Mon.	How, gone so soon?

Ser.	Yes, as his servant told me,
	He was in haste to go; as night comes on,
	And at the evening hour he must take horse,
	To visit some old friend whose lonely mansion
	Stands a short mile beyond the farther wood;
	And, as he loves to wander thro' those wilds
	Whilst yet the early moon may light his way,
	He sends his horses round the usual road,
	And crosses it alone.
	I would not walk thro' those wild dens alone
	For all his wealth. For there, as I have heard,
	Foul murders have been done, and ravens scream;
	And things unearthly, stalking through the night,
	Have scar'd the lonely trav'ller from his wits.
	(De Monfort *stands fixed in thought*.)
	I've ta'en your steed, an' please you, from her field,
	And wait your farther orders.
	(De Monfort *heeds him not*.)
	His hoofs are sound, and where the saddle gall'd,
	Begins to mend. What further must be done?
	(De Monfort *still heeds him not*.)
	His honour heeds me not. Why should I stay?
De Mon.	(*Eagerly, as he is going*.) He goes alone, saidst thou?
Ser.	His servant told me so.
De Mon.	And at what hour?
Ser.	He 'parts from Amberg by the fall of eve.
	Save you, my lord? how chang'd your count'nance is!
	Are you not well?
De Mon.	Yes, I am well: begone!
	And wait my orders by the city wall:
	I'll that way bend, and speak to thee again.

[EXIT Servant.

(De Monfort *walks rapidly two or three times across the stage; then seizes his dagger from the wall, looks steadfastly at its point, and* EXIT, *hastily*.)

ACT IV.—SCENE I.

Moon-light. A wild path in a wood, shaded with trees. Enter De Monfort, *with a strong expression of disquiet, mixed with fear, upon his face, looking behind him, and bending his ear to the ground, as if he listened to something.*

De Mon.   How hollow groans the earth beneath my tread!
      Is there an echo here? Methinks it sounds
      As tho' some heavy footstep follow'd me.
      I will advance no farther.
      Deep settled shadows rest across the path,
      And thickly-tangled boughs o'er-hang this spot.
      O that a tenfold gloom did cover it!
      That 'midst the murky darkness I might strike;
      As in the wild confusion of a dream,
      Things horrid, bloody, terrible do pass,
      As tho' they pass'd not; nor impress the mind
      With the fix'd clearness of reality.
      (*An owl is heard screaming near him.*)
      (*Starting.*) What sound is that?
      (*Listens, and the owl cries again.*)
                       It is the screech-owl's cry.
      Foul bird of night! what spirit guides thee here?
      Art thou instinctive drawn to scenes of horrour?
      I've heard of this. (*Pauses and listens.*)
      How those fall'n leaves so rustle on the path,
      With whisp'ring noise, as though the earth around me
      Did utter secret things!
      The distant river, too, bears to mine ear
      A dismal wailing. O mysterious night!
      Thou art not silent; many tongues hast thou.
      A distant gath'ring blast sounds through the wood,
      And dark clouds fleetly hasten o'er the sky:
      O! that a storm would rise, a raging storm;
      Amidst the roar of warring elements;
      I'd lift my hand and strike: but this pale light,
      The calm distinctness of each stilly thing,
      Is terrible. (*Starting.*) Footsteps, are near—
      He comes, he comes! I'll watch him farther on—
      I cannot do it here.

                                       [Exit.

Enter Rezenvelt, *and continues his way slowly across the stage:but just as he is going off the owl screams, he stops and listens, and the owl screams again.*

Rez.   Ha! does the night-bird greet me on my way?
      How much his hooting is in harmony
      With such a scene as this! I like it well.
      Oft when a boy, at the still twilight hour,

I've leant my back against some knotted oak,
And loudly mimick'd him, till to my call
He answer would return, and, thro' the gloom,
We friendly converse held.
Between me and the star-bespangl'd sky,
Those aged oaks their crossing branches wave,
And through them looks the pale and placid moon.
How like a crocodile, or winged snake,
Yon sailing cloud bears on its dusky length!
And now transformed by the passing wind,
Methinks it seems a flying Pegasus.
Ay, but a shapeless band of blacker hue
Comes swiftly after. —
A hollow murm'ring wind sounds through the trees;
I hear it from afar; this bodes a storm.
I must not linger here —
(*A bell heard at some distance.*) What bell is this?
It sends a solemn sound upon the breeze.
Now, to a fearful superstitious mind,
In such a scene, 'twould like a death-knell come:
For me it tells but of a shelter near,
And so I bid it welcome.

[Exit.

SCENE II.

The inside of a Convent Chapel, of old Gothick architecture, almost dark; two torches only are seen at a distance, burning over a new-made grave. The noise of loud wind, beating upon the windows and roof, is heard. Enter two MONKS.

1st *Monk.*   The storm increases: hark how dismally
               It howls along the cloisters. How goes time?
2d *Monk*   It is the hour: I hear them near at hand;
               And when the solemn requiem has been sung
               For the departed sister, we'll retire.
               Yet, should this tempest still more violent grow,
               We'll beg a friendly shelter till the morn.
1st *Monk.*   See, the procession enters: let us join.

(*The organ strikes up a solemn prelude. Enter a procession of* Nuns, *with the* Abbess, *bearing torches. After compassing the grave twice, and remaining there some time, the organ plays a grand dirge, they advance to the front of the stage.*)

SONG, BY THE NUNS.

Departed soul, whose poor remains
This hallow'd lowly grave contains;
Whose passing storm of life is o'er,

Whose pains and sorrows are no more!
Bless'd be thou with the bless'd above!
Where all is joy, and purity, and love.

Let him, in might and mercy dread,
Lord of the living and the dead;
In whom the stars of heav'n rejoice,
To whom the ocean lifts his voice,
Thy spirit purified to glory raise,
To sing with holy saints his everlasting praise.

Departed soul, who in this earthly scene
Hast our lowly sister been.
Swift be thy way to where the blessed dwell!
Until we meet thee there, farewell! farewell!

Enter a LAY SISTER, *with a wild terrified look, her hair and dress all scattered, and rushes forward amongst them.*

Abb.	Why com'st thou here, with such disorder'd looks,
	To break upon our sad solemnity?
Sist.	Oh! I did hear thro' the receding blast,
	Such horrid cries! they made my blood run chill.
Abb.	'Tis but the varied voices of the storm,
	Which many times will sound like distant screams:
	It has deceiv'd thee.
Sist.	O no, for twice it call'd, so loudly call'd,
	With horrid strength, beyond the pitch of nature;
	And murder! murder! was the dreadful cry.
	A third time it return'd with feeble strength,
	But o' the sudden ceas'd, as though the words
	Were rudely smother'd in the grasped throat;
	And all was still again, save the wild blast
	Which at a distance growl'd —
	Oh! it will never from my mind depart!
	That dreadful cry, all I' the instant still'd,
	For then, so near, some horrid deed was done,
	And none to rescue.
Abb.	Where didst thou hear it?
Sist.	In the higher cells,
	As now a window, open'd by the storm,
	I did attempt to close.
1st Monk.	I wish our brother Bernard were arriv'd;
	He is upon his way.
Abb.	Be not alarm'd; it still may be deception.
	'Tis meet we finish our solemnity,
	Nor show neglect unto the honour'd dead.
	(*Gives a sign, and the organ plays again: just as it ceases a loud knocking is heard without.*)

Abb.	Ha! who may this be? hush!
	(*Knocking heard again.*)
2d Monk.	It is the knock of one in furious haste,
	Hush! hush! What footsteps come? Ha! brother Bernard.

Enter BERNARD *bearing a lantern.*

1st Monk.	See, what a look he wears of stiffen'd fear!
	Where hast thou been, good brother?
Bern.	I've seen a horrid sight!
	(*All gathering round him and speaking at once.*)
	What hast thou seen?
Bern.	As on I hasten'd, bearing thus my light,
	Across the path, not fifty paces off,
	I saw a murther'd corse stretch'd on his back,
	Smear'd with new blood, as though but freshly slain.
Abb.	A man or woman?
Bern.	A man, a man!
Abb.	Didst thou examine if within its breast
	There yet is lodg'd some small remains of life?
	Was it quite dead?
	Nought in the grave is deader.
Bern.	I look'd but once, yet life did never lodge
	In any form so laid.
	A chilly horror seiz'd me, and I fled.
1st Monk.	And does the face seem all unknown to thee?
Bern.	The face! I would not on the face have look'd
	For e'en a kingdom's wealth, for all the world.
	O no! the bloody neck, the bloody neck!
	(*Shaking his head, and shuddering with horrour. Loud knocking heard without.*)
Sist.	Good mercy! who comes next?
Bern.	Not far behind
	I left our brother Thomas on the road;
	But then he did repent him as he went,
	And threatened to return.
2d Monk.	See, here he comes.
	Enter brother THOMAS, *with a wild terrified look.*
1st Monk.	How wild he looks!
Bern.	(*Going up to him eagerly.*) What, hast thou seen it too?
Thom.	Yes, yes! it glar'd upon me as it pass'd.
Bern.	What glar'd upon thee?
	(*All gathering round* Thomas *and speaking at once.*)
	O! what hast thou seen?
Thom.	As, striving with the blast, I onward came,
	Turning my feeble lantern from the wind,
	Its light upon a dreadful visage gleam'd,
	Which paus'd, and look'd upon me as it pass'd.
	But such a look, such wildness of despair,

	Such horror-strain'd features never yet
	Did earthly visage show. I shrank and shudder'd.
	If damned spirits may to earth return
	I've seen it.
Bern.	Was there any blood upon it?
Thom.	Nay, as it pass'd, I did not see its form;
	Nought but the horrid face.
Bern.	It is the murderer.
1st Monk.	What way went it?
Thom.	I durst not look till I had pass'd it far,
	Then turning round, upon the rising bank,
	I saw, between me and the paly sky,
	A dusky form, tossing and agitated.
	I stopp'd to mark it, but, in truth, I found
	'Twas but a sapling bending to the wind,
	And so I onward hied, and look'd no more.
1st Monk.	But we must look to't; we must follow it:
	Our duty so commands. (*To* 2d Monk.) Will you go, brother?
	(*To* Bernard.) And you, good Bernard?
Bern.	If I needs must go.
1st Monk.	Come, we must all go.
Abb.	Heaven be with you, then!

[EXEUNT *Monks.*

Sist.	Amen! amen! Good heav'n, be with us all!
	O what a dreadful night!
Abb.	Daughters retire; peace to the peaceful dead!
	Our solemn ceremony now is finish'd.

[EXEUNT.

SCENE III.

A large room in the Convent, very dark. Enter the ABBESS, *Lay Sister bearing a light, and several* Nuns; Sister *sets down the light on a table at the bottom of the stage, so that the room is still very gloomy.*

Abb.	They have been longer absent than I thought:
	I fear he has escap'd them.
1st Nun.	Heaven forbid!
Sist.	No, no, found out foul murder ever is,
	And the foul murd'rer too.
2d Nun.	The good Saint Francis will direct their search;
	The blood so near this holy convent shed
	For threefold vengeance calls.
Abb.	I hear a noise within the inner court,
	They are return'd; (*listening;*) and Bernard's voice I hear:
	They are return'd.
Sist.	Why do I tremble so?
	It is not I who ought to tremble thus.

2d *Nun.*	I hear them at the door.
Bern.	(*Without.*) Open the door, I pray thee, brother Thomas;
	I cannot now unhand the prisoner.
	(*All speak together, shrinking back from the door, and staring upon one*
	another.)
	He is with them!

(*A folding door at the bottom of the stage is opened, and enter* **Bernard, Thomas,** *and the other two* Monks, *carrying lanterns in their hands, and bringing in* De Monfort. *They are likewise followed by other* Monks. *As they lead forward* De Monfort *the light is turned away, so that he is seen obscurely; but when they come to the front of the stage they all turn the light side of their lanterns on him at once, and his face is seen in all the strengthened horrour of despair, with his hands and cloathes bloody.*)

	(Abbess *and* Nuns *speak at once, and starting back.*) Holy saints be with us!
Bern.	(*to* Abb.) Behold the man of blood!
Abb.	Of misery too; I cannot look upon him.
Bern.	(*to* Nuns.) Nay, holy sisters, turn not thus away.
	Speak to him, if, perchance, he will regard you:
	For from his mouth we have no utt'rance heard,
	Save one deep and smother'd exclamation,
	When first we seiz'd him.
Abb.	(*to* De Mon.) Most miserable man, how art thou thus?
	(*Pauses.*)
	Thy tongue is silent, but those bloody hands
	Do witness horrid things. What is thy name?
De Mon.	(*Roused; looks steadfastly at the* Abbess *for some time; then speaking in a*
	short hurried voice.) I have no name.
Abb.	(*to* Bern.) Do it thyself; I'll speak to him no more.
Sist.	O holy saints! that this should be the man,
	Who did against his fellow lift the stroke,
	Whilst he so loudly call'd. —
	Still in mine ear it sounds: O murder! murder!
De Mon.	(*Starting.*) He calls again!
Sist.	No, he did call, but now his voice is still'd.
	'Tis past.
De Mon.	(*In great anguish.*) 'Tis past.
Sist.	Yes, it is past, art thou not he who did it?
	(De Monfort *utters a deep groan, and is supported from falling by the*
	Monks. *A noise is heard without.*)
Abb.	What noise is this of heavy lumb'ring steps,
	Like men who with a weighty burthen come?
Bern.	It is the body: I have orders given
	That here it should be laid.

(*Enter men bearing the body of* Rezenvelt, *covered with a white cloth, and set it down in the middle of the room: they then uncover it.* De Monfort *stands fixed and motionless with horrour, only that a sudden shivering seems to pass over him when they uncover the corps. The* Abbess *and* Nuns *shrink back and retire to some distance; all the rest fixing their eyes steadfastly upon* De Monfort. *A long pause.*)

Bern.	(*to* De Mon.) Seest thou the lifeless corps, those bloody wounds,
	See how he lies, who but so shortly since

134

	A living creature was, with all the powers
	Of sense, and motion, and humanity!
	Oh! what a heart had he who did this deed!
1st Monk.	(*Looking at the body.*) How hard those teeth against the lips are press'd,
	As though he struggled still!
2d Monk	The hands too, clench'd: the last efforts of nature.
	(De Monfort *still stands motionless. Brother* Thomas *then goes to the body,*
	and raising up the head a little, turns it towards De Monfort.)
Thom.	Knowst thou this ghastly face?
De Mon.	(*Putting his hands before his face in violent perturbation.*)
	Oh, do not! do not! Veil it from my sight!
	Put me to any agony but this!
Thom.	Ha! dost thou then confess the dreadful deed?
	Hast thou against the laws of awful heav'n
	Such horrid murder done? What fiend could tempt thee?
	(*Pauses, and looks steadfastly at De Monfort.*)
De Mon.	I hear thy words, but do not hear their sense —
	Hast thou not cover'd it?
Bern.	(*to* Thom.) Forbear, my brother, for thou seest right well
	He is not in a state to answer thee.
	Let us retire and leave him for a while.
	These windows are with iron grated o'er;
	He cannot 'scape, and other duty calls.
Thom.	Then let it be.
Bern.	(*to Monks, &c.*) Come, let us all depart.
	(EXEUNT Abbess *and* Nuns, *followed by the* Monks. *One* Monk *lingering*
	a little behind.)
De Mon.	All gone! (*Perceiving the Monk.*)
	O stay thou here!
Monk	It must not be.
De Mon.	I'll give thee gold; I'll make thee rich in gold,
	If thou wilt stay e'en but a little while.
Monk.	I must not, must not stay.
De Mon.	I do conjure thee!
Monk.	I dare not stay with thee. (*Going.*)
De Mon.	And wilt thou go?
	(*Catching hold of him eagerly.*)
	O! throw thy cloak upon this grizly form!
	The unclos'd eyes do stare upon me still.
	O do not leave me thus!
	[Monk *covers the body, and* EXIT.
De Mon.	(*Alone, looking at the covered body, but at a distance.*)
	Alone with thee! but thou art nothing now,
	'Tis done, 'tis number'd with the things o'erpast,
	Would! would it were to come!
	What fated end, what darkly gathering cloud
	Will close on all this horrour?
	O that dire madness would unloose my thoughts,
	And fill my mind with wildest fantasies,

Dark, restless, terrible! ought, ought but this!
(*Pauses and shudders.*)
How with convulsive life he heav'd beneath me,
E'en with the death's wound gor'd. O horrid, horrid!
Methinks I feel him still. — What sound is that?
I heard a smother'd groan. — It is impossible!
(*Looking steadfastly at the body.*)
It moves! it moves! the cloth doth heave and swell.
It moves again. — I cannot suffer this —
Whate'er it be I will uncover it.
(*Runs to the corps, and tears off the cloth in despair.*)
All still beneath.
Nought is there here but fix'd and grizly death.
How sternly fixed! Oh! those glazed eyes!
They look upon me still.
(*Shrinks back with horrour.*)
Come, madness! come unto me senseless death!
I cannot suffer this! Here, rocky wall,
Seatter these brains, or dull them.
(*Runs furiously, and, dashing his head against the wall, falls upon the floor.*)

Enter two MONKS, *hastily.*

1*st Monk.*	See; wretched man, he hath destroy'd himself.
2*d Monk.*	He does but faint. Let us remove him hence.
1*st Monk.*	We did not well to leave him here alone.
2*d Monk.*	Come, let us bear him to the open air.

[EXEUNT, *bearing out* De Monfort.

ACT V.—SCENE I.

Before the gates of the Convent. Enter JANE DE MONFORT, FREBERG, *and* MANUEL. *As they are proceeding towards the gate,* JANE *stops short and shrinks back.*

Freb.	Ha! wherefore? has a sudden illness seiz'd thee?
Jane.	No, no, my friend.—And yet I am very faint—
	I dread to enter here!
Man.	Ay, so I thought:
	For, when between the trees, that abbey tower
	First shew'd its top, I saw your count'nance change.
	But breathe a little here; I'll go before,
	And make enquiry at the nearest gate.
Freb.	Do so, good Manuel.
	(Manuel *goes and knocks at the gate.*)
	Courage, dear madam: all may yet be well.
	Rezenvelt's servant, frighten'd with the storm,
	And seeing that his master join'd him not,
	As by appointment, at the forest's edge,
	Might be alarm'd, and give too ready ear
	To an unfounded rumour.
	He saw it not; he came not here himself.
Jane.	(*Looking eagerly to the gate, where* Manuel *talks with the* Porter.)
	Ha! see, he talks with some one earnestly.
	And sees't thou not that motion of his hands?
	He stands like one who hears a horrid tale.
	Almighty God!
	(Manuel *goes into the convent.*)
	He comes not back; he enters.
Freb.	Bear up, my noble friend.
Jane.	I will, I will! But this suspense is dreadful.
	(*A long pause.* Manuel *re-enters from the convent, and comes forward slowly, with a sad countenance.*)
	Is this the pace of one who bears good tidings?
	O God! his face doth tell the horrid fact;
	There is nought doubtful here.
Freb.	How is it, Manuel?
Man.	I've seen him through a crevice in his door:
	It is indeed my master.
	(*Bursting into tears.*)
	(Jane *faints, and is supported by* Freberg.—*Enter* ABBESS *and several* NUNS *from the convent who gather about her, and apply remedies. She recovers.*)
1st Nun.	The life returns again.
2d Nun.	Yes, she revives.
Abb. (*to* FREB.)	Let me entreat this noble lady's leave
	To lead her in. She seems in great distress:
	We would with holy kindness soothe her woe,
	And do by her the deeds of christian love.
Freb.	Madam, your goodness has my grateful thanks.
	[EXEUNT, *supporting* Jane *into the convent.*

De Monfort is discovered sitting in a thoughtful posture. He remains so for some time. His face afterwards begins to appear agitated, like one whose mind is harrowed with the severest thoughts; then, starting from his seat, he clasps his hands together, and holds them up to heaven.

De Mon.	O that I ne'er had known the light of day!
	That filmy darkness on mine eyes had hung,
	And clos'd me out from the fair face of nature!
	O that my mind in mental darkness pent,
	Had no perception, no distinction known,
	Of fair or foul, perfection nor defect;
	Nor thought conceiv'd of proud pre-eminence!
	O that it had! O that I had been form'd
	An idiot from the birth! a senseless changeling,
	Who eats his glutton's meal with greedy haste,
	Nor knows the hand which feeds him. —
	(*Pauses; then in a calmer sorrowful voice.*)
	What am I now? how ends the day of life?
	For end it must; and terrible this gloom,
	This storm of horrours that surrounds its close.
	This little term of nature's agony
	Will soon be o'er, and what is past is past:
	But shall I then, on the dark lap of earth
	Lay me to rest, in still unconsciousness,
	Like senseless clod that doth no pressure feel
	From wearing foot of daily passenger;
	Like a steeped rock o'er which the breaking waves
	Bellow and foam unheard? O would I could!

Enter MANUEL, *who springs forward to his master, but is checked upon perceiving* De Monfort *draw back and look sternly at him.*

Man.	My lord, my master! O my dearest master!
	(De Monfort *still looks at him without speaking.*)
	Nay, do not thus regard me; good my lord!
	Speak to me: am I not your faithful Manuel?
De Mon.	(*In a hasty broken voice.*) Art thou alone?
Man.	No, Sir, the lady Jane is on her way;
	She is not far behind.
De Mon.	(*Tossing his arm over his head in an agony.*)
	This is too much! All I can bear but this!
	It must not be. — Run and prevent her coming.
	Say, he who is detain'd a prisoner here
	Is one to her unknown. I now am nothing.
	I am a man of holy claims bereft;
	Out from the pale of social kindred cast;
	Nameless and horrible. —
	Tell her De Monfort far from hence is gone
	Into a desolate and distant land,

Ne'er to return again. Fly, tell her this;
For we must meet no more.

Enter JANE DE MONFORT, *bursting into the chamber and followed by* FREBERG, ABBESS, *and several* NUNS.

Jane.   We must! we must! My brother, O my brother!
          (De Monfort *turns away his head and hides his face with his arm.* Jane *stops*
          short, and, making a great effort, turns to Freberg, *and the others who followed*
          her, and with an air of dignity stretches out her hand, beckoning them to retire.
          All retire but Freberg, *who seems to hesitate.*)
      And thou too, Freberg: call it not unkind.
                       [EXIT Freberg: Jane *and* De Monfort *only remain.*

Jane.   My hapless Monfort!
          (De Monfort *turns round and looks sorrowfully upon her; she opens her arms*
          to him, and he, rushing into them, hides his face upon her breast, and weeps.)

Jane.   Ay, give thy sorrow vent: here mayst thou weep.

De Mon.   (*In broken accents.*) Oh! this, my sister, makes me feel again
      The kindness of affection.
      My mind has in a dreadful storm been tost;
      Horrid and dark. — I thought to weep no more. —
      I've done a deed — But I am human still.

Jane.   I know thy suff'rings: leave thy sorrow free:
      Thou art with one who never did upbraid;
      Who mourns, who loves thee still.

De Mon.   Ah! sayst thou so? no, no; it should not be.
      (*Shrinking from her.*) I am a foul and bloody murderer,
      For such embrace unmeet: O leave me! leave me!
      Disgrace and publick shame abide me now;
      And all, alas! who do my kindred own,
      The direful portion share. — Away, away!
      Shall a disgrac'd and publick criminal
      Degrade thy name, and claim affinity
      To noble worth like thine? — I have no name —
      I'm nothing now, not e'en to thee; depart.
      (*She takes his hand, and grasping it firmly, speaks with a determined voice.*)

Jane.   De Monfort, hand in hand we have enjoy'd
      The playful term of infancy together;
      And in the rougher path of ripen'd years
      We've been each other's stay. Dark lowers our fate,
      And terrible the storm that gathers over us;
      But nothing, till that latest agony
      Which severs thee from nature, shall unloose
      This fix'd and sacred hold. In thy dark prison-house;
      In the terrifick face of armed law;
      Yea, on the scaffold, if it needs must be,
      I never will forsake thee.

De Mon.   (*Looking at her with admiration.*)
      Heav'n bless thy gen'rous soul, my noble Jane!
      I thought to sink beneath this load of ill,

	Depress'd with infamy and open shame;
	I thought to sink in abject wretchedness:
	But for thy sake I'll rouse my manhood up,
	And meet it bravely; no unseemly weakness,
	I feel my rising strength, shall blot my end,
	To clothe thy cheek with shame.
Jane.	Yes, thou art noble still.
De Mon.	With thee I am; who were not so with thee?
	But, ah, my sister! short will be the term:
	Death's stroke will come, and in that state beyond,
	Where things unutterable wait the soul,
	New from its earthly tenement discharg'd,
	We shall be sever'd far.
	Far as the spotless purity of virtue
	Is from the murd'rer's guilt, far shall we be.
	This is the gulf of dread uncertainty
	From which the soul recoils.
Jane.	The God who made thee is a God of mercy;
	Think upon this.
De Mon.	(*Shaking his head.*) No, no! this blood! this blood!
Jane.	Yea, e'en the sin of blood may be forgiv'n,
	When humble penitence hath once aton'd.
De Mon.	(*Eagerly.*)What, after terms of lengthen'd misery,
	Imprison'd anguish of tormented spirits,
	Shall I again, a renovated soul,
	Into the blessed family of the good
	Admittance have? Thinkst thou that this may be?
	Speak, if thou canst: O speak me comfort here!
	For dreadful fancies, like an armed host,
	Have push'd me to despair. It is most horrible —
	O speak of hope! if any hope there be.
	(Jane *is silent, and looks sorrowfully upon him; then clasping her hands, and*
	turning her eyes to heaven, seems to mutter a prayer.)
De Mon.	Ha! dost thou pray for me? heav'n hear thy prayer!
	I fain would kneel. — Alas! I dare not do it.
Jane.	Not so; all by th' Almighty Father form'd
	May in their deepest mis'ry call on him.
	Come kneel with me, my brother.
	(*She kneels and prays to herself; he kneels by her, and clasps his hands fervently,*
	but speaks not. A noise of chains clanking is heard without, and they both rise.)
De Mon.	Hear'st thou that noise? They come to interrupt us.
Jane.	(*Moving towards a side door.*) Then let us enter here.
De Mon.	(*Catching hold of her with a look of horror.*)
	Not there — not there — the corps — the bloody corps!
Jane.	What, lies he there? — Unhappy Rezenvelt!
De Mon.	A sudden thought has come across my mind;
	How came it not before? Unhappy Rezenvelt!
	Sayst thou but this?
Jane.	What should I say? he was an honest man;
	I still have thought him such, as such lament him.

(De Monfort *utters a deep groan*.)
What means this heavy groan?

De Mon.   It hath a meaning.

Enter ABBESS *and* MONKS, *with two* OFFICERS *of justice carrying fetters in their hands to put upon* DE MONFORT.

Jane.   (*Starting*.) What men are these?

1st Off.   Lady, we are the servants of the law,
             And bear with us a power, which doth constrain
             To bind with fetters this our prisoner.
             (*Pointing to* De Monfort.)

Jane.   A stranger uncondemn'd? this cannot be.

1st Off.   As yet, indeed, he is by law unjudg'd,
             But is so far condemn'd by circumstance,
             That law, or custom sacred held as law,
             Doth fully warrant us, and it must be.

Jane.   Nay, say not so; he has no power to escape:
             Distress hath bound him with a heavy chain;
             There is no need of yours.

1st Off.   We must perform our office.

Jane.   O! do not offer this indignity!

1st Off.   Is it indignity in sacred law
             To bind a murderer? (*To* 2d *Officer*.) Come, do thy work.

Jane.   Harsh are thy words, and stern thy harden'd brow;
             Dark is thine eye; but all some pity have
             Unto the last extreme of misery.
             I do beseech thee! if thou art a man —
             (*Kneeling to him*.)
             (De Monfort, *roused at this, runs up to* Jane, *and raises her hastily from the ground; then stretches himself up proudly*.)

De Mon.   (*to* Jane.) Stand thou erect in native dignity;
             And bend to none on earth the suppliant knee,
             Though cloth'd in power imperial. To my heart
             It gives a feller gripe than many irons.
             (*Holding out his hands*.)
             Here, officers of law, bind on those shackles,
             And, if they are too light bring heavier chains.
             Add iron to iron, load, crush me to the ground;
             Nay, heap ten thousand weight upon my breast,
             For that were best of all.
             (*A long pause, whilst they put irons upon him. After they are on,* Jane *looks a thim sorrowfully, and lets her head sink on her breast.* De Monfort *stretches out his hand, looks at them, and then at* Jane; *crosses them over his breast, and endeavours to suppress his feelings*.)

1st Off.   I have it, too, in charge to move you hence,
             (*To* De Monfort.)
             Into another chamber, more secure.

De Mon.   Well, I am ready, sir.
             (*Approaching* Jane, *whom the* Abbess *is endeavouring to comfort, but to no purpose*.)
             Ah! wherefore thus, most honour'd and most dear?

Shrink not at the accoutrements of ill,
Daring the thing itself.
(*Endeavouring to look cheerful.*)
Wilt thou permit me with a gyved hand?
(*She gives him her hand, which he raises to his lips.*)
This was my proudest office.

[EXEUNT, De Monfort *leading out* Jane.

SCENE III.

An long narrow gallery in the convent, with the doors of the cells on each side. The stage darkened. A Nun is discovered at a distance listening. Enter another Nun at the front of the stage, and starts back.

1st Nun.	Ha! who is this not yet retir'd to rest?
	My sister, is it you?
	(*To the other who advances.*)
2d Nun.	Returning from the sister Nina's cell,
	Passing yon door where the poor pris'ner lies,
	The sound of one who struggl'd with despair
	Struck on me as I went: I stopp'd and listen'd;
	Oh God! such piteous groans!
1st Nun.	Yes, since the ev'ning sun it hath been so.
	The voice of mis'ry oft hath reach'd mine ear,
	E'en in the cell above.
2d Nun.	How is it thus?
	Methought he brav'd it with a manly spirit,
	And led, with shakl'd hands, his sister forth,
	Like one resolv'd to bear misfortune boldly.
1st Nun.	Yes, with heroic courage, for a while
	He seem'd inspir'd; but, soon depress'd again,
	Remorse and dark despair o'erwhelm'd his soul,
	And so he hath remain'd.

Enter Father BERNARD, *advancing from the further end of the gallery, bearing a crucifix.*

1st Nun.	How goes it, father, with your penitent?
	We've heard his heavy groans.
Bern.	Retire, my daughters; many a bed of death,
	With all its pangs and horror I have seen,
	But never ought like this.
2d Nun.	He's dying, then?
Bern.	Yes, death is dealing with him.
	From violent agitation of his mind,
	Some stream of life within his breast has burst;
	For many a time, within a little space,
	The ruddy-tide has rush'd into his mouth.
	God grant his pains be short!
1st Nun.	Amen, amen!
2d Nun.	How does the lady?

142

Bern.	She sits and bears his head upon her lap;
	And like a heaven-inspir'd angel, speaks
	The word of comfort to his troubled soul:
	Then does she wipe the cold drops from his brow,
	With such a look of tender wretchedness,
	It wrings the heart to see her.
1st Nun.	Ha! hear ye nothing?
2d Nun.	(*Alarmed.*) Yes, I heard a noise.
1st Nun.	And see'st thou nothing?
	(*Creeping close to her sister.*)
Bern.	'Tis a nun in white.

Enter LAY SISTER *in her night cloathes, advancing from the dark end of the gallery.*
(*To* Sister.) Wherefore, my daughter, hast thou left thy cell?
It is not meet at this untimely hour.

Sist.	I cannot rest. I hear such dismal sounds,
	Such wailings in the air, such shrilly shrieks,
	As though the cry of murder rose again
	From the deep gloom of night. I cannot rest:
	I pray you let me stay with you, good sisters!
	(*Bell tolls.*)
Nuns.	(*Starting.*) What bell is that?
Bern.	It is the bell of death.
	A holy sister was upon the watch
	To give this notice. (*Bell tolls again.*) Hark! Another knell!
	The wretched struggler hath his warfare clos'd;
	May heaven have mercy on him.
	(*Bell tolls again.*)
	Retire, my daughters; let us all retire,
	For scenes like this to meditation call.
	[EXEUNT, *bell tolling again.*

SCENE IV.

A hall or large room in the convent. The bodies of DE MONFORT *and* REZENVELT *are discovered laid out upon a low table or platform, covered with black.* FREBERG, BERNARD, ABBESS, MONKS, *and* NUNS *attending.*

Abb.	(*to* Freb.) Here must they lie, my lord, until we know
	Respecting this the order of the law.
Freb.	And you have wisely done, my rev'rend mother.
	(*Goes to the table, and looks at the bodies, but without uncovering them.*)
	Unhappy men! ye, both in nature rich,
	With talents and with virtues were endu'd.
	Ye should have lov'd, yet deadly rancour came,
	And in the prime and manhood of your days
	Ye sleep in horrid death. O direful hate!
	What shame and wretchedness his portion is,
	Who, for a secret inmate, harbours thee!

	And who shall call him blameless who excites,
	Ungen'rously excites, with careless scorn,
	Such baleful passion in a brother's breast,
	Whom heav'n commands to love. Low are ye laid:
	Still all contention now. — Low are ye laid:
	I lov'd you both, and mourn your hapless fall.

Abb. They were your friends, my lord?

Freb. I lov'd them both. How does the Lady Jane?

Abb. She bears misfortune with intrepid soul.
I never saw in woman bow'd with grief
Such moving dignity.

Freb.   Ay, still the same.
I've known her long; of worth most excellent;
But in the day of woe she ever rose
Upon the mind with added majesty,
As the dark mountain more sublimely tow'rs
Mantled in clouds and storm.

Enter MANUEL *and* JEROME.

Man. (*Pointing.*) Here, my good Jerome, there's a piteous sight.

Jer. A piteous sight! yet I will look upon him:
I'll see his face in death. Alas, alas!
I've seen him move a noble gentleman;
And when with vexing passion undisturb'd,
He look'd most graciously.
(*Lifts up in mistake the cloth from the body of* Rezenvelt, *and starts back
with horrour.*)
Oh! this was the bloody work! Oh, oh! oh, oh!
That human hands could do it!
(*Drops the cloth again.*)

Man. That is the murder'd corps; here lies De Monfort.
(*Going to uncover the other body.*)

Jer. (*Turning away his head.*) No, no! I cannot look upon him now.

Man. Didst thou not come to see him?

Jer. Fy! cover him — inter him in the dark —
Let no one look upon him.

Bern. (*to* Jer.) Well dost thou show the abhorrence nature feels
For deeds of blood, and I commend thee well.
In the most ruthless heart compassion wakes
For one who, from the hand of fellow man,
Hath felt such cruelty.
(*Uncovering the body of* Rezenvelt.)
This is the murder'd corse:
(*Uncovering the body of* De Monfort.)
               But see, I pray!
Here lies the murderer. What think'st thou here?
Look on those features, thou hast seen them oft,
With the last dreadful conflict of despair,
So fix'd in horrid strength.

	See those knit brows; those hollow sun'ken eyes;

See those knit brows; those hollow sun'ken eyes;
The sharpen'd nose, with nostrils all distent;
That writhed mouth, where yet the teeth appear,
In agony, to gnash the nether lip.
Thinkst thou, less painful than the murd'rer's knife
Was such a death as this?
Ay, and how changed too those matted locks!

Jer.   Merciful heaven! his hair is grisly grown,
Chang'd to white age, that was, but two days since,
Black as the raven's plume. How may this be?

Bern.   Such change, from violent conflict of the mind,
Will sometimes come.

Jer.   Alas, alas! most wretched!
Thou wert too good to do a cruel deed,
And so it kill'd thee. Thou hast suffer'd for it.
God rest thy soul! I needs must touch thy hand,
And bid thee long farewell.
(*Laying his hand on* De Monfort.)

Bern.   Draw back, draw back! see where the lady comes.

Enter JANE DE MONFORT. FREBERG, *who has been for sometime retired by himself at the bottom of the stage, now steps forward to lead her in, but checks himself on seeing the fixed sorrow of her countenance, and draws back respectfully.* JANE *advances to the table, and looks attentively at the covered bodies.* MANUEL *points out the body of* DE MONFORT, *and she gives a gentle inclination of the head, to signify that she understands him. She then bends tenderly over it, without speaking.*

Man.   (*to* Jane, *as she raises her head.*) Oh, madam! my good lord.

Jane.   Well says thy love, my good and faithful Manuel;
But we must mourn in silence.

Man.   Alas! the times that I have followed him!

Jane.   Forbear, my faithful Manuel. For this love
Thou hast my grateful thanks; and here's my hand:
Thou hast lov'd him, and I'll remember thee:
Where'er I am, in whate'er spot of earth
I linger out the remnant of my days,
I will remember thee.

Man.   Nay, by the living God! where'er you are,
There will I be. I'll prove a trusty servant:
I'll follow you, even to the world's end.
My master's gone; and I, indeed, am mean,
Yet will I show the strength of nobler men,
Should any dare upon your honour'd worth
To put the slightest wrong. Leave you, dear lady!
Kill me, but say not this!
(*Throwing himself at her feet.*)

Jane.   (*Raising him.*) Well, then! be thou my servant, and my friend.
Art thou, good Jerome, too, in kindness come?
I see thou art. How goes it with thine age?

Jer.   Ah, madam! woe and weakness dwell with age:

	Would I could serve you with a young man's strength!
	I'd spend my life for you.
Jane.	Thanks, worthy Jerome.
	O! who hath said, the wretched have no friends?
Freb.	In every sensible and gen'rous breast
	Affliction finds a friend; but unto thee,
	Thou most exalted and most honourable,
	The heart in warmest adoration bows,
	And even a worship pays.
Jane.	Nay, Freberg! Freberg! grieve me not, my friend.
	He, to whose ear my praise most welcome was,
	Hears it no more; and, oh, our piteous lot!
	What tongue will talk of him? Alas, alas!
	This more than all will bow me to the earth;
	I feel my misery here.
	The voice of praise was wont to name us both:
	I had no greater pride.

(*Covers her face with her hands, and bursts into tears. Here they all hang about her*: Freberg *supporting her tenderly,* Manuel *embracing her knees, and old* Jerome *catching hold of her robe affectionately.* Bernard, Abbess, Monks, *and* Nuns *likewise gather round her, with looks of sympathy.*)

Enter Two OFFICERS *of law.*

1st Off.	Where is the prisoner?
	Into our hands he straight must be consign'd.
Bern.	He is not subject now to human laws;
	The prison that awaits him is the grave.
1st Off.	Ha! sayst thou so? there is foul play in this.
Man.	(*to* Off.) Hold thy unrighteous tongue, or hie thee hence,
	Nor in the presence of this honour'd dame,
	Utter the slightest meaning of reproach.
1st Off.	I am an officer on duty call'd,
	And have authority to say, how died?

(*Here* Jane *shakes off the weakness of grief, and repressing* Manuel, *who is about to reply to the* Officer, *steps forward with dignity.*)

Jane.	Tell them by whose authority you come,
	He died that death which best becomes a man,
	Who is with keenest sense of conscious ill
	And deep remorse assail'd, a wounded spirit.
	A death that kills the noble and the brave,
	And only them. He had no other wound.
1st Off.	And shall I trust to this.
Jane.	Do as thou wilt:
	To one who can suspect my simple word
	I have no more reply. Fulfil thine office.
1st Off.	No, lady. I believe your honour'd word,
	And will no further search.
Jane.	I thank your courtesy: thanks, thanks to all!
	My rev'rend mother, and ye honour'd maids;
	Ye holy men, and you, my faithful friends;

The blessing of the afflicted rest with you:
And he, who to the wretched is most piteous,
Will recompense you. — Freberg, thou art good;
Remove the body of the friend you lov'd,
'Tis Rezenvelt I mean. Take thou this charge:
'Tis meet, that with his noble ancestors,
He lie entomb'd in honourable state.
And now, I have a sad request to make,
Nor will these holy sisters scorn my boon;
That I, within these sacred cloister walls,
May raise a humble, nameless tomb to him,
Who, but for one dark passion, one dire deed,
Had claim'd a record of as noble worth,
As e'er enrich'd the sculptur'd pedestal.

[EXEUNT.

FINIS.

THE
LAY
OF
THE LAST MINSTREL
A POEM.
BY
WALTER SCOTT, ESQ.

Cum relego, scripsisse pudet, quia plurima cerno,
Me quoque, qui feci, judice, digna limi.[1]

THE SECOND EDITION.

LONDON:
PRINTED FOR LONGMAN, HURST, REES, AND ORMS, PATERNOS-
TER-ROW, AND A. CONSTABLE AND CO. EDINBURGH
By James Ballantyne, Edinburgh.
1805

TO THE
RIGHT HONOURABLE
CHARLES,
EARL OF DALKEITH,[2]
THIS POEM
IS INSCRIBED BY
THE
AUTHOR.

THE Poem, now offered to the Public, is intended to illustrate the customs and manners which anciently prevailed on the borders of Scotland and England. The inhabitants, living in a state partly pastoral and partly warlike, and combining habits of constant depredation with the influence of a rude spirit of chivalry, were often engaged in scenes highly susceptible of poetical ornament. As the description of scenery and manners was more the object of the Author, than a combined and regular narrative, the plan of the ancient metrical romance was adopted, which allows greater latitude in this respect than would be consistent with the dignity of a regular poem. The same model offered other facilities, as it permits an occasional alteration of measure, which, in some degree, authorises the change of rhythm in the text. The machinery also, adopted from popular belief, would have seemed puerile in a poem, which did not partake of the rudeness of the old ballad, or metrical romance.

---

1   From Ovid (43 B.C.–17/18 A.D.), *Letters from the Black Sea* book I ch. v, ll.15–16, but also familiar from its use in Michel de Montaigne's *Essays* book II ch.xvii: 'When I re-read, I shame I write; for much I see, / My selfe, who made them, being judge, blotted to be' (from John Florio's 1603 translation of the *Essays*).

2   Charles Scott, eldest son of the 4th Duke of Buccleuch (to whom Scott had dedicated his *Minstrelsy of the Scottish Border*); he succeeded to the Dukedom in 1812.

For these reasons, the poem was put into the mouth of an ancient Minstrel, the last of the race, who, as he is supposed to have survived the Revolution,[3] might have caught somewhat of the refinement of modern poetry, without losing the simplicity of his original model. The date of the tale is about the middle of the 16th century, when most of the personages actually flourished. The time occupied by the action is three nights and three days.

INTRODUCTION.

THE way was long, the wind was cold,
The Minstrel was infirm and old;
His withered cheek, and tresses gray,
Seemed to have known a better day;
The harp, his sole remaining joy,   5
Was carried by an orphan boy.
The last of all the bards was he,
Who sung of Border chivalry;
For, well-a-day! their date was fled,
His tuneful brethren all were dead;   10
And he, neglected and oppressed,
Wished to be with them and at rest.
No more, on prancing palfrey borne,
He carolled, light as lark at morn;
No longer courted and carressed,   15
High placed in hall, a welcome guest,
He poured, to lord and lady gay,
The unpremeditated lay:
Old times were changed, old manners gone,
A stranger filled the Stuarts' throne;   20
The bigots of the iron time
Had called his harmless art a crime.[4]
A wandering Harper, scorn'd and poor,
He begg'd his bread from door to door.
And tuned, to please a peasant's ear,   25
The harp, a King had loved to hear.

He passed where Newark's stately tower
Looks out from Yarrow's birchen bower:
The Minstrel gazed with wishful eye—
No humbler resting-place was nigh.   30
With hesitating step, at last,
The embattled portal arch he passed,
Whose ponderous grate, and massy bar,
Had oft rolled back the tide of war,

---

3   The 'Revolution' was the deposition of James Stuart, VII of Scotland and II of England, in 1688; and accession of his Protestant sister Mary and her husband William Prince of Orange.
4   The 'iron time' refers to Puritan rule under Cromwell in the 1650s, when various popular entertainments were suppressed.

But never closed the iron door   35
Against the desolate and poor.
The Duchess[5] marked his weary pace,
His timid mien, and reverend face,
And bade her page the menials tell,
That they should tend the old man well: 40
For she had known adversity,
Though born in such a high degree;
In pride of power, in beauty's bloom,
Had wept o'er Monmouth's bloody tomb![6]

    When kindness had his wants supplied,   45
And the old man was gratified,
Began to rise his minstrel pride:
And he began to talk anon,
Of good Earl Francis,[7] dead and gone,
And of Earl Walter,[8] rest him, God!   50
A braver ne'er to battle rode:
And how full many a tale he knew,
Of the old warriors of Buccleuch;
And, would the noble Duchess deign
To listen to an old man's strain,   55
Though stiff his hand, his voice though weak,
He thought even yet, the sooth to speak,
That, if she loved the harp to hear,
He could make music to her ear.

    The humble boon was soon obtained;   60
The aged Minstrel audience gained.
But, when he reached the room of state,
Where she, with all her ladies, sate
Perchance he wished his boon denied:
For, when to tune his harp he tried,   65
His trembling hand had lost the ease,
Which marks security to please;
And scenes, long past, of joy and pain,
Came wildering o'er his aged brain —
He tried to tune his harp in vain.   70

---

5   Anne, duchess of Buccleuch and Monmouth, representative of the ancient Lords of Buccleuch, and widow of the unfortunate James, Duke of Monmouth, who was beheaded in 1685. [Scott's footnote. As well as footnotes, usually explaining archaic words and all of which are included here, the last third of the original volume is taken up with endnotes, usually expanding on the histories of persons or places mentioned in the poem. Extracts or summaries from these endnotes are included here only where particularly interesting or relevant. Where not accredited to Scott, footnotes are the editor's.]

6   The Protestant Monmouth, the eldest illegitimate son of Charles II, led a rebellion against his uncle James on the latter's succession. It failed, with the outcome noted above.

7   Francis Scot, earl of Buccleuch, father to the duchess. [Scott's footnote]

8   Walter, earl of Buccleuch, grandfather to the duchess, and a celebrated warrior. [Scott's footnote]

The pitying Duchess praised its chime,
And gave him heart, and gave him time,
Till every string's according glee
Was blended into harmony.
And then, he said, he would full fain   75
He could recal an ancient strain,
He never thought to sing again.
It was not framed for village churles,
But for high dames and mighty earls;
He played it to King Charles the Good,   80
When he kept court at Holyrood;[9]
And much he wished, yet feared, to try
The long forgotten melody.

        Amid the strings his fingers strayed,
And an uncertain warbling made,   85
And oft he shook his hoary head.
But when he caught the measure wild,
The old man raised his face, and smiled;
And lightened up his faded eye,
With all a poet's extacy!   90
In varying cadence, soft or strong,
He swept the sounding chords along:
The present scene, the future lot,
His toils, his wants, were all forgot:
Cold diffidence, and age's frost,   95
In the full tide of song were lost;
Each blank, in faithless memory void,
The poet's glowing thought supplied;
And, while his harp responsive rung,
'Twas thus the LATEST MINSTREL sung.   100

---

9   Charles I stayed at Holyrood on his one trip to Scotland in 1633: the last monarch to do so
    until George IV in 1822.

CANTO FIRST

I.

THE feast was over in Branksome tower,[1]
And the Ladye had gone to her secret bower;
Her bower, that was guarded by word and by spell,
Deadly to hear, and deadly to tell—
Jesu Maria, shield us well!
No living wight, save the Ladye alone,
Had dared to cross the threshold stone.

II.

The tables were drawn, it was idlesse all;
    Knight, and page, and household squire,
Loitered through the lofty hall,
    Or crowded round the ample fire:
The stag-hounds, weary with the chase,
    Lay stretched upon the rushy floor,
And urged, in dreams, the forest race,
    From Teviot-stone to Eskdale-moor.

III.

Nine-and-twenty knights of fame
    Hung their shields in Branksome-Hall;
Nine-and-twenty squires of name
    Brought them their steeds to bower from stall;
      Nine-and-twenty yeomen tall
      Waited, duteous, on them all:
      They were all knights of mettle true,
      Kinsmen to the bold Buccleuch.

IV.

Ten of them were sheathed in steel,
With belted sword, and spur on heel:
They quitted not their harness bright,
Neither by day, nor yet by night:
    They lay down to rest
    With corslet laced,
Pillowed on buckler cold and hard;
    They carved at the meal
    With gloves of steel,
And they drank the red wine through the helmet barred.

---

1   Branxsholme Castle, on the Teviot, south of Hawick. An endnote describes its situation and history: 'Branksome Castle continued to be the principal seat of the Buccleuch family, while security was any object in their choice of mansion [...] The extent of the ancient edifice can still be traced by some vestiges of its foundation, and its strength is obvious from the situation, on a deep bank surrounded by the Teviot [...]'. Anne Scott was brought up at the more modern Newark, on the Yarrow.

V.

Ten squires, ten yeomen, mail-clad men,
Waited the beck of the warders ten.
Thirty steeds, both fleet and wight,
Stood saddled in stable day and night,
Barbed with frontlet of steel, I trow,
And with Jedwood-axe at saddle bow;
A hundred more fed free in stall —
Such was the custom of Branksome Hall.

VI.

Why do these steeds stand ready dight?
Why watch these warriors, armed, by night?
They watch, to hear the blood-hound baying;
They watch, to hear the war-horn braying;
To see St George's red cross streaming,
To see the midnight beacon gleaming;
   They watch, against Southern force and guile,
    Lest Scroop, or Howard, or Percy's powers,
    Threaten Branksome's lordly towers,
From Warkworth, or Naworth, or merry Carlisle.[2]

VII.

Such is the custom of Branksome Hall.
   Many a valiant knight is here;
But he, the Chieftain of them all,
His sword hangs rusting on the wall,
   Beside his broken spear.
Bards long shall tell
How Lord Walter fell![3]
When startled burghers fled, afar,
The furies of the Border war;
When the streets of high Dunedin
Saw lances gleam, and falchions redden,
And heard the slogan's[4] deadly yell
Then the Chief of Branksome fell.

---

2   Northern English barons and castles.
3   In an endnote Scott explains the origins of the feud between the Scotts and the Kerrs in the attempted rescue of the young James V, at his request, from the Douglas family, then ruling in his name, at Melrose in 1526. In the battle the Laird of Cessford, a Kerr, was killed by an Elliot in Buccleuch's retinue (see stanza XXX of this canto). '[T]he most signal act of violence, to which this quarrel gave rise, was, the murder of Sir Walter himself, who was slain by the Kerrs in the streets of Edinburgh, in 1552. [...] [T]he poem is supposed to open shortly after it had taken place' [Scott's endnote].
4   The war-cry, or gathering word, of a Border clan. [Scott's footnote]

Can piety the discord heal,
    Or stanch the death-feud's enmity?
Can Christian lore, can patriot zeal,
    Can love of blessed charity?
No! vainly to each holy shrine,
    In mutual pilgrimage, they drew;
Implored, in vain, the grace divine
    For chiefs, their own red falchions slew:
While Cessford owns the rule of Car[5]
    While Ettrick boasts the line of Scott,
The slaughtered chiefs, the mortal jar,
The havoc of the feudal war,
    Shall never, never be forgot!

IX.

In sorrow o'er Lord Walter's bier
    The warlike foresters had bent;[6]
And many a flower, and many a tear,
    Old Teviot's maids and matrons lent:
But o'er her warrior's bloody bier
The Ladye dropped nor flower nor tear!
Vengeance, deep-brooding o'er the slain,
    Had locked the source of softer woe;
And burning pride, and high disdain,
    Forbade the rising tear to flow;
Until, amid his sorrowing clan,
    Her son lisped from the nurse's knee—
"And if I live to be a man,
    "My father's death revenged shall be!"
    Then fast the mother's tears did seek
    To dew the infant's kindling cheek.

X.

All loose her negligent attire,
    All loose her golden hair,
Hung Margaret o'er her slaughtered sire,
    And wept in wild despair,
But not alone the bitter tear
    Had filial grief supplied;
For hopeless love, and anxious fear,
    Had lent their mingled tide:
Nor in her mother's altered eye
Dared she to look for sympathy.
    Her lover, 'gainst her father's clan,

---

5   In a later endnote Scott comments, 'The name is spelt differently [Ker, Kerr, or Car] by the various families who bear it. Car is selected, not as the most correct, but as the most poetical reading.'

6   I.e. the inhabitants of the Forest of Ettrick, the Scott heartland.

With Car in arms had stood,
When Mathouse burn to Melrose ran,
   All purple with their blood;
And well she knew, her mother dread,
Before lord Cranstoun she should wed,
Would see her on her dying bed.

XI.

Of noble race the Lady came,
Her father was a clerk of fame,[7]
   Of Bethune's line of Picardie:
He learned the art, that none may name,
   In Padua, far beyond the sea.[8]
Men said, he changed his mortal frame
   By feat of magic mystery;
For when, in studious mood, he paced
   St Andrew's cloistered hall,
His form no darkening shadow traced
   Upon the sunny wall!

XII.

And, of his skill, as bards avow,
   He taught that Ladye fair,
Till to her bidding she could bow
   The viewless forms of air.
And now she sits in secret bower,
In old Lord David's western tower,
And listens to a heavy sound,
That moans the mossy turrets round.
Is it the roar of Teviot's tide,
That chafes against the scaur's[9] red side?
Is it the wind, that swings the oaks?
Is it the echo from the rocks?
What may it be, the heavy sound,
That moans old Branksome's turrets round?

XIII.

At the sullen, moaning sound,
   The ban-dogs bay and howl;
And, from the turrets round,
   Loud whoops the startled owl.
In the hall, both squire and knight
   Swore that a storm was near,
And looked forth to view the night;
   But the night was still and clear!

---

7   'Clerk' here meaning churchman or learned man.
8   Padua was long supposed by the Scottish peasants to be the principal school of necromancy.
    [Scott's endnote]
9   *Scaur*, a precipitous bank of earth. [Scott's footnote]

XIV.

From the sound of Teviot's tide,
Chafing with the mountain's side,
From the groan of the wind-swung oak,
From the sullen echo of the rock,
From the voice of the coming storm,
    The Ladye knew it well!
It was the Spirit of the Flood that spoke,
And he called on the Spirit of the Fell.

XV.
RIVER SPIRIT.

"Sleepest thou, brother?"

MOUNTAIN SPIRIT.
——"Brother, nay —

On my hills the moon-beams play.
From Craik-cross to Skelfhill-pen,
By every rill, in every glen,
    Merry elves, their morrice pacing,
      To aerial minstrelsy,
    Emerald rings on brown heath tracing,
      Trip it deft and merrily.
    Up, and mark their nimble feet!
    Up, and list their music sweet!"

XVI.
RIVER SPIRIT.

"Tears of an imprisoned maiden
    Mix with my polluted stream;
Margaret of Branksome, sorrow-laden,
    Mourns beneath the moon's pale beam.
Tell me, thou, who viewest the stars,
When shall cease these feudal jars?
What shall be the maiden's fate?
Who shall be the maiden's mate?"

XVII.
MOUNTAIN SPIRIT.

"Arthur's slow wain his course doth roll,
In utter darkness, round the pole;
The Northern Bear lowers black and grim;
Orion's studded belt is dim;
Twinkling faint, and distant far,
Shimmers through mist each planet star;
    Ill may I read their high decree:
But no kind influence deign they shower
On Teviot's tide, and Branksome's tower,
    Till pride be quelled, and love be free."

XVIII.

The unearthly voices ceast,
    And the heavy sound was still;
It died on the river's breast,
    It died on the side of the hill. —
But round Lord David's tower
    The sound still floated near;
For it rung in the Ladye's bower,
    And it rung in the Ladye's ear.
She raised her stately head,
    And her heart throbbed high with pride:
"Your mountains shall bend,
And your streams ascend,
    Ere Margaret be our foeman's bride!"

XIX.

The Ladye sought the lofty hall,
    Where many a bold retainer lay,
And, with jocund din, among them all,
    Her son pursued his infant play.
A fancied moss-trooper, the boy
    The truncheon of a spear bestrode,
And round the hall, right merrily,
    In mimic foray[10] rode.
Even bearded knights, in arms grown old,
    Share in his frolic gambols bore,
Albeit their hearts, of rugged mould,
    Were stubborn as the steel they wore.
For the grey warriors prophesied,
    How the brave boy, in future war,
Should tame the Unicorn's pride,
    Exalt the Crescent and the Star.[11]

XX.

The Ladye forgot her purpose high,
    One moment, and no more;
One moment gazed with a mother's eye,
    As she paused at the arched door.
Then from amid the armed train,
She called to her William of Deloraine.

XXI.

A stark moss-trooping Scott was he,
As e'er couched border lance by knee;
Through Solway sands, through Tarras moss,
Blindfold, he knew the paths to cross;
By wily turns, by desperate bounds,

---

10 *Foray*, a predatory inroad. [Scott's footnote]
11 Alluding to the armorial bearings of the Scotts and Cars. [Scott's footnote]

Had baffled Percy's best blood-hounds;
In Eske or Liddel, fords were none,
But he would ride them one by one;
Alike to him was time, or tide,
December's snow, or July's pride;
Alike to him was tide or time,
Moonless midnight, or mattin prime:
Steady of heart, and stout of hand,
As ever drove prey from Cumberland;
Five times outlawed had he been,
By England's king, and Scotland's Queen.[12]

XXII.

"Sir William of Deloraine, good at need,
Mount thee on the wightest steed;
Spare not to spur, nor stint to ride,
Until thou come to fair Tweedside;
And in Melrose's holy pile
Seek thou the Monk of St. Mary's aisle.
    Greet the father well from me;
        Say, that the fated hour is come,
    And to-night he shall watch with thee,
        To win the treasure of the tomb:
For this will be St Michael's night,[13]
And, though stars be dim the moon is bright;
And the cross of bloody red,
Will point to the grave of the mighty dead.

XXIII.

"What he gives thee, see thou keep;
Stay not thou for food or sleep.
Be it scroll, or be it book,
Into it, knight, thou must not look;
If thou readest thou art lorn!
Better hadst thou ne'er been born."

XXIV.

"O swiftly can speed my dapple-grey steed,
    Which drinks of the Teviot clear;
Ere break of day," the Warrior 'gan say,
    "Again will I be here:
And safer by none may thy errand be done,
    Than, noble dame, by me;
Letter nor line know I never a one,
    Wer't my neck-verse at Hairibee."[14]

12 England's king in 1552 is Edward IV. Scotland's Queen is the ten-year-old Mary, and any
    outlawing is being done by the Regent, James Hamilton, Earl of Arran (see Canto III, stanza
    XXIX, and Canto IV, stanza XXX).
13 I.e. Michaelmas, 29 September.
14 *Hairibee*, the place of executing the Border marauders at Carlisle. The *neck-verse* is the

XXV.

Soon in his saddle sate he fast,
And soon the steep descent he past;
Soon crossed the sounding barbican,[15]
And soon the Teviot side he won.
Eastward the wooded path he rode;
Green hazels o'er his basnet nod:
He passed the Peel of Goldiland,[16]
And crossed old Borthwick's roaring strand;
Dimly he view'd the Moat-hill's mound,
Where Druid shades still flitted round:
In Hawick twinkled many a light;
Behind him soon they set in night;
And soon he spurred his courser keen
Beneath the Tower of Hazledean.

XXVI.

The clattering hoofs the watchmen mark;
"Stand, ho! thou courier of the dark."
"For Branksome, ho!" the knight rejoined,
And left the friendly tower behind.
He turned him now from Teviot side,
    And guided by the tinkling rill,
Northward the dark ascent did ride,
    And gained the moor at Horsliehill;
Broad on the left before him lay,
For many a mile, the Roman way.[17]

XXVII.

A moment now he slacked his speed,
A moment breathed his panting steed;
Drew saddle-girth and corslet-band,
And loosen'd in the sheath his brand.
On Minto-crags the moon-beams glint,
Where Barnhill hew'd his bed of flint;
Who flung his outlawed limbs to rest,
Where falcons hang their giddy nest,
Mid cliffs, from whence his eagle eye
For many a league his prey could spy;
Cliffs doubling, on their echoes borne,
The terrors of the robber's horn;
Cliffs, which, for many a later year,

---

beginning of the 51st psalm, *Miserere mei*, &c. anciently read by criminals claiming the benefit of clergy. [Scott's footnote. Pleading 'benefit of clergy' could overturn a conviction: it depended on the pleader being able to read and write.]

15 *Barbican*, the defences of the outer gate of a feudal castle. [Scott's footnote]

16 *Peel*, a Border tower. [Scott's footnote. A *basnet* is a light helmet with a visor.]

17 An ancient Roman road, crossing through part of Roxburghshire. [Scott's footnote]

The warbling Doric reed shall hear,[18]
When some sad swain shall teach the grove,
Ambition is no cure for love.

XXVIII.

Unchallenged, thence past Deloraine
To ancient Riddel's fair domain,
    Where Aill, from mountains freed,
Down from the lakes did raving come;
Each wave was crested with tawny foam,
    Like the mane of a chestnut steed.
In vain! no torrent, deep or broad,
Might bar the bold moss-trooper's road.

XXIX.

At the first plunge the horse sunk low,
And the water broke o'er the saddle-bow;
Above the foaming tide, I ween,
Scarce half the charger's neck was seen;
For he was barded from counter to tail,[19]
And the rider was armed complete in mail;
Never heavier man and horse
Stemmed a midnight torrent's force;
The warrior's very plume, I say,
Was daggled by the dashing spray;
Yet, through good heart, and Our Ladye's grace,
At length he gain'd the landing place.

XXX.

Now Bowden Moor the march-man won,
    And sternly shook his plumed head,
As glanced his eye o'er Halidon;[20]
    For on his soul the slaughter red
Of that unhallowed morn arose
When first the Scott and Car were foes;
When royal James beheld the fray,
Prize to the victor of the day;
When Home and Douglas, in the van,
Bore down Buccleuch's retiring clan,
Till gallant Cessford's heart-blood dear
Reek'd on dark Elliot's Border spear.[21]

---

18 Doric: rustic.
19 *Barded*,or barbed, applied to a horse accoutered with defensive armour. [Scott's footnote]
20 Halidon-hill, on which the battle of Melrose was fought. [Scott's footnote]
21 See note 3 above for the significance of this encounter.

In bitter mood he spurred fast,
And soon the hated heath was past;
And far beneath, in lustre wan,
Old Melros' rose, and fair Tweed ran:
Like some tall rock, with lichens grey,
Seemed dimly huge, the dark Abbaye.
When Hawick he passed, had curfew rung,
Now midnight lauds[22] were in Melrose sung.
The sound, upon the fitful gale,
In solemn wise, did rise and fail,
Like that wild harp, whose magic tone
Is wakened by the winds alone:
But when Melrose he reached, 'twas silence all;
He meetly stabled his steed in stall,
And sought the convent's lonely wall.

————

HERE paused the harp; and with its swell
The Master's fire and courage fell:
Dejectedly, and low, he bowed,
And, gazing timid on the crowd,
He seemed to seek, in every eye,
If they approved his minstrelsy;
And, diffident of present praise,
Somewhat he spoke of former days,
And how old age, and wandering long,
Had done his hand and harp some wrong.

   The Duchess, and her daughters fair,
And every gentle lady there,
Each after each, in due degree,
Gave praises to his melody;
His hand was true, his voice was clear,
And much they longed the rest to hear.
Encouraged thus, the Aged Man,
After meet rest, again began.

———

22 *Lauds*, the midnight service of the Catholic church. [Scott's footnote]

CANTO SECOND

I.

IF thou would'st view fair Melrose aright,
Go visit it by the pale moon-light;
For the gay beams of lightsome day
Gild, but to flout, the ruins gray.
When the broken arches are black in night,
And each shafted oriel glimmers white;
When the cold light's uncertain shower
Streams on the ruined central tower;
When the buttress and buttress, alternately,
Seem framed of ebon and ivory;
When silver edges the imagery,
And the scrolls that teach thee to live and die;
When distant Tweed is heard to rave,
And the owlet to hoot o'er the dead man's grave,
Then go — but go alone the while —
Then view St David's ruined pile;
And, home returning, soothly swear,
Was never scene so sad and fair!

II.

Short halt did Deloraine make there;
Little recked he of the scene so fair;
With dagger's hilt, on the wicket strong,
He struck full loud, and struck full long.
The porter hurried to the gate —
"Who knocks so loud, and knocks so late?"
"From Branksome I," the warrior cried;
And straight the wicket open'd wide:
For Branksome's chiefs had in battle stood,
    To fence the rights of fair Melrose;
And lands and livings, many a rood,
    Had gifted the shrine for their souls' repose.

III.

Bold Deloraine his errand said;
The porter bent his humble head;
With torch in hand, and feet unshod,
And noiseless step, the path he trod,
The arched cloisters, far and wide,
Rang to the warrior's clanking stride;
Till, stooping low his lofty crest,
He entered the cell of the ancient priest,
And lifted his barred aventayle,[1]
To hail the Monk of St Mary's aisle.

---

1 *Aventayle*, visor of the helmet. [Scott's footnote]

IV.

"The Ladye of Branksome greets thee by me,
    Says, that the fated hour is come,
And that to-night I shall watch with thee,
    To win the treasure of the tomb."
From sackcloth couch the Monk arose,
    With toil his stiffened limbs he reared;
A hundred years had flung their snows
    On his thin locks and floating beard.

V.

And strangely on the Knight looked he,
    And his blue eyes gleamed wild and wide;
"And, darest thou, warrior! seek to see
    What heaven and hell alike would hide?
My breast, in belt of iron pent,
    With shirt of hair and scourge of thorn;
For threescore years, in penance spent,
    My knees those flinty stones have worn;
Yet all too little to atone
    For knowing what should ne'er be known.
Would'st thou thy every future year
      In ceaseless prayer and penance drie,
Yet wait thy latter end with fear—
      Then, daring warrior, follow me!"

VI.

"Penance, father, will I none;
Prayer know I hardly one;
For mass or prayer can I rarely tarry,
Save to patter an Ave Mary,
When I ride on a Border foray.
Other prayer can I none;
So speed me my errand, and let me begone."

VII.

Again on the Knight looked the Churchman old,
    And again he sighed heavily;
For he had himself been a warrior bold,
    And fought in Spain and Italy.
And he thought on the days that were long since by,
When his limbs were strong, and his courage was high:—
Now, slow and faint, he led the way,
Where, cloistered round, the garden lay;
The pillared arches were over their head,
And beneath their feet were the bones of the dead.

VIII.

Spreading herbs, and flowerets bright,
Glistened with the dew of night;
Nor herb nor floweret, glistened there,
But was carved in the cloister-arches as fair.
    The Monk gazed long on the lovely moon,
        Then into the night he looked forth;
    And red and bright the streamers light
        Were dancing in the glowing north.
    So had he seen, in fair Castile,
        The youth in glittering squadrons start;
Sudden the flying jennet wheel,
        And hurl the unexpected dart.
He knew, by the streamers that shot so bright,
That spirits were riding the northern light.

IX.

By a steel-clenched postern door,
    They entered now the chancel tall;
The darkened roof rose high aloof
    On pillars, lofty, and light, and small:
The key-stone, that locked each ribbed aisle,
Was a fleur-de-lys, or a quatre-feuille;
The corbells[2] were carved grotesque and grim;
And the pillars, with clustered shafts so trim,
With base and with capital flourished around,
Seemed bundles of lances which garlands had bound.

X.

Full many a scutcheon and banner, riven,
Shook to the cold night-wind of heaven,
    Around the screened altar's pale;
And there the dying lamps did burn,
Before thy low and lonely urn,
O gallant Chief of Otterburne,
    And thine, dark knight of Liddesdale![3]
O fading honours of the dead!
O high ambition, lowly laid!

XI.

The moon on the east oriel shone
Through slender shafts of shapely stone,
    By foliaged tracery combined;
Thou would'st have thought some fairy's hand
'Twixt poplars straight, the ozier wand,

---

2   *Corbells*, the projections from which the arches spring, usually cut in a fantastic face, or mask. [Scott's footnote]

3   Two endnotes explain the references to James, Earl of Douglas, killed at Otterburne in 1388; and to William Douglas, another of that family from the reign of David II: both buried in Melrose.

In many a freakish knot, had twined;
Then framed a spell, when the work was done,
And changed the willow wreaths to stone.
    The silver light, so pale and faint,
    Shewed many a prophet, and many a saint,
        Whose image on the glass was dyed;
    Full in the midst, his Cross of Red
    Triumphant Michael brandished,
        And trampled the Apostate's pride.
The moon-beam kissed the hole pane,
And threw on the pavement a bloody stain.

XII.

They sate them down on a marble stone,
    A Scottish monarch slept below;[4]
Thus spoke the Monk, in solemn tone:
    "I was not always a man of woe —
For Paynim countries I have trod,
And fought beneath the cross of God;
Now, strange to my eyes thine arms appear,
And their iron clang sounds strange to my ear.

XIII.

"In these far climes, it was my lot
To meet the wondrous Michael Scott;[5]
    A wizard of such dreaded fame,
That when, in Salamanca's cave,
Him listed his magic wand to wave,
    The bells would ring in Notre Dame!
Some of his skill he taught to me;
And, warrior, I could say to thee
The words that cleft Eildon hills in three,
    And bridled the Tweed with a curb of stone:[6]
But to speak them were a deadly sin;
And for having but thought them my heart within,
    A treble penance must be done.

---

4   An endnote identifies this as Alexander II.
5   Sir Michael Scot of Balwearie flourished during the 13th century; and was one of the
embassadors [sic.] sent to bring the Maid of Norway to Scotland upon the death of Alexander
III. By a poetical anachronism, he is here placed in a later æra. He was a man of much
learning, chiefly acquired in foreign countries. He wrote a commentary upon Aristotle,
printed at Venice in 1496; and several treatises upon natural philosophy, from which he
appears addicted to the abstruse studies of judicial astrology, alchymy, physiognomy,
and chiromancy. Hence he passed among his contemporaries for a skilful magician. [...] A
personage, thus spoken of by biographers and historians, loses little of his mystical fame in
vulgar tradition. Accordingly, the memory of Sir Michael Scott survives in many a legend;
and in the south of Scotland, any work of great labour and antiquity is ascribed, either to the
agency of *Auld Michael*, of Sir William Wallace, or of the devil. Tradition varies concerning
the place of his burial [...] [from Scott's endnote].
6   An endnote explains that these are tasks Scott set a bothersome spirit (the 'curb of stone' is
the weir at Kelso). He is only rid of it when he commands it to make ropes from sea-sand.

XIV.

"When Michael lay on his dying bed,
His conscience was awakened;
He bethought him of his sinful deed,
And he gave me a sign to come with speed:
I was in Spain when the morning rose,
But I stood by his bed ere evening close.
The words may not again be said,
That he spoke to me, on death-bed laid;
They would rend this Abbaye's massy nave,
And pile it in heaps above his grave.

XV.

"I swore to bury his mighty Book,
That never mortal might therein look;
And never to tell where it was hid,
Save at his chief of Branksome's need;
And when that need was past and o'er,
Again the volume to restore.
I buried him on St. Michael's night,
When the bell tolled one, and the moon was bright;
And I dug his chamber among the dead,
When the floor of the chancel was stained red,
That his patron's cross might over him wave,
And scare the fiends from the wizard's grave.

XVI.

"It was a night of woe and dread,
When Michael in the tomb I laid!
Strange sounds along the chancel past,
The banners waved without a blast" —
—Still spoke the Monk, when the bell tolled one!
I tell you, that a braver man
Than William of Deloraine, good at need,
Against a foe ne'er spurred a steed;
Yet somewhat was he chilled with dread,
And his hair did bristle upon his head.

XVII.

"Lo, warrior! now the Cross of Red
Points to the grave of the mighty dead;
Within it burns a wondrous light,
To chase the spirits that love the night:
That lamp shall burn unquenchably,
Until the eternal doom shall be."
Slow moved the Monk to the broad flag-stone,
Which the bloody Cross was traced upon:
He pointed to a secret nook;

An iron bar the warrior took;
And the Monk made a sign with his withered hand,
The grave's huge portal to expand.

XVIII.

With beating heart to the task he went;
His sinewy frame o'er the grave-stone bent;
With bar of iron heaved amain,
Till the toil-drops fell from his brows like rain.
It was by dint of passing strength,
That he moved the massy stone at length.
I would you had been there, to see
How the light broke forth so gloriously,
Streamed upward to the chancel roof,
And through the galleries far aloof!
    No earthly flame blazed e'er so bright:
    It shone like heaven's own blessed light;
    And, issuing from the tomb,
Shewed the Monk's cowl, and visage pale;
Danced on the dark-browed Warrior's mail,
    And kissed his waving plume.

XIX.

Before their eyes the Wizard lay,
As if he had not been dead a day;
His hoary beard in silver rolled,
He seem'd some seventy winters old;
    A palmer's amice wrapp'd him round,
    With a wrought Spanish baldric bound,
      Like a pilgrim from beyond the sea:
    His left hand held his Book of Might;
    A silver cross was in his right;
      The lamp was placed beside his knee:
High and majestic was his look,
At which the fellest fiends had shook;
And all unruffled was his face —
They trusted his soul had gotten grace.

XX.

Often had William of Deloraine
Rode through the battle's bloody plain,
And trampled down the warriors slain,
    And neither known remorse nor awe;
Yet now remorse and awe he own'd;
His breath came thick, his head swam round,
    When this strange scene of death he saw.
Bewildered and unnerved, he stood,
And the priest prayed fervently, and loud:
With eyes averted prayed he,

He might not endure the sight to see,
Of the man he had loved so brotherly.

XXI.

And when the priest his death-prayer had prayed,
Thus unto Deloraine he said —
"Now, speed thee what thou hast to do,
Or, warrior, we may dearly rue;
For those, thou may'st not look upon,
Are gathering fast round the yawning stone!" —
Then Deloraine, in terror, took
From the cold hand the Mighty Book,
With iron clasped, and with iron bound:
He thought, as he took it, the dead man frowned;
But the glare of the sepulchral light,
Perchance, had dazzled the warrior's sight.

XXII.

When the huge stone sunk o'er the tomb,
The night returned, in double gloom;
For the moon had gone down, and the stars were few;
And, as the Knight and Priest withdrew,
With wavering steps and dizzy brain,
They hardly might the postern gain.
'Tis said, as through the aisles they passed,
They heard strange noises on the blast;
And through the cloister-galleries small,
Which at mid-height thread the chancel wall,
Loud sobs, and laughter louder, ran,
And voices unlike the voice of man;
As if the fiends kept holiday,
Because these spells were brought to day.
I cannot tell how the truth may be;
I say the tale as 'twas said to me.

XXIII.

"Now, hie thee hence," the father said,
"And when we are on death-bed laid,
O may our dear Ladye, and sweet St John,
Forgive our souls for the deed we have done!"
    The Monk returned him to his cell,
        And many a prayer and penance sped;
    When the convent met at the noontide bell —
        The Monk of St Mary's aisle was dead!
Before the cross was the body laid,
With hands clasped fast, as if still he prayed.

XXIV.

The knight breathed free in the morning wind,
And strove his hardihood to find;
He was glad when he passed the tomestones gray,
Which girdle round the fair Abbaye;
For the mystic Book, to his bosom prest,
Felt like a load upon his breast;
And his joints, with nerves of iron twined,
Shook, like the aspen leaves in wind.
Full fain was he when the dawn of day
Began to brighten Cheviot grey;
He joyed to see the cheerful light,
And he said Ave Mary, as well as he might.

XXV.

The sun had brightened Cheviot gray,
    The sun had brightened the Carter's side;[7]
And soon beneath the rising day
Smiled Branksome Towers and Teviot's tide.
The wild birds told their warbling tale,
    And waken'd every flower that blows;
And peeped forth the violet pale,
And spread her breast the mountain rose:
And lovelier than the rose so red,
Yet paler than the violet pale,
She early left her sleepless bed,
The fairest maid of Teviotdale.

XXVI.

Why does fair Margaret so early awake,
    And don her kirtle so hastilie;
And the silken knots, which in hurry she would make,
    Why tremble her slender fingers to tie;
Why does she stop, and look often around,
    As she glides down the secret stair;
And why does she pat the shaggy blood-hound,
    As he rouses him up from his lair;
And though she passes the postern alone,
Why is not the watchman's bugle blown?

XXVII.

The ladye steps in doubt and dread,
Lest her watchful mother hear her tread;
The lady caresses the rough blood-hound,
Lest his voice should waken the castle round;
The watchman's bugle is not blown,
For he was her foster-father's son;
And she glides through the greenwood at dawn of light
To meet Baron Henry, her own true knight.

---

7   A mountain on the border of England, above Jedburgh. [Scott's footnote; the Cheviot is another, of course.]

The knight and ladye fair are met,
And under the hawthorn's boughs are set.
A fairer pair were never seen
To meet beneath the hawthorn green.
He was stately, and young, and tall;
Dreaded in battle, and loved in hall:
And she, when love, scarce told, scarce hid,
Lent to her cheek a livelier red;
When the half sigh her swelling breast
Against the silken ribbon pressed;
When her blue eyes their secret told,
Though shaded by her locks of gold —
Where would you find the peerless fair,
With Margaret of Branksome might compare!

XXIX.

And now, fair dames, methinks I see
You listen to my minstrelsy;
Your waving locks ye backward throw,
And sidelong bend your necks of snow: —
Ye ween to hear a melting tale
Of two true lovers in a dale;
    And how the knight, with tender fire,
        To paint his faithful passion strove;
    Swore, he might at her feet expire,
        But never, never cease to love;
And how she blushed, and how she sighed,
And, half consenting, half denied,
And said that she would die a maid —
Yet, might the bloody feud be stayed,
Henry of Cranstoun, and only he,
Margaret of Branksome's choice should be.

XXX.

Alas! fair dames, your hopes are vain!
My harp has lost the enchanting strain;
    Its lightness would my age reprove:
My hairs are grey, my limbs are old,
My heart is dead, my veins are cold —
    I may not, must not, sing of love.

XXXI.

Beneath an oak, mossed o'er by eld,
The Baron's Dwarf his courser held,[8]
    And held his crested helm and spear:
That Dwarf was scarce an earthly man,

---

8   The idea of Lord Cranstoun's Goblin Page is taken from a being called Gilpin Horner, who appeared, and made some stay, at a farm-house among the Border-mountains [...] [Scott's endnote].

If the tales were true that of him ran
　　Through all the Border, far and near.
'Twas said, when the Baron a hunting rode
Through Reedsdale's glens, but rarely trod,
　　He heard a voice cry, "Lost! lost! lost!"
　　And, like tennis-ball by racket tossed,
　　　A leap, of thirty feet and three,
　　Made from the gorse this elfin shape,
　　Distorted like some dwarfish ape,
　　　And lighted at Lord Cranstoun's knee.
　　Lord Cranstoun was some whit dismayed;
　　'Tis said that five good miles he rade,
　　　To rid him of his company;
But where he rode one mile, the Dwarf ran four,
And the Dwarf was first at the castle door.

XXXII.

Use lessens marvel, it is said.
This elvish Dwarf with the Baron staid;
Little he ate, and less he spoke,
Nor mingled with the menial flock:
And oft apart his arms he tossed,
And often muttered "Lost! lost! lost!"
　　He was waspish, arch, and litherlie,
　　But well Lord Cranstoun served he:
And he of his service was full fain;
For once he had been ta'en or slain,
　　An' it had not been for his ministry.
All, between Home and Hermitage,
Talked of Lord Cranstoun's Goblin Page.

XXXIII.

For the Baron went on pilgrimage,
And took with him this elvish Page,
　　To Mary's chapel of the Lowes:
For there, beside Our Ladye's lake,
An offering he had sworn to make,
　　And he would pay his vows.
But the Ladye of Branksome gather'd a band
Of the best that would ride at her command;
　　The trysting place was Newark Lee.
Wat of Harden came thither amain,
And thither came John of Thirlestane,
And thither came William of Deloraine;
　　They were three hundred spears and three.
Through Douglas-burn, up Yarrow stream,
Their horses prance, their lances gleam.
They came to St. Mary's lake ere day;
But the chapel was void, and the Baron away.

They burned the chapel for very rage,
And cursed Lord Cranstoun's Goblin Page.

XXXIV.

And now, in Branksome's good green wood,
As under the aged oak he stood,
The Baron's courser pricks his ears,
As if a distant noise he hears.
The Dwarf waves his long lean arm on high,
And signs to the lovers to part and fly;
No time was then to vow or sigh.
Fair Margaret through the hazel grove,
Flew like the startled cushat-dove:[9]
The Dwarf the stirrup held and rein;
Vaulted the Knight on his steed amain,
And, pondering deep that morning's scene,
Rode eastward through the hawthorns green.

————

WHILE thus he poured the lengthened tale,
The Minstrel's voice began to fail:
Full slyly smiled the observant page,
And gave the withered hand of age
A goblet, crowned with mighty wine,
The blood of Velez' scorched vine.
He raised the silver cup on high,
And, while the big drop filled his eye,
Prayed God to bless the Duchess long,
And all who cheered a son of song.
The attending maidens smiled to see,
How long, how deep, how zealously,
The precious juice the Minstrel quaffed;
And he, emboldened by the draught,
Looked gaily back to them, and laughed.
The cordial nectar of the bowl
Swelled his old veins, and cheered his soul;
A lighter, livelier prelude ran,
Ere thus his tale again began.

---

9   Wood pigeon. [Scott's footnote]

CANTO THIRD.

I.

AND said I that my limbs were old;
And said I that my blood was cold,
And that my kindly fire was fled,
And my poor wither'd heart was dead,
  And that I might not sing of love?—
How could I to the dearest theme,
That ever warm'd a minstrel's dream,
  So foul, so false a recreant prove!
How could I name love's very name,
Nor wake my heart to notes of flame!

II.

In peace, Love tunes the shepherd's reed;
In war, he mounts the warrior's steed;
In halls, in gay attire is seen;
In hamlets, dances on the green.
Love rules the court, the camp, the grove,
And men below, and saints above;
For love is heaven, and heaven is love.

III.

So thought Lord Cranstoun, as I ween,
While, pondering deep the tender scene,
He rode through Branksome's hawthorn green.
  But the Page shouted wild and shrill—
    And scarce his helmet could he don,
  When downward from the shady hill
    A stately knight came pricking on.
That warrior's steed, so dapple-gray,
Was dark with sweat, and splashed with clay;
  His armour red with many a stain:
He seem'd in such a weary plight,
As if he had ridden the live-long night;
  For it was William of Deloraine.

IV.

But no whit weary did he seem,
When, dancing in the sunny beam,
He marked the crane on the Baron's crest;
For his ready spear was in his rest.
  Few were the words, and stern and high,
    That marked the foemen's feudal hate;
  For question fierce, and proud reply,
    Gave signal soon of dire debate.
Their very coursers seem'd to know
That each was other's mortal foe;

And snorted fire, when wheeled around,
To give each knight his vantage ground.

V.

In rapid round the Baron bent;
    He sighed a sigh, and prayed a prayer;
The prayer was to his patron saint,
    The sigh was to his ladye fair.
Stout Deloraine nor sighed, nor prayed,
Nor saint, nor ladye, called to aid;
But he stooped his head, and couched his spear,
And spurred his steed to full career.
The meeting of these champions proud
Seemed like the bursting thunder-cloud.

VI.

Stern was the dint the Borderer lent!
The stately Baron backwards bent;
Bent backwards to his horse's tail,
And his plumes went scattering on the gale;
The tough ash spear, so stout and true,
Into a thousand flinders flew.
But Cranstoun's lance, of more avail,
Pierced through, like silk, the Borderer's mail;
Through shield, and jack, and acton, past,
Deep in his bosom broke at last. —
Still sate the warrior saddle-fast,
Till, stumbling in the mortal shock,
Down went the steed, the girthing broke,
Hurled on a heap lay man and horse.
The Baron onward passed his course;
Nor knew so giddy rolled his brain
His foe lay stretched upon the plain.

VII.

But when he reined his courser round,
And saw his foeman on the ground
    Lie senseless as the bloody clay,
He bade his Page to stanch the wound,
    And there beside the warrior stay,
And tend him in his doubtful state,
And lead him to Branksome castle-gate;
His noble mind was inly moved
For the kinsman of the maid he loved.
"This shalt thou do without delay:
No longer here myself may stay;
Unless the swifter I speed away,
Short shrift will be at my dying day."

VIII.

Away in speed Lord Cranstoun rode;
The Goblin-Page behind abode;
His lord's command he ne'er withstood,
Though small his pleasure to do good.
As the corslet off he took,
The Dwarf espied the Mighty Book!
Much he marvelled a knight of pride,
Like a book-bosomed priest, should ride:
He thought not to search or stanch the wound,
Until the secret he had found.

IX.

The iron band, the iron clasp,
Resisted long the elfin grasp:
For when the first he had undone,
It closed as he the next begun.
Those iron clasps, that iron band,
Would not yield to unchristened hand,
Till he smeared the cover o'er
With the Borderer's curdled gore;
A moment then the volume spread,
And one short spell therein he read.
It had much of glamour[1] might,
Could make a ladye seem a knight;
The cobwebs, on a dungeon wall,
Seem tapestry in lordly hall;
A nut-shell seem a gilded barge,
A sheeling[2] seem a palace large,
And youth seem age, and age seem youth —
All was delusion, nought was truth.

X.

He had not read another spell,
When on his cheek a buffet fell,
So fierce, it stretched him on the plain,
Beside the wounded Deloraine.
From the ground he rose dismayed,
And shook his huge and matted head;
One word he muttered, and no more —
"Man of age, thou smitest sore!"
No more the Elfin Page durst try
Into the wondrous book to pry;
The clasps, though smeared with Christian gore,
Shut faster than they were before.
He hid it underneath his cloak. —

---

1   Magical delusion. [Scott's footnote]. In an endnote, Scott expands: '*Glamour*, in the legends of Scottish superstition, means the magic power of imposing on the eye-sight of spectators, so that the appearance of an object shall be totally different from the reality [...]'.

2   A shepherd's hut. [Scott's footnote]

Now, if you ask who gave the stroke,
I cannot tell, so mot I thrive;
It was not given by man alive.

                                    XI.

Unwillingly himself he addressed,
To do his master's high behest:
He lifted up the living corse,
And laid it on the weary horse;
He led him into Branksome Hall,
Before the beards of the warders all;
And each did after swear and say,
There only passed a wain of hay.
He took him to Lord David's tower,
Even to the Ladye's secret bower;
And, but that stronger spells were spread,
And the door might not be opened,
He had laid him on her very bed.
Whate'er he did of gramarye,[3]
Was always done maliciously.
He flung the warrior on the ground,
And the blood welled freshly from the wound.

                                    XII.

As he repassed the outer court,
He spied the fair young child at sport:
He thought to train him to the wood;
For, at a word, be it understood,
He was always for ill, and never for good.
Seemed to the boy, some comrade gay
Led him forth to the woods to play;
On the draw-bridge the warders stout
Saw a terrier and lurcher passing out.

                                    XIII.

He led the boy o'er bank and fell,
    Until they came to a woodland brook;
The running stream dissolved the spell,
    And his own elvish shape he took.[4]
Could he have had his pleasure vilde,
He had crippled the joints of the noble child;
Or, with his fingers long and lean,
Had strangled him in fiendish spleen:
But his awful mother he had in dread,
And also his power was limited;
So he but scowled on the startled child,
And darted through the forest wild:

---

3   Magic. [Scott's footnote]
4   Scott's endnote points out the analogy with Burns's *Tam O'Shanter* here.

The woodland brook he bounding crossed
And laughed, and shouted, "Lost! lost! lost!"

XIV.

Full sore amazed at the wondrous change,
    And frightened as a child might be,
At the wild yell and visage strange,
    And the dark words of gramarye,
The child, amidst the forest bower,
Stood rooted like a lily flower;
    And when at length, with trembling pace,
        He sought to find where Branksome lay,
    He feared to see that grisly face
        Glare from some thicket on his way.
Thus, starting oft, he journeyed on,
And deeper in the wood is gone:
For aye the more he sought his way,
The farther still he went astray,
Until he heard the mountains round
Ring to the baying of a hound.

XV.

And hark! and hark! the deep-mouthed bark
    Comes nigher still, and nigher;
Bursts on the path a dark blood-hound,
His tawny muzzle tracked the ground,
    And his red eye shot fire.
Soon as the wildered child saw he,
He flew at him right furiouslie.
I ween you would have seen with joy
The bearing of the gallant boy,
When, worthy of his noble sire,
His wet cheek glowed 'twixt fear and ire!
He faced the blood-hound manfully,
And held his little bat on high;
So fierce he struck, the dog, afraid,
At cautious distance hoarsely bayed,
    But still in act to spring;
When dashed an archer through the glade,
And when he saw the hound was stay'd,
    He drew his tough bow-string;
But a rough voice cried, "Shoot not, hoy!
Ho! shoot not, Edward—'Tis a boy!"

XVI.

The speaker issued from the wood,
And checked his fellow's surly mood,
    And quelled the ban-dog's ire:
He was an English yeoman good,

And born in Lancashire;
Well could be hit a fallow deer
   Five hundred feet him fro;
With hand more true, and eye more clear,
   No archer bended bow.
His coal-black hair, shorn round and close,
 Set off his sun-burned face;
Old England's sign, St George's cross,
 His barret-cap did grace;
His bugle horn hung by his side,
  All in a wolf-skin baldric tied;
And his short falchion, sharp and clear,
Had pierced the throat of many a deer.

XVII.

His kirtle, made of forest green,
   Reached scantly to his knee;
And, at his belt, of arrows keen
   A furbished sheaf bore he;
His buckler scarce in breadth a span,
   No larger fence had he;
He never counted him a man,
   Would strike below the knee;[5]
His slackened bow was in his hand,
And the leash that was his blood-hound's band.

XVIII.

He would not do the fair child harm,
But held him with his powerful arm,
That he might neither fight nor flee;
For when the Red-Cross spied he,
The boy strove long and violently.
"Now, by St. George," the archer cries,
"Edward, methinks we have a prize!
This boy's fair face, and courage free,
Shews he is come of high degree."

XIX.

"Yes! I am come of high degree,
   For I am the heir of bold Buccleuch;
And, if thou dost not set me free,
   False Suthron, thou shalt dearly rue!
For Walter of Harden shall come with speed,
And William of Deloraine, good at need,
And every Scott from Esk to Tweed;
And if thou dost not let me go,
Despite thy arrows, and thy bow,
I'll have thee hanged to feed the crow!"

5   Scott's model for the Lancastrian archer comes as no surprise: 'Imitated from Drayton's account of Robin Hood and his followers in *Poly-Albion* [1612–22] song 26' [endnote].

"Gramercy, for thy good will, fair boy!
My mind was never set so high;
But if thou art chief of such a clan,
And art the son of such a man,
And ever comest to thy command,
    Our wardens had need to keep good order:
My bow of yew to a hazel wand,
    Thou'lt make them work upon the Border.
Meantime, be pleased to come with me,
For good Lord Dacre shalt thou see;
I think our work is well begun,
When we have taken thy father's son."

XXI.

Although the child was led away,
In Branksome still he seemed to stay,
For so the Dwarf his part did play;
And, in the shape of that young boy,
He wrought the castle much annoy.
The comrades of the young Buccleuch
He pinched, and beat, and overthrew;
Nay, some of them he well nigh slew.
He tore Dame Maudlin's silken tire;
And, as Sym Hall stood by the fire,
He lighted the match of his bandelier,[6]
And wofully scorched the hackbuteer.[7]
It may be hardly thought, or said,
The mischief that the urchin made,
Till many of the castle guessed,
That the young Baron was possessed!

XXII.

Well I ween the charm he held
The noble Ladye had soon dispelled;
But she was deeply busied then
To tend the wounded Deloraine.
    Much she wondered to find him lie,
        On the stone threshold stretched along;
    She thought some spirit of the sky
        Had done the bold moss-trooper wrong;
Because, despite her precept dread,
Perchance he in the book had read;
But the broken lance in his bosom stood,
And it was earthly steel and wood.

---

6   *Bandelier*, belt for carrying ammunition. [Scott's footnote]
7   *Hackbutteer*, musketeer. [Scott's footnote]

She drew the splinter from the wound,
    And with a charm she stanched the blood;
She bade the gash be cleansed and bound:
    No longer by his couch she stood;
But she has ta'en the broken lance,
    And washed it from the clotted gore,
    And salved the splinter o'er and o'er.[8]
William of Deloraine, in trance,
      Whene'er she turn'd it round and round,
    Twisted as if she gall'd his wound.
      Then to her maidens she did say,
    That he should be whole man and sound,
      Within the course of a night and day.
Full long she toiled; for she did rue
Mishap to friend so stout and true.

XXIV.

So passed the day — the evening fell,
'Twas near the time of curfew bell;
The air was mild, the wind was calm,
The stream was smooth, the dew was balm;
E'en the rude watchman, on the tower,
Enjoyed and blessed the lovely hour.
Far more fair Margaret loved and blessed
The hour of silence and of rest.
On the high turret, sitting lone,
She waked at times the lute's soft tone;
Touched a wild note, and all between
Thought of the bower of hawthorns green;
Her golden hair streamed free from band,
Her fair cheek rested on her hand,
Her blue eyes sought the west afar,
For lovers love the western star.

XXV.

Is yon the star, o'er Penchryst-Pen,
That rises slowly to her ken,
And, spreading broad its wavering light,
Shakes its loose tresses on the night?
Is yon red glare the western star? —
O, 'tis the beacon-blaze of war!
Scarce could she draw her tightened breath,
For well she knew the fire of death!

XXVI.

The warder viewed it blazing strong,
And blew his war-note loud and long,

---

8   In an endnote Scott gives pages of examples of this traditional treatment for a wound.

Till, at the high and haughty sound,
Rock, wood, and river, rung around;
The blast alarmed the festal hall,
And startled forth the warriors all;
Far downward, in the castle-yard,
Full many a torch and cresset glared;
And helms and plumes, confusedly tossed,
Were in the blaze half-seen, half-lost;
And spears in wild disorder shook,
Like reeds beside a frozen brook.

XXVII.

The Seneschal, whose silver hair
Was reddened by the torches' glare,
Stood in the midst, with gesture proud,
And issued forth his mandates loud. —
"On Penchryst glows a bale[9] of fire,
And three are kindling on Priesthaughswire;
    Ride out, ride out,
    The foe to scout!
Mount, mount for Branksome,[10] every man!
Thou, Todrig, warn the Johnstone clan,
    That ever are true and stout. —
Ye need not send to Liddesdale;
For when they see the blazing bale,
Elliots and Armstrongs never fail. —
Ride, Alton, ride, for death and life!
And warn the Warden of the strife.
Young Gilbert, let our beacon blaze,
Our kin, and clan, and friends, to raise."

XXVIII.

Fair Margaret, from the turret head,
Heard, far below, the coursers' tread,
    While loud the harness rung,
As to their seats, with clamour dread,
    The ready horsemen sprung;
And trampling hoofs, and iron coats,
And leaders' voices, mingled notes,
    And out! and out!
    In hasty route,
    The horsemen galloped forth;
Dispersing to the south to scout,
    And east, and west, and north,
To view their coming enemies,
And warn their vassals and allies.

---

9   *Bale*, beacon-faggot. [Scott's footnote]
10 *Mount for Branksome* was the gathering word of the Scotts. [Scott's footnote]

The ready page, with hurried hand,
Awaked the need-fire's[11] slumbering brand,
    And ruddy blushed the heaven:
For a sheet of flame, from the turret high,
Waved like a blood-flag on the sky,
    All flaring and uneven;
And soon a score of fires, I ween,
From height, and hill, and cliff, were seen;
Each with warlike tidings fraught;
Each from each the signal caught;
Each after each they glanced to sight,
As stars arise upon the night.
They gleamed on many a dusky tarn,[12]
Haunted by the lonely earn;[13]
On many a cairn's grey pyramid,[14]
Where urns of mighty chiefs lie hid;
Till high Dunedin the blazes saw,
From Soltra and Dumpender Law;
And Lothian heard the regent's order,
That all should bowne[15] them for the Border.

XXX.

The livelong night in Branksome rang
The ceaseless sound of steel;
The castle-bell, with backward clang,
    Sent forth the larum peal;
Was frequent heard the heavy jar,
Where massy stone and iron bar
Were piled on echoing keep and tower,
To whelm the foe with deadly shower;
Was frequent heard the changing guard,
And watch-word from the sleepless ward;
While, wearied by the endless din,
Blood-hound and ban-dog yelled within.

XXXI.

The noble Dame, amid the broil,
Shared the gray Seneschal's high toil,
And spoke of danger with a smile;
    Cheered the young knights, and council sage
Held with the chiefs of riper age
No tidings of the foe were brought,
Nor of his numbers knew they aught,
Nor what in time of truce he sought.

---

11 *Need-fire,* beacon. [Scott's footnote]
12 *Tarn,* a mountain lake. [Scott's footnote]
13 *Earn,* a Scottish eagle. [Scott's footnote]
14 *Cairn,* a pile of stones. [Scott's footnote]
15 *Bowne,* make ready. [Scott's footnote]

Some said, that there were thousands ten;
And others weened that it was nought
    But Leven Clans, or Tynedale men,
Who came to gather in black-mail;[16]
And Liddlesdale, with small avail,
    Might drive them lightly back agen.
So passed the anxious night away,
And welcome was the peep of day.

————

CEASED the high sound—the listening throng
Applaud the Master of the Song;
And marvel much, in helpless age,
So hard should be his pilgrimage.
Had he no friend—no daughter dear,
His wandering toil to share and cheer;
No son to be his father's stay,
And guide him on the rugged way?—
"Ay! once he had—but he was dead!"
Upon the harp he stooped his head,
And busied himself the strings withal,
To hide the tear, that fain would fall.
In solemn measure, soft and slow,
Arose a father's notes of woe.

————

16 Protection-money exacted by free-booters. [Scott's footnote]

CANTO FOURTH.

I.

SWEET Teviot! on thy silver tide
    The glaring bale-fires blaze no more;
No longer steel-clad warriors ride
    Along thy wild and willowed shore;
    Where'er thou wind'st, by dale or hill,
All, all is peaceful, all is still,
    As if thy waves, since Time was born,
Since first they rolled upon the Tweed,
Had only heard the shepherd's reed,
    Nor started at the bugle-horn.

II.

Unlike the tide of human time,
    Which, though it change in ceaseless flow,
Retains each grief, retains each crime
    Its earliest course was doomed to know;
And, darker as it downward bears,
Is stained with past and present tears.
    Low as that tide has ebbed with me,
It still reflects to memory's eye
The hour, my brave, my only boy,
    Fell by the side of great Dundee.
Why, when the volleying musket played
Against the bloody Highland blade,
Why was not I beside him laid!—
Enough—he died the death of fame;
Enough—he died with conquering Graeme.[1]

III.

Now over Border dale and fell,
    Full wide and far, was terror spread;
For pathless marsh, and mountain cell,
    The peasant left his lowly shed.
The frightened flocks and herds were pent
Beneath the peel's rude battlement;
And maids and matrons dropped the tear,
While ready warriors seized the spear.
From Branksome's towers, the watchman's eye
Dun wreaths of distant smoke can spy,
Which, curling in the rising sun,
Shewed southern ravage was begun.

---

1   Scott in his endnote observes only that this refers to John Graham of Claverhouse, Viscount Dundee, and the battle of Killiecrankie. At the deposition of James (whom he had served so well in the suppression of the Covenanters) Claverhouse raised an army for him in the Highlands which defeated government forces at the Pass of Killiecrankie in Perthshire in 1689. It is in this battle that the minstrel's son has died. Claverhouse himself was killed, and the rebellion fizzled out.

Now loud the heedful gate-ward cried—
    "Prepare ye all for blows and blood!
Watt Tinlinn, from the Liddle-side,
    Comes wading through the flood.
Full oft the Tynedale snatchers knock
    At the lone gate, and prove the lock;
It was but last St Barnabright
They sieged him a whole summer night,
But fled at morning; well they knew,
In vain he never twanged the yew.
Right sharp has been the evening shower,
That drove him from his Liddle tower;
And, by my faith," the gate-ward said,
"I think 'twill prove a warden raid."[2]

V.

While thus he spoke, the bold yeoman
Entered the echoing barbican.
He led a small and shaggy nag,
That through a bog, from hag to hag,[3]
Could bound like any Billhope stag;
It bore his wife and children twain;
A half-clothed serf[4] was all their train:
His wife, stout, ruddy, and dark-browed,
Of silver brooch and bracelet proud,
Laughed to her friends among the crowd.
He was of stature passing tall,
But sparely formed, and lean withal;
A battered morion on his brow;
A leather jack, as fence enow,
On his broad shoulders loosely hung;
A border-axe behind was slung;
    His spear, six Scottish ells in length,
Seem'd newly dyed with gore;
    His shafts and bow, of wonderous strength,
His hardy partner bore.

VI.

Thus to the Ladye did Tinlinn shew
The tidings of the English foe—
"Belted Will Howard is marching here,
And hot Lord Dacre, with many a spear,
And all the German hackbut-men,[5]

---

2   An inroad commanded by the warden in person. [Scott's footnote]
3   The broken ground in a bog. [Scott's footnote]
4   Bonds-man. [Scott's footnote]
5   Musketeers. [Scott's footnote]

Who have long lain at Askerten:
They cross'd the Liddle at curfew hour,
And burn'd my little lonely tower;
The fiend receive their souls therefor!
It had not been burnt this year and more.
Barn-yard and dwelling, blazing bright,
Served to guide me on my flight;
But I was chased the live-long night.
Black John of Akeshaw, and Fergus Graeme,
Fast upon my traces came,
Until I turn'd at Priesthaugh-Scrogg,
And shot their horses in the bog,
Slew Fergus with my lance outright;
I had him long at high despite:
He drove my cows last Fastern's night."

VII.

Now weary scouts from Liddesdale,
Fast hurrying in, confirmed the tale;
    As far as they could judge by ken,
        Three hours would bring to Teviot's strand
    Three thousand armed Englishmen;
        Meanwhile, full many a warlike band,
From Teviot, Aill, and Ettrick shade,
Came in, their Chief's defence to aid.

VIII.

From fair St Mary's silver wave,
    From dreary Gamescleugh's dusky height,
His ready lances Thirlestane brave
    Arrayed beneath a banner bright.
The tressured fleur-de-luce he claims,
To wreathe his shield, since royal James,
Encamped by Fala's mossy wave,
The proud distinction grateful gave,
    For faith mid feudal jars;
What time, save Thirlestane alone,
Of Scotland's stubborn barons none
    Would march to southern wars;[6]
And hence, in fair remembrance worn,
Yon sheaf of spears his crest has borne;
Hence his high motto shines revealed
"Ready, aye ready," for the field.

IX.

An aged knight, to danger steeled,
    With many a moss-trooper, came on;
And azure in a golden field,
The stars and crescent graced his shield,

---

6   An endnote describes another instance of James V's inability to control his nobles.

Without the bend of Murdieston.
Wide lay his lands round Oakwood tower,
And wide round haunted Castle-Ower;
High over Borthwick's mountain flood,
His wood-embosomed mansion stood;
In the dark glen, so deep below,
The herds of plundered England low;
His bold retainers' daily food,
And bought with danger, blows, and blood.
Marauding chief! his sole delight
The moonlight raid, the morning fight;
Not even the Flower of Yarrow's charms,
In youth, might tame his rage for arms;
And still, in age, he spurned at rest,
And still his brows the helmet pressed,
Albeit the blanched locks below
Were white as Dinlay's spotless snow;
    Five stately warriors drew the sword
      Before their father's band;
    A braver knight than Harden's lord
      Ne'er belted on a brand.

X.

Whitslade the Hawk, and Headshaw came,
And warriors more than I may name;
From Yarrow-cleugh to Hindhaugh-swair,
    From Woodhouselie to Chester-glen,
Trooped man and horse, and bow and spear;
    Their gathering word was Bellenden.
And better hearts o'er Border sod
To seige or rescue never rode.
    The Ladye marked the aids come in,
      And high her heart of pride arose;
    She bade her youthful son attend,
    That he might know his father's friend,
      And learn to face his father's foes.
    "The boy is ripe to look on war;
      I saw him draw a cross-bow stiff,
    And his true arrow struck afar
      The raven's nest upon the cliff;
The Red Cross, on a southern breast,
Is broader than the raven's nest:
Thou, Whitslade, shalt teach him his weapon to wield,
And o'er him hold his father's shield."

XI.

Well may you think the wily Page
Cared not to face the Ladye sage.
He counterfeited childish fear,

And shrieked, and shed fully many a tear,
    And moaned and plained in manner wild.
        The attendants to the Ladye told,
    Some fairy, sure, had changed the child,
        That wont to be so free and bold.
Then wrathful was the noble dame;
She blushed blood-red for every shame —
"Hence! ere the clan his faintness view;
Hence with the weakling to Buccleuch;
Watt Tinlinn, thou shalt be his guide
To Rangleburn's lonely side.
Sure some fell fiend has cursed our line,
That coward should e'er be son of mine!"

XII.

A heavy task Watt Tinlinn had
To guide the counterfeited lad.
Soon as the palfrey felt the weight
Of that ill-omen'd elfish freight,
He bolted, sprung, and reared amain,
Nor heeded bit, nor curb, nor rein.
It cost Watt Tinlinn mickle toil
To drive him but a Scottish mile;
    But, as a shallow brook they crossed,
The elf, amid the running stream,
His figure changed, like form in dream,
    And fled, and shouted, "Lost! lost! lost!"
Full fast the urchin ran and laughed,
But faster still a cloth-yard shaft
Whistled from startled Tinlinn's yew,
And pierced his shoulder through and through.
Although the imp might not be slain,
And though the wound soon healed again,
Yet, as he ran, he yelled for pain;
And Wat of Tinlinn, much aghast,
Rode back to Branksome fiery fast.

XIII.

Soon on the hill's steep verge he stood,
That looks o'er Branksome's towers and wood;
And martial murmurs, from below,
Proclaimed the approaching southern foe.
Through the dark wood, in mingled tone,
Were Border-pipes and bugles blown;
The coursers' neighing he could ken,
A measured tread of marching men;
While broke at times the solemn hum,
The Almayn's sullen kettle-drum;
    And banners tall, of crimson sheen,

Above the copse appear;
And, glistening through the hawthorns green,
Shine helm, and shield, and spear.

XIV.

Light forayers, first, to view the ground,
Spurred their fleet coursers loosely round;
    Behind, in close array and fast,
        The Kendal archers, all in green,
    Obedient to the bugle-blast,
        Advancing from the wood were seen.
To back and guard the archer band,
Lord Dacre's bill-men were at hand;
A hardy race, on Irthing bred,
With kirtles white, and crosses red,
Arrayed beneath the banner tall,
That streamed o'er Acre's conquered wall;
And minstrels, as they marched in order,
Played "Noble Lord Dacre, he dwells on the Border."

XV.

Behind the English bill and bow,
The mercenaries, firm and slow,
    Moved on to fight, in dark array,
By Conrad led of Wolfenstein,
Who brought the band from distant Rhine,
    And sold their blood for foreign pay.
The camp their home, their law the sword,
They knew no country, owned no lord;
They were not armed like England's sons,
But bore the levin-darting guns;
Buff-coats, all frounced and 'broidered o'er,
And morsing-horns[7] and scarfs they wore;
Each better knee was bared, to aid
The warriors in the escalade;
All, as they marched in rugged tongue,
Songs of Teutonick feuds they sung.[8]

XVI.

But louder still the clamour grew,
And louder still the minstrels blew,
When, from beneath the greenwood tree,
Rode forth Lord Howard's chivalry;
His men-at-arms, with glaive and spear,
Brought up the battle's glittering rear.
There many a youthful knight, full keen
To gain his spurs, in arms was seen;

---

7   Powder flasks. [Scott's footnote]
8   In an endnote, Scott comments on the extensive use of German mercenaries by Henry VIII
     and his successors in campaigns against Scotland.

With favour in his crest, or glove,
Memorial of his ladye-love.
So rode they forth in fair array,
Till full their lengthened lines display;
Then call'd a halt, and made a stand,
And cried, "St George, for merry England!"

XVII.

Now every English eye, intent,
On Branksome's armed towers was bent;
So near they were, that they might know
The straining harsh of each cross-bow;
On battlement and bartizan
Gleamed axe, and spear, and partizan;
Falcon and culver,[9] on each tower,
Stood prompt, their deadly hail to shower;
And flashing armour frequent broke
From eddying whirls of sable smoke,
Where, upon tower and turret head,
The seething pitch and molten lead
Reeked, like a witch's caldron red.
While yet they gaze, the bridges fall,
The wicket opes, and from the wall
Rides forth the hoary Seneschal.

XVIII.

Armed he rode, all save the head,
His white beard o'er his breast-plate spread;
Unbroke by age, erect his seat,
He ruled his eager courser's gait;
Forced him, with chastened fire, to prance,
And, high curvetting, slow advance:
In sign of truce, his better hand
Displayed a peeled willow wand;
His squire, attending in the rear,
Bore high a gauntlet on a spear.
When they espied him riding out,
Lord Howard and Lord Dacre stout
Sped to the front of their array,
To hear what this old knight should say.

XIX.

"Ye English warden lords, of you
Demands the Ladye of Buccleuch,
Why, 'gainst the truce of Border tide,
In hostile guise ye dare to ride,
With Kendal bow, and Gilsland brand,
And all you mercenary band,

---

9   Ancient pieces of artillery. [Scott's footnote]

Upon the bounds of fair Scotland?
My Ladye reads you swith return;
And, if but one poor straw you burn,
Or do our towers so much molest,
As scare one swallow from her nest,
St. Mary! but we'll light a brand,
Shall warm your hearths in Cumberland."

XX.

A wrathful man was Dacre's lord,
But calmer Howard took the word—
"May't please thy Dame, Sir Seneschal,
To seek the castle's outward wall;
Our pursuivant-at-arms shall shew,
Both why we came, and when we go."
The message sped, the noble Dame
To the wall's outward circle came;
Each chief around leaned on his spear,
To see the pursuivant appear.
All in Lord Howard's livery dressed,
The lion argent decked his breast;
He led a boy of blooming hue—
O sight to meet a mother's view!
It was the heir of great Buccleuch.
Obeisance meet the herald made,
And thus his master's will he said.

XXI.

"It irks, high Dame, my noble Lords,
'Gainst ladye fair to draw their swords;
But yet they may not tamely see,
All through the western wardenry,
Your law-contemning kinsmen ride,
And burn and spoil the Border-side;
And ill beseems your rank and birth
To make your towers a flemens-firth.[10]
We claim from thee William of Deloraine,
That he may suffer march-treason[11] pain:
It was but last St Cuthbert's even
He pricked to Stapleton on Leven,
Harried[12] the lands of Richard Musgrave,
And slew his brother by dint of glaive;
Then, since a lone and widow'd Dame
These restless riders may not tame,
Either receive within thy towers
Two hundred of my master's powers,

10 An asylum for outlaws. [Scott's footnote]
11 Border treason. [Scott's footnote]
12 Plundered. [Scott's footnote]

Or straight they sound their warison,[13]
And storm and spoil thy garrison;
And this fair boy, to London led,
Shall good King Edward's page be bred."

XXII.

He ceased—and loud the boy did cry,
And stretched his little arms on high;
Implored for aid each well-known face,
And strove to seek the Dame's embrace.
A moment changed that Ladye's cheer,
Gushed to her eye the unbidden tear;
She gazed upon the leaders round,
And dark and sad each warrior frowned;
Then, deep within her sobbing breast
She locked the struggling sigh to rest;
Unaltered and collected stood,
And thus replied, in dauntless mood:

XXIII.

"Say to your Lords of high emprize,
Who war on women and on boys,
That either William of Deloraine
Will cleanse him, by oath, of march-treason stain;
Or else he will the combat take
'Gainst Musgrave, for his honour's sake.
No knight in Cumberland so good,
But William may count with him kin and blood;
Knighthood he took of Douglas' sword,
When English blood swelled Ancram ford;
And but Lord Dacre's steed was wight,
And bare him ably in the flight,
Himself had seen him dubbed a knight.
For the young heir of Branksome's line,
God be his aid, and God be mine;
Through me no friend shall meet his doom;
Here, while I live, no foe finds room.
    Then if thy lords their purpose urge,
      Take our defiance loud and high;
    Our slogan is their lyke-wake[14] dirge,
      Our moat the grave where they shall lie."

XXIV.

Proud she looked round, applause to claim—
Then lightened Thirlestane's eye of flame;
    His bugle Wat of Harden blew;
Pensils and pennons wide were flung,

---

13 Note of assault. [Scott's footnote]
14 *Lyke-wake,* the watching a corpse previous to interment. [Scott's footnote]

To heaven the Border slogan rung,
    "St Mary for the young Buccleuch!"
The English war-cry answered wide,
    And forward bent each southern spear;
Each Kendal archer made a stride,
    And drew the bowstring to his ear;
Each minstrel's war-note loud was blown;
But, ere a gray-goose shaft had flown,
        A horseman galloped from the rear.

                                    XXV.

"Ah! noble Lords!" he, breathless, said,
"What treason has your march betrayed?
What make you here, from aid so far,
Before you walls, around you war?
Your foemen triumph in the thought,
That in the toils the lion's caught.
Already on dark Ruberslaw
The Douglas holds his weapon-schaw;[15]
The lances waving in his train,
Clothe the dun heath like autumn grain;
And on the Liddle's northern strand,
To bar retreat to Cumberland,
Lord Maxwell ranks his merry-men good,
Beneath the eagle and the rood;
    And Jedwood, Eske, and Teviotdale,
        Have to proud Angus come;
    And all the Merse and Lauderdale
        Have risen with haughty Home.
    An exile from Northumberland,
        In Liddesdale I've wandered long;
    But still my heart was with merry England,
        And cannot brook my country's wrong;
And hard I've spurred all night, to shew
The mustering of the coming foe."

                                    XXVI.

"And let them come!" fierce Dacre cried;
"For soon yon crest, my father's pride,
That swept the shores of Judah's sea,
And waved in gales of Galilee,
From Branksome's highest towers displayed,
Shall mock the rescue's lingering aid! —
Level each harquebuss on row;
Draw, merry archers, draw the bow;
Up, bill-men, to the walls, and cry,
Dacre for England, win or die!"

---

15 *Weapon-schaw*, the military array of a county. [Scott's footnote]

XXVII.

"Yet hear," quoth Howard, "calmly hear,
Nor deem my words the words of fear:
For who, in field or foray slack
Saw the blanche lion e'er fall back?
But thus to risk our Border flower
In strife against a kingdom's power,
Ten thousand Scots 'gainst thousands three,
Certes, were desperate policy.
Nay, take the terms the Ladye made,
E're conscious of the advancing aid:
Let Musgrave meet fierce Deloraine
In single fight; and if he gain,
He gains for us; but if he's crossed,
'Tis but a single warrior lost:
The rest, retreating as they came,
Avoid defeat, and death, and shame."

XXVIII.

Ill could the haughty Dacre brook
His brother-warden's sage rebuke;
And yet his forward step he staid,
And slow and sullenly obeyed.
But ne'er again the Border side
Did these two lords in friendship ride;
And this slight discontent, men say,
Cost blood upon another day.

XXIX.

The pursuivant-at-arms again
    Before the castle took his stand;
His trumpet called, with parleying strain,
    The leaders of the Scottish band;
And he defied, in Musgrave's right,
Stout Deloraine to single fight;
A gauntlet at their feet he laid,
And thus the terms of fight he said:—
"If in the lists good Musgrave's sword
    Vanquish the Knight of Deloraine,
Your youthful chieftain, Branksome's lord,
    Shall hostage for his clan remain:
If Deloraine foil good Musgrave,
The boy his liberty shall have.
    Howe'er it falls, the English band,
Unharming Scots, by Scots unharmed,
In peaceful march, like men unarmed,
    Shall straight retreat to Cumberland."

Unconscious of the near relief,
The proffer pleased each Scottish chief,
   Though much the Ladye sage gainsayed:
For though their hearts were brave and true,
From Jedwood's recent sack they knew,
   How tardy was the regent's aid;[16]
And you may guess the noble Dame
   Durst not the secret prescience own,
Sprung from the art she might not name,
   By which the coming help was known.
Closed was the compact, and agreed
That lists should be enclosed with speed
   Beneath the castle, on a lawn,
They fix'd the morrow for the strife,
On foot, with Scottish axe and knife,
   At the fourth hour from peep of dawn;
When Deloraine, from sickness freed,
Or else a champion in his stead,
Should for himself and chieftain stand,
Against stout Musgrave, hand to hand.

XXXI.

I know right well, that, in their lay,
Full many minstrels sing and say,
   Such combat should be made on horse,
On foaming steed, in full career,
With brand to aid, when as the spear
   Should shiver in the course:
But he, the jovial Harper, taught
Me, yet a youth, how it was fought,
   In the guise which now I say;
He knew each ordinance and clause
Of black Lord Archibald's battle-laws,
   In the old Douglas' day.
He brooked not, he, that scoffing tongue
Should tax his minstrelsy with wrong,
   Or call his song untrue:
For this, when they the goblet plied,
And such rude taunt had chafed his pride,
   The Bard of Reull he slew.
On Teviot's side, in fight, they stood,
And tuneful hands were stain'd with blood;
Where still the thorn's white branches wave,
Memorial o'er his rival's grave.

---

16 I.e. that of the Scottish crown: see note 12 to Canto I.

Why should I tell the rigid doom,
That dragg'd my master to his tomb;
    How Ousenam's maidens tore their hair,
Wept till their eyes were dead and dim,
And wrung their hands for love of him,
    Who died at Jedwood Air?
He died!—his scholars, one by one,
To the cold silent grave are gone;
And I, alas! survive alone,
To muse o'er rivalries of yore,
And grieve that I shall hear no more
The strains, with envy heard before;
For, with my minstrel brethren fled,
My jealousy of song is dead.

———

HE paused—the listening dames again
Applaud the hoary Minstrel's strain;
With many a word of kindly cheer,
In pity half, and half sincere,
Marvelled the Duchess how so well
His legendary song could tell
Of ancient deeds, so long forgot;
Of feuds, whose memory was not;
Of forests, now laid waste and bare;
Of towers, which harbour now the hare;
Of manners, long since changed and gone;
Of chiefs, who under their grey stone
So long had slept, that fickle Fame
Had blotted from her rolls their name,
And twined round some new minion's head
The fading wreath for which they bled—
In sooth, 'twas strange, this old man's verse
Could call them from their marble hearse.

    The Harper smiled, well-pleased; for ne'er
Was flattery lost on poet's ear:
A simple race! they waste their toil
For the vain tribute of a smile;
E'en when in age their flame expires,
Her dulcet breath can fan its fires;
Their drooping fancy wakes at praise,
And strives to trim the short-lived blaze.

    Smiled then, well pleased, the Aged Man,
And thus his tale continued ran.

CANTO FIFTH.

I.

CALL it not vain—they do not err,
    Who say, that, when the poet dies,
Mute Nature mourns her worshipper,
    And celebrates his obsequies:
Who say, tall cliff, and cavern lone,
For the departed bard make moan;
That mountains weep in crystal rill;
That flowers in tears of balm distil;
Through his loved groves that breezes sigh,
And oaks, in deeper groan, reply;
And rivers teach their rushing wave
To murmur dirges round his grave.

II.

Not that, in sooth, o'er mortal urn
Those things inanimate can mourn;
But that the stream, the wood, the gale,
Is vocal with the plaintive wail
Of those, who, else forgotten long,
Lived in the poet's faithful song,
And, with the poet's parting breath,
Whose memory feels a second death.
The maid's pale shade, who wails her lot,
That love, true love, should be forgot
From rose and hawthorn shakes the tear
Upon the gentle minstrel's bier:
The phantom knight, his glory fled,
Mourns o'er the field he heaped with dead;
Mounts the wild blast that sweeps amain,
And shrieks along the battle-plain;
The chief, whose antique crownlet long
Still sparkled in the feudal song,
Now, from the mountain's misty throne,
Sees, in the thanedom once his own,
His ashes undistinguished lie,
His place, his power, his memory die:
His groans the lonely caverns fill,
His tears of rage impel the rill;
All mourn the minstrel's harp unstrung,
Their name unknown, their praise unsung.

III.

Scarcely the hot assault was staid,
The terms of truce were scarcely made,
When they could spy, from Branksome's towers,
The advancing march of martial powers;

Thick clouds of dust afar appeared,
And trampling steeds were faintly heard;
Bright lances, above the columns dun,
Glanced momentary to the sun;
And feudal banners fair displayed
The bands that moved to Branksome's aid.

IV.

Vails not to tell each hardy clan,
    From the fair Middle Marches came;
The Bloody Heart blazed in the van,
    Announcing Douglas, dreaded name!
Vails not to tell what steeds did spurn,
Where the Seven Spears of Wedderburne
    Their men in battle order set;
And Swinton laid the lance in rest,
That tamed of yore the sparkling crest
    Of Clarence's Plantagenet.
Nor list I say what hundreds more,
From the rich Merse and Lammermore,
And Tweed's fair borders, to the war,
Beneath the crest of Old Dunbar,
    And Hepburn's mingled banners, come,
Down the steep mountain glittering far,
    And shouting still, "A Home! a Home!"

V.

Now squire and knight, from Branksome sent,
On many a courteous message went;
To every chief and lord they paid
Meet thanks for prompt and powerful aid;
And told them, — how a truce was made,
    And how a day of fight was ta'en
    'Twixt Musgrave and stout Deloraine;
        And how the Ladye prayed them dear,
    That all would stay the fight to see,
    And deign, in love and courtesy,
        To taste of Branksome cheer.
Nor, while they bade to feast each Scot,
Were England's noble Lords forgot;
Himself, the hoary Seneschal,
Rode forth, in seemly terms to call
Those gallant foes to Branksome Hall.
Accepted Howard, than whom knight
Was never dubbed, more bold in fight;
Nor, when from war and armour free,
More famed for stately courtesy:
But angry Dacre rather chose
In his pavilion to repose.

VI.

Now, noble Dame, perchance you ask,
    How these two hostile armies met?
Deeming it were no easy task
    To keep the truce which here was set;
Where martial spirits, all on fire,
Breathed only blood and mortal ire. —
— By mutual inroads, mutual blows,
By habit, and by nation, foes,
    They met on Teviot's strand;
They met and sate them mingled down,
Without a threat, without a frown,
    As brothers meet in foreign land.
The hands, the spear that lately grasped
Still in the mailed gauntlet clasped,
    Were interchanged in greeting dear;
Visors were raised, and faces shown,
And many a friend, to friend made known,
    Partook of social cheer.
Some drove the jolly bowl about;
    With dice and draughts some chased the day;
And some, with many a merry shout,
In riot, revelry, and rout,
    Pursued the foot-ball play.[1]

VII.

Yet, be it known, had bugles blown,
    Or sign of war been seen;
Those bands, so fair together ranged,
Those hands, so frankly interchanged,
    Had dyed with gore the green:
The merry shout by Teviot-side
Had sunk in war-cries wild and wide,
    And in the groan of death;
And whingers,[2] now in friendship bare,
The social meal to part and share,
    Had found a bloody sheath.
'Twixt truce and war, such sudden change
Was not infrequent, nor held strange,
    In the old Border-day:
But yet on Branksome's towers and town,
In peaceful merriment, sunk down
    The sun's declining ray.

---

1   In an endnote Scott observes that "The foot-ball was anciently a very favourite sport all
through Scotland" and that "very serious accidents have sometimes taken place" in matches.
2   A sort of knife, or poniard. [Scott's footnote]

VIII.

The blithsome signs of wassel gay
Decayed not with the dying day;
Soon through the latticed windows tall,
Of lofty Branksome's lordly hall,
Divided square by shafts of stone,
Huge flakes of ruddy lustre shone;
Nor less the gilded rafters rang
With merry harp and beakers' clang;
    And frequent, on the darkening plain,
      Loud hollo, whoop, or whistle ran,
    As bands, their stragglers to regain,
      Give the shrill watch-word of their clan;
And revellers, o'er their bowls, proclaim
Douglas or Dacre's conquering name.

IX.

Less frequent heard, and fainter still,
    At length the various clamours died;
And you might hear, from Branksome hill,
    No sound but Teviot's rushing tide;
Save when the changing centinel
The challenge of his watch could tell;
And save, where, through the dark profound,
The clanging axe and hammer's sound
    Rung from the nether lawn;
For many a busy hand toiled there,
Strong pales to shape, and beams to square,
The lists' dread barriers to prepare
    Against the morrow's dawn.

X.

Margaret from hall did soon retreat,
    Despite the Dame's reproving eye;
Nor marked she, as she left her seat,
    Full many a stifled sigh;
For many a noble warrior strove
To win the Flower of Teviot's love,
    And many a bold ally.
With throbbing head and anxious heart,
All in her lonely bower apart,
    In broken sleep she lay:
By times, from silken couch she rose,
While yet the bannered hosts repose,
    She viewed the dawning day.
Of all the hundreds sunk to rest,
First woke the loveliest and the best.

She gazed upon the inner court,
    Which in the tower's tall shadow lay;
Where coursers' clang, and stamp, and snort,
    Had rung the live-long yesterday;
Now still as death—till stalking slow—
    The jingling spurs announced his tread—
A stately warrior passed below;
    But when he raised his plumed head—
Blessed Mary! can it be?
Secure, as if in Ousenam bowers,
He walks through Branksome's hostile towers,
    With fearless step and free.
She dared not sign, she dared not speak—
Oh! if one page's slumbers break,
    His blood the price must pay!
Not all the pearls Queen Mary wears,
Not Margaret's yet more precious tears,
    Shall buy his life a day.

Yet was his hazard small—for well
You may bethink you of the spell
    Of that sly urchin Page;
This to his lord he did impart,
And made him seem, by glamour art,
    A knight from Hermitage.
Unchallenged thus, the warder's post,
The court, unchallenged, thus he crossed,
    For all the vassalage:
But, O what magic's quaint disguise
Could blind fair Margaret's azure eyes!
    She started from her seat;
While with surprise and fear she strove,
And both could scarcely master love—
    Lord Henry's at her feet.

Oft have I mused, what purpose bad
That foul malicious urchin had
    To bring this meeting round;
For happy love's a heavenly sight,
And by a vile malignant sprite
    In such no joy is found;
And oft I've deemed, perchance he thought
Their erring passion might have wrought
    Sorrow, and sin, and shame;
And death to Cranstoun's gallant Knight,
And to the gentle Ladye bright,

Disgrace, and loss of fame.
But earthly spirit could not tell
The heart of them that loved so well.
True love's the gift which God has given
To man alone beneath the heaven:
    It is not fantasy's hot fire,
      Whose wishes, soon as granted, fly;
    It liveth not in fierce desire,
      With dead desire it doth not die;
It is the secret sympathy,
The silver link, the silken tie,
Which heart to heart, and mind to mind,
In body and in soul can bind. —
Now leave we Margaret and her Knight,
To tell you of the approaching fight.

XIV.

Their warning blasts the bugles blew,
    The pipes shrill port[3] aroused each clan;
In haste the deadly strife to view,
    The trooping warriors eager ran.
Thick round the lists their lances stood,
Like blasted pines in Ettricke wood;
To Branksome many a look they threw,
The combatants' approach to view,
And bandied many a word of boast,
About the knight each favour'd most.

XV.

Meantime full anxious was the Dame;
For now arose disputed claim,
Of who should fight for Deloraine,
'Twixt Harden and 'twixt Thirlestaine:
    They 'gan to reckon kin and rent,
    And frowning brow on brow was bent;
      But yet not long the strife — for, lo!
    Himself, the Knight of Deloraine,
    Strong, as it seemed, and free from pain,
      In armour sheathed from top to toe,
Appeared, and craved the combat due.
The Dame her charm successful knew,[4]
And the fierce chiefs their claims withdrew.

XVI.

When for the lists they sought the plain,
The stately Ladye's silken rein
    Did noble Howard hold;
Unarmed by her side he walked,

---

3   A martial piece of music, adapted to the bagpipes. [Scott's footnote]
4   See Canto III, Stanza XXIII. [Scott's footnote]

And much, in courteous phrase, they talked
    Of feats of arms of old.
Costly his garb—his Flemish ruff
Fell o'er his doublet, shaped of buff,
    With satin slashed and lined;
Tawny his boot, and gold his spur,
His cloak was all of Poland fur,
    His hose with silver twined;
His Bilboa blade, by Marchmen felt,
Hung in a broad and studded belt;
Hence, in rude phrase, the Borderers still
Called Noble Howard, Belted Will.

XVII.

Behind Lord Howard and the Dame,
Fair Margaret on her palfrey came,
    Whose foot-cloth swept the ground;
White was her wimple, and her veil,
And her loose locks a chaplet pale
    Of whitest roses bound;
The lordly Angus, by her side,
In courtesy to cheer her tried;
Without his aid, her hand in vain
Had strove to guide her broidered rein.
He deemed, she shuddered at the sight
Of warriors met for mortal fight;
But cause of terror, all unguessed,
Was fluttering in her gentle breast,
When, in their chairs of crimson placed,
The Dame and she the barriers graced.

XVIII.

Prize of the field, the young Buccleuch,
An English knight led forth to view;
Scarce rued the boy his present plight,
So much he longed to see the fight.
Within the lists, in knightly pride,
High Home and haughty Dacre ride;
Their leading staffs of steel they wield,
As marshals of the mortal field;
While to each knight their care assigned
Like vantage of the sun and wind:
Then heralds hoarse did loud proclaim,
In king and queen, and warden's name,
    That none, while lasts the strife,
Should dare, by look, or sign, or word,
Aid to a champion to afford,
    On peril of his life;
And not a breath the silence broke,
Till thus the alternate Heralds spoke:

XIX
ENGLISH HERALD.

Here standeth Richard of Musgrave,
   Good knight and true, and freely born,
Amends from Deloraine to crave,
   For foul despiteous scathe and scorn.
He sayeth, that William of Deloraine
   Is traitor false by Border laws;
This with his sword he will maintain,
   So help him God, and his good cause!

XX.
SCOTTISH HERALD.

Here standeth William of Deloraine,
Good knight and true, of noble strain,
Who sayeth, that foul treason's stain,
   Since he bore arms, ne'er soiled his coat,
   And that, so help him God above!
   He will on Musgrave's body prove,
He lyes most foully in his throat.
LORD DACRE.
Forward, brave champions, to the fight!
Sound trumpets!—
LORD HOME.
————God defend the right!—
Then, Teviot! how thine echoes rang,
When bugle-sound and trumpet-clang
   Let loose the mortal foes,
And in mid list, with shield poised high,
And measured step and wary eye,
   The combatants did close.

XXI.

Ill would it suit your gentle ear,
Ye lovely listeners, to hear
How to the axe the helms did sound,
And blood poured down from many a wound;
For desperate was the strife, and long,
And either warrior fierce and strong.
But, were each dame a listening knight,
I well could tell how warriors fight;
For I have seen war's lightning flashing,
Seen the claymore with bayonet clashing,
Seen through red blood the war-horse dashing,
And scorned, amid the reeling strife,
To yield a step for death or life.

XXII.

'Tis done, 'tis done! that fatal blow
    Has stretched him on the bloody plain;
He strives to rise—Brave Musgrave, no!
    Thence never shalt thou rise again!
He chokes in blood—some friendly hand
Undo the visor's barred band,
Unfix the gorget's iron clasp,
And give him room for life to gasp!—
O, bootless aid—haste, holy friar,
Haste, ere the sinner shall expire!
Of all his guilt let him be shriven,
And smooth his path from earth to heaven!

XXIII.

In haste the holy friar sped,
His naked foot was dyed with red,
    As through the lists he ran;
Unmindful of the shouts on high,
That hailed the conqueror's victory,
    He raised the dying man;
Loose waved his silver beard and hair,
As o'er him he kneeled down in prayer;
And still the crucifix on high
He holds before his darkening eye,
His faultering penitence to hear;
    Still props him from the bloody sod,
Still, even when soul and body part,
Pours ghostly comfort on his heart,
    And bids him trust in God!
Unheard he prays; the death pang's o'er!
Richard of Musgrave breathes no more.

XXIV.

As if exhausted in the fight,
Or musing o'er the piteous sight,
    The silent victor stands;
His beaver did he not unclasp,
Marked not the shouts, felt not the grasp
    Of gratulating hands.
When lo! strange cries of wild surprise,
Mingled with seeming terror, rise
    Among the Scottish bands;
And all, amid the throng'd array,
In panic haste gave open way
To a half-naked ghastly man,
Who downward from the castle ran;
He crossed the barriers at a bound,
    And wild and haggard looked around,

As dizzy, and in pain;
And all, upon the armed ground,
Knew William of Deloraine!
Each ladye sprung from seat with speed;
Vaulted each marshal from his steed;
"And who art thou," they cried,
"Who hast this battle fought and won?"
His plumed helm was soon undone —
"Cranstoun of Teviot-side!
For this fair prize I've fought and won," —
And to the Ladye led her son.

XXV.

Full oft the rescued boy she kissed,
And often pressed him to her breast;
For, under all her dauntless show,
Her heart had throbbed at every blow;
Yet not Lord Cranstoun deigned she greet,
Though low he kneeled at her feet. —
Me lists not tell what words were made,
What Douglas, Home, and Howard, said —
— For Howard was a generous foe —
And how the clan united prayed
The Ladye would the feud forego,
And deign to bless the nuptial hour
Of Cranstoun's Lord and Teviot's Flower.

XXVI.

She looked to river, looked to hill,
Thought on the Spirit's prophecy,
Then broke her silence stern and still, —
"Not you, but Fate, has vanquished me;
Their influence kindly stars may shower
On Teviot's tide and Branksome's tower,
For pride is quelled, and love is free."
She took fair Margaret by the hand,
Who, breathless, trembling, scarce might stand;
That hand to Cranstoun's lord gave she:
"As I am true to thee and thine,
Do thou be true to me and mine!
This clasp of love our bond shall be;
For this is your betrothing day,
And all these noble lords shall stay,
To grace it with their company."

XXVII.

All as they left the listed plain,
Much of the story she did gain;
How Cranstoun fought with Deloraine,

And of his Page, and of the Book,
Which from the wounded knight he took;
And how he sought her castle high,
That morn, by help of gramarye;
How, in Sir William's armour dight,
Stolen by his Page, while slept the knight,
He took on him the single fight.
But half his tale he left unsaid,
And linger'd till he joined the maid. —
Cared not the Ladye to betray
Her mystic arts in view of day;
But well she thought, ere midnight came,
Of that strange Page the pride to tame,
From his foul hands the Book to save,
And send it back to Michael's grave. —
Needs not to tell each tender word
'Twixt Margaret and 'twixt Cranstoun's lord;
Nor how she told of former woes,
And how her bosom fell and rose,
While he and Musgrave bandied blows—
Needs not these lovers' joys to tell;
One day, fair maids, you'll know them well.

XXVIII.

William of Deloraine, some chance
Had wakened from his deathlike trance;
    And taught that, in the listed plain,
Another, in his arms and shield,
Against fierce Musgrave axe did wield,
    Under the name of Deloraine.
Hence to the field, unarmed, he ran,
And hence his presence scared the clan,
Who held him for some fleeting wraith,[5]
And not a man of blood and breath.
    Not much this new ally he loved,
    Yet when he saw what hap had proved,
        He greeted him right heartilie:
    He would not waken old debate,
    For he was void of rancorous hate,
        Though rude, and scant of courtesy;
In raids he spilt but seldom blood,
Unless when men at arms withstood,
Or, as was meet, for deadly feud.
He ne'er bore grudge for stalwart blow,
Ta'en in fair fight from gallant foe:
    And so 'twas seen of him, e'en now,
        When on dead Musgrave he look'd down;
    Grief darkened on his rugged brow,

---

5   The spectral apparition of a living person. [Scott's footnote]

Though half-disguised with a frown;
And thus, while sorrow bent his head,
His foeman's epitaph he made.

XXIX.

"Now, Richard Musgrave, liest thou here!
    I ween, my deadly enemy;
For, if I slew thy brother dear,
    Thou slewest a sister's son to me;
And when I lay in dungeon dark,
    Of Naworth Castle, long months three,
Till ransom'd for a thousand mark,
    Dark Musgrave, it was long of thee.
And, Musgrave, could our fight be tried,
    And thou wert now alive, as I,
No mortal man should us divide,
    Till one, or both of us, did die:
Yet, rest thee God! for well I know,
I ne'er shall find a nobler foe!
In all the northern counties here,
Whose word is Snaffle, spur, and spear,[6]
Thou wert the best to follow gear.
'Twas pleasure, as we looked behind,
To see how thou the chase couldst wind,
Cheer the dark blood-hound on his way,
And with the bugle rouse the fray!
I'd give the lands of Deloraine,
Dark Musgrave were alive again."

XXX.

So mourned he, till Lord Dacre's band
Were bowning back to Cumberland.
They raised brave Musgrave from the field,
And laid him on his bloody shield;
On levelled lances, four and four,
By turns, the noble burden bore.
Before, at times, upon the gale,
Was heard the Minstrel's plaintive wail;
Behind, four priests, in sable stole,
Sung requiem for the warrior's soul:
Around, the horsemen slowly rode;
With trailing pikes the spearmen trod;
And thus the gallant knight they bore,
Through Liddesdale, to Leven's shore;
Thence to Holme Coltrame's lofty nave,
And laid him in his father's grave.

---

6   'The lands, that over Ouse to Berwick forth do bear / Have for their blazon had, the snafle,
    spur, and spear.' *Poly-Albion*, Song xxxiii. [Scott's footnote]

THE harp's wild notes, though hushed the song,
The mimic march of death prolong;
Now seems it far, and now a-near,
Now meets, and now eludes, the ear;
Now seems some mountain side to sweep,
Now faintly dies in valley deep;
Seems now as if the Minstrel's wail,
Now the sad requiem loads the gale;
Last, o'er the warrior's closing grave,
Rung the full choir in choral stave.

After due pause, they bade him tell,
Why he, who touch'd the harp so well,
Should thus, with ill-rewarded toil,
Wander a poor and thankless soil,
When the more generous southern land
Would well requite his skilful hand.

The Aged Harper, howsoe'er
His only friend, his harp, was dear,
Liked not to hear it rank'd so high
Above his flowing poesy:
Less liked he still, that scornful jeer
Misprised the land, he loved so dear;
High was the sound, as thus again
The Bard resumed his minstrel strain.

CANTO SIXTH

I.

BREATHES there the man, with soul so dead,
Who never to himself hath said,
    This is my own, my native land!
Whose heart hath ne'er within him burned,
As home his footsteps he hath turned,
    From wandering on a foreign strand!
If such there breathe, go, mark him well;
For him no Minstrel raptures swell;
High though his titles, proud his name,
Boundless his wealth as wish can claim;
Despite those titles, power, and pelf,
The wretch, concentred all in self,
Living, shall forfeit fair renown,
And, doubly dying, shall go down
To the vile dust, and whence he sprung,
Unwept, unhonour'd, and unsung.

II.

O Caledonia! stern and wild,
Meet nurse for a poetic child!
Land of brown heath and shaggy wood,
Land of the mountain and the flood,
Land of my sires! what mortal hand
Can e'er untie the filial band,
That knits me to thy rugged strand!
Still, as I view each well known scene,
Think what is now, and what hath been,
Seems as, to me, of all bereft,
Sole friends thy woods and streams were left;
And thus I love them better still,
Even in extremity of ill.
By Yarrow's streams still let me stray,
Though none should guide my feeble way;
Still feel the breeze down Ettricke break,
Although it chill my withered cheek;
Still lay my head by Teviot Stone,
Though there, forgotten and alone,
The Bard may draw his parting groan.

III.

Not scorned like me! to Branksome Hall
The Minstrels came, at festive call;
Trooping they came, from near and far,
The jovial priests of mirth and war;
Alike for feast and fight prepared,
Battle and banquet both they shared.

Of late, before each martial clan,
They blew their death-note in the van,
But now, for every merry mate,
Rose the Portcullis' iron grate;
They sound the pipe, they strike the string,
They dance, they revel, and they sing,
Till the rude turrets shake and ring.

IV.

Me lists not at this tide declare
    The splendour of the spousal rite,
How mustered in the chapel fair
    Both maid and matron, squire and knight;
Me lists not tell of owches rare,
Of mantles green, and braided hair,
And kirtles furred with miniver;
What plumage waved the altar round,
How spurs, and ringing chainlets, sound:
And hard it were for bard to speak
The changeful hue of Margaret's cheek;
That lovely hue, which comes and flies,
As awe and shame alternate rise!

V.

Some bards have sung, the Ladye high
Chapel or altar came not nigh;
Nor durst the rites of spousal grace,
So much she feared each holy place.
False slanders these — I trust right well
She wrought not by forbidden spell;
For mighty words and signs have power
O'er sprites in planetary hour:
Yet scarce I praise their venturous part,
Who tamper with such dangerous art.
    But this for faithful truth I say,
    The Ladye by the altar stood,
    Of sable velvet her array,
    And on her head a crimson hood,
With pearls embroidered and entwined,
Guarded with gold, with ermine lined;
A merlin sat upon her wrist
Held by a leash of silken twist.

VI.

The spousal rites were ended soon;
'Twas now the merry hour of noon,
And in the lofty-arched hall
Was spread the gorgeous festival:
Steward and squire, with heedful haste,
Marshalled the rank of every guest;

Pages, with ready blade, were there,
The mighty meal to serve and share:
O'er capon, heron-shew, and crane,
And princely peacock's gilded train,
And o'er the boar-head, garnish'd brave,
And cygnet from St. Mary's wave;
O'er ptarmigan and venison,
The priest had spoke his benison.
Then rose the riot and the din,
Above, beneath, without, within!
For, from the lofty balcony,
Rung trumpet, shalm, and psaltery:
Their clanging bowls old warriors quaffed,
Loudly they spoke, and loudly laughed;
Whispered young knights, in tone more mild,
To ladies fair, and ladies smiled.
The hooded hawks, high perched on beam,
The clamour joined with whistling scream,
And flapped their wings, and shook their bells,
In concert with the staghounds' yells.
Round go the flasks of ruddy wine,
From Bourdeaux, Orleans, or the Rhine;
Their tasks the busy sewers ply,
And all is mirth and revelry.

VII.

The Goblin Page, omitting still
No opportunity of ill,
Strove now, while blood ran hot and high,
To rouse debate and jealousy;
Till Conrad, lord of Wolfenstein,
By nature fierce, and warm with wine,
And now in humour highly cross'd,
About some steeds his band had lost,
High words to words succeeding still,
Smote, with his gauntlet, stout Hunthill;
A hot and hardy Rutherford,
Whom men called Dickon Draw-the-sword.
He took it on the Page's saye,
Hunthill had driven these steeds away.
Then Howard, Home, and Douglas rose,
The kindling discord to compose:
Stern Rutherford right little said,
But bit his glove, and shook his head.
A fortnight thence, in Inglewood,
Stout Conrad, cold, and drenched in blood,
His bosom gored with many a wound,
Was by a woodman's lyme-dog found;
Unknown the manner of his death,

Gone was his brand, both sword and sheath;
But ever from that time, 'twas said,
That Dickon wore a Cologne blade.

VIII.

The Dwarf, who feared his master's eye
Might his foul treachery espie,
Now sought the castle buttery,
Where many a yeoman, bold and free,
Revelled as merrily and well
As those, that sat in lordly selle.
Watt Tinlinn, there, did frankly raise
The pledge to Arthur Fire-the-braes;
And he, as by his breeding bound,
To Howard's merry-men sent it round.
To quit them, on the English side,
Red Roland Forster loudly cried,
"A deep carouse to yon fair bride!"
At every pledge, from vat and pail,
Foamed forth, in floods, the nut-brown ale;
While shout the riders every one,
Such day of mirth ne'er cheered their clan,
Since old Buccleuch the name did gain,
When in the cleuch the buck was ta'en.[1]

IX.

The wily Page, with vengeful thought,
    Remember'd him of Tinlinn's yew,
And swore, it should be dearly bought
    That ever he the arrow drew.
First, he the yeoman did molest,
With bitter gibe and taunting jest;
Told, how he fled at Solway strife,
And how Hob Armstrong cheered his wife;
Then, shunning still his powerful arm,
At unawares he wrought him harm;
From trencher stole his choicest cheer,
Dash'd from his lips his can of beer,
Then, to his knee sly creeping on,
With bodkin pierced him to the bone:
The venomed wound, and festering joint,
Long after rued that bodkin's point.
The startled yeoman swore and spurned,
And board and flagons overturned;
Riot and clamour wild began;
Back to the hall the urchin ran;
Took in a darkling nook his post,
And grinned and muttered, "Lost! lost! lost!"

---

1   An incident recounted in an endnote.

213

By this, the Dame, lest farther fray
Should mar the concord of the day,
Had bid the Minstrels tune their lay.
And first stept forth old Albert Graeme,
The Minstrel of that ancient name:
Was none who struck the harp so well,
Within the Land Debateable;
Well friended, too, his hardy kin,
Whoever lost, were sure to win;
They sought the beeves, that made their broth,
In Scotland and in England both.
In homely guise, as nature bade,
His simple song the Borderer said.

XI.
ALBERT GRÆME

It was an English ladye bright,
    The sun shines fair on Carlisle wall,
And she would marry a Scottish knight,
    For Love will still be lord of all![2]

Blithely they saw the rising sun,
    When he shone fair on Carlisle wall,
But they were sad ere day was done,
    Though Love was still the lord of all!

Her sire gave brooch and jewel fine,
    Where the sun shines fair on Carlisle wall,
Her brother gave but a flask of wine,
    For ire that Love was lord of all!

For she had lands, both meadow and lea,
    Where the sun shines fair on Carlisle wall,
And he swore her death, ere he would see
    A Scottish knight the lord of all!

XII.

That wine she had not tasted well,
    The sun shines fair on Carlisle wall;
When dead, in her true love's arms, she fell,
    For Love was still the lord of all!

He pierced her brother to the heart,
    Where the sun shines fair on Carlisle wall!
So perish all, would true love part,
    That Love may still be lord of all!

---

2   This burden is adopted, with some alteration, from an old Scottish song, beginning thus:
'She leaned her back against a thorn, / The sun shines fair on Carlisle wa'; / And there she
has her young babe born, / And the lyon shall be lord of a'.' [Scott's endnote]

And then he took the cross divine,
    Where the sun shines fair on Carlisle wall,
And died for her sake in Palestine,
    So Love was still the lord of all!

Now all ye lovers, that faithful prove,
    The sun shines fair on Carlisle wall,
    Pray for their souls who died for love,
    For Love shall still be lord of all!

                                        XIII.

As ended Albert's simple lay,
    Arose a bard of loftier port;
For sonnet, rhyme, and roundelay,
    Renowned in haughty Henry's court:
There rung thy harp, unrivalled long,
Fitztraver of the silver song!
    The gentle Surrey loved his lyre —
        Who has not heard of Surrey's fame?[3]
    His was the hero's soul of fire,
        And his the bard's immortal name,
And his was love, exalted high
By all the glow of chivalry.

                                        XIV.

They sought, together, climes afar,
    And oft, within some olive grove,
When evening came with twinkling star,
    They sung of Surrey's absent love.
His step the Italian peasant staid,
    And deemed, that spirits from on high,
Round where some hermit saint was laid,
    Were breathing heavenly melody;
So sweet did harp and voice combine,
To praise the name of Geraldine.

                                        XV.

Fitztraver! O what tongue may say
    The pangs thy faithful bosom knew,
When Surrey, of the deathless lay,
    Ungrateful Tudor's sentence slew?
Regardless of the tyrant's frown,
His harp called wrath and vengeance down.
He left, for Naworth's iron towers,
Windsor's green glades, and courtly bowers,
And, faithful to his patron's name,

---

3   Henry Howard, Earl of Surrey, poet and courtier, beheaded on Tower Hill in 1546. Scott's
endnote says that the story told about him in the song is a traditional one.

With Howard still Fitztraver came;
Lord William's foremost favourite he,
And chief of all his minstrelsy.

XVI.
FITZTRAVER.

Twas All-souls' eve, and Surrey's heart beat high;
　　He heard the midnight-bell with anxious start,
Which told the mystic hour, approaching nigh,
　　When wise Cornelius promised, by his art,
To show to him the ladye of his heart,
　　Albeit betwixt them roared the ocean grim;
Yet so the sage had hight to play his part,
　　That he should see her form in life and limb,
And mark, if still she loved, and still she thought of him.

XVII.

Dark was the vaulted room of gramarye,
　　To which the wizard led the gallant knight,
Save that before a mirror, huge and high,
　　A hallowed taper shed a glimmering light
On mystic implements of magic might,
　　On cross, and character, and talisman,
And almagest, and altar, nothing bright:
　　For fitful was the lustre, pale and wan,
As watch-light by the bed of some departing man.

XVIII.

But soon within that mirror, huge and high,
　　Was seen a self-emitted light to gleam;
And forms upon its breast the earl 'gan spy,
　　Cloudy and indistinct, as feverish dream;
Till, slow arranging, and defined, they seem
　　To form a lordly and a lofty room,
Part lighted by a lamp with silver beam,
　　Placed by a couch of Agra's silken loom,
And part by moonshine pale, and part was hid in gloom.

XIX.

Fair all the pageant—but how passing fair
　　The slender form, which lay on couch of Ind!
O'er her white bosom strayed her hazel hair,
　　Pale her dear cheek, as if for love she pined;
All in her night-robe loose, she lay reclined,
　　And, pensive, read from tablet eburnine,
Some strain, that seemed her inmost soul to find—
　　That favoured strain was Surrey's raptured line,
That fair and lovely form, the Lady Geraldine.

XX.

Slow rolled the clouds upon the lovely form,
    And swept the goodly vision all away
So royal envy rolled the murky storm
    O'er my beloved Master's glorious day.
Thou jealous, ruthless tyrant! Heaven repay
    On thee, and on thy children's latest line,
The wild caprice of thy despotic sway,
    The gory bridal bed, the plundered shrine,
The murder'd Surrey's blood, the tears of Geraldine!

XXI.

Both Scots, and Southern chiefs, prolong
Applauses of Fitztraver's song;
These hated Henry's name as death,
And those still held the ancient faith. —
Then, from his seat, with lofty air,
Rose Harold, bard of brave St. Clair;
St. Clair, who, feasting high at Home,
Had with that lord to battle come.
Harold was born where restless seas
Howl round the storm-swept Orcades;
Where erst St. Clairs held princely sway
O'er isle and islet, strait and bay;
Still nods their palace to its fall,
Thy pride and sorrow, fair Kirkwall! —
Thence oft he mark'd fierce Pentland rave,
As if grim Odin rode her wave;
And watched, the whilst, with visage pale,
And throbbing heart, the struggling sail;
For all of wonderful and wild
Had rapture for the lonely child.

XXII.

And much of wild and wonderful,
In these rude isles, might Fancy cull;
For thither came, in times afar,
Stern Lochlin's sons of roving war,
The Norsemen, trained to spoil and blood,
Skilled to prepare the raven's food;
Kings of the main their leaders brave,
Their barks the dragons of the wave.
And there, in many a stormy vale,
The Scald had told his wondrous tale;
And many a Runic column high
Had witnessed grim idolatry.
And thus had Harold, in his youth,
Learned many a Saga's rhime uncouth,
Of that Sea-Snake, tremendous curled,

Whose monstrous circle girds the world;
Of those dread Maids, whose hideous yell
Maddens the battle's bloody swell;
Of chiefs, who, guided through the gloom
By the pale death-lights of the tomb,
Ransacked the graves of warriors old,
Their faulchions wrenched from corpses' hold,
Waked the deaf tomb with war's alarms,
And bade the dead arise to arms!
With war and wonder all on flame,
To Roslin's bowers young Harold came,
Where, by sweet glen and greenwood tree,
He learned a milder minstrelsy;
Yet something of the Northern spell
Mixed with the softer numbers well.

XXIII.
HAROLD.

O listen, listen, ladies gay!
   No haughty feat of arms I tell;
Soft is the note, and sad the lay,
   That mourns the lovely Rosabelle.

  —"Moor, moor the barge, ye gallant crew!
   And, gentle ladye, deign to stay!
Rest thee in Castle Ravensheuch,
   Nor tempt the stormy firth to-day.

"The blackening wave is edged with white:
   To inch and rock the sea-mews fly;
The fishers have heard the Water Sprite,
   Whose screams forbode that wreck is nigh.

"Last night the gifted seer did view
   A wet shroud swathed round ladye gay;
Then stay thee, Fair, in Ravensheuch:
   Why cross the gloomy firth to-day?" —

"'Tis not because Lord Lindesay's heir
   To-night at Roslin leads the ball,
But that my Ladye-mother there
   Sits lonely in her castle-hall.

"'Tis not because the ring they ride,
   And Lindesay at the ring rides well,
But that my sire the wine will chide,
   If 'tis not filled by Rosabelle."

O'er Roslin all that dreary night,
  A wondrous blaze was seen to gleam;
'Twas broader than the watch-fire light,
  And redder than the bright moon-beam.

It glared on Roslin's castled rock,
  It ruddied all the copse-wood glen;
'Twas seen from Dryden's groves of oak,
  And seen from caverned Hawthornden.

Seemed all on fire that chapel proud,
  Where Roslin's chiefs uncoffined lie,
Each Baron, for a sable shroud,
  Sheathed in his iron panoply.

Seemed all on fire within, around,
  Deep sacristy and altar's pale;
Shone every pillar foliage-bound,
  And glimmered all the dead men's mail.

Blazed battlement and pinnet high,
  Blazed every rose-carved buttress fair —
So still they blaze, when fate is nigh
  The lordly line of high St. Clair.

There are twenty of Roslin's barons bold
  Lie buried within that proud chapelle;
Each one the holy vault doth hold —
  But the sea holds lovely Rosabelle!

And each St. Clair was buried there,
  With candle, with book, and with knell;
But the sea-caves rung, and the wild winds sung,
  The dirge of lovely Rosabelle.

XXIV.

So sweet was Harold's piteous lay,
  Scarce marked the guests the darkened hall,
Though, long before the sinking day,
  A wondrous shade involved them all:
It was not eddying mist or fog,
Drained by the sun for fen or bog;
  Of no eclipse had sages told;
And yet, as it came on apace,
Each one could scarce his neighbour's face,
  Could scarce his own stretched hand, behold.
A secret horror checked the feast,
And chilled the soul of every guest;
Even the high Dame stood half aghast,

She knew some evil on the blast;
The elfish Page fell to the ground,
And, shuddering, muttered, "Found! found! found!"

XXV.

Then sudden through the darkened air
    A flash of lightning came;
So broad, so bright, so red the glare,
    The castle seemed on flame:
Glanced every rafter of the hall,
Glanced every shield upon the wall,
Each trophied beam, each sculptured stone,
Were instant seen, and instant gone;
Full through the guests' bedazzled band
Resistless flashed the levin-brand,
And filled the hall with smouldering smoke,
As on the elvish Page it broke;
    It broke, with thunder long and loud,
    Dismayed the brave, appalled the proud,
        From sea to sea the larum rung;
    On Berwick wall, and at Carlisle withal,
        To arms the startled warders sprung.
When ended was the dreadful roar,
The elvish Dwarf was seen no more!

XXVI.

Some heard a voice in Branksome Hall,
Some saw a sight, not seen by all;
That dreadful voice was heard by some,
Cry, with loud summons, "GYLBIN, COME!"
    And on the spot where burst the brand,
        Just where the Page had flung him down,
    Some saw an arm, and some a hand,
        And some the waving of a gown.
The guests in silence prayed and shook,
And terror dimmed each lofty look:
But none of all the astonished train
Was so dismayed as Deloraine;
His blood did freeze, his brain did burn,
'Twas feared his mind would ne'er return;
    For he was speechless, ghastly, wan,
    Like him, of whom the story ran,
    Who spoke the spectre-hound in Man.[4]
        At length, by fits, he darkly told,
        With broken hint, and shuddering cold —
        That he had seen, right certainly,
    A shape with amice wrapped around,
    With a wrought Spanish baldric bound,

---

4   An endnote fills in the ghost story of Peel Castle.

Like pilgrim from beyond the sea;
And knew — but how it mattered not —
It was the wizard, Michael Scott.

XXVII.

The anxious crowd, with horror pale,
All trembling, heard the wondrous tale;
   No sound was made, no word was spoke,
   Till noble Angus silence broke;
    And he a solemn sacred plight
   Did to St Bryde of Douglas make,
   That he a pilgrimage would take
   To Melrose Abbey, for the sake
    Of Michael's restless sprite.
Then each, to ease his troubled breast,
To some blessed saint his prayers addressed:
Some to St Modan made their vows,
Some to St Mary of the Lowes,
Some to the Holy Rood of Lisle,
Some to our Lady of the Isle;
Each did his patron witness make,
That he such pilgrimage would take,
And monks should sing, and bells should toll,
All for the weal of Michael's soul.
While vows were ta'en, and prayers were prayed,
'Tis said the noble Dame, dismayed,
Renounced, for aye, dark magic's aid.

XXVIII.

Nought of the bridal will I tell,
Which after in short space befel;
Nor how brave sons and daughters fair
Blessed Teviot's Flower, and Cranstoun's heir:
After such dreadful scene, 'twere vain
To wake the note of mirth again;
   More meet it were to mark the day
    Of penitence and prayer divine,
   When pilgrim-chiefs, in sad array,
    Sought Melrose' holy shrine.

XXIX.

With naked foot, and sackcloth vest,
And arms enfolded on his breast,
   Did every pilgrim go;
The standers-by might hear uneath,
Footstep, or voice, or high-drawn breath,
   Through all the lengthened row:
No lordly look, nor martial stride,
Gone was their glory, sunk their pride,

Forgotten their renown;
Silent and slow, like ghosts, they glide
To the high altar's hallowed side,
    And there they kneeled them down:
Above the suppliant chieftains wave
The banners of departed brave.
Beneath the lettered stones were laid
The ashes of their fathers dead;
From many a garnished nich around,
Stern saints, and tortured martyrs, frowned.

XXX.

And slow up the dim aisle afar,
With sable cowl and scapular,
And snow-white stoles, in order due,
The holy fathers, two and two,
    In long procession came;
Taper, and host, and book they bare,
And holy banner, flourished fair
    With the Redeemer's name.
Above the prostrate pilgrim band
The mitred abbot stretched his hand,
    And bless'd them as they kneeled;
With holy cross he signed them all,
And prayed they might be sage in hall,
    And fortunate in field.
Then mass was sung, and prayers were said,
And solemn requiem for the dead;
And bells tolled out their mighty peal,
For the departed spirit's weal;
And ever in the office close
The hymn of intercession rose;
And far the echoing aisles prolong
The awful burthen of the song,
    DIES IRÆ, DIES ILLA,
    SOLVET SÆCLUM IN FAVILLA;[5]
While the pealing organ rung;
    Were it meet with sacred strain
    To close my lay, so light and vain,
Thus the holy fathers sung.

HYMN FOR THE DEAD.

That day of wrath, that dreadful day,
When heaven and earth shall pass away,
What power shall be the sinner's stay?
How shall he meet that dreadful day?

---

5   'Day of wrath, this day / that will dissolve the world to ashes': from the Requiem Mass of
     the Catholic church.

When, shriveling like a parched scroll,
The flaming heavens together roll;
When louder yet, and yet more dread,
Swells the high trump that wakes the dead;

O! on that day, that wrathful day,
When man to judgment wakes from clay,
By THOU the trembling sinner's stay,
Though heaven and earth shall pass away!

————

HUSH'D is the harp—the Minstrel gone.
And did he wander forth alone?
Alone, in indigence and age,
To linger out his pilgrimage?
No—close beneath proud Newark's tower,
Arose the Minstrel's lowly bower;
A simple hut; but there was seen
The little garden hedged with green,
The cheerful hearth, and lattice clean.
There sheltered wanderers, by the blaze,
Oft heard the tale of other days;
For much he loved to ope his door,
And give the aid he begged before.
So passed the winter's day—but still,
When summer smiled on sweet Bowhill,
And July's eve, with balmy breath,
Waved the blue-bells on Newark heath;
When throstles sung in Hare-head shaw,
And corn was green on Carterhaugh,
And flourished, broad, Blackandro's oak,
The aged Harper's soul awoke!
Then would he sing achievements high,
And circumstance of chivalry,
Till the rapt traveller would stay,
Forgetful of the closing day;
And noble youths, the strain to hear,
Forsook the hunting of the deer;
And Yarrow, as he rolled along,
Bore burden to the Minstrel's song.

ANNALS OF THE PARISH;

OR THE

CHRONICLE OF DALMAILING

DURING THE MINISTRY OF

THE REV. MICAH BALWHIDDER

WRITTEN BY HIMSELF.

WRITTEN AND ARRANGED

BY THE AUTHOR OF "THE AYRSHIRE LEGATEES," &c[1]

EDINBURGH:
PRINTED FOR WILLIAM BLACKWOOD, EDINBURGH;
AND T. CADELL, STRAND, LONDON.

1821.

INTRODUCTION.

IN the same year, and on the same day of the same month, that his Sacred Majesty King George, the third of the name, came to his crown and kingdom, I was placed and settled as the minister of Dalmailing.[2] When about a week thereafter this was known in the parish, it was thought a wonderful thing, and every body spoke of me and the new king as united in our trusts and temporalities, marvelling how the same should come to pass, and thinking the hand of Providence was in it, and that surely we were pre-ordained to fade and flourish in fellowship together; which has really been the case, for in the same season that his Most Excellent Majesty, as he was very properly styled in the proclamations for the general fasts and thanksgivings, was set by as a precious vessel which had received a crack or a flaw, and could only be serviceable in the way of an ornament,[3] I was obliged, by reason of age and the growing infirmities of my recollection, to consent to the earnest entreaties of the Session,[4] and to accept of Mr Amos to be my helper. I was long reluctant to do so, but the great respect that my people had for me, and the love that I bore towards them, over and above the sign that

---

1   That is, John Galt. *The Ayrshire Legatees* had been serialised in *Blackwood's Edinburgh Magazine* the previous year.

2   George III acceded to the throne on the sudden death of his grandfather, George II, on 25th October 1760.

3   By late 1810, George's recurring mental illness made him permanently incapable of carrying out his duties as monarch. Parliament therefore conferred the status of Prince Regent on his eldest son in early 1811. The Regent took his father's constitutional place until the latter's death in 1820 allowed his coronation as George IV in his own right. The period 1810–1820 is often referred to as 'The Regency'.

4   The Kirk Session is the body, consisting of the elders elected by the congregation, to which the minister is answerable in the day-to-day running of a Church of Scotland parish.

was given to me in the removal of the royal candlestick from its place, worked upon my heart and understanding, and I could not stand out. So, on the last Sabbath of the year 1810, I preached my last sermon, and it was a moving discourse. There were few dry eyes in the kirk that day, for I had been with the aged from the beginning—the young considered me as their natural pastor—and my bidding them all farewell was, as when of old among the heathen, an idol was taken away by the hands of the enemy.

At the close of the worship, and before the blessing, I addressed them in a fatherly manner, and although the kirk was fuller than ever I saw it before, the fall of a pin might have been heard—at the conclusion there was a sobbing and much sorrow. I said,

"My dear friends, I have now finished my work among you forever. I have often spoken to you from this place the words of truth and holiness, and, had it been in poor frail human nature to practise the advice and counselling that I have given in this pulpit to you, there would not need to be any cause for sorrow on this occasion—the close and latter end of my ministry. But, nevertheless, I have no reason to complain, and it will be my duty to testify, in that place where I hope we are all one day to meet again, that I found you a docile and a tractable flock, far more than at first I could have expected. There are among you still a few, but with grey heads and feeble hands now, that can remember the great opposition that was made to my placing, and the stout part they themselves took in the burly, because I was appointed by the patron;[5] but they have lived to see the error of their way, and to know that preaching is the smallest portion of the duties of a faithful minister. I may not, my dear friends, have applied my talent in the pulpit so effectually as perhaps I might have done, considering the gifts that it pleased God to give me in that way, and the education that I had in the Orthodox University of Glasgow, as it was in the time of my youth, nor can I say that, in the works of peace-making and charity, I have done all that I should have done. But I have done my best, studying no interest but the good that was to rise according to the faith in Christ Jesus.

"To my young friends I would, as a parting word, say, look to the lives and conversation of your parents[6]—they were plain, honest, and devout Christians, fearing God and honouring the King. They believed the Bible was the word of God, and when they practised its precepts, they found, by the good that came from them, that it was truly so. They bore in mind the tribulation and persecution of their forefathers for righteousness-sake, and were thankful for the quiet and protection of the government in their day and generation.[7] Their land was tilled with industry, and they ate the bread of carefulness with a contented spirit, and, verily, they had the reward of well-doing even in this world, for they beheld on all sides the blessing of God upon the nation, and

---

5   The 'patron' was a local landowner who inherited the right in civil law, as set down in the Patronage Act of 1712, to appoint a minister to a local parish. According to the Presbyterian system of church government established for the Kirk in the seventeenth century, however, this ought to have been the right of the parish Session alone. Balwhidder's patron is the Laird of Breadland, he tells us at the end of the next chapter.

6   Conversation here means 'behaviour', as used in the King James bible's version of Paul's epistles; e.g. 'Let no man despise thy youth; but be thou an example of the believers, in word, in conversation, in charity, in spirit, in faith, in purity' (I Timothy 4.12).

7   The 'forefathers' mentioned here are the 'Covenanters' of the seventeenth century's civil wars (see Introduction): the movement was particularly staunch in the south west of Scotland, including Ayrshire, where Rev. Balwhidder has his fictional parish. In Balwhidder's following words, Presbyterianism is the 'ark of the tabernacle', defence of which alone justifies revolt against the state; in contrast to the 'hypothetical' *social* politics troubling Dalmailing in the early nineteenth century.

the tree growing, and the plough going, where the banner of the oppressor was planted of old, and the war-horse trampled in the blood of martyrs. Reflect on this, my young friends, and know, that the best part of a Christian's duty in this world of much evil, is to thole[8] and suffer with resignation, as lang as it is possible for human nature to do. I do not counsel passive obedience; that is a doctrine that the Church of Scotland can never abide; but the divine right of resistance, which, in the days of her trouble, she so bravely asserted against popish and prelatic usurpations, was never resorted to till the attempt was made to remove the ark of the tabernacle from her. I therefore counsel you, my young friends, no to lend your ears to those that trumpet forth their hypothetical politics, but to believe that the laws of the land are administered with a good intent, till in your own homes and dwellings ye feel the presence of the oppressor—then, and not till then, are ye free to gird your loins for battle—and woe to him, and woe to the land where that is come to, if the sword be sheathed till the wrong be redressed.

"As for you, my old companions, many changes have we seen in our day, but the change that we ourselves are soon to undergo will be the greatest of all. We have seen our bairns grow to manhood[9]—we have seen the beauty of youth pass away—we have felt our backs become unable for the burthen, and our right hand forget its cunning—Our eyes have become dim, and our heads grey—we are now tottering with short and feckless steps towards the grave;[10] and some, that should have been here this day, are bed-rid, lying, as it were, at the gates of death, like Lazarus at the threshhold of the rich man's door, full of ails and sores, and having no enjoyment but in the hope that is in hereafter.[11] What can I say to you but farewell! Our work is done—we are weary and worn out, and in need of rest—may the rest of the blessed be our portion!—and, in the sleep that all must sleep, beneath the cold blanket of the kirkyard grass, and on that clay pillow where we must shortly lay our heads, may we have pleasant dreams, till we are awakened to partake of the everlasting banquet of the saints in glory."

When I had finished, there was for some time a great solemnity throughout the kirk, and, before giving the blessing, I sat down to compose myself, for my heart was big, and my spirit oppressed with sadness.

As I left the pulpit, all the elders stood on the steps to hand me down, and the tear was in every eye, and they helped me into the session-house; but I could not speak to them, nor them to me. Then Mr Dalziel, who was always a composed and sedate man, said a few words of prayer, and I was comforted therewith, and rose to go home to the manse; but in the church-yard all the congregation was assembled, young and old, and they made a lane for me to the back-yett[12] that opened into the manse-garden—Some of them put out their hands and touched me as I passed, followed by the elders, and some of them wept. It was as if I was passing away, and to be no more—verily, it was the reward of my ministry—a faithful account of which, year by year, I now sit down, in the evening of my days, to make up, to the end that I may bear witness to the work of a beneficent Providence, even in the narrow sphere of my parish, and the concerns of that flock of which it was His most gracious pleasure to make me the unworthy shepherd.

---

8   Thole (Sc.): endure.
9   Bairns (Sc.): children.
10   Feckless: throughout this text in the older sense of 'feeble', without any hint of the modern sense of 'irresponsible, shiftless' (*OED*).
11   The Lazarus referred to is the exemplary figure of Jesus's parable in Luke 16.19–31, who suffers in this life to be rewarded in the next; not the dead man resurrected by Jesus in John 11–12.
12   Yett (Sc.): gate.

CHAPTER I.—YEAR 1760.

The placing of Mr Balwhidder—The resistance of the parishioners—Mrs Malcolm, the widow—Mr Balwhidder's marriage.

THE An. Dom. one thousand seven hundred and sixty,[13] was remarkable for three things in the parish of Dalmailing.—First and foremost, there was my placing; then the coming of Mrs Malcolm with her five children to settle among us; and next, my marriage upon my own cousin, Miss Betty Lanshaw, by which the account of this year naturally divides itself into three heads or portions.

First, of the placing.—It was a great affair; for I was put in by the patron, and the people knew nothing whatsoever of me, and their hearts were stirred into strife on the occasion, and they did all that lay within the compass of their power to keep me out, insomuch, that there was obliged to be a guard of soldiers to protect the presbytery;[14] and it was a thing that made my heart grieve when I heard the drum beating and the fife playing as we were going to the kirk. The people were really mad and vicious, and flung dirt upon us as we passed, and reviled us all, and held out the finger of scorn at me; but I endured it with a resigned spirit, compassionating their wilfulness and blindness. Poor old Mr Kilfuddy of the Braehill got such a clash of glar on the side of his face,[15] that his eye was almost extinguished.

When we got to the kirk door, it was found to be nailed up, so as by no possibility to be opened. The serjeant of the soldiers wanted to break it, but I was afraid that the heritors[16] would grudge and complain of the expence of a new door, and I supplicated him to let it be as it was; we were, therefore, obligated to go in by a window, and the crowd followed us, in the most unreverent manner, making the Lord's house like an inn on a fair day, with their grievous yellyhooing. During the time of the psalm and the sermon, they behaved themselves better, but when the induction came on, their clamour was dreadful; and Thomas Thorl the weaver, a pious zealot in that time, he got up and protested, and said, "Verily, verily, I say unto you, he that entereth not by the door into the sheepfold, but climbeth up some other way, the same is a thief and a robber."[17] And I thought I would have a hard and sore time of it with such an outstrapolous people. Mr Given, that was then the minister of Lugton, was a jocose man,[18] and would have his joke even at a solemnity. When the laying of the hands upon me was a-doing, he could not get near enough to put on his, but he stretched out his staff and touched my head, and said, to the great diversion of the rest,—"This will do well enough, timber to timber;" but it was an unfriendly saying of Mr Given, considering the time and the place, and the temper of my people.

After the ceremony, we then got out at the window, and it was a heavy day to me, but we went to the manse, and there we had an excellent dinner, which Mrs Watts of the new inns of Irville prepared at my request, and sent her chaise-driver to serve, for he was

---

13   An. Dom., sometimes Ann. Dom.: Anno Domini, i.e. in the year of our Lord.

14   The Presbytery is the level of church government above the Session: the ministers of all the churches in a particular area, along with their elders. Such a body would have attended a particular church for the induction of a new minister there, and participated in the 'laying on of hands' that confirmed him in his post.

15   Clash of glar (Sc.): lump of mud.

16   The heritors are the local property-owners who pay for the upkeep of the church, manse, and parish school, and pay the stipend of the minister and the school-teacher.

17   Thomas is quoting John 10.1.

18   Jocose: full of jokes.

likewise her waiter, she having then but one chaise, and that no often called for. [19]

But, although my people received me in this unruly manner, I was resolved to cultivate civility among them; and therefore, the very next morning I began a round of visitations; but oh, it was a steep brae that I had to climb, and it needed a stout heart.[20] For I found the doors in some places barred against me; in others, the bairns, when they saw me coming, ran crying to their mothers, "Here's the feckless Mess-John;"[21] and then when I went in into the houses, their parents would no ask me to sit down, but with a scornful way, said, "Honest man, what's your pleasure here?" Nevertheless, I walked about from door to door, like a dejected beggar, till I got the almous deed[22] of a civil reception, and who would have thought it, from no less a person than the same Thomas Thorl that was so bitter against me in the kirk on the foregoing day.

Thomas was standing at the door with his green duffle apron, and his red Kilmarnock nightcap — I mind him as well as if it was but yesterday — and he had seen me going from house to house, and in what manner I was rejected, and his bowels were moved, and he said to me in a kind manner, "Come in, sir, and ease yoursel; this will never do, the clergy are God's gorbies,[23] and for their Master's sake it behoves us to respect them. There was no ane in the whole parish mair against you than mysel, but this early visitation is a symptom of grace that I couldna have expectit from a bird out the nest of patronage." I thanked Thomas, and went in with him, and we had some solid conversation together, and I told him that it was not so much the pastor's duty to feed the flock, as to herd them well; and that although there might be some abler with the head than me, there was na a he within the bounds of Scotland more willing to watch the fold by night and by day. And Thomas said he had not heard a mair sound observe for some time, and that if I held to that doctrine in the poopit, it would na be lang till I would work a change. — "I was mindit," quoth he, "never to set my foot within the kirk door while you were there; but to testify, and no to condemn without a trial, I'll be there next Lord's day, and egg my neighbours to be likewise, so ye'll no have to preach just to the bare walls and the laird's family."[24]

I have now to speak of the coming of Mrs Malcolm. She was the widow of a Clyde shipmaster, that was lost at sea with his vessel. She was a genty body, calm and methodical. From morning to night she sat at her wheel, spinning the finest lint,[25] which suited well with her pale hands. She never changed her widow's weeds, and she was aye as if she had just been ta'en out of a bandbox. The tear was often in her e'e when the bairns were at the school; but when they came home, her spirit was lighted up with gladness, although, poor woman, she had many a time very little to give them. They were, however, wonderful well-bred things, and took with thankfulness whatever she

---

19   'Irville' is Galt's fictionalised version of his birthplace, Irvine, the Royal Burgh and port on the Ayrshire coast. A chaise is a small horse-drawn carriage, available (in this case) to rent.

20   Balwhidder adapts the traditional Scottish exhortation to effort: 'pit a stout hert tae a stey brae' (put a stout heart to a steep slope).

21   Mess John (Sc.): 'A jocular or contemptuous name for a Scottish Presbyterian minister' (*DOST*). 'Mess' is from 'Master', as in 'Master of Arts': Church of Scotland clergy traditionally took the MA before studying divinity.

22   Almous deed: alms, charitable donation.

23   His bowels were moved: that is, he was moved with pity. This usage is borrowed from the King James bible; e.g. I John 3.17: 'But whoso hath this world's good, and seeth his brother have need, and shutteth up his bowels [of compassion] from him, how dwelleth the love of God in him?' Gorbies (Sc.): chicks or nestlings.

24   Laird (Sc.): landowner; in this case, the patron who has appointed Balwhidder.

25   A genty body (Sc.): a 'neat, dainty, graceful' (*SND*) person. Lint: flax (for linen).

set before them, for they knew that their father, the breadwinner, was away, and that she had to work sore for their bit and drap.[26] I dare say, the only vexation that ever she had from any of them, on their own account, was when Charlie, the eldest laddie, had won fourpence at pitch and toss at the school, which he brought home with a proud heart to his mother. I happened to be daunrin' bye at the time,[27] and just looked in at the door to say gude night: It was a sad sight. There was she sitting with the silent tear on her cheek, and Charlie greeting as if he had done a great fault,[28] and the other four looking on with sorrowful faces. Never, I am sure, did Charlie Malcolm gamble after that night.

I often wondered what brought Mrs Malcolm to our clachan, instead of going to a populous town, where she might have taken up a huxtry-shop, as she was but of a silly constitution,[29] the which would have been better for her than spinning from morning to far in the night, as if she was in verity drawing the thread of life. But it was, no doubt, from an honest pride to hide her poverty; for when her daughter Effie was ill with the measles—the poor lassie was very ill—nobody thought she could come through, and when she did get the turn, she was for many a day a heavy handful;—our session being rich, and nobody on it but cripple Tammy Daidles, that was in that time known through all the country side for begging on a horse, I thought it my duty to call upon Mrs Malcolm, in a sympathizing way, and offer her some assistance, but she refused it.[30]

"No, sir," said she, "I canna take help from the poor's-box, although it's very true that I am in great need; for it might hereafter be cast up to my bairns,[31] whom it may please God to restore to better circumstances when I am no to see't; but I would fain borrow five pounds, and if, sir, you will write to Mr Maitland, that is now the Lord Provost of Glasgow, and tell him that Marion Shaw would be obliged to him for the lend of that soom, I think he will not fail to send it."[32]

I wrote the letter that night to Provost Maitland, and, by the retour of the post, I got an answer, with twenty pounds for Mrs Malcolm, saying, "that it was with sorrow he heard so small a trifle could be serviceable." When I took the letter and the money, which was in a bank-bill, she said, "this is just like himsel'." She then told me, that Mr Maitland had been a gentleman's son of the east country, but driven out of his father's house, when a laddie, by his step-mother; and that he had served as a servant lad with her father, who was the Laird of Yillcogie,[33] but ran through his estate, and left her, his only daughter, in little better than beggary with her auntie, the mother of Captain Malcolm, her husband that was. Provost Maitland in his servitude had ta'en a notion of her, and when he recovered his patrimony, and had become a great Glasgow merchant, on hearing how she was left by her father, he offered to marry her, but she had promised herself to her cousin the Captain, whose widow she was. He then married a rich lady, and in time grew, as he was, Lord Provost of the city; but his letter with the twenty pounds to me, shewed that he had not forgotten his first love. It was a short, but a well-written letter, in a fair hand of write, containing much of the true gentleman; and Mrs Malcolm said, "Who knows but out of the regard he once had for their mother, he may do something for my five helpless orphans."

---

26   Bit and drap (Sc.): food and drink.
27   Dauner, dawner (Sc.): stroll or saunter.
28   Greet (Sc.): weep.
29   Clachan (Sc.): hamlet. Huxtry-shop: general store. Silly: delicate.
30   The Session was responsible for distributing poor-relief to the needy in the parish.
31   Be cast up to: bring shame on.
32   Soom (Sc.): sum. The Lord Provost of a Scottish town or city is the equivalent of a mayor.
33   'Yillcogie' means 'ale-jug' in Scots.

Thirdly, upon the subject of taking my cousin, Miss Betty Lanshaw, for my first wife, I have little to say. It was more out of a compassionate habitual affection, than the passion of love. We were brought up by our grandmother in the same house, and it was a thing spoken of from the beginning, that Betty and me were to be married. So when she heard that the Laird of Breadland had given me the presentation of Dalmailing, she began to prepare for the wedding. And as soon as the placing was well over, and the manse in order, I gaed to Ayr,[34] where she was, and we were quietly married, and came home in a chaise, bringing with us her little brother Andrew, that died in the East Indies, and he lived and was brought up by us.

Now, this is all, I think, that happened in that year, worthy of being mentioned, except that at the sacrament, when old Mr Kilfuddie was preaching in the tent,[35] it came on such a thunder-plump, that there was not a single soul stayed in the kirkyard to hear him; for the which he was greatly mortified, and never after came to our preachings.

CHAPTER II.—YEAR 1761.

The great increase of smuggling—Mr Balwhidder disperses a tea-drinking party of gossips—He records the virtues of Nanse Banks, the school-mistress—The servant of a military man, who had been prisoner in France, comes into the parish, and opens a dancing-school.

IT was in this year that the great smuggling trade corrupted all the west coast, especially the Laigh Lands about the Troon and the Loans.[36] The tea was going like the chaff, the brandy like well-water, and the wastrie of all things was terrible. There was nothing minded but the riding of cadgers by day,[37] and excisemen by night—and battles between the smugglers and the King's men, both by sea and land. There was a continual drunkenness and debauchery; and our Session, that was but on the lip of this whirlpool of iniquity, had an awful time o't. I did all that was in the power of nature to keep my people from the contagion; I preached sixteen times from the text, Render to Cæsar the things that are Cæsar's.[38] I visited and I exhorted; I warned and I prophesied; I told them, that, although the money came in like sclate stones, it would go like the snow off the dyke.[39] But for all I could do, the evil got in among us, and we had no less than three contested bastard bairns upon our hands at one time, which was a thing never heard of in a parish of the shire of Ayr, since the Reformation. Two of the bairns, after no small sifting and searching, we got fathered at last; but the third, that was by Meg Glaiks, and given to one Rab Rickerton, was utterly refused, though the fact was not denied; but he was a termagant fellow,[40] and snappit his fingers at the elders. The

34　Gaed (Sc.): went.
35　In the tent: outdoors. The sacrament is Holy Communion, traditionally held three or four times a year, sometimes in services bringing together several parish congregations, necessitating the move outside the church at which it was held.
36　The flat lands around the Troon promontory and Loans, a village a few miles inland; the area is half-way between Ayr and Irvine.
37　Wastrie: extravagance. Cadgers: peddlers (both Sc.).
38　Jesus's injunction to his followers when asked about the lawfulness of paying Roman taxes: this text is from Mark 12.17, but the same advice appears in Matthew 22.21 and Luke 20.25.
39　Sclate stones (Sc.): roofing slates. 'Like snaw aff a dyke' (wall) is an conventional Scottish simile for transience.
40　Fact: in this text, usually has the old sense of evil deed or crime. Termagant: violent,

next day he listed in the Scotch Greys,[41] who were then quartered at Ayr, and we never heard more of him, but thought he had been slain in battle, till one of the parish, about three years since, went up to London to lift a legacy from a cousin, that died among the Hindoos;[42] when he was walking about, seeing the curiosities, and among others Chelsea Hospital,[43] he happened to speak to some of the invalids, who found out from his tongue that he was a Scotchman; and speaking to the invalids, one of them, a very old man, with a grey head, and a leg of timber, inquired what part of Scotland he was come from; and when he mentioned my parish, the invalid gave a great shout, and said he was from the same place himself; and who should this old man be, but the very identical Rab Rickerton, that was art and part in Meg Glaik's disowned bairn. Then they had a long converse together, and he had come through many hardships, but had turned out a good soldier; and so, in his old days, was an in-door pensioner, and very comfortable; and he said that he had, to be sure, spent his youth in the devil's service, and his manhood in the king's, but his old age was given to that of his Maker, which I was blithe and thankful to hear; and he inquired about many a one in the parish, the blooming and the green of his time, but they were all dead and buried; and he had a contrite and penitent spirit, and read his Bible every day, delighting most in the Book of Joshua, the Chronicles, and the Kings.

Before this year, the drinking of tea was little known in the parish, saving among a few of the heritors' houses on a Sabbath evening, but now it became very rife, yet the commoner sort did not like to let it be known that they were taking to the new luxury, especially the elderly women, who, for that reason, had their ploys in out-houses and by-places, just as the witches lang syne had their sinful possets and galravitchings;[44] and they made their tea for common in the pint-stoup, and drank it out of caps and luggies,[45] for there were but few among them that had cups and saucers. Well do I remember one night in harvest, in this very year, as I was taking my twilight dawner aneath the hedge along the back side of Thomas Thorl's yard, meditating on the goodness of Providence, and looking at the sheaves of victual on the field, that I heard his wife, and two three other carlins, with their bohea in the inside of the hedge, and no doubt but it had a lacing of the conek, for they were all cracking like pen-guns.[46] But I gave them a sign by a loud host, that Providence sees all, and it skailed the bike;[47] for I heard them, like guilty creatures, whispering and gathering up their truck-pots and trenchers, and cowering away home.

It was in this year that Patrick Dilworth, (he had been schoolmaster of the parish from the time, as his wife said, of Anna Regina,[48] and before the Rexes came to the

---

quarrelsome.

41   The Scots Greys were the Royal North British Dragoons, a cavalry regiment in the British Army. To list is to *enlist*.

42   From its takeover of Bengal in the 1760s, service in the East India Company became a popular career for ambitious Scots with more education than money. Such service could be very lucrative, but also, and more often, fatal, as the climate and diseases of the subcontinent took their toll.

43   The home for pensioned soldiers in West London.

44   Ploys: parties; lang syne: long ago; posset: hot milk curdled with ale or wine; galravitchings: drinking sessions (all Sc.).

45   Stoup: pitcher; caps and luggies: wooden bowls (all Sc.).

46   Carlin (Sc.): old woman; Bohea: a type of black tea; Conek: 'cogniac' (Galt's footnote); crack (Sc.): chat or gossip; pen-gun: pop-gun, made from a quill pen. 'To crack like a pen-gun' was a (punning) expression meaning 'to be very talkative'.

47   Host: cough; skaill: scatter; bike: wasp's nest (all Sc.).

48   Queen Anne reigned 1702–1714, the last Stuart monarch.

crown,) was disabled by a paralytic, and the heritors, grudging the cost of another school-master as long as he lived, would not allow the Session to get his place supplied, which was a wrong thing, I must say of them; for the children of the parishioners were obliged, therefore, to go to the neighbouring towns for their schooling, and the custom was to take a piece of bread and cheese in their pockets for dinner, and to return in the evening always voracious for more, the long walk helping the natural crave of their young appetites. In this way Mrs Malcolm's two eldest laddies, Charlie and Robert, were wont to go to Irville, and it was soon seen that they kept themselves aloof from the other callans in the clachan, and had a genteeler turn than the grulshy bairns of the cotters.[49] Her bit lassies, Kate and Effie, were better off; for, some years before, Nanse Banks had taken up a teaching in a garret-room of a house, at the corner where John Bayne has biggit the sclate-house for his grocery-shop.[50] Nanse learnt them reading and working stockings, and how to sew the semplar, for twal-pennies a-week.[51] She was a patient creature, well cut out for her calling, with bleer eyn, a pale face, and a long neck, but meek and contented withall, tholing the dule of this world with a Christian submission of the spirit;[52] and her garret-room was a cordial of cleanliness, for she made the scholars set the house in order, time and time about, every morning; and it was a common remark for many a day, that the lassies, who had been at Nanse Banks's school, were always well spoken of, both for their civility, and the trigness of their houses, when they were afterwards married.[53] In short, I do not know, that in all the long epoch of my ministry, any individual body did more to improve the ways of the parishioners, in their domestic concerns, than did that worthy and innocent creature, Nanse Banks, the schoolmistress; and she was a great loss when she was removed, as it is to be hoped, to a better world; but anent this I shall have to speak more at large hereafter.[54]

It was in this year that my patron, the Laird of Breadland, departed this life, and I preached his funeral-sermon; but he was none beloved in the parish, for my people never forgave him for putting me upon them, although they began to be more on a familiar footing with myself. This was partly owing to my first wife, Betty Lanshaw, who was an active through-going woman, and wonderfu' useful to many of the cotters' wives at their lying-in; and when a death happened among them, her helping hand, and any thing we had at the Manse, was never wanting; and I went about myself to the bed-sides of the frail, leaving no stone unturned to win the affections of my people, which, by the blessing of the Lord, in process of time, was brought to a bearing.

But a thing happened in this year, which deserves to be recorded, as manifesting what effect the smuggling was beginning to take in the morals of the country side. One Mr Macskipnish, of Highland parentage, who had been a valet-de-chambre with a Major in the campaigns, and taken a prisoner with him by the French, he having come home in a cartel,[55] took up a dancing-school at Irville, the which art he had learnt in the genteelest fashion, in the mode of Paris, at the French court. Such a thing as a dancing-

---

49   Callan, callant: lad, teenage boy; grulshy: 'sturdy, fat and clumsy-looking' (*SND*); cotter (more usually cottar): farm-tenant (all Sc.).

50   Biggit: built; sclate-house: house with a slated roof, as opposed to the thatch more usual in country districts (both Sc.)

51   Semplar: sampler; twal: twelve (both Sc.).

52   Eyn: eyes; dule: grief, suffering (both Sc.).

53   Trig (Sc.): neat and tidy.

54   Anent (Sc.): with respect to.

55   A 'cartel' was an exchange of prisoners; the 'campaigns' referred to are those of the Seven Years' War (1756–63), being fought in Europe, North America, the Caribbean and India by Britain and its German allies against France and Spain.

school had never, in the memory of man, been known in our country side; and there was such a sound about the steps and cottillions of Mr Macskipnish, that every lad and lass, that could spare time and siller, went to him, to the great neglect of their work.[56] The very bairns on the loan, instead of their wonted play, gaed linking and louping in the steps of Mr Macskipnish, who was, to be sure, a great curiosity, with long spindle legs, his breast shot out like a duck's, and his head powdered and frizzled up like a tappit-hen.[57] He was, indeed, the proudest peacock that could be seen, and he had a ring on his finger, and when he came to drink his tea at the Breadland, he brought no hat on his head, but a droll cockit thing under his arm, which, he said, was after the manner of the courtiers at the petty suppers of one Madam Pompadour, who was, at that time, the concubine of the French king.

I do not recollect any other remarkable thing that happened in this year. The harvest was very abundant, and the meal so cheap, that it caused a great defect in my stipend, so that I was obligated to postpone the purchase of a mahogany scrutoire for my study, as I had intended.[58] But I had not the heart to complain of this; on the contrary, I rejoiced thereat, for what made me want my scrutoire till another year, had carried blitheness into the hearth of the cotter, and made the widow's heart sing with joy; and I would have been an unnatural creature, had I not joined in the universal gladness, because plenty did abound.

CHAPTER III.—YEAR 1762.

Havoc produced by the small-pox—Charles Malcolm is sent off a cabin-boy, on a voyage to Virginia—Mizy Spaewell dies on Halloween—Tea begins to be admitted at the Manse, but the Minister continues to exert his authority against smuggling.

THE third year of my ministry was long held in remembrance for several very memorable things. William Byres of the Loan-head had a cow that calved two calves at one calving; Mrs Byres, the same year, had twins, male and female; and there was such a crop on his fields, testifying that the Lord never sends a mouth into the world without providing meat for it. But what was thought a very daunting sign of something, happened on the Sacrament Sabbath at the conclusion of the action sermon, when I had made a very suitable discourse.[59] The day was tempestuous, and the wind blew with such a pith and birr, that I thought it would have twirled the trees in the kirk-yard out by the roots, and, blowing in this manner, it tirled the thack from the rigging of the Manse stable;[60] and the same blast that did that, took down the lead that was on the kirk-roof, which hurled off, as I was saying, at the conclusion of the action sermon, with such a dreadful sound, as the like was never heard, and all the congregation thought that it betokened a mutation to me. However, nothing particular happened to me; but the small-pox came in among the weans of the parish, and the smashing that it made of the poor bits

---

56 Cottillion, usually cotillion: a type of dance, of French origin. Siller (Sc.): silver: i.e. money.
57 Loan: village green; linking and louping: gliding and jumping; tappit-hen: in this case, a hen with a crest on its head (all Sc.).
58 Scrutoire: writing-desk. Part of a minister's income came from the produce of agricultural land attached to the manse, called the glebe. A plentiful harvest is good for the cottars who grow their crops primarily to eat; but the resultant fall in prices means less income for Balwhidder, who is selling most of his on the market.
59 The 'action sermon' is that preached on the Sunday of Holy Communion; in distinction to the 'preparation sermon' preached the Sunday before.
60 Birr: vigour; tirl: strip; thack: thatch; rigging: roof (all Sc.).

o' bairns was indeed woeful.[61]

One Sabbath, when the pestilence was raging, I preached a sermon about Rachel weeping for her children,[62] which Thomas Thorl, who was surely a great judge of good preaching, said "was a monument of divinity whilk searched the heart of many a parent that day;" a thing I was well pleased to hear, for Thomas, as I have related at length, was the most zealous champion against my getting the parish; but, from this time, I set him down in my mind for the next vacancy among the elders. Worthy man! it was not permitted him to arrive at that honour. In the fall of that year he took an income in his legs,[63] and could no go about, and was laid up for the remainder of his days, a perfect Lazarus, by the fireside. But he was well supported in his affliction. In due season, when it pleased Him that alone can give and take, to pluck him from this life, as the fruit ripened and ready for the gathering, his death, to all that knew him, was a gentle dispensation, for truly he had been in sore trouble.

It was in this year that Charlie Malcolm, Mrs Malcolm's eldest son, was sent to be a cabin-boy in the Tobacco trader, a three masted ship, that sailed between Port-Glasgow and Virginia in America.[64] She was commanded by Captain Dickie, an Irville man; for at that time the Clyde was supplied with the best sailors from our coast, the coal-trade with Ireland being a better trade for bringing up good mariners than the long voyages in the open sea;[65] which was the reason, as I often heard said, why the Clyde shipping got so many of their men from our country-side. The going to sea of Charlie Malcolm was, on divers accounts, a very remarkable thing to us all, for he was the first that ever went from our parish, in the memory of man, to be a sailor, and every body was concerned at it, and some thought it was a great venture of his mother to let him, his father having been lost at sea. But what could the forlorn widow do? She had five weans and little to give them; and, as she herself said, he was aye in the hand of his Maker, go where he might, and the will of God would be done in spite of all earthly wiles and devices to the contrary.

On the Monday morning, when Charlie was to go away to meet the Irville carrier on the road, we were all up, and I walked by myself from the Manse to the clachan to bid him farewell, and I met him just coming from his mother's door, as blithe as a bee, in his sailor's dress, with a stick, and a bundle tied in a Barcelona silk handkerchief hanging o'er his shoulder, and his two little brothers were with him, and his sisters, Kate and Effie, looking out from the door all begreeten;[66] but his mother was in the house, praying to the Lord to protect her orphan, as she afterwards told me. All the weans of the clachan were gathered at the kirk-yard yett to see him pass, and they gave him three shouts as he was going bye; and every body was at their doors, and said something encouraging to him; but there was a great laugh when auld Mizy Spaewell came hirpling with her bachle in her hand, and flung it after him for gude luck.[67] Mizy had a wonderful faith in freats, and was just an oracle of sagacity at expounding dreams, and bodes of every sort and description—besides, she was reckoned one of

---

61 Weans: children; smashing, smash, smashery: destruction (both Sc.).
62 In Jeremiah 31.15, alluded to in the gospels at Matthew 2.18.
63 Income (Sc.): 'An illness or infirmity not due to any apparent external cause' (*SND*). A *financial* income is an 'incoming' in Galt's Scots.
64 The tobacco trade with North America was the basis of Glasgow's rise as a metropolis in the eighteenth century, decades before it became an industrial centre.
65 Irvine's economy as a port was based on the trade in coal from the Scottish coalfields across the North Channel to Ireland.
66 Begreeten, more usually begrutten: tear-stained.
67 Hirple: limp, hobble; bachle, more usually bauchle: an old shoe (both Sc.).

the best howdies in her day;[68] but by this time she was grown frail and feckless, and she died the same year on Hallowe'en, which made every body wonder, that it should have so fallen out for her to die on Hallowe'en.

Shortly after the departure of Charlie Malcolm, the Lady of Breadland, with her three daughters, removed to Edinburgh, where the young laird, that had been my pupil, was learning to be an advocate, and the Breadland house was set to Major Gilchrist, a nabob from India;[69] but he was a narrow ailing man, and his maiden-sister, Miss Girzie, was the scrimpetest creature that could be; so that, in their hands, all the pretty policy of the Breadlands,[70] that had cost a power of money to the old laird, that was my patron, fell into decay and disorder; and the bonny yew trees, that were cut into the shape of peacocks, soon grew out of all shape, and are now doleful monuments of the Major's tack,[71] and that of Lady Skim-milk, as Miss Girzie Gilchrist, his sister, was nicknamed by every ane that kent her.

But it was not so much on account of the neglect of the Breadland, that the incoming of Major Gilchrist was to be deplored. The old men, that had a light labour in keeping the policy in order, were thrown out of bread, and could do little; and the poor women, that whiles got a bit and a drap from the kitchen of the family, soon felt the change, so that, by little and little, we were obligated to give help from the Session; insomuch, that before the end of the year, I was necessitated to preach a discourse on almsgiving, specially for the benefit of our own poor, a thing never before known in the parish.

But one good thing came from the Gilchrists to Mrs Malcolm. Miss Girzie, whom they called Lady Skim-milk, had been in a very penurious way as a seamstress, in the Gorbals of Glasgow, while her brother was making the fortune in India, and she was a clever needle-woman—none better, as it was said; and she having some things to make, took Kate Malcolm to help her in the coarse work; and Kate, being a nimble and birky thing,[72] was so useful to the lady, and the complaining man the Major, that they invited her to stay with them at the Bread-land for the winter, where, although she was holden to her seam from morning to night, her food lightened the hand of her mother, who, for the first time since her coming into the parish, found the penny for the day's dark more than was needed for the meal-basin;[73] and the tea-drinking was beginning to spread more openly, insomuch, that by the advice of the first Mrs Balwhidder, Mrs Malcolm took in tea to sell, and in this way was enabled to eke something to the small profits of her wheel. Thus the tide, that had been so long ebbing to her, began to turn; and here I am bound in truth to say, that although I never could abide the smuggling, both on its own account, and the evils that grew therefrom to the country-side, I lost some of my dislike to the tea, after Mrs Malcolm began to traffic in it, and we then had it for our breakfast in the morning at the Manse, as well as in the afternoon. But what I thought most of it for, was, that it did no harm to the head of the drinkers, which was not always the case with the possets that were in fashion before. There is no meeting now in the summer evenings, as I remember often happened in my younger days, with decent ladies coming home with red faces, tozy and cosh from a posset masking;[74] so, both for its temperance, and on account of Mrs Malcolm's sale, I refrained from

68   Freats or freits: superstitions; howdie: midwife (both Sc.).
69   Set: leased; nabob: a rich returnee from India, from Urdu *nawab* meaning viceroy.
70   Scrimpet, usually scrimpit (Sc.): mean, niggardly (*SND* 'scrimp' IV.3). Policy: ornamental grounds.
71   Tack (Sc.): here, period of a lease.
72   Birky (Sc.): lively, alert.
73   Day's dark, usually darg: day's work.
74   Tozy: tipsy, flushed; cosh: merry; masking: brewing (all Sc.).

the November in this year to preach against tea; but I never lifted the weight of my displeasure from off the smuggling trade, until it was utterly put down by the strong hand of government.

There was no other thing of note in this year, saving only that I planted in the garden the big pear-tree, which had the two great branches that we call the Adam and Eve. I got the plant, then a sapling, from Mr Graft, that was Lord Eglesham's head-gardener; and he said it was, as indeed all the parish now knows well, a most juicy sweet pear, such as was not known in Scotland till my lord brought down the father plant from the King's garden in London, in the forty-five, when he went up to testify his loyalty to the House of Hanover.[75]

CHAPTER IV.—YEAR 1763.

Charles Malcolm's return from sea—Kate Malcolm is taken to live with Lady Macadam—Death of the first Mrs Balwhidder.

THE An. Dom. 1763, was, in many a respect, a memorable year, both in public and in private. The King granted peace to the French,[76] and Charlie Malcolm, that went to sea in the Tobacco trader, came home to see his mother. The ship, after being at America, had gone down to Jamaica, an island in the West Indies, with a cargo of live lumber, as Charlie told me himself, and had come home with more than a hundred and fifty hoggits of sugar, and sixty-three puncheons full of rum;[77] for she was, by all accounts, a stately galley, and almost two hundred tons in the burden, being the largest vessel then sailing from the creditable town of Port-Glasgow. Charlie was not expected; and his coming was a great thing to us all, so I will mention the whole particulars.

One evening, towards the gloaming, as I was taking my walk of meditation, I saw a brisk sailor laddie coming towards me. He had a pretty green parrot, sitting on a bundle, tied in a Barcelona silk handkerchief, which he carried with a stick over his shoulder, and in this bundle was a wonderful big nut, such as no one in our parish had ever seen. It was called a cocker-nut. This blithe callant was Charlie Malcolm, who had come all the way that day his leaful lane,[78] on his own legs from Greenock, where the Tobacco trader was then 'livering her cargo. I told him how his mother, and his brothers, and his sisters were all in good health, and went to convoy him home; and as we were going along he told me many curious things, and he gave me six beautiful yellow limes, that he had brought in his pouch all the way across the seas, for me to make a bowl of punch with, and I thought more of them than if they had been golden guineas, it was so mindful of the laddie.

When we got to the door of his mother's house, she was sitting at the fire-side, with her three other bairns at their bread and milk, Kate being then with Lady Skimmilk at the Breadland sewing. It was between the day and dark, when the shuttle stands still till the lamp is lighted. But such a shout of joy and thankfulness as rose from that hearth, when Charlie went in! The very parrot, ye would have thought, was a participator, for

---

75   By 'the forty-five' Balquidder refers to the Jacobite rebellion of 1745: see Introduction.
76   The Treaty of Paris which ended the Seven Years' War left Britain the world's dominant imperial power.
77   Hoggit: hogsheads; puncheon: a size of barrel. Both the tobacco and sugar were of course grown on plantations worked by slave labour.
78   His leaful lane (Sc): quite alone (SND 'Lief' 4).

he beast gied a skraik that made my whole head dirl;[79] and the neighbours came flying and flocking to see what was the matter, for it was the first parrot ever seen within the bounds of the parish, and some thought it was but a foreign hawk, with a yellow head and green feathers.

In the midst of all this, Effie Malcolm had run off to the Breadland for her sister Kate, and the two lassies came flying breathless, with Miss Girzie Gilchrist, the Lady Skimmilk pursuing them like desperation, or a griffon, down the avenue; for Kate, in her hurry, had flung down her seam, a new printed gown, that she was helping to make, and it had fallen into a boyne of milk that was ready for the creaming,[80] by which ensued a double misfortune to Miss Girzie, the gown being not only ruined, but licking up the cream. For this, poor Kate was not allowed ever to set her face in the Breadland again.

When Charlie Malcolm had staid about a week with his mother, he returned to his birth in the Tobacco trader,[81] and shortly after his brother Robert was likewise sent to serve his time to the sea, with an owner that was master of his own bark, in the coal trade at Irville. Kate, who was really a surprising lassie for her years, was taken off her mother's hands by the old Lady Macadam, that lived in her jointure house,[82] which is now the Cross Keys Inns. Her ladyship was a woman of high-breeding, her husband having been a great general, and knighted by the King for his exploits; but she was lame, and could not move about in her dining-room without help, so hearing from the first Mrs Balwhidder how Kate had done such an unatonable deed to Miss Girzie Gilchrist, she sent for Kate, and finding her sharp and apt, she took her to live with her as a companion. This was a vast advantage, for the lady was versed in all manner of accomplishments, and could read and speak French with more ease than any professor at that time would do in the College of Glasgow; and she had learnt to sew flowers on satin, either in a nunnery abroad, or a boarding-school in England, and took pleasure in teaching Kate all she knew, and how to behave herself like a lady.

In the summer of this year, old Mr Patrick Dilworth, that had so long been doited with the paralytics,[83] died, and it was a great relief to my people, for the heritors could no longer refuse to get a proper schoolmaster; so we took on trial Mr Loremore, who has ever since the year after, with so much credit to himself, and usefulness to the parish, been schoolmaster, session-clerk, and precentor[84]—a man of great mildness, and extraordinary particularity. He was then a very young man, and some objection was made on account of his youth, to his being session-clerk, especially as the smuggling immorality still gave us much trouble in the making up of irregular marriages; but his discretion was greater than could have been hoped for from his years; and after a twelvemonth's probation in the capacity of schoolmaster, he was installed in all the offices that had belonged to his predecessor, old Mr Patrick Dilworth that was.

But the most memorable thing that befell among my people this year, was the burning of the lint-mill on the Lugton Water,[85] which happened, of all the days of

---

79   Gied: gave; skraik: screech (of birds); dirl: vibrate, ring (all Sc.).
80   Boyne (Sc.): 'a plate for pouring milk to let cream rise' (SND).
81   Birth: i.e. berth.
82   Among the wealthy, the terms of a marriage agreement would settle a 'jointure', that is, an income or property or both, on the bride, for her support in the event of her husband's death.
83   Doited (Sc.): of unsound mind.
84   The Kirk regarded musical instruments inside the church as sinful; in the absence of an organ, the precentor's job was to lead the singing. This is still the practice in some churches in the islands today.
85   That is, a water-powered 'scutching' mill for removing the bark from the flax fibres. Linen

the year, on the very self-same day that Miss Girzie Gilchrist, better known as Lady Skim-milk, hired the chaise from Mrs Watts of the New Inns of Irville, to go with her brother the Major, to consult the faculty in Edinburgh,[86] concerning his complaints. For, as the chaise was coming by the mill, William Huckle, the miller that was, came flying out of the mill like a demented man, crying fire!—and it was the driver that brought the melancholy tidings to the clachan—and melancholy they were; for the mill was utterly destroyed, and in it not a little of all that year's crop of lint in our parish. The first Mrs Balwhidder lost upwards of twelve stone, which we had raised on the glebe with no small pains, watering it in the drouth, as it was intended for sarking to ourselves, and sheets and napery.[87] A great loss indeed it was, and the vexation thereof had a visible effect on Mrs Balwhidder's health, which from the spring had been in a dwining way.[88] But for it, I think she might have wrestled through the winter; however, it was ordered otherwise, and she was removed from mine to Abraham's bosom on Christmas day, and buried on Hogmanae, for it was thought uncanny to have a dead corpse in the house on the new-year's day. She was a worthy woman, studying with all her capacity to win the hearts of my people towards me—in the which good work she prospered greatly; so that when she died, there was not a single soul in the parish that was not contented with both my walk and conversation.[89] Nothing could be more peaceable than the way we lived together. Her brother Andrew, a fine lad, I had sent to the College at Glasgow, at my own cost, and when he came out to the burial, he staid with me a month, for the Manse after her decease was very dull, and it was during this visit that he gave me an inkling of his wish to go out to India as a cadet, but the transactions anent that fall within the scope of another year—as well as what relates to her headstone, and the epitaph in metre, which I indicted myself thereon; John Truel the mason carving the same, as may be seen in the kirk-yard, where it wants a little reparation and setting upright, having settled the wrong way when the second Mrs Balwhidder was laid by her side.—But I must not here enter upon an anticipation.

CHAPTER V.—YEAR 1764.

He gets a marble headstone for Mrs Balwhidder, and writes an Epitaph for it—He is afflicted with melancholy, and thinks of writing a book—Nichol Snipe the gamekeeper's device when reproved in church.

THIS year well deserved the name of the monumental year in our parish; for the young Laird of the Breadland, that had been my pupil, being learning to be an advocate among the faculty in Edinburgh, with his lady mother, who had removed thither with the young ladies her daughters, for the benefit of education, sent out to be put up in the kirk, under the loft over the family vault, an elegant marble headstone, with an epitaph engraven thereon, in fair Latin, setting forth many excellent qualities which the old laird, my patron that was, the inditer thereof, said he possessed. I say the inditer, because it could no have been the young laird himself, although he got the credit o't on the stone, for he was nae daub in my aught at the Latin or any other language.[90]

---

was still spun and woven by hand in cottages, power looms not spreading until the 1820s. Lint-mills were very prone to burning down.

86   That is, the medical faculty.

87   Drouth: drought; sarking: linen for shirts etc. (all Sc.).

88   Dwine (Sc.): pine or waste away.

89   Walk: here, 'manner of behaviour, conduct of life' (*OED* IV.18).

90   Nae daub in my aught: James Kinsley, editor of the Oxford World's Classics edition of

However, he might improve himself at Edinburgh, where a' manner of genteel things were then to be got at an easy rate, and doubtless, the young laird got a probationer at the College to write the epitaph; but I have often wondered sin' syne, how he came to make it in Latin, for assuredly his dead parent, if he could have seen it, could not have read a single word o't, notwithstanding it was so vaunty about his virtues,[91] and other civil and hospitable qualifications.

The coming of the laird's monumental stone had a great effect on me, then in a state of deep despondency, for the loss of the first Mrs Balwhidder; and I thought I could not do a better thing, just by way of diversion in my heavy sorrow, than to get a well-shapen headstone made for her—which, as I have hinted at in the record of the last year, was done and set up. But a headstone without an epitaph, is no better than a body without the breath of life in't; and so it behoved me to make a posey for the monument,[92] the which I conned and pondered upon for many days. I thought as Mrs Balwhidder, worthy woman as she was, did not understand the Latin tongue, it would not do to put on what I had to say, in that language, as the laird had done—nor indeed would it have been easy, as I found upon the experimenting, to tell what I had to tell in Latin, which is naturally a crabbed language, and very difficult to write properly. I therefore, after mentioning her age and the dates of her birth and departure, composed in sedate poetry, the following epitaph, which may yet be seen on the tomb-stone.

EPITAPH.

A lovely Christian, spouse, and friend,
Pleasant in life, and at her end. —
A pale consumption dealt the blow
That laid her here, with dust below.
Sore was the cough that shook her frame;
That cough her patience did proclaim —
And as she drew her latest breath,
She said, "The Lord is sweet in death."
O pious reader, standing by,
Learn like this gentle one to die.
The grass doth grow and fade away,
And time runs out by night and day;
The King of Terrors has command
To strike us with his dart in hand.
Go where we will by flood or field,
He will pursue and make us yield.
But though to him we must resign
The vesture of our part divine,
There is a jewel in our trust,
That will not perish in the dust,
A pearl of price, a precious gem,
Ordain'd for Jesus' diadem;
Therefore, be holy while you can,

this novel, glosses this as 'no adept in my estimation' (Oxford 1986, p.219), but there is no support for this in *SND*.

91   Sin syne: since then; vaunty: proud, boastful (both Sc.).
92   Posey: Balwhidder means 'poesy', poetry.

And think upon the doom of man.
Repent in time and sin no more,
That when the strife of life is o'er,
On wings of love your soul may rise,
To dwell with angels in the skies,
Where psalms are sung eternally,
And martyrs ne'er again shall die;
But with the saints still bask in bliss,
And drink the cup of blessedness.

This was greatly thought of at the time, and Mr Loremore, who had a nerve for poesy himself in his younger years, was of opinion, that it was so much to the purpose and suitable withal, that he made his scholars write it out for their examination copies, at the reading whereof before the heritors, when the examination of the school came round, the tear came into my eye, and every one present sympathised with me in my great affliction for the loss of the first Mrs Balwhidder.

Andrew Lanshaw, as I have recorded, having come from the Glasgow College to the burial of his sister, my wife that was, staid with me a month to keep me company; and staying with me, he was a great cordial, for the weather was wet and sleety, and the nights were stormy, so that I could go little out, and few of the elders came in, they being at that time old men in a feckless condition, not at all qualified to warsle with the blasts of winter.[93] But when Andrew left me to go back to his classes, I was eirie and lonesome,[94] and but for the getting of the monument ready, which was a blessed entertainment to me in these dreary nights, with consulting anent the shape of it with John Truel, and meditating on the verse for the epitaph, I might have gone altogether demented. However, it pleased HIM, who is the surety of the sinner, to help me through the Slough of Despond,[95] and to get my feet on a fair land, establishing my way thereon.

But the work of the monument, and the epitaph, could not endure for a constancy, and after it was done, I was again in great danger of sinking into the hypochonderies a second time. However, I was enabled to fight with my affliction, and by and by, as the spring began to open her green lattice, and to set out her flower-pots to the sunshine, and the time of the singing of birds was come, I became more composed, and like myself, so I often walked in the fields, and held communion with nature, and wondered at the mysteries thereof.

On one of these occasions, as I was sauntering along the edge of Eglesham-wood, looking at the industrious bee going from flower to flower, and the idle butterfly, that layeth up no store, but perisheth ere it is winter, I felt as it were a spirit from on high descending upon me, a throb at my heart, and a thrill in my brain, and I was transported out of myself, and seized with the notion of writing a book—but what it should be about, I could not settle to my satisfaction: Sometimes I thought of an orthodox poem, like Paradise Lost, by John Milton, wherein I proposed to treat more at large of Original Sin, and the great mystery of Redemption; at others, I fancied that a connect treatise on the efficacy of Free Grace,[96] would be more taking; but although I

---

93   Wastle (Sc.): wrestle.
94   Eirie, usually eerie (Sc.): gloomy, dismal, melancholy (*SND* 3). In this sense, there is no association with the supernatural.
95   Slough of Despond: a bog, representing despair, traversed by John Bunyan's allegorical hero Christian in *The Pilgrim's Progress* (1678).
96   Connect: systematic. Balwhidder's proposed theme, the ability of God's grace alone to

made divers beginnings in both subjects, some new thought ever came into my head, and the whole summer passed away, and nothing was done. I therefore postponed my design of writing a book till the winter, when I would have the benefit of the long nights. Before that, however, I had other things of more importance to think about: My servant lasses, having no eye of a mistress over them, wastered every thing at such a rate, and made such a galravitching in the house,[97] that, long before the end of the year, the year's stipend was all spent, and I did not know what to do. At lang and length I mustered courage to send for Mr Auld, who was then living, and an elder. He was a douce and discreet man,[98] fair and well-doing in the world, and had a better handful of strong common sense than many even of the heritors. So I told him how I was situate, and conferred with him, and he advised me, for my own sake, to look out for another wife, as soon as decency would allow, which, he thought, might very properly be after the turn of the year, by which time the first Mrs Balwhidder would be dead more than twelve months; and when I mentioned my design to write a book, he said, (and he was a man of good discretion,) that the doing of the book was a thing that would keep, but wasterful servants were a growing evil; so, upon his counselling, I resolved not to meddle with the book till I was married again, but employ the interim, between then and the turn of the year, in looking out for a prudent woman to be my second wife, strictly intending, as I did perform, not to mint a word about my choice,[99] if I made one, till the whole twelve months and a day, from the date of the first Mrs Balwhidder's interment, had run out.

In this the hand of Providence was very visible, and lucky for me it was that I had sent for Mr Auld when I did send, as the very week following, a sound began to spread in the parish, that one of my lassies had got herself with bairn, which was an awful thing to think had happened in the house of her master, and that master a minister of the Gospel. Some there were, for backbiting appertaineth to all conditions, that jealoused and wondered if I had not a finger in the pye;[100] which, when Mr Auld heard, he bestirred himself in such a manful and godly way in my defence, as silenced the clash,[101] telling that I was utterly incapable of any such thing, being a man of a guileless heart, and a spiritual simplicity, that would be ornamental in a child. We then had the latheron summoned before the Session,[102] and was not long of making her confess, that the father was Nichol Snipe, Lord Glencairn's game-keeper; and both her and Nichol were obligated to stand in the kirk,[103] but Nichol was a graceless reprobate, for he came with two coats, one buttoned behind him, and another buttoned before him, and two wigs of my lord's, lent him by the valet-de-chamer; the one over his face, and the other in the right way; and he stood with his face to the church-wall. When I saw him from the pu'-pit, I said to him—"Nichol, you must turn your face towards me!" At the which, he turned round to be sure, but there he presented the same show as his back. I was confounded, and did not know what to say, but cried out, with a voice of anger—"Nichol, Nichol! if ye had been a' back, ye would nae hae been there

---

97   Galravitch, usually gilravage (Sc.): 'to indulge in high living' (*SND*).
98   Douce (Sc.): 'Sedate, sober, quiet, respectable' (*SND*).
99   Mint (Sc.): hint, imply.
100   Jealouse, usually jalouse (Sc.): suspect. Nothing to do with the modern meaning of 'jealousy'.
101   Clash (Sc.): here, gossip, scandal.
102   Latheron, laidron (Sc.): here, slattern.
103   That is, stand at the 'stool of repentance', to be publicly rebuked by the minister on a succession of Sundays as a punishment for fornication.

this day;"[104] which had such an effect on the whole congregation, that the poor fellow suffered afterwards more derision, than if I had rebuked him in the manner prescribed by the Session.

This affair, with the previous advice of Mr Auld, was, however, a warning to me, that no pastor of his parish should be long without a helpmate. Accordingly, as soon as the year was out, I set myself earnestly about the search for one, but as the particulars fall properly within the scope and chronicle of the next year, I must reserve them for it; and I do not recollect that any thing more particular befell in this, excepting that William Mutchkins, the father of Mr Mutchkins, the great spirit-dealer in Glasgow, set up a change house in the clachan, which was the first in the parish, and which, if I could have helped, it would have been the last; for it was opening a howf to all manner of wickedness,[105] and was an immediate get and offspring of the smuggling trade, against which I had so set my countenance. But William Mutchkins himself was a respectable man, and no house could be better ordered than his change. At a stated hour he made family worship, for he brought up his children in the fear of God and the Christian religion; and although the house was full, he would go into the customers, and ask them if they would want any thing for half an hour, for that he was going to make exercise with his family; and many a wayfaring traveller has joined in the prayer. There is no such thing, I fear, now-a-days, of publicans entertaining travellers in this manner.

CHAPTER VI.—YEAR 1765.

Establishment of a whisky distillery—He is again married to Miss Lizy Kibbock—Her industry in the dairy—Her example diffuses a spirit of industry through the parish.

As there was little in the last year that concerned the parish, but only myself, so in this the like fortune continued; and saving a rise in the price of barley, occasioned, as was thought, by the establishment of a house for brewing whisky in a neighbouring parish, it could not be said that my people were exposed to the mutations and influences of the stars, which ruled in the seasons of Ann. Dom. 1765. In the winter there was a dearth of fuel, such as has not been since; for when the spring loosened the bonds of the ice, three new coal-heughs were shanked in the Douray moor,[106] and ever since there has been a great plenty of that necessary article. Truly, it is very wonderful to see how things come round; when the talk was about the shanking of thir heughs, and a paper to get folk to take shares in them, was carried through the circumjacent parishes, it was thought a gowk's errand;[107] but no sooner were the coal reached, but up sprung such a traffic, that it was a God-send to the parish, and the opening of a trade and commerce, that has, to use an old bye-word, brought gold in gowpins amang us.[108] From that time my stipend has been on the regular increase, and therefore I think that the incoming of the heritors must have been in like manner augmented.

---

104 Nae hae (Sc.): not have.
105 A change-house, (a change for short) is a pub. Howf (Sc.): a pub can be a howff in the sense of 'A place of resort, a favourite haunt, a meeting place' (SND 3); but Balwhidder is punning here on its sense of 'shelter or refuge' (SND 4), the sense in which it is also used in chapter IX.
106 Heughs: pits; shanked: sunk (both Sc.).
107 Thir: these; gowk: fool (both Sc.).
108 Gowpin (Sc.): 'The fill of the two hands held out together in the form of a bowl' (DOST).

Soon after this, the time was drawing near for my second marriage. I had placed my affections, with due consideration, on Miss Lizy Kibbock, the well-brought up daughter of Mr Joseph Kibbock, of the Gorbyholm, who was the first that made a speculation in the farming way in Ayrshire, and whose cheese were of such an excellent quality, that they have, under the name of Delap-cheese,[109] spread far and wide over the civilized world. Miss Lizy and me were married on the 29th day of April, with some inconvenience to both sides, on account of the dread that we had of being married in May, for it is said,

> "Of the marriages in May,
> The bairns die of a decay."

However, married we were, and we hired the Irville stage, and with Miss Jenny her sister, and Becky Cairns her niece, who sat on a portmanty at our feet, we went on a pleasure jaunt to Glasgow, where we bought a miracle of useful things for the Manse, that neither the first Mrs Balwhidder nor me ever thought of; but the second Mrs Balwhidder that was, had a geni for management, and it was extraordinary what she could go through. Well may I speak of her with commendations, for she was the bee that made my honey, although at first things did not go so clear with us. For she found the Manse rookit and herrit,[110] and there was such a supply of plenishing of all sort wanted, that I thought myself ruined and undone by her care and industry. There was such a buying of wool to make blankets, with a booming of the meikle wheel to spin the same, and such birring of the little wheel for sheets and napery, that the Manse was for many a day like an organ kist.[111] Then we had milk cows, and the calves to bring up, and a kirning of butter, and a making of cheese; in short, I was almost by myself with the jangle and din,[112] which prevented me from writing a book as I had proposed, and I for a time thought of the peaceful and kindly nature of the first Mrs Balwhidder with a sigh; but the out-coming was soon manifest. The second Mrs Balwhidder sent her butter on the market-days to Irville, and her cheese from time to time to Glasgow, to Mrs Firlot, that kept the huxtry in the Saltmarket, and they were both so well made, that our dairy was just a coining of money, insomuch, that after the first year, we had the whole tot of my stipend to put untouched into the bank.

But I must say, that although we were thus making siller like sclate stones, I was not satisfied in my own mind, that I had got the Manse merely to be a factory of butter and cheese, and to breed up veal calves for the slaughter; so I spoke to the second Mrs Balwhidder, and pointed out to her what I thought the error of our way; but she had been so ingrained with the profitable management of cows and grumphies in her father's house,[113] that she could not desist, at the which I was greatly grieved. By and by, however, I began to discern that there was something as good in her example, as the giving of alms to the poor folk. For all the wives of the parish were stirred up by it into a wonderful thrift, and nothing was heard of in every house, but of quiltings and wabs to weave;[114] insomuch, that before many years came round, there was not a better stocked parish, with blankets and napery, than mine was, within the bounds of Scotland.

---

109   Galt has in mind Dunlop cheese, developed in Ayrshire in the eighteenth century: the
      name 'Kibbock' is a version of kebbock or kebbuck, another type of cheese.
110   Rookit: literally, moulted, but here, bare; herrit, herried: plundered, harried (both Sc.).
111   Meikle: big; birr: whirr; organ-kist: organ-loft, as in an (Episcopalian) church.
112   Kirn: churn; by myself: we would now say, beside myself (both Sc.).
113   Grumphies (Sc.): pigs.
114   Wabs (Sc.): webs, textiles.

It was about the Michaelmas of this year that Mrs Malcolm opened her shop, which she did chiefly on the advice of Mrs Balwhidder, who said it was far better to allow a little profit on the different haberdasheries that might be wanted, than to send to the neighbouring towns an end's errand on purpose for them,[115] none of the lasses that were so sent ever thinking of making less than a day's play on every such occasion. In a word, it is not to be told how the second Mrs Balwhidder, my wife, shewed the value of flying time, even to the concerns of this world, and was the mean of giving a life and energy to the housewifery of the parish, that has made many a one beak his shins in comfort,[116] that would otherwise have had but a cold coal to blow at. Indeed, Mr Kibbock, her father, was a man beyond the common, and had an insight of things, by which he was enabled to draw profit and advantage, where others could only see risk and detriment. He planted mounts of fir-trees on the bleak and barren tops of the hills of his farm, the which every body, and I among the rest, considered as a thrashing of the water, and raising of bells.[117] But as his tack ran his trees grew, and the plantations supplied him with stabs to make stake and rice between his fields,[118] which soon gave them a trig and orderly appearance, such as had never before been seen in the west country; and his example has, in this matter, been so followed, that I have heard travellers say, who have been in foreign countries, that the shire of Ayr, for its bonny round green plantings on the tops of the hills, is above comparison either with Italy or Switzerland, where the hills are, as it were, in a state of nature.

Upon the whole, this was a busy year in the parish, and the seeds of many great improvements were laid. The king's road, which then ran through the Vennel,[119] was mended; but it was not till some years after, as I shall record by and by, that the trust-road,[120] as it was called, was made, the which had the effect of turning the town inside out.

Before I conclude, it is proper to mention, that the kirk-bell, which had to this time, from time immemorial, hung on an ash-tree, was one stormy night cast down by the breaking of the branch, which was the cause of the heritors agreeing to build the steeple. The clock was a mortification to the parish from the Lady Breadland,[121] when she died some years after.

CHAPTER VII.—YEAR 1766.

The burning of the Breadland—a new bell, and also a steeple—Nanse Birrel found drowned in a well—The parish troubled with wild Irishmen.

It was in this An. Dom. that the great calamity happened, the which took place on a Sabbath evening in the month of February. Mrs Balwhidder had just infused or masket the tea, and we were set round the fire-side, to spend the night in an orderly and religious manner, along with Mr and Mrs Petticrew, who were on a friendly visitation

---

115   End's errand (Sc.): 'anes errand', a journey with a single purpose.

116   Beak, beek (Sc.): warm, bask.

117   Bells (Sc.): bubbles. The whole expression is proverbial for pointless effort.

118   Stabs: stakes; stake and rice: uprights interwoven with branches etc. to make a fence (both Sc.).

119   'Vennel' (Sc.) usually names a narrow passage between buildings.

120   Eighteenth-century road improvements were often initiated by groups of local landowners combining in a 'trust', which could then charge a toll for carriage over the new road, rather than by central government.

121   A 'mortification' is a charitable donation, left in a will.

to the Manse, the mistress being full cousin to Mrs Balwhidder—Sitting, as I was saying at our tea, one of the servant lasses came into the room with a sort of a panic laugh, and said, "What are ye all doing there when the Breadland's in a low?" "The Breadland in a low! cried I." —"O, aye," cried she; "bleezing at the windows and the rigging, and out at the lum, like a killogie."[122] Upon the which we all went to the door, and there, to be sure, we did see that the Breadland was burning, the flames crackling high out o'er the trees, and the sparks flying like a comet's tail in the firmament.

Seeing this sight, I said to Mr Petticrew that, in the strength of the Lord, I would go and see what could be done, for it was as plain as the sun in the heavens, that the ancient place of the Breadlands would be destroyed; whereupon he accorded to go with me, and we walked at a lively course to the spot,[123] and the people from all quarters were pouring in, and it was an awsome scene. But the burning of the house, and the droves of the multitude, were nothing to what we saw when we got forenent the place.[124] There was the rafters crackling, the flames raging, the servants running, some with bedding, some with looking-glasses, and others with chamber utensils, as little likely to be fuel to the fire, but all testifications to the confusion and alarm. Then there was a shout, "Whar's Miss Girzie? whar's the Major?" The Major, poor man, soon cast up, lying upon a feather-bed, ill with his complaints, in the garden; but Lady Skim-milk was nowhere to be found. At last, a figure was seen in the upper-flat, pursued by the flames, and that was Miss Grizy. O! it was a terrible sight to look at her in that jeopardy at the window, with her gold watch in the one hand and the silver tea-pot in the other, skreighing like desperation for a ladder and help.[125] But, before a ladder or help could be found, the floor sunk down, and the roof fell in, and poor Miss Grizy, with her idols, perished in the burning. It was a dreadful business; I think to this hour, how I saw her at the window, how the fire came in behind her, and claught her like a fiery Belzebub,[126] and bore her into perdition before our eyes. The next morning the atomy of the body was found among the rubbish, with a piece of metal in what had been each of its hands, no doubt the gold watch and the silver tea-pot. Such was the end of Miss Grizy, and the Breadland, which the young laird, my pupil that was, by growing a resident at Edinburgh, never rebuilt. It was burnt to the very ground, nothing was spared but what the servants in the first flaught gathered up in a hurry and ran with,[127] but no one could tell how the Major, who was then, as it was thought by the faculty, past the power of nature to recover, got out of the house, and was laid on the feather-bed in the garden. However, he never got the better of that night, and before Whitsunday he was dead too,[128] and buried beside his sister's bones at the south side of the kirk-yard dyke, where his cousin's son, that was his heir, erected the handsome monument, with the three urns and weeping cherubims, bearing witness to the great valour of the Major among the Hindoos, as well as other commendable virtues, for which, as the epitaph says, he was universally esteemed and beloved by all who knew him, in his public and private capacity.

But although the burning of the Breadland-House was justly called the great calamity, on account of what happened to Miss Girzy with her gold watch and silver teapot, yet, as Providence never fails to bring good out of evil, it turned out a catastrophe

---

122 In a low: on fire; lum: chimney; killogie: kiln for drying grain, a proverbially smoky operation (all Sc.).
123 Course (Sc.): pace.
124 Forenent (Sc.): opposite, across from.
125 Skreighing: shrieking.
126 Claught (Sc.): grasp, clutch. Belzebub: Satan.
127 Flaught, usually flaucht (Sc.): flight.
128 Whitsunday: the seventh after Easter; Pentecost.

that proved advantageous to the parish; for the laird, instead of thinking to build it up, was advised to let the policy out as a farm, and the tack was taken by Mr Coulter, than whom there had been no such man in the agriculturing line among us before, not even excepting Mr Kibbock of the Gorbyholm, my father-in-law that was. Of the stabling, Mr Coulter made a comfortable dwelling-house, and having rugget out the evergreens and other unprofitable plants, saving the twa ancient yew-trees which the near-begun Major and his sister had left to go to ruin about the mansion-house,[129] he turned all to production, and it was wonderful what an increase he made the land bring forth. He was from far beyond Edinburgh, and had got his insight among the Lothian farmers,[130] so that he knew what crop should follow another, and nothing could surpass the regularity of his rigs and furrows. — Well do I remember the admiration that I had, when, in a fine sunny morning of the first spring after he took the Breadland, I saw his braird on what had been the cows' grass,[131] as even and pretty as if it had been worked and stripped in the loom with a shuttle. Truly, when I look back at the example he set, and when I think on the method and dexterity of his management, I must say, that his coming to the parish was a great God's-send, and tended to do far more for the benefit of my people, than if the young laird had rebuilded the Breadland-house in a fashionable style, as was at one time spoken of.

But the year of the great calamity was memorable for another thing: In the December foregoing, the wind blew, as I have recorded in the chronicle of the last year, and broke down the bough of the tree, whereon the kirk-bell had hung from the time, as was supposed, of the Persecution, before the bringing over of King William.[132] Mr Kibbock, my father-in-law then that was, being a man of a discerning spirit, when he heard of the unfortunate fall of the bell, advised me to get the heritors to big a steeple,[133] but which, when I thought of the expence, I was afraid to do. He, however, having a great skill in the heart of man, gave me no rest on the subject, but told me, that if I allowed the time to go by, till the heritors were used to come to the kirk without a bell, I would get no steeple at all. I often wondered what made Mr Kibbock so fond of a steeple, which is a thing that I never could see a good reason for, saving that it is an ecclesiastical adjunct, like the gown and bands. However, he set me on to get a steeple proposed, and after no little argolbargling with the heritors, it was agreed to. This was chiefly owing to the instrumentality of Lady Moneyplack, who, in that winter, was much subjected to the rheumatics, she having, one cold and raw Sunday morning, there being no bell to announce the time, come half an hour too soon to the kirk, made her bestir herself to get an interest awakened among the heritors in behalf of a steeple.

But when the steeple was built, a new contention arose. It was thought that the bell, which had been used in the ash-tree, would not do in a stone and lime fabric, so, after great agitation among the heritors, it was resolved to sell the old bell to a foundry in Glasgow, and buy a new bell suitable to the steeple, which was a very comely fabric. The buying of the new bell led to other considerations, and the old Lady Breadland, being at the time in a decaying condition, and making her will, she left a mortification

---

129 A coulter is the blade of a plough. Rugget: pulled; near-begun, ne'er-begun: 'miserly, greedy, close-fisted' (*SND*) (both Sc.).
130 East Lothian was at the forefront of the agricultural revolution in Scotland, where landowners encouraged tenants to try modern techniques such as field enclosure and crop-rotation.
131 Braird: the first shoots of a crop.
132 That is, the persecution of the Covenanters, before the accession of William of Orange in 1688.
133 Big (Sc.): build.

to the parish, as I have intimated, to get a clock, so that, by the time the steeple was finished, and the bell put up, the Lady Breadland's legacy came to be implemented, according to the ordination of the testatrix.

Of the casualties that happened in this year, I should not forget to put down, as a thing for remembrance, that an aged woman, one Nanse Birrel, a distillator of herbs, and well skilled in the healing of sores, who had a great repute among the quarriers and coalliers,—she having gone to the physic well in the sandy hills, to draw water, was found with her feet uppermost in the well, by some of the bairns of Mr Loremore's school; and there was a great debate whether Nanse had fallen in by accident head foremost, or, in a temptation, thrown herself in that position, with her feet sticking up to the evil one; for Nanse was a curious discontented blear-eyed woman, and it was only with great ado that I could get the people keepit from calling her a witch wife.

I should, likewise, place on record, that the first ass, that had ever been seen in this part of the country, came in the course of this year with a gang of tinklers, that made horn-spoons, and mended bellows.[134] Where they came from never was well made out, but being a blackaviced crew, they were generally thought to be Egyptians.[135] They tarried about a week among us, living in tents, with their little ones squattling among the litter; and one of the older men of them set and tempered to me two razors, that were as good as nothing, but which he made better than when they were new.

Shortly after, but I am not quite sure whether it was in the end of this year, or the beginning of the next, although I have a notion that it was in this, there came over from Ireland a troop of wild Irish, seeking for work as they said, but they made free quarters,[136] for they herrit the roosts of the clachan, and cutted the throat of a sow of ours, the carcase of which they no doubt intended to steal, but something came over them, and it was found lying at the backside of the Manse, to the great vexation of Mrs Balwhidder, for she had set her mind on a clecking of pigs,[137] and only waited for the China boar, that had been brought down from London by Lord Eglesham, to mend the breed of pork—a profitable commodity, that her father, Mr Kibbock, cultivated for the Glasgow market. The destruction of our sow, under such circumstances, was therefore held to be a great crime and cruelty, and it had the effect to raise up such a spirit in the clachan, that the Irish were obligated to decamp; and they set out for Glasgow, where one of them was afterwards hanged for a fact, but the truth concerning how he did it, I either never heard, or it has passed from my mind, like many other things I should have carefully treasured.

CHAPTER VIII.—YEAR 1767.

Lord Eglesham meets with an accident, which is the means of getting the parish a new road—I preach for the benefit of Nanse Banks, the schoolmistress, reduced to poverty.

ALL things in our parish were now beginning to shoot up into a great prosperity. The spirit of farming began to get the upper hand of the spirit of smuggling, and the coal-heughs that had been opened in the Douray, now brought a pour of money among us. In the Manse, the thrift and frugality of the second Mrs Balwhidder throve exceedingly, so that we could save the whole stipend for the bank.

---

134   Tinklers: tinkers, gypsies.
135   Blackaviced: dark-skinned.
136   That is, behaved like government soldiers billeted on a community, from which they had a right to free food and board.
137   Clecking (Sc.): brood, litter.

The king's highway, as I have related in the foregoing, ran through the Vennel, which was a narrow and a crooked street, with many big stones here and there, and every now and then, both in the spring and the fall, a gathering of middens for the fields, insomuch that the coal carts from the Dowray-moor were often reested in the middle of the causeway, and on more than one occasion some of them laired altogether in the middens,[138] and others of them broke down. Great complaint was made by the carters anent these difficulties, and there was, for many a day, a talk and sound of an alteration and amendment, but nothing was fulfilled in the matter till the month of March in this year, when the Lord Eglesham was coming from London to see the new lands that he had bought in our parish. His lordship was a man of a genteel spirit, and very fond of his horses, which were the most beautiful creatures of their kind that had been seen in all the country side. Coming, as I was noting, to see his new lands, he was obliged to pass through the clachan one day, when all the middens were gathered out reeking and sappy in the middle of the causeway.[139] Just as his lordship was driving in with his prancing steeds like a Jehu at the one end of the Vennel,[140] a long string of loaded coal carts came in at the other, and there was hardly room for my lord to pass them. What was to be done? his lordship could not turn back, and the coal carts were in no less perplexity. Every body was out of doors to see and to help, when, in trying to get his lordship's carriage over the top of a midden, the horses gave a sudden loup, and couped the coach,[141] and threw my lord, head foremost, into the very scent-bottle of the whole commodity, which made him go perfect mad, and he swore like a trooper, that he would get an act of parliament to put down the nuisance—the which now ripened in the course of this year into the undertaking of the trust road.

His lordship being in a woeful plight, left the carriage and came to the Manse, till his servant went to the Castle for a change for him; but he could not wait nor abide himself, so he got the lend of my best suit of clothes, and was wonderful jocose both with Mrs Balwhidder and me, for he was a portly man, and I but a thin body, and it was really a droll curiosity to see his lordship clad in my garments.

Out of this accident grew a sort of a neighbourliness between that Lord Eglesham and me, so that when Andrew Lanshaw, the brother that was of the first Mrs Balwhidder, came to think of going to India, I wrote to my lord for his behoof, and his lordship got him sent out as a cadet, and was extraordinary discreet to Andrew when he went up to London to take his passage,[142] speaking to him of me as if I had been a very saint, which the Searcher of Hearts knows I am far from thinking myself.

But to return to the making of the trust-road, which, as I have said, turned the town inside out. It was agreed among the heritors, that it should run along the back-side of the south houses; and that there should be steadings fewed off on each side,[143] according to a plan that was laid down, and this being gone into, the town gradually, in the course of years, grew up into that orderlyness which makes it now a pattern to the country-side—all which was mainly owing to the accident that befel the Lord

---

138   Middens: dung heaps; reested: stalled or stuck; laired: bogged down (all Sc.).

139   Reeking and sappy (Sc.): smoking and wet.

140   Like a Jehu: that is, 'he driveth furiously', as Jehu does in 2 Kings 9.20.

141   Coup (Sc.): overturn.

142   Cadet: that is, a junior officer in the East India Company's army (the company had its own armed forces of Indian soldiers with European officers); discreet: here in the specifically Scottish sense of polite, attentive.

143   Steading: building plots; fewed off: divided into feus, individual pieces of real-estate (both Sc.). The building of planned villages was a common feature of Scotland's 'Age of Improvement' in the countryside.

Eglesham, which is a clear proof how improvements came about, as it were, by the immediate instigation of Providence, which should make the heart of man humble, and change his eyes of pride and haughtiness into a lowly demeanour.

But, although this making of the trust-road was surely a great thing for the parish, and of an advantage to my people, we met, in this year, with a loss not to be compensated, — that was the death of Nanse Banks, the schoolmistress. She had been long in a weak and frail state, but, being a methodical creature, still kept on the school, laying the foundation for many a worthy wife and mother. However, about the decline of the year her complaints increased, and she sent for me to consult about her giving up the school; and I went to see her on a Saturday afternoon, when the bit lassies, her scholars, had put the house in order, and gone home till the Monday.

She was sitting in the window-nook, reading THE WORD to herself, when I entered, but she closed the book, and put her spectacles in for a mark when she saw me; and, as it was expected I would come, her easy chair, with a clean cover, had been set out for me by the scholars, by which I discerned that there was something more than common to happen, and so it appeared when I had taken my seat.

"Sir," said she, "I hae sent for you on a thing troubles me sairly. I have warsled with poortith in this shed, which it has pleased the Lord to allow me to possess, but my strength is worn out, and I fear I maun yield in the strife;"[144] and she wiped her eye with her apron. I told her, however, to be of good cheer; and then she said, "that she could no longer thole the din of the school, and that she was weary, and ready to lay herself down to die whenever the Lord was pleased to permit. But," continued she, "what can I do without the school; and, alas! I can neither work nor want; and I am wae to go on the Session, for I am come of a decent family."[145] I comforted her, and told her, that I thought she had done so much good in the parish, that the Session was deep in her debt, and that what they might give her was but a just payment for her service. "I would rather, however, sir," said she, "try first what some of my auld scholars will do, and it was for that I wanted to speak with you. If some of them would but just, from time to time, look in upon me, that I may not die alane; and the little pick and drap that I require would not be hard upon them[146] — I am more sure that in this way their gratitude would be no discredit, than I am of having any claim on the Session."

As I had always a great respect for an honest pride, I assured her that I would do what she wanted, and accordingly, the very morning after, being Sabbath, I preached a sermon on the helplessness of them that have no help of man, meaning aged single women, living in garret-rooms, whose forlorn state, in the gloaming of life,[147] I made manifest to the hearts and understandings of the congregation, in such a manner that many shed tears, and went away sorrowful.

Having thus roused the feelings of my people, I went round the houses on the Monday morning, and mentioned what I had to say more particularly about poor old Nanse Banks the schoolmistress, and truly I was rejoiced at the condition of the hearts of my people. There was a universal sympathy among them; and it was soon ordered that, what with one and another, her decay should be provided for. But it was not ordained that she should be long heavy on their good will. On the Monday the school was given up, and there was nothing but wailing among the bit lassies, the scholars, for getting the vacance,[148] as the poor things said, because the mistress was

144 Sairly: sorely; poortith: poverty; maun: must (all Sc.).
145 Wae (Sc.): grieved.
146 Pick and drap (Sc.): food and drink.
147 Gloaming (Sc.): twilight.
148 Vacance: vacation.

going to lie down to dee. And, indeed, so it came to pass, for she took to her bed the same afternoon, and, in the course of the week, dwindled away, and slippet out of this howling wilderness into the kingdom of heaven, on the Sabbath following, as quietly as a blessed saint could do. And here I should mention, that the Lady Macadam, when I told her of Nanse Banks's case, inquired if she was a snuffer, and, being answered by me that she was, her ladyship sent her a pretty French enamel box full of Macabaw, a fine snuff that she had in a bottle; and, among the Macabaw, was found a guinea, at the bottom of the box, after Nanse Banks had departed this life, which was a kind thing of Lady Macadam to do.

About the close of this year there was a great sough of old prophecies,[149] foretelling mutations and adversities, chiefly on account of the canal that was spoken of to join the rivers of the Clyde and the Forth,[150] it being thought an impossible thing to be done; and the Adam and Eve pear-tree, in our garden, budded out in an awful manner, and had divers flourishes on it at Yule, which was thought an ominous thing, especially as the second Mrs Balwhidder was at the downlying with my eldest son Gilbert, that is the merchant in Glasgow, but nothing came o't, and the howdie said she had an easy time when the child came into the world,[151] which was on the very last day of the year, to the great satisfaction of me, and of my people, who were wonderful lifted up because their minister had a man-child born unto him.

CHAPTER IX.—YEAR 1768.

Lord Eglesham uses his interest in favour of Charles Malcolm —The finding of a new Schoolmistress—Miss Sabrina Hooky gets the place—Change of fashions in the parish.

IT'S a surprising thing how time flieth away, carrying off our youth and strength, and leaving us nothing but wrinkles and the ails of old age. Gilbert, my son, that is now a corpulent man, and a Glasgow merchant, when I take up my pen to record the memorables of this An. Dom., seems to me yet but a suckling in swaddling clothes, mewing and peevish in the arms of his mother, that has been long laid in the cold kirk-yard, beside her predecessor, in Abraham's bosom. It is not, however, my design to speak much anent my own affairs, which would be a very improper and uncomely thing, but only of what happened in the parish, this book being for a witness and testimony of my ministry. Therefore, setting out of view both me and mine, I will now resuscitate the concerns of Mrs Malcolm and her children; for, as I think, never was there such a visible preordination seen in the lives of any persons, as was seen in that of this worthy decent woman, and her well-doing offspring. Her morning was raw, and a sore blight fell upon her fortunes, but the sun looked out on her mid-day, and her evening closed loun and warm,[152] and the stars of the firmament, that are the eyes of Heaven, beamed, as it were, with gladness, when she lay down to sleep the sleep of rest.

Her son Charles was by this time grown up into a stout buirdly lad, and it was expected that before the return of the Tobacco trader, he would have been out of his

---

149   Sough: 'rushing or murmuring sound, as of wind or water' (*OED*).
150   Construction of the Forth and Clyde canal, running across central Scotland's waist between the River Clyde west of Glasgow and the River Carron near its junction with the Firth of Forth, began in 1768; financial problems delayed completion until 1790.
151   Downlying (Sc.): lying-in.
152   Loun (Sc.): here, calm, quiet.

time,[153] and a man afore the mast, which was a great step of preferment, as I heard say by persons skilled in sea-faring concerns. But this was not ordered to happen; for, when the Tobacco trader was lying in the harbour of Virginia in the North Americas, a press-gang, that was in need of men for a man of war, came on board, and pressed poor Charles and sailed away with him on a cruize, nobody, for many a day, could tell where, till I thought of the Lord Eglesham's kindness. His lordship having something to say with the King's government, I wrote to him, telling him who I was, and how jocose he had been when buttoned in my clothes, that he might recollect me, thanking him, at the same time, for his condescension and patronage to Andrew Lanshaw, in his way to the East Indies. I then slipped in, at the end of the letter, a bit nota bene concerning the case of Charles Malcolm, begging his lordship, on account of the poor lad's widow mother, to inquire at the government if they could tell us any thing about Charles. In the due course of time, I got a most civil reply from his lordship, stating all about the name of the man of war, and where she was; and at the conclusion his lordship said, that I was lucky in having the brother of a Lord of the Admiralty on this occasion for my agent, as otherwise, from the vagueness of my statement, the information might not have been procured; which remark of his lordship was long a great riddle to me, for I could not think what he meant about an agent, till, in the course of the year, we heard that his own brother was concerned in the Admiralty; so that all his lordship meant was only to crack a joke with me, and that he was ever ready and free to do, as shall be related in the sequel, for he was an excellent man.

There being a vacancy for a school-mistress, it was proposed to Mrs Malcolm, that, under her superintendance, her daughter Kate, that had been learning great artifices in needle-work so long with Lady Macadam, should take up the school, and the Session undertook to make good to Kate the sum of five pounds sterling per annum, over and above what the scholars were to pay. But Mrs Malcolm said she had not strength herself to warsle with so many unruly brats, and that Kate, though a fine lassie, was a tempestuous spirit, and might lame some of the bairns in her passion; and that self-same night, Lady Macadam wrote me a very complaining letter, for trying to wile away her companion; but her ladyship was a canary-headed woman,[154] and given to flights and tantrums, having in her youth been a great toast among the quality. It would, however, have saved her from a sore heart, had she never thought of keeping Kate Malcolm. For this year her only son, who was learning the art of war at an academy in France, came to pay her, his lady mother, a visit. He was a brisk and light-hearted stripling, and Kate Malcolm was budding into a very rose of beauty; so between them a hankering began, which, for a season, was productive of great heaviness of heart to the poor old cripple lady; indeed, she assured me herself, that all her rheumatics were nothing to the heart-ache which she suffered in the progress of this business. But that will be more treated of hereafter; suffice it to say for the present, that we have thus recorded how the plan for making Kate Malcolm our school-mistress came to nought. It pleased however Him, from whom cometh every good and perfect gift, to send at this time among us a Miss Sabrina Hookie, the daughter of old Mr Hookie, who had been schoolmaster in a neighbouring parish. She had gone, after his death, to live with an auntie in Glasgow, that kept a shop in the Gallowgate. It was thought that the old woman would have left her heir to all her gatherings, and so she said she would, but

---

153 Buirdly (Sc.): 'stalwart, well-built, powerful' (SND); out of his time: finished his apprenticeship.

154 'To canary' in this period meant to do a lively dance: Galt's usage here may derive from this.

alas! our life is but within our lip.[155] Before her testament was made, she was carried suddenly off by an apoplectick,[156] an awful monument of the uncertainty of time, and the nearness of eternity, in her own shop, as she was in the very act of weighing out an ounce of snuff to a Professor of the College, as Miss Sabrina herself told me. Being thus destitute, it happened that Miss Sabrina heard of the vacancy in our parish, as it were, just by the cry of a passing bird, for she could not tell how; although I judge myself that William Keckle the elder had a hand in it, as he was at the time in Glasgow; and she wrote me a wonderful well-penned letter, bespeaking the situation, which letter came to hand on the morn following Lady Macadam's stramash to me about Kate Malcolm,[157] and I laid it before the Session the same day; so that by the time her auntie's concern was taken off her hands, she had a home and a howff among us to come to,[158] in the which she lived upwards of thirty years in credit and respect, although some thought she had not the art of her predecessor, and was more uppish in her carriage than befitted the decorum of her vocation. Her's, however, was but a harmless vanity; and, poor woman, she needed all manner of graces to set her out, for she was made up of odds and ends, and had but one good eye, the other being blind, and just like a blue bead; at first she plainly set her cap for Mr Loremore, but after ogling and gogling at him every Sunday in the kirk for a whole half year and more, Miss Sabrina desisted in despair.

But the most remarkable thing about her coming into the parish, was the change that took place in Christian names among us. Old Mr Hookie, her father, had, from the time he read his Virgil, maintained a sort of intromission with the Nine Muses, by which he was led to baptize her Sabrina, after a name mentioned by John Milton in one of his works.[159] Miss Sabrina began by calling our Jennies, Jessies, and our Nannies, Nancies; alas! I have lived to see even these likewise grow old-fashioned. She had also a taste in the mantua-making line,[160] which she had learnt in Glasgow, and I could date from the very Sabbath of her first appearance in the kirk, a change growing in the garb of the younger lassies, who from that day began to lay aside the silken plaidie over the head, the which had been the pride and bravery of their grandmothers, and instead of the snood, that was so snod and simple, they hided their heads in round-eared bees-cap mutches,[161] made of gauze and catgut, and other curious contrivances of French millendery; all which brought a deal of custom to Miss Sabrina, over and above the incomings and Candlemas offerings of the school;[162] insomuch, that she saved money, and in the course of three years had ten pounds to put in the bank.

At the time, these alterations and revolutions in the parish were thought a great advantage; but now when I look back upon them, as a traveller on the hill over the road he has passed, I have my doubts. For with wealth come wants, like a troop of clamorous beggars at the heels of a generous man, and it's hard to tell wherein the benefit of improvement in a country parish consists, especially to those who live by the sweat of their brow. But it is not for me to make reflections, my task and duty is to note the changes of time and habitudes.

155   I.e., only certain within each breath. Gatherings: savings.
156   I.e. a stroke.
157   Stramash (Sc.): Uproar, commotion.
158   Howff (Sc.): in this case, refuge.
159   'Intromission' means 'dealings with': a term in Scots law. Sabrina: John Milton, *Comus* (1634) ll.824 ff.
160   Mantua: loose gown.
161   Snood: 'the distinctive hair-band worn by young unmarried women' in Scotland and the North of England (*OED*); snod (Sc.): neat, trim. A mutch is a close-fitting cap, usually linen.
162   At Candlemas (2nd February) pupils traditionally gave a gratuity to their teacher.

CHAPTER X.—YEAR 1769.

A toad found in the heart of a stone—Robert Malcolm, who had been at sea, returns from a northern voyage—Kate Malcolm's clandestine correspondence with Lady Macadam's son.

I HAVE my doubts whether it was in the beginning of this year, or in the end of the last, that a very extraordinar thing came to light in the parish; but howsoever that may be, there is nothing more certain than the fact, which it is my duty to record. I have mentioned already how it was that the toll, or trust-road, was set a-going, on account of the Lord Eglesham's tumbling on the midden in the vennel. Well, it happened to one of the labouring men, in breaking the stones to make metal for the new road, that he broke a stone that was both large and remarkable, and in the heart of it, which was boss,[163] there was found a living creature, that jumped out the moment it saw the light of heaven, to the great terrification of the man, who could think it was nothing but an evil spirit that had been imprisoned therein for a time. The man came to me like a demented creature, and the whole clachan gathered out, young and old, and I went at their head, to see what the miracle could be, for the man said it was a fiery dragon, spuing smoke and flames. But when we came to the spot, it was just a yird toad, and the laddie weans nevelled it to death with stones,[164] before I could persuade them to give over. Since then I have read of such things coming to light in the Scots Magazine, a very valuable book.[165]

Soon after the affair of "the wee deil in the stane," as it was called,[166] a sough reached us that the Americas were seized with the rebellious spirit of the ten tribes, and were snapping their fingers in the face of the King's government.[167] The news came on a Saturday night, for we had no newspapers in those days, and was brought by Robin Modewort, that fetched the letters from the Irville post. Thomas Fullarton (he has been dead many a day) kept the grocery-shop in Irville, and he had been in at Glasgow, as was his yearly custom, to settle his accounts, and to buy a hogshead of tobacco, with sugar and other spiceries; and being in Glasgow, Thomas was told by the merchant of a great rise in tobacco, that had happened by reason of the contumacity of the plantations, and it was thought that blood would be spilt before things were ended, for that the King and Parliament were in a great passion with them. But as Charles Malcolm, in the King's ship, was the only one belonging to the parish that was likely to be art or part in the business, we were in a manner little troubled at the time with this first gasp of the monster of war, who, for our sins, was ordained to swallow up, and devour so many of our fellow-subjects, before he was bound again in the chains of mercy and peace.

I had, in the mean time, written a letter to the Lord Eglesham, to get Charles Malcolm out of the clutches of the press-gang in the man of war; and about a month after, his

---

163   Boss (Sc.): hollow.

164   Yird toad: 'earth toad', the common toad; nevel: pummel, batter (both Sc.).

165   Published monthly in Edinburgh from 1739 to 1826, the Scots Magazine combined news with reviews and extracts from recent books.

166   Deil (Sc.): devil.

167   On Solomon's death, most of the people of Israel reject his son as their king and choose Jeroboam instead in I Kings 12; I Kings 11.31 suggests that the rebels constitute 10 of the 12 tribes of Israel. American protests at taxes imposed on various commodities by the government led to the occupation of Boston by government troops in 1768.

lordship sent me an answer, wherein was inclosed a letter from the captain of the ship, saying, that Charles Malcolm was so good a man, that he was reluctant to part with him, and that Charles himself was well contented to remain aboard. Anent which, his lordship said to me, that he had written back to the captain to make a midshipman of Charles, and that he would take him under his own protection, which was great joy on two accounts to us all, especially to his mother; first, to hear that Charles was a good man, although in years still but a youth; and, secondly, that my lord had, of his own free will, taken him under the wing of his patronage.

But the sweet of this world is never to be enjoyed without some of the sour. The coal bark between Irville and Belfast, in which Robert Malcolm, the second son of his mother, was serving his time to be a sailor, got a charter, as it was called, to go with to Norway for deals,[168] which grieved Mrs Malcolm to the very heart, for there was then no short cut by the canal, as now is, between the rivers of the Forth and Clyde, but every ship was obligated to go far away round by the Orkneys, which, although a voyage in the summer not overly dangerous, there being long days and short nights then, yet in the winter it was far otherwise, many vessels being frozen up in the Baltic till the spring; and there was a story told at the time, of an Irville bark coming home in the dead of the year, that lost her way altogether, and was supposed to have sailed north into utter darkness, for she was never more heard of; and many an awful thing was said of what the auld mariners about the shore thought concerning the crew of that misfortunate vessel. However, Mrs Malcolm was a woman of great faith, and having placed her reliance on Him who is the orphan's stay and widow's trust, she resigned her bairn into His hands, with a religious submission to His pleasure, though the mother's tear of weak human nature was on her cheek and in her e'e. And her faith was well rewarded, for the vessel brought him safe home, and he had seen such a world of things, that it was just to read a story-book to hear him tell of Elsineur and Gottenburgh, and other fine and great places that we had never heard of till that time; and he brought me a bottle of Riga balsam, which for healing cuts was just miraculous, besides a clear bottle of Rososolus for his mother, a spirit which for cordiality could not be told; for though since that time we have had many a sort of Dantzick cordial,[169] I have never tasted any to compare with Robin Malcolm's Rososolus. The Lady Macadam, who had a knowledge of such things, declared it was the best of the best sort; for Mrs Malcolm sent her ladyship some of it in a doctor's bottle, as well as to Mrs Balwhidder, who was then at the down-lying with our daughter Janet—a woman now in the married state, that makes a most excellent wife, having been brought up with great pains, and well educated, as I shall have to record by and by.

About the Christmas of this year, Lady Macadam's son having been perfected in the art of war at a school in France, had, with the help of his mother's friends, and his father's fame, got a stand of colours in the Royal Scots regiment;[170] he came to shew himself in his regimentals to his lady mother, like a dutiful son, as he certainly was. It happened that he was in the kirk in his scarlets and gold, on the same Sunday that Robert Malcolm came home from the long voyage to Norway for deals; and I thought when I saw the soldier and the sailor from the pulpit, that it was an omen of war, among our harmless country folks, like swords and cannon amidst ploughs and sickles, coming upon us, and I became laden in spirit, and had a most weighty prayer upon the

---

168   Deals: pine planking.
169   Dantzick: i.e. from Danzig on the Baltic, at this period in Prussia, now Gdańsk in Poland.
170   Its 'stand of colours' are a regiment's flags: young Macadam has been commissioned into the Royal Scots.

occasion, which was long after remembered, many thinking, when the American war broke out, that I had been gifted with a glimmering of prophecy on that day.

It was during this visit to his lady mother, that young Laird Macadam settled the correspondence with Kate Malcolm, which, in the process of time, caused us all so much trouble; for it was a clandestine concern, but the time is not yet ripe for me to speak of it more at large. I should however mention, before concluding this annal, that Mrs Malcolm herself was this winter brought to death's door by a terrible host that came on her in the kirk, by taking a kittling in her throat.[171] It was a terrification to hear her sometimes; but she got the better of it in the spring, and was more herself thereafter than she had been for years before; and her daughter Effie, or Euphemia, as she was called by Miss Sabrina, the schoolmistress, was growing up to be a gleg and clever quean; she was, indeed, such a spirit in her way, that the folks called her Spunkie;[172] while her son William, that was the youngest of the five, was making a wonderful proficiency with Mr Loremore. He was indeed a douce, well-doing laddie, of a composed nature; insomuch, that the master said he was surely chosen for the ministry. In short, the more I think on what befell this family, and of the great meekness and Christian worth of the parent, I verily believe there never could have been in any parish such a manifestation of the truth, that they who put their trust in the Lord, are sure of having a friend that will never forsake them.

CHAPTER XI.—YEAR 1770.

This year a happy and tranquil one—Lord Eglesham establishes a fair in the village—The show of Punch appears for the first time in the parish.

THIS blessed An. Dom. was one of the Sabbaths of my ministry; when I look back upon it, all is quiet and good order; the darkest cloud of the smuggling had passed over, at least from my people, and the rumours of rebellion in America, were but like the distant sound of the bars of Ayr.[173] We sat, as it were, in a lown and pleasant place,[174] beholding our prosperity, like the apple-tree adorned with her garlands of flourishes, in the first fair mornings of the spring, when the birds are returning thanks to their Maker for the coming again of the seed-time, and the busy bee goeth forth from her cell, to gather honey from the flowers of the field, and the broom of the hill, and the blue-bells and gowans,[175] which Nature, with a gracious and a gentle hand, scatters in the valley, as she walketh forth in her beauty, to testify to the goodness of the Father of all mercies.

Both at the spring and the harvest sacraments, the weather was as that which is in Paradise; there was a glad composure in all hearts, and the minds of men were softened towards each other. The number of communicants was greater than had been known for many years, and the tables were filled by the pious from many a neighbouring parish; those of my hearers who had opposed my placing, declared openly for a testimony of satisfaction and holy thankfulness, that the tent, so surrounded as it was on both occasions, was a sight they never had expected to see. I was, to be sure, assisted by some of the best divines then in the land, but I had not been a sluggard myself in the vineyard.

---

171   Kittle (Sc.): tickle.
172   Gleg: quick-witted; quean: girl; Spunkie: 'a smart, lively young person' (*SND* 3.1) (all Sc.).
173   Bars: sandbars.
174   Lown (Sc.): here, sheltered.
175   Gowans (Sc.): daisies.

Often, when I think on this year, so fruitful in pleasant intimacies, has the thought come into my mind, that as the Lord blesses the earth from time to time with a harvest of more than the usual increase, so, in like manner, he is sometimes for a season pleased to pour into the breasts of mankind a larger portion of good will and charity, disposing them to love one another, to be kindly to all creatures, and filled with the delight of thankfulness to himself, which is the greatest of blessings.

It was in this year that the Earl of Eglesham ordered the fair to be established in the village; and it was a day of wonderful festivity to all the bairns, and lads and lassies, for miles round. I think, indeed, that there has never been such a fair as the first since; for although we have more mountebanks and Merry Andrews now, and richer cargoes of groceries and packman's stands, yet there has been a falling off in the light-hearted daffing, while the hobble-shows in the change-houses have been awfully augmented.[176] It was on this occasion that Punch's opera was first seen in our country side, and surely never was there such a funny curiosity; for although Mr Punch himself was but a timber idol, he was as droll as a true living thing, and napped with his head so comical;[177] but O he was a sorrowful contumacious captain, and it was just a sport to see how he rampaged, and triumphed, and sang. For months after, the laddie weans did nothing but squeak and sing like Punch. In short, a blithe spirit was among us throughout this year, and the briefness of the chronicle bears witness to the innocency of the time.

CHAPTER XII.—YEAR 1771.

The nature of Lady Macadam's amusements—She intercepts letters from her Son to Kate Malcolm.

IT was in this year that my troubles with Lady Macadam's affair began. She was a woman, as I have by a hint here and there intimated, of a prelatic disposition, seeking all things her own way, and not overly scrupulous about the means, which I take to be the true humour of prelacy. She was come of a high episcopal race in the east country,[178] where sound doctrine had been long but little heard, and she considered the comely humility of a presbyter as the wickedness of hypocrisy; so that, saving in the way of neighbourly visitation, there was no sincere communion between us. Nevertheless, with all her vagaries, she had the element of a kindly spirit, that would sometimes kythe in actions of charity,[179] that showed symptoms of a true Christian grace, had it been properly cultivated; but her morals had been greatly neglected in her youth, and she would waste her precious time in the long winter nights, playing at the cards with her visitors; in the which thriftless and sinful pastime, she was at great pains to instruct Kate Malcolm, which I was grieved to understand. What, however, I most misliked in her ladyship, was a lightness and juvenility of behaviour, altogether unbecoming her years, for she was far past three score, having been long married without children. Her son, the soldier officer, came so late, that it was thought she would have been taken up as an evidence in the Douglas cause.[180] She was, to be sure, crippled with the

176   Merry Andrews: clowns; daffing (Sc.): joking, fooling around; hobble-shows, or hubbleshew (Sc.): 'a mob, an unruly gathering, a disorderly crowd' (*SND* 2).
177   Napped (Sc.): knocked, rapped.
178   Episcopal: see Introduction. What Balwhidder interprets as characteristically Episcopalian look like attitudes typical of the aristocracy.
179   Kythe, kithe (Sc.): reveal itself, become manifest.
180   A battle in the law-courts over the rightful heir of the Duke of Douglas, who died in 1761,

rheumatics, and no doubt the time hung heavy on her hands; but the best friends of recreation and sport must allow, that an old woman, sitting whole hours jingling with that paralytic chattel a spinnet,[181] was not a natural object! What then could be said for her singing Italian songs, and getting all the newest from Vauxhall in London,[182] a boxful at a time, with new novel-books, and trinkum-trankum flowers and feathers,[183] and sweet-meats, sent to her by a lady of the blood royal of Paris? As for the music, she was at great pains to instruct Kate, which, and the other things she taught, were sufficient, as my lady said herself, to qualify poor Kate for a duchess or a governess, in either of which capacities, her ladyship assured Mrs Malcolm, she would do honour to her instructor, meaning her own self; but I must come to the point anent the affair.

One evening, early in the month of January, as I was sitting by myself in my closet studying the Scots Magazine, which I well remember the new number had come but that very night, Mrs Balwhidder being at the time busy with the lasses in the kitchen, and superintending, as her custom was, for she was a clever woman, a great wool-spinning we then had, both little wheel and meickle wheel,[184] for stockings and blankets—sitting, as I was saying, in the study, with the fire well gathered up, for a night's reflection, a prodigious knocking came to the door, by which the book was almost startled out of my hand, and all the wheels in the house were silenced at once. This was her ladyship's flunkey, to beg me to go to her, whom he described as in a state of desperation. Christianity required that I should obey the summons; so, with what haste I could, thinking that perhaps, as she had been low-spirited for some time about the young laird's going to the Indies, she might have got a cast of grace,[185] and been wakened in despair to the state of darkness in which she had so long lived, I made as few steps of the road between the Manse and her house as it was in my ability to do.

On reaching the door, I found a great light in the house—candles burning up stairs and down stairs, and a sough of something extraordinar going on. I went into the dining-room, where her ladyship was wont to sit; but she was not there—only Kate Malcolm all alone, busily picking bits of paper from the carpet. When she looked up, I saw that her eyes were red with weeping, and I was alarmed, and said, "Katty, my dear, I hope there is no danger?" Upon which the poor lassie rose, and flinging herself in a chair, covered her face with her hands, and wept bitterly.

"What is the old fool doing with the wench?" cried a sharp angry voice from the drawing-room—"why does not he come to me?" It was the voice of Lady Macadam herself, and she meant me. So I went to her; but, O, she was in a far different state from what I had hoped. The pride of this world had got the upper-hand of her, and was playing dreadful antics with her understanding. There was she, painted like a Jezebel, with gum-flowers on her head, as was her custom every afternoon, sitting on a settee, for she was lame, and in her hand she held a letter. "Sir," said she, as I came into the room, "I want you to go instantly to that young fellow, your clerk, (meaning Mr

---

centred on a litigant's claim to be the son of the Duke's sister: if true, he was born when she was 50 years old. The Court of Session decided this was impossible; the British House of Lords overturned this decision.

181   Spinnet (now spinet): a type of small harpsichord.

182   Italian music, and opera in particular, were hugely popular in 18th century London; Vauxhall gardens was a pleasure ground south of the Thames and a centre for the more popular end of this musical culture. In Scotland, a similar popularity was accompanied by some resentment at the 'corruption' of Scottish song by the Italian style.

183   Trinkum-trankum: from trinkums (Sc.), 'trinkets, nick-nacks, gew-gaws' (SND).

184   Meickle, usually muckle (Sc.): big.

185   Cast: in this sense, 'a stroke, a touch' (OED I.9).

Loremore, the schoolmaster, who was likewise session-clerk and precentor,) and tell him I will give him a couple of hundred pounds to marry Miss Malcolm without delay, and undertake to procure him a living from some of my friends."[186]

"Softly, my lady, you must first tell me the meaning of all this haste of kindness," said I, in my calm methodical manner. At the which she began to cry and sob, like a petted bairn, and to bewail her ruin, and the dishonour of her family. I was surprised, and beginning to be confounded, at length out it came. The flunkie had that night brought two London letters from the Irville post, and Kate Malcolm being out of the way when he came home, he took them both into her ladyship on the silver server, as was his custom; and her ladyship, not jealousing that Kate could have a correspondence with London, thought both the letters were for herself, for they were franked, so, as it happened, she opened the one that was for Kate, and this, too, from the young laird, her own son. She could not believe her eyes when she saw the first words in his hand of write, and she read, and she better read, till she read all the letter, by which she came to know that Kate and her darling were trysted,[187] and that this was not the first love-letter which had passed between them. She, therefore, tore it in pieces, and sent for me, and screamed for Kate; in short, went, as it were, off at the head, and was neither to bind nor to hold on account of this intrigue, as she, in her wrath, stigmatized the innocent gallanting of poor Kate and the young laird.

I listened in patience to all she had to say anent the discovery, and offered her the very best advice; but she derided my judgment, and because I would not speak outright to Mr Loremore, and get him to marry Kate off hand, she bade me good night with an air, and sent for him herself. He, however, was on the brink of marriage with his present worthy helpmate, and declined her ladyship's proposals, which angered her still more. But although there was surely a great lack of discretion in all this, and her ladyship was entirely overcome with her passion, she would not part with Kate, nor allow her to quit the house with me, but made her sup with her as usual that night, calling her sometimes a perfidious baggage, and at other times, forgetting her delirium, speaking to her as kindly as ever. At night, Kate as usual helped her ladyship into her bed, (this she told me with tears in her eyes next morning) and when Lady Macadam, as was her wont, bent to kiss her for good night, she suddenly recollected "the intrigue," and gave Kate such a slap on the side of the head, as quite dislocated for a time the intellects of the poor young lassie. Next morning, Kate was solemnly advised never to write again to the laird, while the lady wrote him a letter, which, she said, would be as good as a birch to the breech of the boy. Nothing, therefore, for some time, indeed throughout the year, came of this matter, but her ladyship, when Mrs Balwhidder soon after called on her, said that I was a nose of wax,[188] and that she never would speak to me again, which surely was not a polite thing to say to Mrs Balwhidder, my second wife.

This stramash was the first time that I had interposed in the family concerns of my people, for it was against my nature to make or meddle with private actions, saving only such as, in course of nature, came before the Session; but I was not satisfied with the principles of Lady Macadam, and I began to be weary about Kate Malcolm's situation with her ladyship,[189] whose ways of thinking I saw were not to be depended on, especially

186   A living: that is, an appointment as an Episcopalian priest.
187   Trysted (Sc.): Kinsley (1986) thinks this means the couple are engaged (following *SND* II.2.1.ii). The context perhaps suggests something slightly less than this: 'innocent gallanting' is no more than 'stepping out' (see *OED* 'gallant' 5).
188   A nose of wax: 'a person easily influenced, or of a weak character' (*OED* 'nose' 9).
189   Weary: in Scottish usage, 'referring to sadness and dispiritedness, rather than exhaustion

in those things wherein her pride and vanity were concerned. But the time ran on—the butterflies and the blossoms were succeeded by the leaves and the fruit, and nothing of a particular nature farther molested the general tranquillity of this year; about the end of which, there came on a sudden frost, after a tack of wet weather.[190] The roads were just a sheet of ice, like a frozen river; insomuch, that the coalcarts could not work; and one of our cows, (Mrs Balwhidder said after the accident it was our best, but it was not so much thought of before,) fell in coming from the glebe to the byre, and broke its two hinder legs, which obligated us to kill it, in order to put the beast out of pain. As this happened after we had salted our mart,[191] it occasioned us to have a double crop of puddings, and such a show of hams in the kitchen, as was a marvel to our visitors to see.

CHAPTER XIII.—YEAR 1772.

The detection of Mr Heckletext's guilt—He threatens to prosecute the Elders for defamation—The Muscovy duck gets an operation performed on it.

ON New-Year's night, this year, a thing happened, which, in its own nature, was a trifle, but it turned out as a mustard-seed that grows into a great tree.[192] One of the elders, who has long been dead and gone, came to the Manse about a fact that was found out in the clachan, and after we had discoursed on it some time, he rose to take his departure. I went with him to the door with the candle in my hand—it was a clear frosty night, with a sharp wind, and the moment I opened the door, the blast blew out the candle, so that I heedlessly, with the candlestick in my hand, walked with him to the yett without my hat, by which I took a sore cold in my head, that brought on a dreadful tooth-ache; insomuch, that I was obliged to go into Irville to get the tooth drawn, and this caused my face to swell to such a fright, that, on the Sabbath-day, I could not preach to my people. There was, however, at that time, a young man, one Mr Heckletext, tutor in Sir Hugh Montgomerie's family, and who had shortly before been licenced.[193] Finding that I would not be able to preach myself, I sent to him, and begged he would officiate for me, which he very pleasantly consented to do, being like all the young clergy, thirsting to shew his light to the world. 'Twixt the fore and afternoon's worship, he took his check of dinner at the Manse,[194] and I could not but say, that he seemed both discreet and sincere. Judge, however, what was brewing, when the same night Mr Loremore came and told me, that Mr Heckletext was the suspected person anent the fact, that had been instrumental in the hand of a chastising Providence, to afflict me with the tooth-ache, in order, as it afterwards came to pass, to bring the hidden hypocrisy of the ungodly preacher to light. It seems that the donsie lassie,[195] who was in fault, had gone to the kirk in the afternoon, and seeing who was in the pulpit, where she expected to see me, was seized with the hystericks, and taken with her crying on the spot,[196] the which being untimely, proved the death of both mother and bairn, before the thing was properly laid to the father's charge.

---

      as in England' (*SND*).
190   Tack (Sc.): period.
191   Mart (Sc.): a cow killed at the end of the year to provide the winter's salted meat.
192   Matthew 13.31–32, where the seed and the tree are the Kingdom of Heaven.
193   Licenced: that is, to preach; this was a probationary stage before appointment to a parish.
194   Check, usually chack (Sc.): snack.
195   Donsie (Sc.): 'Unfortunate, luckless, hapless […] often in reference to sexual lapses' (*SND*).
196   Taken with her crying: went into labour.

This caused a great uproar in the parish. I was sorely blamed to let such a man as Mr Heckletext go up into my pulpit, although I was as ignorant of his offences as the innocent child that perished; and, in an unguarded hour, to pacify some of the elders, who were just distracted about the disgrace, I consented to have him called before the Session. He obeyed the call, and in a manner that I will never forget, for he was a sorrow of sin and audacity, and demanded to know why and for what reason he was summoned. I told him the whole affair in my calm and moderate way, but it was oil cast upon a burning coal. He flamed up in a terrible passion, threapit at the elders that they had no proof whatever of his having had any trafficking in the business,[197] which was the case, for it was only a notion, the poor deceased lassie never having made a disclosure; called them libellous conspirators against his character, which was his only fortune, and concluded by threatening to punish them, though he exempted me from the injury which their slanderous insinuations had done to his prospects in life. We were all terrified, and allowed him to go away without uttering a word; and sure enough he did bring a plea in the courts of Edinburgh against Mr Loremore and the elders for damages, laid at a great sum.

What might have been the consequence, no one can tell; but soon after he married Sir Hugh's house-keeper, and went with her into Edinburgh, where he took up a school, and, before the trial came on, that is to say, within three months of the day that I myself married them, Mrs Heckletext was delivered of a thriving lad bairn, which would have been a witness for the elders, had the worst come to the worst. This was, indeed, we all thought, a joyous deliverance to the parish, and it was a lesson to me never to allow any preacher to mount my pulpit, unless I knew something of his moral character.

In other respects, this year passed very peaceably in the parish; there was a visible increase of worldly circumstances, and the hedges which had been planted along the toll-road, began to put forth their branches, and to give new notions of orderlyness and beauty to the farmers. Mrs Malcolm heard from time to time from her son Charles, on board the man of war the Avenger, where he was midshipman, and he had found a friend in the captain, that was just a father to him. Her second son Robert, being out of his time at Irville, went to the Clyde to look for a birth, and was hired to go to Jamaica, in a ship called the Trooper. He was a lad of greater sobriety of nature than Charles; douce, honest, and faithful; and when he came home, though he brought no limes to me to make punch, like his brother, he brought a Muscovy duck to Lady Macadam, who had, as I have related, in a manner educated his sister Kate. That duck was the first of the kind we had ever seen, and many thought it was of the goose species, only with short bowly legs. It was however, a tractable and homely beast, and after some confabulation, as my lady herself told Mrs Balwhidder, it was received into fellowship by her other ducks and poultry. It is not, however, so much on account of the rarity of the creature, that I have introduced it here, as for the purpose of relating a wonderful operation that was performed on it by Miss Sabrina, the schoolmistress.

There happened to be a sack of beans in our stable, and Lady Macadam's hens and fowls, which were not overly fed at home, through the inattention of her servants, being great stravaggers for their meat,[198] in passing the door, went in to pick, and the Muscovy seeing a hole in the bean-sack, dabbled out a crap full before she was disturbed. The beans swelled on the poor bird's stomach, and her crap bellied out like the kyte of a Glasgow magistrate,[199] until it was just a sight to be seen with its head back on its

---

197 Threapit (Sc.): nagged at, was insistent with.
198 Stravagger, usually stravaiger (Sc.): wanderer.
199 Crap: crop (i.e., a bird's gullet); kyte: belly (both Sc.).

shoulders. The bairns of the clachan followed it up and down, crying, the lady's muckle jock's ay growing bigger,[200] till every heart was wae for the creature. Some thought it was afflicted with a tympathy,[201] and others, that it was the natural way for such like ducks to cleck their young. In short, we were all concerned, and my lady having a great opinion of Miss Sabrina's skill, had a consultation with her on the case, at which Miss Sabrina advised, that what she called the Cæsarian operation should be tried, which she herself performed accordingly, by opening the creature's crap, and taking out as many beans as filled a mutchkin stoup,[202] after which she sewed it up, and the Muscovy went its way to the water-side, and began to swim, and was as jocund as ever; insomuch, that in three days after it was quite cured of all the consequences of its surfeit.

I had at one time a notion to send an account of this to the Scots Magazine, but something always came in the way to prevent me; so that it has been reserved for a place in this chronicle, being, after Mr Heckletext's affair, the most memorable thing in our history of this year.

CHAPTER XIV.—YEAR 1773.

The new school-house—Lord Eglesham comes down to the Castle—I refuse to go and dine there on Sunday, but go on Monday, and meet with an English dean.

IN this Ann. Dom. there was something like a plea getting to a head, between the Session and some of the heritors, about a new school-house; the thatch having been torn from the rigging of the old one by a blast of wind, on the first Monday of February, by which a great snow storm got admission, and the school was rendered utterly uninhabitable. The smaller sort of lairds were very willing to come into the plan with an extra contribution, because they respected the master, and their bairns were at the school; but the gentlemen, who had tutors in their own houses, were not so manageable, and some of them even went so far as to say, that the kirk being only wanted on Sunday, would do very well for a school all the rest of the week, which was a very profane way of speaking, and I was resolved to set myself against any such thing, and to labour according to the power and efficacy of my station, to get a new school built.

Many a meeting the Session had on the subject, and the heritors debated and discussed, and revised their proceedings, and still no money for the needful work was forthcoming. Whereupon it happened one morning, as I was rummaging in my scrutoire, that I laid my hand on the Lord Eglesham's letter anent Charles Malcolm, and it was put into my head at that moment, that if I was to write his lordship, who was the greatest heritor, and owned now the major part of the parish,[203] that by his help and influence, I might be an instrument to the building of a comfortable new school; accordingly I sat down and wrote my lord all about the accident, and the state of the school-house, and the divisions and seditions among the heritors, and sent the letter to him at London by the post the same day, without saying a word to any living soul on the subject.

This in me was an advised thought, for, by the return of post, his lordship, with his own hand, in a most kind manner, authorized me to say that he would build a new

---

200   Muckle jock: in this context just means a big bird. A turkey is a 'bubbly-jock'; ay: always, continually (both Sc.).

201   Tympathy: Balwhidder's mistake for tympany, the 18th century word for tumour.

202   Mutchkin stoup (Sc.): mug holding ¾ of an imperial pint.

203   Note that the really big landowner, the one who sits in the House of Lords in London, is not in the parish most of the time and thus not part of these everyday discussions.

school at his own cost, and bade me go over and consult about it with his steward, at the Castle, to whom he had written by the same post the necessary instructions. Nothing could exceed the gladness which the news gave to the whole parish, and none said more in behalf of his lordship's bounty and liberality, than the heritors; especially those gentry who grudged the undertaking, when it was thought that it would have to come out of their own pock-nook.[204]

In the course of the summer, just as the roof was closing in of the school-house, my lord came to the castle with a great company, and was not there a day till he sent for me to come over on the next Sunday, to dine with him; but I sent him word that I could not do so, for it would be a transgression of the Sabbath,[205] which made him send his own gentleman, to make his apology for having taken so great a liberty with me, and to beg me to come on the Monday, which I accordingly did, and nothing could be better than the discretion with which I was used. There was a vast company of English ladies and gentlemen, and his lordship, in a most jocose manner, told them all how he had fallen on the midden, and how I had clad him in my clothes, and there was a wonder of laughing and diversion; but the most particular thing in the company, was a large, round-faced man, with a wig, that was a dignitary in some great Episcopalian church in London, who was extraordinary condescending towards me, drinking wine with me at the table, and saying weighty sentences in a fine style of language, about the becoming grace of simplicity and innocence of heart, in the clergy of all denominations of Christians, which I was pleased to hear; for really he had a proud red countenance, and I could not have thought he was so mortified to humility within, had I not heard with what sincerity he delivered himself, and seen how much reverence and attention was paid to him by all present, particularly by my lord's chaplain, who was a pious and pleasant young divine, though educated at Oxford for the Episcopalian persuasion.

One day soon after, as I was sitting in my closet conning a sermon for the next Sunday, I was surprised by a visit from the dean, as the dignitary was called. He had come, he said, to wait on me as rector of the parish, for so it seems they call a pastor in England, and to say, that, if it was agreeable, he would take a family dinner with us before he left the castle. I could make no objection to this kindness, but said I hoped my lord would come with him, and that we would do our best to entertain them with all suitable hospitality. About an hour or so after he had returned to the castle, one of the flunkies brought a letter from his lordship to say, that not only he would come with the dean, but that they would bring his other guests with them, and that, as they could only drink London wine, the butler would send me a hamper in the morning, assured, as he was pleased to say, that Mrs Balwhidder would otherwise provide good cheer.

This notification, however, was a great trouble to my wife, who was only used to manufacture the produce of our glebe and yard to a profitable purpose, and not used to the treatment of deans and lords, and other persons of quality. However, she was determined to stretch a point on this occasion, and we had, as all present declared, a charming dinner; for fortunately one of the sows had a litter of pigs a few days before, and, in addition to a goose, that is but a boss bird, we had a roasted pig, with an apple in its mouth, which was just a curiosity to see; and my lord called it a tythe pig,[206] but I told him it was one of Mrs Balwhidder's own clecking, which saying of mine made no little sport when expounded to the dean.

---

204   Pock-nook, usually -neuk (Sc.): bottom of a bag, especially one used to hold money.
205   The Kirk was strict in its observation of the Sabbath, as the Church of England was not.
206   The English clergy continued to collect a share of the agricultural output of their parish as part of their income, called a tithe. For the Scottish equivalent see note 331 (chapter XXVII).

But, och how![207] this was the last happy summer that we had for many a year in the parish; and an omen of the dule that ensued, was in a sacrilegious theft that a daft woman, Jenny Gaffaw, and her idiot daughter, did in the kirk, by tearing off and stealing the green serge lining of my lord's pew, to make, as they said, a hap for their shoulders in the cold weather[208] — saving, however, the sin, we paid no attention at the time to the mischief and tribulation that so unheard of a trespass boded to us all. It took place about Yule, when the weather was cold and frosty, and poor Jenny was not very able to go about seeking her meat as usual. The deed, however, was mainly done by her daughter, who, when brought before me, said, "her poor mother's back had mair need of claes than the kirk-boards,"[209] which was so true a thing, that I could not punish her, but wrote anent it to my lord, who not only overlooked the offence, but sent orders to the servants at the castle to be kind to the poor woman, and the natural, her daughter.[210]

CHAPTER XV.—YEAR 1774.

The murder of Jean Glaikit—The young Laird Macadam comes down and marries Kate Malcolm— The ceremony performed by me, and I am commissioned to break the matter to Lady Macadam— Her behaviour.

WHEN I look back on this year, and compare what happened therein with the things that had gone before, I am grieved to the heart, and pressed down with an afflicted spirit. We had, as may be read, trials and tribulations in the days that were past, and in the rank and boisterous times of the smuggling there was much sin and blemish among us, but nothing so dark and awful as what fell out in the course of this unhappy year. The evil omen of daft Jenny Gaffaw, and her daughter's sacrilege, had soon a bloody verification.

About the beginning of the month of March in this year, the war in America was kindling so fast, that the government was obligated to send soldiers over the sea, in the hope to quell the rebellious temper of the plantations, and a party of a regiment that was quartered at Ayr was ordered to march to Greenock, to be there shipped off. The men were wild and wicked profligates, without the fear of the Lord before their eyes, and some of them had drawn up with light women in Ayr, who followed them on their march. This the soldiers did not like, not wishing to be troubled with such gear in America; so the women, when they got the length of Kilmarnock, were ordered to retreat, and go home, which they all did, but one Jean Glaikit, who persisted in her intent to follow her jo,[211] Patrick O'Neil, a catholic Irish corporal. The man did, as he said, all in his capacity to persuade her to return, but she was a contumacious limmer,[212] and would not listen to reason, so that, in passing along our toll-road, from less to more, the miserable wretches fell out, and fought, and the soldier put an end to her, with a hasty knock on the head with his firelock,[213] and marched on after his comrades.

The body of the woman was, about half an hour after, found by the scholars of Mr

---

207 Och how! (Sc.): 'an exclamation expressive of weariness or sorrow' (*SND*).
208 Hap (Sc.): 'a wrap, shawl or plaid' (*SND* II).
209 Mair: more; claes: clothes (both Sc.).
210 Natural (Sc.): half-witted person, simpleton.
211 Jo (Sc.): sweetheart. Jean's surname means 'thoughtless, irresponsible [...] (gen. applied to women)' (*SND*).
212 Limmer (Sc.): 'a woman of loose or disreputable character' (*SND* 2).
213 Firelock: musket.

Loremore's school, who had got the play to see the marching,[214] and to hear the drums of the soldiers. Dreadful was the shout and the cry throughout the parish at this foul work. Some of the farmer lads followed the soldiers on horseback, and others ran to Sir Hugh, who was a justice of the peace, for his advice. — Such a day as that was!

However, the murderer was taken, and, with his arms tied behind him with a cord, he was brought back to the parish, where he confessed before Sir Hugh the deed, and how it happened. He was then put in a cart, and being well guarded by six of the lads, was taken to Ayr jail.

It was not long after this that the murderer was brought to trial, and, being found guilty on his own confession, he was sentenced to be executed, and his body to be hung in chains near the spot where the deed was done. I thought that all in the parish would have run to desperation with horror when the news of this came, and I wrote immediately to the Lord Eglesham to get this done away by the merciful power of the government, which he did, to our great solace and relief.

In the autumn, the young Laird Macadam, being ordered with his regiment for the Americas, got leave from the king to come and see his lady-mother, before his departure. But it was not to see her only, as will presently appear.

Knowing how much her ladyship was averse to the notion he had of Kate Malcolm, he did not write of his coming, lest she would send Kate out of the way, but came in upon them at a late hour, as they were wasting their precious time, as was the nightly wont of my lady, with a pack of cards; and so far was she from being pleased to see him, that no sooner did she behold his face, but like a tap of tow,[215] she kindled upon both him and Kate, and ordered them out of her sight and house. The young folk had discretion: Kate went home to her mother, and the laird came to the Manse, and begged us to take him in. He then told me what had happened, and that having bought a Captain's commission,[216] he was resolved to marry Kate, and hoped I would perform the ceremony, if her mother would consent. "As for mine," said he, "she will never agree; but, when the thing is done, her pardon will not be difficult to get, for, with all her whims and caprice, she is generous and affectionate." In short, he so wiled and beguiled me, that I consented to marry them, if Mrs Malcolm was agreeable. "I will not disobey my mother," said he, "by asking her consent, which I know she will refuse; and, therefore, the sooner it is done the better." So we then stepped over to Mrs Malcolm's house, where we found that saintly woman, with Kate, and Effie, and Willie, sitting peacefully at their fire-side, preparing to read their bibles for the night. When we went in, and when I saw Kate, that was so lady-like there, with the decent humility of her parent's dwelling, I could not but think she was destined for a better station; and when I looked at the Captain, a handsome youth, I thought surely their marriage is made in Heaven; and so I said to Mrs Malcolm, who after a time consented, and likewise agreed that her daughter should go with the Captain to America, for her faith and trust in the goodness of Providence was great and boundless, striving, as it were, to be even with its tender mercies. Accordingly, the Captain's man was sent to bid the chaise wait that had taken him to the lady's, and the marriage was sanctified by me before we left Mrs Malcolm's. No doubt, they ought to have been proclaimed three several Sabbaths, but I satisfied the Session, at our first meeting, on account of the necessity of the case. The young couple went in the chaise travelling to Glasgow, authorising me to break the matter to Lady Macadam, which was a sore task, but I

214 Got the play: got a day off school.
215 Tap of tow: tuft of flax (proverbially inflammable).
216 Promotion in the army was bought, rather than on merit.

was spared from the performance. For her ladyship had come to herself, and thinking on her own rashness in sending away Kate and the Captain in the way she had done, she was like one by herself; all the servants were scattered out and abroad in quest of the lovers, and some of them, seeing the chaise drive from Mrs Malcolm's door, with them in it, and me coming out, jealoused what had been done, and told their mistress outright of the marriage, which was to her like a clap of thunder; insomuch, that she flung herself back in her settee, and was beating and drumming with her heels on the floor, like a mad woman in Bedlam, when I entered the room. For some time she took no notice of me, but continued her din; but, by and by, she began to turn her eyes in fiery glances upon me, till I was terrified lest she would fly at me with her claws in her fury. At last she stopped all at once, and in a calm voice, said, "But it cannot now be helped, where are the vagabonds?" — "They are gone," replied I. — "Gone?" cried she, "gone where?" — "To America, I suppose," was my answer; upon which she again threw herself back in the settee, and began again to drum and beat with her feet as before. But not to dwell on small particularities, let it suffice to say, that she sent her coachman on one of her coach horses, which being old and stiff, did not overtake the fugitives till they were in their bed at Kilmarnock, where they stopped that night; but when they came back to the lady's in the morning, she was as cagey and meikle taken up with them,[217] as if they had gotten her full consent and privilege to marry from the first. Thus was the first of Mrs Malcolm's children well and creditably settled. I have only now to conclude with observing, that my son Gilbert was seized with the smallpox, about the beginning of December, and was blinded by them for seventeen days; for the inoculation was not in practice yet among us, saving only in the genteel families, that went into Edinburgh for the education of their children, where it was performed by the faculty there.[218]

CHAPTER XVI.—YEAR 1775.

Captain Macadam provides a house and an annuity for old Mrs Malcolm—Miss Betty Wadrife brings from Edinburgh a new-fashioned silk mantle, but refuses to give the pattern to old Lady Macadam—Her revenge.

THE regular course of nature is calm and orderly, and tempests and troubles are but lapses from the accustomed sobriety with which Providence works out the destined end of all things. From Yule till Pace-Monday there had been a gradual subsidence of our personal and parochial tribulations,[219] and the spring, which, though late, set in bright and beautiful, was accompanied with the spirit of contentment, so that, excepting the great concern that we all began to take in the American rebellion, especially on account of Charles Malcolm that was in the man of war, and of Captain Macadam that had married Kate, we had throughout the better half of the year but little molestation of any sort. I should, however, note the upshot of the marriage.

By some cause that I do not recollect, if I ever heard it properly told, the regiment wherein the Captain had bought his commission was not sent to the plantations, but only over to Ireland, by which the Captain and his lady were allowed to prolong their

---

217   Cagey, usually cadgy: cheerful, friendly; meikle: much (both Sc.).
218   Inoculation against smallpox had been available since the 1720s, after its introduction from Turkey. But it was still rare, and misunderstood, in many parts of Scotland at the end of the century.
219   Pace-Monday: Easter Monday (Pace is a version of Pasch, meaning Easter).

stay in the parish with his mother, and he, coming of age, while he was among us, in making a settlement on his wife, bought the house at the braehead, which was then just built by Thomas Shivers the mason, and he gave that house, with a judicious income, to Mrs Malcolm, telling her that it was not becoming, he having it in his power to do the contrary, that she should any longer be dependent on her own industry. For this the young man got a name like a sweet odour in all the country-side; but that whimsical and prelatic lady his mother, just went out of all bounds, and played such pranks, for an old woman, that cannot be told. To her daughter-in-law, however, she was wonderful kind; and in fitting her out for going with the Captain to Dublin, it was extraordinary to hear what a parapharnalia she provided her with. But who could have thought that in this kindness a sore trial was brewing for me!

It happened that Miss Betty Wadrife, the daughter of an heritor, had been on a visit to some of her friends in Edinburgh; and, being in at Edinburgh, she came out with a fine mantle,[220] decked and adorned with many a ribbon-knot, such as had never been seen in the parish. The Lady Macadam, hearing of this grand mantle, sent to beg Miss Betty to lend it to her, to make a copy for young Mrs Macadam. But Miss Betty was so vogie with her gay mantle,[221] that she sent back word, it would be making it o'er common; which so nettled the old courtly lady, that she vowed revenge, and said the mantle would not be long seen on Miss Betty. Nobody knew the meaning of her words; but she sent privately for Miss Sabrina, the schoolmistress, who was ay proud of being invited to my lady's, where she went on the Sabbath night to drink tea, and read Thomson's Seasons and Harvey's Meditations for her ladyship's recreation.[222] Between the two, a secret plot was laid against Miss Betty and her Edinburgh mantle; and Miss Sabrina, in a very treacherous manner, for the which I afterwards chided her severely, went to Miss Betty, and got a sight of the mantle, and how it was made, and all about it, until she was in a capacity to make another like it; by which my lady and her, from old silk and satin negligées which her ladyship had worn at the French court,[223] made up two mantles of the self-same fashion as Miss Betty's, and, if possible, more sumptuously garnished, but in a flagrant fool way. On the Sunday morning after, her ladyship sent for Jenny Gaffaw, and her daft daughter Meg, and shewed them the mantles, and said she would give them half-a-crown if they would go with them to the kirk, and take their place in the bench beside the elders, and, after worship, walk home before Miss Betty Wadrife. The two poor natural things were just transported with the sight of such bravery, and needed no other bribe; so, over their bits of ragged duds,[224] they put on the pageantry, and walked away to the kirk like peacocks, and took their place on the bench, to the great diversion of the whole congregation.

I had no suspicion of this, and had prepared an affecting discourse about the horrors of war, in which I touched, with a tender hand, on the troubles that threatened families and kindred in America; but all the time I was preaching, doing my best, and expatiating till the tears came into my eyes, I could not divine what was the cause of the inattention of my people. But the two vain haverels were on the bench under me, and I could not see

220   Mantle: cloak.
221   Vogie (Sc.): vain.
222   James Thomson, *The Seasons*, four very popular descriptive poems published between 1726 and 1746, and a touchstone of eighteenth-century 'polite reading'; William Harvey, *Divine Meditations upon Some of the Virtuous, and Vitious Women, in the Scriptures: Wherein, as in a Glass, everyone may see their own Faces; whether Fair, or Foul; Deformed, or Comely. A Work worthy their Spare-Hours* (1661).
223   Negligée: in this period, a loose gown.
224   Natural: simple-minded; bravery (from braw): finery; duds: clothes (all Sc.).

them; where they sat, spreading their feathers and picking their wings, stroking down and setting right their finery, with such an air as no living soul could see and withstand; while every eye in the kirk was now on them, and now at Miss Betty Wadrife, who was in a worse situation than if she had been on the stool of repentance.[225]

Greatly grieved with the little heed that was paid to my discourse, I left the pulpit with a heavy heart; but when I came out into the kirk-yard, and saw the two antics linking like ladies,[226] and aye keeping in the way before Miss Betty, and looking back and around in their pride and admiration, with high heads and a wonderful pomp, I was really overcome, and could not keep my gravity, but laughed loud out among the graves, and in the face of all my people, who, seeing how I was vanquished in that unguarded moment by my enemy,[227] made a universal and most unreverent breach of all decorum, at which Miss Betty, who had been the cause of all, ran into the first open door, and almost fainted away with mortification.

This affair was regarded by the elders as a sinful trespass on the orderlyness that was needful in the Lord's house, and they called on me at the Manse that night, and said it would be a guilty connivance, if I did not rebuke and admonish Lady Macadam of the evil of her way; for they had questioned daft Jenny, and had got at the bottom of the whole plot and mischief. But I, who knew her ladyship's light way, would fain have had the elders to overlook it, rather than expose myself to her tantrums; but they considered the thing as a great scandal, so I was obligated to conform to their wishes. I might, however, have as well stayed at home, for her ladyship was in one of her jocose humours when I went to speak to her on the subject; and it was so far from my power to make a proper impression on her of the enormity that had been committed, that she made me laugh, in spite of my reason, at the fantastical drollery of her malicious prank on Miss Betty Wadrife.

It, however, did not end here; for the Session, knowing that it was profitless to speak to the daft mother and daughter, who had been the instruments, gave orders to Willy Howking, the betheral,[228] not to let them again so far into the kirk, and Willy having scarcely more sense than them both, thought proper to keep them out next Sunday altogether. They twa said nothing at the time, but the adversary was busy with them;[229] for, on the Wednesday following, there being a meeting of the Synod at Ayr,[230] to my utter amazement, the mother and daughter made their appearance there in all their finery, and raised a complaint against me and the Session, for debarring them from church privileges. No stage play could have produced such an effect; I was perfectly dumb-foundered, and every member of the Synod might have been tied with a straw, they were so overcome with this new device of that endless woman, when bent on provocation—the Lady Macadam; in whom the saying was verified, that old

---

225 See note 103 (chapter V).

226 Linking: going arm-in-arm.

227 Although Galt did not correct this in the second edition, Kinsley, in his edition of *Annals*, changes 'my enemy' to 'the enemy', i.e., the Devil (as in 'the adversary' at note 229 below). That is almost certainly what Balwhidder consciously means here; but 'my enemy' leaves open the possibility that, at some level, he has the Devil confused with Lady Macadam.

228 Betheral, bedral (Sc.): a minister's general attendant, usually also acting as bell-ringer and grave-digger.

229 Adversary: i.e., the Devil.

230 The Synod was the third level (now abolished) of church authority, above the Presbytery of an area and the Session of a parish, imposing ecclesiastical discipline on the other two. The only higher authority was the annual General Assembly of the whole Kirk (see chapter XX).

folk are twice bairns, for in such plays, pranks, and projects, she was as playrife as a very lassie at her sampler, and this is but a swatch to what lengths she would go.[231] The complaint was dismissed, by which the Session and me were assoilzied;[232] but I'll never forget till the day of my death, what I suffered on that occasion, to be so put to the wall by two born idiots.

CHAPTER XVII.—YEAR 1776.

A recruiting party comes to Irville—Thomas Wilson and some others enlist—Charles Malcolm's return.

IT belongs to the chroniclers of the realm, to describe the damage and detriment which fell on the power and prosperity of the kingdom, by reason of the rebellion that was fired into open war against the name and authority of the king in the plantations of America; for my task is to describe what happened within the narrow bound of the pasturage of the Lord's flock, of which, in his bounty and mercy, he made me the humble, willing, but, alas! the weak and ineffectual shepherd.

About the month of February, a recruiting party came to our neighbour town of Irville, to beat up for men to be soldiers against the rebels; and thus the battle was brought, as it were, to our gates, for the very first man that took on with them was one Thomas Wilson, a cotter in our clachan, who, up to that time, had been a decent and creditable character. He was at first a farmer lad, but had foregathered with a doited tawpy,[233] whom he married, and had offspring three or four. For some time it was noticed, that he had a down and thoughtful look, that his cleeding was growing bare,[234] and that his wife kept an untrig house, which, it was feared by many, was the cause of Thomas going o'er often to the change-house; he was, in short, during the greater part of the winter, evidently a man foregone in the pleasures of this world,[235] which made all that knew him compassionate his situation.

No doubt, it was his household ills that burdened him past bearing, and made him go into Irville, when he heard of the recruiting, and take on to be a soldier. Such a wally wallying as the news of this caused at every door; for the red-coats, from the persecuting days, when the black-cuffs rampaged through the country,[236] soldiers that fought for hire, were held in dread and as a horror among us, and terrible were the stories that were told of their cruelty and sinfulness; indeed, there had not been wanting in our own time a sample of what they were, as witness the murder of Jean Glaikit by Patrick O'Neal, the Irish corporal, anent which I have treated at large in the memorables of the year 1774.

A meeting of the Session was forthwith held; for here was Thomas Wilson's wife and all his weans, an awful cess,[237] thrown upon the parish; and it was settled outright among us, that Mr Docken, who was then an elder, but is since dead, a worthy man,

231 Playrife: playful, frolicsome; swatch: typical piece, example (both Sc.).
232 Assoilzie (Scots Law): find not guilty.
233 Forgather, forgaither: here, marry (SND I.4); Tawpy, taupie: giddy or scatter-brained person, usually a young woman (both Sc.).
234   Cleeding, usually cleeds (Sc.): clothes.
235   Foregone: '? Weary, disconsolate; abandoned in despair, forsaken' suggests SND, but this is its only example, and comments, 'the word may be a usage of Galt's own invention.'
236 Wally wallying: lamentation. British soldiers traditionally wore red tunics, hence the name 'red coats'; the black cuffs belonged to 17th century dragoons, sent to suppress the Covenanters.
237 Cess (Sc.): tax (here, upon the Session's funds).

with a soft tongue and a pleasing manner, should go to Irville, and get Thomas, if possible, released from the recruiters. But it was all in vain, the serjeant would not listen to him, for Thomas was a strapping lad; nor would the poor infatuated man himself agree to go back, but cursed like a cadger,[238] and swore that if he staid any longer among his plagues, he would commit some rash act; so we were saddled with his family, which was the first taste and preeing of what war is when it comes into our hearths,[239] and among the breadwinners.

The evil, however, did not stop here. Thomas, when he was dressed out in the King's clothes, came over to see his bairns, and take a farewell of his friends, and he looked so gallant, that the very next market-day, another lad of the parish listed with him; but he was a ramplor,[240] roving sort of a creature, and, upon the whole, it was thought he did well for the parish when he went to serve the King.

The listing was a catching distemper.[241] Before the summer was over, other three of the farming lads went off with the drum, and there was a wailing in the parish, which made me preach a touching discourse. I likened the parish to a widow woman with a small family, sitting in their cottage by the fire-side, herself spinning with an eydent wheel, ettling her best to get them a bit and a brat, and the poor weans all canty about the hearth-stane— the little ones at their playocks,[242] and the elder at their tasks—the callans working with hooks and lines to catch them a meal of fish in the morning—and the lassies working stockings to sell at the next Marymas fair.[243]—And then I likened war to a calamity coming among them—the callans drowned at their fishing—the lassies led to a misdoing —and the feckless wee bairns laid on the bed of sickness, and their poor forlorn mother sitting by herself at the embers of a cauldrife fire; her tow done, and no a bodle to buy more;[244] dropping a silent and salt tear for her babies, and thinking of days that war gone, and, like Rachel weeping for her children, she would not be comforted. With this I concluded, for my own heart filled full with the thought, and there was a deep sob in the church, verily, it was Rachel weeping for her children.

In the latter end of the year, the man of war, with Charles Malcolm in her, came to the tail of the Bank at Greenock,[245] to press men as it was thought, and Charles got leave from his captain to come and see his mother; and he brought with him Mr Howard, another midshipman, the son of a great Parliament man in London, which, as we had tasted the sorrow, gave us some insight into the pomp of war. Charles was now grown up into a fine young man, rattling,[246] light-hearted, and just a cordial of gladness, and his companion was every bit like him. They were dressed in their fine gold-laced garbs, and nobody knew Charles when he came to the clachan, but all wondered, for they were on horseback, and rode to the house where his mother lived when he went away, but which was then occupied by Miss Sabrina and her school. Miss Sabrina had never seen Charles, but she had heard of him, and when he inquired for his mother, she guessed who he was, and shewed him the way to the new house that the Captain had bought for her.

---

238 Cadger (Sc.): pedlar.
239 Preeing (Sc.): a small quantity or sample.
240 Ramplor: to rample (Sc.) is to romp or sport.
241 Distemper: illness, suggesting an imbalance in the body's constitution.
242 Eydent, usually eident: industrious, continuously busy; ettling: intending; a bit and a brat: food and clothing; canty: lively, cheerful; playocks, playoks: playthings (all Sc.).
243 Marymas is the Feast of the Assumption (15 August).
244 Cauldrife: cold; bodle: a copper coin worth one-sixth of an English penny (both Sc.).
245 The Tail of the Bank is the anchorage at Greenock, named after the sandbank that restricts access further up the Clyde estuary.
246 Rattling: chatty.

Miss Sabrina, who was a little overly perjinct at times,[247] behaved herself on this occasion with a true spirit, and gave her lassies the play immediately, so that the news of Charles's return was spread by them like wild-fire, and there was a wonderful joy in the whole town. When Charles had seen his mother, and his sister Effie, with that douce and well-mannered lad William, his brother, for of their meeting I cannot speak, not being present, he then came with his friend to see me at the Manse, and was most jocose with me, and in a way of great pleasance, got Mrs Balwhidder to ask his friend to sleep at the Manse. In short, we had just a ploy the whole two days they staid with us, and I got leave from Lord Eglesham's steward to let them shoot on my lord's land, and I believe every laddie wean in the parish attended them to the field. As for old Lady Macadam, Charles being, as she said, a near relation, and she having likewise some knowledge of his comrade's family, she was just in her element with them, though they were but youths, for she was a woman naturally of a fantastical, and, as I have narrated, given to comical devices and pranks to a degree.[248] She made for them a ball, to which she invited all the bonniest lassies, far and near, in the parish, and was out of the body with mirth, and had a fiddler from Irville; and it was thought by those that were there, that had she not been crippled with the rheumatics, she would have danced herself. But I was concerned to hear both Charles and his friend, like hungry hawks, rejoicing at the prospect of the war, hoping thereby, as soon as their midship term was out, to be made lieutenants; saving this, there was no allay in the happiness they brought with them to the parish, and it was a delight to see how auld and young of all degrees made of Charles,[249] for we were proud of him, and none more than myself, though he began to take liberties with me, calling me old governor; it was, however, in a warm-hearted manner, only I did not like it when any of the elders heard. As for his mother, she deported herself like a saint on the occasion. There was a temperance in the pleasure of her heart, and in her thankfulness, that is past the compass of words to describe. Even Lady Macadam, who never could think a serious thought all her days, said, in her wild way, that the gods had bestowed more care in the making of Mrs Malcolm's temper, than on the bodies and souls of all the saints in the calendar. On the Sunday the strangers attended divine worship, and I preached to them a sermon purposely for them, and enlarged at great length and fullness on how David overcame Goliah; and they both told me that they had never heard such a good discourse, but I do not think they were great judges of preachings.[250] How, indeed, could Mr Howard know any thing of sound doctrine, being educated, as he told me, at Eton school, a prelatic establishment. Nevertheless, he was a fine lad, and though a little given to frolic and diversion, he had a principle of integrity, that afterwards kithed into much virtue; for, during this visit, he took a notion of Effie Malcolm, and the lassie of him, then a sprightly and blooming creature, fair to look upon, and blithe to see; and he kept up a correspondence with her till the war was over, when, being a captain of a frigate, he came down among us, and they were married by me, as shall be related in its proper place.

---

247   Perjinct, elsewhere perjink: exact, precise.

248   Fantastical: Kinsley glosses this as 'grotesque, extravagant fancy'. 'To a degree' means 'to the highest degree'; not, as it usually does today, 'to *some* degree, partially'.

249   Made of: anglicising Sc. to mak o', meaning 'to fuss over, to pet, to make much of' (*SND* 'mak' I.B.8).

250   Balwhidder *seems* oblivious to the possible parallel between the story of David and Goliath in 1 Samuel 17 and the war between the American colonists and the British Empire; yet it is not clear on what other grounds he would preach on this text 'purposely' for the navy men.

CHAPTER XVIII.—YEAR 1777.

Old Widow Mirkland—Bloody accounts of the war—He gets a newspaper—Great flood.

THIS may well be called the year of the heavy heart, for we had sad tidings of the lads that went away as soldiers to America. First, there was a boding in the minds of all their friends that they were never to see them more, and their sadness, like a mist spreading from the waters and covering the fields, darkened the spirit of the neighbours. Secondly, a sound was bruited about,[251] that the King's forces would have a hot and a sore struggle before the rebels were put down, if they were ever put down. Then came the cruel truth of all the poor lads' friends had feared; but it is fit and proper that I should relate at length, under their several heads, the sorrows and afflictions as they came to pass.

One evening, as I was taking my walk alone, meditating my discourse for the next Sabbath—it was shortly after Candlemas—it was a fine clear pretty evening, just as the sun was setting. Taking my walk alone, and thinking of the dreadfulness of Almighty Power, and how that if it was not tempered and restrained by infinite goodness, and wisdom, and mercy, the miserable sinner man, and all things that live, would be in a woeful state, I drew near the beild[252] where old widow Mirkland lived by herself, who was grandmother to Jock Hempy, the ramplor lad that was the second who took on for a soldier. I did not mind of this at the time, but passing the house, I heard the croon, as it were, of a laden soul, busy with the Lord, and, not to disturb the holy workings of grace, I paused, and listened. It was old Mizy Mirkland herself, sitting at the gable of the house, looking at the sun setting in all his glory beyond the Arran hills; but she was not praying—only moaning to herself,—an oozing out, as it might be called, of the spirit from her heart, then grievously oppressed with sorrow, and heavy bodements of grey-hairs and poverty.—"Yonder it slips awa'," she was saying, "and my poor bairn, that's o'er the seas in America, is maybe looking on its bright face, thinking of his hame, and aiblins of me,[253] that did my best to breed him up in the fear of the Lord; but I couldna warsle wi' what was ordained. Ay, Jock! as ye look at the sun gaun down, as many a time, when ye were a wee innocent laddie at my knee here, I hae bade ye look at him as a type of your Maker, you will hae a sore heart; for ye hae left me in my need, when ye should hae been near at hand to help me, for the hard labour and industry with which I brought you up. But it's the Lord's will,—blessed be the name of the Lord, that makes us to thole the tribulations of this world, and will reward us, through the mediation of Jesus, hereafter." She wept bitterly as she said this, for her heart was tried, but the blessing of a religious contentment was shed upon her; and I stepped up to her, and asked about her concerns, for, saving as a parishioner, and a decent old woman, I knew little of her. Brief was her story, but it was one of misfortune.—"But I will not complain," she said, "of the measure that has been meted unto me. I was left myself an orphan; when I grew up, and was married to my gudeman, I had known but scant and want. Our days of felicity were few, and he was ta'en awa' from me shortly after my Mary was born—a wailing baby, and a widow's heart, was a' he left me. I nursed her with my salt tears, and bred her in straits, but the favour of God was with us, and she grew up to womanhood, as lovely as the rose, and as blameless as the lily. In her

---

251   I.e., word went round.
252   Beild (Sc.): shelter, home.
253   Aiblins (Sc.): perhaps.

^time she was married to a farming lad; there never was a brawer pair in the kirk, than on that day when they gaed there first as man and wife. My heart was proud, and it pleased the Lord to chastize my pride — to nip my happiness even in the bud. The very next day he got his arm crushed. It never got well again, and he fell into a decay, and died in the winter, leaving my Mary far on in the road to be a mother.

"When her time drew near, we both happened to be working in the yard. She was delving to plant potatoes, and I told her it would do her hurt, but she was eager to provide something, as she said, for what might happen. O, it was an ill-omened word. The same night her trouble came on, and before the morning she was a cauld corpse, and another wee wee fatherless baby was greeting at my bosom — It was him that's noo awa' in America. He grew up to be a fine bairn, with a warm heart, but a light head, and, wanting the rein of a father's power upon him, was no sae douce as I could have wished; but he was no man's foe save his own. I thought, and hoped, as he grew to years of discretion, he would have sobered, and been a consolation to my old age; but he's gone, and he'll never come back — disappointment is my portion in this world, and I have no hope; while I can do, I will seek no help, but threescore and fifteen can do little, and a small ail is a great evil to an aged woman, who has but the distaff for her bread-winner."[254]

I did all that I could to bid her be of good cheer, but the comfort of a hopeful spirit was dead within her; and she told me, that by many tokens she was assured, her bairn was already slain. — "Thrice," said she, "I have seen his wraith — The first time he was in the pride of his young manhood, the next he was pale and wan, with a bloody and a gashy wound in his side, and the third time there was a smoke, and when it cleared away, I saw him in a grave, with neither winding-sheet nor coffin."

The tale of this pious and resigned spirit dwelt in mine ear, and when I went home, Mrs Balwhidder thought that I had met with an o'ercome,[255] and was very uneasy; so she got the tea soon ready to make me better but scarcely had we tasted the first cup when a loud lamentation was heard in the kitchen. This was from that tawpy the wife of Thomas Wilson, with her three weans. They had been seeking their meat among the farmer houses, and, in coming home, forgathered on the road with the Glasgow carrier,[256] who told them, that news had come in the London Gazette, of a battle, in which the regiment that Thomas had listed in was engaged, and had suffered loss both in rank and file; none doubting that their head was in the number of the slain, the whole family grat aloud,[257] and came to the Manse, bewailing him as no more; and it afterwards turned out to be the case, making it plain to me that there is a farseeing discernment in the spirit, that reaches beyond the scope of our incarnate senses.

But the weight of the war did not end with these afflictions; for, instead of the sorrow that the listing caused, and the anxiety after, and the grief of the bloody tidings, operating as wholesome admonition to our young men, the natural perversity of the human heart was more and more manifested. A wonderful interest was raised among us all to hear of what was going on in the world, insomuch, that I myself was no longer contented with the relation of the news of the month in the Scots Magazine, but joined with my father-in-law, Mr Kibbock, to get a newspaper twice a-week from Edinburgh. As for Lady Macadam, who being naturally an impatient woman, she had one sent to

---

254 That is, depends on spinning for a living (a distaff is the spindle on which the thread is spun).

255   O'ercome, owercome (Sc.): a sudden attack of illness.

256   Forgather, forgaither (Sc.): here, encounter, meet with (*SND* I.2).

257   Grat (Sc.): wept.

her three times a-week from London, so that we had something fresh five times every week; and the old papers were lent out to the families who had friends in the wars. This was done on my suggestion, hoping it would make all content with their peaceable lot, but dominion for a time had been given to the power of contrariness, and it had quite an opposite effect. It begot a curiosity, egging on to enterprize, and, greatly to my sorrow, three of the brawest lads in the parish, or in any parish, all in one day took on with a party of the Scots Greys that were then lying in Ayr; and nothing would satisfy the callans at Mr Loremore's school, but, instead of their innocent plays with girs and shintys, and sicklike,[258] they must go ranking like soldiers, and fight sham-fights in bodies. In short, things grew to a perfect hostility, for a swarm of weans came out from the schools of Irville on a Saturday afternoon, and, forgathering with ours, they had a battle with stones on the toll-road, such as was dreadful to hear of, for many a one got a mark that day he will take to the grave with him.

It was not, however, by accidents of the field only, that we were afflicted; those of the flood, too, were sent likewise against us. In the month of October, when the corn was yet in the holms,[259] and on the cold land by the river side, the water of Irville swelled to a great speat, from bank to brae, sweeping all before it, and roaring, in its might, like an agent of divine displeasure, sent forth to punish the inhabitants of the earth. The loss of the victual was a thing reparable, and those that suffered did not greatly complain; for, in other respects, their harvest had been plenteous; but the river, in its fury, not content with overflowing the lands, burst through the sandy hills with a raging force, and a riving asunder of the solid ground, as when the fountains of the great deep were broken up. All in the parish was a-foot, and on the hills, some weeping and wringing their hands, not knowing what would happen, when they beheld the landmarks of the waters deserted, and the river breaking away through the country, like the war-horse set loose in his pasture, and glorying in his might.[260] By this change in the way and channel of the river, all the mills in our parish were left more than half a mile from dam or lade; and the farmers, through the whole winter, till the new mills were built, had to travel through a heavy road with their victual, which was a great grievance, and added not a little to the afflictions of this unhappy year, which to me were not without a particularity, by the death of a full cousin of Mrs Balwhidder, my first wife; she was grievously burnt by looting over a candle.[261] Her mutch, which was of the high structure then in vogue, took fire, and being fastened with corking pins to a great toupee,[262] it could not be got off until she had sustained a deadly injury, of which, after lingering long, she was kindly eased by her removal from trouble. This sore accident was to me a matter of deep concern and cogitation; but as it happened in Tarbolton,[263] and no in our parish, I have only alluded to it to shew, that when my people were chastised by the hand of Providence, their pastor was not spared, but had a drop from the same vial.

---

258   Girs and shintys: hoops and shinty-sticks; sicklike, usually siclike: suchlike (all Sc.).
259   Holm (Sc.): 'low-lying land beside a river' (*DOST*).
260   Job 38.21.
261   Loot, usually lout (Sc.): bend, stoop.
262   Toupee: a feature on top of the large wigs worn by well-off ladies in the eighteenth century.
263   Tarbolton is seven miles north-east of Ayr.

CHAPTER XIX.—YEAR 1778.

Revival of the smuggling trade—Betty and Janet Pawkie, and Robin Bicker, an exciseman, come to the parish—Their doings—Robin is succeeded by Mungo Argyle—Lord Eglesham assists William Malcolm.

THIS year was as the shadow of the bygane;[264] there was less actual suffering, but what we came through cast a gloom among us, and we did not get up our spirits till the spring was far advanced; the corn was in the ear, and the sun far towards Midsummer height, before there was any regular shew of gladness in the parish.

It was clear to me that the wars were not to be soon over, for I noticed, in the course of this year, that there was a greater christening of lad bairns, than had ever been in any year during my incumbency; and grave and wise persons, observant of the signs of the times, said, that it had been long held as a sure prognostication of war, when the births of male children outnumbered that of females.

Our chief misfortune in this year, was a revival of that wicked mother of many mischiefs, the smuggling trade, which concerned me greatly; but it was not allowed to it to make any thing like a permanent stay among us, though in some of the neighbouring parishes, its ravages, both in morals and property, was very distressing, and many a mailing was sold to pay for the triumphs of the cutters and gaugers;[265] for the government was by this time grown more eager, and the war caused the King's ships to be out and about, which increased the trouble of the smugglers, whose wits in their turn were thereby much sharpened.

After Mrs Malcolm, by the settlement of Captain Macadam, had given up her dealing, two maiden-women, that were sisters, Betty and Janet Pawkie,[266] came in among us from Ayr, where they had friends in league with some of the laigh land folk, that carried on the contraband with the Isle of Man, which was the very eye of the smuggling. They took up the tea-selling, which Mrs Malcolm had dropped, and did business on a larger scale, having a general huxtry, with parliament-cakes,[267] and candles, and pincushions, as well as other groceries, in their window. Whether they had any contraband dealings, or were only back-bitten, I cannot take it upon me to say, but it was jealoused in the parish, that the meal in the sacks, that came to their door at night, and was sent to the Glasgow market in the morning, was not made of corn. They were, however, decent women, both sedate and orderly; the eldest, Betty Pawkie, was of a manly stature, and had a long beard, which made her have a coarse look, but she was, nevertheless, a worthy, well-doing creature, and, at her death, she left ten pounds to the poor of the parish, as may be seen in the mortification board,[268] that the Session put up in the kirk as a testification and an example.

Shortly after the revival of the smuggling, an exciseman was put among us, and the first was Robin Bicker, a very civil lad, that had been a flunkie with Sir Hugh Montgomerie, when he was a residenter in Edinburgh, before the old Sir Hugh's death. He was a queer fellow, and had a coothy way of getting in about folk, the which was

264   I.e., the shadow of the previous one.
265   Mailing (Sc.): leased land, a smallholding (*SND* II.2). Gaugers: customs men; cutters: their patrol-vessels.
266   Pawkie means 'witty, sly, cunning, crafty' (*SND*).
267   Parliament cake: 'a thin flat type of gingerbread' (*OED*).
268   Mortification board: 'a wooden panel in a church on which charitable donations and requests were recorded' (*SND* 'mortify'). See note 121 (chapter VI).

very serviceable to him in his vocation; nor was he overly gleg,[269] but when a job was ill done, and he was obliged to notice it, he would often break out on the smugglers for being so stupid, so that for an exciseman he was wonderful well liked, and did not object to a waught of brandy at a time,[270] when the auld wives ca'd it well-water. It happened, however, that some unneighbourly person sent him notice of a clecking of tea chests, or brandy kegs, at which both Jenny and Betty Pawkie were the howdies. Robin could not but therefore enter their house; however, before going in, he just cried at the door to somebody on the road, so as to let the twa industrious lassies hear he was at hand. They were not slack in closing the trance-door,[271] and putting stoups and stools behind it, so as to cause trouble, and give time before any body could get in. They then emptied their chaff-bed, and filled the tikeing with tea,[272] and Betty went in on the top, covering herself with the blanket, and graining like a woman in labour. It was thought that Robin Bicker himself would not have been overly particular in searching the house, considering there was a woman seemingly in the dead thraws; but a sorner, an incomer from the east country, and that hung about the change-house as a divor hostler,[273] that would rather gang a day's journey in the dark than turn a spade in day-light, came to him as he stood at the door, and went in with him to see the sport. Robin, for some reason, could not bid him go away, and both Betty and Janet were sure he was in the plot against them; indeed, it was always thought he was an informer, and no doubt he was something not canny, for he had a down look.

It was some time before the door-way was cleared of the stoups and stools, and Janet was in great concern, and flustered, as she said, for her poor sister, who was taken with a heart-cholic. "I'm sorry for her," said Robin, "but I'll be as quiet as possible;" and so he searched all the house, but found nothing, at the which his companion, the divor east-country hostler, swore an oath that could not be misunderstood, so, without more ado, but as all thought against the grain, Robin went up to sympathize with Betty in the bed, whose groans were loud and vehement. "Let me feel your pulse," said Robin, and he looted down as she put forth her arm from aneath the clothes, and laying his hand on the bed, cried, "Hey! what's this? this is a costly filling." Upon which Betty jumpet up quite recovered, and Janet fell to the wailing and railing, while the hostler from the east country took the bed of tea on his back, to carry it to the change-house, till a cart was gotten to take it into the custom-house at Irville.

Betty Pawkie being thus suddenly cured, and grudging the loss of property, took a knife in her hand, and as the divor was crossing the burn at the stepping-stones, that lead to the back of the change-house, she ran after him, and ripped up the tikeing, and sent all the tea floating away on the burn, which was thought a brave action of Betty, and the story not a little helped to lighten our melancholy meditations.

Robin Bicker was soon after this affair removed to another district, and we got in his place one Mungo Argyle, who was as proud as a provost, being come of Highland parentage. Black was the hour he came among my people, for he was needy and greedy, and rode on the top of his commission. Of all the manifold ills in the train of

---

269 Queer: here probably in Sc. sense of humorous, comical; coothy, usually couthie: agreeable, sociable; gleg: quick of perception (both Sc.).
270 Waught, usually waucht: a long pull at a drink, as in Burns's 'We'll tak a right good-willie-waught/For auld lang syne'.
271 Trance-door: the inner door, between the street-door and the lobby (the trance).
272 Mattresses and pillows were commonly made of a strong linen or cotton called tick, and stuffed with chaff.
273 Graining: groaning; dead thraws: death-throes; sorner: a scrounger, particularly an intimidating one; divor: bankrupt (all Sc.).

smuggling, surely the excisemen are the worst, and the setting of this rabiator over us was a severe judgment for our sins.[274] But he suffered for't, and peace be with him in the grave, where the wicked cease from troubling.

Willie Malcolm, the youngest son of his mother, had by this time learnt all that Mr Loremore, the schoolmaster, could teach, and, as it was evidenced to every body, by his mild manners and saintliness of demeanour, that he was a chosen vessel, his mother longed to fulfil his own wish, which was doubtless the natural working of the act of grace that had been shed upon him; but she had not the where withal to send him to the college of Glasgow, where he was desirous to study, and her just pride would not allow her to cess his brother-in-law, the Captain Macadam, whom, I should now mention, was raised, in the end of this year, as we read in the newspapers, to be a Major. I thought her in this somewhat unreasonable, for she would not be persuaded to let me write to the Captain; but when I reflected on the good that Willie Malcolm might in time do as a preacher, I said nothing more to her, but indited a letter to the Lord Eglesham,[275] setting forth the lad's parts, telling who he was, and all about his mother's scruples; and, by the retour of the post from London,[276] his lordship sent me an order on his steward, to pay me twenty pounds towards equipping my protegée, as he called Willie, with a promise to pay for his education, which was such a great thing for his lordship to do off-hand on my recommendation, that it won him much affection throughout the country side; and folk began to wonder, rehearsing the great things, as was said, that I had gotten my lord at different times, and on divers occasions, to do, which had a vast of influence among my brethren of the presbytery,[277] and they grew into a state of greater cordiality with me, looking on me as a man having authority; but I was none thereat lifted up, for not being gifted with the power of a kirk-filling eloquence, I was but little sought for at sacraments and fasts, and solemn days, which was doubtless well ordained, for I had no motive to seek fame in foreign pulpits, but was left to walk in the paths of simplicity within my own parish. To eschew evil myself, and to teach others to do the same, I thought the main duties of the pastoral office, and with a sincere heart endeavoured what in me lay to perform them with meekness, sobriety, and a spirit wakeful to the inroads of sin and Satan. But O the sordidness of human nature! —The kindness of the Lord Eglesham's own disposition, was ascribed to my influence, and many a dry answer I was obliged to give to applicants that would have me trouble his lordship, as if I had a claim upon him. In the ensuing year, the notion of my cordiality with him came to a great head, and brought about an event, that could not have been forethought by me as a thing within the compass of possibility to bring to pass.

---

274 Rabiator (Sc.): 'a plunderer, a violent ruthless person' (*SND*).
275 Indite: compose.
276 Retour (Sc.): return.
277 A vast of influence: 'vast' can still be used as noun in the nineteenth century where we would use e.g. 'vast amount'. Balwhidder's 'brethren of the presbytery' are his fellow ministers in the area.

CHAPTER XX.—YEAR 1779.

He goes to Edinburgh to attend the General Assembly—Preaches before the Commissioner.

I WAS named in this year for the General Assembly,[278] and Mrs Balwhidder, by her continual thrift, having made our purse able to stand a shake against the wind, we resolved to go into Edinburgh in a creditable manner. Accordingly, in conjunct with Mrs Dalrymple, the lady of a Major of that name, we hired the Irville chaise, and we put up in Glasgow at the Black Boy, where we staid all night. Next morning, by seven o'clock, we got into the fly coach for the capital of Scotland,[279] which we reached after a heavy journey, about the same hour in the evening, and put up at the public where it stopped, till the next day; for really both me and Mrs Balwhidder were worn out with the undertaking, and found a cup of tea a vast refreshment.

Betimes, in the morning, having taken our breakfast, we got a caddy to guide us and our wallise to widow McVicar's, at the head of the Covenanter's Close.[280] She was a relation to my first wife, Betty Lanshaw, my own full cousin that was, and we had advised her, by course of post, of our coming, and intendment to lodge with her, as uncos and strangers.[281] But Mrs McVicar kept a cloth shop, and sold plaidings and flannels, besides Yorkshire superfines, and was used to the sudden incoming of strangers, especially visitants, both from the West and the North Highlands, and was withal a gawsy furthy woman,[282] taking great pleasure in hospitality, and every sort of kindliness and discretion. She would not allow of such a thing as our being lodgers in her house, but was so cagey to see us, and to have it in her power to be civil to a minister, as she was pleased to say, of such repute, that nothing less would content her, but that we must live upon her, and partake of all the best that could be gotten for us within the walls of "the gude town."

When we found ourselves so comfortable, Mrs Balwhidder and me waited on my patron's family, that was, the young ladies, and the laird, who had been my pupil, but was now an advocate high in the law. They likewise were kind also. In short, every body in Edinburgh were in a manner wearisome kind, and we could scarcely find time to see the Castle and the palace of Holyrood-house, and that more sanctified place, where that Maccabeus of the Kirk of Scotland, John Knox,[283] was wont to live.

---

278   The General Assembly is the highest governing body of the Kirk, meeting annually in Edinburgh: Balwhidder has been chosen to represent his Presbytery there.

279   Fly coach: the stage coach, a scheduled public service.

280   Balwhidder is misremembering Covenant Close (still there, on the south side of the High Street, between the Tron and St. Giles), named after the National Covenant that defied Charles I's authority in 1638 (which was kept in this close) rather than the later martyrs of Balwhidder's own west country. A caddy is a street porter. Wallise, usually walise (Sc.): valise, travelling case.

281   Unco (Sc.): here, just means stranger (*SND* III.2). The point is that the Balwhidders are proposing to pay for their lodging as they would if they were not related to their landlady.

282   Gawsy, usually gawsie: plump and fresh-complexioned; furthy, furthie: generous, hospitable (both Sc.).

283   John Knox (c.1510–1572), preacher, theologian and historian, and leader of the Scottish Reformation. Balwhidder compares him to Judas Maccabeus, leader of a Jewish revolt against the Persian rulers of Judea in 167–160 BC, in the course of which he purified and re-consecrated the Temple in Jerusalem (defiled with pagan idols) as Knox purified the Scottish church. The house at 43/45 High Street is celebrated as Knox's: it is not clear that he ever lived there.

Upon my introduction to his Grace the Commissioner, I was delighted and surprised to find the Lord Eglesham at the levee, and his lordship was so glad on seeing me, that he made me more kentspeckle than I could have wished to have been in his Grace's presence;[284] for, owing to the same, I was required to preach before his Grace, upon a jocose recommendation of his lordship; the which gave me great concern, and daunted me, so that in the interim I was almost bereft of all peace and studious composure of mind. Fain would I have eschewed the honour that was thus thrust upon me, but both my wife and Mrs McVicar were just lifted out of themselves with the thought.

When the day came, I thought all things in this world were loosened from their hold, and that the sure and steadfast earth itself was grown coggly beneath my feet,[285] as I mounted the pulpit. With what sincerity I prayed for help that day, and never stood man more in need of it, for through all my prayer the congregation was so watchful and still, doubtless to note if my doctrine was orthodox, that the beating of my heart might have been heard to the uttermost corners of the kirk.

I had chosen as my text, from Second Samuel, xixth chapter, and 35th verse, these words — "Can I hear any more the voice of singing men and singing women? Wherefore, then, should thy servant be yet a burden to the King." And hardly had I with a trembling voice read the words, when I perceived an awful stir in the congregation, for all applied the words to the state of the church, and the appointment of his Grace the Commissioner. Having paused after giving out the text, the same fearful and critical silence again ensued, and every eye was so fixed upon me, that I was for a time deprived of courage to look about; but Heaven was pleased to compassionate my infirmity, and as I proceeded, I began to warm as in my own pulpit. I described the gorgeous Babylonian harlot riding forth in her chariots of gold and silver, with trampling steeds, and a hurricane of followers, drunk with the cup of abominations, all shouting with revelry, and glorying in her triumph, treading down in their career those precious pearls, the saints and martyrs, into the mire beneath their swinish feet. "Before her you may behold Wantonness playing the tinkling cymbal, Insolence beating the drum, and Pride blowing the trumpet. Every vice is there with his emblems, and the seller of pardons, with his crucifix and triple crown, is distributing his largess of perdition.[286] The voices of men shout to set wide the gates, to give entrance to the Queen of nations, and the gates are set wide, and they all enter. The avenging gates close on them — they are all shut up in hell."

There was a sough in the kirk as I said these words, for the vision I described seemed to be passing before me as I spoke, and I felt as if I had witnessed the everlasting destruction of Antichrist, and the worshippers of the beast. But soon recovering myself, I said, in a soft and gentle manner, "Look at yon lovely creature in virgin-raiment, with the Bible in her hand. See how mildly she walks along, giving alms to the poor as she passes on towards the door of that lowly dwelling — Let us follow her in — She takes her seat in the chair at the bed-side of the poor old dying sinner, and as he tosses in the height of penitence and despair, she reads to him the promise of the Saviour. — 'This night thou shalt be with me in Paradise;'[287] and he embraces her with transports, and

---

284 The Commissioner represents the monarch at the General Assembly. A levee is, in this case, a reception held by the monarch or his representative, for the purposes of introductions, paying court etc. Kentspeckle, usually kenspeckle (Sc.): conspicuous.

285 Coggly (Sc.): unsteady.

286 This stuff is of course from the Book of Revelation, chapters 17–18, describing the Day of Judgement, not from 2 Samuel. The seller of pardons in the triple crown is the Pope (equated with the Antichrist of Revelation in Protestant interpretations).

287 On the cross, Jesus assures one of the criminals executed alongside him, 'To day shalt thou be with me in paradise'.

falling back on his pillow, calmly closes his eyes in peace. She is the true religion; and when I see what she can do even in the last moments of the guilty, well may we exclaim, when we think of the symbols and pageantry of the departed superstition, Can I hear any more the voice of singing men and singing women? No; let us cling to the simplicity of the Truth that is now established in our native land."

At the conclusion of this clause of my discourse, the congregation, which had been all so still and so solemn, never coughing, as was often the case among my people, gave a great rustle, changing their positions, by which I was almost overcome; however, I took heart, and ventured on, and pointed out, that with our Bible and an orthodox priesthood, we stood in no need of the King's authority, however bound we were in temporal things to respect it, and I shewed this at some length, crying out, in the words of my text, "Wherefore, then, should thy servant be yet a burden to the King?" in the saying of which I happened to turn my eyes towards his Grace the Commissioner, as he sat on the throne, and I thought his countenance was troubled, which made me add, that he might not think I meant him any offence, That the King of the Church[288] was one before whom the great, and the wise, and the good, — all doomed and sentenced convicts — implore his mercy. "It is true," said I, "that in the days of his tribulation he was wounded for our iniquities, and died to save us; but, at his death, his greatness was proclaimed by the quick and the dead. There was sorrow, and there was wonder, and there was rage, and there was remorse; but there was no shame there — none blushed on that day at that sight but yon glorious luminary." The congregation rose, and looked round, as the sun that I pointed at shone in at the window. I was disconcerted by their movement, and my spirit was spent, so that I could say no more.

When I came down from the pulpit, there was a great pressing in of acquaintance and ministers, who lauded me exceedingly; but I thought it could be only in derision, therefore I slipped home to Mrs McVicar's as fast as I could.

Mrs McVicar, who was a clever, hearing-all sort of a neighbour, said my sermon was greatly thought of, and that I had surprised every body; but I was fearful there was something of jocularity at the bottom of this, for she was a flaunty woman,[289] and liked well to give a good-humoured jibe or jeer. However, his Grace the Commissioner was very thankful for the discourse, and complimented me on what he called my apostolical earnestness; but he was a courteous man, and I could not trust to him, especially as my Lord Eglesham had told me in secrecy before — it's true, it was in his gallanting way, — that, in speaking of the King's servant as I had done, I had rather gone beyond the bounds of modern moderation.[290] Altogether, I found neither pleasure nor profit in what was thought so great an honour, but longed for the privacy of my own narrow pasture, and little flock.

It was in this visit to Edinburgh that Mrs Balwhidder bought her silver tea-pot, and other ornamental articles; but this was not done, as she assured me, in a vain spirit of bravery, which I could not have abided, but because it was well known, that tea draws better in a silver pot, and drinks pleasanter in a china cup, than out of any other kind of cup or tea-pot.

---

288   The King of the Church: Christ.
289   Flaunty, flauntie (Sc.): capricious, giddy, flighty.
290   By 'gallanting' Balwhidder seems to mean merely 'light-hearted': all examples in *OED* imply an element of flirtation. 'Modern moderation' was the stance of the dominant party in the eighteenth-century Kirk, a readiness to compromise with secular authority in matters of church government (such as patronage), and to acknowledge the importance of new types of secular learning: many important figures in the Scottish Enlightenment were moderate clergy. Balwhidder's pulpit rhetoric is his inheritance from an older, more fundamentalist Presbyterianism.

By the time I got home to the Manse, I had been three whole weeks and five days absent, which was more than all my absences together, from the time of my placing, and my people were glowing with satisfaction, when they saw us driving in a Glasgow chaise through the clachan to the Manse.

The rest of the year was merely a quiet succession of small incidents, none of which are worthy of notation, though they were all severally, no doubt, of aught somewhere,[291] as they took up both time and place in the coming to pass, and nothing comes to pass without helping onwards some great end; each particular little thing that happens in the world, being a seed sown by the hand of Providence to yield an increase, which increase is destined, in its turn, to minister to some higher purpose, until at last the issue affects the whole earth. There is nothing in all the world that doth not advance the cause of goodness; no, not even the sins of the wicked, though through the dim casement of her mortal tabernacle, the soul of man cannot discern the method thereof.

CHAPTER XXI.—YEAR 1780.

Lord George Gordon—Report of an illumination.

THIS was, among ourselves, another year of few events. A sound, it is true, came among us of a design on the part of government in London, to bring back the old harlotry of papistry; but we spent our time in the lea of the hedge, and the lown of the hill. Some there were that a panic seized upon, when they heard of Lord George Gordon, that zealous protestant, being committed to the Tower;[292] but for my part, I had no terror upon me, for I saw all things around me going forward improving, and I said to myself, it is not so when Providence permits scathe and sorrow to fall upon a nation.[293] Civil troubles, and the casting down of thrones, is always forewarned by want and poverty striking the people. What I have, therefore, chiefly to record as the memorables of this year, are things of small import, — the main of which are, that some of the neighbouring lairds, taking example by Mr Kibbock, my father-in-law that was, began in this fall to plant the tops of their hills with mounts of fir-trees; and Mungo Argyle, the exciseman, just herried the poor smugglers to death, and made a power of prize-money,[294] which, however, had not the wonted effect of riches; for it brought him no honour, and he lived in the parish like a leper, or any other kind of excommunicated person.

But I should not forget a most droll thing that took place with Jenny Gaffaw, and her daughter. They had been missed from the parish for some days, and folk began to be uneasy about what could have become of the two silly creatures; till one night, at the dead hour, a strange light was seen beaming and burning at the window of the bit

---

291   Of aught: 'of importance, consequence', but this is the only example cited in SND.
292   The plan to 'bring back [...] papistry' was no more than the Catholic Relief Act of 1778, which had allowed Catholics in England, Ireland, and Wales to own property, inherit land, and join the army; the first revocation of the Penal Laws in place against them since 1698. Lord George Gordon, a Protestant demagogue, started a campaign to have the Act revoked, encouraging the sorts of fears Balwhidder alludes to here: in 1780 its demonstrations ended in riots, and the looting and burning of Catholic chapels, homes, and businesses; the riot in London lasted for six days before the army was called out and Lord George arrested (and later found not guilty of high treason).
293   Scathe: hurt, harm, damage.
294   Customs officers, like sailors in the navy, were awarded a share in the value of captured vessels and their cargos.

hole where they lived. It was first observed by Lady Macadam, who never went to bed at any Christian hour, but sat up reading her new French novels and play books with Miss Sabrina, the school-mistress. She gave the alarm, thinking that such a great and continuous light from a lone house, where never candle had been seen before, could be nothing less than the flame of a burning. And sending Miss Sabrina and the servants to see what was the matter, they beheld daft Jenny, and her as daft daughter, with a score of candle doups,[295] (Heaven only knows where they got them!) placed in the window, and the twa fools dancing, and linking, and admiring before the door. "What's all this about, Jenny," said Miss Sabrina. — "Awa' wi' you, awa' wi' you — ye wicked pope, ye whore of Babylon — Is na it for the glory of God, and the Protestant religion? d'ye think I will be a pope as long as light can put out darkness?" — And with that the mother and daughter began again to leap and dance as madly as before.

It seems, that poor Jenny having heard of the luminations that were lighted up through the country, on the ending of the Popish Bill,[296] had, with Meg, travelled by themselves into Glasgow, where they had gathered or begged a stock of candles, and coming back under the cloud of night, had surprised and alarmed the whole clachan, by lighting up their window in the manner that I have described. Poor Miss Sabrina, at Jenny's uncivil salutation, went back to my lady with her heart full, and would fain have had the idiots brought to task before the Session, for what had been said to her. But I would not hear tell of such a thing, for which Miss Sabrina owed me a grudge, that was not soon given up. At the same time, I was grieved to see the testimonies of joyfulness for a holy victory, brought into such disrepute by the ill-timed demonstrations of the two irreclaimable naturals, that had not a true conception of the cause for which they were triumphing.

CHAPTER XXII.—YEAR 1781.

Argyle, the exciseman, grows a gentleman—Lord Eglesham's concubine—His death—The parish children afflicted with the measles.

IF the two last years passed o'er the heads of me and my people without any manifest dolour, which is a great thing to say for so long a period in this world, we had our own trials and tribulations in the one of which I have now to make mention. Mungo Argyle, the exciseman, waxing rich, grew proud and petulant, and would have ruled the country side with a rod of iron. Nothing less would serve him than a fine horse to ride on, and a world of other conveniencies and luxuries, as if he had been on an equality with gentlemen. And he bought a grand gun, which was called a fowling-piece; and he had two pointer dogs, the like of which had not been seen in the parish since the planting of the Eglesham-wood on the moorland, which was four years before I got the call. Every body said the man was fay,[297] and truly, when I remarked him so gallant

---

295 Doups (Sc.): stumps, butts.
296 Scotland's separate legal system required a Scottish version of the Catholic Relief Act. But the Scottish version of Gordon's organisation got their pogroms in first, in 1779, while also compiling mass petitions against relief: the Synod of Glasgow and Ayr raised 20,000 signatures in only three weeks. It is the victory of these tactics that are being celebrated here: no Scottish Relief Bill was put before parliament, and no civil penalties for Catholics were lifted in Scotland until 1793, by which time Catholics had been replaced by republican revolutionaries as the bogeymen of the loyalist imagination.
297 Fay, usually fey (Sc.): fated to die, doomed.

and gay on the Sabbath at the kirk, and noted his glowing face and gleg e'en, I thought at times there was something no canny about him. It was, indeed, clear to be seen, that the man was hurried out of himself, but nobody could have thought that the death he was to dree,[298] would have been what it was.

About the end of summer, my Lord Eglesham came to the castle, bringing with him an English madam, that was his Miss. Some days after he came down from London, as he was riding past the Manse, his lordship stopped to inquire for my health, and I went to the door to speak to him. I thought that he did not meet me with that blithe countenance he was wont, and in going away, he said with a blush, "I fear I dare not ask you to come to the castle." I had heard of his concubine, and I said, "In saying so, my lord, you shew a spark of grace, for it would not become me to see what I have heard; and I am surprised, my lord, you will not rather take a lady of your own." He looked kindly, but confused, saying, he did not know where to get one; so seeing his shame, and not wishing to put him out of conceit entirely with himself, I replied, "Na, na, my lord, there's nobody will believe that, for there never was a silly Jock, but there was as silly a Jenny," at which he laughed heartily, and rode away. But I know not what was in't, I was troubled in mind about him, and thought, as he was riding away, that I would never see him again; and sure enough it so happened, for the next day, being airing in his coach with Miss Spangle, the lady he had brought, he happened to see Mungo Argyle with his dogs and his gun, and my lord being as particular about his game as the other was about boxes of tea and kegs of brandy, he jumped out of the carriage, and run to take the gun. Words passed, and the exciseman shot my lord.[299] Never shall I forget that day; such riding, such running, the whole country side afoot; but the same night my lord breathed his last, and the mad and wild reprobate, that did the deed, was taken up and sent off to Edinburgh. This was a woeful riddance of that oppressor, for my lord was a good landlord and a kind-hearted man; and albeit, though a little thoughtless, was aye ready to make his power, when the way was pointed out, minister to good works. The whole parish mourned for him, and there was not a sorer heart in all its bounds than my own. Never was such a sight seen as his burial: The whole country side was there, and all as solemn as if they had been assembled in the valley of Jehoshaphat in the latter day.[300] The hedges where the funeral was to pass were clad with weans, like bunches of hips and haws, and the kirk-yard was as if all its own dead were risen. Never, do I think, was such a multitude gathered together. Some thought there could not be less than three thousand grown men, besides women and children.

Scarcely was this great public calamity past, for it could be reckoned no less, when one Saturday afternoon, as Miss Sabrina, the schoolmistress, was dining with Lady Macadam, her ladyship was stricken with the paralytics, and her face so thrown in the course of a few minutes, that Miss Sabrina came flying to the Manse for the help and advice of Mrs Balwhidder. A doctor was gotten with all speed by express, but her ladyship was smitten beyond the reach of medicine. She lived, however, some time after; but O she was such an object, that it was a grief to see her. She could only mutter when she tried to speak, and was as helpless as a baby. Though she never liked me, nor could I say there was many things in her demeanour that pleased me, yet she was a free-handed woman to the needful, and when she died she was more missed than it was thought she could have been.

298 Dree (Sc.): suffer.
299 This is based on a true Ayrshire story: the shooting, in 1769, of the Earl of Eglinton by a Highland exciseman, Mungo Campbell, poaching on his land. See Kinsley (1986) pp.231–32.
300 Joel 3.2: the scene of another passage in the apocalypse.

Shortly after her funeral, which was managed by a gentleman sent from her friends in Edinburgh, that I wrote to about her condition, the Major, her son, with his lady, Kate Malcolm, and two pretty bairns, came and stayed in her house for a time, and they were a great happiness to us all, both in the way of drinking tea, and sometimes taking a bit dinner, their only mother now, the worthy and pious Mrs Malcolm, being regularly of the company.

Before the end of the year, I should mention, that the fortune of Mrs Malcolm's family got another shove upwards, by the promotion of her second son, Robert Malcolm, who being grown an expert and careful mariner, was made Captain of a grand ship, whereof Provost Maitland of Glasgow, that was kind to his mother in her distresses, was the owner. But that douce lad Willie, her youngest son, who was at the University of Glasgow, under the Lord Eglesham's patronage, was like to have suffered a blight; however, Major Macadam, when I spoke to him anent the young man's loss of his patron, said, with a pleasant generosity, he should not be stickit;[301] and, accordingly, he made up, as far as money could, for the loss of his lordship, but there was none that made up for the great power and influence, which, I have no doubt, the Earl would have exerted in his behalf, when he was ripened for the church. So that, although in time William came out a sound and heart-searching preacher, he was long obliged, like many another unfriended saint, to cultivate sand, and wash Ethiopians in the shape of an east-country gentleman's camstrairy weans;[302] than which, as he wrote me himself, there cannot be on earth a greater trial of temper. However, in the end, he was rewarded, and is not only now a placed minister, but a doctor of divinity.

The death of Lady Macadam was followed by another parochial misfortune, for, considering the time when it happened, we could count it as nothing less: Auld Thomas Howkings, the betherel, fell sick, and died in the course of a week's illness, about the end of November, and the measles coming at that time upon the parish, there was such a smashing of the poor weans, as had not been known for an age; insomuch, that James Banes, the lad who was Thomas Howkings's helper, rose in open rebellion against the Session, during his superior's illness, and we were constrained to augment his pay, and to promise him the place, if Thomas did not recover, which it was then thought he could not do. On the day this happened, there were three dead children in the clachan, and a panic and consternation spread about the burial of them, when James Banes's insurrection was known, which made both me and the Session glad to hush up the affair, that the heart of the public might have no more than the sufferings of individuals to hurt it. — Thus ended a year, on many accounts, heavy to be remembered.

CHAPTER XXIII.—YEAR 1782.

News of the victory over the French fleet—He has to inform Mrs Malcolm of the death of her son Charles in the engagement.

ALTHOUGH I have not been particular in noticing it, from time to time, there had been an occasional going off, at fairs and on market-days, of the lads of the parish as soldiers, and when Captain Malcolm got the command of his ship, no less than four young men sailed with him from the clachan; so that we were deeper and deeper interested in the proceedings of the doleful war, that was raging in the plantations. By one post we

301 Sticket (Sc.): 'of persons: halted in their trade or profession' (SND).
302 Camstrairy: Kinsley has 'unmanageable, riotous', which fits the context, but is not in SND.

heard of no less than three brave fellows belonging to us being slain in one battle, for which there was a loud and general lamentation.

Shortly after this, I got a letter from Charles Malcolm, a very pretty letter it indeed was; he had heard of my Lord Eglesham's murder, and grieved for the loss, both because his lordship was a good man, and because he had been such a friend to him and his family. "But," said Charles, "the best way that I can shew my gratitude for his patronage, is to prove myself a good officer to my King and country." Which I thought a brave sentiment, and was pleased thereat; for somehow Charles, from the time he brought me the limes to make a bowl of punch, in his pocket from Jamaica, had built a nest of affection in my heart. But, oh! the wicked wastry of life in war. In less than a month after, the news came of a victory over the French fleet,[303] and by the same post I got a letter from Mr Howard, that was the midshipman who came to see us with Charles, telling me that poor Charles had been mortally wounded in the action, and had afterwards died of his wounds. "He was a hero in the engagement," said Mr Howard, "and he died as a good and a brave man should." — These tidings gave me one of the sorest hearts I ever suffered, and it was long before I could gather fortitude to disclose the tidings to poor Charles's mother. But the callants of the school had heard of the victory, and were going shouting about, and had set the steeple bell a-ringing, by which Mrs Malcolm heard the news; and knowing that Charles's ship was with the fleet, she came over to the Manse in great anxiety, to hear the particulars, somebody telling her that there had been a foreign letter to me by the post-man.

When I saw her I could not speak, but looked at her in pity, and the tear fleeing up into my eyes, she guessed what had happened. After giving a deep and sore sigh, she inquired, "How did he behave? I hope well, for he was aye a gallant laddie!" — and then she wept very bitterly. However, growing calmer, I read to her the letter, and when I had done, she begged me to give it to her to keep, saying, "It's all that I have now left of my pretty boy; but it's mair precious to me than the wealth of the Indies;" and she begged me to return thanks to the Lord, for all the comforts and manifold mercies with which her lot had been blessed, since the hour she put her trust in Him alone, and that was when she was left a pennyless widow, with her five fatherless bairns.

It was just an edification of the spirit, to see the Christian resignation of this worthy woman. Mrs Balwhidder was confounded, and said, there was more sorrow in seeing the deep grief of her fortitude, than tongue could tell.

Having taken a glass of wine with her, I walked out to conduct her to her own house, but in the way we met with a severe trial. All the weans were out parading with napkins and kail-blades on sticks,[304] rejoicing and triumphing in the glad tidings of victory. But when they saw me and Mrs Malcolm coming slowly along, they guessed what had happened, and threw away their banners of joy; and, standing all up in a row, with silence and sadness, along the kirk-yard wall as we passed, shewed an instinct of compassion that penetrated to my very soul. The poor mother burst into fresh affliction, and some of the bairns into an audible weeping; and, taking one another by the hand, they followed us to her door, like mourners at a funeral. Never was such a sight seen in any town before. The neighbours came to look at it, as we walked along, and the men turned aside to hide their faces, while the mothers pressed their babies fondlier to their bosoms, and watered their innocent faces with their tears.

---

303 France had entered the war on the side of the American rebels in 1778. The victory referred to here was at the Battle of the Saintes, in the Caribbean, in April 1782. This kept Jamaica in British hands, but the continental war had already been lost: the same French fleet had forced the British surrender at Yorktown, Virginia, the previous October.

304 Kail-blades (Sc.): cabbage-leaves.

I prepared a suitable sermon, taking as the words of my text, "Howl, ye ships of Tarshish, for your strength is laid waste."[305] But when I saw around me so many of my people, clad in complimentary mourning for the gallant Charles Malcolm, and that even poor daft Jenny Gaffaw, and her daughter, had on an old black ribbon; and when I thought of him, the spirited laddie, coming home from Jamaica, with his parrot on his shoulder, and his limes for me, my heart filled full, and I was obliged to sit down in the pulpit, and drop a tear.

After a pause, and the Lord having vouchsafed to compose me, I rose up, and gave out that anthem of triumph, the 124th Psalm; the singing of which brought the congregation round to themselves; but still I felt that I could not preach as I had meant to do, therefore I only said a few words of prayer, and singing another psalm, dismissed the congregation.

CHAPTER XXIV.—YEAR 1783.

Janet Gaffaw's death and burial.

THIS was another Sabbath year of my ministry. It has left me nothing to record, but a silent increase of prosperity in the parish. I myself had now in the bank more than a thousand pounds, and every thing was thriving around. My two bairns, Gilbert, that is now the merchant in Glasgow, was grown into a sturdy ramplor laddie, and Janet, that is married upon Dr Kittleword, the minister of Swappington, was as fine a lassie for her years, as the eye of a parent could desire to see.

Shortly after the news of the peace,[306] an event at which all gave themselves up to joy, a thing happened among us, that at the time caused much talk; but although very dreadful, was yet not so serious, some how or other, as such an awsome doing should have been. Poor Jenny Gaffaw happened to take a heavy cold, and soon thereafter died. Meg went about from house to house, begging dead-clothes, and got the body straighted in a wonderful decent manner,[307] with a plate of earth and salt placed upon it — an admonitory type of mortality and eternal life, that has ill-advisedly gone out of fashion. When I heard of this, I could not but go to see how a creature that was not thought possessed of a grain of understanding, could have done so much herself. On entering the door, I beheld Meg sitting with two or three of the neighbouring kimmers,[308] and the corpse laid out on a bed. "Come awa', sir," said Meg, "this is an altered house; they're gane that keepit it bein;[309] but, sir, we maun a' come to this — we maun pay the debt o' nature — death is a grim creditor, and a doctor but brittle bail[310] when the hour of reckoning's at han'! What a pity it is, mother, that you're now dead, for here's the minister come to see you. O, sir, but she would have had a proud heart to see you in her dwelling, for she had a genteel turn, and would not let me, her only daughter, mess or mell we the lathron lasses of the clachan.[311] Ay, ay, she brought me up with care, and edicated me for a lady; nae coarse wark darkened my lilly-white hands. But I maun work now, I maun dree the penalty of man."[312]

---

305   Isaiah 23.1.
306   The American war ended with another Treaty of Paris, 3 September 1783.
307   To straight or straucht a body is to lay it out, to arrange it for burial (Sc.).
308   Kimmers (Sc.): gossips, that is, older local women.
309   Gane that keepit it bien (Sc.): gone that kept it cosy.
310   Brittle bail: Kinsley (1986) gives 'brief, temporary release' for this; obscure.
311   Mess or mell: mix or have dealings with; we, usually wi': with (both Sc.).
312   The penalty of man is work, the sentence passed on Adam after his expulsion from the

Having stopped some time, listening to the curious maunnering of Meg,[313] I rose to come away, but she laid her hand on my arm, saying, "No, sir, ye maun taste before ye gang! My mother had aye plenty in her life, nor shall her latter day be needy."

Accordingly, Meg, with all the due formality common on such occasions, produced a bottle of water, and a dram glass, which she filled and tasted, then presented to me, at the same time offering me a bit of bread on a slate. It was a consternation to every body how the daft creature had learnt all the ceremonies, which she performed in a manner past the power of pen to describe, making the solemnity of death, by her strange mockery, a kind of merriment, that was more painful than sorrow; but some spirits are gifted with a faculty of observation, that, by the strength of a little fancy, enables them to make a wonderful and truth-like semblance of things and events, which they never saw, and poor Meg seemed to have this gift.

The same night the Session having provided a coffin, the body was put in, and removed to Mr Mutchkin's brew-house, where the lads and lassies kept the late wake.

Saving this, the year flowed in a calm, and we floated on in the stream of time towards the great ocean of eternity, like ducks and geese in the river's tide, that are carried down without being sensible of the speed of the current. Alas! we have not wings like them, to fly back to the place we set out from.

CHAPTER XXV.—YEAR 1784.

A Year of sunshine and pleasantness.

I HAVE ever thought, that this was a bright year, truly an An. Dom., for in it many of the lads came home that had listed to be soldiers; and Mr Howard, that was the midshipman, being now a captain of a man of war, came down from England and married Effie Malcolm, and took her up with him to London, where she wrote to her mother, that she found his family people of great note, and more kind to her than she could write. By this time, also, Major Macadam was made a Colonel, and lived with his lady in Edinburgh, where they were much respected by the genteeler classes, Mrs Macadam being considered a great unco among them for all manner of ladylike ornaments,[314] she having been taught every sort of perfection in that way by the old lady, who was educated at the court of France, and was, from her birth, a person of quality. In this year, also, Captain Malcolm, her brother, married a daughter of a Glasgow merchant, so that Mrs Malcolm, in her declining years, had the prospect of a bright setting; but nothing could change the sober Christianity of her settled mind; and although she was strongly invited, both by the Macadams and the Howards, to see their felicity, she ever declined the same, saying—"No! I have been long out of the world, or rather, I have never been in it; my ways are not as theirs; and although I ken their hearts would be glad to be kind to me, I might fash their servants,[315] or their friends might think me unlike other folk, by which, instead of causing pleasure, mortification might ensue; so I will remain in my own house, trusting that when they can spare the time, they will come and see me."

There was a spirit of true wisdom in this resolution, for it required a forbearance, that in weaker minds would have relaxed; but though a person of a most slender and

---

Garden of Eden: 'In the sweat of thy face shalt thou eat bread' (Genesis 3.19).

313 Maunnering (Sc.): incoherent rambling.

314 Unco (Sc.): here, a rarity or novelty.

315 Fash (Sc.): here, trouble or inconvenience (*SND* I.2).

delicate frame of body, she was a Judith in fortitude,[316] and in all the fortune that seemed now smiling upon her, she never was lifted up, but bore always that pale and meek look, which gave a saintliness to her endeavours in the days of her suffering and poverty.

But when we enjoy most, we have least to tell. I look back on this year as on a sunny spot in the valley, amidst the shadows of the clouds of time; and I have nothing to record, save the remembrance of welcomings and weddings, and a meeting of bairns and parents, that the wars and the waters had long raged between. Contentment within the bosom, lent a livelier grace to the countenance of Nature, and every body said, that in this year the hedges were greener than common, the gowans brighter on the brae,[317] and the heads of the statelier trees adorned with a richer coronal of leaves and blossoms. All things were animated with the gladness of thankfulness, and testified to the goodness of their Maker.

CHAPTER XXVI.—YEAR 1785.

Mr Cayenne comes to the parish—A passionate character—His outrageous behaviour at the Session-house.

WELL may we say, in the pious words of my old friend and neighbour, the Reverend Mr Keekie of Loupinton, that the world is such a wheel-carriage, that it might very properly be called the WHIRL'D. This reflection was brought home to me in a very striking manner, while I was preparing a discourse for my people, to be preached on the anniversary day of my placing, in which I took a view of what had passed in the parish during the five-and-twenty years that I had been, by the grace of God, the pastor thereof. The bairns, that were bairns when I came among my people, were ripened into parents, and a new generation was swelling in the bud around me. But it is what happened that I have to give an account of.

This year the Lady Macadam's jointure-house that was, having been long without a tenant, a Mr Cayenne and his family, American loyalists,[318] came and took it, and settled among us for a time. His wife was a clever woman, and they had two daughters, Miss Virginia and Miss Carolina; but he was himself an etter-cap, a perfect spunkie of passion,[319] as ever was known in town or country. His wife had a terrible time o't with him, and yet the unhappy man had a great share of common sense, and, saving the exploits of his unmanageable temper, was an honest and creditable gentleman. Of his humour we soon had a sample, as I shall relate at length all about it.

Shortly after he came to the parish, Mrs Balwhidder and me waited upon the family, to pay our respects, and Mr Cayenne, in a free and hearty manner, insisted on us staying to dinner. His wife, I could see, was not satisfied with this, not being, as I discerned afterwards, prepared to give an entertainment to strangers; however, we fell into the misfortune of staying, and nothing could exceed the happiness of Mr Cayenne.

316 Judith is the heroine of the Book of Judith in the Catholic and Orthodox versions of the Old Testament. Like Mrs Malcolm she is a widow.
317 Gowans (Sc.): daisies.
318 That is, American colonists who had sided with the British government during the war. The American Revolution was, like all revolutions, also a civil war. The vast majority of Loyalists stayed in the new United States afterwards. Of those who emigrated, most went to what remained British North America (i.e. Canada); probably around 7,000, like the Cayennes, came to Britain.
319 Etter-cap, usually ettercap: spiteful, bad-tempered person; spunkie: here, 'a fiery, irascible person' (SND 3.2) (both Sc.).

I thought him one of the blithest bodies I had ever seen, and had no notion that he was such a tap of tow as in the sequel he proved himself.

As there was something extra to prepare, the dinner was a little longer of being on the table than usual, at which he began to fash,[320] and every now and then took a turn up and down the room, with his hands behind his back, giving a short melancholious whistle. At length the dinner was served, but it was more scanty than he had expected, and this upset his good humour altogether. Scarcely had I asked the blessing when he began to storm at his blackamoor servant,[321] who was, however, used to his way, and did his work without minding him; but by some neglect there was no mustard down, which Mr Cayenne called for in the voice of a tempest, and one of the servant lassies came in with the pot, trembling. It happened that, as it had not been used for a day or two before, the lid was clagged, and, as it were, glewed in, so that Mr Cayenne could not get it out, which put him quite wud, and he attempted to fling it at Sambo, the black lad's head, but it stottit against the wall,[322] and the lid flying open, the whole mustard flew in his own face, which made him a sight not to be spoken of. However it calmed him; but really, as I had never seen such a man before, I could not but consider the accident as a providential reproof, and trembled to think what greater evil might fall out in the hands of a man so left to himself in the intemperance of passion.

But the worst thing about Mr Cayenne was his meddling with matters in which he had no concern, for he had a most irksome nature, and could not be at rest, so that he was truly a thorn in our side.[323] Among other of his strange doings, was the part he took in the proceedings of the Session, with which he had as little to do, in a manner, as the man of the moon; but, having no business in his hands, he attended every sederunt,[324] and from less to more, having no self-government, he began to give his opinion in our deliberations; and often bred us trouble, by causing strife to arise.

It happened, as the time of the summer occasion was drawing near, that it behoved us to make arrangements about the assistance;[325] and upon the suggestion of the elders, to which I paid always the greatest deference, I invited Mr Keekie of Loupinton, who was a sound preacher, and a great expounder of the kittle parts of the Old Testament,[326] being a man well versed in the Hebrew and etymologies, for which he was much reverenced by the old people that delighted to search the Scriptures. I had also written to Mr Sprose of Annock, a preacher of another sort, being a vehement and powerful thresher of the word, making the chaff and vain babbling of corrupt commentators to fly from his hand. He was not, however, so well liked, as he wanted that connect method which is needful to the enforcing of doctrine. But he had never been among us, and it was thought it would be a godly treat to the parish to let the people hear him. Besides Mr Sprose, Mr Waikle of Gowanry, a quiet hewer out of the image of holiness in the heart, was likewise invited, all in addition to our old stoops from the adjacent parishes.

None of these three preachers were in any estimation with Mr Cayenne, who had only heard each of them once; and he happening to be present in the Session-house at the time, inquired how we had settled. I thought this not a very orderly question, but I gave him a civil answer, saying, that Mr Keekie of Loupinton would preach on

---

320   Fash (Sc.): here, 'fret, be angry' (*SND* I.1).
321   Mr Cayenne's black servant may have been his slave in the colonies; he ceased to be so on arriving in Britain itself, where slavery had no legal reality.
322   Clagged: clogged; wud, wuid: mad; stottit: bounced (all Sc.).
323   Numbers 33.55.
324   Sederunt: sitting.
325   Summer occasion: summer communion. See note 35 (chapter I).
326   Kittle (Sc.): 'Hard to deal with, intractable, intricate' (*SND* III.5).

the morning of the fast-day, Mr Sprose of Annock in the afternoon, and Mr Waikle of Gowanry on the Saturday. Never shall I or the elders, while the breath of life is in our bodies, forget the reply. Mr Cayenne struck the table like the clap of thunder, and cried, "Mr Keekie of Loupinton, and Mr Sprose of Annock, and Mr Waikle of Gowanry, and all such trash, may go to—and be—!" and out of the house he bounced, like a hand-ball stotting on a stone.

The elders and me were confounded, and for some time we could not speak, but looked at each other, doubtful if our ears heard aright. At long and length I came to myself, and, in the strength of God, took my place at the table, and said, this was an outrageous impiety not to be borne, which all the elders agreed to; and we thereupon came to a resolve, which I dictated myself, wherein we debarred Mr Cayenne from ever after entering, unless summoned, the Session-house, the which resolve we directed the Session-clerk to send to him direct, and thus we vindicated the insulted privileges of the church.

Mr Cayenne had cooled before he got home, and our paper coming to him in his appeased blood, he immediately came to the Manse, and made a contrite apology for his hasty temper, which I reported, in due time and form, to the Session, and there the matter ended. But here was an example plain to be seen of the truth of the old proverb, that as one door shuts another opens; for scarcely were we in quietness by the decease of that old light-headed woman, the Lady Macadam, till a full equivalent for her was given in this hot and fiery Mr Cayenne.

CHAPTER XXVII.—YEAR 1786.

Repairs required for the Manse—By the sagacious management of Mr Kibbock, the heritors are made to give a new Manse altogether—They begin, however, to look upon me with a grudge, which provokes me to claim an augmentation, which I obtain.

FROM the day of my settlement, I had resolved, in order to win the affections of my people, and to promote unison among the heritors, to be of as little expence to the parish as possible; but by this time the Manse had fallen into a sore state of decay—the doors were wormed on the hinges—the casements of the windows chattered all the winter, like the teeth of a person perishing with cold, so that we had no comfort in the house; by which, at the urgent instigations of Mrs Balwhidder, I was obligated to represent our situation to the Session. I would rather, having so much saved money in the bank, paid the needful repairs myself, than have done this, but she said it would be a rank injustice to our own family; and her father, Mr Kibbock, who was very long-headed,[327] with more than a common man's portion of understanding, pointed out to me, that as my life was but in my lip, it would be a wrong thing towards whomsoever was ordained to be my successor, to use the heritors to the custom of the minister paying for the reparations of the Manse, as it might happen he might not be so well able to afford it as me. So in a manner, by their persuasion, and the constraint of the justice of the case, I made a report of the infirmities both of doors and windows, as well as of the rotten state of the floors, which were constantly in want of cobbling. Over and above all, I told them of the sarking of the roof, which was as frush as a puddock stool;[328] insomuch, that in every blast, some of the pins lost their grip, and the slates came hurling off.

---

327 Long-headed, lang-heidit (Sc.): 'of great foresight or judgement, discerning, sagacious' (*SND*).
328 Cobbling: patching-up; sarking (Sc.): the wooden lining of a roof to which the slates are fixed; frush (Sc.): brittle, liable to disintegrate; puddock-stool (Sc.): toadstool.

The heritors were accordingly convened, and, after some deliberation, they proposed that the house should be seen to, and whitewashed and painted; and I thought this might do, for I saw they were terrified at the expence of a thorough repair; but when I went home and repeated to Mrs Balwhidder what had been said at the meeting, and my thankfulness at getting the heritors consent to do so much, she was excessively angry, and told me, that all the painting and white washing in the world would avail nothing, for that the house was as a sepulchre full of rottenness; and she sent for Mr Kibbock, her father, to confer with him on the way of getting the matter put to rights.

Mr Kibbock came, and hearing of what had passed, pondered for some time, and then said, "All was very right! The minister (meaning me) has just to get tradesmen to look at the house, and write out their opinion of what it needs. There will be plaster to mend; so, before painting, he will get a plasterer. There will be a slater wanted; he has just to get a slater's estimate, and a wright's, and so forth, and when all is done, he will lay them before the Session and the heritors, who, no doubt, will direct the reparations to go forward."

This was very pawkie counselling of Mr Kibbock, but I did not see through it at the time, but did as he recommended, and took all the different estimates, when they came in, to the Session. The elders commended my prudence exceedingly for so doing, before going to work; and one of them asked me what the amount of the whole would be, but I had not cast it up. Some of the heritors thought that a hundred pounds would be sufficient for the outlay, but judge of our consternation, when, in counting up all the sums of the different estimates together, we found them well on towards a thousand pounds. "Better big a new house at once, than do this!" cried all the elders, by which I then perceived the draughtiness of Mr Kibbock's advice.[329] Accordingly, another meeting of the heritors was summoned, and, after a great deal of controversy, it was agreed, that a new Manse should be erected; and, shortly after, we contracted with Thomas Trowel, the mason, to build one for six hundred pounds, with all the requisite appurtenances, by which a clear gain was saved to the parish, by the foresight of Mr Kibbock, to the amount of nearly four hundred pounds. But the heritors did not mean to have allowed the sort of repair that his plan comprehended. He was, however, a far forecasting man, the like of him for natural parts not being in our country side, and nobody could get the whip-hand of him, either in a bargain or an improvement, when he once was sensible of the advantage. He was, indeed, a blessing to the shire, both by his example as a farmer, and by his sound and discreet advice in the contentions of his neighbours, being a man, as was a saying among the commonality, "wiser than the law and the fifteen Lords of Edinburgh."[330]

The building of the new Manse occasioned a heavy cess on the heritors, which made them overly ready to pick holes in the coats of me and the elders; so that, out of my forbearance and delicacy in time past, grew a lordliness on their part, that was an ill return for the years that I had endured no little inconveniency for their sake. It was not in my heart or principles to harm the hair of a dog; but when I discerned the austerity with which they were disposed to treat their minister, I bethought me, that, for the preservation of what was due to the establishment and the upholding of the decent administration of religion, I ought to set my face against the sordid intolerance by which they were actuated. This notion I weighed well before divulging it to any

329 Draughty (Sc.): cunning, crafty.
330 The fifteen Lords are the Senators of the College of Justice, who together make up the Court of Session, the highest court within Scotland (there are more than 15 today, including a few Ladies).

person, but when I had assured myself as to the rectitude thereof, I rode over one day to Mr Kibbock's, and broke my mind to him about claiming out of the tiends an augmentation of my stipend,[331] not because I needed it, but in case, after me, some bare and hungry gorbie of the Lord should be sent upon the parish, in no such condition to plea with the heritors as I was. Mr Kibbock highly approved of my intent, and by his help, after much tribulation, I got an augmentation, both in glebe and income; and to mark my reason for what I did, I took upon me to keep and clothe the wives and orphans of the parish, who lost their bread-winners in the American war. But, for all that, the heritors spoke of me as an avaricious Jew, and made the hard won fruits of Mrs Balwhidder's great thrift and good management a matter of reproach against me. Few of them would come to the church, but stayed away, to the detriment of their own souls hereafter, in order, as they thought, to punish me; so that, in the course of this year, there was a visible decay of the sense of religion among the better orders of the parish, and, as will be seen in the sequel, their evil example infected the minds of many of the rising generation.

It was in this year that Mr Cayenne bought the mailing of the Wheatrigs, but did not begin to build his house till the following spring; for being ill to please with a plan, he fell out with the builders, and on one occasion got into such a passion with Mr Trowel the mason, that he struck him a blow in the face, for which he was obligated to make atonement. It was thought the matter would have been carried before the Lords; but, by the mediation of Mr Kibbock, with my helping hand, a reconciliation was brought about, Mr Cayenne indemnifying the mason with a sum of money to say no more anent it; after which, he employed him to build his house, a thing that no man could have thought possible, who reflected on the enmity between them.

CHAPTER XXVIII.—YEAR 1787.

Lady Macadam's house is changed into an Inn—The making of jelly becomes common in the parish—Meg Gaffaw is present at a payment of victual—Her behaviour.

THERE had been, as I have frequently observed, a visible improvement going on in the parish. From the time of the making of the toll-road, every new house that was built in the clachan was built along that road. Among other changes thereby caused, the Lady Macadam's jointure-house that was, which stood in a pleasant parterre,[332] inclosed within a stone-wall and an iron-gate, having a pillar with a pine-apple head on each side, came to be in the middle of the town. While Mr Cayenne inhabited the same, it was maintained in good order, but on his flitting to his own new house on the Wheatrigs, the parterre was soon over-run with weeds, and it began to wear the look of a waste place. Robert Toddy, who then kept the change-house, and who had from the lady's death rented the coach-house byre for stabling, in this juncture thought of it for an inn; so he set his own house to Thomas Treddles, the weaver, whose son, William, is now the great Glasgow manufacturer, that has cotton-mills and steam-engines; and took "the Place," as it was called, and had a fine sign, THE CROSS KEYS, painted and put

---

331   Tiends (Sc.): tithes. After the Reformation, the one-tenth of all agricultural produce (a tithe) that was supposed to go to the support of a parish church was taken over by the Crown, rather than paid directly to the clergy, who were instead paid a fixed stipend in money plus the produce of the glebe. But this remained a resource on which a minister could claim.

332   Parterre: area of flower-beds.

up in golden characters, by which it became one of the most noted inns any where to be seen; and the civility of Mrs Toddy was commended by all strangers. But although this transmutation from a change-house to an inn was a vast amendment, in a manner, to the parish, there was little amendment of manners thereby, for the farmer lads began to hold dancings, and other riotous proceedings there, and to bring, as it were, the evil practices of towns into the heart of the country. All sort of licence was allowed as to drink and hours, and the edifying example of Mr Mutchkins, and his pious family, was no longer held up to the imitation of the wayfaring man.

Saving the mutation of "the Place" into an inn, nothing very remarkable happened in this year. We got into our new Manse about the middle of March, but it was rather damp, being new plastered, and it caused me to have a severe attack of the rheumatics in the fall of the year.

I should not, in my notations, forget to mark a new luxury that got in among the commonality at this time. By the opening of new roads, and the traffic thereon with carts and carriers, and by our young men that were sailors going to the Clyde, and sailing to Jamaica and the West Indies, heaps of sugar and coffee-beans were brought home, while many, among the kail-stocks and cabbages in their yards, had planted grozet and berry bushes;[333] which two things happening together, the fashion to make jam and jelly, which hitherto had been only known in the kitchens and confectionaries of the gentry, came to be introduced into the clachan. All this, however, was not without a plausible pretext, for it was found that jelly was an excellent medicine for a sore throat, and jam a remedy as good as London candy for a cough, or cold, or a shortness of breath. I could not, however, say, that this gave me so much concern as the smuggling trade, only it occasioned a great fasherie to Mrs Balwhidder;[334] for, in the berry time, there was no end to the borrowing of her brass-pan, to make jelly and jam, till Mrs Toddy, of the Cross Keys, bought one, which, in its turn, came into request, and saved ours.

It was in the Martinmas quarter of this year that I got the first payment of my augmentation. Having no desire to rip up old sores, I shall say no more anent it, the worst being anticipated in my chronicle of the last year; but there was a thing happened in the payment, that occasioned a vexation at the time of a very disagreeable nature. Daft Meg Gaffaw, who, from the tragical death of her mother, was a privileged subject, used to come to the Manse on the Saturdays for a meal of meat; and it so fell out, that as, by some neglect of mine, no steps had been taken to regulate the disposal of the victual that constituted the means of the augmentation, some of the heritors, in an ungracious temper, sent what they called the tythe-boll (the Lord knows it was not the fiftieth) to the Manse,[335] where I had no place to put it. This fell out on a Saturday night, when I was busy with my sermon, thinking not of silver or gold, but of much better; so that I was greatly molested and disturbed thereby. Daft Meg, who sat by the kitchen chimlay-lug hearing a',[336] said nothing for a time, but when she saw how Mrs Balwhidder and me were put to, she cried out with a loud voice, like a soul under the inspiration of prophecy — "When the widow's creuse had filled all the vessels in the house, the Lord stopped the increase;[337] verily, verily, I say unto you, if your barns be filled, and your

---

333 Grozet (Sc): gooseberry.
334 Fasherie (Sc.): trouble, bother.
335 Tythe-boll, Sc. teind-boll: 'a boll of threshed corn' paid as the tithe. Tithes had long been paid only in grain; from 1808 they were replaced with cash. A boll is a measure of grain, equal to six bushels.
336 Chimlay-lug: the recess of a wide old-fashioned chimney.
337 The prophet Elijah does a trick with a widow's oil-cruse (earthen vessel) and meal-barrel

garnelkests can hold no more, seek till ye shall find the tume basins of the poor, and therein pour the corn, and the oil, and the wine of your abundance;[338] so shall ye be blessed of the Lord." The which words I took for an admonition, and directing the sacks to be brought into the dining-room, and other chambers of the Manse, I sent off the heritors' servants, that had done me this prejudice, with an unexpected thankfulness. But this, as I afterwards was informed, both them and their masters attributed to the greedy grasp of avarice, with which they considered me as misled; and having said so, nothing could exceed their mortification on Monday, when they heard (for they were of those who had deserted the kirk), that I had given by the precentor notice, to every widow in the parish that was in need, to come to the Manse, and she would receive her portion of the partitioning of the augmentation. Thus, without any offence on my part, saving the strictness of justice, was a division made between me and the heritors; but the people were with me, and my own conscience was with me; and though the fronts of the lofts and the pews of the heritors were but thinly filled, I trusted that a good time was coming, when the gentry would see the error of their way. So I bent the head of resignation to the Lord, and, assisted by the wisdom of Mr Kibbock, adhered to the course I had adopted; but, at the close of the year, my heart was sorrowful for the schism, and my prayer on Hogmanay was one of great bitterness of soul, that such an evil had come to pass.

CHAPTER XXIX.—YEAR 1788.

A cotton-mill is built—The new spirit which it introduces among the people.

IT had been often remarked by ingenious men, that the Brawl burn, which ran through the parish, though a small, was yet a rapid stream, and had a wonderful capability for damming, and to turn mills. From the time that the Irville water deserted its channel this brook grew into repute, and several mills and dams had been erected on its course. In this year a proposal came from Glasgow to build a cotton-mill on its banks, beneath the Witch-linn,[339] which being on a corner of the Wheatrig, the property of Mr Cayenne, he not only consented thereto, but took a part in the profit or loss therein; and, being a man of great activity, though we thought him, for many a day, a serpent plague sent upon the parish,[340] he proved thereby one of our greatest benefactors. The cotton-mill was built, and a spacious fabric it was—nothing like it had been seen before in our day and generation—and, for the people that were brought to work in it, a new town was built in the vicinity, which Mr Cayenne, the same being founded on his land, called Cayenneville, the name of the plantation in Virginia that had been taken from him by the rebellious Americans. From that day Fortune was lavish of her favours upon him; his property swelled, and grew in the most extraordinary manner, and the whole country-side was stirring with a new life. For, when the mill was set a-going, he got weavers of muslin established in Cayenneville;[341] and shortly after, but that did not take

---

at I Kings 17.8–16 very similar to the one performed by Jesus with the loaves and fishes.
338   Garnel: granary; kests, usually kists: chests; tume: empty (all Sc.). Corn, wine and oil appear in several places in the Old Testament as a representation of the wealth bestowed by God on those who stay true to him, but nowhere attached to a demand for redistribution such as Meg makes here (Nehemiah chapter 5 comes closest).
339   A linn is a deep pool, usually one below a waterfall (Sc.).
340   Such as that sent by God against the Israelites for complaining, in Numbers 21.5–9.
341   The work of the cotton mill at this point was the production of yarn through mechanised

place till the year following, he brought women all the way from the neighbourhood of Manchester in England, to teach the lassie bairns in our old clachan tambouring.[342] Some of the ancient families, in their turretted houses, were not pleased with this innovation, especially when they saw the handsome dwellings that were built for the weavers of the mills, and the unstinted hand that supplied the wealth required for the carrying on of the business. It sank their pride into insignificance, and many of them would almost rather have wanted the rise that took place in the value of their lands,[343] than have seen this incoming of what they called o'er-sea speculation. But, saving the building of the cotton-mill, and the beginning of Cayenneville, nothing more memorable happened in this year, still it was nevertheless a year of a great activity. The minds of men were excited to new enterprizes; a new genius, as it were, had descended upon the earth, and there was an erect and out-looking spirit abroad that was not to be satisfied with the taciturn regularity of ancient affairs. Even Miss Sabrina Hookie, the schoolmistress, though now waned from her meridian, was touched with the enlivening rod, and set herself to learn and to teach tambouring, in such a manner as to supersede by precept and example that old time-honoured functionary, as she herself called it, the spinning-wheel, proving, as she did one night, to Mr Kibbock and me, that, if more money could be made by a woman tambouring than by spinning, it was better for her to tambour than to spin.

But, in the midst of all this commercing and manufacturing, I began to discover signs of decay in the wonted simplicity of our country ways. Among the cotton-spinners and muslin-weavers of Cayenneville, were several unsatisfied and ambitious spirits, who clubbed together, and got a London newspaper to the Cross-keys, where they were nightly in the habit of meeting and debating about the affairs of the French, which were then gathering towards a head. They were represented to me as lads by common in capacity,[344] but with unsettled notions of religion. They were, however, quiet and orderly, and some of them since, at Glasgow, Paisley, and Manchester, even, I am told, in London, have grown into a topping way.[345]

It seems they did not like my manner of preaching, and on that account absented themselves from public worship; which, when I heard, I sent for some of them, to convince them of their error, with regard to the truth of divers points of doctrine; but they confounded me with their objections, and used my arguments, which were the old and orthodox proven opinions of the Divinity Hall,[346] as if they had been the light sayings of a vain man. So that I was troubled, fearing that some change would ensue to my people, who had hitherto lived amidst the boughs and branches of the gospel unmolested by the fowler's snare,[347] and I set myself to watch narrowly, and with a vigilant eye, what would come to pass.

There was a visible increase among us of worldly prosperity in the course of this year; insomuch, that some of the farmers who were in the custom of taking their vendibles to the neighbouring towns on the Tuesdays, the Wednesdays, and Fridays, were led to open a market on the Saturdays in our own clachan, the which proved a great convenience. But I cannot take it upon me to say, whether this can be said

carding and spinning; weaving this into cloth continued to be done in private houses on hand-looms. Power looms did not displace these until the 1810s.
342   Tambouring: embroidery.
343   'Wanted' here meaning 'gone without'.
344   By common (Sc.): out of the ordinary.
345   Topping way: superior position.
346   That is, in theological college.
347   The fowler's snare as an image of evil is from Psalms 91.3.

to have well began in the present Ann. Dom., although I know that in the summer of the ensuing year it was grown into a settled custom; which I well recollect by the Macadams coming with their bairns to see Mrs Malcolm their mother, suddenly on a Saturday afternoon; on which occasion me and Mrs Balwhidder were invited to dine with them, and Mrs Malcolm bought in the market for the dinner that day, both mutton and fowls, such as twenty years before could not have been got for love or money on such a pinch.[348] Besides, she had two bottles of red and white wine from the Cross Keys, luxuries which, saving in the Breadland house in its best days, could not have been had in the whole parish, but must have been brought from a borough town; for Eglesham Castle is not within the bounds of Dalmailing, and my observe does not apply to the stock and stores of that honourable mansion, but only to the dwellings of our own heritors, who were in general straitened in their circumstances, partly with upsetting, and partly by the eating rust of family pride, which hurt the edge of many a clever fellow among them, that would have done well in the way of trade, but sunk into divors for the sake of their genteelity.[349]

CHAPTER XXX.—YEAR 1789.

William Malcolm comes to the parish and preaches—The opinions upon his sermon.

THIS I have always reflected upon as one of our blessed years. It was not remarkable for any extraordinary occurrence, but there was a hopefulness in the minds of men, and a planning of new undertakings, of which, whatever may be the upshot, the devising is ever rich in the cheerful anticipations of good.

Another new line of road was planned, for a shorter cut to the cotton-mill, from the main road to Glasgow, and a public-house was opened in Cayenneville; the latter, however, was not an event that gave me much satisfaction, but it was a convenience to the inhabitants, and the carriers that brought the cotton-bags and took away the yarn twice a-week, needed a place of refreshment. And there was a stage-coach set up thrice every week from Ayr, that passed through the town, by which it was possible to travel to Glasgow between breakfast and dinner-time, a thing that could not, when I came to the parish, have been thought within the compass of man.

This stage-coach I thought one of the greatest conveniencies that had been established among us; and it enabled Mrs Balwhidder to send a basket of her fresh butter into the Glasgow market, by which, in the spring and the fall of the year, she got a great price, for the Glasgow merchants are fond of excellent eatables, and the payment was aye ready money—Tam Whirlit the driver paying for the one basket when he took up the other.

In this year William Malcolm, the youngest son of the widow, having been sometime a tutor in a family in the east country, came to see his mother, as indeed he had done every year from the time he went to the College, but this occasion was made remarkable by his preaching in my pulpit. His old acquaintance were curious to hear him, and I myself had a sort of a wish likewise, being desirous to know how far he was orthodox; so I thought fit, on the suggestion of one of the elders, to ask him to preach one day for me, which, after some fleeching,[350] he consented to do. I think, however, there was a true modesty in his diffidence, although his reason was a weak one, being lest he might

---

348 That is, at such short notice.
349 Upsetting: 'dislocation, disturbance, upset' (*OED*); divors (Sc.): bankrupts. Balwhidder notes the perception of some landowners that going into commerce would undermine their status as 'gentlemen'.
350 Fleeching (Sc.): coaxing, wheedling, flattery.

not satisfy his mother, who had as yet never heard him. Accordingly, on the Sabbath after, he did preach, and the kirk was well packed, and I was not one of the least attentive of the congregation. His sermon assuredly was well put together, and there was nothing to object to in his doctrine; but the elderly people thought his language rather too Englified, which I thought likewise, for I never could abide that the plain auld Kirk of Scotland, with her sober presbyterian simplicity, should borrow, either in word or in deed, from the language of the prelatic hierarchy of England. Nevertheless, the younger part of the congregation were loud in his praise, saying, there had not been heard before such a style of language in our side of the country. As for Mrs Malcolm, his mother, when I spoke to her anent the same, she said but little, expressing only her hope that his example would be worthy of his precepts; so that, upon the whole, it was a satisfaction to us all, that he was likely to prove a stoop and upholding pillar to the Kirk of Scotland.[351] His mother, however, had the satisfaction, before she died, to see him a placed minister, and his name among the authors of his country; for he published at Edinburgh a volume of Moral Essays, of which he sent me a pretty bound copy, and they were greatly creditable to his pen, though lacking somewhat of that birr and smeddum, that is the juice and flavour of books of that sort.[352]

CHAPTER XXXI.—YEAR 1790.

A bookseller's shop is set up among the houses of the weavers at Cayenne-ville.

THE features of this Ann. Dom. partook of the character of its predecessor. Several new houses were added to the clachan; Cayenneville was spreading out with weavers' shops, and growing up fast into a town. In some respects it got the start of our's, for one day, when I was going to dine with Mr Cayenne, at Wheatrig-house, not a little to my amazement, did I behold a bookseller's shop opened there, with sticks of red and black wax, pouncet-boxes, pens, pocket-books,[353] and new publications, in the window, such as the like of was only to be seen in cities and borough towns. And it was lighted at night by a patent lamp, which shed a wonderful beam, burning oil, and having no smoke.[354] The man sold likewise perfumery, powder-puffs, trinkets, and Dublin dolls, besides pen-knives, Castile soap, and walking-sticks, together with a prodigy of other luxuries too tedious to mention.

Upon conversing with the man, for I was enchanted to go into this phenomenon, for as no less could I regard it, he told me that he had a correspondence with London, and could get me down any book published there within the same month in which it came out, and he shewed me divers of the newest come out,[355] of which I did not read even in the Scots Magazine, till more than three months after, although I had till then always considered that work as most interesting for its early intelligence. But what I was most

---

351 Stoop (Sc.): pillar or prop.
352 Birr: 'force, energy, enthusiasm' (*SND*); smeddum: 'spirit, mettle, [...] vigorous common sense' (*SND*) (both Sc.). In lacking these in his writing, as in his anglicised rhetoric, William Malcolm reveals himself as an example of the 'modern moderation' mentioned in chapter XX.
353 Pouncet box: a small box with a perforated lid, for holding perfumes. Pocket-book: simply a small printed book, or a note book.
354 As opposed to the wall-lamp, made of iron with a wick made of rush, still usual at this point.
355 Divers meaning here 'diverse examples of' (Sc.).

surprised to hear, was that he took in a daily London newspaper for the spinners and weavers, who paid him a penny a-week a piece for the same; they being all greatly taken up with what, at the time, was going on in France.

This bookseller in the end, however, proved a whowp in our nest,[356] for he was in league with some of the English reformers, and when the story took wind three years after, concerning the plots and treasons of the Corresponding Societies and democrats,[357] he was fain to make a moonlight flitting, leaving his wife for a time to manage his affairs. I could not, however, think any ill of the man notwithstanding; for he had very correct notions of right and justice, in a political sense, and when he came into the parish, he was as orderly and well-behaved as any other body; and conduct is a test that I have always found as good for a man's principles, as professions. Nor, at the time of which I am speaking, was there any of that dread or fear of reforming the government, that has since been occasioned by the wild and wasteful hand which the French employed in their Revolution.

But, among other improvements, I should mention, that a Doctor Marigold came and settled in Cayenneville, a small, round, happy-tempered man, whose funny stories were far better liked than his drugs. There was a doubt among some of the weavers, if he was a skilful Esculapian,[358] and this doubt led to their holding out an inducement to another medical man, Dr Tanzey, to settle there likewise, by which it grew into a saying, that at Cayenneville there was a doctor for health as well as sickness. For Dr Marigold was one of the best hands in the country at a pleasant punch-bowl, while Dr Tanzey had all the requisite knowledge of the faculty for the bed-side.

It was in this year, that the hour-plate and hand on the kirk steeple were renewed, as indeed may yet be seen by the date, though it be again greatly in want of fresh gilding; for it was by my advice that the figures of the Ann. Dom. were placed one in each corner. In this year, likewise, the bridge over the Brawl burn was built, a great convenience, in the winter time, to the parishioners that lived on the north side; for when there happened to be a speat on the Sunday, it kept them from the kirk, but I did not find that the bridge mended the matter, till after the conclusion of the war against the democrats, and the beginning of that which we are now waging with Boney,[359] their child and champion. It is, indeed, wonderful to think of the occultation of grace that was taking place about this time, throughout the whole bound of Christendom; for I could mark a visible darkness of infidelity spreading in the corner of the vineyard committed to my keeping, and a falling away of the vines from their wonted props and confidence in the truths of Revelation. But I said nothing. I knew that the faith could not be lost, and that it would be found purer and purer the more it was tried; and this I have lived to see, many now being zealous members of the church, that were abundantly lukewarm at the period of which I am now speaking.

---

356 'A whaup in the nest' is a proverbial expression meaning 'something, gen. of a vexatious or unpleasant nature, which is likely to make its presence felt, something brewing, hatching, or afoot'. A whaup is a curlew, a moorland bird; the expression may combine this with another sense of 'whaup', that used in the expression 'a whaup in the rape', a hitch or fault in the rope (all *SND*).

357 Balwhidder refers to the sedition trials of 1793: see Introduction.

358 Esculapian: healer (from Asclepius, the Greek god of medicine).

359 The war with the (notionally democratic) French Republic seemed to have ended with the Treaty of Amiens in March 1802, but hostilities resumed in May 1803. Napoleon Bonaparte ('Boney') had ruled France as 'First Consul' since a coup in 1799. In December 1804 he crowned himself emperor, ending the (first) French Republic. The war against him continued until 1814.

CHAPTER XXXII.—YEAR 1791.

I place my son Gilbert in a counting-house at Glasgow—My observations on Glasgow—On my return I preach against the vanity of riches, and begin to be taken for a Black-neb.

IN the spring of this year, I took my son Gilbert into Glasgow, to place him in a counting-house.[360] As he had no inclination for any of the learned professions, and not having been there from the time when I was sent to the General Assembly, I cannot express my astonishment at the great improvements, surpassing far all that was done in our part of the country, which I thought was not to be paralleled. When I came afterwards to reflect on my simplicity in this, it was clear to me that we should not judge of the rest of the world by what we see going on around ourselves, but walk abroad into other parts, and thereby enlarge our sphere of observation, as well as ripen our judgment of things.

But although there was no doubt a great and visible increase of the city, loftier buildings on all sides, and streets that spread their arms far into the embraces of the country, I thought the looks of the population were impaired, and that there was a greater proportion of long white faces in the Trongate, than when I attended the Divinity class. These, I was told, were the weavers and others concerned in the cotton trade, which I could well believe, for they were very like in their looks to the men of Cayenneville; but from living in a crowded town, and not breathing a wholesome country air between their tasks, they had a stronger cast of unhealthy melancholy. I was, therefore, very glad, that Providence had placed in my hand the pastoral staff of a country parish, for it cut me to the heart to see so many young men, in the rising prime of life, already in the arms of a pale consumption.[361] "If, therefore," said I to Mrs Balwhidder, when I returned home to the Manse, "we live, as it were, within the narrow circle of ignorance, we are spared from the pain of knowing many an evil; and, surely, in much knowledge, there is sadness of heart."

But the main effect of this was to make me do all in my power to keep my people contented with their lowly estate; for in that same spirit of improvement, which was so busy every where, I could discern something like a shadow, that shewed it was not altogether of that pure advantage, which avarice led all so eagerly to believe. Accordingly, I began a series of sermons on the evil and vanity of riches, and, for the most part of the year, pointed out in what manner they led the possessor to indulge in sinful luxuries, and how indulgence begat desire, and desire betrayed integrity and corrupted the heart, making it evident, that the rich man was liable to forget his unmerited obligations to God, and to oppress the laborious and the needful when he required their services.

Little did I imagine, in thus striving to keep aloof the ravenous wolf Ambition from my guileless flock, that I was giving cause for many to think me an enemy to the king and government, and a perverter of Christianity, to suit levelling doctrines. But so it was. Many of the heritors considered me a black-neb,[362] though I knew it not, but went on in the course of my duty, thinking only how best to preserve peace on earth, and good will towards men. I saw, however, an altered manner in the deportment of

---

360 That is, a merchant's office.
361 Consumption is tuberculosis; but the cotton dust filling the mills caused various other respiratory diseases.
362 Levelling: that is, radical or democratic. Black-neb (Sc.): 'A person charged with democratic sympathies at the time of the French Revolution' (*OED*).

several, with whom I had long lived in friendly terms. It was not marked enough to make me inquire the cause, but sufficiently plain to affect my ease of mind. Accordingly, about the end of this year, I fell into a dull way: My spirit was subdued, and at times I was aweary of the day, and longed for the night, when I might close my eyes in peaceful slumbers. I missed my son Gilbert, who had been a companion to me in the long nights, while his mother was busy with the lasses, and their ceaseless wheels and cardings, in the kitchen. Often could I have found it in my heart to have banned that never-ceasing industry, and to tell Mrs Balwhidder, that the married state was made for something else than to make napery, and bittle blankets;[363] but it was her happiness to keep all at work, and she had no pleasure in any other way of life, so I sat many a night by the fire-side with resignation; sometimes in the study, and sometimes in the parlour, and, as I was doing nothing, Mrs Balwhidder said it was needless to light the candle. Our daughter Janet was in this time at a boarding-school in Ayr, so that I was really a most solitary married man.

CHAPTER XXXIII.—YEAR 1792.

Troubled with low spirits—Accidental meeting with Mr Cayenne, who endeavours to remove the prejudices entertained against me.

WHEN the spring in this year began to brighten on the brae, the cloud of dulness, that had darkened and oppressed me all the winter, somewhat melted away, and I could now and then joke again at the never-ending toil and trouble of that busiest of all bees, the second Mrs Balwhidder. But still I was far from being right, a small matter affected me, and I was overly given to walking by myself, and musing on things that I could tell nothing about—my thoughts were just the rack of a dream without form, and driving witlessly as the smoke that mounteth up, and is lost in the airy heights of the sky.

Heeding little of what was going on in the clachan, and taking no interest in the concerns of any body, I would have been contented to die, but I had no ail about me. An accident, however, fell out, that, by calling on me for an effort, had the blessed influence of clearing my vapours almost entirely away.

One morning, as I was walking on the sunny side of the road, where the foot-path was in the next year made to the cotton-mill, I fell in with Mr Cayenne, who was seemingly much fashed—a small matter could do that at any time; and he came up to me with a red face and an angry eye. It was not my intent to speak to him, for I was grown loth to enter into conversation with any body, so I bowed and passed on. "What," cried Mr Cayenne, "and will you not speak to me?" I turned round, and said meekly, "Mr Cayenne, I have no objections to speak to you; but having nothing particular to say, it did not seem necessary just now."

He looked at me like a gled,[364] and in a minute exclaimed, "Mad, by Jupiter! as mad as a March hare!" He then entered into conversation with me, and said, that he had noticed me an altered man, and was just so far on his way to the Manse, to inquire what had befallen me. So, from less to more, we entered into the marrow of my case; and I told him how I had observed the estranged countenances of some of the heritors; at which he swore an oath, that they were a parcel of the damn'dest boobies in the country,[365] and told me how they had taken it into their heads that I was a leveller.

363 Bittle (Sc.): beat.
364 Gled: red kite, a bird of prey.
365 'Booby' was a contemptuous (English) term for a petty landowner, stereotypically heavy-

"But I know you better," said Mr Cayenne, "and have stood up for you as an honest conscientious man, though I don't much like your humdrum preaching. However, let that pass; I insist upon your dining with me to-day, when some of these arrant fools are to be with us, and the devil's in't, if I don't make you friends with them." I did not think Mr Cayenne, however, very well qualified for a peace-maker, but, nevertheless, I consented to go; and having thus got an inkling of the cause of that cold back-turning which had distressed me so much, I made such an effort to remove the error that was entertained against me, that some of the heritors, before we separated, shook me by the hands with the cordiality of renewed friendship; and, as if to make amends for past neglect, there was no end to their invitations to dinner, which had the effect of putting me again on my mettle, and removing the thick and muddy melancholious humour out of my blood.

But what confirmed my cure, was the coming home of my daughter Janet from the Ayr boarding-school, where she had learnt to play on the spinet, and was become a conversible lassie, with a competent knowledge, for a woman, of geography and history; so that when her mother was busy with the wearyful booming wheel, she entertained me sometimes with a tune, and sometimes with her tongue, which made the winter nights fly cantily by.

Whether it was owing to the malady of my imagination, throughout the greatest part of this year, or that really nothing particular did happen to interest me, I cannot say, but it is very remarkable that I have nothing remarkable to record—farther, than that I was at the expence myself of getting the Manse rough cast, and the window cheeks painted, with roans put up, rather than apply to the heritors; for they were always sorely fashed when called upon for outlay.

CHAPTER XXXIV.—YEAR 1793.

I dream a remarkable dream, and preach a Sermon in consequence, applying to the events of the times—Two democratical weaver lads brought before Mr Cayenne, as justice of peace.

ON the first night of this year, I dreamt a very remarkable dream, which, when I now recal to mind, at this distance of time, I cannot but think that there was a cast of prophecy in it. I thought that I stood on the tower of an old popish kirk, looking out at the window upon the kirk-yard, where I beheld ancient tombs, with effigies and coats of arms on the wall thereof, and a great gate at the one side, and a door that led into a dark and dismal vault, at the other. I thought all the dead, that were lying in the common graves, rose out of their coffins; at the same time, from the old and grand monuments, with the effigies and coats of arms, came the great men, and the kings of the earth with crowns on their heads, and globes and sceptres in their hands.

I stood wondering what was to ensue, when presently I heard the noise of drums and trumpets, and anon I beheld an army with banners entering in at the gate; upon which the kings and the great men came also forth in their power and array, and a dreadful battle was foughten; but the multitude, that had risen from the common graves, stood afar off, and were but lookers on.

The kings and their host were utterly discomfited. They were driven within the doors of their monuments, their coats of arms were broken off, and their effigies cast down, and the victors triumphed over them with the flourishes of trumpets and the waving of banners. But while I looked, the vision was changed, and I then beheld

drinking, ignorant, and conservative.

a wide and a dreary waste, and far off the steeples of a great city, and a tower in the midst, like the tower of Babel, and on it I could discern written in characters of fire, "Public Opinion." While I was pondering at the same, I heard a great shout, and presently the conquerors made their appearance, coming over the desolate moor. They were going in great pride and might towards the city, but an awful burning rose, far as it were in the darkness, and the flames stood like a tower of fire that reached unto Heaven. And I saw a dreadful hand and an arm stretched from out of the cloud, and in its hold was a besom made of the hail and the storm, and it swept the fugitives like dust;[366] and in their place I saw the churchyard, as it were, cleared and spread around, the graves closed, and the ancient tombs, with their coats of arms and their effigies of stone, all as they were in the beginning. I then awoke, and behold it was a dream.

This vision perplexed me for many days, and when the news came that the King of France was beheaded by the hands of his people,[367] I received, as it were, a token in confirmation of the vision that had been disclosed to me in my sleep, and I preached a discourse on the same, and against the French Revolution, that was thought one of the greatest and soundest sermons that I had ever delivered in my pulpit.

On the Monday following, Mr Cayenne, who had been some time before appointed a justice of the peace, came over from Wheatrig-house to the Cross Keys, where he sent for me and divers other respectable inhabitants of the clachan, and told us that he was to have a sad business, for a warrant was out to bring before him two democratic weaver lads, on a suspicion of high treason. Scarcely were the words uttered, when they were brought in, and he began to ask them how they dared to think of dividing, with their liberty and equality principles, his and every other man's property in the country. The men answered him in a calm manner, and told him they sought no man's property, but only their own natural rights; upon which he called them traitors and reformers. They denied they were traitors, but confessed they were reformers, and said they knew not how that should be imputed to them as a fault, for that the greatest men of all times had been reformers. — "Was not," they said, "our Lord Jesus Christ a reformer?" — "And what the devil did he make of it?" cried Mr Cayenne, bursting with passion; "Was he not crucified?"

I thought, when I heard these words, that the pillars of the earth sunk beneath me, and that the roof of the house was carried away in a whirlwind. The drums of my ears crackit, blue starns danced before my sight,[368] and I was fain to leave the house and hie me home to the Manse, where I sat down in my study, like a stupified creature awaiting what would betide. Nothing, however, was found against the weaver lads; but I never, from that day, could look on Mr Cayenne as a Christian, though surely he was a true government-man.

Soon after this affair, there was a pleasant re-edification of a gospel-spirit among the heritors, especially when they heard how I had handled the regicides of France; and on the following Sunday, I had the comfortable satisfaction to see many a gentleman in their pews, that had not been for years within a kirk-door. The democrats, who

---

366   Besom: broom. Writing in 1811, when Napoleon's empire was at its maximum extent, Balwhidder cannot know how fully the latter part of this dream will be realised. Napoleon invaded Russia in June 1812, but Moscow, evacuated and lawless, burnt down, denying his army winter quarters and supplies. The army was forced to retreat through the Russian winter (sent, in Balwhidder's dream, by God). Of over 600,000 men who invaded Russia, perhaps only 80,000 returned to the west, and these losses were the beginning of the end of French dominance in Europe.

367   Louis XVI was guillotined on 21 January 1793; France declared war on Britain on 1 February.

368   Crackit: cracked; starns: stars (both Sc.).

took a world of trouble to misrepresent the actions of the gentry, insinuated that all this was not from any new sense of grace, but in fear of their being reported as suspected persons to the King's government. But I could not think so, and considered their renewal of communion with the church as a swearing of allegiance to the King of Kings, against that host of French atheists, who had torn the mortcloth from the coffin, and made it a banner, with which they were gone forth to war against the Lamb.[369] The whole year was, however, spent in great uneasiness, and the proclamation of the war was followed by an appalling stop in trade. We heard of nothing but failures on all hands,[370] and among others that grieved me, was that of Mr Maitland of Glasgow, who had befriended Mrs Malcolm in the days of her affliction, and gave her son Robert his fine ship. It was a sore thing to hear of so many breakings, especially of old respected merchants like him, who had been a Lord Provost, and was far declined into the afternoon of life. He did not, however, long survive the mutation of his fortune, but bending his aged head in sorrow, sunk down beneath the stroke, to rise no more.

CHAPTER XXXV.—YEAR 1794.

The condition of the parish, as divided into Government-men and Jacobins—I endeavour to prevent Christian charity from being forgotten in the phraseology of utility and philanthropy.

THIS year had opened into all the leafiness of midsummer before any thing memorable happened in the parish, farther than that the sad division of my people into government-men and jacobins was perfected.[371] This calamity, for I never could consider such heart-burning among neighbours as any thing less than a very heavy calamity, was assuredly occasioned by faults on both sides, but it must be confessed that the gentry did nothing to win the commonality from the errors of their way. A little more condescension on their part would not have made things worse, and might have made them better; but pride interposed, and caused them to think that any show of affability from them would be construed by the democrats into a terror of their power. While the democrats were no less to blame; for hearing how their compeers were thriving in France and demolishing every obstacle to their ascendency, they were crouse and really insolent,[372] evidencing none of that temperance in prosperity that proves the possessors worthy of their good fortune.

As for me, my duty in these circumstances was one plain and simple. The Christian religion was attempted to be brought into disrepute; the rising generation were taught to jibe at its holiest ordinances; and the kirk was more frequented as a place to while away the time on a rainy Sunday, than for any insight of the admonitions and revelations in the sacred book. Knowing this, I perceived that it would be of no effect to handle much the mysteries of the faith; but as there was at the time a bruit and a sound about universal benevolence, philanthropy, utility, and all the other disguises with which an infidel philosophy appropriated to itself the charity, brotherly love, and

---

369   The Lamb is of course Christ. In its struggle for authority with the French church, the Republic became explicitly atheist, for example celebrating a 'Festival of Reason' in Notre Dame Cathedral on 10 November 1793 in repudiation of religion.

370   That is, commercial failures, bankruptcies.

371   The Jacobins were the most radical party of the French Revolution, effectively in power from the summer of 1793, and responsible for 'The Terror', large-scale executions of enemies of the regime. But in Britain, all sympathisers with the revolution, however appalled by its violent turn, were labelled 'jacobins' by their reactionary antagonists.

372   Crouse (Sc.): arrogant, proud.

well-doing inculcated by our holy religion,[373] I set myself to task upon these heads, and thought it no robbery to use a little of the stratagem employed against Christ's Kingdom, to promote the interests thereof in the hearts and understandings of those whose ears would have been sealed against me, had I attempted to expound higher things. Accordingly, on one day it was my practice to shew what the nature of Christian charity was, comparing it to the light and warmth of the sun that shines impartially on the just and the unjust[374]—shewing that man, without the sense of it as a duty, was as the beasts that perish,[375] and that every feeling of his nature was intimately selfish, but that, when actuated by this divine impulse, he rose out of himself and became as a god, zealous to abate the sufferings of all things that live.—And, on the next day, I demonstrated that the new benevolence which had come so much into vogue, was but another version of this Christian virtue.—In like manner I dealt with brotherly love, bringing it home to the business and bosoms of my hearers, that the Christianity of it was neither enlarged nor bettered by being baptized with the Greek name of philanthropy. With well-doing, however, I went more roundly to work. I told my people that I thought they had more sense than to secede from Christianity to become Utilitarians, for that it would be a confession of ignorance of the faith they deserted, seeing that it was the main duty inculcated by our religion to do all in morals and manners, to which the new-fangled doctrine of utility pretended.

These discourses, which I continued for some time, had no great effect on the men; but being prepared in a familiar household manner, they took the fancies of the young women, which was to me an assurance that the seed I had planted would in time shoot forth; for I reasoned with myself, that if the gudemen of the immediate generation should continue free-thinkers, their wives will take care that those of the next shall not lack that spunk of grace;[376] so I was cheered under that obscurity which fell upon Christianity at this time, with a vista beyond, in which I saw, as it were, the children unborn, walking in the bright green, and in the unclouded splendour of the faith.

But, what with the decay of trade, and the temptation of the King's bounty,[377] and, over all, the witlessness that was in the spirit of man at this time, the number that enlisted in the course of the year from the parish was prodigious. In one week no less than three weavers and two cotton-spinners went over to Ayr, and took the bounty for the Royal Artillery. But I could not help remarking to myself, that the people were grown so used to changes and extraordinary adventures, that the single enlistment of Thomas Wilson, at the beginning of the American war, occasioned a far greater grief and work among us, than all the swarms that went off week after week in the months of November and December of this year.

---

373 Balwhidder sets out to counter the secularisation of morality that was an important part of Enlightenment thought, grounding right and wrong on principles of human nature rather than revealed religion. As such, he sets himself as much against the 'sympathy' of David Hume and Adam Smith as against the 'utility' of Jeremy Bentham.

374 Matthew 5.45: God 'maketh his sun to rise on the evil and on the good, and sendeth rain on the just and on the unjust'.

375 Psalms 49.12.

376 Spunk (Sc.): spark.

377 That is, the shilling paid on enlisting.

CHAPTER XXXVI.—YEAR 1795.

A recruiting party visits the town—After them, players—then preaching quakers—the progress of philosophy among the weavers.

THE present Ann. Dom. was ushered in with an event that I had never dreaded to see in my day, in our once sober and religious country parish. The number of lads that had gone over to Ayr to be soldiers from among the spinners and weavers of Cayenneville had been so great, that the government got note of it, and sent a recruiting party to be quartered in the town; for the term clachan was beginning by this time to wear out of fashion; indeed the place itself was outgrowing the fitness of that title. Never shall I forget the dunt that the first tap of the drum gied to my heart,[378] as I was sitting, on Hansel Monday, by myself, at the parlour fireside, Mrs Balwhidder being throng with the lasses looking out a washing,[379] and my daughter at Ayr, spending a few days with her old comrades of the boarding-school. I thought it was the enemy,[380] and then anon the sound of the fife came shrill to the ear; for the night was lown and peaceful. My wife and all the lasses came flying in upon me, crying all, in the name of Heaven, what could it be? by which I was obligated to put on my big-coat, and, with my hat and staff, go out to inquire. The whole town was aloof,[381] the aged at the doors in clusters, and the bairns following the tattoo, as it was called, and at every doubling beat of the drum, shouting as if they had been in the face of their foemen.

Mr Archibald Dozendale, one of my elders, was saying to several persons around him, just as I came up, "Hech, sirs! but the battle draws near our gates," upon which there was a heavy sigh from all that heard him; and then they told me of the serjeant's business, and we had a serious communing together anent the same. But, while we were thus standing discoursing on the causeway, Mrs Balwhidder and the servant lasses could thole no longer, but in a troop came in quest of me, to hear what was doing. In short, it was a night both of sorrow and anxiety. Mr Dozendale walked back to the Manse with us, and we had a sober tumbler of toddy together, marvelling exceedingly where these fearful portents and changes would stop, both of us being of opinion, that the end of the world was drawing nearer and nearer.

Whether it was, however, that the lads belonging to the place did not like to shew themselves with the enlistment cockades among their acquaintance, or that there was any other reason, I cannot take it upon me to say, but certain it is, the recruiting party came no speed,[382] and in consequence were removed about the end of March.

Another thing happened in this year, too remarkable for me to neglect to put on record, as it strangely and strikingly marked the rapid revolutions that were going on. In the month of August, at the time of the fair, a gang of play-actors came, and hired Thomas Thacklan's barn for their enactments. They were the first of that clanjamfrey who had ever been in the parish,[383] and there was a wonderful excitement caused by the rumours concerning them. Their first performance was Douglas Tragedy, and the

---

378 Dunt: blow; gied: gave (both Sc.).
379 Hansel (or Handsel) Monday: the first Monday of the year, on which a present (Handsel) is given e.g. on visiting friends. Throng, thrang (Sc.): fully occupied (*DOST* A.3.c).
380 The enemy: it is not clear here whether Balwhidder means the devil or the French. Cf. note 227 (chapter XVI).
381 Aloof: obscure. Kinsley takes this as the English word; but the children of the town, included here, are not 'standing at a distance' (Kinsley p.149). It may just mean 'alive' in the sense of wide awake and on the streets.
382 Came no speed (Sc.): had no success.
383 Clanjamfrey, clamjamfry (Sc.): bunch of riff-raff.

Gentle Shepherd;[384] and the general opinion was, that the lad who played Norval in the play, and Patie in the farce, was an English lord's son, who had run away from his parents, rather than marry an old cracket lady,[385] with a great portion. But, whatever truth there might be in this notion, certain it is, the whole pack was in a state of perfect beggary; and yet, for all that, they not only in their parts, as I was told, laughed most heartily, but made others do the same; for I was constrained to let my daughter go to see them, with some of her acquaintance, and she gave me such an account of what they did, that I thought I would have liked to have gotten a keek at them myself.[386] At the same time, I must own this was a sinful curiosity, and I stifled it to the best of my ability. Among other plays that they did, was one called Macbeth and the Witches, which the Miss Cayennes had seen performed in London, when they were there in the winter time, with their father, for three months, seeing the world, after coming from the boarding-school. But it was no more like the true play of Shakespeare the poet, according to their account, than a duddy betherel,[387] set up to fright the sparrows from the pease, is like a living gentleman. The hungry players, instead of behaving like guests at the royal banquet, were voracious on the needful feast of bread, and the strong ale, that served for wine in decanters; but the greatest sport of all, was about a kail-pot, that acted the part of a cauldron, and which should have sunk with thunder and lightning into the earth; however, it did quite as well, for it made its exit, as Miss Virginia said, by walking quietly off, being pulled by a string fastened to one of its feet. No scene of the play was so much applauded as this one; and the actor who did the part of King Macbeth, made a most polite bow of thankfulness to the audience, for the approbation with which they had received the performance of the pot.

We had likewise, shortly after the "omnes exeunt" of the players,[388] an exhibition of a different sort in the same barn. This was by two English quakers, and a quaker lady, tanners from Kendal, who had been at Ayr on some leather business, where they preached, but made no proselytes. The travellers were all three in a whisky,[389] drawn by one of the best ordered horses, as the hostler at the Cross-keys told me, ever seen. They came to the inns to their dinner, and meaning to stay all night, sent round, to let it be known that they would hold a meeting in friend Thacklan's barn; but Thomas denied they were either kith or kin to him; this, however, was their way of speaking.

In the evening, owing to the notice, a great congregation was assembled in the barn, and I myself, along with Mr Archibald Dozendale, went there likewise, to keep the people in awe; for we feared the strangers might be jeered and insulted. The three were seated aloft, on a high stage, prepared on purpose, with two mares and scaffold-deals,[390] borrowed from Mr Trowel the mason. They sat long, and silent; but at last the spirit moved the woman, and she rose, and delivered a very sensible exposition of Christianity. I was really surprised to hear such sound doctrine; and Mr Dozendale

384 Eighteenth-century Scotland's two most famous stage-plays: *The Gentle Shepherd* by Allan Ramsay (1725) and *Douglas; a Tragedy* by John Home (1757).
385 Cracket, usually crackit (Sc.): crazy.
386 Keek (Sc.): peek. The Kirk traditionally regarded the theatre as sinful; it was instrumental in closing Ramsay's theatre in Edinburgh, though another opened later; it banned ministers from attending Home's play, but Home was himself a (moderate) minister; by Balwhidder's generation it had given up this institutional opposition, but maintained its moral disapproval.
387 Duddy betheral (Sc.): scarecrow.
388 Omnes exeunt: the stage direction, all leave (the stage).
389 Whisky: a small carriage.
390 Mare, mear (Sc.): wooden trestle; deals: planks.

said, justly, that it was more to the purpose than some that my younger brethren from Edinburgh endeavoured to teach. So, that those who went to laugh at the sincere simplicity of the pious quakers, were rebuked by a very edifying discourse on the moral duties of a Christian's life.

Upon the whole, however, this, to the best of my recollection, was another unsatisfactory year. In this we were, doubtless, brought more into the world, but we had a greater variety of temptation set before us, and there was still jealousy and estrangement in the dispositions of the gentry, and the lower orders, particularly the manufacturers.[391] I cannot say, indeed, that there was any increase of corruption among the usual portion of my people; for their vocation calling them to work apart, in the purity of the free air of Heaven, they were kept uncontaminated by that seditious infection which fevered the minds of the sedentary weavers, and working like flatulence in the stomachs of the cotton-spinners, sent up into their heads a vain and diseased fume of infidel philosophy.

CHAPTER XXXVII.—YEAR 1796.

Death of second Mrs Balwhidder—I look out for a third, and fix upon Mrs Nugent, a widow—Particulars of the courtship.

THE prosperity of fortune is like the blossoms of spring, or the golden hue of the evening cloud. It delights the spirit, and passes away.

In the month of February my second wife was gathered to the Lord. She had been very ill for some time with an income in her side, which no medicine could remove. I had the best doctors in the country-side to her, but their skill was of no avail, their opinions being, that her ail was caused by an internal abscess, for which physic has provided no cure. Her death was to me a great sorrow, for she was a most excellent wife, industrious to a degree, and managed every thing with so brisk a hand, that nothing went wrong that she put it to. With her I had grown richer than any other minister in the presbytery; but above all, she was the mother of my bairns, which gave her a double claim upon me.

I laid her by the side of my first love, Betty Lanshaw, my own cousin that was, and I inscribed her name upon the same headstone; but time had drained my poetical vein, and I have not yet been able to indite an epitaph on her merits and virtues, for she had an eminent share of both. Her greatest fault—the best have their faults—was an over-earnestness to gather geer;[392] in the doing of which I thought she sometimes sacrificed the comforts of a pleasant fire-side, for she was never in her element but when she was keeping the servants eydent at their work. But, if by this she substracted something from the quietude that was most consonant to my nature,[393] she has left cause, both in bank and bond, for me and her bairns to bless her great household activity.

She was not long deposited in her place of rest till I had occasion to find her loss. All my things were kept by her in a most perjinct and excellent order, but they soon fell into an amazing confusion, for, as she often said to me, I had a turn for heedlessness; insomuch, that although my daughter Janet was grown up, and able to keep the house, I saw that it would be necessary, as soon as decency would allow, for me to take

---

391   Note that Balwhidder often uses 'manufacturers' to refer to the factory workers, not the factory owners or managers as we would now.
392   Geer, usually gear (Sc.): wealth.
393   Substract: take away.

another wife. I was moved to this chiefly by foreseeing that my daughter would in time be married, and taken away from me, but more on account of the servant lasses, who grew out of all bounds, verifying the proverb, "Well kens the mouse when the cat's out of the house." Besides this, I was now far down in the vale of years, and could not expect to be long without feeling some of the penalties of old age, although I was still a hail and sound man. It therefore behoved me to look in time for a helpmate, to tend me in my approaching infirmities.

Upon this important concern I reflected, as I may say, in the watches of the night, and, considering the circumstances of my situation, I saw it would not do for me to look out for an overly young woman, nor yet would it do for one of my ways to take an elderly maiden, ladies of that sort being liable to possess strong-set particularities. I therefore resolved that my choice should lie among widows of a discreet age; and I had a glimmer in my mind of speaking to Mrs Malcolm, but when I reflected on the saintly steadiness of her character, I was satisfied it would be of no use to think of her. Accordingly, I bent my brows, and looked towards Irville, which is an abundant trone for widows and other single women;[394] and I fixed my purpose on Mrs Nugent, the relic of a Professor in the University of Glasgow, both because she was a well-bred woman, without any children to plea about the interest of my own two, and likewise because she was held in great estimation by all who knew her, as a lady of a Christian principle.

It was sometime in the summer, however, before I made up my mind to speak to her on the subject; but one afternoon, in the month of August, I resolved to do so, and, with that intent, walked leisurely over to Irville, and after calling on the Rev. Dr Dunwiddie, the minister, I stepped in, as if by chance, to Mrs Nugent's. I could see that she was a little surprised at my visit; however, she treated me with every possible civility, and her servant lass bringing in the tea things, in a most orderly manner, as punctually as the clock was striking, she invited me to sit still, and drink my tea with her; which I did, being none displeased to get such encouragement. However, I said nothing that time, but returned to the Manse, very well content with what I had observed, which made me fain to repeat my visit. So, in the course of the week, taking Janet, my daughter, with me, we walked over in the forenoon, and called at Mrs Nugent's first, before going to any other house; and Janet saying, as we came out to go to the minister's, that she thought Mrs Nugent an agreeable woman, I determined to knock the nail on the head without farther delay.

Accordingly, I invited the minister and his wife to dine with us on the Thursday following; and before leaving the town, I made Janet, while the minister and me were handling a subject, as a sort of thing of common civility, go to Mrs Nugent, and invite her also. Dr Dunwiddie was a gleg man, of a jocose nature; and he, guessing something of what I was ettling at, was very mirthful with me, but I kept my own counsel till a meet season.

On the Thursday, the company, as invited, came, and nothing extraordinary was seen, but in cutting up, and helping a hen, Dr Dunwiddie put one wing on Mrs Nugent's plate, and the other wing on my plate, and said, there have been greater miracles than these two wings flying together, which was a sharp joke, that caused no little merriment, at the expence of Mrs Nugent and me. I, however, to show that I was none daunted, laid a leg also on her plate, and took another on my own, saying, in the words of the Reverend Doctor, there have been greater miracles than that these two legs should lie in the same nest, which was thought a very clever come off; and at the same time, I gave Mrs Nugent a kindly nip on her sonsy arm,[395] which was breaking

394 Trone, usually tron (Sc.): here, market-place.
395 Sonsy (Sc.): comely, attractive, plump.

the ice in as pleasant a way as could be. In short, before any thing passed between ourselves on the subject, we were set down for a tristed pair;[396] and this being the case, we were married as soon as a twelvemonth and a day had passed from the death of the second Mrs Balwhidder; and neither of us have had occasion to rue the bargain. It is, however, but a piece of justice due to my second wife to say, that this was not a little owing to her good management; for she had left such a well plenished house, that her successor said, we had nothing to do but to contribute to one another's happiness.

In this year nothing more memorable happened in the parish, saving that the cotton-mill dam burst, about the time of the Lammas flood,[397] and the waters went forth like a deluge of destruction, carrying off much victual, and causing a vast of damage to the mills that are lower down the stream. It was just a prodigy to see how calmly Mr Cayenne acted on that occasion; for being at other times as crabbed as a wud terrier, folk were afraid to tell him, till he came out himself in the morning, and saw the devastation; at the sight of which he gave only a shrill whistle, and began to laugh at the idea of the men fearing to take him the news, as if he had not fortune and philosophy enough, as he called it, to withstand much greater misfortunes.

CHAPTER XXXVIII.—YEAR 1797.

Mr Henry Melcomb comes to the parish to see his uncle, Mr Cayenne—From some jocular behaviour on his part, Meg Gaffaw falls in love with him—The sad result of the adventure when he is married.

WHEN I have seen, in my walks, the irrational creatures of God, the birds and the beasts, governed by a kindly instinct in attendance on their young, often has it come into my head, that love and charity, far more than reason or justice, formed the tie that holds the world, with all its jarring wants and woes, in social dependance and obligation together; and, in this year, a strong verification of the soundness of this notion, was exemplified in the conduct of the poor haverel lassie Meg Gaffaw, whose naturality on the occasion of her mother's death,[398] I have related at length in this chronicle.

In the course of the summer, Mr Henry Melcomb, who was a nephew to Mr Cayenne, came down from England to see his uncle. He had just completed his education at the College of Christ Church, in Oxford, and was the most perfect young gentleman that had ever been seen in this part of the country.

In his appearance he was a very paragon, with a fine manly countenance, frank-hearted, blithe, and, in many points of character, very like my old friend the Lord Eglesham, who was shot. Indeed, in some respects, he was even above his lordship, for he had a great turn at ready wit, and could joke and banter in a most agreeable manner. He came very often to the Manse to see me, and took great pleasure in my company, and really used a freedom that was so droll, I could scarcely keep my composity and decorum with him. Among others that shared in his attention, was daft Meg Gaffaw, whom he had forgathered with one day in coming to see me, and after conversing with her for some time, he handed her, as she told me herself, over the kirk-stile, like a lady of high degree, and came with her to the Manse-door linking by the arm.

From the ill-timed daffin of that hour,[399] poor Meg fell deep in love with Mr

396   Tristed (Sc.): here, engaged.
397   Lammas: 1 August.
398   Haverel: foolish; naturality: simple-mindedness.
399   Daffin (Sc.): jesting.

Melcomb, and it was just a play-acting to see the arts and antics she put in practice to win his attention. In her garb, she had never any sense of a proper propriety, but went about the country asking for shapings of silks and satins, with which she patched her duds, calling them by the divers names of robes and negligées. All hitherto, however, had been moderation, compared to the daffadile of vanity which she was now seen, when she had searched, as she said, to the bottom of her coffer. I cannot take it upon me to describe her, but she kithed in such a variety of cuffs and ruffles,[400] feathers and flowers, old gumflowers, painted paper knots, ribbans, and furs, and laces, and went about gecking and simpering with an old fan in her hand,[401] that it was not in the power of nature to look at her with sobriety.

Her first appearance in this masquerading, was at the kirk on the Sunday following her adventure with Mr Melcomb, and it was with a sore difficulty that I could keep my eyes off her, even in prayer; and when the kirk skailed,[402] she walked before him, spreading all her grandeur to catch his eye in such a manner as had not been seen or heard of since the prank that Lady Macadam played Miss Betty Wadrife.

Any other but Mr Melcomb would have been provoked by the fool's folly, but he humoured her wit, and, to the amazement of the whole people, presented her his hand, and allemanded her along in a manner that should not have been seen in any street out of a king's court,[403] and far less on the Lord's day. But alas! this sport did not last long. Mr Melcomb had come from England to be married to his cousin, Miss Virginia Cayenne, and poor daft Meg never heard of it till the banns for their purpose of marriage was read out by Mr Loremore on the Sabbath after. The words were scarcely out of his mouth, when the simple and innocent natural gave a loud shriek, that terrified the whole congregation, and ran out of the kirk demented. There was no more finery for poor Meg; but she went and sat opposite to the windows of Mr Cayenne's house, where Mr Melcomb was, with clasped hands and beseeching eyes, like a monumental statue in alabaster, and no entreaty could drive her away. Mr Melcomb sent her money, and the bride many a fine thing, but Meg flung them from her, and clasped her hands again, and still sat. Mr Cayenne would have let loose the house-dog on her, but was not permitted.

In the evening it began to rain, and they thought that and the coming darkness would drive her away, but when the servants looked out before barring the doors, there she was in the same posture. I was to perform the marriage ceremony at seven o'clock in the morning, for the young pair were to go that night to Edinburgh; and when I went, there was Meg sitting looking at the windows with her hands clasped. When she saw me she gave a shrill cry, and took me by the hand, and wised me to go back,[404] crying out in a heart-breaking voice, "O, sir! No yet—no yet! He'll may be draw back, and think of a far truer bride." I was wae for her, and very angry with the servants for laughing at the fond folly of the ill-less thing.

When the marriage was over, and the carriage at the door, the bridegroom handed in the bride. Poor Meg saw this, and jumping up from where she sat, was at his side like a spirit, as he was stepping in, and taking him by the hand, she looked in his face so piteously, that every heart was sorrowful, for she could say nothing. When he pulled away his hand, and the door was shut, she stood as if she had been charmed to the

400   Kithed (Sc.): here, simply appeared.
401   Geck (Sc.): here, 'lift the head proudly' (*SND* 3).
402   Skail (Sc.): disperse.
403   An allemande was a type of dance, originating in Germany; Melcomb leads Meg as in a dance (this is *OED*'s only instance of the word used as a verb in this way).
404   Wise (Sc.): 'advise, counsel, instruct' (*SND* 3).

spot, and saw the chaise drive away. All that were about the door then spoke to her, but she heard us not. At last she gave a deep sigh, and the water coming into her eye, she said, "The worm—the worm is my bonny bridegroom, and Jenny with the many feet my bridal maid.[405] The mill-dam water's the wine o' the wedding, and the clay and the clod shall be my bedding. A lang night is meet for a bridal, but none shall be langer than mine." In saying which words, she fled from among us, with heels like the wind. The servants pursued, but long before they could stop her, she was past redemption in the deepest plumb of the cotton-mill dam.

Few deaths had for many a day happened in the parish, to cause so much sorrow as that of this poor silly creature. She was a sort of household familiar among us, and there was much like the inner side of wisdom in the pattern of her sayings, many of which are still preserved as proverbs.

CHAPTER XXXIX.—YEAR 1798.

A dearth—Mr Cayenne takes measures to mitigate the evil—he receives kindly some Irish refugees—his daughter's marriage.

THIS was one of the heaviest years in the whole course of my ministry. The spring was slow of coming, and cold and wet when it did come; the dibs were full,[406] the roads foul, and the ground that should have been dry at the seed time, was as claggy as clay and clung to the harrow. The labour of man and beast was thereby augmented, and all nature being in a state of sluggish indisposition, it was evident to every eye of experience that there would be a great disappointment to the hopes of the husbandman. Foreseeing this, I gathered the opinion of all the most sagacious of my parishioners, and consulted with them for a provision against the evil day, and we spoke to Mr Cayenne on the subject, for he had a talent by common in matters of mercantile management. It was amazing, considering his hot temper, with what patience he heard the grounds of our apprehension, and how he questioned and sifted the experience of the old farmers, till he was thoroughly convinced that all similar seed-times were ever followed by a short crop. He then said, that he would prove himself a better friend to the parish than he was thought. Accordingly, as he afterwards told me himself, he wrote off that very night to his correspondents in America to buy for his account all the wheat and flour they could get, and ship it to arrive early in the fall; and he bought up likewise in countries round the Baltic great store of victual, and brought in two cargos to Irville on purpose for the parish, against the time of need, making for the occasion a garnel of one of the warehouses of the cotton-mill.

The event came to pass as had been fore-told; the harvest fell short, and Mr Cayenne's cargos from America and the Baltic came home in due season, by which he made a terrible power of money, clearing thousands on thousands by post after post—making more profit, as he said himself, in the course of one month, he believed, than ever was made by any individual within the kingdom of Scotland in the course of a year.—He said, however, that he might have made more if he had bought up the corn at home, but being convinced by us that there would be a scarcity, he thought it his duty as an honest man to draw from the stores and granaries of foreign countries, by which he was sure he would serve his country and be abundantly rewarded. In short,

---

405 Jenny with the many feet (Sc): centipede.
406 Dib (Sc.): puddle.

we all reckoned him another Joseph when he opened his garnels at the cotton-mill,[407] and, after distributing a liberal portion to the poor and needy, selling the remainder at an easy rate to the generality of the people. Some of the neighbouring parishes, however, were angry that he would not serve them likewise, and called him a wicked and extortionate forestaller; but he made it plain to the meanest capacity that if he did not circumscribe his dispensation to our own bounds it would be as nothing. So that, although he brought a wonderful prosperity in by the cotton-mill, and a plenteous supply of corn in a time of famine, doing more in these things for the people than all the other heritors had done from the beginning of time, he was much reviled; even his bounty was little esteemed by my people, because he took a moderate profit on what he sold to them. Perhaps, however, these prejudices might be partly owing to their dislike of his hasty temper, at least I am willing to think so, for it would grieve me if they were really ungrateful for a benefit that made the pressure of the time lie but lightly on them.

The alarm of the Irish rebellion in this year was likewise another source of affliction to us, for many of the gentry coming over in great straights, especially ladies and their children, and some of them, in the hurry of their flight having but little ready money, were very ill off.[408] Some four or five families came to the Cross Keys in this situation, and the conduct of Mr Cayenne to them was most exemplary. He remembered his own haste with his family from Virginia, when the Americans rebelled; and immediately on hearing of these Irish refugees, he waited on them with his wife and daughter, supplied them with money, invited them to his house, made ploys to keep up their spirits, while the other gentry stood back till they knew something of the strangers.

Among these destitute ladies was a Mrs Desmond and her two daughters, a woman of a most august presence, being indeed more like one ordained to reign over a kingdom, than for household purposes. The Miss Desmonds were only entering their teens, but they also had no ordinary stamp upon them. What made this party the more particular, was on account of Mr Desmond, who was supposed to be a united man with the rebels, and it was known his son was deep in their plots; yet although this was all told to Mr Cayenne, by some of the other Irish ladies who were of the loyal connexion, it made no difference with him, but, on the contrary, he acted as if he thought the Desmonds the most of all the refugees entitled to his hospitable civilities. This was a wonderment to our strait-laced narrow lairds, as there was not a man of such strict government principles in the whole country-side as Mr Cayenne: but he said he carried his political principles only to the camp and the council. "To the hospital and the prison," said he, "I take those of a man" — which was almost a Christian doctrine, and from that declaration Mr Cayenne and me began again to draw a little more cordially together; although he had

407 Joseph in Egypt (Genesis 41) predicts seven years of plenty followed by seven years of famine, allowing Pharaoh to stockpile during the former against the latter.

408 Prompted by the terrorization of the countryside by the troops of a paranoid government following a French invasion attempt, the United Irishmen, a republican group affiliated to the Paris regime, rose in rebellion against British rule in 1798. In Ulster the movement was non-sectarian, with Presbyterians prominent in its leadership; in Wexford, the other centre of rebellion, it took on a sectarian, anti-protestant character. French military forces arrived too late to help, and the rebellion was crushed, with brutal reprisals. 30,000 people died in the 3½ months the rebellion lasted; as one historian of the French Revolution points out, 'a similar number to the Terror in France, but over a shorter period, and from a population one-sixth the size' (William Doyle, *Oxford History of the French Revolution* p.343). The (Anglican) Anglo-Irish landowning class who ruled Ireland were deeply shaken, and most of the refugees Balwhidder mentions would have belonged to this group.

still a very imperfect sense of religion, which I attributed to his being born in America, where even as yet, I am told, they have but a scanty sprinkling of grace.

But before concluding this year, I should tell the upshot of the visitation of the Irish, although it did not take place until some time after the peace with France.[409]

In the putting down of the rebels Mr Desmond and his son made their escape to Paris, where they staid till the Treaty was signed, by which, for several years after the return to Ireland of the grand lady and her daughters, as Mrs Desmond was called by our commonality, we heard nothing of them. The other refugees repaid Mr Cayenne his money with thankfulness, and on their restoration to their homes, could not sufficiently express their sense of his kindness. But the silence and seeming ingratitude of the Desmonds vexed him; and he could not abide to hear the Irish rebellion mentioned without flying into a passion against the rebels, which every body knew was owing to the ill return he had received from that family. However, one afternoon, just about half an hour before his wonted dinner hour, a grand equipage, with four horses and outriders, stopped at his door, and who was in it but Mrs Desmond and an elderly man, and a young gentleman with an aspect like a lord. It was her husband and son. They had come from Ireland in all their state on purpose to repay with interest the money Mr Cayenne had counted so long lost, and to express in person the perpetual obligation which he had conferred upon the Desmond family, in all time coming. The lady then told him, that she had been so straightened in helping the poor ladies that it was not in her power to make repayment till Desmond, as she called her husband, came home; and not choosing to assign the true reason, lest it might cause trouble, she rather submitted to be suspected of ingratitude than do an improper thing.

Mr Cayenne was transported with this unexpected return, and a friendship grew up between the families which was afterwards cemented into relationship by the marriage of the young Desmond with Miss Caroline Cayenne: Some in the parish objected to this match, Mrs Desmond being a papist; but as Miss Caroline had received an Episcopalian education, I thought it of no consequence, and married them after their family chaplain from Ireland, as a young couple, both from beauty and fortune, well matched, and deserving of all conjugal felicity.

CHAPTER XL.—YEAR 1799.

My Daughter's marriage—Her large portion—Mrs Malcolm's death.

THERE are but two things to make me remember this year; the first was the marriage of my daughter Janet with the Reverend Dr Kittleword of Swappington, a match in every way commendable, and on the advice of the third Mrs Balwhidder, I settled a thousand pounds down, and promised five hundred more at my own death, if I died before my spouse, and a thousand at her death, if she survived me; which was the greatest portion ever minister's daughter had in our country side. In this year, likewise, I advanced fifteen hundred pounds for my son in a concern in Glasgow, — all was the gathering of that indefatigable engine of industry the second Mrs Balwhidder, whose talents her successor said were a wonder, when she considered the circumstances in which I had been left at her death, and made out of a narrow stipend.

The other memorable was the death of Mrs Malcolm. If ever there was a saint on this earth she was surely one. She had been for some time bedfast, having all her days

---

409   I.e. after the Treaty of Amiens in March 1802.

from the date of her widowhood been a tender woman;[410] but no change made any alteration on the Christian contentment of her mind. She bore adversity with an honest pride, she toiled in the day of penury and affliction with thankfulness for her earnings, although ever so little. She bent her head to the Lord in resignation when her first-born fell in battle; nor was she puffed up with vanity when her daughters were married, as it was said, so far above their degree, though they shewed it was but into their proper sphere by their demeanour after. She lived to see her second son, the Captain, rise into affluence, married, and with a thriving young family; and she had the very great satisfaction, on the last day she was able to go to church, to see her youngest son, the Clergyman, standing in my pulpit, a doctor of divinity, and the placed minister of a richer parish than mine. Well indeed might she have said on that day, "Lord, let thy servant depart in peace, for mine eyes have seen thy salvation."

For some time it had been manifest to all who saw her that her latter end was drawing nigh; and therefore, as I had kept up a correspondence with her daughters, Mrs Macadam and Mrs Howard, I wrote them a particular account of her case, which brought them to the clachan. They both came in their own carriages, for Col. Macadam was now a general, and had succeeded to a great property by an English uncle, his mother's brother; and Capt. Howard, by the death of his father, was also a man, as it was said, with a lord's living. Robert Malcolm, her son the captain, was in the West Indies at the time, but his wife came on the first summons, as did William the minister.

They all arrived about four o'clock in the afternoon, and at seven a message came for me and Mrs Balwhidder to go over to them, which we did, and found the strangers seated by the heavenly patient's bedside. On my entering she turned her eyes towards me and said, "Bear witness, sir, that I die thankful for an extraordinary portion of temporal mercies. The heart of my youth was withered like the leaf that is seared with the lightning, but in my children I have received a great indemnification for the sorrows of that trial." She then requested me to pray, saying, "No, let it be a thanksgiving. My term is out, and I have nothing more to hope or fear from the good or evil of this world. But I have had much to make me grateful; therefore, sir, return thanks for the time I have been spared, for the goodness granted so long unto me, and the gentle hand with which I feel the way from this world smoothed for my passing."

There was something so sweet and consolatory in the way she said this, that although it moved all present to tears, they were tears without the wonted bitterness of grief. Accordingly, I knelt down and did as she had required, and there was a great stillness while I prayed; at the conclusion we looked to the bed, but the spirit had in the meantime departed, and there was nothing remaining but the clay tenement.

It was expected by the parish, considering the vast affluence of the daughters, that there would have been a grand funeral, and Mrs Howard thought it was necessary; but her sister, who had from her youth upward a superior discernment of propriety, said, "No, as my mother has lived so shall be her end." Accordingly, every body of any respect in the clachan was invited to the funeral; but none of the gentry, saving only such as had been numbered among the acquaintance of the deceased. But Mr Cayenne came unbidden, saying to me, that although he did not know Mrs Malcolm personally, he had often heard she was an amiable woman, and therefore he thought it a proper compliment to her family, who were out of the parish, to shew in what respect she was held among us; for he was a man that would take his own way, and do what he thought was right, heedless alike of blame or approbation.

If, however, the funeral was plain, though respectable, the ladies distributed a

---

410   Tender (Sc.): in delicate health.

liberal sum among the poor families; but before they went away, a silent token of their mother's virtue came to light, which was at once a source of sorrow and pleasure. Mrs Malcolm was first well provided by the Macadams, afterwards the Howards settled on her an equal annuity, by which she spent her latter days in great comfort. Many a year before, she had repaid Provost Maitland the money he sent her in the day of her utmost distress, and at this period he was long dead, having died of a broken heart at the time of his failure. From that time his widow and her daughters had been in very straightened circumstances, but unknown to all but herself, and Him from whom nothing is hid, Mrs Malcolm from time to time had sent them, in a blank letter, an occasional note to the young ladies to buy a gown. After her death, a bank bill for a sum of money, her own savings, was found in her scrutoire, with a note of her own writing pinned to the same, stating, that the amount being more than she had needed for herself, belonged of right to those who had so generously provided for her, but as they were not in want of such a trifle, it would be a token of respect to her memory, if they would give the bill to Mrs Maitland and her daughters, which was done with a most glad alacrity; and, in the doing of it, the private kindness was brought to light.

Thus ended the history of Mrs Malcolm, as connected with our Parish Annals. Her house was sold, and is the same now inhabited by the mill-wright, Mr Periffery, and a neat house it still is, for the possessor is an Englishman, and the English have an uncommon taste for snod houses and trim gardens; but, at the time it was built, there was not a better in the town, though it's now but of the second class. Yearly we hear both from Mrs Macadam and her sister, with a five-pound note from each to the poor of the parish, as a token of their remembrance; but they are far off, and were any thing ailing me, I suppose the gift will not be continued. As for Captain Malcolm, he has proved, in many ways, a friend to such of our young men as have gone to sea. He has now left it off himself, and settled at London, where he latterly sailed from, and I understand is in a great way as a ship-owner. These things I have thought it fitting to record, and will now resume my historical narration.

CHAPTER XLI.—YEAR 1800.

Return of an inclination towards political tranquillity—Death of the Schoolmistress.

THE same quietude and regularity that marked the progress of the last year, continued throughout the whole of this. We sowed and reaped in tranquillity, though the sough of distant war came heavily from a distance. The cotton-mill did well for the company, and there was a sobriety in the minds of the spinners and weavers, which shewed that the crisis of their political distemperature was over;—there was something more of the old prudence in men's reflections; and it was plain to me that the elements of reconciliation were coming together throughout the world. The conflagration of the French Revolution was indeed not extinguished, but it was evidently burning out; and their old reverence for the Grand Monarque was beginning to revive among them, though they only called him a Consul.[411] Upon the king's fast I preached on this subject; and when the peace was concluded, I got great credit for my foresight, but there was no merit in't. I had only lived longer than the most of those around me, and had been all my days a close observer of the signs of the times; so that what was lightly called prophecy and prediction, were but a probability that experience had taught me to discern.

In the affairs of the parish, the most remarkable generality (for we had no particular

411   I.e. Napoleon: see note 359 (chapter XXXI).

catastrophe) was a great death of old people in the spring. Among others, Miss Sabrina, the schoolmistress, paid the debt of nature, but we could now better spare her than we did her predecessor; for at Cayenneville there was a broken manufacturer's wife, an excellent teacher, and a genteel and modernized woman, who took the better order of children; and Miss Sabrina having been long frail (for she was never stout), a decent and discreet carlin, Mrs McCaffie, the widow of a custom-house officer, that was a native of the parish, set up another for plainer work. Her opposition, Miss Sabrina did not mind, but she was sorely displeased at the interloping of Mrs Pirn at Cayenneville; and some said it helped to kill her — of that, however, I am not so certain, for Dr Tanzey had told me in the winter, that he thought the sharp winds in March would blow out her candle, as it was burnt to the snuff; accordingly, she took her departure from this life, on the twenty-fifth day of that month, after there had, for some days prior, been a most cold and piercing east wind.

Miss Sabrina, who was always an oddity and aping grandeur, it was found, had made a will, leaving her gatherings to her favourites, with all regular formality. To one she bequeathed a gown, to another this, and a third that, and to me, a pair of black silk stockings. I was amazed when I heard this; but judge what I felt, when a pair of old marrowless stockings, darned in the heel, and not whole enough in the legs to make a pair of mittens to Mrs Balwhidder, were delivered to me by her executor, Mr Caption, the lawyer. Saving, however, this kind of flummery, Miss Sabrina was a harmless creature, and could quote poetry in discourse, more glibly than texts of Scripture — her father having spared no pains on her mind; as for her body, it could not be mended; but that was not her fault.

After her death, the Session held a consultation, and we agreed to give the same salary that Miss Sabrina enjoyed to Mrs McCaffie; which angered Mr Cayenne, who thought it should have been given to the head mistress; and it made him give Mrs Pirn, out of his own pocket, double the sum. But we considered that the parish funds were for the poor of the parish, and therefore, it was our duty to provide for the instruction of the poor children. Saving, therefore, those few notations, I have nothing further to say concerning the topics and progress of this Ann. Dom.

CHAPTER XLII.—YEAR 1801.

An Account of Colin Mavis, who becomes a poet.

IT is often to me very curious food for meditation, that as the parish increased in population, there should have been less cause for matter to record. Things that in former days would have occasioned great discourse and cogitation, are forgotten, with the day in which they happen; and there is no longer that searching into personalities which was so much in vogue during the first epoch of my ministry, which I reckon the period before the American war; nor has there been any such germinal changes among us, as these which took place in the second epoch, counting backward from the building of the cotton-mill that gave rise to the town of Cayenneville. But still we were not, even at this era, of which this Ann. Dom. is the beginning, without occasional personality, or an event that deserved to be called a germinal.[412]

412 'Germinal', as an adjective, means in the earliest stage of development, the seed of something. Early nineteenth-century English and Scots sometimes use an adjective alone where we would add a noun (see 'a vast' meaning a vast *amount* in chapter XIX; 'divers' meaning diverse *things* in chapter XXXI); but germinal as a noun only exists elsewhere, ironically

Some years before, I had noted among the callans at Mr Loremore's school, a long soople laddie, who, like all bairns that grow fast and tall, had but little smeddum. He could not be called a dolt, for he was observant and thoughtful, and given to asking sagacious questions; but there was a sleepiness about him, especially in the kirk, and he gave, as the master said, but little application to his lessons, so that folk thought he would turn out a sort of gaunt-at-the-door,[413] more mindful of meat than work. He was, however, a good-natured lad; and, when I was taking my solitary walks of meditation, I sometimes fell in with him, sitting alone on the brae by the water-side, and sometimes lying on the grass, with his hands under his head, on the sunny green knolls where Mr Cylindar, the English engineer belonging to the cotton-work, has built the bonny house that he calls Dairy-hill Cottage. This was when Colin Mavis was a laddie at the school,[414] and when I spoke to him, I was surprised at the discretion of his answers, so that gradually I began to think and say, that there was more about Colin than the neighbours knew. Nothing, however, for many a day, came out to his advantage; so that his mother, who was by this time a widow woman, did not well know what to do with him, and folk pitied her heavy handful of such a droud.[415]

By and by, however, it happened that one of the young clerks at the cotton-mill shattered his right-hand thumb by a gun bursting; and, being no longer able to write, was sent into the army to be an ensign, which caused a vacancy in the office; and, through the help of Mr Cayenne, I got Colin Mavis into the place, where, to the surprise of every body, he proved a wonderful eydent and active lad, and, from less to more, has come at the head of all the clerks, and deep in the confidentials of his employers. But although this was a great satisfaction to me, and to the widow woman his mother, it somehow was not so much so to the rest of the parish, who seemed, as it were, angry that poor Colin had not proved himself such a dolt as they had expected and foretold.

Among other ways that Colin had of spending his leisure, was that of playing music on an instrument, in which it was said he made a wonderful proficiency; but being long and thin, and of a delicate habit of body, he was obligated to refrain from this recreation; so he betook himself to books, and from reading, he began to try writing; but, as this was done in a corner, nobody jealoused what he was about, till one evening in this year, he came to the Manse, and asked a word in private with me. I thought that perhaps he had fallen in with a lass, and was come to consult me anent matrimony; but when we were by ourselves, in my study, he took out of his pocket a number of the Scots Magazine, and said, "Sir, you have been long pleased to notice me more than any other body, and when I got this, I could not refrain from bringing it, to let you see't. Ye maun ken, sir, that I have been long in secret given to trying my hand at rhyme, and, wishing to ascertain what others thought of my power in that way, I sent, by the post, twa three verses to the Scots Magazine, and they have not only inserted them, but placed them in the body of the book, in such a way, that I kenna what to think."[416] So I looked at the Magazine, and read his verses, which were certainly very well made verses, for one who had no regular education. But I said to him, as the Greenock magistrates said to John Wilson, the author of Clyde, when they stipulated with him to give up the art,[417]

---

enough, as the name of a month in the French Revolutionary calendar (corresponding to 21 March to 19 April).

413   Gaunt-at-the-door (Sc.): loafer, a work-shy person (from gant: yawn).
414   Mavis is the Scots name for the song-thrush.
415   Droud (Sc.): a useless, slovenly person.
416   Kenna (Sc.): don't know.
417   John Wilson (1720–89), author of *Clyde: A Descriptive Poem* (1764). A teacher by profession, in 1767 he was offered the job of Master of Greenock Grammar School by the local

that poem-making was a profane and unprofitable trade, and he would do well to turn his talent to something of more solidity, which he promised to do; but he has since put out a book, whereby he has angered all those that had foretold he would be a donae-gude. Thus has our parish walked sidy for sidy with all the national improvements,[418] having an author of its own, and getting a literary character in the ancient and famous republic of letters.

CHAPTER XLIII.—YEAR 1802.

The political condition of the world felt in the private concerns of individuals—Mr Cayenne comes to ask my advice, and acts according to it.

"EXPERIENCE teaches fools," was the first moral apothegm that I wrote in small text, when learning to write at the school, and I have ever since thought it was a very sensible reflection. For assuredly, as year after year has flown away on the swift wings of time, I have found my experience mellowing, and my discernment improving; by which I have, in the afternoon of life, been enabled to foresee what kings and nations would do, by the symptoms manifested within the bounds of the society around me. Therefore, at the beginning of the spring in this Ann. Dom., I had misgivings at the heart, a fluttering in my thoughts, and altogether a strange uneasiness as to the stability of the peace and harmony that was supposed to be founded upon a stedfast foundation between us and the French people. What my fears principally took the rise from, was a sort of compliancy, on the part of those in power and authority, to cultivate the old relations and parts between them and the commonalty.[419] It did not appear to me that this proceeded from any known or decided event, for I read the papers at this period daily, but from some general dread and fear, that was begotten, like a vapour, out of the fermentation of all sorts of opinions; most people of any sagacity, thinking that the state of things in France being so much of an antic, poetical, and play-actor like guise, that it would never obtain that respect, far less that reverence from the world, which is necessary to the maintenance of all beneficial government. The consequence of this was a great distrust between man and man, and an aching restlessness among those who had their bread to bake in the world. Persons possessing the power to provide for their kindred, forcing them, as it were, down the throats of those who were dependent on them in business, a bitter morsel.

But the pith of these remarks chiefly applies to the manufacturing concerns of the new town of Cayenneville, for in the clachan we lived in the lea of the dike, and were more taken up with our own natural rural affairs, and the markets for victual, than the craft of merchandize. The only man interested in business, who walked in a steady

---

magistrates and minister on condition that he gave up 'the profane and unprofitable art of poem-making'; he agreed, and burnt his manuscripts (*DNB*). The incident was still notorious in Galt's day as the last occasion when presbyterian hostility to the creative imagination was able to wield such power in Scotland.

418 Donae-gude (Sc.): ne'er-do-well; sidy for sidy: side by side, in step.

419 Balwhidder's point here is a little difficult to grasp: 'compliancy' is not a word in either *OED* or *SND*. From what follows, 'the old relations and parts' between the ruling elite and the commonality appear to include the patronage system, which threatens to force Mr Cayenne to give up part of his share in the business to a relation of the mill's directors; and this implied criticism is rather at odds with Balwhidder's previous success in *using* the patronage system to help various parishioners, through his relationship with Lord Eglesham.

manner at his old pace, though he sometimes was seen, being of a spunkie temper, grinding the teeth of vexation, was Mr Cayenne himself.

One day, however, he came to me at the Manse. "Doctor," says he, for so he always called me, "I want your advice. I never choose to trouble others with my private affairs, but there are times when the word of an honest man may do good. I need not tell you, that when I declared myself a Royalist in America, it was at a considerable sacrifice. I have, however, nothing to complain of against government on that score, but I think it damn'd hard that those personal connections, whose interests I preserved, to the detriment of my own, should, in my old age, make such an ungrateful return. By the steps I took prior to quitting America, I saved the property of a great mercantile concern in London. In return for that, they took a share with me, and for me, in the cotton-mill; and being here on the spot, as manager, I have both made and saved them money. I have, no doubt, bettered my own fortune in the meantime. Would you believe it, doctor, they have written a letter to me, saying, that they wish to provide for a relation, and requiring me to give up to him a portion of my share in the concern—a pretty sort of providing this, at another man's expence. But I'll be damn'd if I do any such thing. If they want to provide for their friend, let them do so from themselves, and not at my cost—What is your opinion?"

This appeared to me a very weighty concern, and not being versed in mercantile dealing, I did not well know what to say; but I reflected for some time, and then I replied, "As far, Mr Cayenne, as my observation has gone in this world, I think that the giffs and the gaffs nearly balance one another;[420] and when they do not, there is a moral defect on the failing side. If a man long gives his labour to his employer, and is paid for that labour, it might be said that both are equal, but I say no. For it's in human nature to be prompt to change; and the employer, having always more in his power than his servant or agent, it seems to me a clear case, that in the course of a number of years, the master of the old servant is the obligated of the two; and, therefore, I say, in the first place, in your case there is no tie or claim, by which you may, in a moral sense, be called upon to submit to the dictates of your London correspondents; but there is a reason, in the nature of the thing and case, by which you may ask a favour from them— So, the advice I would give you would be this, write an answer to their letter, and tell them, that you have no objection to the taking in of a new partner, but you think it would be proper to revise all the copartnery, especially as you have, considering the manner in which you have advanced the business, been of opinion, that your share should have been considerably enlarged."

I thought Mr Cayenne would have louped out of his skin with mirth at this notion, and being a prompt man, he sat down at my scrutoire, and answered the letter which gave him so much uneasiness. No notice was taken of it for some time; but, in the course of a month, he was informed, that it was not considered expedient at that time to make any change in the Company. I thought the old man was gone by himself when he got this letter. He came over instantly in his chariot, from the cotton-mill office, to the Manse, and swore an oath, by some dreadful name, that I was a Solomon.[421] However, I only mention this to shew how experience had instructed me, and as a sample of that sinister provisioning of friends that was going on in the world at this time—all owing, as I do verily believe, to the uncertain state of governments and national affairs.

Besides these generalities, I observed another thing working to effect—mankind read more, and the spirit of reflection and reasoning was more awake than at any

---

420 Giffs and gaffs (Sc.): gains and losses (from giff-gaff, give-and-take).
421 Solomon: the proverbially wise king of I Kings; see e.g. 4.29–30.

time within my remembrance. Not only was there a handsome bookseller's shop in Cayenneville, with a London newspaper daily, but Magazines, and Reviews, and other new publications.[422]

Till this year, when a chaise was wanted, we had to send to Irville; but Mr Toddy of the Cross-keys being in at Glasgow, he bought an excellent one at the second hand, being a portion of the effects of a broken merchant, by which, from that period, we had one of our own; and it proved a great convenience, for I, who never but twice in my life before hired that kind of commodity, had it thrice during the summer, for a bit jaunt with Mrs Balwhidder, to divers places and curiosities in the country, that I had not seen before, by which our ideas were greatly enlarged; indeed, I have always had a partiality for travelling, as one of the best means of opening the faculty of the mind, and giving clear and correct notions of men and things.

CHAPTER XLIV.—YEAR 1803.

Fear of an invasion—Raising of volunteers in the parish—The young ladies embroider a stand of colours for the regiment.

DURING the tempestuous times that ensued, from the death of the King of France, by the hands of the executioner, in 1793, there had been a political schism among my people that often made me very uneasy. The folk belonging to the cotton-mill, and the muslin-weavers in Cayenneville, were afflicted with the itch of jacobinism, but those of the village were staunch and true to King and Country; and some of the heritors were desirous to make volunteers of the young men of them, in case of any thing like the French anarchy and confusion rising on the side of the manufacturers. I, however, set myself, at that time, against this, for I foresaw that the French business was but a fever which would soon pass off, but no man could tell the consequence of putting arms in the hands of neighbour against neighbour, though it was but in the way of policy.

But when Bonaparte gathered his host fornent the English coast, and the government at London were in terror of their lives for an invasion,[423] all in the country saw that there was danger, and I was not backward in sounding the trumpet to battle. For a time, however, there was a diffidence among us somewhere. The gentry had a distrust of the manufacturers, and the farming lads were wud with impatience, that those who should be their leaders would not come forth. I, knowing this, prepared a sermon suitable to the occasion, giving out from the pulpit myself, the Sabbath before preaching it, that it was my intent, on the next Lord's day, to deliver a religious and political exhortation on the present posture of public affairs. This drew a vast congregation of all ranks.

I trow that the stoor had no peace in the stuffing of the pulpit in that day,[424] and the effect was very great and speedy, for, next morning the weavers and cotton-mill folk held a meeting, and they, being skilled in the ways of committees and associating together, had certain resolutions prepared, by which a select few was appointed to take an enrolment of all willing in the parish to serve as volunteers in defence of their King and country, and to concert with certain gentlemen named therein, about the

---

422 The *Edinburgh Review* was founded in 1802.
423 Between the resumption of war in 1803 and the summer of 1805 Napoleon massed an army along the channel and North Sea coasts of mainland Europe in preparation for an invasion of southern England. But the seas remained in the control of the Royal Navy and the plan was abandoned.
424 Stoor (Sc.): dust.

formation of a corps, of which, it was an understood thing, the said gentlemen were to be the officers. The whole of this business was managed with the height of discretion, and the weavers, and spinners, and farming lads, vied with one another who should be first on the list. But that which the most surprised me, was the wonderful sagacity of the committee in naming the gentlemen that should be the officers. I could not have made a better choice myself, for they were the best built, the best bred, and the best natured, in the parish. In short, when I saw the bravery that was in my people, and the spirit of wisdom by which it was directed, I said in my heart, the Lord of Hosts is with us,[425] and the adversary shall not prevail.

The number of valiant men which at that time placed themselves around the banners of their country was so great, that the government would not accept of all who offered; so, like as in other parishes, we were obligated to make a selection, which was likewise done in a most judicious manner, all men above a certain age being reserved for the defence of the parish, in the day when the young might be called to England, to fight the enemy.

When the corps was formed, and the officers named, they made me their chaplain, and Dr Marigold their doctor. He was a little man with a big belly, and was as crouse as a bantum cock; but it was not thought he could do so well in field exercises, on which account he was made the doctor, although he had no repute in that capacity, in comparison with Dr Tanzey, who was not however liked, being a stiff-mannered man, with a sharp temper.

All things having come to a proper head, the young ladies of the parish resolved to present the corps with a stand of colours, which they embroidered themselves, and a day was fixed for the presentation of the same. Never was such a day seen in Dalmailing. The sun shone brightly on that scene of bravery and grandeur, and far and near the country folk came flocking in, and we had the regimental band of music hired from the soldiers that were in Ayr barracks. The very first sound o't made the hair on my old grey head to prickle up, and my blood to rise and glow, as if youth was coming again in to my veins.

Sir Hugh Montgomery was the commandant, and he came in all the glory of war, on his best horse, and marched at the head of the men, to the green-head. The doctor and me were the rear-guard, not being able, on account of my age, and his fatness, to walk so fast as the quick-step of the corps. On the field, we took our place in front, near Sir Hugh, and the ladies with the colours; and, after some salutations according to the fashion of the army, Sir Hugh made a speech to the men, and then Miss Maria Montgomery came forward, with her sister Miss Eliza, and the other ladies, and the banners were unfurled, all glittering with gold, and the King's arms in needle-work. Miss Maria then made a speech, which she had got by heart, but she was so agitated, that it was said she forgot the best part of it; however, it was very well considering. When this was done, I then stepped forward, and laying my hat on the ground, every man and boy taking off theirs, I said a prayer, which I had conned most carefully, and which I thought the most suitable I could devise, in unison with Christian principles, which are averse to the shedding of blood; and I particularly dwelt upon some of the specialities of our situation.

When I had concluded, the volunteers gave three great shouts, and the multitude answered them to the same tune, and all the instruments of music sounded, making such a bruit,[426] as could not be surpassed for grandeur—a long, and very circumstantial

---

425 Psalms 41.7.
426 Bruit: 'din, clamour' (*OED*). This is Galt's correction in the second edition; the first has

account of all which may be read in the newspapers of that time.

The volunteers, at the word of command, then shewed us the way they were to fight with the French, in the doing of which a sad disaster happened; for when they were charging bayonets, they came towards us like a flood, and all the spectators ran, and I ran, and the doctor ran, but being laden with his belly, he could not run fast enough, so he lay down, and being just before me at the time, I tumbled over him, and such a shout of laughter shook the field, as was never heard.

When the fatigues of the day were at an end, we marched to the cotton-mill, where, in one of the warehouses, a vast table was spread, and a dinner, prepared at Mr Cayenne's own expence, was sent in from the Cross-keys, and the whole corps, with many of the gentry of the neighbourhood, dined with great jollity, the band of music playing beautiful airs all the time. At night, there was a universal dance, gentle and semple mingled together.[427] All which made it plain to me, that the Lord, by this union of spirit,[428] had decreed our national preservation; but I kept this in my own breast, lest it might have the effect to relax the vigilance of the kingdom. And I should note, that Colin Mavis, the poetical lad, of whom I have spoken in another part, made a song for this occasion, that was very mightily thought of, having in it a nerve of valiant genius, that kindled the very souls of those that heard it.

CHAPTER XLV.—YEAR 1804.

The Session agrees that church censures shall be commuted with fines—Our parish has an opportunity of seeing a turtle, which is sent to Mr Cayenne—Some fears of popery—Also about a preacher of universal redemption—Report of a French ship appearing in the west, which sets the volunteers astir.

IN conformity with the altered fashions of the age, in this year the Session came to an understanding with me, that we should not inflict the common church censures for such as made themselves liable thereto;[429] but we did not formally promulge our resolution as to this, wishing as long as possible to keep the deterring rod over the heads of the young and thoughtless. Our motive, on the one hand, was the disregard of the manufacturers in Cayenneville, who were, without the breach of truth, an irreligious people, and, on the other, a desire to preserve the ancient and wholesome admonitory and censorian jurisdiction of the minister and elders. We therefore laid it down as a rule to ourselves, that, in the case of transgressions on the part of the inhabitants of the new district of Cayenneville, we should subject them rigorously to a fine; but that for the farming lads, we would put it to their option to pay the fine, or stand in the kirk.

We conformed also in another matter to the times, by consenting to baptize occasionally in private houses. Hitherto it had been a strict rule with me only to baptize from the pulpit. Other places, however, had long been in the practice of this relaxation of ancient discipline.

But all this, on my part, was not done without compunction of spirit; for I was of opinion, that the principle of Presbyterian integrity should have been maintained to the uttermost. Seeing, however, the elders set on an alteration, I distrusted my own judgment, and yielded myself to the considerations that weighed with them; for they

---

'show' here.
427 Semple (Sc.): commoners, those without birth or rank.
428 In the second edition of 1822, Galt changes 'union' to 'unison'.
429 Including, most notably, the stool of repentance for fornication: see note 103 (chapter V).

were true men, and of a godly honesty, and took the part of the poor in all contentions with the heritors, often to the hazard and damage of their own temporal welfare.

I have now to note a curious thing, not on account of its importance, but to shew to what lengths a correspondence had been opened in the parish with the farthest parts of the earth. Mr Cayenne got a turtle-fish sent to him from a Glasgow merchant, and it was living when it came to Wheatrig-house, and was one of the most remarkable beasts that had ever been seen in our country side. It weighed as much as a well-fed calf, and had three kinds of meat in its body, fish, flesh, and fowl, and it had four water-wings, for they could not be properly said to be fins; but what was little short of a miracle about the creature, happened after the head was cutted off, when, if a finger was offered to it, it would open its mouth and snap at it, and all this after the carcase was divided for dressing.

Mr Cayenne made a feast on the occasion to many of the neighbouring gentry, to the which I was invited, and we drank lime-punch as we ate the turtle, which, as I understand, is the fashion in practice among the Glasgow West Indy merchants, who are famed as great hands with turtles and lime-punch. But it is a sort of food that I should not like to fare long upon. I was not right the next day; and I have heard it said, that, when eaten too often, it has a tendency to harden the heart, and make it crave for greater luxuries.

But the story of the turtle is nothing to that of the Mass, which, with all its mummeries and abominations, was brought into Cayenneville by an Irish priest of the name of Father O'Grady, who was confessor to some of the poor deluded Irish labourers about the new houses and the cotton-mill. How he had the impudence to set up that memento of Satan, the crucifix, within my parish and jurisdiction, was what I never could get to the bottom of; but the soul was shaken within me, when, on the Monday after, one of the elders came to the Manse, and told me, that the old dragon of Popery, with its seven heads and ten horns,[430] had been triumphing in Cayenneville on the foregoing Lord's day! I lost no time in convening the Session to see what was to be done; much, however, to my surprise, the elders recommended no step to be taken, but only a zealous endeavour to greater christian excellence on our part, by which we should put the beast and his worshippers to shame and flight. I am free to confess, that, at the time, I did not think this the wisest counsel which they might have given; for, in the heat of my alarm, I was for attacking the enemy in his camp. But they prudently observed, that the days of religious persecution were past, and it was a comfort to see mankind cherishing any sense of religion at all, after the vehement infidelity that had been sent abroad by the French Republicans; and to this opinion, now that I have had years to sift its wisdom, I own myself a convert and proselyte.

Fortunately, however, for my peace of mind, there proved to be but five Roman Catholics in Cayenneville; and Father O'Grady, not being able to make a living there, packed up his Virgin Marys, saints, and painted Agnuses in a portmanteau,[431] and went off in the Ayr Fly one morning for Glasgow, where I hear he has since met with all the encouragement that might be expected from the ignorant and idolatrous inhabitants of that great city.

Scarcely were we well rid of Father O'Grady, when another interloper entered the parish. He was more dangerous, in the opinion of the Session, than even the Pope of

---

430 'A great red dragon, with seven heads and ten horns' first makes his entrance in Revelation 12.3, and reappears at intervals in the verses that follow: interpreted as a figure for the Catholic Church by Protestant commentators.

431 The Agnus Dei ('Lamb of God'), an image of a lamb bearing a cross or a flag, is part of Catholic iconography.

Rome himself; for he came to teach the flagrant heresy of Universal Redemption, a most consolatory doctrine to the sinner that is loth to repent, and who loves to troll his iniquity like a sweet morsel under his tongue.[432] Mr Martin Siftwell, who was the last ta'en on elder, and who had received a liberal and judicious education, and was, moreover, naturally possessed of a quick penetration, observed, in speaking of this new doctrine, that the grossest papist sinner might have some qualms of fear after he had bought the Pope's pardon, and might thereby be led to a reformation of life; but that the doctrine of universal redemption was a bribe to commit sin, the wickedest mortal, according to it, being only liable to a few thousand years, more or less, of suffering, which, compared with eternity, was but a momentary pang, like having a tooth drawn for the toothache. Mr Siftwell is a shrewd and clear-seeing man in points of theology, and I would trust a great deal to what he says, as I have not, at my advanced age, such a mind for the kittle crudities of polemical investigation that I had in my younger years,[433] especially when I was a student in the Divinity-Hall of Glasgow.

It will be seen from all I have herein recorded, that, in the course of this year, there was a general resuscitation of religious sentiments; for what happened in my parish was but a type and index to the rest of the world. We had, however, one memorable that must stand by itself; for although neither death nor bloodshed happened, yet was it cause of the fear of both.

A rumour reached us from the Clyde, that a French man of war had appeared in a Highland loch, and that all the Greenock volunteers had embarked in merchant-vessels to bring her in for a prize. Our volunteers were just jumping and yowling, like chained dogs, to be at her too; but the colonel, Sir Hugh, would do nothing without orders from his superiors. Mr Cayenne, though an aged man, above seventy, was as bold as a lion, and came forth in the old garb of an American huntsman, like, as I was told, a Robin Hood in the play is; and it was just a sport to see him, feckless man, trying to march so crously with his lean shaking shanks.[434] But the whole affair proved a false alarm, and our men, when they heard it, were as well pleased that they had been constrained to sleep in their warm beds at home, instead of lying on coils of cables, like the gallant Greenock sharpshooters.

CHAPTER XLVI.—YEAR 1805.

Retrenchment of the extravagant expences usual at burials—I use an expedient for putting even the second service out of fashion.

For some time I had meditated a reformation in the parish, and this year I carried the same into effect. I had often noticed with concern, that, out of a mistaken notion of paying respect to the dead, my people were wont to go to great lengths at their burials, and dealt round short-bread and sugar biscuit, with wine and other confections, as if

---

432 Troll: roll. 'Universal Redemption' is the doctrine that Christ died to save all people without exception: it is therefore always within the individual sinner's power to accept this salvation or reject it. Calvinist theology (such as that adopted by the Kirk) is different from protestant theology more generally precisely in denying this: on the Calvinist view, Christ died to save only those already chosen by God (the elect).

433 Crudity: here, having 'the quality of being indigestible' (*OED* 2).

434 I adopt 'shanks' from Kinsley's edition. Both first and second editions have 'hands' here, which makes no sense; it is just about imaginable that the printer might have misread a manuscript 'shanks' in this way.

there had been no ha'd in their hands;[435] which straightened many a poor family, making the dispensation of the Lord a heavier temporal calamity than it should naturally have been. Accordingly, on consulting with Mrs Balwhidder, who has a most judicious judgment, it was thought that my interference would go a great way to lighten the evil. I therefore advised with those whose friends were taken from them, not to make that amplitude of preparation which used to be the fashion, nor to continue handing about as long as the folk would take, but only at the very most to go no more than three times round with the service. Objections were made to this, as if it would be thought mean; but I put on a stern visage, and told them, that if they did more I would rise up and rebuke and forbid the extravagance. So three services became the uttermost modicum at all burials. This was doing so much, but it was not all that I wished to do.

I considered that the best reformations are those which proceed step by step, and stop at that point where the consent to what has been established becomes general; and so I governed myself, and therefore interfered no farther; but I was determined to set an example. Accordingly, at the very next draigie,[436] after I partook of one service, I made a bow to the servitors and they passed on, but all before me had partaken of the second service; some, however, of those after me did as I did, so I foresaw that in a quiet canny way I would bring in the fashion of being satisfied with one service. I therefore, from that time, always took my place as near as possible to the door, where the chief mourner sat, and made a point of nodding away the second service, which has now grown into a custom, to the great advantage of surviving relations.

But in this reforming business I was not altogether pleased with our poet; for he took a pawkie view of my endeavours, and indited a ballad on the subject, in the which he makes a clattering carlin describe what took place,[437] so as to turn a very solemn matter into a kind of derision. When he brought his verse and read it to me, I told him that I thought it was overly natural; for I could not find another term to designate the cause of the dissatisfaction that I had with it; but Mrs Balwhidder said that it might help my plan if it were made public, so upon her advice we got some of Mr Loremore's best writers to make copies of it for distribution, which was not without fruit and influence. But a sore thing happened at the very next burial. As soon as the nodding away of the second service began, I could see that the gravity of the whole meeting was discomposed, and some of the irreverent young chiels almost broke out into even-down laughter,[438] which vext me exceedingly. Mrs Balwhidder, however, comforted me by saying, that custom in time would make it familiar, and by and by the thing would pass as a matter of course, until one service would be all that folk would offer; and truly the thing is coming to that, for only two services are now handed round, and the second is regularly nodded by.

---

435 Ha'd (Sc.): 'Restraint, check, power of retention; used with the neg. "to denote prodigality"' (*SND* 'haud' II.7).
436 Draigie, usually dredgy (Sc.): funeral feast.
437 Clattering (Sc.): gossiping.
438 Chiels: fellows, (young) men; even-down, usually evendoon: absolute, downright (both Sc.).

CHAPTER XLVII.—YEAR 1806.

The death-bed behaviour of Mr Cayenne—A schism in the parish, and a subscription to build a meeting house.

MR CAYENNE of Wheatrig having for several years been in a declining way, partly brought on by the consuming fire of his furious passion, and partly by the decay of old age, sent for me on the evening of the first Sabbath of March in this year. I was surprised at the message, and went to the Wheatrig-house directly, where, by the lights in the windows as I gaed up through the policy to the door, I saw something extraordinary was going on. Sambo, the blackamoor servant, opened the door, and without speaking shook his head; for it was an affectionate creature, and as fond of his master as if he had been his own father. By this sign I guessed that the old gentleman was thought to be drawing near his latter end, so I walked softly after Sambo up the stair, and was shewn into the chamber where Mr Cayenne, since he had been confined to the house, usually sat. His wife had been dead some years before.

Mr Cayenne was sitting in his easy chair, with a white cotton night-cap on his head, and a pillow at his shoulders to keep him straight. But his head had fallen down on his breast, and he breathed like a panting baby. His legs were swelled, and his feet rested on a footstool. His face, which was wont to be the colour of a peony rose, was of a yellow hue, with a patch of red on each cheek like a wafer, and his nose was shirpet and sharp,[439] and of an unnatural purple. Death was evidently fighting with Nature for the possession of the body. "Heaven have mercy on his soul," said I to myself, as I sat me down beside him.

When I had been seated some time, the power was given him to raise his head as it were ajee,[440] and he looked at me with the tail of his eye, which I saw was glittering and glassy. "Doctor," for he always called me doctor, though I am not of that degree, "I am glad to see you," were his words, uttered with some difficulty.

"How do you find yourself, sir?" I replied in a sympathising manner.

"Damned bad," said he, as if I had been the cause of his suffering. I was daunted to the very heart to hear him in such an unregenerate state; but after a short pause I addressed myself to him again, saying, that "I hoped he would soon be more at ease, and he should bear in mind that the Lord chasteneth whom he loveth."[441]

"The devil take such love," was his awful answer, which was to me as a blow on the forehead with a mell.[442] However, I was resolved to do my duty to the miserable sinner, let him say what he would. Accordingly, I stooped towards him with my hands on my knees, and said in a compassionate voice, "It's very true, sir, that you are in great agony, but the goodness of God is without bound."

"Curse me if I think so, doctor," replied the dying uncircumcised Philistine. But he added at whiles, his breathlessness being grievous, and often broken by a sore hiccup, "I am however no saint, as you know, doctor; so I wish you to put in a word for me, doctor; for you know that in these times, doctor, it is the duty of every good subject to die a Christian."

This was a poor account of the state of his soul, but it was plain I could make no better o't, by entering into any religious discourse or controversy with him, he being then in the last gasp; so I knelt down and prayed for him with great sincerity, imploring

---

439   Shirpet (Sc.): thin, emaciated.
440   Ajee (Sc.): to one side.
441   Hebrews 12.6.
442   Mell (Sc.): mallet.

the Lord, as an awakening sense of grace to the dying man, that it would please him to lift up, though it were but for the season of a minute, the chastening hand which was laid so heavily upon his aged servant; at which Mr Cayenne, as if indeed the hand had been then lifted, cried out, "None of that stuff, doctor; you know that I cannot call myself his servant."

Was ever a minister in his prayer so broken in upon by a perishing sinner! However, I had the weight of a duty upon me, and made no reply, but continued, "Thou hearest, O Lord! how he confesses his unworthiness — Let not thy compassion, therefore, be withheld, but verify to him the words that I have spoken in faith, of the boundlessness of thy goodness, and the infinite multitude of thy tender mercies." I then calmly, but sadly, sat down, and presently, as if my prayer had been heard, relief was granted; for Mr Cayenne raised his head, and, giving me a queer look, said, "that last clause of your petition, doctor, was well put, and I think, too, it has been granted, for I am easier," — adding, "I have, no doubt, doctor, given much offence in the world, and oftenest when I meant to do good; but I have wilfully injured no man, and as God is my judge, and His goodness, you say, is so great, He may perhaps take my soul into His holy keeping." In saying which words, Mr Cayenne dropped his head upon his breast, his breathing ceased, and he was wafted away out of this world with as little trouble as a blameless child.

This event soon led to a change among us. In the settling of Mr Cayenne's affairs in the Cotton-mill Company, it was found that he had left such a power of money, that it was needful to the concern, in order that they might settle with the doers under his testament,[443] to take in other partners. By this Mr Speckle came to be a resident in the parish, he having taken up a portion of Mr Cayenne's share. He likewise took a tack of the house and policy of Wheatrig. But although Mr Speckle was a far more conversible man than his predecessor, and had a wonderful plausibility in business, the affairs of the Company did not thrive in his hands. Some said this was owing to his having owre many irons in the fire;[444] others, to the circumstances of the times; in my judgment, however, both helped; but the issue belongs to the events of another year. In the meanwhile, I should here note, that in the course of this current Ann. Dom. it pleased Heaven to visit me with a severe trial; the nature of which I will here record at length — the upshot I will make known hereafter.

From the planting of inhabitants in the cotton-mill town of Cayenneville, or, as the country folk, not used to such lang-nebbit words, now call it, Canaille,[445] there had come in upon the parish various sectarians among the weavers, some of whom were not satisfied with the gospel as I preached it, and endeavoured to practise it in my walk and conversation; and they began to speak of building a kirk for themselves, and of getting a minister that would give them the gospel more to their own ignorant fancies. I was exceedingly wroth and disturbed when the thing was first mentioned to me; and I very earnestly, from the pulpit, next Lord's day, lectured on the growth of newfangled doctrines; which, however, instead of having the wonted effect of my discourses, set up the theological weavers in a bleeze,[446] and the very Monday following they named a committee, to raise money by subscription, to build a meeting-house. This was the first overt-act of insubordination, collectively manifested in the parish; and it was

---

443 Doer (Sc.): agent, factor (here seems to mean executor).
444 Owre many (Sc.): too many.
445 Lang-nebbit (Sc.): long-nosed, here just meaning fancy or foreign; canaille: literally, 'pack of dogs' (French), 'a contemptuous name given to the populace [...] the rabble, the mob' (*OED*).
446 Bleeze (Sc.): blaze.

conducted with all that crafty dexterity, with which the infidel and jacobin spirit of the French Revolution had corrupted the honest simplicity of our good old hameward fashions.[447] In the course of a very short time, the Canaille folk had raised a large sum, and seduced not a few of my people into their schism, by which they were enabled to set about building their kirk; the foundations thereof were not, however, laid till the following year, but their proceedings gave me a het heart,[448] for they were like an open rebellion to my authority, and a contemptuous disregard of that religious allegiance which is due from the flock to the pastor.

On Christmas day, the wind broke off the main arm of our Adam and Eve peartree, and I grieved for it more as a type and sign of the threatened partition, than on account of the damage, though the fruit was the juiciest in all the country-side.

CHAPTER XLVIII.—YEAR 1807.

Numerous marriages—Account of a pay-wedding, made to set up a shop.

THIS was a year to me of satisfaction, in many points, for a greater number of my younger flock married in it, than had done for any one of ten years prior. They were chiefly the offspring of the marriages that took place at the close of the American war; and I was pleased to see the duplification of well-doing, as I think marrying is, having always considered the command, to increase and multiply, a holy ordinance, which the circumstances of this world but too often interfere to prevent.

It was also made manifest to me, that in this year there was a very general renewal in the hearts of men, of a sense of the utility, even in earthly affairs, of a religious life: In some, I trust it was more than prudence, and really a birth of grace. Whether this was owing to the upshot of the French Revolution, all men being pretty well satisfied in their minds, that uproar and rebellion make but an ill way of righting wrongs, or that the swarm of unruly youth, the offspring, as I have said, of the marriages after the American war, had grown sobered from their follies, and saw things in a better light, I cannot take upon me to say. But it was very edifying to me, their minister, to see several lads, who had been both wild and free in their principles, marrying with sobriety, and taking their wives to the kirk, with the comely decorum of heads of families.

But I was now growing old, and could go seldomer out among my people than in former days, so that I was less a partaker of their ploys and banquets, either at birth, bridal, or burial. I heard, however, all that went on at them, and I made it a rule, after giving the blessing at the end of the ceremony, to admonish the bride and bridegroom to ca' canny, and join trembling with their mirth.[449] It behoved me on one occasion, however, to break through a rule, that age and frailty had imposed upon me, and to go to the wedding of Tibby Banes, the daughter of the betherel, because she had once been a servant in the Manse, besides the obligation upon me from her father's part, both in the kirk and kirk-yard. Mrs Balwhidder went with me, for she liked to countenance the pleasantries of my people; and, over and above all, it was a pay-wedding,[450] in order to set up the bridegroom in a shop.

---

447 Hameward (Sc.): native.
448 Het (Sc.): hot. A 'het hert' is one 'suffering from a bitter disappointment' (*SND* 'het' 2).
449 Ca' canny (Sc.): take care; trembling: here, fear of the Lord.
450 Pleasantries: pleasures; pay-wedding, also penny wedding (Sc.): 'a wedding at which the guests contribute to their own entertainment and to give a start in life to the young couple' (*SND* 'pey').

There was, to be sure, a great multitude, gentle and semple, of all denominations, with two fiddles and a bass, and the volunteers' fife and drum, and the jollity that went on was a perfect feast of itself, though the wedding-supper was a prodigy of abundance. The auld carles kecklet with fainness, as they saw the young dancers; and the carlins sat on forms, as mim as May puddocks, with their shawls pinned apart, to shew their muslin napkins. But, after supper, when they had got a glass of the punch, their heels shewed their mettle, and grannies danced with their oes, holding out their hands as if they had been spinning with two rocks.[451] I told Colin Mavis, the poet, that an Infare was a fine subject for his muse,[452] and soon after, he indited an excellent ballad under that title, which he projects to publish with other ditties by subscription;[453] and I have no doubt a liberal and discerning public will give him all manner of encouragement, for that is the food of talent of every kind, and without it, no one can say what an author's faculty naturally is.

CHAPTER XLIX.—YEAR 1808.

Failure of Mr Speckle, the proprietor of the cotton-mill—the melancholy end of one of the overseers and his wife.

THROUGH all the wars that have raged from the time of the King's accession to the throne, there has been a gradually coming nearer and nearer to our gates, which is a very alarming thing to think of. In the first, at the time he came to the crown, we suffered nothing. Not one belonging to the parish was engaged in the battles thereof, and the news of victories, before they reached us, which was generally by word of mouth, were old tales. In the American war, as I have related at length, we had an immediate participation, but those that suffered were only a few individuals, and the evil was done at a distance, and reached us not until the worst of its effects were spent. And during the first term of the present just and necessary contest for all that is dear to us as a people, although, by the offswarming of some of our restless youth,[454] we had our part and portion in common with the rest of the Christian world; yet still there was at home a great augmentation of prosperity, and every thing had thriven in a surprising manner; somewhat, however, to the detriment of our country simplicity. By the building of the cotton-mill, and the rising up of the new town of Cayenneville, we had intromitted so much with concerns of trade,[455] that we were become a part of the great web of commercial reciprocities, and felt in our corner and extremity, every touch or stir that was made on any part of the texture. The consequence of this I have now to relate.

Various rumours had been floating about the business of the cotton manufacturers not being so lucrative as it had been; and Bonaparte, as it is well known, was a perfect limb of Satan against our prosperity, having recourse to the most wicked means and

---

451　Auld carles: old men; kecklet: cackled; fainness: gladness (all Sc.); form: bench; mim (Sc.): prim; puddocks (Sc.): toads; napkins: neckerchiefs. Oes (Sc.): grandchildren. Rocks (Sc.): distaffs, the spindles used in spinning thread.

452　Infare (Sc.): 'The coming of the bride to her new home and the feast given by the bridegroom to celebrate this' (*SND*).

453　By subscription: that is, by collecting purchasers before publication, who are then listed in the volume itself; as opposed to publishing at the author's or publisher's own risk. Burns's Kilmarnock *Poems* were published by subscription in 1786. By the start of the nineteenth century this was quite an old-fashioned way of doing things.

454　Offswarming: this seems to be Balwhidder's own coinage.

455　Intromit: here, have *financial* dealings with (Scots law).

purposes to bring ruin upon us as a nation. His cantrips, in this year, began to have a dreadful effect.[456]

For some time it had been observed in the parish, that Mr Speckle, of the cotton-mill, went very often to Glasgow, and was sometimes off at a few minutes warning to London, and the neighbours began to guess and wonder at what could be the cause of all this running here, and riding there, as if the littlegude was at his heels.[457] Sober folk augured ill o't; and it was remarked, likewise, that there was a haste and confusion in his mind, which betokened a foretaste of some change of fortune. At last, in the fulness of time, the babe was born.

On a Saturday night, Mr Speckle came out late from Glasgow; on the Sabbath he was with all his family at the kirk, looking as a man that had changed his way of life; and on the Monday, when the spinners went to the mill, they were told that the company had stopped payment. Never did a thunder-clap daunt the heart like this news, for the bread in a moment was snatched from more than a thousand mouths. It was a scene not to be described, to see the cotton-spinners and the weavers, with their wives and children, standing in bands along the road, all looking and speaking as if they had lost a dear friend or parent. For my part, I could not bear the sight, but hid myself in my closet, and prayed to the Lord to mitigate a calamity, which seemed to me past the capacity of man to remedy; for what could our parish fund do in the way of helping a whole town, thus suddenly thrown out of bread.

In the evening, however, I was strengthened, and convened the elders at the Manse to consult with them on what was best to be done, for it was well known that the sufferers had made no provision for a sore foot.[458] But all our gathered judgments could determine nothing; and therefore we resolved to wait the issue, not doubting but that He who sends the night, would bring the day in His good and gracious time, which so fell out. Some of them who had the largest experience of such vicissitudes, immediately began to pack up their ends and their awls, and to hie them in to Glasgow and Paisley in quest of employ; but those who trusted to the hopes that Mr Speckle himself still cherished, lingered long, and were obligated to submit to sore distress. After a time, however, it was found that the company was ruined, and the mill being sold for the benefit of the creditors, it was bought by another Glasgow company, who, by getting it a good bargain, and managing well, have it still, and have made it again a blessing to the country. At the time of the stoppage, however, we saw that commercial prosperity, flush as it might be, was but a perishable commodity, and from thence, both by public discourse and private exhortation, I have recommended to the workmen to lay up something for a reverse; and shewed that, by doing with their bawbees and pennies, what the great do with their pounds, they might in time get a pose to help them in the day of need. This advice they have followed, and made up a Savings Bank, which is a pillow of comfort to many an industrious head of a family.[459]

But I should not close this account of the disaster that befell Mr Speckle, and the

---

456 Cantrips (Sc.): magic charms or spells. Balwhidder is referring to the effects of the 'Continental System', Napoleon's ban on any of the nations conquered by or allied with France (almost the entire European continent, at this point) trading with Britain. This was inaugurated in 1806, after the abandonment of any plan for invading the UK.

457 Littlegude (Sc.): Devil. 'Freq. in Galt' notes SND.

458 Sore foot: 'to keep something for the sore foot' meant to keep a reserve in case of misfortune.

459 Galt has in mind the invention of the first Trustee Savings Bank by a real west of Scotland minister, the Rev. Henry Duncan of Dumfriesshire, in 1810. Accepting very small deposits from the local poor, TSBs were co-operative enterprises, owned by those depositors (like modern mutual building societies), not by wealthy shareholders.

cotton-mill company, without relating a very melancholy case that was the consequence. Among the overseers, there was a Mr Dwining, an Englishman from Manchester, where he had seen better days, having had himself there of his own property, once as large a mill, according to report, as the Cayenneville mill. He was certainly a man above the common, and his wife was a lady in every point; but they held themselves by themselves, and shunned all manner of civility, giving up their whole attention to their two little boys, who were really like creatures of a better race than the callans of our clachan.

On the failure of the company, Mr Dwining was observed by those who were present, to be particularly distressed, his salary being his all; but he said little, and went thoughtfully home. Some days after he was seen walking by himself with a pale face, a heavy eye, and a slow step—all tokens of a sorrowful heart. Soon after he was missed altogether; nobody saw him. The door of his house was however open, and his two pretty boys were as lively as usual, on the green before the door. I happened to pass when they were there, and I asked them how their father and mother were. They said they were still in bed, and would not waken, and the innocent lambs took me by the hand, to make me waken their parents. I know not what was in it, but I trembled from head to foot, and I was led in by the babies, as if I had not power to resist. Never shall I forget what I saw in that bed *   *   *   *   *   *   *

*   *   *   *   *   *   *   *   *   *   *

I found a letter on the table; and I came away, locking the door behind me, and took the lovely prattling orphans home. I could but shake my head and weep, as I gave them to the care of Mrs Balwhidder, and she was terrified, but said nothing. I then read the letter. It was to send the bairns to a gentleman, their uncle, in London. Oh it is a terrible tale, but the winding-sheet and the earth is over it. I sent for two of my elders. I related what I had seen. Two coffins were got, and the bodies laid in them; and the next day, with one of the fatherless bairns in each hand, I followed them to the grave, which was dug in that part of the kirk-yard where unchristened babies are laid. We durst not take it upon us to do more, but few knew the reason, and some thought it was because the deceased were strangers, and had no regular lair.[460]

I dressed the two bonny orphans in the best mourning at my own cost, and kept them in the Manse till we should get an answer from their uncle, to whom I sent their father's letter. It stung him to the quick, and he came down all the way from London, and took the children away himself. O he was a vext man, when the beautiful bairns, on being told he was their uncle, ran into his arms, and complained that their papa and mamma had slept so long, that they would never waken.

CHAPTER L.—YEAR 1809.

Opening of a Meeting-house—The elders come to the Manse, and offer me a helper.

As I come towards the events of these latter days, I am surprised to find myself not at all so distinct in my recollection of them, as in those of the first of my ministry; being apt to confound the things of one occasion with those of another, which Mrs Balwhidder says is an admonishment to me to leave off my writing. But, please God, I will endeavour to fulfil this as I have through life tried, to the best of my capacity, to do every other duty; and with the help of Mrs Balwhidder, who has a very clear understanding, I think I may get through my task in a creditable manner, which is all I aspire after; not writing for a

---

460   Lair (Sc.): burial plot. Suicides were traditionally not buried in the consecrated ground of the graveyard.

vain world, but only to testify to posterity anent the great changes that have happened in my day and generation—a period which all the best informed writers say, has not had its match in the history of the world, since the beginning of time.

By the failure of the cotton-mill company, whose affairs were not settled till the spring of this year, there was great suffering during the winter; but my people, those that still adhered to the establishment, bore their share of the dispensation with meekness and patience, nor was there wanting edifying monuments of resignation even among the strayvaggers.[461]

On the day that the Canaille Meeting-house was opened, which was in the summer, I was smitten to the heart to see the empty seats that were in my kirk, for all the thoughtless, and some that I had a better opinion of, went to hear the opening discourse. Satan that day had power given to him to buffet me as he did Job of old; and when I looked around and saw the empty seats, my corruption rose,[462] and I forgot myself in the remembering prayer; for when I prayed for all denominations of Christians, and worshippers, and infidels, I could not speak of the schismatics with patience, but entreated the Lord to do with the hobbleshow at Cayenneville, as he saw meet in his displeasure, the which, when I came afterwards to think upon, I grieved at with a sore contrition.

In the course of the week following, the elders, in a body, came to me in the Manse, and after much commendation of my godly ministry, they said, that seeing I was now growing old, they thought they could not testify their respect for me in a better manner, than by agreeing to get me a helper. But I would not at that time listen to such a proposal, for I felt no falling off in my powers of preaching; on the contrary, I found myself growing better at it, as I was enabled to hold forth, in an easy manner, often a whole half hour longer than what I could do a dozen years before. Therefore nothing was done in this year anent my resignation; but during the winter, Mrs Balwhidder was often grieved, in the bad weather, that I should preach, and, in short, so worked upon my affections, that I began to think it was fitting for me to comply with the advice of my friends. Accordingly, in the course of the winter, the elders began to cast about for a helper, and during the bleak weather in the ensuing spring, several young men spared me from the necessity of preaching. But this relates to the concerns of the next and last year of my ministry. So I will now proceed to give an account of it, very thankful that I have been permitted, in unmolested tranquillity, to bring my history to such a point.

CHAPTER LI.—YEAR 1810.

Conclusion—I repair to the church for the last time—Afterwards receive a silver server from the parishioners—And still continue to marry and baptize.

MY tasks are all near a close; and in writing this final record of my ministry, the very sound of my pen admonishes me that my life is a burden on the back of flying time, that he will soon be obliged to lay down in his great store-house, the grave. Old age has, indeed, long warned me to prepare for rest, and the darkened windows of my sight shew that the night is coming on, while deafness, like a door fast barred, has shut out all the pleasant sounds of this world, and inclosed me, as it were, in a prison, even from the voices of my friends.

I have lived longer than the common lot of man, and I have seen, in my time, many

---

461   I.e. those who have 'wandered' from the established Church of Scotland, and now attend the Meeting House instead.
462   Corruption: 'evil nature, "the old Adam"; anger, "temper"' (*OED* II.5).

mutations and turnings, and ups and downs, notwithstanding the great spread that has been in our national prosperity. I have beheld them that were flourishing like the green bay trees,[463] made desolate, and their branches scattered. But, in my own estate, I have had a large and liberal experience of goodness.

At the beginning of my ministry I was reviled and rejected, but my honest endeavours to prove a faithful shepherd, were blessed from on high, and rewarded with the affection of my flock. Perhaps, in the vanity of doting old age, I thought in this there was a merit due to myself, which made the Lord to send the chastisement of the Canaille schism among my people, for I was then wroth without judgment, and by my heat hastened into an open division the flaw that a more considerate manner might have healed. But I confess my fault, and submit my cheek to the smiter; and I now see that the finger of Wisdom was in that probation, and it was far better that the weavers meddled with the things of God, which they could not change, than with those of the king, which they could only harm. In that matter, however, I was like our gracious monarch in the American war; for though I thereby lost the pastoral allegiance of a portion of my people, in like manner as he did of his American subjects; yet, after the separation, I was enabled so to deport myself, that they shewed me many voluntary testimonies of affectionate respect, and which it would be a vain glory in me to rehearse here. One thing I must record, because it is as much to their honour as it is to mine.

When it was known that I was to preach my last sermon, every one of those who had been my hearers, and who had seceded to the Canaille meeting, made it a point that day to be in the parish kirk, and to stand in the crowd, that made a lane of reverence for me to pass from the kirk door to the back-yett of the Manse. And shortly after a deputation of all their brethren, with their minister at their head, came to me one morning, and presented to me a server of silver, in token, as they were pleased to say, of their esteem for my blameless life, and the charity that I had practised towards the poor of all sects in the neighbourhood; which is set forth in a well-penned inscription, written by a weaver lad that works for his daily bread. Such a thing would have been a prodigy at the beginning of my ministry, but the progress of book learning and education has been wonderful since, and with it has come a spirit of greater liberality than the world knew before, bringing men of adverse principles and doctrines, into a more humane communion with each other, shewing, that it's by the mollifying influence of knowledge, the time will come to pass, when the tiger of papistry shall lie down with the lamb of reformation, and the vultures of prelacy be as harmless as the presbyterian doves; when the independent, the anabaptist, and every other order and denomination of Christians, not forgetting even these poor wee wrens of the Lord, the burghers and anti-burghers,[464] who will pick from the hand of patronage, and dread no snare.

On the next Sunday, after my farewell discourse, I took the arm of Mrs Balwhidder, and with my cane in my hand, walked to our own pew, where I sat some time, but owing to my deafness, not being able to hear, I have not since gone back to the church. But my people are fond of having their weans still christened by me, and the young folk, such as are of a serious turn, come to be married at my hands, believing, as they say, that there is something good in the blessing of an aged gospel minister. But even

---

463   This seems to be a reference to Psalms 37.35–36: 'I have seen the wicked in great power, and spreading himself like a green bay tree. Yet he passed away, and, lo, he was not.' But Balwhidder is not talking here about the wicked, just the people of his parish. Perhaps Galt wants us to recall Psalm 37, and think of Napoleon, whom he, and his readers (but not Balwhidder, in 1811) have seen pass away, defeated for the final time at Waterloo in 1815.

464   Those who split from the Kirk over patronage in 1732 themselves split over a similar issue in 1747: these are the names of the contending parties in this, later, schism.

this remnant of my gown I must lay aside, for Mrs Balwhidder is now and then obliged to stop me in my prayers, as I sometimes wander — pronouncing the baptismal blessing upon a bride and bride-groom, talking as if they were already parents. I am thankful, however, that I have been spared with a sound mind to write this book to the end; but it is my last task, and, indeed, really I have no more to say, saving only to wish a blessing on all people from on High, where I soon hope to be, and to meet there all the old and long-departed sheep of my flock, especially the first and second Mrs Balwhidders.

FINIS

Selected short fiction by James Hogg (1770–1835)

THE BROWNIE OF THE BLACK HAGGS.
BY THE ETTRICK SHEPHERD.[1]

WHEN the Sprots were Lairds of Wheelhope, which is now a long time ago, there was one of the ladies who was very badly spoken of in the country. People did not just openly assert that Lady Wheelhope was a witch, but every one had an aversion even at hearing her named; and when by chance she happened to be mentioned, old men would shake their heads and say. "Ah! let us alane o' her! The less ye meddle wi' her the better." Auld wives would give over spinning, and, as a pretence for hearing what might be said about her, poke in the fire with the tongs, cocking up their ears all the while; and then, after some meaning coughs, hems, and haws, would haply say, "Hech-wow, sirs! An a' be true that's said!" or something equally wise and decisive as that.

In short, Lady Wheelhope was accounted a very bad woman. She was an inexorable tyrant in her family, quarrelled with her servants, often cursing them, striking them, and turning them away; especially if they were religious, for these she could not endure, but suspected them of every thing bad. Whenever she found out any of the servant men of the Laird's establishment for religious characters, she soon gave them up to the military, and got them shot; and several girls that were regular in their devotions, she was supposed to have popped off with poison. She was certainly a wicked woman, else many good people were mistaken in her character, and the poor persecuted Covenanters were obliged to unite in their prayers against her.[2]

As for the Laird, he was a stump. A big, dun-faced, pluffy body,[3] that cared neither for good nor evil, and did not well know the one from the other. He laughed at his lady's tantrums and barley-hoods;[4] and the greater the rage that she got into, the Laird thought it the better sport. One day, when two servant maids came running to him, in great agitation, and told him that his lady had felled one of their companions, the Laird laughed heartily at them, and said he did not doubt it.

"Why sir, how can you laugh?" said they. "The poor girl is killed."

"Very likely, very likely," said the Laird. "Well, it will teach her to take care who she angers again."

"And, sir, your lady will be hanged."

"Very likely; well, it will learn her how to strike so rashly again—Ha, ha, ha! Will it not, Jessy?"

But when this same Jessy died suddenly one morning, the Laird was greatly confounded, and seemed dimly to comprehend that there had been unfair play going. There was little doubt that she was taken off by poison; but whether the lady did it through jealousy or not, was never divulged; but it greatly bamboozled and astonished the poor Laird, for his nerves failed him, and his whole frame became paralytic. He seems to have been exactly in the same state of mind with a colley that I once had. He was extremely fond of the gun as long as I did not kill anything with her, (there being

---

1 From *Blackwood's Edinburgh Magazine* XXIV (Oct. 1828): 489–96. This is Hogg's usual periodical *nom de plume*.

2 The repression of the Covenanters (see Introduction) included the sort of summary execution mentioned in this paragraph. This reference locates the story in the 1680s.

3 Pluffy body (Sc.): chubby person.

4 Barley-hood: 'a fit of obstinacy or violent ill-temper' (*SND*).

no game laws in Ettrick Forest in those days,) and he got a grand chase after the hares when I missed them. But there was one day that I chanced for a marvel to shoot one dead, a few paces before his nose. I'll never forget the astonishment that the poor beast manifested. He stared one while at the gun, and another while at the dead hare, and seemed to be drawing the conclusion, that if the case stood thus, there was no creature sure of its life. Finally, he took his tail between his legs, and ran away home, and never would face a gun all his life again.

So was it precisely with Laird Sprot of Wheelhope. As long as his lady's wrath produced only noise and splutter among the servants, he thought it fine sport; but when he saw what he believed the dreadful effects of it, he became like a barrel organ out of tune, and could only discourse one note, which he did to every one he met. "I wish she maunna hae gotten something she has been the waur of."[5] This note he repeated early and late, night and day, sleeping and waking, alone and in company, from the moment that Jessy died till she was buried; and on going to the churchyard as chief mourner, he whispered it to her relations by the way. When they came to the grave, he took his stand at the head, nor would he give place to the girl's father; but there he stood, like a huge post, as though he neither saw nor heard; and when he had lowered her late comely head into the grave, and dropped the cord, he slowly lifted his hat with one hand, wiped his dim eyes with the back of the other, and said, in a deep tremulous tone, "Poor lassie! I wish she didna get something she had been the waur of."

This death made a great noise among the common people; but there was no protection for the life of the subject in those days; and provided a man or woman was a true loyal subject, and a real Anti-Covenanter, any of them might kill as many as they liked. So there was no one to take cognizance of the circumstances relating to the death of poor Jessy.[6]

After this, the lady walked softly for the space of two or three years. She saw that she had rendered herself odious, and had entirely lost her husband's countenance, which she liked worst of all. But the evil propensity could not be overcome; and a poor boy, whom the Laird, out of sheer compassion, had taken into his service, being found dead one morning, the country people could no longer be restrained; so they went in a body to the Sheriff, and insisted on an investigation. It was proved that she detested the boy, had often threatened him, and had given him brose and butter the afternoon before he died;[7] but the cause was ultimately dismissed, and the pursuers fined.

No one can tell to what height of wickedness she might now have proceeded, had not a check of a very singular kind been laid upon her. Among the servants that came home at the next term, was one who called himself Merodach;[8] and a strange person he was. He had the form of a boy, but the features of one a hundred years old, save that his eyes had a brilliancy and restlessness, which was very extraordinary, bearing a strong resemblance to the eyes of a well-known species of monkey. He was froward and perverse in all actions,[9] and disregarded the pleasure or displeasure of any person; but he performed his work well, and with apparent ease. From the moment that he entered the house, the lady conceived a mortal antipathy against him, and besought the Laird to turn him away. But the Laird, of himself, never turned away any body, and moreover he had hired him for a trivial wage, and the fellow neither wanted

---

5   That is, 'I wish she may not have taken something she has been the worse for.'
6   'Cognizance' here carrying the legal meaning of judicial recognition that there is a case to answer.
7   Brose is oatmeal with boiling water poured on it.
8   Merodach is a god of the Babylonians mentioned in passing in Jeremiah 50.2.
9   Froward: hard to please, refractory.

activity nor perseverance. The natural consequence of this arrangement was, that the lady instantly set herself to make Merodach's life as bitter as it was possible, in order to get early quit of a domestic every way so disgusting. Her hatred of him was not like a common antipathy entertained by one human being against another, — she hated him as one might hate a toad or an adder; and his occupation of jottery-man (as the Laird termed his servant of all work) keeping him always about her hand, it must have proved highly disagreeable.

She scolded him, she raged at him, but he only mocked her wrath, and giggled and laughed at her, with the most provoking derision. She tried to fell him again and again, but never, with all her address, could she hit him; and never did she make a blow at him, that she did not repent it. She was heavy and unwieldy, and he as quick in his motions as a monkey: besides, he generally had her in such an ungovernable rage, that when she flew at him, she hardly knew what she was doing. At one time she guided her blow towards him, and he at the same instant avoided it with such dexterity, that she knocked down the chief hind, or foresman; and then Merodach giggled so heartily, that, lifting the kitchen poker, she threw it at him with a full design of knocking out his brains; but the missile only broke every plate and ashet on the kitchen dresser.[10]

She then hasted to the Laird, crying bitterly, and telling him she would not suffer that wretch Merodach, as she called him, to stay another night in the family. "Why, then, put him away, and trouble me no more about him," said the Laird.

"Put him away!" exclaimed she; "I have already ordered him away a hundred times, and charged him never to let me see his horrible face again; but he only flouts me, and tells me he'll see me at the devil first."

The pertinacity of the fellow amused the Laird exceedingly; his dim eyes turned upwards into his head with delight; he then looked two ways at once, turned round his back, and laughed till the tears ran down his dun cheeks, but he could only articulate "You're fitted now."[11]

The lady's agony of rage still increasing from this derision, she flew on the Laird, and said he was not worthy the name of a man, if he did not turn away that pestilence, after the way he had abused her.

"Why, Shusy, my dear, what has he done to you?"

"What done to me! has he not caused me to knock down John Thomson, and I do not know if ever he will come to life again?"

"Have you felled your favourite John Thomson?" said the Laird, laughing more heartily than before; "you might have done a worse deed than that. But what evil has John done?"

"And has he not broke every plate and dish on the whole dresser?" continued the lady, disregarding the Laird's question; "and for all this devastation, he only mocks at my displeasure, — absolutely mocks me, — and if you do not have him turned away, and hanged or shot for his deeds, you are not worthy the name of man."

"O alack! What a devastation among the china metal!" said the Laird; and calling on Merodach, he said, "Tell me, thou evil Merodach of Babylon, how thou dared'st knock down thy lady's favourite servant, John Thomson?"

"Not I, your honour. It was my lady herself, who got into such a furious rage at me, that she mistook her man, and felled Mr Thomson; and the good man's skull is fractured."

"That was very odd," said the Laird, chuckling; "I do not comprehend it. But then,

---

10 An ashet is a type of large plate.
11 Fit (Sc.): 'To suit, serve with what is wanted, to satisfy one's requirements' (*SND*).

what the devil set you on smashing all my lady's delft and china ware? — That was a most infamous and provoking action."

"It was she herself, your honour. Sorry would I have been to have broken one dish belonging to the house. I take all the house-servants to witness, that my lady smashed all the dishes with a poker, and now lays the blame on me."

The Laird turned his dim and delighted eyes on his lady, who was crying with vexation and rage, and seemed meditating another personal attack on the culprit, which he did not at all appear to shun, but rather encourage. She, however, vented her wrath in the threatenings of the most deep and desperate revenge, the creature all the while assuring her that she would be foiled, and that in all her encounters and contests with him, she would uniformly come to the worst. He was resolved to do his duty, and there before his master he defied her.

The Laird thought more than he considered it prudent to reveal; but he had little doubt that his wife would wreak that vengeance on his jottery-man which she avowed, and as little of her capability. He almost shuddered when he recollected one who had taken *something that she had been the waur of.*

In a word, the Lady of Wheelhope's inveterate malignity against this one object, was like the rod of Moses, that swallowed up the rest of the serpents. All her wicked and evil propensities seemed to be superseded by it, if not utterly absorbed in its virtues. [12] The rest of the family now lived in comparative peace and quietness; for early and late her malevolence was venting itself against the jotteryman, and him alone. It was a delirium of hatred and vengeance, on which the whole bent and bias of her inclination was set. She could not stay from the creature's presence, for in the intervals when absent from him, she spent her breath in curses and execrations, and then not able to rest, she ran again to seek him, her eyes gleaming with the anticipated delights of vengeance, while, ever and anon, all the scaith, the ridicule, and the harm, redounded on herself.

Was it not strange that she could not get quit of this sole annoyance of her life? One would have thought she easily might. But by this time there was nothing farther from her intention; she wanted vengeance, full, adequate, and delicious vengeance, on her audacious opponent. But he was a strange and terrible creature, and the means of retaliation came always, as it were, to his hand.

Bread and sweet milk was the only fare that Merodach cared for, and he having bargained for that, would not want it, though he often got it with a curse and with ill will. The lady having intentionally kept back his wonted allowance for some days, on the Sabbath morning following, she set him down a bowl of rich sweet milk, well drugged with a deadly poison, and then she lingered in a little anteroom to watch the success of her grand plot, and prevent any other creature from tasting of the potion. Merodach came in, and the house-maid says to him, "There is your breakfast, creature."

"Oho! my lady has been liberal this morning," said he; "but I am beforehand with her. — Here, little Missie, you seem very hungry to-day — take you my breakfast." And with that he set the beverage down to the lady's little favourite spaniel. It so happened that the lady's only son came at that instant into the anteroom, seeking her, and teazing his mamma about something which took her attention from the hall-table for a space. When she looked again, and saw Missie lapping up the sweet milk, she burst from her lobby like a dragon, screaming as if her head had been on fire, kicked the bowl and the remainder of its contents against the wall, and lifting Missie in her bosom, she

---

12 Alluding to the miracle before Pharaoh in Exodus 7.8–13 (although the rod is Aaron's, not his brother Moses's). 'Virtue' here means 'a particular power or efficacy inherent in something' (*OED*).

retreated hastily, crying all the way.

"Ha, ha, ha—I have you now!" cried Merodach, as she vanished from the hall.

Poor Missie died immediately, and very privately; indeed, she would have died and been buried, and never one have seen her, save her mistress, had not Merodach, by a luck that never failed him, popped his nose over the flower garden wall, just as his lady was laying her favourite in a grave of her own digging. She, not perceiving her tormentor, plied on at her task, apostrophizing the insensate little carcass,—"Ah! poor dear little creature, thou hast had a hard fortune, and hast drank of the bitter potion that was not intended for thee; but he shall drink it three times double, for thy sake!"

"Is that little Missie?" said the eldrich voice of the jotteryman, close at the lady's ear.[13] She uttered a loud scream, and sunk down on the bank. "Alack for poor little Missie!" continued the creature in a tone of mockery, "My heart is sorry for Missie. What has befallen her—whose breakfast cup did she drink?"

"Hence with thee, thou fiend!" cried the lady; "what right hast thou to intrude on thy mistress's privacy? Thy turn is coming yet, or may the nature of woman change within me."

"It is changed already," said the creature, grinning with delight; "I have thee now, I have thee now! And were it not to shew my superiority over thee, which I do every hour, I should soon see thee strapped like a mad cat, or a worrying bratch.[14] What wilt thou try next?"

"I will cut thy throat, and if I die for it, will rejoice in the deed; a deed of charity to all that dwell on the face of the earth. Go about thy business."

"I have warned thee before, dame, and I now warn thee again, that all thy mischief meditated against me will fall double on thine own head."

"I want none of your warning, and none of your instructions, fiendish cur. Hence with your elvish face, and take care of yourself."

It would be too disgusting and horrible to relate or read all the incidents that fell out between this unaccountable couple. Their enmity against each other had no end, and no mitigation; and scarcely a single day passed over on which her acts of malevolent ingenuity did not terminate fatally for some favourite thing of the lady's, while all these doings never failed to appear as her own act. Scarcely was there a thing, animate or inanimate, on which she set a value, left to her, that was not destroyed; and yet scarcely one hour or minute could she remain absent from her tormentor, and all the while, it seems, solely for the purpose of tormenting him.

But while all the rest of the establishment enjoyed peace and quietness from the fury of their termagant dame, matters still grew worse and worse between the fascinated pair. The lady haunted the menial, in the same manner as the raven haunts the eagle, for a perpetual quarrel, though the former knows that in every encounter she is to come off the loser. But now noises were heard on the stairs by night, and it was whispered among the menials, that the lady had been seeking Merodach's bed by night, on some horrible intent. Several of them would have sworn that they had seen her passing and repassing on the stair after midnight, when all was quiet; but then it was likewise well known, that Merodach slept with well fastened doors, and a companion in another bed in the same room, whose bed, too, was nearest the door. Nobody cared much what became of the jotteryman, for he was an unsocial and disagreeable person; but some one told him what they had seen, and hinted a suspicion of the lady's intent. But the creature only bit his upper lip, winked with his eyes, and said, "She had better let

---

13 Eldritch (Sc.): uncanny, elfin.
14 Bratch: bitch.

alone; she will be the first to rue that."

Not long after this, to the horror of the family and the whole country side, the Laird's only son was found murdered in his bed one morning, under circumstances that manifested the most fiendish cruelty and inveteracy on the part of his destroyer. As soon as the atrocious act was divulged, the lady fell into convulsions, and lost her reason; and happy had it been for her had she never recovered either the use of reason, or her corporeal functions any more, for there was blood upon her hand, which she took no care to conceal, and there was too little doubt that it was the blood of her own innocent and beloved boy, the sole heir and hope of the family.

This blow deprived the Laird of all power of action; but the lady had a brother, a man of the law, who came and instantly proceeded to an investigation of this unaccountable murder; but before the Sheriff arrived, the housekeeper took the lady's brother aside, and told him he had better not go on with the scrutiny, for she was sure the crime would be brought home to her unfortunate mistress; and after examining into several corroborative circumstances, and viewing the state of the raving maniac, with the blood on her hand and arm, he made the investigation a very short one, declaring the domestics all exculpated.

The Laird attended his boy's funeral, and laid his head in the grave, but appeared exactly like a man walking in a trance, an automaton, without feelings or sensations, often times gazing at the funeral procession, as on something he could not comprehend. And when the death-bell of the parish church fell a-tolling, as the corpse approached the kirk-stile, he cast a dim eye up towards the belfry, and said hastily, "What, what's that? Och ay, we're just in time, just in time." And often was he hammering over the name of "Evil Merodach, King of Babylon," to himself.[15] He seemed to have some far-fetched conception that his unaccountable jotteryman had a hand in the death of his only son, and other lesser calamities, although the evidence in favour of Merodach's innocence was as usual quite decisive.

This grievous mistake of Lady Wheelhope (for every landward Laird's wife was then styled Lady)[16] can only be accounted for, by supposing her in a state of derangement, or rather under some evil influence, over which she had no control; and to a person in such a state, the mistake was not so very unnatural. The mansion-house of Wheelhope was old and irregular. The stair had four acute turns, all the same, and four landing-places, all the same. In the uppermost chamber slept the two domestics, — Merodach in the bed farthest in, and in the chamber immediately below that, which was exactly similar, slept the young Laird and his tutor, the former in the bed farthest in; and thus, in the turmoil of raging passions, her own hand made herself childless.

Merodach was expelled the family forthwith, but refused to accept of his wages, which the man of law pressed upon him, for fear of farther mischief; but he went away in apparent sullenness and discontent, no one knowing whither.

When his dismissal was announced to the lady, who was watched day and night in her chamber, the news had such an effect on her, that her whole frame seemed electrified; the horrors of remorse vanished, and another passion, which I neither can comprehend nor define, took the sole possession of her distempered spirit. "He *must* not go! — He *shall* not go!" she exclaimed. "No, no, no — he shall not — he shall not — he shall not!" and then she instantly set herself about making ready to follow him, uttering all the while the most diabolical expressions, indicative of anticipated vengeance. — "Oh, could I but snap his nerves one by one, and birl among his vitals!

---

15 Mentioned in II Kings 25.27.
16 Landward (Sc.): rural.

Could I but slice his heart off piecemeal in small messes, and see his blood lopper and bubble, and spin away in purple slays;[17] and then to see him grin, and grin, and grin, and grin! Oh — oh — oh — How beautiful and grand a sight it would be to see him grin, and grin, and grin!" And in such a style would she run on for hours together.

She thought of nothing, she spake of nothing, but the discarded jotteryman, whom most people now began to regard as a creature that was not canny. They had seen him eat, and drink, and work like other people; still he had that about him that was not like other men. He was a boy in form, and an antediluvian in feature. Some thought he was a mule, between a Jew and an ape; some a wizard, some a kelpie, or a fairy, but most of all, that he was really and truly a Brownie.[18] What he was I do not know, and therefore will not pretend to say; but be that as it may, in spite of locks and keys, watching and waking, the Lady of Wheelhope soon made her escape and eloped after him. The attendants, indeed, would have made oath that she was carried away by some invisible hand, for that it was impossible she could have escaped on foot like other people; and this edition of the story took in the country; but sensible people viewed the matter in another light.

As for instance, when Wattie Blythe, the Laird's old shepherd, came in from the hill one morning, his wife Bessie thus accosted him. — "His presence be about us, Wattie Blythe! have ye heard what has happened at the ha'? Things are aye turning waur and waur there, and it looks like as if Providence had gi'en up our Laird's house to destruction. This grand estate maun now gang frae the Sprots,[19] for it has finished them."

"Na, na, Bessie, it isna the estate that has finished the Sprots, but the Sprots that hae finished it an' themsells into the boot. They hae been a wicked and degenerate race, an' ay the langer the waur, till they hae reached the utmost bounds o' earthly wickedness; an' it's time the deil were looking after his ain."[20]

"Ah, Wattie Blythe, ye never said a truer say. An' that's just the very point where your story ends, and mine commences; for hasna the deil, or the fairies, or the brownies, ta'en away our lady bodily, an' the haill country is running and riding in search o' her; and there is twenty hunder merks[21] offered to the first that can find her, an' bring her safe back. They hae ta'en her away, skin an' bane, body an' soul, an' a', Wattie!"

"Hech-wow! but that is awsome! And where is it thought they have ta'en her to, Bessie?"

"O, they hae some guess at that frae her ain hints afore. It is thought they hae carried her after that Satan of a creature, wha wrought sae muckle wae about the house. It is for him they are a' looking, for they ken weel, that where they get the tane they will get the tither." [22]

"Whew! Is that the gate o't, Bessie? Why, then, the awfu' story is nouther mair nor less than this, that the leddy has made a lopment, as they ca't, and run away after a blackgaird jotteryman. Hech-wow! wae's me for human frailty! But that's just the gate! When aince the deil gets in the point o' his finger,[23] he will soon have in his haill hand.

---

17 Birl (Sc.): spin; lopper: coagulate; slays (Sc.): worms (?).

18 A kelpie is a water-spirit; a brownie is a goblin, usually one associated with a household, performing tasks if rewarded but vengeful if not.

19 Aye: always; waur: worse; maun: must; gang: go; frae: from (all Sc.).

20 Ay the langer the waur: they got worse as they went on; deil: devil (all Sc.).

21 The Merk was a silver coin worth two-thirds of a Pound Scots; Wattie and Bessie belong to the last generation in which it was in circulation.

22 Sae muckle wae: so much woe; ken weel: know well; tane [...] tither: one [...] other (all Sc..)

23 Gate: way; aince: once (both Sc.).

Ay, he wants but a hair to make a tether of, ony day. I hae seen her a braw sonsy lass,[24] but even then I feared she was devoted to destruction, for she aye mockit at religion, Bessie, an' that's no a good mark of a young body. An' she made a' its servants her enemies; an' think you these good men's prayers were a' to blaw away i' the wind, and be nae mair regarded? Na, na, Bessie, my woman, take ye this mark baith o' our ain bairns and ither folk's[25] — If ever ye see a young body that disregards the Sabbath, and makes a mock at the ordinances o' religion, ye will never see that body come to muckle good. A braw hand she had made o' her gibes an' jeers at religion, an' her mockeries o' the poor persecuted hill-folk![26] — sunk down by degrees into the very dregs o' sin and misery! run away after a scullion!"

"Fy, fy, Wattie, how can ye say sae? It was weel kenn'd that she hatit him wi' a perfect an' mortal hatred, an' tried to make away wi' him mae ways nor ane."[27]

"Aha, Bessie; but nipping an' scarting are Scots folk's wooing;[28] an' though it is but right that we suspend our judgments, there will naebody persuade me, if she be found alang wi' the creature, but that she has run away after him in the natural way, on her twa shanks, without help either frae fairy or brownie."

"I'll never believe sic a thing of any woman born, let be a lady weel up in years."

"Od help ye, Bessie! ye dinna ken the stretch o' corrupt nature. The best o' us, when left to oursells, are nae better than strayed sheep, that will never find the way back to their ain pastures; an' of a' things made o' mortal flesh, a wicked woman is the warst."

"Alack-a-day! we get the blame o' muckle that we little deserve. But Wattie, keep ye a gayan sharp look-out about the cleuchs and the caves o' our glen, or hope, as ye ca't; for the lady kens them a' gayan weel; and gin the twenty hunder merks wad come our way, it might gang a waur gate. It wad tocher a' our bonny lasses."[29]

"Ay, weel I wat, Bessie, that's nae lee. And now, when ye bring me amind o't, the L— forgie me gin I didna hear a creature up in Brock-holes this morning, skirling as if something war cutting its throat. It gars a' the hairs stand on my head when I think it may hae been our leddy, an' the droich of a creature murdering her. I took it for a battle of wulcats, and wished they might pu' out ane anither's thrapples;[30] but when I think on it again, they war unco[31] like some o' our leddy's unearthly screams."

"His presence be about us, Wattie! Haste ye. Pit on your bonnet — take your staff in your hand, and gang an' see what it is."

"Shame fa' me, if I daur gang, Bessie."

"Hout, Wattie, trust in the Lord."

"Aweel, sae I do. But ane's no to throw himsell ower a linn,[32] an' trust that the Lord's to kep him in a blanket;[33] nor hing himsell up in a raip, an' expect the Lord to come and cut him down. An' it's nae muckle safer for an auld stiff man to gang away out to a wild remote place, where there is ae body murdering another. — What is that I hear, Bessie? Haud the lang tongue o' you,[34] and rin to the door, an' see what noise that is."

---

24 Braw, sonsy (Sc.): fine, strapping.
25 Bairns: children.
26 I.e. the Covenanters, forced to hold services in secret in the hills for fear of persecution.
27 Mae ways nor ane (Sc.): more ways than one.
28 Scarting (Sc.): scratching.
29 Gayan sharp, gayan weel: pretty sharp, pretty well; gin: if. A tocher is a dowry (all Sc.).
30 I.e. pulled out one another's throats. A droich is a dwarf (all Sc.).
31 Unco (Sc.): here, awfully.
32 I.e. one is not supposed to throw oneself over a waterfall....
33 Kep (Sc.): catch.
34 Haud (Sc.): hold.

Bessie ran to the door, but soon returned an altered creature, with her mouth wide open, and her eyes set in her head.

"It is them, Wattie! it is them! His presence be about us! What will we do?"

"Them? Whaten them?"

"Why, that blackguard creature, coming here, leading our leddy be the hair o' the head, an' yerking her wi' a stick.[35] I am terrified out o' my wits. What will we do?"

"We'll see what they say," said Wattie, manifestly in as great terror as his wife; and by a natural impulse, or as a last resource, he opened the Bible, not knowing what he did, and then hurried on his spectacles; but before he got two leaves turned over, the two entered, a frightful-looking couple indeed. Merodach, with his old withered face, and ferret eyes, leading the Lady of Wheelhope by the long hair, which was mixed with grey, and whose face was all bloated with wounds and bruises, and having stripes of blood on her garments.

"How's this! — How's this, sirs?" said Wattie Blythe.

"Close that book, and I will tell you, goodman," said Merodach.

"I can hear what you hae to say wi' the beuk open, sir," said Wattie, turning over the leaves, as if looking for some particular passage, but apparently not knowing what he was doing. "It is a shamefu' business this, but some will hae to answer for't. My leddy, I am unco grieved to see you in sic a plight. Ye hae surely been dooms sair left to yoursell."[36]

The lady shook her head, uttered a feeble hollow laugh, and fixed her eyes on Merodach. But such a look! It almost frightened the simple aged couple out of their senses. It was not a look of love nor of hatred exclusively; neither was it of desire or disgust, but it was a combination of them all. It was such a look as one fiend would cast on another, in whose everlasting destruction he rejoiced. Wattie was glad to take his eyes from such countenances, and look into the Bible, that firm foundation of all his hopes and all his joy.

"I request that you will shut that book, sir," said the horrible creature; "or if you do not, I will shut it for you with a vengeance;" and with that he seized it, and flung it against the wall. Bessie uttered a scream, and Wattie was quite paralysed; and although he seemed disposed to run after his best friend, as he called it, the hellish looks of the Brownie interposed, and glued him to his seat.

"Hear what I have to say first," said the creature, "and then pore your fill on that precious book of yours. One concern at a time is enough. I came to do you a service. Here, take this cursed, wretched woman, whom you style your lady, and deliver her up to the lawful authorities, to be restored to her husband and her place in society. She is come upon one that hates her, and never said one kind word to her in his life, and though I have beat her like a dog, still she clings to me, and will not depart, so enchanted is she with the laudable purpose of cutting my throat. Tell your master and her brother, that I am not to be burdened with their maniac. I have scourged, I have spurned and kicked her, afflicting her night and day, and yet from my side she will not depart. Take her. Claim the reward in full, and your fortune is made, and so farewell."

The creature bowed and went away, but the moment his back was turned the lady fell a-screaming and struggling like one in an agony, and in spite of all the old couple's exertions, she forced herself out of their hands, and ran after the retreating Merodach. When he saw better would not be, he turned upon her, and, by one blow with his stick, struck her down; and, not content with that, he continued to kick and baste her in such

---

35 Yerk (Sc.): beat.
36 Dooms sair (Sc.): very sore.

a manner as to all appearance would have killed twenty ordinary persons.[37] The poor devoted dame could do nothing but now and then utter a squeak like a half-worried cat, and writhe and grovel on the sward, till Wattie and his wife came up and withheld her tormentor from further violence. He then bound her hands behind her back with a strong cord, and delivered her once more to the charge of the old couple who contrived to hold her by that means and take her home.

Wattie had not the face to take her into the hall, but into one of the outhouses, where he brought her brother to receive her. The man of the law was manifestly vexed at her reappearance, and scrupled not to testify his dissatisfaction; for when Wattie told him how the wretch had abused his sister, and that, had it not been for Bessie's interference and his own, the lady would have been killed outright.

"Why, Walter, it is a great pity that he did not kill her outright," said he. "What good can her life now do to her, or of what value is her life to any creature living? After one has lived to disgrace all connected with them, the sooner they are taken off the better."

The man, however, paid old Walter down his two thousand merks, a great fortune for one like him in those days; and not to dwell longer on this unnatural story, I shall only add, very shortly, that the Lady of Wheelhope soon made her escape once more, and flew, as by an irresistible charm, to her tormentor. Her friends looked no more after; and the last time she was seen alive, it was following the uncouth creature up the water of Daur, weary, wounded, and lame, while he was all the way beating her, as a piece of excellent amusement. A few days after that, her body was found among some wild haggs,[38] in a place called Crook-burn, by a party of the persecuted Covenanters that were in hiding there, some of the very men whom she had exerted herself to destroy, and who had been driven, like David of old, to pray for a curse and earthly punishment upon her.[39] They buried her like a dog at the Yetts of Keppel, and rolled three huge stones upon her grave, which are lying there to this day. When they found her corpse, it was mangled and wounded in a most shocking manner, the fiendish creature having manifestly tormented her to death. He was never more seen or heard of in this kingdom, though all that country-side was kept in terror for him many years afterwards; and to this day, they will tell you of THE BROWNIE OF THE BLACK HAGGS, which title he seems to have acquired after his disappearance.

This story was told to me by an old man, named Adam Halliday, whose great grandfather, Thomas Halliday, was one of those that found the body and buried it. It is many years since I heard it; but, however ridiculous it may appear, I remember it made a dreadful impression on my young mind. I never heard any story like it, save one of an old foxhound that pursued a fox through the Grampians for a fortnight, and when at last discovered by the Duke of Athole's people, neither of them could run, but the hound was still continuing to walk after the fox, and when the latter lay down the other lay down beside him, and looked at him steadily all the while, though unable to do him the least harm. The passion of inveterate malice seems to have influenced these two exactly alike. But, upon the whole, I scarcely believe the tale can be true.

MOUNT BENGER,[40]
    Sept. 10, 1828

---

37 Baste: thrash.
38 Haggs: broken-up peat-moor.
39 In Psalm 109 David calls down various disasters on his enemies.
40 Hogg's farm (rented from the Duke of Buccleuch) on the Yarrow, and his place of residence in 1824–30.

THE MYSTERIOUS BRIDE
BY THE ETTRICK SHEPHERD[1]

A GREAT number of people now-a-days are beginning broadly to insinuate that there are no such things as ghosts, or spiritual beings visible to mortal sight. Even Sir Walter Scott is turned renegade, and, with his stories made up of half-and-half, like Nathaniel Gow's toddy,[2] is trying to throw cold water on the most certain, though most impalpable, phenomena of human nature. The bodies are daft. Heaven mend their wits! Before they had ventured to assert such things, I wish they had been where I have often been; or, in particular, where the Laird of Birkendelly was on St Lawrence's Eve,[3] in the year 1777, and sundry times subsequent to that.

Be it known, then, to every reader of this relation of facts that happened in my own remembrance, that the road from Birkendelly to the great muckle village of Balmawhapple, (commonly called the muckle town, in opposition to the little town that stood on the other side of the burn,)—that road, I say, lay between two thorn hedges, so well kept by the Laird's hedger, so close, and so high, that a rabbit could not have escaped from the highway into any of the adjoining fields. Along this road was the Laird riding on the Eve of St Lawrence, in a careless, indifferent manner, with his hat to one side, and his cane dancing a hornpipe on the curtch of the saddle before him.[4] He was, moreover, chanting a song to himself, and I have heard people tell what song it was too. There was once a certain, or rather uncertain, bard, ycleped[5] Robert Burns, who made a number of good songs; but this that the Laird sung was an amorous song of great antiquity, which like all the said bard's best songs, was sung one hundred and fifty years before he was born. It began thus:

> "I am the Laird of Windy-wa's
> I cam nae here without a cause,
> An' I hae gotten forty fa's
>   In coming o'er the knowe, joe!
>
> The night it is baith wind an weet;
> The morn it will be snaw and sleet;
> My shoon are frozen to my feet;
>   O, rise an' let me in, joe!
>   Let me in this ae night," &c. &c.

This song was the Laird singing, while, at the same time, he was smudging and laughing at the catastrophe, when, ere ever aware, he beheld, a short way before him, an uncommonly elegant and beautiful girl walking in the same direction with him. "Aye," said the Laird to himself, "here is something very attractive indeed! Where the deuce can she have sprung from? She must have risen out of the earth, for I never saw her till this breath. Well, I declare I have not seen such a female figure—I wish I had such an assignation with her as the Laird of Windy-wa's had with his sweetheart."

---

1   From *Blackwood's Edinburgh Magazine* XXVIII (Dec. 1830): 943–50.
2   Nathaniel Gow (1766–1831) was a celebrated fiddler, band-leader, composer and music publisher, but this is the only evidence we have of his sensible drinking-habits.
3   As the story goes on to tell us, this is 9th August.
4   A curch is usually a woman's headscarf: Hogg may mean no more than the covering of the saddle.
5   Ycleped: called. A Spenserian archaism.

As the Laird was half-thinking, half-speaking this to himself, the enchanting creature looked back at him with a motion of intelligence that she knew what he was half-saying, half-thinking, and then vanished over the summit of the rising ground before him, called the Birky Brow. "Aye, go your ways!" said the Laird; "I see by you, you'll not be very hard to overtake. You cannot get off the road, and I'll have a chat with you before you make the Deer's Den."

The Laird jogged on. He did not sing "The Laird of Windy-wa's" any more, for he felt a sort of stifling about his heart; but he often repeated to himself, "She's a very fine woman! — A very fine woman indeed — and to be walking here by herself! I cannot comprehend it."

When he reached the summit of the Birky Brow he did not see her, although he had a longer view of the road than before. He thought this very singular, and began to suspect that she wanted to escape him, although apparently rather lingering on him before. "I shall have another look at her, however," thought the Laird; and off he set at a flying trot. No. He came to one turn, then another. There was nothing of the young lady to be seen. "Unless she take wings and fly away, I shall be up with her," quoth the Laird; and off he set at the full gallop.

In the middle of his career he met with Mr McMurdie of Aulton, who hailed him with, "Hilloa! Birkendelly! where the deuce are you flying at that rate?"

"I was riding after a woman," said the Laird, with great simplicity, reining in his steed.

"Then I am sure no woman on earth can long escape you, unless she be in an air balloon."[6]

"I don't know that. Is she far gone?"

"In which way do you mean?"

"In this."

"Aha-ha-ha! Hee-hee-hee!" nichered McMurdie, misconstruing the Laird's meaning.

"What do you laugh at, my dear sir? Do you know her, then?"

"Ho-ho-ho! Hee-hee-hee! How should I, or how can I, know her, Birkendelly, unless you inform me who she is?"

"Why, that is the very thing I want to know of you. I mean the young lady whom you met just now."

"You are raving, Birkendelly. I met no young lady, nor is there a single person on the road I have come by, while you know, that for a mile and a half forward your way, she could not get out of it."

"I know that," said the Laird, biting his lip, and looking greatly puzzled; "but confound me if I understand this; for I was within speech of her just now on the top of the Birky Brow there; and, when I think of it, she could not have been even thus far as yet. She had on a pure white gauze frock, a small green bonnet and feathers, and a green veil, which, flung back over her left shoulder, hung below her waist; and was altogether such an engaging figure, that no man could have passed her on the road without taking some note of her. — Are you not making game of me? Did you really not meet with her?"

"On my word of truth and honour, I did not. Come, ride back with me, and we shall meet her still, depend on it. She has given you the go-by on the road. Let us go; I am only going to call at the mill about some barley for the distillery, and will return with

6   Either Mr McMurdie is very well informed about the experiments of the Montgolfier brothers in France, or Hogg has forgotten that their first public balloon-flight was not until six years later in 1783.

you to the big town."

Birkendelly returned with his friend. The sun was not yet set, yet McMurdie could not help observing that the Laird looked thoughtful and confused, and not a word could he speak about anything save this lonely apparition with the white frock and the green veil; and lo, when they reached the top of the Birky Brow, there was the maiden again before them, and exactly at the same spot where the Laird first saw her before, only walking in the contrary direction.

"Well, this is the most extraordinary thing that I ever knew!" exclaimed the Laird.

"What is it, sir?" said McMurdie.

"How that young lady could have eluded me," returned the Laird; "see, here she is still."

"I beg your pardon, sir, I don't see her. Where is she?"

"There, on the other side of the angle; but you are short-sighted. See, there she is ascending the other eminence in her white frock and green veil, as I told you—What a lovely creature!"

"Well, well, we have her fairly before us now, and shall see what she is like at all events," said McMurdie.

Between the Birky Brow and this other slight eminence, there is an obtuse angle of the road at the part where it is lowest, and in passing this, the two friends necessarily lost sight of the object of their curiosity. They pushed on at a quick pace—cleared the low angle—the maiden was not there! They rode full speed to the top of the eminence from whence a long extent of road was visible before them—there was no human creature in view! McMurdie laughed aloud; but the Laird turned pale as death, and bit his lip. His friend asked at him, good-humouredly, why he was so much affected. He said, because he could not comprehend the meaning of this singular apparition or illusion, and it troubled him the more, as he now remembered a dream of the same nature which he had had, and which terminated in a dreadful manner.

"Why, man, you are dreaming still," said McMurdie; "But never mind. It is quite common for men of your complexion to dream of beautiful maidens, with white frocks and green veils, bonnets, feathers, and slender waists. It is a lovely image, the creation of your own sanguine imagination, and you may worship it without any blame. Were her shoes black or green?—and her stockings, did you note them? The symmetry of the limbs, I am sure you did! Good-bye; I see you are not disposed to leave the spot. Perhaps she will appear to you again."

So saying, McMurdie rode on towards the mill, and Birkendelly, after musing for some time, turned his beast's head slowly round, and began again to move towards the great muckle village.

The Laird's feelings were now in terrible commotion. He was taken beyond measure with the beauty and elegance of the figure he had seen; but he remembered, with a mixture of admiration and horror, that a dream of the same enchanting object had haunted his slumbers all the days of his life; yet how singular that he should never have recollected the circumstance till now! But farther, with the dream there were connected some painful circumstances, which though terrible in their issue, he could not recollect, so as to form them into any degree of arrangement.

As he was considering deeply of these things, and riding slowly down the declivity, neither dancing his cane, nor singing the "Laird of Windywa's," he lifted up his eyes, and there was the girl on the same spot where he saw her first, walking deliberately up the Birky Brow. The sun was down; but it was the month of August, and a fine evening, and the Laird, seized with an unconquerable desire to see and speak with that incomparable creature, could restrain himself no longer, but shouted out to her to stop till he came up. She beckoned acquiescence, and slackened her pace into a slow movement. The Laird turned the corner quickly, but when he had rounded it, the maiden was still there, though on the very summit of the Brow. She turned round, and, with an ineffable smile and curtsy, saluted him, and again moved slowly on. She vanished gradually beyond the summit, and while the green feathers were still nodding in view and so nigh, that the Laird could have touched them with a fishing rod, he reached the top of the Brow himself. There was no living soul there, nor onward, as far as his view reached. He now trembled every limb, and, without knowing what he did, rode straight on to the big town, not daring well to return and see what he had seen for three several times; and, certain that he would see it again when the shades of evening were deepening, he deemed it proper and prudent to decline the pursuit of such a phantom any further.

He alighted at the Queen's Head, called for some brandy and water, quite forgot what was his errand to the great muckle town that afternoon, there being nothing visible to his mental sight but lovely fairy images, with white gauze frocks and green veils. His friend, Mr McMurdie, joined him; they drank deep, bantered, reasoned, got angry, reasoned themselves calm again, and still all would not do. The Laird was conscious that he had seen the beautiful apparition, and, moreover, that she was the very maiden, or the resemblance of her, who, in the irrevocable decrees of Providence, was destined to be his. It was in vain that McMurdie reasoned of impressions on the imagination, and

"Of fancy moulding on the mind
Light visions on the passing wind."[7]

Vain also was a story that he told him of a relation of his own, who was greatly harrassed by the apparition of an officer in a red uniform, that haunted him day and night, and had very nigh put him quite distracted several times; till at length his physician found out the nature of this illusion so well, that he knew, from the state of his pulse, to an hour when the ghost of the officer would appear, and by bleeding, low diet, and emollients, contrived to keep the apparition away altogether.

The Laird admitted the singularity of this incident, but not that it was one in point; for the one, he said, was imaginary, and the other real; and that no conclusions could convince him in opposition to the authority of his own senses. He accepted of an invitation to spend a few days with McMurdie and his family; but they all acknowledged afterwards that the Laird was very much like one bewitched.

As soon as he reached home he went straight to the Birky-Brow, certain of seeing once more the angelic phantom; but she was not there. He took each of his former positions again and again, but the desired vision would in nowise make its appearance. He tried every day, and every hour of the day, all with the same effect, till he grew absolutely desperate, and had the audacity to kneel on the spot, and entreat of Heaven to see her. Yes, he called on Heaven to see her once more, whatever she was, whether a being of earth, heaven, or hell!

He was now in such a state of excitement that he could not exist; he grew listless, impatient, and sickly; took to his bed, and sent for McMurdie and the doctor; and the issue of the consultation was, that Birkendelly consented to leave the country for a

---

7 Hogg his quoting from his own poem, *The Queen's Wake* (1813), the work that established his fame as a poet.

season, on a visit to his only sister in Ireland, whither we must now accompany him for a short space.

His sister was married to Captain Bryan, younger of Scoresby, and they two lived in a cottage on the estate, and the Captain's parents and sisters at Scoresby Hall. Great was the stir and preparation when the gallant young Laird of Birkendelly arrived at the cottage, it never being doubted that he had come to forward a second bond of connection with the family, which still contained seven dashing sisters, all unmarried, and all alike willing to change that solitary and helpless state for the envied one of matrimony — a state highly popular among the young women of Ireland. Some of the Misses Bryan had not reached the years of womanhood, several of them scarcely; but these small disqualifications made no difference in the estimation of the young ladies themselves; each and all of them brushed up for the competition, with high hopes and unflinching resolutions. True, the elder ones tried to check the younger in their good-natured, forthright, Irish way; but they retorted, and persisted in their superior pretentions. Then there was such shopping in the county-town! It was so boundless, that the credit of the Hall was finally exhausted, and the old squire was driven to remark, that "Och and to be sure it was a dreadful and tirrabell concussion, to be put upon the equipment of seven daughters all at the same moment, as if the young gentleman could marry them all! Och, then, poor dear shoul, he would be after finding that one was sufficient, if not one too many. And, therefore, there was no occasion, none at all, at all, and that there was not, for any of them to rig out more than one."

It was hinted that the Laird had some reason for complaint at this time; but as the lady sided with her daughters, he had no chance. One of the items of his account was, thirty-seven buckling-combs, then greatly in vogue.[8] There were black combs, pale combs, yellow combs, and gilt ones, all to suit or set off various complexions; and if other articles bore any proportion at all to these, it had been better for the Laird and all his family that Birkendelly had never set foot in Ireland.

The plan was all concocted. There was to be a grand dinner at the Hall, at which the damsels were to appear in all their finery. A ball was to follow, and note taken which of the young ladies was their guest's choice, and measures taken accordingly. The dinner and the ball took place, and what a pity I may not describe that entertainment, the dresses, and the dancers for they were all exquisite in their way, and *outré* beyond measure. But such details only serve to derange a winter's evening tale such as this.

Birkendelly having at this time but one model for his choice among womankind, all that ever he did while in the presence of ladies, was to look out for some resemblance to her, the angel of his fancy; and it so happened, that in one of old Bryan's daughters named Luna, or more familiarly, Loony, he perceived, or thought he perceived, some imaginary similarity in form and air to the lovely apparition. This was the sole reason why he was incapable of taking his eyes off from her the whole of that night; and this incident settled the point, not only with the old people, but even the young ladies were forced, after every exertion on their own parts, to "yild the pint to their sister Loony, who certinly was nit the mist ginteelest nor mist handsomest of that guid-lucking fimily."

The next day Lady Luna was dispatched off to the Cottage in grand style, there to live hand and glove with her supposed lover. There was no standing all this. There were the two parrocked together,[9] like a ewe and a lamb, early and late; and though the Laird really appeared to have, and probably had, some delight in her company, it was

---

8   Buckling-combs hold curled hair in place.
9   Parrocked: enclosed in a paddock, often used to name the specific purpose alluded to here of familiarising a ewe with a strange lamb so she will suckle it.

only in contemplating that certain indefinable air of resemblance which she bore to the sole image impressed on his heart. He bought her a white gauze frock, a green bonnet and feathers, with a veil, which she was obliged to wear thrown over her left shoulder; and every day after, six times a-day, was she obliged to walk over a certain eminence at a certain distance before her lover. She was delighted to oblige him; but still when he came up, he looked disappointed and never said, "Luna, I love you; when are we to be married?" No, he never said any such thing, for all her looks and expressions of fondest love; for, alas, in all this dalliance, he was only feeding a mysterious flame, that preyed upon his vitals, and proved too severe for the powers either of reason or religion to extinguish. Still time flew lighter and lighter by, his health was restored, the bloom of his cheek returned, and the frank and simple confidence of Luna had a certain charm with it, that reconciled him to his sister's Irish economy.[10] But a strange incident now happened to him which deranged all his immediate plans.

He was returning from angling one evening, a little before sunset, when he saw Lady Luna awaiting him on his way home. But instead of brushing up to meet him as usual, she turned, and walked up the rising ground before him. "Poor sweet girl! how condescending she is!" said he to himself, "and how like she is in reality to the angelic being whose form and features are so deeply impressed on my heart! I now see it is no fond or fancied resemblance. It is real! real! real! How I long to clasp her in my arms, and tell her how I love her; for, after all, that is the girl that is to be mine, and the former a vision to impress this the more on my heart."

He posted up the ascent to overtake her. When at the top she turned, smiled, and curtsied. Good Heavens! it was the identical Lady of his fondest adoration herself, but lovelier, far lovelier than ever. He expected every moment that she would vanish as was her wont; but she did not—she awaited him, and received his embraces with open arms. She was a being of real flesh and blood, courteous, elegant, and affectionate. He kissed her hand, he kissed her glowing cheek, and blessed all the powers of love who had thus restored her to him again, after undergoing pangs of love such as man never suffered.

"But, dearest heart, here we are standing in the middle of the high way," said he; "suffer me to conduct you to my sister's house, where you shall have an apartment with a child of nature having some slight resemblance to yourself." She smiled, and said, "No, I will not sleep with Lady Luna to-night. Will you please to look round you, and see where you are." He did so, and behold they were standing on the Birky Brow, on the only spot where he had ever seen her. She smiled at his embarrassed look, and asked if he did not remember aught of his coming over from Ireland. He said he thought he did remember something of it, but love with him had long absorbed every other sense. He then asked her to his own house, which she declined, saying she could only meet him on that spot till after their marriage, which could not be before St Lawrence's Eve come three years. "And now," says she, "we must part. My name is Jane Ogilvie, and you were betrothed to me before you were born. But I am come to release you this evening, if you have the slightest objection."

He declared he had none; and, kneeling, swore the most solemn oath to be hers for ever, and to meet her there on St Lawrence's Eve next, and every St. Lawrence's Eve until that blessed day on which she had consented to make him happy, by becoming his own for ever. She then asked him affectionately to exchange rings with her, in pledge of their faith and troth, in which he joyfully acquiesced; for she could not have then asked any conditions, which, in the fulness of his heart's love, he would not have granted; and after one fond and affectionate kiss, and repeating all their engagements over again, they parted.

---

10 I.e. domestic economy, housekeeping.

Birkendelly's heart was now melted within him, and all his senses overpowered by one overwhelming passion. On leaving his fair and kind one, he got bewildered, and could not find the road to his own house, believing sometimes that he was going there, and sometimes to his sister's, till at length he came, as he thought, upon the Liffey, at its junction with Loch Allan; and there, in attempting to call for a boat, he awoke from a profound sleep, and found himself lying in his bed within his sister's house, and the day sky just breaking.

If he was puzzled to account for some things in the course of his dream, he was much more puzzled to account for them now that he was wide awake. He was sensible that he had met his love, had embraced, kissed, and exchanged vows and rings with her, and in token of the truth and reality of all these, her emerald ring was on his finger, and his own away; so there was no doubt that they had met, — by what means it was beyond the power of man to calculate.

There was then living with Mrs Bryan an old Scotswoman commonly styled Lucky Black. She had nursed Birkendelly's mother and been dry-nurse to himself and sister; and having more than a mother's attachment for the latter, when she was married, old Lucky left her country to spend the last of her days in the house of her beloved young lady. When the Laird entered the breakfast parlour that morning, she was sitting in her black velvet hood, as usual, reading "The Fourfold State of Man,"[11] and being paralytic and somewhat deaf, she seldom regarded those who went out or came in. But chancing to hear him say something about the ninth of August, she quitted reading, turned round her head to listen, and then asked, in a hoarse tremulous voice, "What's that he's saying? What's the unlucky callant saying about the ninth of August?[12] Aih? To be sure it is St Lawrence's Eve, although the tenth be his day. It is ower true, ower true![13] ower true for him an' a' his kin, poor man! Aih? What was he saying then?"

The men smiled at her incoherent earnestness, but the lady, with true feminine condescension, informed her, in a loud voice, that Allan had an engagement in Scotland on St Lawrence's Eve. She then started up, extended her shrivelled hands, that shook like the aspen, and panted out, "Aih, aih? Lord preserve us! whaten an engagement has he on St Lawrence's Eve? Bind him! Bind him! Shackle him wi' bands of steel, and of brass, and of iron! — O, may He whose blessed will was pleased to leave him an orphan sae soon, preserve him from the fate which I tremble to think on!"

She then tottered round the table, as with supernatural energy, and seizing the Laird's right hand she drew it close to her unstable eyes, and then, perceiving the emerald ring chased in blood, she threw up her arms with a jerk, opened her skinny jaws with a fearful gape, and uttering a shriek, that made all the house yell, and every one within it to tremble, she fell back lifeless and rigid on the floor. The gentlemen both fled, out of sheer terror; but a woman never deserts her friends in extremity. The lady called her maids about her, had her old nurse conveyed to bed, where every means were used to restore animation. But, alas! life was extinct! The vital spark had fled for ever, which filled all their hearts with grief, disappointment, and horror, as some dreadful tale of mystery was now sealed up from their knowledge, which in all likelihood no other could reveal. But to say the truth, the Laird did not seem greatly disposed to probe it to the bottom.

Not all the arguments of Captain Bryan and of his lady, nor the simple entreaties of

---

11 Thomas Boston, *Human Nature in its Fourfold State* (1730), a classic of Calvinist theology in the eighteenth century. Its author was long a minister in Ettrick.

12 Callant: boy or young man.

13 Ower true: too true.

Lady Luna, could induce Birkendelly to put off his engagement to meet with his love on the Birky Brow on the evening of the 9th of August; but he promised soon to return, pretending that some business of the utmost importance called him away. Before he went, however, he asked his sister if ever she had heard of such a lady in Scotland as Jane Ogilvie? Mrs Bryan repeated the name many times to herself, and said that name undoubtedly was once familiar to her, although she thought not for good, but at that moment she did not recollect one single individual of the name. He then showed her the emerald ring that had been the death of old Lucky Black; but the moment the lady looked at it, she made a grasp at it to take it off by force, which she had very nearly effected. "O, burn it, burn it!" cried she; "it is not a right ring! Burn it!"

"My dear sister, what fault is in the ring?" said he. "It is a very pretty ring, and one that I set great value by."

"O, for Heaven's sake, burn it, and renounce the giver!" cried she. "If you have any regard for your peace here, or your soul's welfare hereafter, burn that ring! If you saw with your own eyes, you would easily perceive that that is not a ring befitting a Christian to wear."

This speech confounded Birkendelly a good deal. He retired by himself and examined the ring, and could see nothing in it unbecoming a Christian to wear. It was a chased gold ring, with a bright emerald, which last had a red foil, in some lights giving it a purple gleam, and inside was engraved "*Elegit*," much defaced, but that his sister could not see;[14] therefore he could not comprehend her vehement injunctions concerning it. But that it might no more give her offence, or any other, he sewed it within his vest, opposite his heart, judging that there was something in it which his eyes were withholden from discerning.

Thus he left Ireland with his mind in great confusion, groping his way, as it were, in a hole of mystery, yet the passion that preyed on his heart and vitals more intense than ever. He seems to have had an impression all his life that some mysterious fate awaited him, which the correspondence of his dreams and day visions tended to confirm. And though he gave himself wholly up to the sway of one overpowering passion, it was not without some yearnings of soul, manifestations of terror, and so much earthly shame that he never more mentioned his love, or his engagements, to any human being, not even to his friend McMurdie, whose company he forthwith shunned.

It is on this account that I am unable to relate what passed between the lovers thenceforward. It is certain that they met at the Birky Brow that St. Lawrence's Eve, for they were seen in company together; but of the engagements, vows, or dalliance, that passed between them, I can say nothing; nor of all their future meetings, until the beginning of August 1781, when he began decidedly to make preparations for his approaching marriage; yet not as if he and his betrothed had been to reside at Birkendelly, all his provision rather bespeaking a premeditated journey.

On the morning of the 9th, he wrote to his sister, and then arraying himself in his new wedding suit, and putting the emerald ring on his finger, he appeared all impatience, until towards evening, when he sallied out on horseback to his appointment. It seems that his mysterious inamorata had met him, for he was seen riding through the Big Town before sunset, with a young lady behind him, dressed in white and green, and the villagers affirmed that they were riding at the rate of fifty miles an hour! They were seen to pass a cottage called Mosskilt, ten miles farther on, where there was no highway, at the same tremendous speed; and I could never hear that they were any

14   An 'elegit' is a writ granting a creditor the goods and lands of a debtor to the value of the debt.

more seen; until the following morning, when Birkendelly's fine bay horse was found lying dead at his own stable door; and shortly after, his master was likewise discovered lying a blackened corpse on the Birky Brow, at the very spot where the mysterious, but lovely dame, had always appeared to him. There was neither wound, bruise, nor dislocation, in his whole frame; but his skin was of a livid colour, and his features terribly distorted.

This woful catastrophe struck the neighbourhood with great consternation, so that nothing else was talked of. Every ancient tradition and modern incident were raked together, compared, and combined; and certainly a most rare concatenation of misfortunes was elicited. It was authenticated that his father had died on the same spot that day twenty years, and his grandfather that day forty years, the former, as was supposed, by a fall from his horse when in liquor, and the latter, nobody knew how; and now this Allan was the last of his race for Mrs Bryan had no children.

It was moreover now remembered by many, and among the rest, the Rev. Joseph Taylor, that he had frequently observed a young lady, in white and green, sauntering about that spot on a St Lawrence's Eve.

When Captain Bryan and his lady arrived to take possession of the premises, they instituted a strict enquiry into every circumstance; but nothing further than what was related to them by Mr McMurdie could be learned of this Mysterious Bride, beside what his own letter bore. It ran thus:—

"DEAREST SISTER,

"I shall, before this time to-morrow, be the most happy, or most miserable, of mankind, having solemnly engaged myself this night to wed a young and beautiful lady, named Jane Ogilvie, to whom it seems I was betrothed before I was born. Our correspondence has been of a most private and mysterious nature; but my troth is pledged, and my resolution fixed. We set out on a far journey to the place of her abode on the nuptial eve, so that it will be long before I see you again.

"Yours till death,

"ALLAN GEORGE SANDISON.

"*Birkendelly, August* 8th, 1781."

That very same year, an old woman, named Marrion Haw, was returned upon that, her native parish, from Glasgow. She had led a migratory life with her son—who was what he called a bell-hanger, but in fact a tinker of the worst grade—for many years, and was at last returned to the muckle town in a state of great destitution.[15] She gave the parishioners a history of the Mysterious Bride, so plausibly correct, but withal so romantic, that every body said of it, (as is often said of my narratives, with the same narrow-minded prejudice and injustice,) that it was *a made story*. There were, however, some strong testimonies of its veracity.

She said the first Allan Sandison, who married the great heiress of Birkendelly, was previously engaged to a beautiful young lady, named Jane Ogilvie, to whom he gave any thing but fair play; and, as she believed, either murdered her, or caused her to be murdered, in the midst of a thicket of birch and broom, at a spot which she mentioned; that she had good reasons for believing so, as she had seen the red blood and the new grave, when she was a little girl, and ran home and mentioned it to her grandfather, who charged her as she valued her life never to mention that again, as it was only the

---

15 Under the old Poor Law, provision for the destitute was a matter for the parish in which they were born and could only be made if they returned there.

numbles and hide of a deer, which he himself had buried there.[16] But when, twenty years subsequent to that, the wicked and unhappy Allan Sandison was found dead on that very spot, and lying across the green mound, then nearly level with the surface, which she had once seen a new grave, she then for the first time ever thought of a Divine Providence; and she added, "for my grandfather, Neddy Haw, he dee'd too; there's naebody kens how, nor ever shall."

As they were quite incapable of conceiving from Marrion's description, any thing of the spot, Mr McMurdie caused her to be taken out to the Birky Brow in a cart, accompanied by Mr Taylor, and some hundreds of the townsfolk; but whenever she saw it, she said "Aha, birkies! the hale kintra's altered now. There was nae road here then; It gaed straight ower the tap o' the hill. An' let me see—there's the thorn where the cushats biggit;[17] an' there's the auld birk that I aince fell off an' left my shoe stickin' i' the cleft. I can tell ye, birkies, either the deer's grave, or bonny Jane Ogilvie's, is no twa yards off the place where that horse's hind feet are standin'; sae ye may howk, an' see if there be ony remains."

The minister, and McMurdie, and all the people, stared at one another, for they had purposely caused the horse to stand still on the very spot where both the father and son had been found dead. They digged, and deep, deep below the road, they found part of the slender bones and skull of a young female, which they deposited decently in the churchyard. The family of the Sandisons is extinct—the Mysterious Bride appears no more on the Eve of St Lawrence—and the wicked people of the great muckle village have got a lesson on Divine justice written to them in lines of blood.

---

16 Numbles: innards. Penalties for poaching included death, so the grandfather's pretence (if that's what it is) works to silence the child.
17 I.e. where the pigeons made their nests.

SEEKING THE HOUDY.
BY THE ETTRICK SHEPHERD.[1]

THERE was a shepherd on the lands of Meggat-dale,[2] who once set out riding with might and main, under cloud of night, for that most important and necessary personage in a remote and mountainous country, called by a different name in every country of the world, excepting perhaps Egypt and England; but by the Highlanders most expressively termed beanglhuine or te she toctor.

The mare that Robin rode was a black one, with a white face like a cow. She had a great big belly, a switch tail, and a back, Robin said, as sharp as a knife; but perhaps this part of the description was rather exaggerated. However, she was laziness itself personified, and the worst thing of all, her foal was closed in at home; for Robin had wiled the mare and foal into the bire with a piece of bread, which he did not give her after all, but put in his pocket in case of farther necessity: he then whipped a hair halter on the mare's head, and the straw sunks on her back,[3] these being the only equipment within his reach; and it having cost Robin a great deal of trouble to get the foal into the bire, he now eyed him with an exulting, and at the same time a malicious, look. 'Ye mischievous rascal,' said he, 'I think I have you now; stand you there an' chack flees till I come back to teach you better manners.'[4]

Robin then hurried out the mare to the side of the kail-yeard dike, and calling out to Jean his wife not to be in ower grit a hurry, and to exercise all the patience she was mistress of, he flew on the yaud's back,[5] and off he went at full gallop.

The hair halter that Robin rode with had a wooden snibbelt upon the end of it, as all hair halters had erewhile, when there were no other bridles in Meggat, saving branks and hair halters annexed;[6] consequently with the further end of this halter one could hit an exceeding hard stroke. Indeed, I never saw anything in my life that hurt so sore as a hair halter and wooden snibbelt at the end of it; and I may here mention, as an instance of its efficacy, that there was once a boy at Hartwood mires, near Selkirk, who killed with a snibbelt two Highland soldiers, who came to press his horses in the forty-five.[7]

Well, to this halter and snibbelt Robin had trusted for a rod, there being no wood in Meggat-dale, not so much as a tree; and a more unlucky and dangerous goad he could scarcely have possessed, and that the black mare, with a white face like a cow, felt to her experience. Robin galloped by the light of the full moon down by the Butt-haugh and Glengaber-foot about as fast as a good horse walks; still he was galloping, and could make no more of it, although he was every now and then lending the yaud a yerk on the flank with the snibbelt. But when he came to Henderland, to which place the mare was accustomed to go every week to meet the eggler,[8] then Robin and the mare split in their opinions. Robin thought it the most natural and reasonable thing in the world that the mare should push on to the sandbed, about eight miles further, to bring

---

1   From *The Forget Me Not for 1830*. This was one of several series that appeared annually, consisting of collections of stories, poems and other improving material, designed to be given as presents and marketed specifically at female readers.

2   Megget Water feeds Saint Mary's Loch on the Yarrow. The places referred to in this story are all real.

3   Sunks (Sc.): saddle.

4   Chack: bite, snap.

5   Yaud (Sc.): jade, old horse.

6   Snibbelt: a piece of wood on a halter used to help tether an animal; branks: bridle (both Sc.).

7   I.e. in the Jacobite rebellion of 1745.

8   Yerk: blow; eggler: egg merchant (both Sc.).

home the wise woman to his beloved wife's assistance. The mare thought exactly the reverse, being inwardly convinced that the most natural and reasonable path she could take was the one straight home again to her foal; and without any farther ceremony, save giving a few switches with her long illshapen tail, she set herself with all her might to dispute the point with Robin.

Then there was such a battle commenced as never was fought at the foot of Henderland-bank at midnight either before or since. O my beloved and respected editor and readers! I wish I could make you understand the humour of this battle as well as I do. The branks were two sticks hung by a headsteel, which, when one drew the halter hard, nipped the beast's nose most terribly; but when they were all made in one way, and could only turn the beast to the nearside. Now the black mare did not, or could not, resist this agency of the branks; she turned round as often as Robin liked, but not one step farther would she proceed on the road to Sandbed. So roundabout and roundabout the two went; and the mare, by a very clever expedient, contrived at every circle to work twice her own length nearer home. Saint Sampson! how Robin did lay on with the halter and snibbelt whenever he got her head round towards the way he wanted her to go! No—round she came again! He cursed her, he flattered her, he reminded her of the precarious state of her mistress, who had so often filled her manger; but all would not do: she thought only of the precarious state of her foal, closed in an old void smearing-house.[9]

Robin at last fell upon a new stratagem, which was this, that as the mare wheeled round whenever her head reached the right point, he hit her a yerk with the wooden snibbelt on the near cheek, to stop that millstone motion of hers. This occasioned some furious plunges, but no advancement the right way, till at length he hit her such a pernicious blow somewhere near about the ear, that he brought her smack to the earth in a moment; and so much was he irritated, that he laid on her when down, and nodding like ane falling asleep. After two or three prolonged groans, she rose again, and, thus candidly admonished, made no further resistance for the present, but moved on apace to the time of the halter and the snibbelt. In reaching a ravine called Capper Cleuch, the mare, coming again in some degree to her senses, perceived that she was not where she ought to have been, at least where it was her interest, and the interest of her foal, that she should have been; and, raising her white face, she uttered a tremendous neigh. The hills to the left are there steep and rocky; and the night being calm and frosty, first one fine echo neighed out of the hill, then another, and then another. 'There are plenty of foals here,' thought the old mare; and neighing again even louder than before, she was again answered in the same way; and, perceiving an old crabbed thorn-tree among the rocks, in the direction whence the echo proceeded, it struck her obtuse head that it was her great lubber of a foal standing on very perilous ground;[10] and off she set at a right angle from the road, or rather a left one, with her utmost speed, braying as she went, while every scream was returned by her shaggy colt with interest. It was in vain that Robin pulled by the hair halter, and smote her on the cheek with the wooden snibbelt: away she ran, through long heath and large stones, with a tremendous and uncultivated rapidity, neighing as she flew. 'Wo! ye jaud! Hap-wo! chywooo!' shouted Robin; 'Hap-wo! hap-wo! Devil confound the beast, for I'm gone!'

Nothing would stay her velocity till she stabled herself against a rock over which she could not win, and then Robin lost no time in throwing himself from her back. Many and bitter were the epithets he there bestowed on his old mare, and grievous was the

9   'Smearing' is treating sheep with tar to kill parasites.
10   Lubber: lazy thing.

lamentation he made for his wife, as endeavouring to lead back the mare from the rocky hill into the miserable track of a road. No; the plague o' one foot would the mare move in that direction! She held out her long nose, with her white muslin face, straight up to heaven, as if contemplating the moon. She weened that her foal was up among the crags, and put on a resolution not to leave him a second time for any man's pleasure. After all, Robin confessed that he had some excuse for her, for the shadow of the old thorn was so like a colt, that he could scarcely reason himself out of the belief that it was one.

Robin was now hardly set indeed, for the mare would not lead a step; and when he came back to her side to leather her with the snibbelt, she only galloped round him and round him, and neighed. 'O plague on you for a beast that ever you were foaled!' exclaimed Robin; 'I shall lose a dearly beloved wife, and perhaps a couple of babies at least, and all owing to your stupidity and obstinacy! I could soon run on foot to the Sandbed, but then I cannot carry the midwife home on my back; and could I once get you there, you would not be long in bringing us both home again. Plague on you for a beast, if I winna knock your brains out!'

Robin now attacked the mare's white face with the snibbelt, yerk for yerk, so potently, that the mare soon grew madly crazed, and came plunging and floundering from the hill at a great rate. Robin thus found out a secret not before known in this country, on which he acted till the day of his death; namely, 'that the best way to make a horse spring forward is to strike it on the face.'

Once more on the path, Robin again mounted, sparing neither the mare nor the halter; while the mare, at every five or six paces, entertained him with a bray so loud, with its accompanying nicker, that every one made the hills ring again.

There is scarcely any thing a man likes worse than this constant neighing of the steed he rides upon, especially by night. It makes him start as from a reverie, and puts his whole frame in commotion. Robin did not like it more than other men. It caused him inadvertently to utter some imprecations on the mare, that he confessed he should not have uttered; but it also caused him to say some short prayers for preservation; and to which of these agencies he owed the following singular adventure he never could divine.

Robin had got only about half a mile farther on his road, when his mare ceased her braying, and all at once stood stone-still, cocking her large ears, and looking exceedingly frightened. 'Oho, madam! what's the matter now?' said Robin; 'is this another stratagem to mar my journey, for all the haste that you see me in? Get on, my fine yaud, get on! There is nothing uncanny there.'

Robin coaxed thus, as well to keep up his own spirits, as to encourage his mare; for the truth is, that his hair began to stand on end with affright. The mare would neither ride, lead, nor drive, one step further; but there she stood, staring, snuffing the wind, and snorting so loud, that it was frightsome to hear as well as to see her. This was the worst dilemma of all. What was our forlorn shepherd to do now? He averred that the mare would not go on either by force or art; but I am greatly deceived, if by this time he durst for his life have gone on, even though the mare could have been induced to proceed. He took the next natural expedient, which was that of shouting out as loud as he could bellow, 'Hilloa! who's there? Be ye devils, be ye witches, or be ye Christian creatures, rise an' shaw yoursels. I say, hilloa! who's there?'

Robin was at this time standing hanging by the mare's hair halter with both his hands, for she was capering and flinging up her white face with such violence, that she sometimes made him bob off the ground; when, behold! at his last call, a being like a woman rose from among some deep heather bushes about twenty yards before him. She was like an elderly female, dressed in a coarse country garb, tall and erect; and there she stood for a space, with her pale face, on which the moon shone full, turned straight towards Robin. He then heard her muttering something to herself; and, with a half-stifled laugh, she stooped down, and lifted something from among the heath, which Robin thought resembled a baby. 'There the gipsy yaud has been murdering that poor bairn!' thought Robin to himself: 'it was nae wonder my auld yaud was frighted! she kens what's what, for as contrarysome as she is. And murderess though the hizzy be, it is out o' my power to pursue her wi' this positive auld hack, for no another foot nearer her will she move.'

Robin never thought but that the mysterious being was to fly from him, or at least go off the road to one side; but in place of that she rolled her baby, or bundle, or whatever it was, deliberately up in a blanket, fastened it between her shoulders, and came straight up to the place where Robin stood hanging by his mare's head. The mare was perfectly mad. She reared, snorted, and whisked her long ill-shaped tail; but Robin held her, for he was a strong young man, and the hair halter must have been proportionably so, else it never could have stood the exercise of that eventful night.

Though I have heard Robin tell the story oftener than once when I was a boy, there was always a confusion here which I never understood. This may be accounted for, in some measure, by supposing that Robin was himself in such perplexity and confusion, that he neither knew well what passed, nor remembered it afterwards. As far as I recollect, the following was the dialogue that passed between the two.

'Wha's this?'

'What need ye speer, goodman? kend fo'k, gin it war daylight.'[11]

'I think I'm a wee bit at a loss. I dinna ken ye.'

'May be no, for ye never saw me afore. An' yet it is a queer thing for a father no to ken his ain daughter.'

'Ay, that wad be a queer thing indeed. But where are you gaun at this time o' the night?'

'Where am I gaun? where but up to the Craigyrigg to get part o' my ain blithemeat.[12] But where are you riding at sic a rate?'

'Why, I'm just riding my whole might for the houdy: an' that's very true, I hae little need to stand claverin here wi' you.'[13]

'Ha, ha, ha, ha! daddy Robin! It is four hours sin' ye came frae hame, an' ye're no won three miles yet. Why, man, afore ye get to the Sandbed an' hame again, your daughter will be ready for spaining.'[14]

'Daughter! what's a' this about a daughter! Has my dear Jean really a daughter?'

'You may be sure she has, else I could not have been here.'

'An' has she only ane? for, od! ye maun ken wifie that I expectit twa at the fewest. But I dinna understand you. I wish ye may be canny enough, for my white-faced yaud seems to jalouse otherwise.'[15]

'Ye dinna ken me, Robin, but ye will ken me. I am Helen Grieve. I was weel brought up, and married to a respectable farmer's son; but he turned out a villain, and, among other qualifications, was a notorious thief; so that I have been reduced to this that you see, to travel the country with a pack, and lend women a helping-hand in their hour o' need. An', Robin, when you and I meet here again, you may be preparing for another world.'

'I dinna comprehend ye at a', wifie. No; a' that I can do, I canna comprehend ye. But I understand thus far. It seems ye are a houdy, or a meedwife, as the grit fo'ks will ca'

---

11 Speer: ask; kend: known; 'You'd recognise me if it were daylight' (all Sc.).
12 Blithemeat (Sc.): meal celebrating birth of a child.
13 Clavering (Sc.): chattering.
14 Spaining (Sc.): weaning.
15 Jalouse (Sc.): suspect.

you. Now that's the very thing I want at present, for your helping hand may be needfu' yonder. Come on ahint me, and we'll soon be hame.'[16]

I must give the expedition home in Robin's own words.

'Weel, I forces my yaud into the Cleuch-brae, contrary as she was, wi' her white face, for she had learned by this time to take a wee care o' the timmer snibbelt. I was on her back in a jiffey; an', to say truth, the kerling wi' the pale round face,[17] and the bit lang bundle on her back, wasna slack; for she was on ahint me, bundle an' a', ere ever I kend I was on mysel. But, Gude forgie us! sickan a voyage as we gat! I declare my yaud gae a snore that gart a' the hills ring, an' the verra fire flew frae her snirls.[18] Out of the Cleuch-brae she sprang, as there hadna been a bane or a joint within her hide, but her hale carcass made o' steel springs; an' ower bush, ower breer, ower stock, an' ower stane she flew, I declare, an' so be it, faster than ever an eagle flew through the firmament of the heavens.

'I kend then that I had either a witch or a mermaid on ahint me; but how was I now to get quit o' her? The hair halter had lost a' power, an' I had no other shift left, than to fix by instinct on the mane wi' baith hands, an' cry out to the mare to stop. "Wo ye auld viper o' the pit! wo, ye beast o' Bashan!"[19] I cries in outer desperation; but ay the louder I cried, the faster did the glyde flee. She snored, an' she grained, an' she reirdit baith ahint an' afore;[20] an' on she dashed, regardless of a' danger.

'I soon lost sight o' the ground—off gaed my bonnet, an' away i' the wind—off gaed my plaid, an' away i' the wind; an' there was I sitting lootching forret, cleaving the wind like an arrow out of a bow, an' my een rinning pouring like streams of water from the south.[21] At length we came to the Birk-bush Linn! and alangst the very verge of that awsome precipice there was my dementit beast scouring like a fiery dragon. "Lord preserve me!" cried I loud out; an' I hadna weel said the word, till my mare gae a tremendous plunge ower something, I never kend what it was, and then down she came on her nose. No rider could stand this concussion, an' I declare, a' so be it, the meed-wife lost her haud, and ower the precipice she flew head foremost. I just gat ae glisk[22] o' her as she was gaun ower the top o' the birk-bush like a shot stern,[23] an' I heard her gie a waw like a cat; an' that was the last sight I saw o' her.

'I was then hanging by the mane an' the right hough; an', during the moment that my mare took to gather hersel' up, I recovered my seat, but only on the top o' the shoulder, for I couldna win to the right place. The mare flew on as madly as ever; and frae the shoulder I came on to the neck, an' forret, an' forret,[24] piecemeal, till, just as I came to my ain door, I had gotten a grip o' baith the lugs. The foal gae a screed of a nicher; on which the glyde threw up her white face wi' sic a vengeance, that she gart me play at pick-an'-toss up in the air. The foal nichered, an' the mare nichered, an' out came the kimmers;[25] an' I declare, an' so be it, there was I lying in the gutter senseless, wanting the plaid, an' wanting the bonnet, an' nae meedwife at a'; an' that's the truth, sir, I declare, an' so be it.

16 Ahint (Sc.): behind.
17 Kerling (more usually carline) (Sc.): old woman.
18 Sickan: such; gart: made; snirls: sniggers (all Sc.).
19 In the King James Bible, David's complaint in Psalm 22 is that 'Many bulls have compassed me: strong bulls of Bashan have beset me round.'
20 Glyde is another word for an old horse. Ahint an' afore: behind and in front (all Sc.).
21 Een: eyes; gaed: went; looching forret: lurching forward (all Sc.).
22 Ae glisk (Sc.): one glimpse.
23 Shot stern (Sc.): shooting-star.
24 Forret (Sc.): forwards.
25 Kimmers: gossips, old women of the town.

'Then they carried me in, an' they washed me, an' they bathed me, an' at last I came to mysel'; an', to be sure, I had gotten a bonny doughter, an' a' things war gaun on as weel as could be expectit. "What hae ye made o' your plaid, Robin?" says ane. "Whare's your bonnet, Robin?" says another. 'But, gudeness guide us! what's come o' the houdy, Robin? Whare's the meedwife, Robin?' cried they a' at aince. I trow this question gart me glower as I had seen a ghaist. "Och! huh! cried the wives, an' held up their hands; "something has happened! something has happened! We see by his looks! — Robin! what has happened? Whare's the meedwife?"

'"Haud your tongue, Janet Reive; an' haud ye your tongue too, Eppie Dickson," says I, "an' dinna speer that question at me again; for the houdy is where the Lord will, an' where my white-faced yaud was pleased to pit her, and that's in the howe o' the Birk-bush Linn. Gin she be a human creature, she's a' dashed to pieces: but an she be nae a human creature she may gang where she like for me; an' that's true, I declare, an' so be it."'

Now it must strike every reader, as it did me at first and for many years afterwards, that this mysterious nocturnal wanderer gave a most confused and unintelligible account of herself. She was Robin's daughter; her name was Helen Grieve; she was married to such and such a man; and had now become a pedlar, and acted occasionally as a midwife: and finally, when they two met there again, it would be time for Robin to be preparing for another state of existence. Now, in the first place, Robin never had a daughter till that very hour and instant when the woman rose out of the heather-bush and accosted him. All the rest appeared to him like a confused dream, of which he had no comprehension, save that he could never again be prevailed on to pass that way alone at night; for he had an impression that at some time or other he should meet with her again.

But by far the most curious part of this story is yet to come, and it shall be related in few words. Robin went with some others, as soon as it was day, to the Birk-bush Linn, but there was neither body nor blood to be seen, nor any appearance of a person having been killed or hurt. Robin's daughter was christened by the name of Helen, after her maternal grandmother, so that her name was actually Helen Grieve: and from the time that Robin first saw his daughter, there never was a day on which some of her looks did not bring the mysterious midwife to his mind. Thus far the story had proceeded when I heard it related; for I lived twelve months in the family, and the girl was then only about seven years of age. But, strange to relate, the midwife's short history of herself has turned out the exact history of this once lovely girl's life; and Robin, a few days before his death, met her at the Kirk Cleuch, with a bundle on her back, and recognized his old friend in every lineament and article of attire. He related this to his wife as a secret, but added, that 'he did not know whether it was his real daughter whom he met or not.'

Many are the traditions remaining in the country, relative to the seeking of midwives, or houdies, as they are universally denominated all over the south of Scotland; and strange adventures are related as having happened in these precipitate excursions, which were proverbially certain to happen by night. Indeed it would appear, that there hardly ever was a midwife brought, but some incident occurred indicative of the fate or fortunes of the little forthcoming stranger; but, amongst them all, I have selected this as the most remarkable.

I am exceedingly grieved at the discontinuance of midwifery, that primitive and original calling, in this primitive and original country; for never were there such merry groups in Scotland as the midwives and their kimmers in former days, and never was there such store of capital stories and gossip circulated as on these occasions. But those days are over! and alack, and wo is me! no future old shepherd shall tell another tale of SEEKING THE HOUDY!

THE UNEARTHLY WITNESS.[1]
BY THE ETTRICK SHEPHERD.

SIR,

WITH regard to the story which has reached you of the late consternation caused at Castle Gower, by the return of William Tibbers from the grave, and the events following on that phenomenon, I am without doubt enabled to write you at great length. And if a man is allowed to take the evidence of his own senses, I am entitled to vouch for the truth of a part of my narrative.

You knew Mr. William Tibbers, at least I remember of your having met with him. He was a man of that specious cast, of that calm reasoning demeanour, that he had great influence with all the gentlemen of the county, and could have carried any public measure almost that he pleased among them, so purely disinterested did all his motives and arguments appear. He was employed by them all, as a factor, a valuator, a land-letter, and an umpire in all debates. And then such general satisfaction he gave in all cases. O, there was no man like old Willie Tibbers! He was quite a public benefit to the country, and a credit to the class to which he belonged.

So far, so well. This was the opinion of the gentlemen concerning him, at least of all, save one or two, and their shakes of the head, and hems and haws, were quite drowned in the general buzz of approbation. But the sentiments of the common people relating to him differed widely from those of their superiors. They detested him; accounting him a hollow-hearted deceitful person; an extortioner, and one who stuck at no means, provided he could attain his own selfish purposes. They even accused him of some of the worst and most flagrant of crimes heard of among men; and I have heard them say they could prove them. This may, however, have originated in the violence of their prejudices; but there is one thing I know, and there is no worse mark of a man—he was abhorred by his servants, and I do not think one of them would ever have staid a second season with him for double wages. Such was the man, of whose fate you are pleased to enquire, and of whose singular destinies I am now to give you an account.

When the good Sir John died, Mr. Tibbers was chosen by the relatives as acting trustee or factor, on the estate of which he got his will, for the young baronet was abroad in the army; and the rest of the trustees, knowing the late Sir John's embarrassments, cared not to trouble their heads much about it. And, in short, after an altercation of six or seven years, between the young laird and the old factor, the estate was declared bankrupt, and sold, and William Tibbers became the purchaser of the best part of it. The common people of our district made a terrible outcry about this; but the thing was not so extraordinary after all. It is rather a common occurrence for the factor to become the Laird, and I know six or seven very prominent instances of it as having occurred in my own remembrance.

But the young baronet was neither to be holden nor bound. He came home in a great rage to expose the factor and get him hanged, and reverse all the sales of his father's property. As a prelude to this bold undertaking, he summoned a meeting of the friends and trustees of the family, before whom compeared the calm and specious William Tibbers. But the fury, the extravagance, and the utter defiance contained in the young soldier's accusations, had no weight when laid in the balance against the calm

1   From *Fraser's Magazine for Town and Country* II, no. viii (Sept. 1830): 171–8. *Fraser's* was founded in 1830 by William Maginn and Hugh Fraser as, in some ways, a London version of **Blackwood's**. Hogg having fallen out with William Blackwood, it provided a valuable market for his fiction in these later years.

and strong reasoning of Tibbers, who concluded every statement by regretting, with tears, that the case was so, but he made it plain to them that it could not be otherwise. The friends only smiled at the indignation of the young baronet; but acquitted, on every charge, their respected friend, Mr. Tibbers. This decision drove the young soldier beyond all bounds. He threatened his ruinator with the High Court of Justiciary, of which Tibbers highly approved. He threatened him with every sort of vengeance which it is possible for one to inflict on another; and, finally, with a flogging every day when they met, until he should render him up his just rights.

This last threat the soldier was not long in putting in execution, for no sooner had they left the court, than he began and gave him a good lashing with his hunting-whip, cursing him most potently all the while. Tibbers replied to all with a grin of despite, and these words, "O, how sweetly you shall repent of this!" He flogged him afterwards at the market of our county town, and another time at church, or at least on the way from it; on both of which times Tibbers resisted unto blood, which was fine diversion for the soldier, and made him double his stripes.

The country gentlemen deprecated these outrages in unmeasured terms, and said it was a shame to see an old man maltreated in that manner, and that this young bully ought to be legally restrained, for it did not behove that he should be suffered to come among them and take the law into his own hand. Some of them ventured to expostulate with him, but he only sneered at them, and answered, that no body knew how he had been used but himself, and that the old villain had not got one third of what he intended for him as yet; but he hoped he would live to see him hanged, that would be some comfort.

The common people viewed the matter quite in a different light. They were grieved at the violence of the young baronet, who, for his father's sake, was their darling; but it was for his own safety alone that they feared, for they were sure that Tibbers was studying some secret and consummate vengeance upon him. He never in his life, they said, bore a grudge at any one whom he did not ruin, and yet the deed never appeared to proceed from him; and never had he got such cause of offence as from the young baronet. Their predictions were too soon fulfilled, though, in all probability, not in the way Tibbers premeditated. At this time an event happened, which seems to have changed the vantage ground of the parties in a very particular manner.

Here there is a great hole in the ballad, as the old singers were wont to say. My narrative must grow confused, because the real events are not known to me, nor, as far as I can gather, to mortal man. All that was certainly known, is as follows: —

The soldier, who had been watching his opportunity, nay, straining every nerve to discover something that would show the man in his true colours, now gained his purpose. He discovered him in some deadly crime, with full proof of its commission; of this there is no doubt. But what that crime was, or whether committed at that time or on a former day, I declare I know not. Reports were various and contradictory. It was said, and believed, that the young baronet got his cue from a man who had once been a servant with Tibbers, and that he followed it out with such persistency, as to watch his enemy night and day till he made the discovery he wanted. I have examined this man oftener than once, and though he admits that "he has a gayan guid guess" what the offence was with which the captain charged Tibbers,[2] he will not so much as give a hint concerning it; but, on the contrary, always try to mislead from one thing to another. This then is the first great blank in the narrative, for I dare not even mention some of the reports that were current among the common people.

But one day, as Tibbers was standing among his harvest workers, the young baronet

---

2   Gayan guid (Sc.): pretty good.

and Mr. Alexander McGill, a friend of his, and a relation of my own, came briskly up to him on foot. He, suspecting some new outrage, drew close to his work-people, and thus addressed his determined persecutor, "You had better refrain from any of your mad pranks to-day, spark; else, depend on it, I have those about me, will chastise you."

"I don't regard these a pin," returned he; "but I am come to-day with a different intention, namely, to make you a full and final recompense for all the favours you have so liberally bestowed upon my late father and me."

"I have never done ought either to you or your father which the laws of my country will not support me in," said he; "and while I have the law on my side, I defy you, and will yet revisit all your outrages upon your head seven-fold."

"O, it is a noble thing, the law of our country," exclaimed the soldier; "it is that which protects the innocent against the fangs of the oppressor, and bestows the due awards of justice on the villain and the wretch. And now to that blessed and infallible establishment I cheerfully resign you, old fellow. I have you on the hip now, and may honour blast my name if I do not follow up my advantage till I see you strapped like a worrying colley!"

The young baronet then with a face of the most inveterate exultation, stepped forward, and in an under voice informed Mr. Tibbers of something, appealing to McGill as a witness. The old fellow drew himself up with a shiver that shook his whole frame; his countenance changed into the blue and pallid hue of death, his jaws fell down, and his whole frame became rigid, and there he stood gazing on his accusers as if in the phrenzy of despair, until the malignant turned on his heel, and desired his humbled enemy to go to dinner with what stomach he had.

This scene was witnessed by twenty people, although none of them heard the accusation. Tibbers spoke not a word; his spirit shrunk within him like that of a man going to execution. He drew his cloak closer about him, and hasted home to his house, in which were none but his two daughters. When there, he threw himself upon the bed, and exclaimed, "O, girls, I am ruined, I am ruined! I am gone! gone! gone! I am ruined and undone for ever, and you are ruined and undone for ever! We must fly from our country this night, this very night, or hide our faces where they can never be seen again! O death, death! I dare not cross your dark threshold of my own accord! And yet I would hide me in the depths of the grave."

In this way he continued raving on till towards the evening, and, as the girls declared afterwards, would tell them nothing, save that they were all three undone. At night he sent express for his attorney, who had conducted all his legal business, knew his parents, and was suspected to be even a greater villain than himself. The two consulted together the whole night, counted over a great deal of money, and early the next morning set off for the county town. The young baronet and Mr. McGill followed some hours after, as Tibbers well knew they would, to deliver him into the hands of justice. But he was before hand with them for that day, for when they arrived none of the functionaries were to be found, and nothing could be done.

Tibbers must now have been put to his last shift; for it was perceived, that when the two gentlemen went up to the sheriff's house, that Tibbers was watching them; and as they returned disappointed, he immediately made up to them and desired to speak with them. At first, they looked at him with disdain, mixed with abhorrence, as men look upon a reptile; but on hearing what he said, they retired with him into an angle of the church which stands in the middle of the main street, where all the three stood debating for nearly an hour. There were hundreds of eyes saw this; for it was market-day, and all their motions were well remembered afterwards. They were manifestly entering into some agreement, for it was noted that the fiery and impatient soldier, after turning several times on his heel, as if to go away, at length held out his hand to Tibbers, which the latter, after a good deal of hesitation, struck, as people do on concluding a bargain. They went through the same motion a second and a third time, and then it appeared that the agreement was settled, for all the three went away together towards the river which runs not above two bow-shots from the spot where they were standing. They were seen to go all three into a boat by some people who were at that instant crossing the ferry to the market. The boat had a sail, and was managed by two seamen whom none of the party knew, and she immediately bore down the river before the wind.

I have been the more minute in those particulars, because they are the only ones known on which positive conjectures could be grounded. It was judged probable by those who witnessed the transaction, that, in order to get quit of the young man's insolence and upbraidings, Tibbers might have proffered him a good part of his father's estate again, in order to enjoy the rest in tranquillity. But then these people knew nothing of the hideous discovery made, and which it is quite manifest could not then, nor ever after, have been revealed. But what strengthened the people's conjecture most, was this. The sheriff was known to be that day down at the village on the quay, five miles below the town, taking evidence on some disputed goods, and the greyhounds and terriers of the law along with him; and it was thought that, in order to strike the iron while it was hot, the parties had gone down forthwith to have their agreement ratified.

They did not, however, call either on the sheriff or any of the writers, nor has the young baronet or his friend ever been more heard of, either alive or dead, unto this day. Their horses remained at the hotel, which created some alarm; but no person could perceive any danger to which the young gentleman could have been exposed. At what time Tibbers returned to his own house, was not known; but it was nearly a week before he was discovered there, and then so frightfully altered was he in his appearance, that scarcely any person could have recognised him for the same man. He had, moreover, a number of wounds upon him. Strong suspicions were raised against him. The common people were clamorous beyond measure; and the consequence was, that he was seized and examined, but nothing could be made out against him to warrant his commitment. In his declaration, he stated, that he had bribed the young man with almost every farthing he himself was worth, to go once more abroad, and not to return to Scotland again during his (Mr. Tibbers's) life, and that he had gone accordingly. He stated farther, that he had gone and seen him abroad before paying him the money, and that Alexander McGill was with him when he left him; whether he went abroad with him he could not tell; but they had plenty of money to carry them both to any part of the known world.

There was a plausibility in this statement, as there was in every statement that Tibbers made. Still it was far from being satisfactory to the friends of the young gentleman. He could neither tell the name of the ship nor the name of the captain with whom they sailed, but pretended that they made choice of the vessel themselves; and he took no heed to either the ship or the master. A reward was offered for the discovery of the two boatmen. They were never discovered; and with this vague statement and suspicious detail of circumstances, people were obliged to rest satisfied for the present, presuming, that in the common course of events, the darkest shades in which they were involved would be brought to light.

They never have as yet been disclosed by any of those common concatenations of circumstances which so often add infallibly to the truth. But the hand of the Almighty, whose eye never either slumbers or sleeps, was manifestly extended to punish William Tibbers, though for what crime or crimes I dare not infer. The man became a terror to himself and to all who beheld him; and certainly, if he was not haunted, as the people said, by a ghost, or some vengeful spirit, he was haunted by an evil conscience, whose persecutions were even more horrible to endure. There were two men hired to watch with him every night, and his cries during that season were often dreadful to hear. These men did sometimes speak of sayings that tended to criminate him, more ways than one; but the words of a person in that state of excitement, or rather derangement, no man can lay hold of. By day he was composed, and walked about by himself, and sometimes made a point of attending to his secular concerns. But wherever he showed his face, all were struck with dumb amazement, an indefinable feeling of terror which words cannot describe. It was as if a cold tremor had seized on the vitals, and frozen up the genial currents of their souls. He was a Magur-missabub; an alien in the walks of humanity from whom the spirits of the living revolted, and the spirits of the dead attached themselves.

But one day it so happened that this man of horrors was missing, and could no where be found; nor could any one be found who had seen him, save a crazy old woman, named Bessy Rieves, and of her account the keepers could make nothing.

"Did you see aught of our master going this way, Bessy?"

"Aye, aye! the dead tells nae tales, or there wad be plenty o' news o' Willie Tibbers, the day. There wad be a sister an' a daughter, a baronet and a young gentleman, an' a poor harmless gardener-lad into the bargain; a' huddled out o' sight to hide the crimes o' ane! Aye, aye, the grave's a good silencer for tell-tales, an' a deposite for secrets that winna keep;[3] but a voice may come frae the grave, an' a lesson frae the depths of the sea to teach the sinner his errors. I saw Willie Tibbers; an' I saw a' thae waitin' on him. He's in braw company the day! But he had better hae been in the lions' den or on the mountains of the leopards. Aye, he had better hae been in the claws o' the teegar than in yon bonny company. The pains o' the body are naething, but it is an awfu' thing to hae the soul sawn asunder! Ye may gang up the hill an' down the hill, ower the hill an' roun' the hill, but ye'll never find the poor castaway that gate. Gang ye to McArrow's grave the night, and note the exact spot that the moon rises at; and when ye gang there ye will either find Willie Tibbers or ane unco like him."

The men took no notice of this raving, but continued the search; and all the domestics and retainers of the family were soon scattered over the country, and sought till the next night, but found nothing. That night the words of daft Bessy came to be discussed, and some of those present judged it worth while to take a note of the place, which they did. But McArrow's grave being on the top of the little hill behind the manse that bears his name, the rising of the moon was so distant that they said Mr. Tibbers could not, without wings, have travelled to that spot. Yet, incredible as it may appear to you, nearly about that spot was Tibbers's body found, but so distorted and bloated that but for the clothes no one could have recognized it. I request you to pay particular attention to this. About forty-six miles from his own house, in the county adjoining ours to the southward, and on the lands of Easter Tulloch, there was a body found, which was clothed in Mr. Tibbers's apparel from crown to toe; but farther than this, no man could depose, or even say that there was a likeness between the body found and the one lost. However, the body was taken home and interred as the body of William Tibbers, and his two handsome daughters were declared joint heiresses of his property and great wealth.

---

3   Winna (Sc.): will not.

The astonishment that now reigned among the country people was extreme, and the saying of old crazy Betty Rieves caused the most amazement of all; and it was averred, without a dissentient voice, that spirits had carried off Willie Tibbers through the air, and tortured him to death, and strange lights were reported to have been seen that day he was lost; but you may conceive how this amazement was magnified, when, immediately subsequent to these alarms, it was as confidently reported that the ghost of Tibbers walked, and had been seen and spoke with about his late habitation!

I never remember of any sensation like the one that prevailed in our district at that period. I had lived to see the war come to our doors, our chapel burnt, and our cattle driven off with impunity;[4] but the consternation then was not half so great as at the period of which I am writing. I preached against it, I prayed publicly that the Almighty would moderate it; yet I thought that all this only made matters the worse. People actually left off their necessary labour, and gathered in crowds to gape, stare, talk and listen about ghosts; and of murdered people returning from the grave and the bottom of the sea, to which they had been sunk with a hundred pounds weight of lead at every foot, to wreak the vengeance of God on a monster of humanity.

Matters now went all topsy-turvy at Castle-Gower together. The heir was lost — totally lost; for he had never joined his regiment, nor been heard of at any port; and the next heir of entail arrived from Lower Canada to take possession of the titles and emoluments of the estate. The latter of these was much reduced, for all the land had been of late sold, except the entailed part, and that was considerably burdened.[5] But now that Tibbers was out of the way, he had great hopes of reducing the late sale, and recovering the whole of the family property. Accordingly, an action was raised against the heirs of the late Mr. Tibbers, who defended, and the cause was tried in the High Court of Justiciary, among the records of which you will find it; for I do not know the particulars, and can only define the feelings that prevailed here.

Mr. Tibbers's two daughters had retired to Edinburgh, to escape the confusion and terror that prevailed at home. They were amiable girls, and as much beloved by the common people as their father was hated. On the other hand, the upstart, Sir Thomas, as he now called himself, was a low-bred, vulgar, and disagreeable person, and was as much hated by the gentry as the commoners; so that the feeling with us was wholly in favour of the two young ladies, and it is amazing what anxiety was manifested on their account. The people said they could not tell whether the defenders' late father had played false in his trusteeship or not. His employers had judged otherwise, and, at all events, the lovely and innocent young girls had no hand in his guilt, but had been tyrannized over all their lives. All parties, however, agreed in this, that if Johnnie Gaskirk, who had acted as attorney for Mr. Tibbers all his lifetime, and knew of every transaction, stood as true to the cause of the daughters as he had always done to that of the father, they were invincible; but if he was bribed to take the other side, all was lost, and of this every one saw the danger; for the other party had been dangling with him and consulting him.

What side Johnie Gaskirk had resolved to take, will never be known. Probably the one that paid him best, had not an incident happened that turned the scale in favour

---

4 Given the date of the letter mentioned in the end note, this must refer to the Jacobite rebellion of 1745–6. As the writer is there described as an Episcopalian minister, his chapel would have been burned by government soldiers: the rebellion drew support from Episcopal as well as Catholic communities.

5 Entails were legal arrangements determining the order of succession to an estate, and protecting it for the future inheritors: as such entailed land could not be sold off by the present proprietor.

of his old employer. I know nothing about law, or law terms, and the less, perhaps, the better. But the success of the plea turned eventually on the want of a duplicate of a disposition. The pursuers denied the possession of it, arguing, that the one produced by the counsel of the defenders was a forgery, and the latter could find no proof of its delivery. Three times there were cunning men dispatched all the way from Edinburgh to our county town, 145 miles, to consult Johnie Gaskirk, but neither of the parties were much the wiser.

One night, however, as Johnie was sitting alone in his office with all the late Mr. Tibbers's papers before him, comparing dates, and taking notes, who should enter but Mr. Tibbers himself, and that in a guise which would have struck any man dead, save Johnie Gaskirk, who seems to have had nerves of steel. But be it considered that this frightful apparition opened the door of the office and came in like another man. It was dressed in the deceased's every-day suit, the same in which the corpse had been found, but its features were what Johnie called "unco gast!"[6]

"Lord preserve us! Mr. Tibbers!" said Johnie.

"Amen! if you be honest," said the apparition, standing straight up with its back to the door, and its eyes turned on the floor.

"Honest, sir?" said Johnie Gaskirk, hesitating. "Ye ken the folks said that neither you nor I were very singular for honesty. But God be wi' us, Mr. Tibbers, we thought you had been dead, but it seems you have been only in hiding."

"Only in hiding," responded the figure.

"Aye, aye! Ye war ay a queer man a' your days, an' had queer gates,"[7] said Johnie. "But this is the strangest manoover of a'. This alters the case very materially."

"Yes, in so far as that, if you dare to pursue your present plans, I'll hang you;" said the apparition. "That duplicate—Dare you for your neck, for you never set your soul at a farthing's value, deny the subscribing and delivery of that paper in this office?"

"A man may be allowed to forget a thing, ye ken, sir," said Johnie. "And truly, though I think it natural that there should have been a duplicate, else the transaction wasna worth a doit; yet I canna say that I remember ought about it."

"You do, you dog. It was signed by you and James Anderson, now in Montrose, and given to Mr. Baillie, who now thinks proper to deny it, and who has likely put it out of the way. But your three oaths will prove its existence. If you shuffle and decline doing this, I will first hang you, and then produce the paper in court to the proper authorities."

Having said this, the stern and haggard figure of William Tibbers withdrew, and left his little attorney in an indescribable state. He declared till his death that he was not frightened, believing it to be the real William Tibbers, but that he was awfully confused and stupid. When he learned, a few minutes thereafter, that the street door had never been opened nor unbolted, then did his flesh begin to creep, his hairs to stand on end, and he knew not what to think. The first idea that then struck him, was that the hideous figure was concealed in his own house, an inmate of whose vicinity he little approved.

The ghost of Tibbers, or himself, continued frequently to be seen; for, till this day, I cannot calculate with certainty, whether it was the one or the other. I certainly would have judged it to have been an apparition, had it not been for the most extraordinary scene that ever was witnessed in this or any other country; and of which I myself was an ear and eye witness, and even that was no decisive proof either ways.—It was as follows:

There were some official men sent from Edinburgh to take a precognition relating to

---

6 Gast (Sc.): terrifying.
7 Gates (Sc.): ways.

facts before our sheriff,[8] to save expenses to the litigants. Fifty or sixty were summoned that day, but in fact the main evidence depended on the statement of Johnie Gaskirk, and it being that day quite the reverse of all his former statements, and decisive in behalf of the Misses Tibbers, the deputy advocate and the sheriff got both into a high fever at his inconsistency, and persisted in knowing from whence he had got this new light; insomuch, that after a great deal of sharp recrimination, Johnie was obliged to tell them flatly that he had it from very good authority — from Mr. Tibbers himself! They asked him if it was from his ghost: he said he could not tell; he took it for himself at the time. He came into his office and conversed with him, and brought facts clearly to his remembrance.

The sheriff and his compeers laughed Johnie Gaskirk to scorn; and the pursuers' counsel said they would have none of this dreamy evidence related at second-hand. If the said William Tibbers had any thing of that sort to communicate, he must come into court himself, or answer by his deputy from the other world. The sheriff acquiesced, and granted rule, half out of spite at the equivocation of Johnie Gaskirk. The counsel wrote out the summons, of the words of which I have an indistinct recollection, weening them at the time a little blasphemous. The name was three times called in court by the proper officer, who then read the summons aloud. "In the name of God and the King, we their liege subjects and lawful officers, warn, summon, and charge you, William Tibbers, to appear here in court, either in your own person or by proxy, to answer upon oath such questions as may be asked of you."

The man had scarce done bawling or the crowded assembly with laughing at the ludicrous nature of the summons, nor had a single remark been made, save one by Johnie Gaskirk, who was just saying to the sheriff, "Ods sir, ye had better hae letten him alane. He was never muckle to lippen to a' his days,[9] and he's less sae now than ever."

Ere this sentence was half said, Tibbers stepped into the witnesses' bench! But such a sight may human eyes never again look on. No corpse risen from the vaults of a charnel house — no departed spirit returning from the valley of terrors, could present a form or a look so appalling. It is impossible to describe it. A shuddering howl of terror pealed through the house. The sheriff, who was well acquainted with Tibbers, flung himself from his seat, and on his hands and knees escaped by the private door, while the incorrigible Johnie Gaskirk called to him to stay and take the witness's evidence.

A scene now ensued, the recollection of which still makes my heart cold. The court-room of our old town-house is ample but ill lighted. It was built in days of old, for a counsel chamber to the kings of Scotland. The entry is dark and narrow, and from the middle of this entry a stair as dark and narrow leads to what is still termed the ladies' gallery. The house was crowded, and the moment the horrid figure made its appearance, the assembly made one simultaneous rush to gain the door. They were instantly heaped above each other to suffocation. Yells and cries of *murder*! resounded from every quarter. The rush from the stair quite overwhelmed those beneath, and trode them to death. Such scenes have been often witnessed, but never by me; and when the ominous cause was taken into consideration, it was a most impressive and judgment-looking catastrophe. The one half of that numerous assembly were wounded or maimed, many of them for life, and nine were killed outright, so that it was with us a season of lamentation, and mourning, and great wo!

From that hour forth, the apparition of William Tibbers was no more seen on earth, that ever I heard of. But it was the general impression that it was the devil who appeared that day in court, and wreaked such vengeance on the simple and credulous

8 Precognition: the preliminary investigation to determine if there is a case to answer.
9 I.e. he could never be trusted.

natives. William Tibbers was indeed a Samson to us,[10] for at this his last appearance, he did us more evil than all the rest of his life. His daughters gained the property, but I cannot say they have enjoyed it. The old adage seems to be realized in their case, that "a narrow gathering gets ay a wide scattering," for their great wealth appears to be melting away like snow from the dike.*

*The date of the above letter is 1749, and is supposed to have been written by the Rev. R. Walker, of the Episcopal communion, to a brother in office. If so, it must have been from some chapel in Morayshire, for undoubtedly Elgin must be the county town alluded to. The distance from Edinburgh. The ancient town house in the middle of the street, with the village and quay, five miles down the river. All these, with other coinciding circumstances, fully warrant such a supposition. The original letter is directed to The Rev. J—— S—n—n, Carubber's Close, Edinburgh.

---

10 Referring of course to Samson's bringing down the temple on the heads of the Philistines in Judges 16.

THE BARBER OF DUNCOW. — A REAL GHOST STORY.[1]
BY THE ETTRICK SHEPHERD.

As Will Gordon, the tinkler,[2] was sitting with his family in his original but wretched cottage, called Thief's Hole, one winter night, the dialogue chanced to turn on the subject of apparitions, when his son-in-law, Hob, remarked, that he wondered how any reasonable being could be so absurd as to entertain a dread of apparitions.

"Aye, aye, lad," says old Will, "Nae doubt ye're a verra bauld chiel,[3] but ma courage has been rather longer tried than yours, an' it was never doubtit yet. For a' that, I hae heard the goodwife there tell a story that frightit me sae ill I hardly kend what I was doing. Aye, whether I was fa'ing off the stook, or sitting still on't , or sinkin down through the grund or rising up i' the air."

"Sic nonsense! sickan absurdity!" exclaimed Hobby, "I wad like to hae a touch o' thae kind o' feelings for aince in my life. Ane might be feared for a human creature that has power to hurt ane, but why ony man should be afraid of a shadow, a mere vision of a human creature, I never can comprehend. If my wife, there, war to hae the luck to dee, an' her ghaist to appear on me, I wad be nae mair feared for it than I'm for that shadow o' hers on the wa'."

"O but ye ken there's nae body has ha'f the currage that ye hae. Ye wadna be feared, aw daursay, an' the deil an' aw his awgents war gaun to come in. Goodwife, tell us the story o' the Barber o' Duncow."

"Ohon an' it's een lang sin I tried to tell that tale, Willie,"[4] said old Raighel, with a grin and a snivel, "but sin ye desyre me, I'll e'en try't. It has only ae ill clag till't that story, an' it's this:[5] when any body hears it, an disna believe it, the murdered woman is sure to come in."

"What d'ye say?" cried Hob, in manifest alarm, "plague on the auld randy,[6] gie us nae sickan story as that, for I assure you I winna believe it."

"Aye, but it will make nae odds to you, though the ghaist *war* to come in, ye ken," said old Will, with a malicious grin.

"Weel, ye see, it is a queer town this Duncow, as ever was seen in the world;[7] it was built by a community o' proscribed covenanters, thae auld warld fo'ks, that grane, an' whine, an preach i' tents; an' it's just like a hill congregation to this day, a' jammed thegither without rule or method, but ilk ane stands just as it comes in.[8] When I was young, it was turned a kind o' rendevous to a' the riff raff in the country. There was some o' our ain gang whilk formed the head class; then there were some fiddlers, several witches, three little dram-shops, where there war a grit chat o' fun went on; an' last an' warst of a', there was a great deal o' thae prayin' austere chaps, covenanters. A' the rest hatit them; an' mony a vizit the deil payed on them, sae that the hale town was keepit in a ferment, for there was a constant wrangling and contention whether he or they war to hae the better. I hae seen him gaun to their meetings mysel wi' their bodily

---

1   From *Fraser's Magazine* III, no. xiv (March 1831): 174–80.
2   A tinker, a mender of pots and other metalware; traditionally a low-caste, usually itinerant occupation.
3   Verr bauld chiel: very brave fellow.
4   It's a long time since…
5   Ohon: alas!; een lang sin: even long since; clag (Sc.): flaw.
6   Randy, randie (Sc.): here, 'any foul-mouthed, brawling, bad-tempered woman' (*SND*).
7   Duncow is about five miles north of Dumfries.
8   Thegither: together; ilk ane: each one (all Sc.). Covenanting ministers, locked out of their churches, preached to their congregations in remote open-air (and illegal) assemblies.

een o' mine, wi' his long tail an' his cloven feet, an' it was said, that he sometimes arguit better nor ony that was there.[9]

"Be that as it may; amang the rest there was a barber, a queer chap; he was every thing in nature! beard-shaver, butcher, wig-maker, rat-catcher, catkiller, horse-doctor, cow-doctor, man-doctor, woman-doctor, surgeon an apothecary; that is to say, he keepit a lance, a roostit fleeme, an' a sack fu' o' salts an' sinny-leaf rowed down i' the mouth, an awfu' stollant o' them he did sell;[10] he made a braw livelihood o't, an' took the use o' what he made, for he drank an' sang, an' played on the pipes, an' he was weel named, for they ca'd him Rodger McFun.

"But it happened ill, it happened warse; it happened that Rodger, the barber, married a Cameronian lass for the sake o' a wheen dirty bawbees,[11] an' then his happy days were done. He wadna pray an' sing psalms wi' her, an' she wadna sing an' drink an' haud the gibberidge wi' him. O, sickan a life as they led! it was really funny to see them! but ilka burd mate wi' ane o' its ain feather, or its weel doing days are ower. Let a tinkler marry a tinkler, an' the ane is a king an' the ither a queen; but to mate wi' a dependent being! figh, fie! a crust o' cheese an' moss water to that.

"Rodger seldom now gaed hame, for, as he said himsel, 'it was nae fun that.' When he did gang, it was to wrangle, to hear a hunder grieveous complaints an' religious lectures, an' to mock an' taunt his yammering dame in return, till at length he got sae mad at her, that he sometimes gae the razor a brandish up i' the air afore her, wi' a significant wink. Now this was a warning that the Cameronian wife shouldna awthegither hae neglectit, for they're unlucky things thae razors in the hands o' a rash man.

"Matters came at length to ane cleemasc atween them; she suspectit Rodger o' some fact,[12] but what that fact was, it dizna become me to say. He was muckle employed among the women, bath the young ones an' the auld anes; an' there was some gentlemen that had secrets to keep, employed the barber, who was necessarily *in* these secrets, to carry them on frae year to year. Whether he put ony o' thae luckless lasses to a waur place than genteel service, an' the poor babies to a caulder hame than a nurice's lap, I canna say, an' therefore I winna. But there was ae night that the poor Cameronian wife had gotten some verra doutfu' tidings about her goodman, an' she had been greeting[13] and praying time about for hours thegither, an' a' that she might come to the knowledge o' the truth; when she lifted up her een there was a ghost of a woman standin hinging o'er the back o' the chair, an' glowerin at her wi' its white een. She had na power to rise frae her knees, nor yet to utter a word, an' though she tried to gie a loud yelloch to raise the neighbours, she was na able; for the apparition was clad in a white winding-sheet, an' was ay making motions for her to follow it to the door. It tried to speak too, but its mouth was black, an' the words wadna come up, an' in a short time it elyed away out at the door,[14] making signs for her to follow.

"Grizel wasna sae daft as to obey; she durstna stir off the bit,[15] but opened the

---

9 Nor ony (Sc.): than any. This is a scenario familiar from the tale of the Auchtermuchty preaching included in Hogg's *Private Memoirs and Confessions of a Justified Sinner* (1824).

10 Lance: lancet. Sinny-leaf is the dried leaflets of the senna plant, used as medicine; rowed (Sc.): rolled. Usages here of "fleeme" and "stollant" are obscure.

11 Cameronians: covenanters who, under Richard Cameron, rejected any compromise with the state and declared war on Charles II as an enemy of God in 1683. After the re-establishment of Presbyterianism in 1690 they continued as a dissenting fundamentalist sect. Bawbees are pennies; a 'wheen' are a few.

12 Fact: evil deed or crime.

13 Greeting (Sc.): crying.

14 Elyed away (Sc.): gradually disappeared from sight.

15 Off the bit: on the spot (*SND* 'in or on the bit').

gospels, an' prayed again, till she pretendit her heart was strengthened; she hadna weel said Amen! an' raised her face, till she heard something tirlin at the door-pin,[16] and on looking that way, saw something like a human shape, made o' blue light, but it was flickering and unsteady, like a reflection frae something else. It tirled at the door-pin again, on which Grizel cries, 'If ye be a creature o' this world, lift the latch by the whang an' come in.[17]' It uttered twa or three loud moans, like a person dying, and then was silent. A third time it tirled at the door-pin, an' then Grizel durstna, for her soul, resist ony longer. 'I perceive how it is,' cried she, 'you are not a being of this world, but a messenger frae the grave, or some waur place beyond it. Weel, weel, come in, but dinna tak a shape that will scare poor human reason away frae her earthly habitation awthegither. Come in, come in, poor disturbit spirit, an' deliver your message; all is ane to me! death or life!—all one! all one! come in.' Wi' that, the door began to open slowly—"Oh, mercy, grannie, dinna tell nae mair," cried little Hobby, who sat at her knee on a bucket-stool, 'O, dinna, dinna! dinna tell nae mair!"

"What means the bilch to skreigh that gate?"[18] said old Will, "Are ye frightened, sirra?"

"Na, na, I'm nae frightened; but see, the whalp's turned that frightened, I can hardly haud it. O, grannie, dinna tell nae mair, or else ye'll pit the whalp mad."

"Whisht, my man, an' never say a word, I'm no near the bit when the ghost comes in here," said old Raighel. "Mind, it's only the barber's house, at Duncow, that it is coming into just now, but it will be here belyve.[19] Weel, as I was saying, the door opened slowly, and the same tall ghastly figure with the sheet, an' the white een, an' the black mouth, came in again, an' began to make motions, an' point at its throat, an' its breast, and then to the door.

"Grizel now conjured it to speak out and tell what it had to reveal, on which, it threw up its arms, as wi' joy, at the question, because a ghost canna speak until it be aince spoken to.

"'Blest be the tongue that axes the question,' said the ghost, 'for it has gien me liberty to speak my yirrant.[20] I am sent to thee, highly favoured and beloved, with tidings of your family.'

"'My family!' said Grizel; 'I now perceive that you are a false and lying spirit, for it has'na been the will o' Providence, that I should hae ony family.'

"'O thou froward and purverse woman, dost thou not believe my words?' said the ghost, 'or canst thou deny that thou and thy husband are one flesh; and that whatsoever pertaineth to the one, pertaineth to the other?'

"'I ken that but ower weel,' said Grizel, 'else my tocher good—'[21]

"'Hold thine, sister, and listen,' said the ghost, 'for I tell thee that thou shalt yet see a numerous, a blooming, and a healthy family.'

"'O shall I? shall I indeed—blessings on you, for the messenger of love and joy, and posterity!' cried Grizel; 'when, O tell me when these eyes shall be blessed by the sight of a son.'

"'Both sons and daughters shall thine eyes behold, and that in a shorter time than

---

16   Tirlin (Sc.): causing to vibrate. Instead of a knocker, poor houses had a hole in the door-frame in which an attached stick was rattled.

17   Whang (Sc.): strip of leather.

18   Bilch (Sc.): 'term of disrespect for a child' like 'brat' (*SND*).

19   Belyve (Sc.): by and by, soon enough.

20   Yirrant (Sc.): errand or purpose.

21   Tocher-good (Sc.): property given as a dowry. Grizel's point is perhaps that only the legal fiction of 'one flesh' justifies her husband's possession of the property that she brought into the marriage.

thou canst conceive,' said the ghost, waving its arms sublimely, 'and now for the time and place, and my errand is said. Two in the house of John Halliday, Holm of Tinneld; two in the tailor's house at Kirkmichael; and three in the house of Francis Fiddes, fiddler in Penpont. All thine own darling sons and daughters. And the time — the blessed time — may be — to-morrow!' And with these words the ghost vanished.

"Grizel started up and stared around her in utter confusion; a sort of dim light began to break through her thick stupid head of some dreadful enormity, while her tongue begun to gang at random. 'Francis Fiddes, fiddler in Penpont! My certy, but for a Christian spirit, ye fiddle weel! My sons and daughters — aye in right o' my husband. Did'na the unearthly creature say sae? — I see how it is, I see how it is! O Rodger McFun! Rodger McFun! I shall be unto thee Grizel McGrief.'

"Grizel spent the night in lamentation and grief, and nourishing in her jealous heart the most deadly revenge, while her prayers and anathemas were all of the most lugubrious description. Next morning she took her bap in her lap, and set off for the house of John Halliday, in which she found two pretty boys at board, and after enquiry made, she was told that they were placed there, and their board regularly paid by a barber body about Kirkmahoe.

"Without uttering a word, Grizel flew across the fire, and seizing the twa callants by the hair of the head, began to knock their heads together, and would soon have finished them both, had she not been seized by Mrs. Halliday in the same manner, who brought her down, kicked her weel, an' laid on her wi' the porritch-stick, till she was obliged to 'take the door on her back,' when a terrible scolding match ensued.

"From thence she posted on to the tailor's house, in the hamlet of Kirkmichael, where she found two little blooming daughters, circumstanced in the same way, and no other at home with them, save the tailor. A furious attack commenced on the unoffending children, while the tailor not liking to knock down a woman, was sadly put to it; for though he gave her the length of the needle repeatedly, so intent was she on vengeance, that she disregarded it, until the cries of *murder*! brought in Rob, the smith, who, as he termed it, 'soon gave her up her foot.'

"But the worst business of all fell at Penpont, where she found three children at board, a son and two daughters, and the reckless barber sitting in the house the worse of liquor, with the fiddler's daughter on his knee. Thinking she had him fairly now in Hay's net, she begun with affected mildness, while the barber could only stammer, 'peace be wi' us, wife, where had been sae late?'

"'Where has I been but seeing a' your bonny family, Mr. McFun? I has been at John Halliday's an' the tailor's an' a'; an I'm gien to understand that this house is gayan weel stockit wi' the same respectable connections. Thir will be a' yours,[22] I's warrant. An' this their mother too: hech, man, but ye hae a braw gate o' gangin on through life.'

"'I'll tell ye what, wife, ye're aye meddling wi' things ye hae nought ado wi',' said the barber. 'An I'll tell ye what, I think ye deserve to hae your beard ta'en off. Od, a' ye dinna set away hame an' make me quat o' your din, I'll gie ye a touch o' the strap, I'll gie ye sic a powdering, as your legs hasna gotten these two towmants.'[23]

"A great battle o' words began, which ended in blows, as is common in such cases, and the fray ended by the fiddler's daughter and the barber beating the wife of the latter out at the door, with many stripes.

"But now begins the mystery of my tale, The barber's wife did not go home, and yet the barber, for ought that ever could be learned, remained in the house, where he

22 Thir (Sc.): these.
23 Towmant (Sc.): twelvemonth, a year.

was all that night, and part of next day; but when he went home his wife was wanting, and none of her religious friends had seen her, although it was alleged that Rodger did not look a great deal after her. Dark suspicions began to be harboured against the barber, and at length the community of Cameronians at Duncow, instituted a legal enquiry anent the fate of the poor woman[24]. But nothing could be elicited farther, than what is shortly mentioned above, and the general opinion became, that on the false supposition that all these natural children were Rodger's, for whom he was only the agent, she had deserted from him in disgust and absconded. But there was one illustrious fact came out on this examination, which was that the ghost that revealed the secret of the numerous family to poor Grizel, was no other than a gypsie queen,[25] ca'd Bess the blinker, as arrant a limmer as e'er was born for mischief,[26] and who it was thought had good reason to ken about a part o' the bairns.

"But now take tent,[27] gude-son, o' what I'm gaun to say; an' ye had better no mis-believe any o' my words, or it will be the waur for ye, ye will maybe be convinced o' the truth o' them, in a way that may frise the best blood o' your body, though no three inches frae the heart."

"But what gin I canna help mis-believing you, ye auld roudess that you are,[28] what's to come o' us then? Gie ower your wild auld world stories in time, I sal keep ye atween me an' the door at any rate."

"The lost woman ye maun ken, had an auld aunt in the village, a very religious woman, an' as superstitious as she had lived among spirits a' her life. Grizel had been brought up wi' her, an' they held their religious duties ay together. Ye ken it's no our way to mind sic things a great deal, but we maun conceive sic characters, or else we canna tell the story, not yet comprehend it. The auld woman's name was Janet Black, for I remember of seeing her in the court, and ane liker a witch I never saw, an auld crazed enthusiast she was.

"Weel she had been reading an' praying a hale afternoon of a Sunday, an' greetin sair for her lost niece, and venting her curses on Rodger the barber, and the fiddler's daughter o' Penpont, and a' that kind o' reveries, when in comes her niece and stood straight up forenent her on the other side of the fire.[29] 'His presence be about us!" exclaimed old Janet, 'and are you indeed there? an' do I see my poor ill-used woman come home again? What for do ye no come round the fire, and gie me your hand?'

"'Na, na, dear aunt, I darena come round the fire, an' I darena gie you my hand. The hearth maun bide atween them that death has parted. Dinna stare sae wildly, nor hae any fear o' me, for I am harmless as your own shadow on the wall; and am only sent to reveal to you some dark secrets that may holp to set your loving heart at rest.'

"'Ah, alas! are you then dead, my poor Grizel? and is it only your shade, your departed spirit that I see stare before me?—aye, aye, my poor old head shakes so, that I cannot see distinctly. But, ah! there is a difference indeed, for neither your lips nor your eyes move, and I see the white plates on the dresser through you. O tell me, while I hae the power o' understanding, what death befel you? were you murdered?'

"'Yes, most foully, basely, and cruelly murdered!—Look here!' The old woman looked again, and perceived a wound in the throat of the apparition, which seemed nearly to sever the head from the body.

---

24 Anent (Sc.): regarding.
25 Queen (Sc.): lass.
26 Limmer (Sc.): rogue.
27 Take tent (Sc.): pay attention.
28 Roudess (Sc.): course-looking or ill-natured woman.
29 Forenent (Sc.): across from.

"'O, the murderous ruffian!' exclaimed old Janet. 'The reprobate wretch! — the son of everlasting perdition! May he roast —'

"'Hold, hold!' said the ghost, in a hollow voice; 'they were two women who did the bloody deed. I knew the one for the wretch May Fiddes, but the other I did not know, while in life, and I know nothing further since. Give the wretch up to justice, and she may confess her associate; while this shall be a sign of my verity. You will find my body lying in a deep, deep linn,[30] about two bowshot below the bridge of Scarrs, for there was I cast while still alive, and sunk with a great weight tied to my waist.'

"'Alas, poor wronged spirit, how can I give her up to justice? I cannot crawl to Dumfries, and if I could, they would only laugh at me, and say I was dreaming.'

"'Call in the elders, and declare the matter to them, stating where my body is to be found, and if one of the three dares to disbelieve you, I will come in and confront him to his face. And whenever this secret, transmitted from heaven, is disbelieved, there will I appear and confirm it; — aye, let it be in the palace, in the hall, in the court of judicature, or at the peasant's ingle![31] Farewell, and do as I have bidden you, for it is unmeet and derogatory to the justice of the Almighty, that the murderer of the innocent escape with impunity; for whosoever sheddeth man's blood, by man shall his blood be shed.'

"When the ghost had said this, it seemed to retire backward, keeping its form and face in the same position till it appeared at a great distance, as if some miles away, although necessarily within the walls of the house, through which the old woman's sight could not penetrate, and then it vanished in the distance.

"The next day at noon Janet sent a special message to each of the three Cameronian elders in the village to attend her instantly, as she had a notice to them from heaven. This was incitement sufficient. They all attended on the instant, and the old woman, whose whole frame was shaking with palsy, but more with zeal, related to them all that the spirit had commanded her. Two of the men, John Baird and Adam Turner, appeared much struck with the narrative, and began to say that, out of nature as it was, it deserved to be looked into. But Gavin Veitch, the eldest of them, resisted the proposal at once, for he was a man of true Cameronian obstinacy, who was never known to yield a point in his life, and shaking his head with an air of immovable incredulity, he thus addressed the old paralytic crone:-

"'Sister, sister! we had some hopes that your message from the presence above might relate to the overthrow of the profligate government of this realm, and the destruction of the covenant-breakers who acknowledge it. For they are rulers, not constituted by God, but denied by him, as he is by them. But since it is only a story of a ghost, a dream of dotage and superannuation, it would not become us, as men and christians, to pay any regard to it.'

"'But I say you *shall* pay regard to it, Gavin Veitch,' screamed old Janet, and shaking her right hand above her head, 'and I here charge you, in the name of your Creator and Redeemer, to go or send on the instant, and see if the body of my murdered niece is or is not in the bottom of the pool. If it is not there, I will submit that I have been deceived; but if it be found there with the throat cut to the neck-bone, I will move heaven and earth but I shall have justice on the murderers.'

"'Calm yourself, Janet, and speak like a rational being and a covenanted christian,' said Gavin; 'I tell you that you have thought on the mysterious loss of your niece till you are crazy, and the phantom is one of your own raising, and were we to travel all the way from hence to drag the unfathomed linn of the Scarr on the authority of an

30 A linn is a deep pool on a river usually associated with a waterfall.
31 Ingle (Sc.): fireside.

old woman's dream, three of the supporting pillars of the only true church of Scotland would deserve to be removed.'

"'Gavin, Gavin, ye may hae a ray o' heaven in your soul,' said Janet, 'an I hope you hae, but ye hae a strong spice o' the perversity of hell alang wi't. Think you I durst for my soul come to you with a lie in my mouth an' tell it to you as the words of heaven? Did the ears of man ever hear me utter an untruth? Tell me that. I hae sat the same communion table wi' you these thretty years; aye, and oft have received the sacred aliments from your hand. As sure then as ever I was serious at that holy table, when in the presence of man, of angels, and of God himself, I am so now. Do you not believe me?'

"'No, no, no, Janet, this fervour only convinces me the more of the total derangement of your mental faculties. I *must* not believe you.' said Gavin.

"'Then she maun come hersel and convince you, for I can gang nae farther,' said Janet, her voice altering to a soft and tremulous key. 'Aye, she maun come hersel, an' the Lord preserve us a' in our right senses! Aye, there she comes! there she comes! my ill-used, murdered woman! An' O how will ye answer her, you whose obstinacy has disturbed the peace of the grave?'

"The elders began to eye each other with doubtful looks, fair daylight as it was, for there was something in the old woman's demeanour truly awful. They looked at her steadily for some time, and perceiving her eyes fixed wildly on the door, and her shrivelled hands stretched out in the same direction, they looked instinctively the same way, when in one moment the three elders were all above each other in the nook behind old Janet, uttering incoherent prayers and verses of psalms. The ghost had entered, and there it stood in a far more frightful guise than it was the evening before. Its hands and its face were turned upwards, and the gash in its throat so much exposed, that it seemed as if the head were cut off all to the thickness of a man's thumb. At length it said, in an audible voice, that seemed to issue from the breast or the wound, and which sounded like the creaking of an hinge, 'He that believeth not Moses and the prophets, neither will he believe if one return to him from the dead. But, think you, a sister in faith would return from a world of spirits with a lie? Search and see; for I swear by Him that liveth for ever and ever, that the tale is true, and woe be to him that will not believe it!' The spirit then retreated in the same manner as it did the evening before, leaving a long vista of darkness behind it. The elders returned thanks and sung psalms together for an hour, and the same evening journeyed as far as Penpont, where they made the extraordinary circumstance known to their minister, Mr. Fairly. When they came the length of the ghost's relation to Janet, Mr. Fairly interrupted them with, 'Hout, hout — haud your tongues; I dinna believe ae word o't.'

"'Ye had better tak a wee care, sir, how ye misbelieve it,' said John Baird. But by this time his associates were rushing out at the door, and John after them; for they were all resolved, if their minister would not believe the message, that they would leave him and the ghost to settle it between themselves two; convinced from experience, that she would appear. What passed afterwards, they knew not, but the next morning the minister was a proselyte to the expediency of the research, and assisted in the investigation of the whole affair.

"They dragged several deep pools of the Scarr with loaded nets, but found nothing, till grappling irons arrived from Drumlanrig Castle, and then they found the body of the lost woman in the very pool which they at the first had dragged in the morning, as corresponding with the ghost's directions. The throat of the deceased was cut, and that in such a manner that the surgeons who attended, said it looked like the act of one used to handle his weapons.

"The body was carried into Mr. Fairly's meeting-house, and there being no human evidence against the perpetrators, that original acute divine devised an old experiment, of most powerful effect and decisive consequences, which was no other than to summon a great number of people to come in and touch the body of the murdered woman, which was acquiesced in by every one, as at least furnishing some presumptive evidence that might assist in a further research.

"Every thing was arranged with the utmost gravity and decorum. — The meeting-house was full, and both magistrates and ministers of the gospel were present; and, among others, both the barber and the fiddler's daughter of Penpont, and the great reluctance manifested by these two to attend, seemed to confirm, in part, the ghost's evidence; for though it exculpated the barber, he refused to attend, till compulsion was used, and even tried to escape. Mr. Fairly prayed for a just judgment in such a manner, that it made all the bearers tremble, and then the trial proceeded; and as the corpse was sunk with a large stone and an iron ring in it, that had long lain at the mill door for tying horses to, the people of the mill were tried first, and then many others, all of whom were known to be quite innocent; and all the while the minister stood and put every person's hand upon the breast of the deceased, and of course no marks of guilt, by the bleeding of the body, appeared. When it came to May Fiddes's turn, she refused, and when they went to force her forward, she screamed and fell into hysterics, crying out, 'I did not touch her life, I did not touch her life; and I will not touch her dead carcase, no, not for the power of man!' She then yelled out most tremendously and fainted. They, however, brought her forward in a state of insensibility, and the minister laid her hand upon the body, but of this she was not aware, and no effects following, she was carried into the minister's house, with orders to let none speak to her till he came in. The barber perceiving that no marks of guilt appeared, began to treat the whole business with levity and contempt; but when he came forward, it took the minister's whole force to press down his hand, so as but slightly to touch the body. In a moment the white sheet was bathed in a flood of purple blood that streamed from the wound, as if it had been newly inflicted. The whole assembly then pronounced him the murderer, but he denied it with blustering and oaths, swearing it was the old malicious Whig minister that had pressed his hand too hard down on the chest of the deceased, which had caused the flow of blood.

"This made the sheriff and the parson look at one another, for they still perceived they had no hold of the villain in law, though all were convinced of his atrocious guilt. Mr. Fairly lectured him very hard to confess, telling him that the eye of the Almighty beheld him, that his divine agency had been manifest, not only in bringing the crime to light, but in bringing it home to the guilty; and it would never stop short till due vengeance was executed. But confess he would not, therefore the sheriff made out his mittimus,[32] and sent him to prison.

"Poor May Fiddes was not so firm, she had half confessed ere ever the sheriff and minister went in to her, though it was only in a raving state; but on the sheriff promising her her life, she confessed all. She said that the barber persuaded her to dress herself and him like two witches, of whom his wife stood in great fear, and to go forth and waylay her, and giver her a drubbing and ducking. And that, though the barber was rather drunk, for the fun of the thing she yielded, and they went. That they seized her, and got her down with her face toward the ground, and then sat above her singing a witch song, the barber holding up her head, and the deponent her feet, so that she could not move nor cry. That she (the deponent) hearing a kind of gurgling cry, looked back and

---

32 Mittimus: a warrant for custody pending a trial.

saw that the barber had cut her throat with a razor, and the blood was running. That then she (May Fiddes) got up and ran away, without ever looking over her shoulder. She told also, where the barber's bloody witch-clothes were buried, and there they were found. The barber was condemned and executed, dying without confession, and the fiddler and his daughter left Nithsdale, but none of the three children went with them, a sign that they were not hers.

"This is the hale story of the barber; but the most curious part is, that if the tale be accurately tould, and one of the hearers or more should doubt of its verity, the ghost o' poor Grizel to this day comes in in the same guise, and gives its testimony. An' mair by token, I hae a test to try you a' wi'." She took a lammer bead out o' her pocket,[33] and held it to her own ear, then to the baby's on her knee — the lurcher began to bristle and look frightened, uttering short, smothered barks, the pup followed the example — "Hush! what's that at the door?"————

33 Lammer: amber.

Thomas Carlyle, 'Signs of the Times.' *Edinburgh Review* 49 (June 1829): 439–459.[1]

It is no very good symptom either of nations or individuals, that they deal much in vaticination. Happy men are full of the present, for its bounty suffices them; and wise men also, for its duties engage them. Our grand business undoubtedly is, not to *see* what lies dimly at a distance, but to *do* what lies clearly at hand.

> Know'st thou *Yesterday*, its aim and reason?
> Work'st thou well *To-day*, for worthy things?
> Calmly wait the *Morrow's* hidden season,
> And fear not thou, what hap soe'er it brings![2]

But man's 'large discourse of reason' *will* look 'before and after;' and, impatient of the 'ignorant present time,' will indulge in anticipation far more than profits him.[3] Seldom can the unhappy be persuaded that the evil of the day is sufficient for it;[4] and the ambitious will not be content with present splendour — but paints yet more glorious triumphs, on the cloud-curtain of the future.

The case, however, is still worse with nations. For here the prophets are not one, but many; and each incites and confirms the other — so that the fatidical fury spreads wider and wider, till at last even a Saul must join in it.[5] For there is still a real magic in the action and reaction of minds on one another. The casual deliration of a few becomes, by this mysterious reverberation, the frenzy of many; men lose the use, not only of their understandings, but of their bodily senses; while the most obdurate, unbelieving hearts melt, like the rest, in the furnace where all are cast, as victims and as fuel. It is grievous to think, that this noble omnipotence of Sympathy has been so rarely the Aaron's-rod of Truth and Virtue,[6] and so often the Enchanter's-rod of Wickedness and Folly! No solitary miscreant, scarcely any solitary maniac, would venture on such actions and imaginations, as large communities of sane men have, in such circumstances, entertained as sound wisdom. Witness long scenes of the French Revolution! a whole people drunk with blood and arrogance — and then with terror and cruelty — and with desperation, and blood again! Levity is no protection against such visitations, nor the utmost earnestness of character.

---

1   This essay first appeared as article VII in this issue of the *Edinburgh Review*. Like all *Edinburgh Review* articles, it was ostensibly an anonymous review of other publications; like many *Edinburgh Review* articles, it makes no mention of these whatsoever. In its original form it had no title other than the details of the reviewed books, but 'Signs of the Times' appears as a running head at the top of each page. The title comes from Jesus's words in Matthew 16.3: 'O ye hypocrites, ye can discern the face of the sky; but can ye not discern the signs of the times?'.

2   This translates lines by Johann Wolfgang von Goethe, the German poet of the period, which appear on an engraving sent by Goethe to Carlyle in 1825.

3   This sentence combines a series of fragments from Shakespeare: *Hamlet* IV.iv.36–7 ('large discourse,/Looking before and after') and I.ii.150 ('discourse of reason'); and towards the end of *Macbeth* I.v ('This ignorant present').

4   Jesus again, in the Sermon on the Mount: 'Take therefore no thought for the morrow: for the morrow shall take thought for the thing of itself. Sufficient unto the day is the evil thereof' (Matthew 6.34).

5   Fatidical: prophetic. Before he is made King of Israel, Saul is given the gift of prophesy, and the people ask, 'Is Saul also among the prophets?' (I Samuel 10.11–12).

6   After the flight from Egypt, Aaron is chosen by God to be High Priest when his rod 'bloomed blossoms, and yielded almonds' (Numbers 17.8), and the rods of the other candidates did not.

The New England Puritan burns witches, wrestles for months with the horrors of Satan's invisible world, and all ghastly phantasms, the daily and hourly precursors of the Last Day; then suddenly bethinks him that he is frantic, weeps bitterly, prays contritely — and the history of that gloomy season lies behind him like a frightful dream.

And Old England too has had her share of such frenzies and panics; though happily, like other old maladies, they have grown milder of late: and since the days of Titus Oates, have mostly passed without loss of men's lives,[7] or indeed without much other loss than that of reason, for the time, in the sufferers. In this mitigated form, however, the distemper is of pretty regular recurrence — and may be reckoned on at intervals, like other natural visitations; so that reasonable men deal with it, as the Londoners do with their fogs — go cautiously out into the groping crowd, and patiently carry lanterns at noon; knowing, by a well-grounded faith, that the sun is still in existence, and will one day reappear. How often have we heard, for the last fifty years, that the country was wrecked, and fast sinking; whereas, up to this date, the country is entire and afloat! The 'State in Danger' is a condition of things, which we have witnessed a hundred times; and as for the church, it has seldom been out of 'danger' since we can remember it.

All men are aware, that the present is a crisis of this sort; and why it has become so. The repeal of the Test Acts, and then of the Catholic disabilities,[8] has struck many of their admirers with an indescribable astonishment. Those things seemed fixed and immovable — deep as the foundations of the world; and, lo! in a moment they have vanished, and their place knows them no more! Our worthy friends mistook the slumbering Leviathan for an island[9] — often as they had been assured, that Intolerance was, and could be, nothing but a Monster; and so, mooring under the lee, they had anchored comfortably in his scaly rind, thinking to take good cheer — as for some space they did. But now their Leviathan has suddenly dived under; and they can no longer be fastened in the stream of time; but must drift forward on it, even like the rest of the world — no very appalling fate, we think, could they but understand it; which, however, they will not yet, for a season. Their little island is gone; sunk deep amid confused eddies; and what is left worth caring for in the universe? What is it to them, that the great continents of the earth are still standing; and the polestar and all our loadstars, in the heavens, still shining and eternal? Their cherished little haven is gone, and they will not be comforted! And therefore, day after day, in all manner of periodical or perennial publications, the most lugubrious predictions are sent forth. The king has virtually abdicated; the church is a widow, without jointure;[10] public principle is gone; private honesty is going; society, in short, is fast falling in pieces; and a time of unmixed evil is come on us. At such a period, it was to be expected that the rage of prophecy should be more than usually excited. Accordingly, the Millennarians have come forth on the right hand, and the Millites on the left. The Fifth-monarchy men prophesy from the Bible, and the Utilitarians from Bentham. The one announce that the last of the seals

---

7   Titus Oates was the fabricator of a Catholic conspiracy to assassinate Charles II: between 1678 and 1681 at least 15 men were executed for involvement in this imaginary "Popish Plot" before it was exposed as a fraud.

8   The Test Acts, passed in the 1670s, barred non-conformist (i.e. non Church of England) protestants from various positions in public life in England, Wales and Ireland; draconian restrictions were placed on Catholics from 1698. The Test Act was repealed in 1828, and the last restrictions on Catholics were lifted in 1829.

9   Alluding to an episode in the voyages of St Brendan, in which the monks land on a whale, mistaking it for an island: the whale moves off when they light a cooking-fire.

10 Jointure was the property or income settled on an upper-class woman at her marriage to support her in the event of her husband's death.

is to be opened, positively, in the year 1860; and the other assures us, that 'the greatest happiness principle' is to make a heaven of earth, in a still shorter time.[11] We know these symptoms too well, to think it necessary or safe to interfere with them. Time and the hours will bring relief to all parties. The grand encourager of Delphic or other noises is — the Echo.[12] Left to themselves, they will soon dissipate, and die away in space.

Meanwhile, we too admit that the present is an important time — as all present time necessarily is. The poorest day that passes over us is the conflux of two Eternities! and is made up of currents that issue from the remotest Past, and flow onwards into the remotest Future. We were wise indeed, could we discern truly the signs of our own time; and, by knowledge of its wants and advantages, wisely adjust our own position in it. Let us then, instead of gazing idly into the obscure distance, look calmly around us, for a little, on the perplexed scene where we stand. Perhaps, on a more serious inspection, something of its perplexity will disappear, some of its distinctive characters, and deeper tendencies, more clearly reveal themselves; whereby our own relations to it, our own true aims and endeavours in it, may also become clearer.

Were we required to characterise this age of ours by any single epithet, we should be tempted to call it, not an Heroical, Devotional, Philosophical, or Moral Age, but, above all others, the Mechanical Age. It is the Age of Machinery, in every outward and inward sense of that word; the age which, with its whole undivided might, forwards, teaches and practises the great art of adapting means to ends. Nothing is now done directly, or by hand; all is by rule and calculated contrivance. For the simplest operation, some helps and accompaniments, some cunning, abbreviating process is in readiness. Our old modes of exertion are all discredited, and thrown aside. On every hand, the living artisan is driven from his workshop, to make room for a speedier, inanimate one. The shuttle drops from the fingers of the weaver, and falls into iron fingers that ply it faster.[13] The sailor furls his sail, and lays down his oar, and bids a strong, unwearied servant, on vaporous wings, bear him through the waters. Men have crossed oceans by steam; the Birmingham Fire-king has visited the fabulous East; and the genius of the Cape, were there any Camoens now to sing it, has again been alarmed, and with far stranger thunders than Gamas.[14] There is no end to machinery. Even the horse is stripped of his

---

11 The Evangelical Revival in the protestant churches in Britain in the early nineteenth century included a strong millenarian element: that is, a belief that Christ's return, followed by the end of the world, was imminent. The Book of Revelation mentions a Fifth Monarchy that would rule at this period (following on from the four empires of the ancient world) and a book with seven seals, the breaking of which in turn constitute a count-down to the Final Judgement. Carlyle parallels this with the considerably more rational thought of the political philosophers Jeremy Bentham (1743–1832) and James Mill (1773–1836). They had argued (Mill in a series of articles in the *Edinburgh Review*) that government policy should be determined by 'the greatest happiness of the greatest number' of its subjects, a doctrine known as Utilitarianism.
12 Delphic: prophetic, like the classical Greek oracle at Delphi.
13 Steam-powered looms for weaving cloth had been multiplying and improving since the start of the century: in 1829 they accounted for about half the cloth produced in Britain, and in the following decades would replace the hand-loom completely, and wipe out the cottage-based hand-loom weavers as a class.
14 The first commercial steamship began taking passengers from Glasgow to Greenock in 1812; by 1829 ocean-going ships were using steam-engines to supplement sails on Atlantic crossings, and one made it round Cape Horn to Calcutta in 1825. This sea-route to India was pioneered by the Portuguese sailor Vasco de Gama in 1497–9; he is celebrated, alongside other Portuguese heroes of the period, in the epic poem *The Lusiads* (1573) by Luís de Camões

harness, and finds a fleet fire-horse yoked in his stead.[15] Nay, we have an artist that hatches chickens by steam — the very brood-hen is to be superseded! For all earthly, and for some unearthly purposes, we have machines and mechanic furtherances; for mincing our cabbages; for casting us into magnetic sleep. We remove mountains, and make seas our smooth highway; nothing can resist us. We war with rude nature; and, by our resistless engines, come off always victorious, and loaded with spoils.

What wonderful accessions have thus been made, and are still making, to the physical power of mankind; how much better fed, clothed, lodged, and, in all outward respects, accommodated, men now are, or might be, by a given quantity of labour, is a grateful reflection which forces itself on every one. What changes, too, this addition of power is introducing into the social system; how wealth has more and more increased, and at the same time gathered itself more and more into masses, strangely altering the old relations, and increasing the distance between the rich and the poor, will be a question for Political Economists — and a much more complex and important one than any they have yet engaged with. But leaving these matters for the present, let us observe how the mechanical genius of our time has diffused itself into quite other provinces. Not the external and physical alone is now managed by machinery, but the internal and spiritual also. Here, too, nothing follows its spontaneous course, nothing is left to be accomplished by old, natural methods. Every thing has its cunningly devised implements, its pre-established apparatus; it is not done by hand, but by machinery. Thus we have machines for Education: Lancastrian machines; Hamiltonian machines — monitors, maps and emblems.[16] Instruction, that mysterious communing of Wisdom with Ignorance, is no longer an indefinable tentative process, requiring a study of individual aptitudes, and a perpetual variation of means and methods, to attain the same end; but a secure, universal, straightforward business, to be conducted in the gross, by proper mechanism, with such intellect as comes to hand. Then, we have Religious machines, of all imaginable varieties — the Bible Society, professing a far higher and heavenly structure, is found, on enquiry, to be altogether an earthly contrivance,[17] supported by collection of monies, by fomenting of vanities, by puffing, intrigue and chicane — and yet, in effect, a very excellent machine for converting the heathen. It is the same in all other departments. Has any man, or any society of men, a truth to speak, a piece of spiritual work to do, they can nowise proceed at once, and with the mere natural organs, but must first call a public meeting, appoint committees, issue prospectuses, eat a public dinner; in a word, construct or borrow machinery, wherewith to speak it and do it. Without machinery they were hopeless, helpless — a colony of Hindoo weavers squatting in the heart of Lancashire.[18] Then every machine must have its moving power, in some of the great currents of society: Every

---

(known as Camoens in English). Birmingham appears here as a hotbed of engineering innovation.

15 At the time of Carlyle's writing in 1829, steam locomotives were already used to pull coal and ore from mines to ironworks. The first passenger railway, the Liverpool and Manchester, opened the following year.

16 Carlyle alludes to two educational reformers: Joseph Lancaster (1778–1838), whose methods included the teaching of younger by older pupils (monitors), and James Hamilton (1769–1831), who developed a new method of teaching languages.

17 The British and Foreign Bible Society, an Evangelical missionary organisation, was founded in 1804.

18 As an image of irrelevance, this has a particular poignancy. The Bengali textile industry had expanded vastly since the mid 17th century to meet demand from Britain; it was wiped out by the cheaper produce of steam-powered production in, above all, Lancashire.

little sect among us, Unitarians, Utilitarians, Anabaptists, Phrenologists,[19] must each have its periodical, its monthly or quarterly magazine—hanging out, like its windmill, into the *popularis aura,*[20] to grind meal for the society.

With individuals, in like manner, natural strength avails little. No individual now hopes to accomplish the poorest enterprise single-handed, and without mechanical aids; he must make interest with some existing corporation, and till his field with their oxen. In these days, more emphatically than ever, 'to live, signifies to unite with a party, or to make one.' Philosophy, Science, Art, Literature, all depend on machinery. No Newton, by silent meditation, now discovers the system of the world from the falling of an apple; but some quite other than Newton stands in his Museum, his Scientific Institution, and behind whole batteries of retorts, digesters, and galvanic piles, imperatively 'interrogates Nature,'[21] — who, however, shows no haste to answer. In defect of Raphaels, and Angelos, and Mozarts, we have Royal Academies of Painting, Sculpture, Music;[22] whereby the languishing spirit of Art may be strengthened by the more generous diet of a Public Kitchen. Literature, too, has its Paternoster-row mechanism,[23] its Trade-dinners, its Editorial conclaves, and huge subterranean, puffing bellows; so that books are not only printed, but, in a great measure, written and sold, by machinery. National culture, spiritual benefit of all sorts, is under the same management. No Queen Christina, in these times, needs to send for her Descartes; no King Frederick for his Voltaire,[24] and painfully nourish him with pensions and flattery: But any sovereign of taste, who wishes to enlighten his people, has only to impose a new tax, and with the proceeds establish Philosophic Institutes. Hence the Royal and Imperial Societies, the Bibliothèques, Glypcothèques,[25] Technothèques, which front us in all capital cities, like so many well-finished hives, to which it is expected the stray agencies of Wisdom will swarm of their own accord, and hive and make honey. In like manner, among ourselves, when it is thought that religion is declining, we have only to vote half-a-million's worth of bricks and mortar, and build new churches. In Ireland, it seems they have gone still farther—having actually established a 'Penny-a-week Purgatory Society!' Thus does the Genius of Mechanism stand by to help us in all difficulties and emergencies; and, with his iron back, bears all our burdens.

---

19 The 'sects' mentioned here are a heterogeneous bunch: the Anabaptists are a very old Protestant sect, the Unitarians, as a denomination, a fairly new one. Phrenology was a pseudo-science which held that the shape of the skull was a guide to personality.

20 *Popularis aura*: public opinion.

21 Isaac Newton (1643–1727), mathematician and discoverer of universal laws of motion. 'Galvanic piles' are what we would now call electric batteries.

22 In defect of: 'in default of, for want of' (*OED*). In Britain, the Royal Academy of Arts was founded in 1768; of Music in 1822. In France, the Royal Academy of Painting and Sculpture dates back to 1648.

23 Paternoster Row was a centre of the London publishing trade. The following reference to bellows depends on the colloquial expression for promoting books through good reviews, 'puffing'. The *Edinburgh Review* saw itself as above all that kind of thing.

24 The paradigm cases of Enlightenment thinkers receiving patronage from 'enlightened' absolutist rulers: Queen Christina of Sweden invited Descartes (see below) to her court in 1649 (the Baltic winter killed him within six months); Voltaire (1694–1778) lasted three years (1750–52) with Frederick the Great of Prussia before falling out with his people and fleeing back to France.

25 A bibliothèque is a library: Carlyle invents the two following words analogously with it. Glypcothèques: in ancient Greek, *glyphikos* means 'to do with carving', so Carlyle might be thinking of a sculpture gallery in coining this word.

These things, which we state lightly enough here, are yet of deep import, and indicate a mighty change in our whole manner of existence. For the same habit regulates, not our modes of action alone, but our modes of thought and feeling. Men are grown mechanical in head and in heart, as well as in hand. They have lost faith in individual endeavour, and in natural force, of any kind. Not for internal perfection, but for external combinations and arrangements, for institutions, constitutions — for Mechanism of one sort or other, do they hope and struggle. Their whole efforts, attachments, opinions, turn on mechanism, and are of a mechanical character.

We may trace this tendency, we think, very distinctly, in all the great manifestations of our time; in its intellectual aspect, the studies it most favours, and its manner of conducting them; in its practical aspects, its politics, arts, religion, morals; in the whole sources, and throughout the whole currents, of its spiritual, no less than its material activity.

Consider, for example, the state of Science generally, in Europe, at this period. It is admitted, on all sides, that the Metaphysical and Moral Sciences are falling into decay, while the Physical are engrossing, every day, more respect and attention. In most of the European nations there is now no such thing as a Science of Mind; only more or less advancement in the general science, or the special sciences, of matter. The French were the first to desert this school of Metaphysics; and though they have lately affected to revive it, it has yet no signs of vitality. The land of Malebranche, Pascal, Descartes, and Fenelon, has now only its Cousins and Villemains;[26] while, in the department of Physics, it reckons far other names. Among ourselves, the Philosophy of Mind, after a rickety infancy, which never reached the vigour of manhood, fell suddenly into decay, languished, and finally died out, with its last amiable cultivator, Professor Stewart.[27] In no nation but Germany has any decisive effort been made in psychological science; not to speak of any decisive result.[28] The science of the age, in short, is physical, chemical, physiological, and, in all shapes, mechanical. Our favourite Mathematics, the highly prized exponent of all these other sciences, has also become more and more mechanical. Excellence, in what is called its higher departments, depends less on natural genius, than on acquired expertness in wielding its machinery. Without undervaluing the wonderful results which a Lagrange, or Laplace, educes by means of it,[29] we may remark, that its calculus, differential and integral, is little else than a more cunningly-constructed arithmetical mill, where the factors being put in, are, as it were, ground into the true product, under cover, and without other effort on our part, than steady turning of the handle. We have more Mathematics certainly than ever; but

---

26 Nicolas Malebranche (1638–1715) and Blaise Pascal (1623–62) both combined pioneering work in rationalist philosophy and mathematics with religious piety; René Descartes (1596–1650), whose rationalist philosophy included an attempt to prove the existence of God; François Fénelon (1651–1715), Catholic theologian and critic of the French monarchy. Carlyle contrasts these giants of early modern French thought with the more derivative work of contemporary French writers like philosopher Victor Cousin (1792–1867) and literary historian Abel-François Villemain (1790–1870).

27 Dugald Stewart (1753–1828), influential professor of Moral Philosophy at Edinburgh 1785–1810, but a populariser of the Scottish tradition in philosophy rather than one of its innovators.

28 Carlyle has in mind German idealism, to which his own thinking owes a great deal; especially Immanuel Kant (1724 –1804) and G.W.F. Hegel (1770–1831).

29 Joseph-Louis Lagrange (1736 –1813), pioneer of calculus in its application to mechanics; Pierre-Simon Laplace, author of *Mécanique Céleste* (1799–1825) which applied similar ideas to the solar system.

less Mathesis.[30] Archimedes and Plato could not have read the *Méchanique Céleste*; but neither would the whole French Institute see aught in that saying, 'God geometrises!' but a sentimental rodomontade.[31]

From Locke's time downwards, our whole Metaphysics have been physical; not a spiritual Philosophy, but a material one. The singular estimation in which his Essay was so long held as a scientific work, (for the character of the man entitled all he said to veneration,) will one day be thought a curious indication of the spirit of these times.[32] His whole doctrine is mechanical, in its aim and origin, in its method and its results. It is a mere discussion concerning the origin of our consciousness, or ideas, or whatever else they are called; a genetic history of what we see *in* the mind. But the grand secrets of Necessity and Freewill, of the mind's vital or non-vital dependence on matter, of our mysterious relations to Time and Space, to God, to the universe, are not, in the faintest degree, touched on in their enquiries; and seem not to have the smallest connexion with them.

The last class of our Scotch Metaphysicians had a dim notion that much of this was wrong; but they knew not how to right it. The school of Reid had also from the first taken a mechanical course, not seeing any other. The singular conclusions at which Hume, setting out from their admitted premises, was arriving, brought this school into being; they let loose Instinct, as an undiscriminating bandog, to guard them against these conclusions—they tugged lustily at the logical chain by which Hume was so coldly towing them and the world into bottomless abysses of Atheism and Fatalism.[33] But the chain somehow snapped between them; and the issue has been that nobody now cares about either—any more than about Hartley's, Darwin's, or Priestley's contemporaneous doings in England.[34] Hartley's vibrations and vibratiuncles one would think were material and mechanical enough; but our continental neighbours have gone still farther. One of their philosophers has lately discovered, that 'as the liver secretes bile, so does the brain secrete thought;' which astonishing discovery Dr. Cabanis, more lately still, in his *Rapports du Physique el du Morale de l'Homme*, has pushed into its minutest developements.[35] The metaphysical philosophy of this last enquirer is certainly no shadowy or unsubstantial one. He fairly lays open our moral structure with

---

30 *Mathesis* in Greek means the *action* of learning (*OED*).

31 The phrase is attributed to Plato by the Roman historian Plutarch; the Greek philosopher does equate geometry with a knowledge of the divine in his surviving writings. Rodomontade: 'a vainglorious brag or boast' (*OED*).

32 The English philosopher John Locke (1632–1704) published *An Essay Concerning Human Understanding* in 1690. Where Descartes and his followers ground truth on the operation of reason on its own, Locke finds the origin of knowledge in the world as we experience it through our senses, from which we ultimately derive all the ideas with which we think (empiricism).

33 David Hume (1711–76) in *A Treatise of Human Nature* (1739–40) argued that, on Locke's definition of knowledge, we cannot *know* the existence of the self, or of the world, or of relations of cause and effect. Thomas Reid (1710–1796) attempted to refute Hume's scepticism with a 'Common Sense' school of epistemology. Hume was also a notorious atheist.

34 David Hartley (1705–57) and Joseph Priestley (1733–1804), both, among their various other work, tended to understand human thought and experience in material terms, as a movement of particles, or an analogous 'association of ideas'. Erasmus Darwin (1731–1802) explored the way in which living organisms adapt themselves to their environments: perhaps another instance, for Carlyle, of life being determined by mere material circumstances.

35 Pierre Jean George Cabanis (1757–1808). *On the Relation between the Physical and Moral Aspects of Man* (1802) tries to reduce psychology to a branch of physiology.

his dissecting-knives and real metal probes; and exhibits it to the inspection of mankind, by Leuwenhoek microscopes and inflation with the anatomical blowpipe.[36] Thought, he is inclined to hold, is still secreted by the brain; but then Poetry and Religion (and it is really worth knowing) are 'a product of the smaller intestines!' We have the greatest admiration for this learned doctor: with what scientific stoicism he walks through the land of wonders, unwondering—like a wise man through some huge, gaudy, imposing Vauxhall, whose fire-works, cascades, and symphonies, the vulgar may enjoy and believe in—but where he finds nothing real but the saltpetre, pasteboard and catgut.[37] His book may be regarded as the ultimatum of mechanical metaphysics in our time: a remarkable realisation of what in Martinus Scriblerus was still only an idea, that 'as the jack had a meat-roasting quality, so had the body a thinking quality,'— upon the strength of which the Nurembergers were to build a wood and leather man, 'who should reason as well as most country parsons.'[38] Vaucanson did indeed make a wooden duck, that seemed to eat and digest; but that bold scheme of the Nurembergers remained for a more modern virtuoso.[39]

This condition of the two great departments of knowledge; the outward, cultivated exclusively on mechanical principles—the inward finally abandoned, because, cultivated on such principles, it is found to yield no result— sufficiently indicates the intellectual bias of our time, its all-pervading disposition towards that line of inquiry. In fact, an inward persuasion has long been diffusing itself, and now and then even comes to utterance. That, except the external, there are no true sciences; that to the inward world (if there be any) our only conceivable road is through the outward; that, in short, what cannot be investigated and understood mechanically, cannot be investigated and understood at all. We advert the more particularly to these intellectual propensies, as to prominent symptoms of our age; because Opinion is at all times doubly related to Action, first as cause, then as effect; and the speculative tendency of any age, will therefore give us, on the whole, the best indications of its practical tendency.

Nowhere, for example, is the deep, almost exclusive faith, we have in Mechanism, more visible than in the Politics of this time. Civil government does, by its nature, include much that is mechanical, and must be treated accordingly. We term it indeed, in ordinary language, the Machine of Society, and talk of it as the grand working wheel from which all private machines must derive, or to which they must adapt, their movements. Considered merely as a metaphor, all this is well enough; but here, as in so many other cases, the 'foam hardens itself into a shell,' and the shadow we have wantonly evoked stands terrible before us, and will not depart at our bidding. Government includes much also that is not mechanical, and cannot be treated mechanically; of which latter truth, as appears to us, the political speculations and exertions of our time are taking less and less cognisance.

36 Antony van Leuwenhoek (1632 –1723) was the first microbiologist.
37 Vauxhall was a pleasure garden on the south bank of the Thames in London, which put on the kinds of entertainments mentioned here. Saltpetre is an ingredient in gunpowder (in the fireworks); pasteboard is used to construct stage scenery; and catgut provided the strings for musical instruments.
38 A jack is a machine for turning a spit. *Memoirs of Martinus Scriblerus* (1741) was a satirical pseudo-autobiography written by a group of writers including Jonathan Swift and Alexander Pope. It includes a description of an attempt, at Nuremberg, to construct a mechanical man capable of thought.
39 Virtuoso: here, scientist or scholar. The eighteenth century was fascinated by clockwork automatons: Jacques de Vaucanson (1709–1782) made the most sophisticated ones, including the duck mentioned here.

Nay, in the very outset, we might note the mighty interest taken in *mere political arrangements,* as itself the sign of a mechanical age. The whole discontent of Europe takes this direction. The deep, strong cry of all civilised nations—a cry which, every one now sees, must and will be answered, is, Give us a reform of Government! A good structure of legislation—a proper check upon the executive—a wise arrangement of the judiciary, is *all* that is wanting for human happiness. The Philosopher of this age is not a Socrates, a Plato, a Hooker, or Taylor,[40] who inculcates on men the necessity and infinite worth of moral goodness, the great truth that our happiness depends on the mind which is within us, and not on the circumstances which are without us; but a Smith, a De Lolme,[41] a Bentham, who chiefly inculcates the reverse of this—that our happiness depends entirely on external circumstances; nay that the strength and dignity of the mind within us is itself the creature and consequence of these. Were the laws, the government, in good order, all were well with us; the rest would care for itself! Dissentients from this opinion, expressed or implied, are now rarely to he met with; widely and angrily as men differ in its application, the principle is admitted by all.

Equally mechanical, and of equal simplicity, are the methods proposed by both parties for completing or securing this all-sufficient perfection of arrangement. It is no longer the moral, religious, spiritual condition of the people that is our concern, but their physical, practical, economical condition, as regulated by public laws. Thus is the Body-politic more than ever worshipped and tended: But the Soul-politic less than ever. Love of country, in any high or generous sense, in any other than an almost animal sense, or mere habit, has little importance attached to it in such reforms, or in the opposition shown them. Men are to be guided only by their self-interests. Good government is a good balancing of these: and, except a keen eye and appetite for self-interest, requires no virtue in any quarter. To both parties it is emphatically a machine: to the discontented, a 'taxing-machine;' to the contented, a 'machine for securing property.' Its duties and its faults are not those of a father, but of an active parish constable.[42]

Thus it is by the mere condition of the machine; by preserving it untouched, or else by re-constructing it, and oiling it anew, that man's salvation as a social being is to be insured and indefinitely promoted. Contrive the fabric of law aright, and without farther effort on your part, that divine spirit of freedom which all hearts venerate and long for, will of herself come to inhabit it; and under her healing wings every noxious influence will wither, every good and salutary one more and more expand. Nay, so devoted are we to this principle, and at the same time so curiously mechanical, that a new trade, specially grounded on it, has arisen among us, under the name of 'Codification,' or code-making in the abstract;[43] whereby any people, for a reasonable consideration, may be accommodated with a patent code—more easily than curious individuals with patent breeches, for the people does *not* need to be measured first.

To us who live in the midst of all this, and see continually the faith, hope and practice of every one founded on Mechanism of one kind or other, it is apt to seem quite natural, and as if it could never have been otherwise. Nevertheless, if we recollect or reflect a

---

40 Richard Hooker (1554–1653), Anglican theologian; I cannot find a likely candidate for 'Taylor'.

41 Adam Smith (1723–1790), moral philosopher and political economist; Jean-Louis de Lolme (1741–1804), political theorist, who in 1775 advocated recasting the French constitution along British lines.

42 Carlyle is describing one version of the 'liberal' state, in which government's duties extend no further than to protect property and enforce contracts; often referred to a the 'night watchman' version of the state.

43 'Code' here meaning, of course, *legal* code or constitution.

little, we shall find both that it has been, and might again be otherwise. The domain of Mechanism, — meaning thereby political, ecclesiastical or other outward establishments, — was once considered as embracing, and we are persuaded can at any time embrace, but a limited portion of man's interests, and by no means the highest portion.

To speak a little pedantically, there is a science of *Dynamics* in man's fortunes and nature, as well as of *Mechanics*. There is a science which treats of, and practically addresses, the primary, unmodified forces and energies of man, the mysterious springs of Love, and Fear, and Wonder, of Enthusiasm, Poetry, Religion, all which have a truly vital and *infinite* character; as well as a science which practically addresses the finite, modified developments of these, when they take the shape of immediate 'motives,' as hope of reward, or as fear of punishment.

Now it is certain, that in former times the wise men, the enlightened lovers of their kind, who appeared generally as Moralists, Poets or Priests, did, without neglecting the Mechanical province, deal chiefly with the Dynamical; applying themselves chiefly to regulate, increase and purify the inward primary powers of man; and fancying that herein lay the main difficulty, and the best service they could undertake. But a wide difference is manifest in our age. For the wise men, who now appear as Political Philosophers, deal exclusively with the Mechanical province; and occupying themselves in counting-up and estimating men's motives, strive by curious checking and balancing, and other adjustments of Profit and Loss, to guide them to their true advantage: while, unfortunately, those same 'motives' are so innumerable, and so variable in every individual, that no really useful conclusion can ever be drawn from their enumeration. But though Mechanism, wisely contrived, has done much for man, in a social and moral point of view, we cannot be persuaded that it has ever been the chief source of his worth or happiness. Consider the great elements of human enjoyment, the attainments and possessions that exalt man's life to its present height, and see what part of these he owes to institutions, to Mechanism of any kind; and what to the instinctive, unbounded force, which Nature herself lent him, and still continues to him. Shall we say, for example, that Science and Art are indebted principally to the founders of Schools and Universities? Did not Science originate rather, and gain advancement, in the obscure closets of the Roger Bacons, Keplers, Newtons;[44] in the workshops of the Fausts and the Watts;[45] — wherever, and in what guise soever Nature, from the first times downwards, had sent a gifted spirit upon the earth? Again, were Homer and Shakspeare members of any beneficed guild, or made Poets by means of it? Was Painting and Sculpture created by forethought, brought into the world by institutions for that end? No; Science and Art have, from first to last, been the free gift of Nature; an unsolicited, unexpected gift — often even a fatal one. These things rose up, as it were, by spontaneous growth, in the free soil and sunshine of Nature. They were not planted or grafted, nor even greatly multiplied or improved by the culture or manuring of institutions. Generally speaking, they have derived only partial help from these; often enough have suffered damage. They made constitutions for themselves. They originated in the Dynamical nature of man, not in his Mechanical nature.

Or, to take an infinitely higher instance, that of the Christian Religion, which, under every theory of it, in the believing or unbelieving mind, must ever be regarded

44 Roger Bacon (d.1294), Franciscan friar and one of the first to promulgate the scientific knowledge of the Islamic world in the west; Johannes Kepler (1571–1630), discoverer of the laws of planetary motion.
45 An odd conjunction of the fictional and the contemporary: Faust is the frustrated polymath of the 16th-century German legend who sells his soul to the devil in exchange for knowledge; James Watt (1736–1819) the engineer who first developed practicable steam engines.

as the crowning glory, or rather the life and soul, of our whole modern culture: How did Christianity arise and spread abroad among men? Was it by institutions, and establishments, and well-arranged systems of mechanism? Not so; on the contrary, in all past and existing institutions for those ends, its divine spirit has invariably been found to languish and decay. It arose in the mystic deeps of man's soul; and was spread abroad by the 'preaching of the word,' by simple, altogether natural and individual efforts; and flew, like hallowed fire, from heart to heart, till all were purified and illuminated by it; and its heavenly light shone, as it still shines, and as sun or star will ever shine, through the whole dark destinies of man. Here again was no Mechanism; man's highest attainment was accomplished, Dynamically, not Mechanically. Nay, we will venture to say, that no high attainment, not even any far-extending movement among men, was ever accomplished otherwise. Strange as it may seem, if we read History with any degree of thoughtfulness, we shall find that the checks and balances of Profit and Loss have never been the grand agents with men; that they have never been roused into deep, thorough, all-pervading efforts by any computable prospect of Profit and Loss, for any visible, finite object; but always for some invisible and infinite one. The Crusades took their rise in Religion; their visible object was, commercially speaking, worth nothing. It was the boundless, Invisible world that was laid bare in the imaginations of those men; and in its burning light, the visible shrunk as a scroll. Not mechanical, nor produced by mechanical means, was this vast movement. No dining at Freemasons' Tavern,[46] with the other long train of modern machinery; no cunning reconciliation of 'vested interests,' was required here: only the passionate voice of one man, the rapt soul looking through the eyes of one man;[47] and rugged, steel-clad Europe trembled beneath his words, and followed him whither he listed. In later ages, it was still the same. The Reformation had an invisible, mystic, and ideal aim; the result was indeed to be embodied in external things; but its spirit, its worth, was internal, invisible, infinite. Our English Revolution, too, originated in Religion.[48] Men did battle, even in those days, not for Purse sake, but for Conscience sake. Nay, in our own days, it is no way different. The French Revolution itself had something higher in it than cheap bread and a Habeas-corpus act.[49] Here too was an Idea; a Dynamic, not a Mechanic force. It was a struggle, though a blind and at last an insane one, for the infinite, divine nature of Right, of Freedom, of Country.

Thus does man, in every age, vindicate, consciously or unconsciously, his celestial birthright. Thus does Nature hold on her wondrous, unquestionable course; and all our systems and theories are but so many froth-eddies or sand-banks, which from time to time she casts up and washes away. When we can drain the Ocean into mill-ponds, and bottle up the Force of Gravity, to be sold by retail, in our gas-jars; then may we hope to comprehend the infinitudes of man's soul under formulas of Profit and Loss; and rule over this too, as over a patent engine, by checks, and valves, and balances.

Nay, even with regard to Government itself, can it be necessary to remind any one that Freedom, without which indeed all spiritual life is impossible, depends on

---

46 This was the regular meeting place of a debating society in London.

47 The 'one man' is presumably Pope Urban II, who organised the First Crusade in 1095; but the 'rapt' and 'passionate' voice might more plausibly belong to St. Bernard of Clairvaux, zealous promoter of the Second Crusade in 1146–7.

48 Carlyle is probably thinking of the accession of William III in 1688, commonly referred to as 'the Revolution' in his time. But this was, in England at least, a peaceful process; unlike the Civil Wars of the 1640s, which gave more opportunity for giving 'battle' in the literal sense.

49 'Habeas Corpus' names the right, originating in English Common Law, to freedom from arbitrary detention by the state.

infinitely more complex influences than either the extension or the curtailment of the 'democratic interest?' Who is there that 'taking the high *priori* road,' shall point out what these influences are;[50] what deep, subtle, inextricably entangled influences they have been, and may be? For man is not the creature and product of Mechanism; but, in a far truer sense, its creator and producer: it is the noble people that makes the noble Government; rather than conversely. On the whole, Institutions are much; but they are not all. The freest and highest spirits of the world have often been found under strange outward circumstances: Saint Paul and his brother Apostles were politically slaves; Epictetus was personally one.[51] Again, forget the influences of Chivalry and Religion, and ask, — what countries produced Columbus and Las Casas? Or, descending from virtue and heroism to mere energy and spiritual talent: Cortes, Pizarro, Alba, Ximenes?[52] The Spaniards of the sixteenth century were indisputably the noblest nation of Europe; yet they had the Inquisition and Philip II. They have the same government at this day; and are the lowest nation. The Dutch, too, have retained their old constitution; but no Siege of Leyden, no William the Silent, not even an Egmont or De Witt, any longer appears among them.[53] With ourselves, also, where much has changed, effect has nowise followed cause, as it should have done: two centuries ago, the Commons' Speaker addressed Queen Elizabeth on bended knees, happy that the virago's foot did not even smite him; yet the people were then governed, not by a Castlereagh, but by a Burghley; they had their Shakspeare and Philip Sidney, where we have our Sheridan Knowles and Beau Brummel.[54]

These and the like facts are so familiar, the truths which they preach so obvious, and have in all past times been so universally believed and acted on, that we should almost feel ashamed for repeating them; were it not that, on every hand, the memory of them seems to have passed away, or at best died into a faint tradition, of no value as a practical principle. To judge by the loud clamour of our Constitution-builders,

---

50 An '*a priori*' argument is one from first principles. Carlyle is quoting Pope's couplet on philosophical scepticism in *The Dunciad* book IV ll.471–2: 'We nobly take the high Priori road/ And reason downward, till we doubt of God.'

51 Epictetus (55 –135), Greek Stoic philosopher. The Apostle Paul was in fact a Roman citizen.

52 'Alba' is Fernando, duke of Alba, Spain's ruthless enforcer against the rebels in the Low Countries from 1567. The others are all men involved in the Spanish crown's conquests in the Americas in the 16th Century: Christopher Columbus (d.1506), their Genoese admiral; Hernán Cortes (d.1547) and Francisco Pizarro (d.1541), conquistador generals; Fortún Ximenes (d.1533), first European settler in Baja California. The odd one out is Bartolomé de las Casas (1484–1566), the Dominican priest who campaigned to stop the slaughter and enslavement of the native people.

53 William I, Prince of Orange (d.1584), leader of the Dutch revolt against Spanish rule in the 1560s; Lamoral, Count of Egmont (d.1568), Flemish statesman whose execution by the Duke of Alba helped spark the revolt; Johan de Witt (d.1672), prime minister presiding over the rise of the now independent United Provinces to imperial wealth, involving several wars with England. Leiden held out heroically against a Spanish siege in 1573–4.

54 William Cecil, Baron Burghley (d.1598), one of Elizabeth I's closest ministers for nearly 40 years; Robert Stewart, Viscount Castlereagh, was Secretary of State for War and the Colonies during the conflict with Napoleon, and influential in the post-war reconstruction of the European order, but committed suicide in 1822 by cutting his throat. James Sheridan Knowles (1759–1840) was a successful actor and playwright in the 1820s and 30s. Sir Philip Sidney (1554–86) is best known now as a poet, but figures here as an ideal type of the English gentleman (also a courtier and soldier, he died fighting against the Spanish in the Low Countries), in contrast to George 'Beau' Brummell (d.1840), the quintessential Regency gambler and dandy.

Statists, Economists, directors, creators, reformers of Public Societies; in a word, all manner of Mechanists, from the Cartwright up to the Code-maker; and by the nearly total silence of all Preachers and Teachers who should give a voice to Poetry, Religion and Morality, we might fancy either that man's Dynamical nature was, to all spiritual intents, extinct—or else so perfected, that nothing more was to be made of it by the old means; and henceforth only in his Mechanical contrivances did any hope exist for him.

To define the limits of these two departments of man's activity, which work into one another, and by means of one another, so intricately and inseparably, were by its nature an impossible attempt. Their relative importance, even to the wisest mind, will vary in different times, according to the special wants and dispositions of those times. Meanwhile, it seems clear enough that only in the right co-ordination of the two, and the vigorous forwarding of *both*, does our true line of action lie. Undue cultivation of the inward or Dynamical province leads to idle, visionary, impracticable courses, and, especially in rude eras, to Superstition and Fanaticism, with their long train of baleful and well-known evils. Undue cultivation of the outward, again, though less immediately prejudicial, and even for the time productive of many palpable benefits, must, in the long-run, by destroying Moral Force, which is the parent of all other Force, prove not less certainly, and perhaps still more hopelessly, pernicious. This, we take it, is the grand characteristic of our age. By our skill in Mechanism, it has come to pass that, in the management of external things we excel all other ages; while in whatever respects the pure moral nature, in true dignity of soul and character, we are perhaps inferior to most civilised ages.

In fact, if we look deeper, we shall find that this faith in Mechanism has now struck its roots down into man's most intimate, primary sources of conviction; and is thence sending up, over his whole life and activity, innumerable stems—fruit-bearing and poison-bearing. The truth is, men have lost their belief in the Invisible, and believe, and hope, and work only in the Visible; or, to speak it in other words, This is not a Religious age. Only the material, the immediately practical, not the divine and spiritual, is important to us. The infinite, absolute character of Virtue has passed into a finite, conditional one; it is no longer a worship of the Beautiful and Good; but a calculation of the Profitable. Worship, indeed, in any sense, is not recognised among us, or is mechanically explained into Fear of pain, or Hope of pleasure. Our true Deity is Mechanism. It has subdued external Nature for us, and, we think, it will do all other things. We are Giants in physical power: in a deeper than metaphorical sense, we are Titans,[55] that strive, by heaping mountain on mountain, to conquer Heaven also.

The strong mechanical character, so visible in the spiritual pursuits and methods of this age, may be traced much farther into the condition and prevailing disposition of our spiritual nature itself. Consider, for example, the general fashion of Intellect in this era. Intellect, the power man has of knowing and believing, is now nearly synonymous with Logic, or the mere power of arranging and communicating. Its implement is not Meditation, but Argument. 'Cause and effect' is almost the only category under which we look at, and work with, all Nature. Our first question with regard to any object is not, What is it? but, How is it? We are no longer instinctively driven to apprehend, and lay to heart, what is Good and Lovely, but rather to enquire, as onlookers, how it is produced, whence it comes, whither it goes? Our favourite Philosophers have no love and no hatred; they stand among us not to do, nor to create any thing, but as a sort of Logic-mills, to grind out the true causes and effects of all that is done and created. To

---

55 The Titans, in Greek mythology, were the original gods, against whom the gods of Mount Olympus went to war.

the eye of a Smith, a Hume or a Constant, all is well that works quietly.[56] An Order of Ignatius Loyola, a Presbyterianism of John Knox, a Wickliffe, or a Henry the Eighth,[57] are simply so many mechanical phenomena, caused or causing.

The *Euphuist* of our day differs much from his pleasant predecessors.[58] An intellectual dapperling of these times boasts chiefly of his irresistible perspicacity, his 'dwelling in the daylight of truth,' and so forth; which, on examination, turns out to be a dwelling in the *rush*-light of 'closet-logic,'[59] and a deep unconsciousness that there is any other light to dwell in; or any other objects to survey with it. Wonder, indeed, is, on all hands, dying out: it is the sign of uncultivation to wonder. Speak to any small man of a high, majestic Reformation, of a high, majestic Luther; and forthwith he sets about 'accounting' for it! how the 'circumstances of the time' called for such a character, and found him, we suppose, standing girt and road-ready, to do its errand; how the 'circumstances of the time' created, fashioned, floated him quietly along into the result; how, in short, this small man, had he been there, could have performed the like himself! For it is the 'force of circumstances' that does everything; the force of one man can do nothing. Now all this is grounded on little more than a metaphor. We figure Society as a 'Machine,' and that mind is opposed to mind, as body is to body; whereby two, or at most ten, little minds must be stronger than one great mind. Notable absurdity! For the plain truth, very plain, we think is, that minds are opposed to minds in quite a different way; and *one* man that has a higher Wisdom, a hitherto unknown spiritual Truth in him, is stronger, not than ten men that have it not, or than ten thousand, but than *all* men that have it not; and stands among them with a quite ethereal, angelic power, as with a sword out of Heaven's own armoury, sky-tempered, which no buckler, and no tower of brass, will finally withstand.

But to us, in these times, such considerations rarely occur. We enjoy, we see nothing by direct vision; but only by reflexion, and in anatomical dismemberment. Like Sir Hudibras,[60] for every Why we must have a Wherefore. We have our little *theory* on all human and divine things. Poetry, the workings of genius itself, which in all times, with one or another meaning, has been called Inspiration, and held to be mysterious and inscrutable, is no longer without its scientific exposition. The building of the lofty rhyme is like any other masonry or bricklaying: we have theories of its rise, height, decline and fall — which latter, it would seem, is now near, among all people.[61] Of our 'Theories of Taste,' as they are called, wherein the deep, infinite, unspeakable Love

---

56 Benjamin Constant (1767–1830), French liberal political philosopher. What Constant has in common with Smith and Hume is a belief that the commercial basis of modern society makes its politics completely different from previous historical models: liberty now consists in the secure enjoyment of private goods (family or business) rather that in rights of participation in public politics that must be noisily, often violently, defended (as in the ancient Roman Republic and its French imitator in the 1790s).

57 Ignatius Loyola (1491–1556), founder of the Jesuit order as an intellectual counter-force to the Protestant reformation; John Knox (c.1510–1572), preacher and leader of the Scottish Reformation; John Wycliffe (c.1325–1384), first translator of the Bible into English and critic of the medieval church; Henry VIII of England (1491–1547), the king who forced the English church to split from Rome.

58 A euphuist is 16th-century verbal show-off, delighting in similes and alliteration.

59 Lighting in the homes of the poor consisted in a metal lamp full of oil, with a rush as a wick.

60 The hero of the mock-heroic narrative poem *Hudibras* (1663–4, 1678) by Samuel Butler, who answers every question by asking another one.

61 Carlyle might be thinking of Thomas Love Peacock's *Four Ages of Poetry* (1820) which takes something like this view.

of Wisdom and Beauty, which dwells in all men, is 'explained,' made mechanically visible, from 'Association,' and the like, why should we say anything?[62] Hume has written us a 'Natural History of Religion;'[63] in which one Natural History, all the rest are included. Strangely, too, does the general feeling coincide with Hume's in this wonderful problem; for whether his 'Natural History' be the right one or not, that Religion must have a Natural History, all of us, cleric and laic, seem to be agreed. He indeed regards it as a Disease, we again as Health; so far there is a difference; but in our first principle we are at one.

To what extent theological Unbelief, we mean intellectual dissent from the Church, in its view of Holy Writ, prevails at this day, would be a highly important, were it not, under any circumstances, an almost impossible inquiry. But the Unbelief, which is of a still more fundamental character, every man may see prevailing, with scarcely any but the faintest contradiction, all around him; even in the Pulpit itself. Religion, in most countries, more or less in every country, is no longer what it was, and should be—a thousand-voiced psalm from the heart of Man to his invisible Father, the fountain of all Goodness, Beauty, Truth, and revealed in every revelation of these; but for the most part, a wise prudential feeling grounded on mere calculation; a matter, as all others now are, of Expediency and Utility; whereby some smaller quantum of earthly enjoyment may be exchanged for a far larger quantum of celestial enjoyment. Thus Religion, too, is Profit; a working for wages; not Reverence, but vulgar Hope or Fear. Many, we know, very many, we hope, are still religious in a far different sense; were it not so, our case were too desperate: but to witness that such is the temper of the times, we take any calm observant man, who agrees or disagrees in our feeling on the matter, and ask him whether our *view* of it is not in general well-founded.

Literature, too, if we consider it, gives similar testimony. At no former era has Literature, the printed communication of Thought, been of such importance as it is now. We often hear that the Church is in danger; and truly so it is—in a danger it seems not to know of: For, with its tithes in the most perfect safety,[64] its functions are becoming more and more superseded. The true Church of England, at this moment, lies in the Editors of its Newspapers. These preach to the people daily, weekly; admonishing kings themselves; advising peace or war, with an authority which only the first Reformers, and a long-past class of Popes, were possessed of; inflicting moral censure; imparting moral encouragement, consolation, edification; in all ways, diligently 'administering the Discipline of the Church.' It may be said, too, that in private disposition, the new Preachers somewhat resemble the Mendicant Friars of old times:[65] outwardly full of holy zeal; inwardly not without stratagem, and hunger for terrestrial things. But omitting this class, and the boundless host of watery personages who pipe, as they are able, on so many scrannel straws,[66] let us look at the higher regions of Literature, where, if anywhere, the pure melodies of Poesy and Wisdom should be heard. Of natural talent there is no deficiency: one or two richly-endowed

---

62 The 'association of ideas', a concept long current in philosophy of mind, appears as a basis for poetry in Wordsworth's 1800 'Preface' to *Lyrical Ballads*.

63 This essay was published in 1757 in *Four Dissertations*. It discusses the development of religious belief through history as the product of human nature, putting to one side the possibility of divine agency in the world.

64 Tithes were the proportion of a parish's agricultural produce that went to support the church.

65 Mendicant: that is, one of the orders who lived entirely on charitable donations.

66 Scrannel: thin, meagre. Here, an echo of Milton, *Lycidas* (1637), complaining of other poets that 'their lean and flashy songs / Grate on their scrannel pipes of wretched straw' (ll.123–4).

individuals even give us a superiority in this respect. But what is the song they sing? Is it a tone of the Memnon Statue, breathing music as the *light* first touches it?[67] A 'liquid wisdom,' disclosing to our sense the deep, infinite harmonies of Nature and man's soul? Alas, no! It is not a matin or vesper hymn to the Spirit of Beauty, but a fierce clashing of cymbals, and shouting of multitudes, as children pass through the fire to Moloch![68] Poetry itself has no eye for the Invisible. Beauty is no longer the god it worships, but some brute image of Strength; which we may call an idol, for true Strength is one and the same with Beauty, and its worship also is a hymn. The meek, silent Light can mould, create and purify all nature; but the loud Whirlwind, the sign and product of Disunion, of Weakness, passes on, and is forgotten. How widely this veneration for the physically Strongest has spread itself through Literature, any one may judge, who reads either criticism or poem. We praise a work, not as 'true,' but as 'strong;' our highest praise is that it has 'affected' us, has 'terrified' us. All this, it has been well observed, is the 'maximum of the Barbarous,' the symptom, not of vigorous refinement, but of luxurious corruption. It speaks much, too, for men's indestructible love of truth, that nothing of this kind will abide with them; that even the talent of a Byron cannot permanently seduce us into idol-worship; that he, too, with all his wild syren charming, already begins to be disregarded and forgotten.[69]

Again, with respect to our Moral condition: here also, he who runs may read that the same physical, mechanical influences are everywhere busy. For the 'superior morality,' of which we hear so much, we, too, would desire to be thankful: at the same time, it were but blindness to deny that this 'superior morality' is properly rather an 'inferior criminality,' produced not by greater love of Virtue, but by greater perfection of Police; and of that far subtler and stronger Police, called Public Opinion. This last watches over us with its Argus eyes more keenly than ever;[70] but the 'inward eye' seems heavy with sleep. Of any belief in invisible, divine things, we find as few traces in our Morality as elsewhere. It is by tangible, material considerations that we are guided, not by inward and spiritual. Self-denial, the parent of all virtue, in any true sense of that word, has perhaps seldom been rarer: so rare is it, that the most, even in their abstract speculations, regard its existence as a chimera. Virtue is Pleasure, is Profit; no celestial, but an earthly thing. Virtuous men, Philanthropists, Martyrs, are happy accidents; their 'taste' lies the right way! In all senses, we worship and follow after Power; which may be called a physical pursuit. No man now loves Truth, as Truth must be loved, with an infinite love; but only with a finite love, and as it were *par amours.*[71] Nay, properly speaking, he does not *believe* and know it, but only '*thinks*' it, and that 'there is every probability!' He preaches it aloud, and rushes courageously forth with it — if there is a multitude huzzaing at his back! yet ever keeps looking over his shoulder, and the instant the huzzaing languishes, he too stops short. In fact, what morality we have takes the shape of Ambition, of Honour: beyond money and money's worth, our only rational blessedness is Popularity. It were but a fool's trick to die for conscience. Only for 'character,' by duel, or, in case of extremity, by suicide, is the wise

---

67 In Roman times, one of the colossi at Memnon on the Nile was reputed to issue a musical sound at dawn.

68 Moloch (in the King James bible, Molech) is an idol to whom God bans the Isrealites from giving child sacrifice: see e.g. Leviticus 20.2–5.

69 Byron, by far the most celebrated poet in English of his age, had died in 1824.

70 In Greek myth, Argus is a giant with a hundred eyes.

71 *Par amours*: that is, as a mistress, rather than a wife.

man bound to die.[72] By arguing on the 'force of circumstances,' we have argued away all force from ourselves; and stand leashed together, uniform in dress and movement, like the rowers of some boundless galley. This and that may be right and true; *but we must not do it.* Wonderful 'Force of Public Opinion!' We must act and walk in all points as it prescribes; follow the traffic it bids us, realise the sum of money, the degree of 'influence' it expects of us, *or* we shall be lightly esteemed; certain mouthfuls of articulate wind will be blown at us, and this what mortal courage can front? Thus, while civil Liberty is more and more secured to us, our moral Liberty is all but lost. Practically considered, our creed is Fatalism; and, free in hand and foot, we are shackled in heart and soul, with far straiter than feudal chains. Truly may we say, with the Philosopher, 'the deep meaning of the Laws of Mechanism lies heavy on us;'[73] and in the closet, in the marketplace, in the temple, by the social hearth, encumbers the whole movements of our mind, and over our noblest faculties is spreading a nightmare sleep.

These dark features, we are aware, belong more or less to other ages, as well as to ours. This faith in Mechanism, in the all-importance of physical things, is in every age the common refuge of Weakness and blind Discontent; of all who believe, as many will ever do, that man's true good lies without him, not within. We are aware also, that, as applied to ourselves in all their aggravation, they form but half a picture; that in the whole picture there are bright lights as well as gloomy shadows. If we here dwell chiefly on the latter, let us not be blamed: it is in general more profitable to reckon up our defects than to boast of our attainments.

Neither, with all these evils more or less clearly before us, have we at any time despaired of the fortunes of society. Despair, or even despondency, in that respect, appears to us, in all cases, a groundless feeling. We have a faith in the imperishable dignity of man; in the high vocation to which, throughout this his earthly history, he has been appointed. However it may be with individual nations, whatever melancholic speculators may assert, it seems a well-ascertained fact that, in all times, reckoning even from those of the Heraclides and Pelasgi,[74] the happiness and greatness of mankind at large have been continually progressive. Doubtless this age also is advancing. Its very unrest, its ceaseless activity, its discontent, contains matter of promise. Knowledge, education, are opening the eyes of the humblest — are increasing the number of thinking minds without limit. This is as it should be; for, not in turning back, not in resting, but only in resolutely struggling forward, does our life consist. Nay, after all, our spiritual maladies are but of Opinion; we are but fettered by chains of our own forging, and which ourselves also can rend asunder. This deep, paralysed subjection to physical objects comes not from nature, but from our own unwise mode of *viewing* Nature. Neither can we understand that man wants, at this hour, any faculty of heart, soul or body, that ever belonged to him. 'He who has been born, has been a First Man;' has had lying before his young eyes, and as yet unhardened into scientific shapes, a world

---

72 In this sentence, 'character' means a person's public reputation, rather than their true essence. Duelling was very rare but still occasionally resorted to by aristocratic men to uphold their 'honour'. The Prime Minister, the Duke of Wellington, had fought one earlier in 1829, against the Earl of Winchilsea, who had accused him of 'treacherously plotting the destruction of the Protestant constitution' by enacting Catholic emancipation. It didn't come to much: Wellington shot wide, and Winchilsea held his fire, and later wrote an apology.

73 As often in Carlyle, what appears to be a quote from another writer is just more Carlyle.

74 *Pelasgoí* is used by some ancient Greek writers to name the people who were in Greece before the Greeks arrived. The Dorian Greeks imagined themselves to be descended from the hero Heracles, with ancestors called the Heraclides providing the link.

as plastic, infinite, divine, as lay before the eyes of Adam himself. If Mechanism, like some glass bell, encircles and imprisons us, if the soul looks forth on a fair heavenly country which it cannot reach, and pines, and in its scanty atmosphere is ready to perish—yet the bell is but of glass; 'one bold stroke to break the bell in pieces, and thou art delivered!' Not the invisible world is wanting, for it dwells in man's soul, and this last is still here. Are the solemn temples, in which the Divinity was once visibly revealed among us, crumbling away? We can repair them, we can rebuild them. The wisdom, the heroic worth of our forefathers, which we have lost, we can recover. That admiration of old nobleness, which now so often shows itself as a faint *dilettantism,* will one day become a generous emulation, and man may again be all that he has been, and more than he has been. Nor are these the mere daydreams of fancy—they are clear possibilities; nay, in this time they are even assuming the character of hopes. Indications we do see, in other countries and in our own, signs infinitely cheering to us, that Mechanism is not always to be our hard taskmaster, but one day to be our pliant, all-ministering servant; that a new and brighter spiritual era is slowly evolving itself for all men. But on these things our present course forbids us to enter.

Meanwhile, that great outward changes are in progress can be doubtful to no one. The time is sick and out of joint. Many things have reached their height; and it is a wise adage that tells us, 'the darkest hour is nearest the dawn.' Whenever we can gather indication of the public thought, whether from printed books, as in France or Germany, or from Carbonari rebellions and other political tumults,[75] as in Spain, Portugal, Italy and Greece, the voice it utters is the same. The thinking minds of all nations call for change. There is a deep-lying struggle in the whole fabric of society; a boundless grinding collision of the New with the Old. The French Revolution, as is now visible enough, was not the parent of this mighty movement, but its offspring. Those two hostile influences, which always exist in human things, and on the constant intercommunion of which depends their health and safety, had lain in separate masses, accumulating through generations, and France was the scene of their fiercest explosion; but the final issue was not unfolded in that country: nay, it is not yet anywhere unfolded. Political freedom is hitherto the object of these efforts; but they will not and cannot stop there. It is towards a higher freedom than mere freedom from oppression by his fellow-mortal, that man dimly aims. Of this higher, heavenly freedom, which is 'man's reasonable service,' all his noble institutions, his faithful endeavours and loftiest attainments, are but the body, and more and more approximated emblem.

On the whole, as this wondrous planet, Earth, is journeying with its fellows through infinite Space, so are the wondrous destinies embarked on it journeying through infinite time, under a higher guidance than ours. For the present, as our Astronomy informs us, its path lies towards *Hercules,* the constellation of *Physical Power:* but that is not our most pressing concern. Go where it will, the deep HEAVEN will be around it. Therein let us have hope and sure faith. To reform a world, to reform a nation, no wise man will undertake; and all but foolish men know, that the only solid, though a far slower reformation, is what each begins and perfects on *himself.*

---

75 The Carbonari were an underground liberal nationalist movement in Italy, which in 1820–21 had risen against the various monarchies and empires that divided up the peninsula between them. They were defeated. Similar movements existed in other Mediterranean countries, perpetuating a sense of national identity fostered during the Napoleonic period.

Lightning Source UK Ltd.
Milton Keynes UK
23 September 2010

160263UK00001B/2/P